S0-AUY-150

Property of
Genevieve Kerr A.P.
Secondary Education
San Jose State College
San Jose, Calif.

A FIRST COURSE IN EDUCATION

THE MACMILLAN COMPANY
NEW YORK • CHICAGO
DALLAS • ATLANTA • SAN FRANCISCO
LONDON • MANILA
BRETT-MACMILLAN LTD.
TORONTO

FOURTH EDITION

A First Course in Education

WARD G. REEDER
PROFESSOR EMERITUS OF EDUCATION
THE OHIO STATE UNIVERSITY

The Macmillan Company
NEW YORK

Printed in the United States of America

First Printing

Previous editions © The Macmillan Company 1937, 1943, and 1950

Library of Congress catalog card number: 57-10478

To my thousands of students, from a one-teacher school in Tipton County, Indiana, in 1910, to graduate students in the Ohio State University where I retired from teaching in 1956.

PREFACE

During recent years most colleges which have been engaged in the preparation of teachers have regularly offered, and have usually required, an introductory course in education. This is the most frequently required and offered course in education. From its beginning the course has been designed to serve two purposes: first, to give the students of the course an overview of the history, the aims, the organization, and the procedures of education—in brief, to provide as systematic a view as possible of the whole field of education; second, to give the students rather complete information regarding the opportunities and the requirements in education as a profession, with the hope that the students will be better qualified to decide whether they want to enter the teaching profession, and if they decide to enter it, to select the phase of it which they will pursue.

This book, which is now in its fourth edition—the first appearing in 1937, the second in 1943, and the third in 1950—has been written primarily as a textbook for students in this introductory course in education. Other potential readers who have been kept in mind by the author in preparing the book are the following: students in other college departments who wish an overview of the field of education, but who are not specializing in that field; teachers in service who desire a new orientation in education, or who wish to bring their knowledge of education up-to-date; and laymen such as members of school boards and of Parent-Teacher Associations who are interested in becoming better acquainted with the educational enterprise and with the process of education.

In preparing the book the author, in all four editions, has been guided by the purposes of orientation and guidance mentioned above.

In selecting the topics to be discussed and in deciding upon the emphasis to be given each topic he has attempted to steer between the two extremes which confront every author of an introductory book: first, of discussing too few topics and those topics so briefly that a broad and an intelligible introduction is not given, and second, of discussing too many topics and those topics so exhaustively that further courses wastefully duplicate the introductory course. In other words, the author has tried to avoid shallowness of treatment, but he has not aimed at exhaustiveness of treatment of any topic. His desire has been to give a "bird's-eye view" of the educational enterprise and of the process of education, with the firm belief that if the prospective teacher acquires such a view he will be more competent (1) to proceed to later courses, such as school organization and management, psychology, curriculum, and methods of teaching, and (2) to begin his systematic observation of schools and of teaching procedures.

The frame of reference of the author has been that science and philosophy must work together in the solution of all educational problems. The author has tried to portray the high points of modern educational practice and to help the student to evaluate that practice in terms of a defensible philosophy of education. He has tried to help the student to start developing a defensible philosophy of education for himself, and to begin acquiring teaching tools and methods which will help the student to attack educational problems scientifically.

Since the course, "Introduction to Education," usually comprises one quarter or one semester, the book has been especially designed for a course of such length. By means, however, of the Selected References and the Questions for Discussion which appear at the close of each chapter, the book can be readily adapted to courses of longer duration. The book has been organized into six parts, with several related chapters under each part. The parts are captioned as follows: Part One, "Education and the American Democracy"; Part Two, "Organization and Administration of the Schools"; Part Three, "The Pupils and the Educative Process"; Part Four, "The Materials of Instruction"; Part Five, "Education as a Profession"; and Part Six, "Methods of Studying Educational Problems."

In this—the fourth edition—the organization of the book remains practically the same as that of the first three editions. Attempt, though, has been made to make the book up-to-date in pictures, statistics, bibliographies, and other aspects. Attempt, too, has been made as always to make the book more accurate, more clear, and more interesting.

In the preparation of the book the author wishes to acknowledge the assistance which he has received from many sources. He acknowledges first the stimulation and the other help given him when he was enrolled as a student in one of the earliest courses in "Introduction to Education." The year was 1918, the institution was the University of Chicago, and the instructor of the course was the late Professor Charles H. Judd. In all his teaching Dr. Judd emphasized the need for attacking educational problems with data obtained by means of objective techniques, and that emphasis could hardly have failed to color the views and the future work of his students.

The author is also indebted to some of his former colleagues with whom he collaborated in teaching in The Ohio State University a course entitled, "Introduction to Education." Of those colleagues he is especially indebted to the late Professor Boyd H. Bode with whom he collaborated longest. Dr. Bode emphasized the need for a defensible philosophy of education as a guide to educational effort, and his exposition of what he regarded as such a philosophy—a democratic philosophy—unquestionably colored the views of the author.

The author recognizes that a large debt is due his thousands of students, beginning in 1919, who have enrolled in this course and in other courses that were taught by him. He is especially indebted to Mrs. Virginia Inada, Roscoe Drake, and John Giesy.

The author's largest debts are due Professors William L. Carter and Gordon Hendrickson of Teachers College, University of Cincinnati, who independently read the entire manuscript and made many constructive suggestions for its improvement; Professor Carter also assisted in the reading of the galley proofs.

Ward G. Reeder

Columbus, Ohio

CONTENTS

PART FOUR

THE MATERIALS OF INSTRUCTION

PART FIVE

EDUCATION AS A PROFESSION

PART SIX

METHODS OF STUDYING EDUCATIONAL PROBLEMS

LIST OF TABLES

LIST OF FIGURES

PART ONE

EDUCATION AND THE AMERICAN DEMOCRACY

CHAPTER 1

America's Historic Faith in Education

Definition, Importance, and Agencies of Education

Definition of Education. In any discussion a common understanding is facilitated by beginning with a definition of the topic or the problem which is being discussed. Since this book is a treatise on education, the book should take its departure from a definition of education. A definition of education seems to be in place, in spite of the fact that the universal and everyday use of the term may have made people accustomed to believe that its meaning is clear. What, then, is education?

Many well-known definitions of education are extant, but when the definitions are stripped of their verbiage and are stated clearly in the American language, they are seen to mean essentially the same. They universally regard education as synonymous with learning or acquired experience. In this book that meaning of education will be accepted. A person has been educated, at least to a certain degree, when he has obtained experience of any sort—intellectual, emotional, or physical. Since every waking moment of a person's life gives experience, it is obvious that education constantly proceeds from birth to death. The school is not the only educational agency; it never was and never can be the only agency of education.

In one sense, education may be regarded as a product—a product of experience, and it is impossible for a person to obtain an experience, without obtaining an accretion—good or bad—to his education. In another sense, education may be regarded as a process—a process through which and by which the experience of the race, that is, knowledge, skills, ideals, and attitudes, are transmitted to the members of the community. Probably, the most widely quoted definition of education is that of the late Professor John Dewey, who was one of the most renowned educators of all time. Dewey defined education, especially as a process, as follows:

> . . . education is a constant reorganizing or reconstructing of experience. It has all the time an immediate end, and so far as activity is educative, it reaches that end—the direct transformation of the quality of experience. Infancy, youth, adult life,—all stand on the same educative level in the sense that what is really *learned* at any and every stage of experience constitutes the value of that experience, and in the sense that it is the chief business of life at every point to make living thus contribute to an enrichment of its own perceptible meaning.
>
> We thus reach a technical definition of education: It is that reconstruction or reorganization of experience which adds to the meaning of experience, and which increases ability to direct the course of subsequent experience.[1]

IMPORTANCE OF EDUCATION. Each person is born into the world with a biological heritage which may be excellent, average, or inferior. Whatever its quality, that heritage contains the basis or the starting point for the education of the person. Unless, however, the social heritage—language, customs, discoveries, inventions, literature, art, and other habits, skills, ideals, and knowledge—are combined with the biological heritage, the individual must remain as an uncivilized or uneducated person and be incompetent to adjust himself to civilized man's world. Unless he came into contact with the heritage of the race, the newborn infant would not advance beyond the stage of mere animal. Without education, the individual could not realize his potentialities, and society could not progress. Education is the dynamo as well as the governor of civilization. According to a book by the late Professor Edward L. Thorndike and Arthur I. Gates, the failure of a society to provide education for its members would probably result in unwanted conditions such as the following:

> If all human beings save newborn infants vanished to another planet, and if by miracle the babies were kept alive for a score of years, preserving

[1] John Dewey, *Democracy and Education*, Macmillan, 1916, pp. 89–90. By permission of The Macmillan Company, publishers.

whatever knowledge and skill came from natural inner growth, and lacking only the influence of the educational activities of other men, they would, at the age of twenty-one, resemble a horde of animals. They would get a precarious living from fruits, berries, and small animals, would easily become victims of malaria, yellow fever, smallpox, and plague, and would know little more of language, mechanical arts, or provision of the future than the monkeys. They would be distinguishable from other mammalian species chiefly by a much greater variety of bodily movements, especially of the hands, mouth parts, and face, a much quicker rate of learning, and a very much keener satisfaction in mental life for its own sake. But even under the simple conditions of a primitive environment, the life of the jungle, the learning of a life time would be limited largely to the simplest type of food getting and protective skills with scarcely any real understanding of themselves or the natural world in which they lived.

If these infants grew up in a deserted modern city, they would advance little if any further without education. They would be engaged in the search of food, mates, and organic comforts like other animals. They would use the books, tools, engines, and other innumerable products of civilization as toys somewhat more intelligently than would apes, but they would not learn to read the books, to bake bread, repair tools, or make engines more than spectacles for amusement, wonder, and fear.[2]

AGENCIES OF EDUCATION. Contrary to a common belief among the people, education, that is, the transmission of the social heritage, is not provided by the school alone. During the many centuries before the school was established, the transmission of the social heritage was accomplished by other institutions and by other agencies. Moreover, the work of the school has always been supplemented by many other educational institutions and by many other educational agencies. Before the founding of the school the main conveyors of education were the home, the church, and apprenticeship, and it must be admitted that for those early times those institutions discharged their functions well. They discharged them well, primarily because they kept in mind, and tried to meet, social and individual needs; they prepared the children for life by illuminating the realities of life as the children were experiencing them and as they would probably experience them in adult life. Because it was closer to the people, perhaps the simple school of those early days met the needs of the people even better than the more complex school of today meets the needs of the present generation.

[2] Edward L. Thorndike and Arthur I. Gates, *Elementary Principles of Education,* Macmillan, 1929, pp. 7–8. By permission of The Macmillan Company, publishers.

Even when they were at the bottom of the ladder of civilization, the people always underwent the process of education, and they underwent the process many centuries before the school as we know

Fig. 1. Education before schools began. Education in those early days was provided largely by the home, as will be seen in this illustration. *(Courtesy of the Smithsonian Institution, Washington, D. C.)*

it today was established. The most powerful urge and ambition of man have always been the desire to rear children who could and would successfully make their way in the world and help others. Man early saw the need for the education of his children, and he early took steps to provide that education. The seed of the modern school, therefore, was planted and cultivated by earliest man. In those earlier times the younger members of the community learned the necessary skills, attitudes, ideals, and knowledge by participating in the activities of the adult members of the community. For example, the Indian boy learned from his father how to start a fire, how to grow maize in a dead forest, how to hunt wild game, how to protect himself from his enemies and from the elements, how to co-operate with the members of his family and his tribe, and how to perform other duties necessary for participation in a primitive life. In the same manner the Indian girl was taught by her mother those activities which would enable her to meet the needs of their times.

With the advent of the industrial revolution and with the rapid development of science, life grew much more complex, and the need for education rapidly mounted. The social heritage soon became too large and society soon grew too complex for parents to provide the proper quality and the proper quantity of education for their children. Parents gradually came to see that they did not have the time or the specialized knowledge to organize and to present all of the necessary experiences for their children. When those problems and those handicaps were recognized by parents, schools were established, and teachers were employed to provide some of the preparation which had formerly been given by the parents of the children.

During the more recent years, the influence of the home and of the church as educational and custodial institutions has seriously waned, and this waning has caused a still larger responsibility to be delegated to the school. Moreover, child labor has been largely prohibited; employment opportunities for youth have decreased; and millions of children now come to school, because they have nothing else to do, or because the state laws require school attendance. As the years have rolled by, more and more of the responsibilities of parents for the education of their children have been delegated to the school, and the end of that process of delegation is not yet in sight, because as science and technology advance, education becomes all the more necessary for obtaining happiness and for the control of civilization itself. Not only do the parents send their children to school, but the parents are more and more bringing themselves to school for refresher courses, for vocational preparation, and for various other types of adult education offered during evenings. More and more, the people are realizing that the education of an individual is never complete.

Although the influence of the school has constantly increased, it is apparent that the modern person does not obtain his education wholly from the school. On the contrary, it is seen that most education comes from the "school of life"—from the home, the church, the radio, the newspaper and magazine, the library, the cinema, television, travel, work and play, and all environment—rather than from the school. The school will probably never supplant those institutions and the other educational agencies, but will always be supplemented by them; this is devoutly to be hoped, because there would be real dangers in a complete centralization in one institution or one agency of the total responsibility for providing education. The eight, twelve, sixteen, or other number of years during which the school has the pupil under its tutelage is a short span compared with the number of years which the pupil spends in the "school of life." In general, and at best, the span of the school is only long enough to give the pupil the necessary tools for acquiring skills, attitudes, and some knowledge, and to instill in him an abiding desire to use those tools. Equipped with those tools and that desire, the pupil is better qualified to continue his education throughout his life. Every person is being educated all the time and in whatever environment he may be. Education continues as long as the individual lives, and it continues whether the individual is conscious of the process or not; it often continues, in spite of the individual and in spite of the fact that some of it is worthless and is sometimes vicious. Not all education is good.

Nonschool Agencies Affecting Children and Youth. The relation of the school to other educative agencies has concerned educators during recent years. Although no large-scale study of the effect of one of these agencies upon children and youth has been

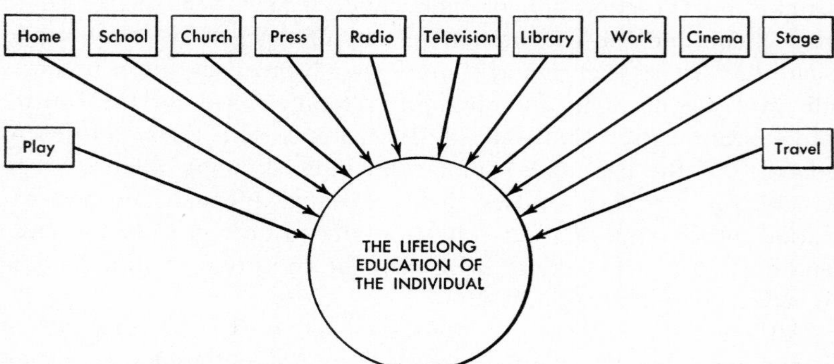

Fig. 2. The chief agencies which now contribute to the education of an individual. Of course, there are many other agencies, and more agencies are being created all the time.

made, since the Payne Fund studies on motion pictures in 1929, the influence of many of the other mass mediums of education is of much concern today. The influence (good or bad) of television, radio, motion pictures, comic books, and newspaper comics has been avidly discussed recently by teachers and by parents of pupils.

Evidences of America's Faith in Education

America's faith in education has been called by a European visitor the "national religion of America." This faith in education appeared almost simultaneously with the first settlements in the early part of the seventeenth century, and it has grown more and more firm as the years have rolled by. It has endured wars, business depressions, and other sorrows and upheavals; it has surmounted every handicap, and it has always moved to greater heights. It has been buttressed by two beliefs: (1) that the welfare, the progress, and the perpetuity of society are determined largely by the education of all the people, and (2) that the individual can best realize his potentialities in happiness and in accomplishment through education. Every civilized parent has shared with Enoch Arden ". . . the noble wish to save all earnings to the uttermost and give his child a better bringing-up than his has been." The good parent asks nothing in return, except good citizenship for his child.

That faith in education has been evidenced in ways too numerous to mention. It was evidenced by the first settlers, in the almost immediate establishment of schools—schools at first private, but shortly afterward public. From the beginning, it has been evidenced by the enactment of thousands of educational laws—laws usually of state-wide or colony-wide application and always calculated to extend and to improve the schools of the state or the colony and to assure universal school attendance by the young. It has been notably evidenced, especially during recent decades, by the large increases in school attendance and in school expenditures. The more important of those evidences of the historic faith of the American people in education will be elaborated upon in the following pages.

The Early Beginning of Schools. The faith of the American people in education was first evidenced by the early date at which schools were established. Schools were established almost immediately after settlements were made in a community. In fact, the availability of schools has always played a prominent part in the promotion of new settlements, as it does in the purchase of a home. According to Reverend Timothy Flint, who was a frontier missionary from 1815 to 1840, "A minister—a church—a school—are words to flourish in an advertisement to sell lots." The first institution to be founded was, of course, the home; immediately after the home came the church; then came the school, almost concurrently with the church. Not only was that the order of the establishment of those institutions by our first settlers, but the same order of establishment continued when settlers pushed westward during the eighteenth and the nineteenth centuries. The attitude of the early settlers toward education is seen from the following quotation (original spelling) from an early New England pamphlet titled "New England's First Fruits," which was printed in London, England in 1643:

> After God had carried us safe to New England
> And wee had builded our houses
> Provided necessaries for our livelihood
> Reard convenient places for Gods worship
> And setled the civill government
> One of the next things we longed for
> And looked after was to advance learning
> And perpetuate it to posterity
> Dreading to leave an illiterate ministry
> To the churches when our present ministers
> Shall lie in the Dust.

The first schools in the United States of America were established upon the initiative of the people of the local communities and without any suggestion or any requirement on the part of the colonial legislatures; in that early period the people could have schools or not have them, as they chose. As a first proof of the early faith of the American people in education, it should be mentioned that private schools were established almost from the time of the first settlement. Moreover, there is evidence that many communities in Massachusetts had established truly public schools as early as 1635,[3] and Harvard College (originally a public institution) was founded by the General Court (legislature today) of Massachusetts

[3] M. W. Jernegan, "The Beginnings of Public Education in New England," *School Review*, Vol. 23 (June, 1915), pp. 361–380.

in 1636 by the granting of £400 "towards a schoale or college" in the colony. The first public schools were established, therefore, only twenty-eight years after the founding in 1607 of Jamestown, Virginia, which was the first permanent English settlement in America, and only fifteen years after the Pilgrims landed on Plymouth rock in Plymouth, Massachusetts.

Compulsory-education Laws. Although the faith in education of our early settlers was widespread, it was by no means universal; it varied from community to community and from colony to colony; it was strongest in the New England colonies. Our forefathers, especially in New England, soon saw that to leave the option of obtaining an education to the children and their parents was resulting in many children growing up in ignorance; they therefore took steps to prevent such situations from occurring. In 1642 the Massachusetts colonial legislature enacted the first compulsory-education law in the English-speaking world. Although the law was poorly enforced, it was colony-wide in operation, and it applied to rich and to poor alike. The law stipulated that "the selectmen in every town [4] shall have power to take account of all parents and masters as to their children's education and employment. . . . They (the selectmen) are to see that the children can read and understand the principles of religion and the capital laws of the country. . . ."

It should be noted that the Massachusetts law of 1642 did not require the establishment of a school, the employment of a teacher, or school attendance on the part of the children; in that law the provision for education was left entirely to the home. Legislation for the establishment of schools and for compulsory school attendance of all pupils came much later as we shall presently see. Parents have continuously delegated their educational functions to the community or to the state, although many of our citizens believe that those functions should remain with the parents and with the church.

Compulsory-school Laws. It was soon found that the Massachusetts law of 1642 was difficult to enforce, because it failed to

[4] A town usually included a small village and the surrounding rural territory. It has always been typically a New England governmental unit. It is generally similar to the township or the county of other sections of the United States. The selectmen were chosen by the people to administer the government of the town. Schools in those days were not separate from other phases of government as they are today.

provide any public means of instruction. It was soon discovered that many parents were educationally incompetent and were financially unable to provide their children with even the rudiments of learning which the law stipulated; many parents then could not teach their children to read, because they themselves could not read, and many parents lacked the financial means to employ a tutor who would provide the instruction. In 1647, therefore, the Massachusetts colonial legislature enacted a law designed to correct the deficiencies just indicated. That law has often been dubbed the "Old Deluder Satan Act." It has also been called the "mother of all school laws." It required all towns having fifty or more families or "householders" to provide an elementary school, and all towns having one hundred or more families or "householders" to provide a secondary school [5] in addition to the elementary school. Because it is one of the most momentous educational acts ever passed in any country, the law of 1647 is quoted (original spelling) herewith *in extenso:*

> It being one chiefe project of that ould deluder, Sathan, to keepe men from the knowledge of the Scriptures, as in former times by keeping them in an unknowne tongue, so in these latter times by perswading from the use of tongues that so at least the true sence and meaning of the originall might be clouded by false glosses of saint seeming deceivers, that learning may not be buried in the grave of our fathers in the church and commonwealth, the Lord assisting our endeavors.
>
> It is therefore ordered, that every township in this jurisdiction, after the Lord hath increased it to the number of fifty householders, shall then forthwith appoint one within their towne to teach all such children as shall resort to him to write and reade, whose wages shall be paid either by the parents or masters of such children, or by the inhabitants in generall, by way of supply, as the major part of those that order the prudentials of the towne shall appoint; provided, those that send their children be not oppressed by paying much more than they can have them taught for in other townes; and it is further ordered, that where any towne shall increase to the number of one hundred families or householders they shall set up a grammer schoole, the master thereof being able to instruct youth so farr as they may be fited for the university; provided, that if any towne neglect the performance hereof above one yeare, that every such towne shall pay 5[s] to the next schoole till they shall perform this order.

[5] As is seen in the quotation from the law, this school was called the grammar school; that school was succeeded by the academy, which was succeeded by the high school. The academy was the dominant secondary school from about 1775 to about 1875. The high school has been the dominant secondary school since about 1875.

Although they appear somewhat trite when they are compared with present school laws, the Massachusetts laws of 1642 and of 1647 embodied the underlying principles of the American school systems; the laws embodied those principles, even though they were then poorly enforced. They were the foundation of all succeeding school laws, not only in Massachusetts, but in other colonies and states as well; they were the genesis of all school laws. In brief, they affirmed, at least by inference, that education was so essential to the well-being and to the progress of society that it could not be left entirely to the whims of the individual, or entirely to the desires of the people of a community. In those early laws the principle of state obligation and of state sovereignty in education was born, and thereafter parents were to know that where education was concerned the children belonged to the state as well as to the parents. On one hand, the laws established the principle that for its progress and its protection the state had the right and the obligation to decide the kind and the amount of education which should be demanded of each individual and of each community; on the other hand, they established the principle that schools could be financed by universal and compulsory taxation. Those principles have never been questioned by any major court in the land. They have never been contradicted by a colonial, a territorial, or a state legislature. They are part of the tradition of America. They are the keystone of our schools.

School-improvement Laws. Following the legislation for the establishment of schools came legislation looking toward the better financing, the constant improvement, and the gradual extension of schools. The Massachusetts law of 1647 was silent regarding any standard which the schools should meet; it merely required the establishment of schools, and the schools could be excellent, mediocre, or inferior. Laws requiring school standards were, however, soon enacted. In fact, since 1647, there has been scarcely a colonial, a territorial, or a state legislature which has not enacted legislation designed to maintain, to improve, or to extend the work of the schools. At first, such legislation has been usually only permissive, that is, the legislatures have empowered local boards of education to take a certain step or steps. Many of these laws have never advanced beyond the permissive stage; however, many of the laws have proved so beneficial that they have been changed from permissive to mandatory and have been given state-wide application. Of course, old laws have been repealed, and new and better ones enacted in their place.

Legislation designed to improve the schools has been enacted on practically every aspect of school organization and administration. As the years have passed, that legislation has prescribed minimum qualifications for teachers and for a few other kinds of school employees; it has set hygienic and safety standards for school plants; it has prescribed a minimum length of school term; it has determined many—perhaps too many—of the school subjects; it has provided for the public transportation of pupils who live more than a certain distance from school and has prescribed standards for the means of pupil transportation; it has established regulations governing the selection of textbooks; it has made provision for kindergartens, libraries, playgrounds, and other school services and conveniences. It has prescribed hundreds of similar standards for the schools and it has constantly raised those standards.[6]

The end of such legislation is not yet in sight. In fact, the end of it can never be reached, because the school will probably always have many defects that need correcting. The school can never be made perfect, because social changes will always occur, and they will require a changed school system. It is the function of legislation to promote, to permit, and even to require that constant change within the school systems which is desirable to meet the needs of a constantly changing society. It is the opportunity and the obligation of school officials, of school employees, and of all other friends of the schools to be aware of and to sponsor desirable changes in school legislation. School officials and school employees must always be alert citizens, interested always in school improvement.

Compulsory School-attendance Laws. The first compulsory school-attendance law was not enacted until 1852, which was more than 200 years after the enactment of the first compulsory-education law (1642). Just as Massachusetts, especially in the early days, has been the leader in innumerable educational movements which have come to be accepted by every state, so she was the first state to enact a compulsory school-attendance law.[7]

In view of the early faith of the American people in education,

[6] This legislation is revised and published periodically, usually under the title of "School Laws," by the state department of education of each state.

[7] A list of the educational movements which Massachusetts started is available in the *Annual Report* of the Massachusetts Department of Education, 1929, Part I, pp. 34–45.

it is difficult to understand why compulsory school-attendance laws came so tardily. As has been said, the first compulsory school-attendance law did not come until more than 200 years after the establishment of schools, and not until 1918 did every American state enact a compulsory school-attendance law. One explanation for the tardiness in enacting such legislation is the fact that the people long deemed that they were not able to finance universal education which compulsory school-attendance laws always prescribe. Such laws were not feasible until the income and the wealth of the people were sufficient to finance the obligations which the laws entailed. Another explanation for the tardiness is the fact that the American people, like the people of all democracies, have historically been somewhat individualistic; they have not relished legislation which would interfere with their right of choice; their faith in rugged individualism and their desire for social co-operation have been difficult to reconcile. In practice, however, they have tended to resolve such conflicts in favor of social co-operation; they have progressively spurned—perhaps too much—the view of Thomas Jefferson, namely, "That government is best which governs least." What the individual should do for himself and what the government should do for him is the eternal problem of democratic governments, and we hope that it will always be a problem in our democracy.

The legislatures came gradually to see that for local communities to be required to establish and to support schools, without all children being required to attend either a public or a private school was incongruous and wasteful. Compulsory school-attendance laws were the outcome of that conclusion—a conclusion fathered by the belief that education was so necessary to the welfare of the individual and of society that it could not be left entirely to the whims of the child and his parents. As has been previously stated, Massachusetts enacted the first compulsory school-attendance law in 1852. Vermont followed in 1867. The next states to enact such legislation were Michigan, New Hampshire, and Washington, all in 1871. By 1910, forty-two states had enacted such laws, and by 1918 all of the forty-eight states had provided such laws.[8]

As would be expected, the early compulsory school-attendance laws

[8] For the dates of the enactment of the first compulsory school-attendance law in each state, the reader may consult U. S. Bureau of Education, *Bulletin*, 1914, No. 2, p. 10. He may consult also H. G. Good, *A History of American Education*, Macmillan, 1956, p. 376.

were very flimsy compared with the present laws. The laws of many of the states were permissive only, leaving to the local communities the decision as to whether compulsory school attendance should be adopted. Moreover, in all states the age span for compulsory school attendance was much less than it is today, and the number of weeks of school each year which the pupil was required to attend was only a small portion of the total school term. For example, the Massachusetts law of 1852 applied only to children between the ages of eight and fourteen and required those children to attend school for at least twelve weeks during the school term; the law further stipulated that six of those twelve weeks should be continuous. Still more, little or no provision was made for enforcing the early laws; as a rule, provisions for school-attendance employees came much later than compulsory school-attendance provisions, and even today, qualifications for school-attendance employees are seldom required by law, although they should be in all states.

The tendency, though, has been to make the compulsory school-attendance laws more rigid, to establish machinery for the enforcement of the laws, and to enforce the laws more rigidly. Several states now require school attendance until the age of eighteen, unless the child has met certain educational standards, or can claim exemption under other provisions of the law. Whereas the earlier laws placed emphasis on age standards, by requiring everyone to attend school until a specified age, the recent tendency has been to place emphasis on educational standards, by requiring everyone, except the mentally or the physically incompetent, to complete a specified grade in school. Moreover, the recent laws make fewer provisions for exemptions than did the earlier laws.

These compulsory school-attendance laws have had far-reaching effects. The most obvious effect has been greatly to increase school enrollment and school attendance. A second effect has been for a better type of education to be demanded, because it has been realized that to require children to attend school, without providing them with the best education possible, was not meeting their highest purposes and their best interests. In the third place, it soon came to be realized that provisions would have to be made for furnishing indigent children with textbooks, clothing, and other necessities of life, if they were to be expected to attend school the same as other children. In the fourth place and finally, it is gradually coming to be realized that to provide a school and to require the pupil to attend that school, without insisting that the pupil be in the best physical condition possible to receive the instruction which the school provides, is incongruous and wasteful; health education has been the outcome of that observation, and in consequence, as Chapter 12 will show, health education is being introduced into more and more school systems. Making all of these provisions has, of course, required larger school expenditures, as we shall presently see.

The Increase in School Enrollment. The people's estimate of the need for or of the worth of any product or service is determined by the extent to which they use that product or service; hence, the people's estimate of the value of education may be measured by the amount of school enrollment. What, then, has been the trend of school enrollment? In brief, the data show a phenomenal increase in school enrollment. If we go back only a few decades,[9] it is observed that since 1870 the total population of the United States has increased approximately fourfold, whereas the enrollment in the public elementary and secondary schools has increased approximately fivefold. In 1870, only 57 per cent of the children five to seventeen years of age inclusive were enrolled in the public schools, whereas at present approximately 85 per cent are enrolled.

The increase in school enrollment has been particularly large during recent decades. Large increases have been noted, especially in the kindergarten, in the secondary school, and in the college. The enrollment in public and private kindergartens increased from 31,337 in 1890 to more than 1,500,000 at present; the enrollment in the public and the private elementary schools and kindergartens increased from 14,181,415 in 1890 to approximately 30,000,000 today; the enrollment in the public and the private secondary schools went from 357,813 in 1890 to approximately 8,000,000 today; and the enrollment in the public and the private colleges and normal schools leaped from 156,756 in 1890 to more than 3,000,000 today. Since 1900 the

[9] Educational statistics, especially on a nation-wide basis, before 1870 are meager and somewhat untrustworthy; hence, most studies of trends of educational development in the United States do not start before 1870. Statistics, by states, on almost every phase of education may be obtained from the statistical reports of the U. S. Office of Education; these statistics are collected and published every two years. Similar statistics are also collected annually or biennially by the state departments of education.

number of youth of secondary school age has increased approximately 60 per cent, but total secondary school enrollment has increased approximately 1100 per cent.

There was an increase of approximately 13 per cent in elementary school enrollment each decade from 1890 to 1930. For a few years after 1930, however—probably because of the decline in the national birth rate—there was a small decrease in elementary school enrollment. The next years, however, showed a large increase, because of the large increase in the birth rate following World War II. The percentage increase in enrollment in the secondary schools has been much larger than that in the elementary schools. The number of pupils in the secondary schools approximately doubled from 1890 to 1900, increased approximately 60 per cent from 1900 to 1910, and approximately doubled each decade from 1910 to 1930; the increase since 1930 has been slower, and in 1941 a decrease was shown for the first time, but is now rapidly increasing again. Likewise, college enrollment has shown gigantic increases; the increase here has been approximately 50 per cent for each of the decades following 1890; of course, decreases were shown during World War I and World War II. Large increases were shown after each war; the increases were gigantic immediately following World War II, partly because of the Federal aid given to former servicemen and women.

It is estimated that in the United States today there are 5,000,000 living college graduates, and 14,000,000 living secondary school graduates who have not continued their education into and through college. It is estimated also that there are approximately 40 college graduates in every 1,000 persons twenty-one years of age and over; approximately 140 more persons in each 1,000 have a secondary school diploma, but not a college diploma; thus, a total of 180 persons in each 1,000 persons twenty-one years of age and over have advanced through secondary school or beyond, and that number is increasing every year.

Today, practically every child of elementary school age is enrolled in school, but there is a large drop-out at the end of the elementary school. A large percentage of pupils who complete the elementary school do not enroll in secondary school and of those pupils who enter secondary school only about two-fifths finish secondary school. More than half of the top quarter of our secondary-school graduates do not go to college; some of them do not attend college, because they lack financial means, but many of them lack motivation to attend college.

These huge increases in school enrollment did not come by chance. They were planned for, and sometimes they were fought for. They represent a growing faith of the American people in education. Our people have increasingly attended school because of their belief that education, more than any other factor, tends to make people equal in opportunity; they have believed that through the proper kind and the proper amount of education the individual may best realize his potentialities for himself and for society.

A second factor which has operated to increase school enrollment has been the enactment of compulsory school-attendance laws in every state, and the tendency to make those laws more rigid. Likewise, many states have enacted child-labor laws which have directed thousands of children into school, instead of into the mines, factories, shops, and other places of labor. Unquestionably, by far the majority of the people of the United States today would attend school of their own free will and accord; there is, however, a small fringe which would probably not attend school in the absence of compulsory school-attendance laws. It has always been observed that when a state enacted a compulsory school-attendance law, or when it made its attendance law more rigid, school attendance increased. A somewhat similar effect has followed the enactment of child-labor legislation. Periods of unemployment bring more pupils to school, especially in the upper school grades.

What is the outlook for further increases in school enrollment? If we knew what would happen to the birth rate, we could come to grips with that question. The birth rate is largely dependent on wars and on economic conditions of the nation. In 1913 the birth rate was 25.8 per 1,000 inhabitants; it decreased to approximately 18 per 1,000 in 1941; the rate increased to 25.9 per 1,000 in 1947, and it is approximately 25 per 1,000 today. If more children are born, the nation will have to look forward to an increase in school facilities and school services in a few years; if fewer children are born, the educational problem will decrease. The large increase in the birth rate, which followed World War II has already catapulted several million more children into the schools, and they must be properly cared for by the schools. In Table 1, Emery M. Foster of

TABLE 1. ACTUAL AND ESTIMATED PUBLIC SCHOOL ENROLLMENT FOR CONTINENTAL UNITED STATES, BY GRADE, 1949–50 THROUGH 1959–60 * [IN THOUSANDS]

	SCHOOL YEAR										
Grade	1949–50†	1950–51	1951–52†	1952–53	1953–54	1954–55	1955–56	1956–57	1957–58	1958–59	1959–60
1	2	3	4	5	6	7	8	9	10	11	12
K	1,034	941	1,272	1,312	1,237	1,237	1,228	1,280	1,308	1,344	1,298
1	3,170	3,053	2,957	3,319	4,152	4,285	4,267	4,250	4,369	4,481	4,602
2	2,645	2,739	2,670	2,978	2,886	3,617	3,741	3,731	3,723	3,834	3,938
3	2,396	2,601	2,718	2,769	2,855	2,767	3,468	3,587	3,578	3,571	3,677
4	2,254	2,358	2,559	2,559	2,700	2,783	2,698	3,382	3,497	3,489	3,482
5	2,151	2,211	2,320	2,397	2,483	2,619	2,700	2,618	3,281	3,394	3,386
6	2,056	2,117	2,166	2,229	2,361	2,447	2,581	2,661	2,580	3,234	3,345
7	1,947	1,995	2,083	2,103	2,180	2,311	2,394	2,526	2,604	2,525	3,165
8	1,752	1,885	1,936	1,906	1,940	2,014	2,138	2,215	2,338	2,410	2,338
K–8	19,405	19,900†	20,681	21,572	22,794	24,080	25,215	26,250	27,278	28,282	29,231
9	1,756	1,781	1,820	1,903	1,964	1,998	2,073	2,199	2,279	2,404	2,479
10	1,512	1,548	1,582	1,661	1,722	1,782	1,815	1,887	2,006	2,079	2,194
11	1,274	1,313	1,338	1,401	1,439	1,500	1,559	1,592	1,660	1,770	1,835
12	1,123	1,127	1,111	1,202	1,264	1,304	1,364	1,423	1,456	1,519	1,624
9–12‡	5,665	5,769†	5,851	6,167	6,389	6,583	6,811	7,101	7,401	7,772	8,132
K–12	25,070	25,669†	26,532	27,739	29,183	30,663	32,026	33,351	34,679	36,054	37,363

* Does not include enrollments in residential schools for exceptional children, noncollegiate departments of colleges (preparatory or training schools), and Federal schools or enrollments in the outlying parts of the United States.

† Reported data; not estimates.

‡ Excludes postgraduates.

the U. S. Office of Education estimates public school enrollment for each school year until 1959–1960.[10]

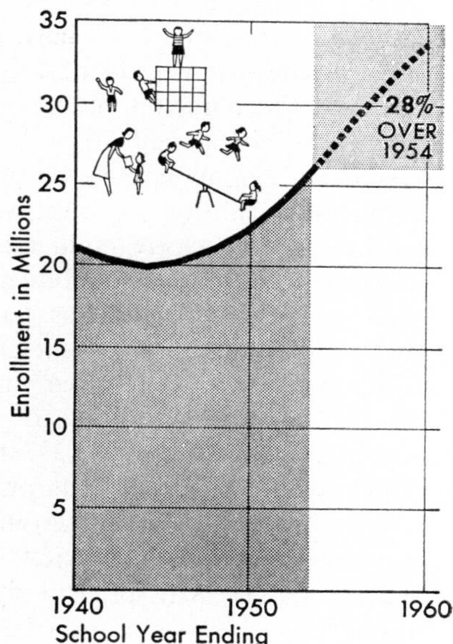

Fig. 3. Past, present, and predicted enrollments in the elementary schools, including kindergarten, of the United States. *(From* Teachers for Tomorrow, *p. 12. Courtesy of The Fund for the Advancement of Education.)*

The Increase in the Length of the School Term. The historic tendency to increase the length of the school term is another evidence of the increasing faith of our people in education. Since 1870, every decade, with the exception of the business-depression decade of 1870–1880, has seen an increase in the average length of the school term; from an average length of school term of 132.2 days in 1870 there has been a gradual increase to more than 178 days at present. Approximately one-half of the states now require and help to finance a school term of at least 180 days in every community.

The Increase in School Expenditures.[11] In no other way is the faith in education of our people better revealed than by their willingness to be taxed larger and larger amounts for schools. When the people have been convinced that more money was needed by

[10] "Elementary and Secondary School Enrollment in the Public School Systems of the United States, by Grade, 1949–50 through 1959–60," *School Life,* Vol. 37 (May, 1955), pp. 126–127.

[11] A detailed discussion of these increases is found in Chapter 6.

the schools, they have somehow found the money. They have not only provided the wherewithal for improving the existing school program, but have furnished additional money for extending the scope of the program. They have made certain that all persons who desired an education could have it, either at public or at private expense, and the tendency has been to provide it at public expense. If they have occasionally regarded schools as expensive, they have always deemed ignorance to be much more expensive.

From the beginning, expenditures for schools in the United States have increased at a very rapid rate, and since 1920, the rate of increase has been almost phenomenal. Whereas since 1870, the total population of the nation has had an estimated fourfold increase and school enrollment has increased approximately fivefold, total expenditures for schools have increased more than one hundredfold. The total expenditures for public elementary and secondary schools have gone from $63,397,000 in 1870 to more than $8,000,000,000 today. On a per capita of population basis, the expenditures have gone from $1.64 in 1870 to more than $50 today; on a per-pupil-in-average-daily-attendance basis the annual expenditures have increased from $15.25 in 1870 to more than $270 today. Moreover, in terms of its wealth the nation has tended to finance its schools on an increasingly better scale; in 1870, $2.89 was expended for public elementary and secondary schools per $1,000 of wealth, whereas today it is estimated that approximately $16 per $1,000 of wealth is so expended.

Another view of the increasing expenditures for schools may be obtained by observing the increase in the value of school property. The value of all property of the public elementary and secondary schools increased from $130,383,000 in 1870 to an estimated $20,000,000,000 today. On the basis of the value of school property per pupil enrolled, there has been an increase from $19 in 1870 to more than $500 today.

AMOUNT OF SCHOOLING OF OUR PEOPLE TODAY. The majority of the people of the United States have obtained some secondary school education. For the first time in history, the United States Census, in 1940, obtained the amount of schooling of its people; similar data were obtained in the 1950 census. Those data show that illiteracy is largely confined to the older portion of our people. The average number of years of schooling of our people above 25 years of age increased from 8.4 in 1940 to 9.3 in 1950. The data for each state and for the District of Columbia are shown in Table 2. The table shows that several states improved their rank between 1940 and 1950. What will happen in the census of 1960? We have only a guess on that, but the guess is a rather confident one.

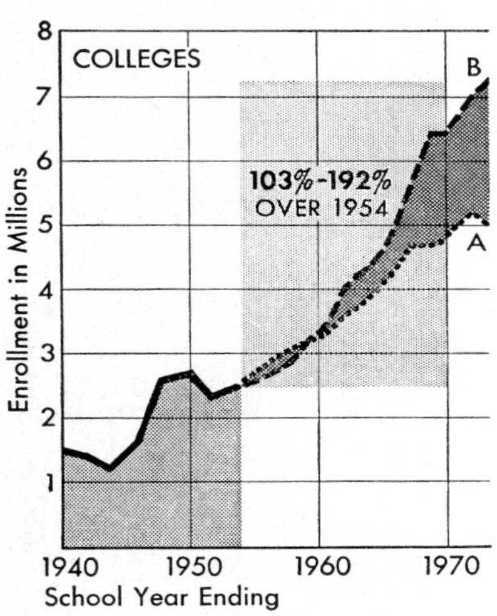

FIG. 4. Past, present, and predicted college enrollments in the United States. (*From* Teachers for Tomorrow, *p. 15. Courtesy of The Fund for the Advancement of Education.*) That source says: "The lower line [A] is based on a recent projection by the U. S. Office of Education, which assumes little rise in the proportion of young people attending college. The top line [B] indicates what will happen if the average trend of the past 15 years continues into the future—that is, if the ratio of college enrollments to the size of the 18–21 age group keeps growing one percentage point each year (from about 30 per cent in 1955 to 48 per cent by 1973)."

PRIVATE INTEREST IN EDUCATION. Private interest in education has always been encouraged in the United States, and a large portion of the educational function of the nation has always been performed by private auspices. Of the approximately 40,000,000 pupils enrolled in all schools and colleges, approximately 5,600,000 are found in private schools and colleges, and of the approximately $9,000,000,000

TABLE 2. AVERAGE AMOUNT OF SCHOOLING, IN YEARS, OF THE PEOPLE OF EACH STATE, ABOVE 25 YEARS OF AGE, 1940*–1950†

	1940		1950	
State	MEDIAN YEARS OF SCHOOLING	RANK OF STATE	MEDIAN YEARS OF SCHOOLING	RANK OF STATE
Dist. of Columbia	10.3	1.00	12.0	1.50
Alabama	7.1	46.33	7.9	45.50
Arizona	8.6	18.33	10.0	15.50
Arkansas	7.5	43.00	8.3	43.00
California	9.9	3.00	11.6	3.00
Colorado	8.9	9.33	10.9	7.33
Connecticut	8.5	21.14	9.8	19.25

State	1940 Median Years of Schooling	1940 Rank of State	1950 Median Years of Schooling	1950 Rank of State
Delaware	8.5	21.14	9.8	19.25
Florida	8.3	31.20	9.6	23.33
Georgia	7.1	46.33	7.8	47.00
Idaho	8.9	9.33	10.6	10.00
Illinois	8.5	21.14	9.3	26.20
Indiana	8.5	21.14	9.6	23.33
Iowa	8.7	14.25	9.8	19.25
Kansas	8.7	14.25	10.2	11.50
Kentucky	7.7	39.33	8.4	40.50
Louisiana	6.6	49.00	7.6	48.50
Maine	8.9	9.33	10.2	11.50
Maryland	8.0	37.00	8.9	34.33
Massachusetts	9.0	8.00	10.9	7.33
Michigan	8.6	18.33	9.9	17.50
Minnesota	8.5	21.14	9.0	33.50
Mississippi	7.1	46.33	8.1	44.00
Missouri	8.3	31.20	8.8	37.00
Montana	8.7	14.25	10.1	13.50
Nebraska	8.8	12.50	10.1	13.50
Nevada	9.6	4.00	11.5	4.00
New Hampshire	8.7	14.25	9.8	19.25
New Jersey	8.4	28.33	9.3	26.20
New Mexico	7.9	37.00	9.3	26.20
New York	8.4	28.33	9.6	23.33
North Carolina	7.4	45.00	7.9	45.50
North Dakota	8.3	31.20	8.7	38.00
Ohio	8.6	18.33	9.9	17.50
Oklahoma	8.4	28.33	9.1	31.00
Oregon	9.1	6.50	10.9	7.33
Pennsylvania	8.2	36.00	9.0	33.50
Rhode Island	8.3	31.20	9.3	26.20
South Carolina	6.7	43.00	7.6	48.50
South Dakota	8.5	21.14	8.9	34.33
Tennessee	7.7	39.33	8.4	41.50
Texas	8.5	21.14	9.3	25.20
Utah	10.2	2.00	12.0	1.50
Vermont	8.8	12.50	10.0	15.50
Virginia	7.7	39.33	8.5	39.50
Washington	9.1	6.50	11.2	5.00
West Virginia	7.8	38.00	8.5	39.50
Wisconsin	8.3	31.20	8.9	34.33
Wyoming	9.2	5.00	11.1	6.00
U. S. Average	8.4		9.3	

* U. S. Department of Commerce, Bureau of The Census, *Statistical Abstract of The United States,* 73rd Edition, p. 114.

† *Ibid.,* 75th Edition, p. 123.

expended by all types of schools and colleges and for all purposes, it is estimated that approximately $850,000,000 is expended by the private schools and colleges.

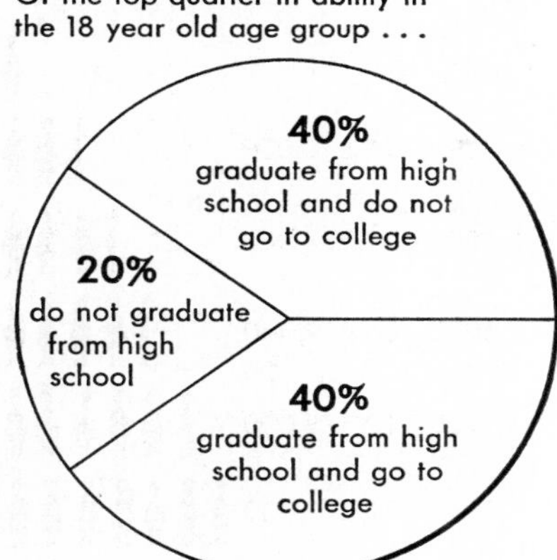

FIG. 5. Something will have to be done to improve the above conditions. *(From* Teachers of Tomorrow, *p. 35. Courtesy of The Fund for the Advancement of Education.)*

Consonant with the policy of encouraging private interest in education—a policy which began in 1636 with John Harvard's gift of approximately £780 and his library of 260 books to Harvard College (University today)—billions of dollars have been given by private individuals to education. As a rule, this money has been given to the private schools and colleges, but during recent years a tendency to make gifts to the public schools and colleges has been observed.[12] At present the public and the private schools and colleges possess endowments amounting to approximately $4,000,000,000, and many millions are being added each year; owing, however, to higher taxes, large profits and big fortunes are gradually decreasing, and gifts to schools are also decreasing in amount.

Perhaps, as has often been said, we have been too much a nation of "dollar chasers," but, if we have possessed too much of that trait, we have also been noted for our philanthropy. No doubt, the philosophy of Andrew Carnegie, the world's greatest endower of libraries, has dominated many of our persons of wealth. Carnegie once said:

[12] For a national survey of gifts to the public schools, see William R. Odell, *Gifts to the Public Schools,* Odell, 1932. Published privately.

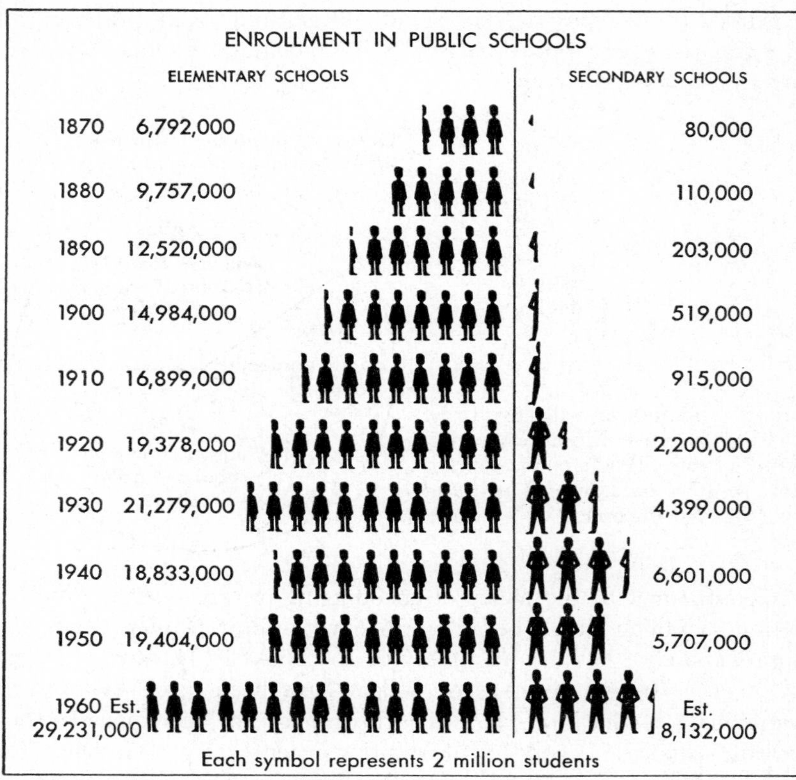

Fig. 6. Actual and estimated enrollment in the public elementary and secondary schools of the United States, each decade, 1870–1960. (The 1960 enrollments are estimated and are based on Table 1.)

This, then, is held to be the duty of the man of wealth; to set an example of modest, unostentatious living, shunning display or extravagance; to provide moderately for the legitimate wants of those dependent upon him; and, after doing so, to consider all surplus revenues which come to him simply as trust funds, which he is called upon to administer in the manner which, in his judgment, is best calculated to provide the most beneficial results for the community.[13]

Private interest in education has also been shown by the creation of dozens of private educational foundations and boards. Many of

[13] *Ibid.*, p. v. By permission of William R. Odell, publisher.

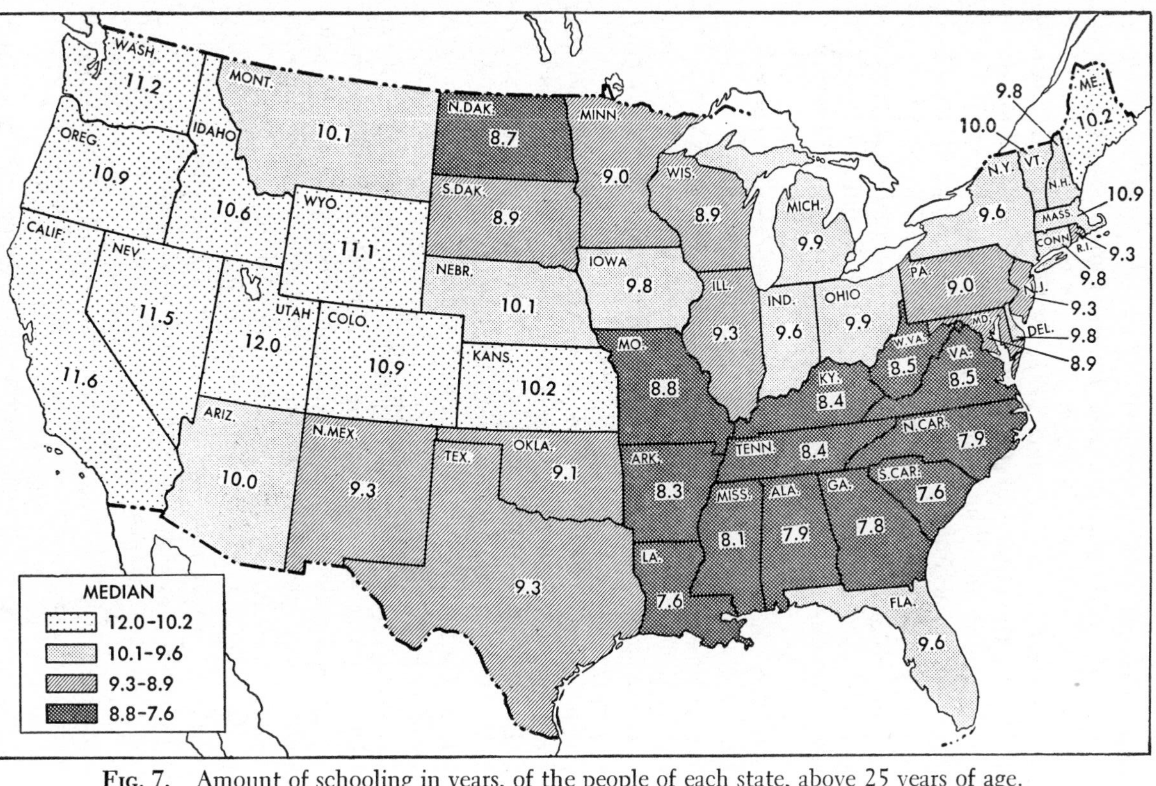

FIG. 7. Amount of schooling in years, of the people of each state, above 25 years of age. (Based on Table 2.)

these agencies have endowments of millions of dollars, and the income from the endowments is used for the stimulation and the improvement of education. Among the larger of those foundations and boards are the following: [14] Anna T. Jeanes Fund, Carnegie Foundation for the Advancement of Teaching, Commonwealth Fund, General Education Board, John F. Slater Fund, Julius Rosenwald Fund, Milbank Memorial Fund, Payne Fund, Phelps-Stokes Fund, Carnegie Corporation, W. K. Kellogg Foundation, Rockefeller Foundation, Ford Foundation, and Russell Sage Foundation. The Ford Foundation, late in 1955, gave several hundred million dollars to colleges; this was the largest sum ever given to higher institutions, up to that date.

As further evidence of private interest in education, there should also be mentioned the church educational boards, the international educational associations and foundations, the National Congress of Parents and Teachers, the American Library Association, the state library associations, and the standardizing and accrediting organizations (Association of American Universities, American Association of Junior Colleges, New England Association of Colleges and Secondary Schools, Middle States Association of Colleges and Secondary Schools, North Central Association of Colleges and Secondary Schools, Western Association of Colleges and Secondary Schools, Southern Association of Colleges and Secondary Schools, American Association of Colleges for Teacher Education, and Northwest Association of Secondary and Higher Schools). In addition to the organizations just mentioned, there are hundreds of local, regional, state, and national educational, civic, and learned societies and associations; among the more important of these are the National Education Association, the American Association of School Administrators, the American Federation of Teachers, the American Psychological Association, the state education associations, and the American Association for the Advancement of Science.[15]

STATEMENTS OF LEADERS ON THE IMPORTANCE OF EDUCATION. That

[14] A complete list of such foundations and boards, together with the names of their officers, may be obtained from the *Educational Directory* which is published annually by the U. S. Office of Education, Washington, D. C.

[15] For a complete list of these hundreds of educational organizations, the interested reader may consult also the annual *Educational Directory* of the U. S. Office of Education, which lists about five hundred national, regional, and state educational organizations.

"an institution is largely the lengthened shadow of an individual" can be observed everywhere. What an industry is, what a school system is, what a government is—in brief, what any institution is—is largely determined by the leaders in thought and action, and especially by the leaders who have administrative responsibility, in those times. Great leaders are not satisfied merely to maintain the *status quo;* they cherish ideals for improving the *status quo,* and they vigorously attempt to reach those ideals. Great leaders have always been known as reformers. A great movement is started by one person.

From the time of the founding of the Republic there has been scarcely a President of the United States or a governor of a state who has failed to make at least one statement on the importance of education. Similar statements have been made by myriad other leaders in our national life. All of these leaders have regarded an educated citizenry as a necessity in a democracy. We shall quote first from a few of the Presidents.[16]

As early as 1787, Thomas Jefferson, who was later (1801–1809) to become our third President, said:

> Above all things, I hope the education of the common people will be attended to, convinced that on this good sense we may rely with the most security for the preservation of a due degree of liberty.

James Madison, our fourth President (1809–1817), had the following to say on the importance of education:

> A satisfactory plan for primary education is certainly a vital desideratum in our republic.
>
> A popular government without popular information or the means of acquiring it is but a prologue to a farce or a tragedy, or perhaps both. Knowledge will forever govern ignorance; and a people who mean to be their own governors must arm themselves with the power which knowledge gives.

Abraham Lincoln, who was our sixteenth President (1861–1865), attended school only a few weeks and probably experienced, as have few other persons, the difficulties and the challenges of climbing up from poverty and ignorance. He was always a warm friend

[16] A more complete collection of such quotations is found in *Expressions on Education by Builders of American Democracy,* U. S. Office of Education, *Bulletin,* 1940, No. 10, pp. 1–90.

of formal education. His earliest, as well as one of his most forceful, pronouncements on education appeared in a letter in the *Sangamon* (Illinois) *Journal*, of March 15, 1832, at which time he was a candidate for the Illinois General Assembly. The letter follows:

To the People of Sangamo(n) County:

Fellow Citizens: Having become a candidate for the honorable office of one of your Representatives in the next General Assembly of this State, in accordance with an established custom and the principles of true republicanism, it becomes my duty to make known to you, the people whom I propose to represent—my sentiments with regard to local affairs. . . .

Upon the subject of education, not presuming to dictate any plan or system respecting it, I can only say that I view it as the most important subject which we as a people can be engaged in. That every man may receive at least a moderate education, and thereby be enabled to read the histories of his own and other countries, by which he may duly appreciate the value of our free institutions, appears to be an object of vital importance, even on this account alone, to say nothing of the advantages and satisfaction to be derived from all being able to read the Scriptures and other works, both of a religious and moral nature, for themselves. For my part, I desire to see the time when education, and by its means, morality, sobriety, enterprise, and industry, shall become much more general than at present, and should be gratified to have it in my power to contribute something to the advancement of any measure which might have a tendency to accelerate the happy period.

A. Lincoln

As Chapters 3 and 6 will show in detail, in this country providing for education has always been a state and territorial function rather than a Federal prerogative. In consequence, the governors of our states and our territories have had a very real responsibility for seeing that provision was made for education. With few exceptions,[17] the governors have been ardent supporters of education. This attitude could be shown by hundreds of quotations from their addresses and their writings, but a few quotations from them will suffice.

DeWitt Clinton, who was for nine years (1817–1823 and 1825–1828) governor of New York, in 1826 made, in a message as governor,

[17] Probably the most famous exception was William Berkeley, who was governor of colonial Virginia from 1641 to 1652 and again from 1660 to 1676. In 1671 Governor Berkeley said, "But I thank God there are no free schools and printing, and I hope we shall not have them these hundred years, for learning has brought disobedience and heresy and sects into this world and printing has divulged them and libels against the best government. God keep us from both."

the following statement in defense of the schools established in that state:

> The first duty of government, and the surest evidence of good government, is the encouragement of education. A general diffusion of knowledge is a precursor and protector of republican institutions, and in it we must confide as the conservative power that will watch over our liberties and guard them against fraud, intrigue, corruption, and violence. I consider the system of our common schools as the palladium of our freedom, for no reasonable apprehension can be entertained of its subversion as long as the great body of the people are enlightened by education.

Although he attended and was always friendly toward church schools, former Governor Alfred E. Smith of New York, who was the candidate of the Democratic Party for President in 1928, was also always friendly toward the public schools. During the very severe business depression of the nineteen-thirties, he said:

> Whatever may be the exigencies, whatever may be the reasons for drastic reductions in appropriations, one thing must not happen. There must be no curtailment of educational facilities. The school systems for the education of our children in every state must be kept up to one hundred per cent efficiency. A state can afford to lose time on the construction of a road, a bridge, or a building and by speeding up construction at a later time possibly catch up, but education must be continuous.

Statements as cogent as those which have just been quoted from Presidents and from governors have been made by thousands of other leaders in the political, economic, educational, social, and religious life of the nation. Space will permit quotations from but a few of those leaders.

In 1835, a proposal was made in the Pennsylvania Legislature to repeal the Free School Law of 1834, and Thaddeus Stevens, then a member of the Legislature, defended that law in the following words:

> If an elective Republic is to endure for any length of time, every elector must have sufficient information not only to accumulate wealth and take care of his pecuniary concerns, but to direct wisely the legislature, the ambassadors, and the Executive of the Nation—for some part of all these things, some agency in approving or disapproving of them, falls to every freeman. If, then, the permanency of our Government depends upon

such knowledge, it is the duty of Government to see that the means of information be diffused to every citizen. This is a sufficient answer to those who deem education a private and not a public duty—who argue that they are willing to educate their own children but not their neighbor's children.

In an address delivered at Madison, Indiana, in 1837, Daniel Webster, eminent statesman and lawyer, said:

> Education, to accomplish the ends of good government, should be universally diffused. Open the doors of the schoolhouses to all the children in the land. Let no man have the excuse of poverty for not educating his offspring. Place the means of education within his reach, and if he remain in ignorance, be it his own reproach. . . . On the diffusion of education among the people rests the preservation and perpetuation of our free institutions.

Thousands of articles and editorials on the importance of education have been published in the newspapers and the magazines. Because of the almost universal interest in it, education has always been one of the most popular subjects to editorialize upon. Those articles and editorials have appeared, especially during crises, such as wars and serious business depressions. Although practically all of those literary contributions have praised the efficiency with which the schools were being managed and have "preached" the importance of education, some of them have been adversely critical of the purposes, the procedures, the cost, and the accomplishments of the schools. Many of them have been responsible for improvements in the schools.

STATEMENTS OF ORGANIZATIONS ON THE IMPORTANCE OF EDUCATION. Certain organizations have always been known as warm supporters of education. This, of course, has always been true of organizations of school officials and school employees. It has usually been true also of labor organizations. During recent years, it has become increasingly true of dozens of other organizations such as the American Legion, the National Association of Manufacturers, the General Federation of Women's Clubs, the National League of Women Voters, the National Congress of Parents and Teachers, and the service clubs such as Rotary and Kiwanis. At countless times and in innumerable ways those organizations have affirmed their faith in the importance of education, and they have done much to implement that faith.

Statements of Law on the Importance of Education. The laws of a state or of a nation, especially of a democracy, such as ours, evince the crystallization of the sentiments of the people on public issues and public problems. Attention has already been called to the fact that laws on education came almost immediately after the first settlements were made. As early as 1642 and 1647, Massachusetts colony enacted statutes requiring certain educational standards of every child and of every community. Since those dates, every state has enacted hundreds of statutes calculated to obtain progressively higher educational standards. Those statutes may be regarded as evidence of the early and ever-growing faith of the people in education.

By the close of the eighteenth century the sentiment for education had become so widespread that the states and the territories began to make pronouncements on the importance, the scope, and the financing of education in their fundamental laws, that is, their constitutions. The people were impelled to write their sentiments on education into their state constitutions, because they could then be more certain that the sentiments would not be forgotten or violated by ephemeral legislatures. North Carolina and Pennsylvania made such pronouncements in 1776; Vermont and Georgia, in 1777; and Massachusetts, in 1780. Of those pronouncements that of the Massachusetts Constitution was unquestionably the strongest; it directed "the legislatures and magistrates to encourage education in all types of schools, including the university at Cambridge" (Harvard). The complete pronouncement of Massachusetts is quoted herewith:

> Wisdom and knowledge, as well as virtue, diffused generally among the body of the people, being necessary for the preservation of their rights and liberties; and as these depend on spreading the opportunities and advantages of education in the various parts of the country, and among the different orders of the people, it shall be the duty of the legislatures and magistrates, in all future periods of this Commonwealth, to cherish the interest of literature and the sciences, and all seminaries of them; especially the university at Cambridge, public schools, and grammar schools in the towns; to encourage private societies and public institutions, by rewards and immunities, for the promotion of agriculture, arts, sciences, commerce, trades, manufactures, and a natural history of the country; to countenance and inculcate the principles of humanity and frugality, benevolence, public and private charity, industry and

frugality, honesty and punctuality in their dealings; sincerity, good humor, and all social affections and generous sentiments among the people.

The Massachusetts pronouncement was soon imitated by other states when they came to frame new constitutions or to amend their old ones. For example, the similarity between the treatment of education in the Ordinance of 1787[18] and the Massachusetts pronouncement of 1780 lends credence to the theory of imitation. In providing for the government of the territory lying north of the Ohio River, that is, the Northwest Territory, Congress affirmed that "Religion, morality, and knowledge being necessary to good government and the happiness of mankind, schools and the means of education shall be forever encouraged" in the states to be formed from that territory.

After the opening of the nineteenth century, pronouncements on education came to be rapidly written into the state and the territorial constitutions, and by the middle of that century they were universal. Moreover, the tendency has been to make those pronouncements stronger as new constitutions have been adopted or old ones amended. The present constitutions almost always affirm the importance of education, and they require the legislatures to make provision for the establishment and the financial support of a system of public schools extending from the elementary school through the university. The pronouncements of the Ohio Constitution may be regarded as typical and are quoted herewith:

ARTICLE I, SECTION 7. . . . Religion, morality, and knowledge, however, being essential to good government, it shall be the duty of the general assembly to pass suitable laws to protect every religious denomination in the peaceable enjoyment of its mode of public worship, and to encourage schools and the means of instruction.

ARTICLE VI, SECTION 1. The principal of all funds, arising from the sale, or other disposition of lands, or other property, granted or entrusted to this state for educational or religious purposes shall forever be preserved inviolate, and undiminished; and, the income arising therefrom, shall be faithfully applied to the specific objects of the original grants, or appropriations.

[18] This was the ordinance for the government of the Northwest Territory, including today the states of Illinois, Indiana, Ohio, Michigan, Wisconsin, and that part of Minnesota which is east of the Mississippi River.

ARTICLE VI, SECTION 2. The general assembly shall make such provisions, by taxation, or otherwise, as, with the income arising from the school trust fund, will secure a thorough and efficient system of common schools throughout the state; but no religious or other sect, or sects, shall ever have any exclusive right to, or control of, any part of the school funds of this state.

In the last analysis, the higher courts make the laws. As former Chief Justice Hughes of the United States Supreme Court once said, "our courts are super legislatures." Legislative bodies enact statutes, but the courts interpret those statutes and have the power to declare any statute to be unconstitutional. In hundreds of decisions the courts have affirmed the importance of education; moreover, they have usually given a liberal interpretation to the statutes as they affect the powers and the duties of school officials. As a rule, school officials have been permitted by the courts to take any steps for the improvement of education, which, of course, the statutes or the constitution of the state did not specifically prohibit.

One of the most famous of the court decisions is that of the Supreme Court of Michigan on the so-called *Kalamazoo Case*. That decision was so trenchant and on such a fundamental aspect of education that it has influenced subsequent court decisions and the development of education down to the present time. Briefly, the decision affirmed that a board of education and the people were not limited in their determination of what the scope of education should be. The case developed from a decision in 1872 of the board of education of the city of Kalamazoo to establish a high school and to employ a superintendent of schools. A citizen by the name of Stuart had brought suit to prevent the collection of taxes for the purposes mentioned, because he claimed that the power of the board to establish "common schools" did not include the power to establish high schools. The case was carried to the Supreme Court of the state, and Chief Justice Thomas M. Cooley wrote in 1874 the decision of the court. The concluding paragraphs of the decision were as follows:

If these facts do not demonstrate clearly and conclusively a general state policy, beginning in 1817 and continuing until after the adoption of the present state constitution, in the direction of free schools in which education, and at their option the elements of classical education, might be brought within the reach of all the children of the State, then, as it seems to us, nothing can demonstrate it. We might follow the subject further and show that the subsequent legislation has all concurred with this policy, but it would be a waste of time and labor. We content ourselves with the statement that neither in our state policy, in our constitution, nor in our laws, do we find the primary school districts restricted in the branches of knowledge which their officers may cause to be taught, or the grade of instruction that may be given, if their voters consent in regular form to bear the expense and raise the taxes for the purpose.

Having reached this conclusion, we shall spend no time upon the objection that the district in question had no authority to appoint a superintendent of schools, and that the duties of the superintendency should be performed by the district board. We think the power to make the appointment was incident to the full control which by law the board and the people of the district have been wisely left by the legislature to follow their own judgment in the premises.[19]

As has already been stated, there have been hundreds of court pronouncements on the importance of education. The following, from the Supreme Court of Tennessee, may be regarded as typical:

We are of the opinion that the legislature, under the constitutional provision, may as well establish a uniform system of schools and a uniform administration of them, as it may establish a uniform system of criminal laws and of courts to execute them. The object of the criminal law is, by punishment, to deter others from the commission of crimes, and thus preserve the peace, morals, good order, and well-being of society; and the object of the public-school system is to prevent crime by educating the people, and thus, by providing and securing a higher state of intelligence and morals, conserve the peace, good order, and well-being of society. The prevention of crime, and preservation of good order and peace, is the highest exercise of the police power of the state, whether done by punishing offenders or educating the children.

Probably the most famous court decision on education was that of the United States Supreme Court on May 17, 1954, which declared racial segregation in the public schools to be unconstitutional. The Southern states and the "border" states had, by their state constitutions, required racial segregation for many years, and it is understandable that they were not pleased with that decision of the U. S. Supreme Court. At this date (February 1, 1957), the decision has been accepted by only a few hundred boards of education in the

[19] Charles E. Stuart, *et al. vs.* School District No. 1 of the Village of Kalamazoo, 30 Michigan, p. 69.

South. When Chief Justice Warren announced the decision, he said that the court realized the decree presented problems "of considerable complexity." Many of those "problems" still remain, and will probably remain for many years, but in time desegregation in the public schools will be everywhere practiced. Desegregation is making rapid progress in the public schools; but, more tolerance is needed over the issue.

Battles Over the Schools

A List of the Battles. The preceding discussion has essayed to give evidences of the early and continuing faith in education of the people of the United States. Although that faith has always triumphed, it has had to undergo many major battles and much guerrilla warfare. As in all social movements, it has often had to combat conservatism, radicalism, penuriousness, selfishness, and similar opposition. Many of its forward-looking beliefs, which later came to be universally adopted, were held in the beginning by only a small minority—often by only "a minority of one." The major battles which have been, or are being, fought over the support, the control, and the extension of the schools may be described as follows:

1. The battle for compulsory education, compulsory schools, and compulsory school attendance. (This three-part battle has been fought and largely won; however, there is still much controversy, especially in a few states, over the extension of compulsory school attendance.)
2. The battle for tax support of schools and for schools that were entirely free. (This battle has been won, although there is still much controversy over the amount of tax support which should be given and over the type of tax to be used.)
3. The battle for state control and state supervision of the schools. (The principle of state control and state supervision has been generally accepted, but there is still much controversy over the amount and the type of control and supervision which the state should exercise.)
4. The battle to eliminate sectarianism. (The teaching of sectarianism in the public schools and the use of public funds for the support of private and sectarian schools are everywhere prohibited by state constitutions; however, a few states have recently made provisions for free textbooks, free health service, and free transportation for pupils in private and sectarian schools. Such aid is given to the "pupils, not to the schools.")
5. The battle to extend the school system, and especially to make it include secondary schools, colleges, and universities. (This battle has

been generally won, although many school districts have not yet made provision for secondary school advantages; moreover, provisions for junior colleges are still meager in most states.)

6. The battle for a reasonable amount of state aid for the elementary and the secondary schools. (This is probably the major battle of today; it has been won in most of the states, but is still being fought in a few of the states.)
7. The battle for Federal financial aid of elementary and secondary schools. (This battle has been in progress for several decades, but as yet no regular Federal subsidies are given for elementary and secondary schools.)
8. The battle for a program of vocational education. (Since 1917, the Federal Government has subsidized vocational departments in the public schools; vocational education should, however, be much further developed.)
9. The battle to eliminate racial segregation. (This battle is not known yet to have been definitely won, in spite of the recent decision of the U. S. Supreme Court, which banned racial segregation in the public schools. There is still much skirmishing over this issue, especially in the Southern states, and there is still much inequality in educational opportunities for the Negroes and the whites, especially in some communities and in some states.)

Argumentative Weapons Used. The late Professor Ellwood P. Cubberley has given an interesting description of the battle for public tax-supported schools. He has listed the opposing forces in the battle, the sectors on which the battle was fought, and the arguments which the opposing forces employed.[20] Because of their historical interest, and especially because many of the arguments are still being used, we are reproducing them herewith:

I. *Arguments for public tax-supported schools:*
   1. That education tends to prevent pauperism and crime.
   2. That education tends to reduce poverty and distress.
   3. That education increases production, and eliminates wrong ideas as to the distribution of wealth.
   4. That a common state school, equally open to all, would prevent that class differentiation so dangerous in a Republic.
   5. That the old church and private school education had proved utterly inadequate to meet the needs of a changed society.
   6. That a system of religious schools is impossible in such a mixed nation as our own.

[20] For this description, see Ellwood P. Cubberley, *Public Education in the United States,* Revised edition, Houghton Mifflin Company, 1934, Chs. 5, 6, and 7.

7. That the pauper-school idea is against the best interests of society, inimical to public welfare, and a constant offense to the poor, many of whom will not send their children because of the stigma attached to such schools.
8. That education as to one's civic duties is a necessity for the intelligent exercise of suffrage, and for the preservation of republican institutions.
9. That the increase of foreign immigration (which became quite noticeable after 1825, and attained large proportions after 1845) is a menace to our free institutions, and that these new elements can be best assimilated in a system of publicly supported and publicly directed common schools.
10. That the free and general education of all children at public expense is the natural right of all children of the Republic.
11. That the social, moral, political, and industrial benefits to be derived from the general education of all compensate many times over for its cost.
12. That a state which has the right to hang has the right to educate.
13. That the taking over of education by the state is not based on considerations of economy, but is the exercise of the state's inherent right to self-preservation and improvement.
14. That only a system of state-controlled schools can be free to teach whatever the welfare of the state may demand.

II. *Arguments against public tax-supported schools:*

1. Impractical, visionary, and "too advanced" legislation.
2. Will make education too common, and will educate people out of their proper position in society.
3. Would not benefit the masses, who are already as well cared for as they deserve.
4. Would tend to break down long-established and very desirable social barriers.
5. Would injure private and parochial schools in which much money has been put and "vested rights" established.
6. Fear of the churches that state schools might injure their church progress and welfare.
7. Fear of the non-English speaking classes that state schools might supplant instruction in their languages.
8. The "conscientious objector" claimed that the state had no right to interfere between a parent and his child in the matter of education.
9. That those having no children to be educated should not be taxed for schools.
10. That taking a man's property to educate his neighbor's child is no more defensible than taking a man's plow to plow his neighbor's field.

11. That the state may be justified in taxing to defend the liberties of the people, but not to support their benevolences.
12. That the industrious would be taxed to educate the indolent.
13. That taxes would be so increased that no state could long meet such a lavish drain on its resources.
14. That there was priestcraft in the scheme, the purpose being first to establish a state school, and then a state church.[21]

Contrasts with Other Countries

The faith in education of the American people has been responsible for their developing probably the best school systems in the world. In no other country is so large a percentage of the population enrolled in school, and in no other country are the educational offerings equal to ours. Although it has been rapidly increasing, the faith in education in no foreign country is yet nearly as strong as in this country. Among the explanations for America's greater faith in education compared with foreign countries are the following:

1. Our early settlers were better educated than the average person of those times, and it was only natural for them to desire excellent educational advantages for their children.
2. Our form of government has always been democratic as contrasted with monarchial and totalitarian forms of government found in many foreign countries. In a democracy the people are sovereign, hence education is more necessary in a democracy.
3. Our people have been blessed with an abundance of natural resources and have fared well in an economic way, and this has made possible the financing of a rapidly expanding school program.

American Schools Truly Public. Whereas the schools of most foreign countries are caste schools, the schools of the United States are truly public and are for all classes—rich and poor alike. In the United States any boy or any girl who has completed the secondary school, then may enter and complete the college, and finally may enter and pursue graduate work in the university; what is of even greater moment, any boy or any girl may have those advantages, without any expenditure for tuition, except the amount in the college and university. Our educational opportunity, which is provided for every boy and every girl alike, has been described as "the educational ladder"; any boy or any girl who has the intellectual ability

[21] *Ibid.*, pp. 165–166. By permission of Houghton Mifflin Company, publishers.

may step on its first rung and climb to the top. Of course, some of our states, mainly because of their larger wealth, provide greater equality of educational opportunity than other states.

In the schools of most foreign countries, on the contrary, there are two systems of schools, and they differ widely in purpose and in scope. One school system is for the common people, and the other is for the aristocracy. In brief, whereas America has only one "educa-

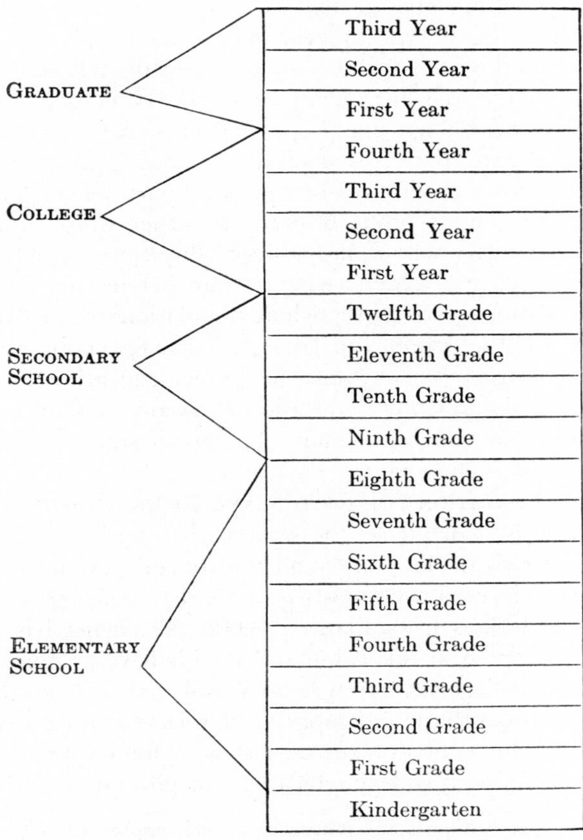

FIG. 8. The "educational ladder" in the schools of the United States. (As Chapter 4 will show, certain changes in the divisions of this ladder are in the process of making.)

tional ladder," most foreign countries have two "educational ladders." One of these two ladders is short and is available only to the common people; the other is longer and more expensively constructed and can be used only by the aristocracy.

American Secondary and Higher Education Free. Whereas in foreign countries only elementary school education is free, in this country all levels of education—elementary, secondary, and higher—are free.[22] The United States has the only secondary schools and the only colleges and universities that are chiefly free. The theory which guides our practice of making secondary school and college education free is that the welfare and the progress of the nation can be best assured by raising the educational level of the whole population. The theory underlying foreign practice is that to make secondary school and college education free is wasteful, because under such a plan many persons avail themselves of free secondary school and college education who cannot profit from it. In other words, the foreign systems of secondary school and college education are calculated to select and to prepare leaders, whereas our systems are designed to raise the educational level of the whole population, in the expectation that leaders for the people will emerge. To make more certain that poor boys of large promise reach the proper educational level—and secondary school and college education is usually available in foreign countries only to the boys—many foreign countries now provide scholarships for such boys.

American Education for Both Sexes. In the United States, college education is available on the same basis to girls as to boys. The enrollment of girls in the public and private colleges and universities of the United States now amounts to more than 936,000, whereas the enrollment of boys is more than 1,784,000. The belief has gradually come to be accepted in this country that girls have as much right to and need for a college education as boys, and that through the education of both, the welfare and progress of society can be made more certain. All of this is in strange contrast with foreign practice which usually frowns upon a college education for girls. It should be men-

[22] Of course, free textbooks and other educational supplies are not always provided, and some tuition is usually required in the colleges and universities. Moreover, students differ greatly in their ability to furnish their living expenses and many other necessary expenses. In the secondary schools and the colleges, students often have several private expenses, such as "activity fees," class dues, gym suits, costumes for their class plays, and musical instruments.

tioned, though, that during recent years more and more foreign countries have increased the opportunities of girls for college education.

9. A foreign language shall *not* be the vehicle of instruction in the schools.

8. Sectarian instruction shall *not* be permitted in the public schools.

7. All children shall attend school until a certain age is reached.

6. Equal educational opportunities shall be provided for both sexes, all races, and all colors.

5. Public schools shall be free.

4. Private as well as public schools shall be required to meet state standards.

3. Private schools shall be permitted and encouraged, but they shall *not* be supported by public funds.

2. Public schools shall be established and supported through universal taxation.

1. *The basic principle:* Efficient democracy requires an educated citizenry.

FIG. 9. The fundamental principles of the school systems of the United States. All of these principles have been crystallized into the laws of every, or practically every, state.

In Retrospect and in Prospect

In Retrospect. In this chapter the historic faith in education of the American people has been noted, and the unfolding of that faith in the phenomenal growth of the school systems has been glimpsed. In every sense the story of this growth constitutes one of the wonder stories of American history; in fact, it constitutes one of the wonder stories of all times and of all lands, because no other country has ever attempted to provide universal education to the extent which the states of the United States are providing it.

From small beginnings, formal education, as provided by the schools, has developed until it has become one of the nation's largest enterprises, public or private. It represents a capital investment in school plant of approximately $20,000,000,000, and only six industries—manufacturing, agriculture, railroads, oil, electricity, and lumber—have larger capital investments. It is managed by more than a million teachers and tens of thousands of other employees, such as school administrators, supervisors, attendance employees, nurses, librarians, janitors, and bus drivers. In only seven occupations—agriculture, construction, manufacturing, transportation, trade and distribution, service industries, and textiles—are more persons employed. But greater than all these facts is the fact that approximately 40,000,000 pupils are enrolled in all public and private schools and colleges. In brief, almost one-fourth of the American people now spend, each school day, five or six hours in school, either as pupils or as employees. Millions of adults also attend school on one or more evenings each week.

The rapid growth of the schools could hardly have happened, without many "growing pains"; it could scarcely have taken place, without many errors and inefficiencies. In extenuation of those shortcomings it should be remembered that school officials have been compelled to work with lightninglike speed to provide a school plant, school employees, and other services and facilities which would serve the increasing hordes of pupils. School officials have faced a practical situation—"a condition, not a theory." Although they have failed to do many things and have made many mistakes, the really surprising phenomenon is that they have been able to accomplish as much as they have. School officials are more deserving of praise than of condemnation.

FIG. 10. A balance between better schools and a better world. (*Courtesy of* Better Schools.)

What have the schools accomplished to justify the faith of the people in them? To what extent have they contributed to the realization of the fundamental ideal of the people, namely, the improvement of the individual and of social well-being? That question is always pertinent, but it is difficult to answer, because of the impossibility of separating the influence of the school from the influence of other educational forces such as the home, the church, the theater, the radio, the television, the newspaper, the library, and social and other contacts. Certain it is that much progress has been made in improving individual and social well-being, and it is reasonable to infer that the schools have been a vital force in stimulating that progress. That progress can be discerned, even through the clouds of economic stress, of internal turmoil, and of international conflict. These clouds would probably be much more black, without the excellent work which the schools have done. The clouds can only be banished through better work of the schools and of the other agencies of education. Some of the changes which the schools have helped to bring in American life are the following:

1. Since 1900, the death rate per inhabitant has decreased approximately one-half, and life expectancy has increased approximately one-half. The death rate is now less than 10 per 1,000 inhabitants.
2. Illiteracy is now only one-third as frequent as it was in 1900. (Although large progress has been made in the elimination of illiteracy and in increasing the amount of education, the 1950 United States Census reports that of each one hundred persons twenty-five years old and over in the United States, three have had no formal schooling. Illiteracy is today confined to the older portion of the population.)
3. Our total national wealth has increased several fold since 1900. It is higher, of course, in good times. Our national income has increased even more than our wealth.
4. The per inhabitant circulation of library books has increased several fold since 1900.
5. The average worker now produces and consumes much more than his parents and his grandparents. Moreover, his standard of living is much higher, and he has much more time for leisure. Education has enabled him to produce machines which now do most of his work.

In Prospect. As we survey the past and peer into the future, no evidence is seen that the historic faith of the American people in education is likely to diminish. On the contrary, there is abundant evidence that education will continue to be regarded as the bulwark of an efficient democracy, as the best guarantee of a progressing society, and as an open-sesame to the individual for the realization of his potentialities. The people will probably continue to demand better, more free, and more equal schools and to increase, if necessary, their financial support for such schools. Before increasing their financial support, however, the people will increasingly exhibit a "show me" attitude, especially because of the increasingly higher taxes for old-age pensions, relief, past wars, defense, and other functions of government; paying for World War I and World War II will place a large strain upon the public purse for many years and make funds for all other public purposes more difficult to obtain. Better schools will have to be fought for in the future as in the past. Better schools will be needed to help meet the problems caused by the tragedies of World War II and the Korean War.

To meet the demand for better schools should be easier, in certain regards, in the future than it has been, because, as has been previously noted, the tide of day-school enrollment will probably level off over the long term. That will not happen for several years, though, because the great number of children born following World War II, and the Korean War, must be educated. The period of rapid expansion in school plant, in school employees, and in other school facilities will sometime run its course. School officials and school employees will then be able to spend more time on improving the quality of education than they have in the past; they can then be more concerned with offering the best education rather than with merely caring for the ever-increasing hordes of pupils; they can emphasize "quality production" rather than "quantity output." They can then become more interested in the improvement of school aims, of subject matter, and of teaching methods; they can then have more time to study the needs of each pupil and of the community; they can become more concerned with the selection of better-qualified teachers and of other school employees and with providing a better school plant; they can then develop the adult-education program of the school. In brief, they can then become engrossed with the task of improving every feature of the school. That is their obligation as well as their opportunity. If that obligation is fully met, our nation will be transformed, and for the first time in history a nation will be thoroughly civilized and be able not only to meet its own problems, but to help other nations meet theirs. That is the challenge of education today and in the future.

QUESTIONS FOR DISCUSSION

1. Is education more necessary today than formerly? Why or why not?

2. Is education more necessary in a democratic form of government than in a totalitarian form? Why or why not?

3. Do you believe that America's faith in education has been built too much on an economic and on a materialistic basis rather than on a social basis? Why or why not? Are the public schools supported primarily to advance the interests of the individual or of those of society? Explain.

4. What effect has the tendency to decrease the length of the working day had on the people's faith in education and on the type of education to be provided? Discuss also the effect of other social and economic changes upon education.

5. Do persons who have attended private schools have as much faith in public education as they should have? Discuss. What attitude should the state take toward private schools? Should such schools be abolished, should they be permitted to exist, provided they meet certain state standards, or should they be permitted to operate without any state regulations? Why or why not?

6. Account for certain communities and certain states having less faith in education than other communities and other states.

7. How do you explain the fact that labor organizations have always been warm supporters of public schools? What groups and organizations are lukewarm toward public schools? Account for the lukewarmness. By what means, if any, could that lukewarmness be changed?

8. Do you discern any evidence that the American people are drifting away from their historic faith in free, public schools? Discuss.

9. Should compulsory school-attendance laws be made more rigid than they are today? Why or why not? What would be the effect on unemployment and economic conditions of raising the upper limits of the compulsory school-attendance laws? Should those limits be raised? Why or why not?

10. What is the outlook for further increases in school enrollment in the elementary school, in the secondary school, and in the college and university? Do you predict that adult evening classes will continue their rapid development? Why?

11. What advantages, if any, are there in comparing our schools with those of foreign countries? When our practices are different from those of most of the other countries, does that prove that our practices are wrong? Explain. Discuss pro and con our policy and the policy of foreign countries with reference to (a) caste schools versus truly public schools, (b) making secondary and college education free, and (c) providing college education for girls as well as for boys.

12. Do you anticipate that our schools and those of foreign countries will become more similar or more dissimilar? In what ways? Why?

13. Does education accomplish the following things: decrease crime,

obtain more competent public officials, raise the standard of living of the people, make the people more productive in economics and in art, and make the people more happy? Why or why not?

SELECTED REFERENCES

NOTE: *Since this book aims to present not only facts but conflicting points of view, all of the lists of Selected References have been selected with that fundamental aim in mind. The annotation, or brief description, which follows each reference, indicates the general content of the reference and the point of view from which the reference is written. The attempt has been made to select the best recent references on each topic, but no attempt has been made to give a* complete *bibliography on any topic. All colleges have libraries, and those libraries have catalogues.*

Carlile, Amos B., "One Hundred Years of Compulsory School-Attendance Laws in Massachusetts," *Educational Administration and Supervision*, Vol. 40 (January, 1954), pp. 1–10.

A brief tracing of the school-attendance laws in the state that pioneered in this area.

Cubberley, Ellwood P., *Public Education in the United States*, Revised edition, Houghton Mifflin Co., Boston, 1934, pp. 120–287.

Discusses the battle to establish, to control, and to extend the school system.

Dewey, John, *Democracy and Education*, The Macmillan Co., New York, 1916, pp. 1–27.

These pages discuss education as a necessity of life and as a social function.

Farley, Belmont, "Meeting the Attacks on Education," *Bulletin of the National Association of Secondary-School Principals*, Vol. 36 (April, 1952), pp. 334–344.

Meets several recent attacks on the schools.

Ginzberg, Eli., and Bray, Douglas W., *The Uneducated*, Columbia University Press, New York, 1953, 200 pp.

Shows the amount of uneducated in this country.

Good, H. G., A *History of American Education*, The Macmillan Co., New York, 1956, 570 pp.

Describes important and recent educational movements in America.

Hechinger, Fred M., *An Adventure in Education*, The Macmillan Co., New York, 1956, 266 pp.

The report of a special Fact-Finding Commission on Education in Connecticut; of interest to other states as well.

Higher Education for American Democracy, Harper and Bros., New York, 1948, 430 pp.

This is the report of President Truman's commission on college education. Recognizes college education as a basic part of democratic education.

Hook, Sidney, "Modern Education and Its Critics," *Seventh Yearbook of the American Association of Colleges for Teacher Education*, 1954, pp. 139–160.

Meets the challenge of the school critics.

Lynd, Albert, *Quackery in the Public Schools*, Little, Brown and Co., Boston, 1953, 282 pp.

States prejudices about the public schools.

Mass Media and Education, Fifty-Third Yearbook of the National Society for the Study of Education, University of Chicago Press, 1954, 290 pp.

A nation-wide study.

McGrath, Earl J., "American Education in Crisis," *School and Society*, Vol. 81 (January 22, 1955), pp. 17–22.

The article presents some of the problems facing education today. Such topics as shortage of teachers and increased school enrollment are discussed at the national level.

Morgan, Joy Elmer, *The School That Built a Nation*, The University of Pittsburgh Press, Pittsburgh, 1954, 104 pp.

An exposition of the public school as the foundation of the American democratic society; a biography of Horace Mann.

Punke, Harold H., "How Free *Is* Free Education?" *School Executive*, Vol. 74 (September, 1954), pp. 58–60.

A study concerning the cost of sending a student through the secondary school. This study was limited to instructional expense and it was found that education in the secondary school is not free but costly in many schools.

Teachers for Tomorrow, The Fund for the Advancement of Education, New York, 1955, 72 pp.

Presents data on the increasing enrollments in the public schools.

Thayer, Vivian T., *Public Education and Its Critics*, The Macmillan Co., New York, 1954, 170 pp.

Answers attacks of the critics of the public schools.

Whitman, Howard, "Speak Out, Silent People," *Colliers*, Vol. 133 (February 5, 1954), pp. 23–25.

Discusses some of the criticisms of the conduct of the schools.

CHAPTER 2

The Philosophy and Aims of the American Democracy's Schools[1]

America's Philosophy of Education

Although it was not thus labeled, the preceding chapter on "America's Historic Faith in Education" was essentially a discussion of America's philosophy of education or of what the American philosophy of life meant for education. The heart of that philosophy was seen to be an abiding faith in education—a faith that education, especially of the right kind, is necessary for the realization of the potentialities of the individual and for the stability and the progress of society. Posited upon and as evidences of that faith were seen to be several universal, and many other almost universal, educational practices. The most worthy and frequently found of these practices is that of providing at public expense a good education from the kindergarten through the university for everyone who is capable and desirous of receiving it.

America unquestionably has a philosophy of education, which is usually called the "democratic philosophy of education." There are, however, as we shall see later, innumerable ways of interpreting what the democratic philosophy is. America's philosophy of education does not have the "oneness" possessed by that of most foreign countries,

[1] Many college instructors, especially of first-year students, have reported to the author that they prefer to have their students read this chapter in connection with Part Six of the book rather than here.

even when the countries profess to follow the democratic philosophy the same as America. This difference in philosophy of education is accounted for by the difference in the relation of the school system to general government. In practically all foreign countries there is a national school system, and there is only one recognized philosophy of education, that formulated by the government functionaries in charge of the educational program. In the United States, on the contrary, education has always been a function of the states and the territories rather than a function of the Federal Government. Since each state and each territory is autonomous in education, and since each has delegated to the separate school districts within it a large amount of freedom in determining the kind of school program, much experimentation with various brands of the democratic philosophy has been conducted among the different school districts.

Since the nature and the importance of educational philosophy do not seem to be sufficiently realized by most teachers and by the general public, it will be the purpose of this chapter to direct attention to those matters and especially to the heart of a philosophy of education, namely, the fundamental aims of education. The chapter will first defend the thesis that a prime requisite for every teacher is a good philosophy. Before defending this thesis, though, it seems desirable to define and to discuss a few educational terms and issues. What is the nature of philosophy? Is philosophy, as many persons apparently believe, something of interest to only a few "long-haired" pedants? Is it a mysterious something beyond the ken of ordinary mortals? Does it have any practical value? Will it beget better schools?

The Nature and the Importance of Philosophy

The Nature of Philosophy. Philosophy, at least in a rudimentary form, is one of the oldest as well as one of the most universal activities of man. It originated as soon as man started to reflect about his status to the end that he might gain greater security and more happiness. Of course, man took this action early in his evolution; he took it as soon as he started to think and to plan his actions. Adam, the first man mentioned in the Bible, took it, and we may therefore call him the world's first philosopher, and by the same token Eve, the first woman, was the world's second philosopher.

Adam and Eve possessed a philosophy, although it was very fragmentary and elementary, and was soon adjudged by the angels to be askew and unholy.

There have always been various views of the purpose, the content, and the method of philosophy. There have always been innumerable and conflicting philosophies. Just as Adam's philosophy was in conflict with that of Eve, at least until Eve won the conflict, so at all succeeding periods of history, there have been conflicting philosophies—conflicting in purpose, in content, and in method. Those conflicting philosophies have often caused schisms in society; they have been responsible for religious crusades; they have led to wars, as witness World War II, and they could lead to World War III and to even later wars. William H. Burton has given the following thumbnail sketch of the evolution of those various views of philosophy from the earliest times to the present:

> *Purposes:* (a) To discover knowledge; (b) to discover the essential nature of things; (c) to discover and present an explanation of the universe in terms of one or more unifying principles; (d) to present a guide to conduct; (e) to solve problems of immediate import in terms of facts and values; (f) to evaluate and interpret the assumptions and findings of science.
>
> *Content:* (a) Speculative knowledge about things, men, and the universe; (b) a system of *a priori* principles explaining the universe; (c) a system of *a priori* principles supplying ethical guides; (d) a system of values, dealing with goodness, truth, and beauty; (e) a system of empirically derived principles explaining the universe, or offering a guide to conduct.
>
> *Methods:* (a) Speculation, intuition, imagination; (b) formal logic based on *a priori* principles; (c) reflective thought in best modern sense of problem-solving and functional logic.[2]

What are the views of the nature of philosophy today? We shall distinguish between and briefly discuss two common views, although there are many others. One fairly large group of present-day philosophers regards philosophy as having essentially the same function, content, and method as metaphysics. That view was held, for example, by the late Professor J. E. Leighton who said, "Every special

[2] William H. Burton, *Introduction to Education*, D. Appleton-Century, 1934, p. 157. By permission of D. Appleton-Century Company, publishers.

science, and special form of practical activity interprets the facts of experience from some limited and one-sided or abstract point of view. Metaphysics aims to correct these abstractions." [3] He said further, "Inasmuch as the special sciences, such as physics, biology, psychology, and sociology, set out from unexamined dogmatic assumptions and issue, severally, in various unco-ordinate results which require synthesis, in order to yield a consistent world view, to metaphysics belongs the two-fold task of critically examining the primary assumptions of the sciences and of synthesizing their conclusions into a harmonious whole." [4]

In other words, according to the view just stated, the purpose of philosophy is to conceive a systematic view of all things. According to that view, philosophy may be defined as the "science which synthesizes all sciences." It assumes, as Ralph Waldo Emerson said, that the philosopher "takes up into himself all arts, sciences, all knowables, as his food," and assimilates them through the process known as thinking. That view of the purpose, the content, and the method of philosophy has been summarized in an interesting and in a clear manner by B. A. G. Fuller:

> To put it all in terms of the detective agency, the sciences are like the individual detectives following up and reporting upon that particular aspect of the case to which each has been assigned, whereas philosophy is like the chief who gathers all their reports together, reflects upon them, tries to harmonize them where they conflict, and to supplement them by reasonable conjecture where they fail to connect or are unable to follow the clue further into the unknown. Thus it constructs, using their reports as its data, a theory regarding the true inwardness of the case which seems to it to throw some light, at least upon the central mystery.[5]

During recent years, however, the concept that philosophy is "a systematic view of all things" or "a theory of ultimate and absolute reality" has suffered an eclipse, and the more realistic and practical concept that philosophy is a "system of values" has largely supplanted it. The former concept has suffered an eclipse, because of the growing recognition that human activities are far too numerous and too

[3] J. E. Leighton, *Man and the Cosmos*, D. Appleton-Century, 1922, p. 3. By permission of D. Appleton-Century Company, publishers.

[4] *Ibid.*, p. 2. By permission of D. Appleton-Century Company, publishers.

[5] B. A. G. Fuller, *History of Greek Philosophy*, Holt, 1923, p. 17. By permission of Henry Holt and Company, publishers.

complex for a single individual to obtain a systematic and integrated view of them. On the impossibility of any modern mortal acquiring a universality of knowledge, if, indeed, such asquisition were ever possible, M. C. Otto says:

> It is recognized by the plain man and by the specialist that universality of knowledge is no longer attainable by any mind. One scarcely reads a book in any special field which does not state this fact or imply it. A chemist, physicist, biologist, mathematician, who should announce that he has mastered the essentials of his field would be thought to have lost his balance. Everywhere it is admitted that the obstacles in the way of arriving at the essentials of knowledge in even a limited field and by those best qualified through training and experience to do so, are practically insuperable. If philosophers rush in where experts fear to tread what reception can they expect for the "total vision" with which they come out? [6]

Although this latter concept, namely, that philosophy is a "system of values," does not gainsay the necessity for a systematic knowledge of as many fields of human activity as possible, it has ceased chasing the will-o'wisp of the impossible. It no longer regards a philosopher as a person who knows everything, or who has "all the answers." It takes its cue from a definition of philosophy by the late Professor William James, one of America's most eminent philosophers. James defined philosophy as "our more or less dumb sense of what life honestly and deeply means." According to the late Professor John Dewey, who is everywhere recognized as one of the outstanding philosophers of all time, philosophy essays to answer the question: "What does our knowledge demand of us?" Science gives us knowledge about our world, but, according to Dewey, "When we ask what sort of permanent disposition or action toward the world the scientific disclosures exact of us, we are raising a philosophic question." [7] For example, science produces a poison gas, but philosophy tells us whether to use that lethal weapon to destroy human beings or to increase their happiness through using it to destroy harmful insects and rodents.

In this book the view of James and Dewey is accepted, that is,

[6] M. C. Otto, *Things and Ideals: Essays in Educational Philosophy,* Holt, 1924, pp. 8–9. By permission of Henry Holt and Company, publishers.

[7] John Dewey, *Democracy and Education,* Macmillan, 1916, p. 379. By permission of The Macmillan Company, publishers.

philosophy is regarded as a way of interpreting life—as a system of values for the solution of life's problems. When that view is accepted, philosophy is seen to be a relatively simple, common-sense, and practical sort of thing, rather than a formidable and abstract thing stated, as it often is, in confusing verbiage. Moreover, it is seen to be a possession to a certain degree and in a certain form, of every normal person, because every normal person has a way of interpreting life—has, according to James, a "more or less dumb sense of what life honestly and deeply means."

Although a philosophy of some kind and of a certain degree of depth is possessed by all normal persons, it must be admitted that most persons do not have a very conscious, related, logical, and deep philosophy. Democracy and Americanism, for example, have a strong emotional appeal to all of us, but investigations show that most of us have difficulty in defining those terms. The outlook of most persons upon life is hazy, haphazard, inconsistent, and without depth. Too often that outlook upon life takes its departure from a foundation of superstition, prejudice, rumor, general ignorance, and selfishness. The tree of philosophy of most persons consists chiefly of undeveloped leaves and branches and lacks adequate roots. But, whatever the stage of the development and the degree of wholesomeness of his philosophy, every normal person possesses a philosophy and as we shall see later, his philosophy possesses him, because it is the mainspring and the governor of his actions.

The discussion thus far has been concerned with general philosophy, and no reference has been made to a philosophy of education. Since the teacher is concerned with preparing human beings to take their proper place in a changing society, the philosophy which determines the nature of that preparation will have essentially the same purpose, content, and method as general philosophy. Its purpose will be to conceive a system of values which will guide the educative process; its content will be the educational problems faced by society and by the individual; and its method will be reflective thinking concerning those problems and values.

The philosophy of education of any teacher must stem from his general philosophy of life. Like general philosophy, it must take account of the problems which people now face and which they will likely face in the future. It must conceive an educational program which will prepare pupils to recognize their problems and to solve them. It must have a well-developed concept of the characteristics of the "good life" and of the means by which the good life may be attained. It must conceive the most desirable aims of education, and with the aid of science it must indicate the best means by which those aims may be accomplished.

It was stated above that a philosophy of education deals with educational problems; it does not operate in a vacuum. Likewise, the science of education deals with educational problems. Philosophy of education unites with science of education to solve those problems. Science contributes facts bearing on the definition and the solution of a problem, and philosophy evaluates those facts according to a system of values. There is always an infinite number of educational problems, and philosophy must have a place in the solution of all of them; it has, of course, a larger place in the solution of certain problems than of others. John Dewey mentioned the following problems as being among those which must be solved partly, largely, or entirely by philosophy:

> . . . Is it the duty of the schools to give indoctrination in the economic and political, including nationalistic principles that are current in contemporary society? Should criticism of the existing social order be permitted? If so, in what ways? . . .
>
> . . . Do students go forth from the school without adequate consciousness of the problems and issues they will have to face? As far as it is true, can this state of affairs be remedied without a realization of responsibility for social planning on the part of the teaching body and administration? . . .
>
> . . . Is the work of administrators too far removed from that of teachers? . . . How much of present administrative procedures is based upon distrust of the intellectual capacities of classroom teachers? . . .
>
> Can the power of independent and critical thinking, said to be an objective, be attained when the field of thought is restricted by exclusion of whatever relates to controverted social questions? . . .
>
> . . . Can such questions as the relation of capital and labor, the history and aims of labor organizations, causes and extent of unemployment . . . , etc., be considered in the schoolroom? . . .
>
> How far is the working purpose of present school work to prepare the individual for personal success? How far are competitive incentives relied upon? How far are these factors compatible with the professed objective of democratic co-operation?
>
> How far can and should the schools deal with such questions as arise from racial color and class contact and prejudice? . . .

. . . Does the teaching of patriotism tend toward antagonism toward other people? . . .[8]

Relation Between Science and Philosophy. When the student of education reflects upon the questions just quoted from Dewey, he will see that the answer to the questions can only be found in terms of his system of educational values, that is, in terms of his philosophy of education. The questions cannot be answered by snap judgment, but only by "stubborn thinking" and the use of all facts which the student can command. In other words, the student must make use of the facts of science in formulating his philosophy of education; unfortunately, however, facts of science are not always available.

In spite of the warm discussions of doctrinaires, there is no conflict between honest science and altruistic philosophy. The purpose of both is the same, namely, to find the truth and to obtain greater security and happiness for mankind. In seeking to accomplish that purpose, science and philosophy make use of somewhat similar content and method. Without the facts which science provides, a philosophy would be purely speculative, and without the evaluations which philosophy provides for the facts of science, those facts might be used, or not used, to decrease the happiness of man.

Difficult though such knowledge is to obtain, the teacher who would develop a sound philosophy must have wide knowledge of the world and of human activities. Without that knowledge, the teacher is not likely to see problems clearly or to possess the facts which contribute to the solution of the problems. Moreover, the teacher needs knowledge of the past as well as of the present, because many practices can be understood and evaluated only in their historical setting. The foundations of new institutions must be built, at least in part, from the materials of old institutions. The teacher who would develop a sound philosophy of education must, therefore, know much about history, especially history of education. George Burton Adams says of the relation between the old and the new:

. . . It is necessary here, and in all institutional history, to distinguish very carefully between two sets of causes or antecedents. First, there is the general cause, or the prevailing condition of things in the society of the time, which renders a new institution necessary; and, second, there

[8] John Dewey, "The Duties and Responsibilities of the Teaching Profession," *School and Society*, Vol. 32 (August 9, 1930), pp. 190–191.

is the old institution, on which the prevailing cause seizes, and which it transforms into a new one. Both these are always present. No institution ever starts into life wholly new. Every new institution has its foundation far in the past in some earlier one. The prevailing necessity transforms it into a new institution, but the character of the new creation is as much conditioned by the character of the old as it is by the new necessity which it is made to meet. The sneer which is sometimes heard against that sort of investigation which seeks the foundations of a new institution in those which have preceded it, as merely antiquarian, is proof only of a very narrow conception of history.[9]

In brief, any attempt to philosophize without having wide and careful knowledge is unscholarly, if not dishonest. When they are not guided by knowledge, so-called "philosophers" are often nothing more than quacks or mountebanks; they build their castles of philosophy upon the sands of guesses and upon snap judgment rather than upon the rock of certainty, which is knowledge. When he lacks sufficient knowledge to guide him, the great philosopher will not philosophize; if he formulates a conclusion which is not supported by sufficient knowledge, he will state his conclusion as only tentative; if he has a doubt, he will not propose or recommend. He must have a deep sense of values. The knowledge which the science of education gives a teacher is so important that Chapter 23 (The Scientific Study of Education) will be entirely devoted to it.

Knowledge alone, though, does not make a philosopher. Coupled with knowledge must be the ability and the disposition to appraise the value of the knowledge in the solution of man's problems. That ability and that disposition are the qualities which distinguish the philosopher from the scientist. The philosopher reflects deeply upon the value of knowledge, and he does not cease in that effort. The scientist is primarily concerned with the discovery and the organization of knowledge, whereas the philosopher is concerned primarily with evaluating the use to which knowledge is put or should be put. Science and philosophy are so closely related that the great scientist is almost sure to be somewhat of a philosopher, and the great philosopher is as certain to be somewhat of a scientist.

IMPORTANCE OF A PROPER PHILOSOPHY. In a previous paragraph of this chapter it was stated that every normal person has a philosophy of some kind and of a certain degree of depth. Moreover, it was

[9] George Burton Adams, *Civilization during the Middle Ages*, Scribner's, 1914, p. 190. By permission of Charles Scribner's Sons, publishers.

stated that a person's philosophy is the most important characteristic of him, because it serves as the mainspring and the governor of his life; it constitutes his innermost thoughts, and "as a man thinketh in his heart, so is he." Since a proper philosophy of life is the most important possession of an individual, every individual should strive to obtain such a philosophy. The most important task of the teacher is to help his pupils to start developing a good philosophy of life, and the teacher should always remember that his example is potent.

Because of the importance of his work, the teacher especially needs a proper philosophy of life and of the educative process. If the teacher does not have a good philosophy of life, his pupils are not likely to be helped to acquire one. Good philosophy would conceive the type of society which is needed and the type of individual which is needed in that society; moreover, it would conceive the function and the processes of education as agencies for achieving that type of society and individual. By providing a frame of reference for evaluating his aims, his materials, and his methods, it would energize and guide the efforts of the teacher to provide the best type of educational program for his pupils; it would direct and control his educational strategy. Thus equipped, the teacher would likely find his work to be the great adventure, rather than a series of chores to be perfunctorily and mechanically performed.

Many teachers fail to accomplish all that they might, because they are not equipped with a proper educational philosophy. In fact, many of those teachers who fail do not possess a conscious educational philosophy of any sort, proper or improper. Many teachers are content to be mere technicians; they do not question why they do what they do; they are oblivious to purposes and values. They have never paid the price required for acquiring a philosophy; that price, according to William James, is "an unusually stubborn effort to think consistently." They are satisfied to worship slogans and to ride hobbies, without considering their meaning and their value—without appraising them according to a fundamental philosophy of education. They are content to drift, and to be blown by the winds of uncritical tradition or by the zephyrs of questionable "isms." Their good ship, "education," does not have a sense of direction, or if it does have a direction, it is the wrong direction. Such teachers fail to arrive at a desirable destination, or if they do arrive, it is only after great travail and effort and at too large an expense to the public, the parents, and the pupils.

A desirable educational philosophy can be acquired only by conscious, assiduous, and profound effort; there is no royal road to a desirable philosophy. As has already been stated, the chief requisites for a good philosophy are wide knowledge of man's activities, and clear and profound thinking concerning the use to be made of that knowledge. The individual cannot acquire those qualifications in a day, a week, a month, or a year; they are the products largely of sound professional preparation, of wide-awake educational experience, and of never-ending reflection on the problems of life and on the aims and the procedures of education. But, they are not impossible to acquire.

The student who aspires to a successful career as a teacher should start early to formulate an educational philosophy. Most colleges for the preparation of teachers aid him in making this start through offering such courses as "Philosophy of Education" or "Principles of Education." Moreover, since all teacher-preparing courses are designed to provide knowledge of the schools and of the educative process, they should also be of great help to the student in formulating his educational philosophy. Unfortunately, though, these courses —whether in philosophy of education or other subject matter—do not always exhibit a conscious educational philosophy, or what is more frequent and more unfortunate, they present only one educational philosophy and insist upon the student adopting it. Strange to say, the teachers of these courses often plead for one philosophy, but they practice another; for example, they inveigh against indoctrination,[10] but they practice indoctrination; they plead for a school which permits the pupil to think, but they seldom give the pupil that opportunity; they argue for a pupil-centered school, but they run a subject-centered school; they preach democracy, but they practice autocracy.

Among the first discoveries which even the casual student of philosophy makes is that there is not one philosophy, but many, and that each philosophy often deems that it contains the last word of wisdom. There are several brands, even of the democratic philosophy.

[10] By indoctrination is meant the attempt to teach for acceptance only one view concerning controversial issues.

The student is here invited to examine those philosophies—past and present, but especially the present—to ascertain their characteristics, and especially to obtain any worth-while suggestions which other philosophies may contain for his own philosophy. As he proceeds with that examination, the student will find that many philosophies are not based on sufficient knowledge of either the present or of the past, that others do not interpret knowledge accurately, and that others are selfish and destructive. He will discover that one philosophy emphasizes the importance of the group and neglects the individual, whereas another philosophy emphasizes the sacredness of the individual and neglects the group; that a second philosophy favors universal education at public expense, whereas another philosophy favors the education of only a few prospective leaders at public expense; that a third philosophy has as its core the postulate that the school should indoctrinate the pupils with certain views, whereas another accepts the postulate that the school should not indoctrinate the

FIG. 11. The results of the lack of an educational philosophy in school affairs. *(From Luther Gulick and Rudolph Modley,* The New York Primer, *Regents Inquiry into the Character and Cost of Public Education in the State of New York.)* School officials, teachers, parents, and the general public are all in the same boat, and all seem to lack a sense of direction and a co-ordinated effort.

pupils with a particular view, but rather should permit them to select their own views.

Since philosophy is fundamentally a belief, a view, or an opinion of what man should do and should not do, and as such cannot be omnipotent, the prospective teacher should not have any particular brand of philosophy, which is not thoroughly democratic, foisted upon him.[11] The tenets of philosophy are controversial and should be treated as such. With the hope and the expectation that the prospective teacher will be better prepared to develop a desirable educational philosophy of his own, he should be given the opportunity of becoming acquainted with the tenets of various educational philosophies. For all of his studies he should arm himself against the "witchery of words." He should not swallow any philosophy "hook, line, and sinker." His attitude toward philosophy should always be examining and critical. Moreover, he should realize that his educational philosophy can never be complete, but that it must change and expand as he obtains further educational and social experience and insight. As new knowledge of the nature of the individual is acquired, as society changes, and as concepts of the nature of the good life change, the teacher's philosophy of education must also change.

CRITERIA FOR EVALUATING A PHILOSOPHY OF EDUCATION. Since philosophy rests finally upon opinion, it is clear that there can be as many philosophies as there are persons who have organized opinions. Every person, of course, selects what he likes, prefers, or values. A philosophy can, therefore, be defended only on basis of opinion. Its merits can be measured only in terms of certain criteria, and in the last analysis criteria rest upon opinions. George S. Counts affirms that a defensible philosophy of education should conform to at least the following five requirements, though he is aware of the subjective nature of these criteria:

1. It should be systematically empirical in its foundations. . . it should be derived from experience. . . it should comprehend and bring into a synthesis, not only science and metaphysics, but ethics and aesthetics as well. . . .
2. It should be comprehensive in its outlook. It must not only derive its substance from the whole range of human experience, but it must

[11] Since the purpose of the schools of our nation is to prepare for democratic living, the foundation and the framework of the philosophy of teachers should be thoroughly democratic. Teachers have the responsibility of indoctrinating their pupils in the spirit and the method of democracy, and persons who do not have a firm faith in democratic principles should never be placed or retained on the payroll of any school.

also face squarely and with some sense of proportion all the problems of education. . . .

3. It should be consistent in its several departments. . . .
4. It should be practicable in its provisions. . . . An educational philosophy for twentieth century America must take into account the existing conditions of life and civilization. Whatever may be its ultimate goals it must articulate with the world as it is.
5. It should be satisfying to its adherents . . . unless it fits experience as the glove fits the hand, it will be acceptable to no individual or group.[12]

Can there be a preferred philosophy? Although the present writer firmly favors the democratic philosophy, he believes as firmly that no brand of democratic philosophy can be given a preferred status. The people are, of course, the final judges of the merit of any educational philosophy which the teacher possesses. If the philosophy of the teacher brings the people justifiable happiness, they will approve it; if it does not bring them that happiness, they will disapprove it. From the beginning, the American people have placed their faith in the democratic philosophy, and they expect all their teachers to operate in the democratic framework. The Educational Policies Commission of the National Education Association has recommended that only those persons who believe in democracy be employed in our schools.[13]

The Democratic Philosophy of Education

This chapter has already indicated that America possesses a philosophy of education and that it is usually called the democratic philosophy. It was stated, though, that there are various interpretations of what the democratic philosophy is; in other words, there are various philosophies which are labeled "democratic," and the teacher should be on his guard, lest he be misled by labels. Those differences in interpretations are characterized primarily by different beliefs regarding the relation between the individual and the social order and those different beliefs will presently be evaluated. William H. Burton gives the following summary of what he considers to be the fundamentals of the democratic philosophy:

[12] George S. Counts, "Criteria for Judging a Philosophy of Education," *School and Society*, Vol. 30 (July 27, 1929), pp. 103–107.

[13] See *American Education and International Tensions*, Educational Policies Commission, National Education Association, Washington, D. C., 1949.

Thus we see that democracy is not equalitarianism, nor majority rule, nor blind conformity, nor ruthless individualism, nor paternalistic guarantee of individual happiness. What, then, is it? . . . Democracy is participatory group life, enjoyed by free individuals possessing maximum opportunities for participation. Its chief characteristic *in regard to individuals* is, in current happy phrase, "respect for personality." *In regard to the group* its chief characteristic is the flexible and evolutionary nature of group institutions. Free participation in co-operative group life under evolutionary institutions and with respect between individuals are the earmarks of democracy. . . .

The keynote is integration. And what is integration? In simplest terms it means unity and absence of conflict. Society will be integrated in that individuals are imbued with the same ideals and concepts of the good life, are motivated by desire for the common good, are contributing each his special ability or skill, are respected therefor. Society thus is not an aggregation or collection of individuals, it is not merely the sum of its parts. It is a unified functioning organism by means of which individuals achieve commonly conceived ends through participatory contributions.[14]

John Dewey was probably the most eminent and the most prolific exponent of the democratic philosophy. All of his numerous literary contributions breathed the spirit of that philosophy, but one of them—*Democracy and Education*—was entirely devoted to its exposition. A paragraph from that noted work, which summarizes Dewey's conception of the democratic philosophy, is quoted herewith:

Since education is a social process, and there are many kinds of societies, a criterion for educational criticism and construction implies a *particular* social ideal. The two points selected by which to measure the worth of a form of social life are the extent to which the interests of the group are shared by all its members and the fullness and freedom with which it interacts with other groups. An undesirable society, in other words, is one which internally and externally sets up barriers to free intercourse and communication of experience. A society which makes provision for participation in its good of all its members on equal terms and which secures flexible readjustment of its institutions through interaction of the different forms of associated life is in so far democratic. Such a society must have a type of education which gives individuals a personal interest in social relationships and control, and the habits of mind which secure social changes without introducing disorder.[15]

[14] Burton, *op. cit.*, pp. 179–180. By permission of D. Appleton-Century Company, publishers.

[15] Dewey, *op. cit.*, p. 115. By permission of The Macmillan Company, publishers.

In brief, Dewey's writings constantly plead for a type of education which will be appropriate for the development of a democratic society. According to him, such a society would provide for free and full participation of all its members in the determination and pursuance of common interests; its essence would be a willingness to share in planning. According to that view, therefore, democracy is more than a theory and a practice of government. It is a way of life and applies to school affairs, church matters, home affairs, economic matters, and all other aspects of life as well as to government. At another place Dewey says that the democratic criterion for education implies "the ideal of a continuous reconstruction or reorganizing of experience, of such a nature as to increase its recognized meaning or social content, and as to increase the capacity of individuals to act as guardians of this reorganization." [16]

The quotations from Burton and from Dewey demonstrate the difficulty of summarizing a philosophy in only a few sentences. In such a summary there is certain to be misunderstanding as to what the author of the quotation means. Even when it is described in detail, as can be done only in a whole book, the philosophy of a person is likely to be somewhat vague and largely platitudinous. Many philosophers "talk to the gods rather than to man." In the foregoing quotations, for example, what does Burton mean by the "common good"? And what does Dewey mean by "continuous reconstruction of experience"? To find that author's definition of those terms the reader would need to consult the complete text in which the terms are found, and even there he would probably encounter much vagueness. Many of the long-winded arguments over the relative merits of various educational philosophies and their educational practices are occasioned by different interpretations of the same terms. After many "heads have been cracked" and when "the smoke of battle" has cleared, the protagonists often discover that they have been arguing fiercely for the same thing, with no one winning the argument.

THE GROUP PATTERN VERSUS THE INDIVIDUAL PATTERN. The most perplexing problem of educational philosophers, as well as of governments, has always been the determination of the best relation between society and the individual. Specifically stated, the problem is:

[16] *Ibid.*, p. 376. By permission of The Macmillan Company, publishers.

Shall educational aims, materials, and methods be determined by the demands of society, or by the demands of the individual? Or, if neither of those extremes is desirable, what is the optimum position between them? That problem has always confronted school officials and teachers. It was perennial, even before the establishment of the school, when all education was given by the family, the tribe, apprenticeship, the church, and other nonschool agencies. During recent years, the problem has been particularly urgent, because, as General Smuts, an eminent South African statesman, has said, "Humanity has struck its tents and is once more on the march." There is scarcely a nation today which is not questioning old values—political, economic, social, and educational—and trying to establish other values which will give the people of the nation greater security and happiness. In that ubiquitous questioning of old values, America has an opportunity to assume world leadership by applying the philosophy of democracy [17] to her relations with other nations and with all groups and individuals within her jurisdiction; that opportunity constitutes her "rendezvous with destiny."

As is true in every other endeavor, it is the extreme or the radically different philosophy which most often attracts attention. The commonly occurring happening does not make news, or does a middle-of-the-road philosophy call attention to itself. The importance of the individual has been stressed by various political and educational theorists to the disparagement of society; likewise, the importance of society has been stressed by other political and educational theorists to the disparagement of the individual. Rousseau (1712–1778) went as far in the former direction as Plato (428–348 B. C.) went in the latter, although as we shall see later, the views of neither, when taken *in toto*, were as extreme as they are usually believed to be. This book presents the view that the welfare of both society and the individual must be kept in mind in the formulation of any political, social, economic, or educational program. The next few pages will first present the case for society, then the case for the individual; the case for an interaction of both will finally be presented.

EDUCATION FOR THE GROUP. The case for keeping in mind the group, that is, society, as the most important element in determining the aims and the procedures of education, was stated more than

[17] That philosophy is embodied in the Golden Rule: "And as ye would that men should do to you, do ye also to them likewise." (Luke, 6:31)

two thousand years ago by Plato in his *Laws:* "Education is, in fact, the drawing and leading of children to the rule which has been pronounced right by the voice of the law, and approved as truly right by the concordant experience of the best and oldest men." At another place in the same famous work Plato affirms that, "He (i.e., the law-giver) need only tax his invention to discover what convictions would be most beneficial to a city, and then contrive all manner of devices to ensure that the whole of such community shall treat the topic in one single and selfsame lifelong tone, alike in song, in story and in discourse." In Plato's ideal society which was created in his *Laws*, laws, policies, and procedures were to be determined not democratically, but by "the best and oldest men." Plato did not indicate, though, how the "best" men were to be selected. According to his view, education would begin only after an ideal state (called "Utopia" by Sir Thomas More) had been erected, and its purpose would be to preserve that state. That ideal state would, of course, be erected by "the best and oldest men," and the public at large—the people—would have no voice in the procedure.

Education for the Individual. Until the time of Rousseau the interests of the individual were entirely subordinated to the interests of the group; the philosophy of Plato was everywhere accepted. It was the practice of making the welfare of the group the only political and educational end which Rousseau inveighed against, and which, at one time, gained for him the sobriquet of "firebrand of the French Revolution." "Liberty, Equality, Fraternity" became the slogan of his followers both in France and in the American colonies. Rousseau wanted to make the welfare of the individual the aim and the end of education. He affirmed that society is a deformer and that the good life comes only when the individual has complete liberty. He believed that education could best be received "according to nature" and without risking contamination of the individual by an ogreish society. A paragraph from his *Emile* gives the heart of his philosophy: "The only man who does his own will is he who has no need, in order to do it, to put the arms of another to it as well as his own; whence it follows that the first of all good things is not authority, but liberty. The man truly free wants only what he can have and does what pleases himself. There you have my fundamental maxim."

Rousseau's doctrine of the all-pervading importance of the individual encountered severe resistance from the long-established order which glorified the group and neglected the individual. Practically all governments of his time were totalitarian, and democracy was hardly a name. It was argued by the proponents of the old order that society was not sufficiently stable to permit the individual to go his own way; group safety required rigid conformity, and non-conformists risked exile, death, or other severe punishment. Any political, economic, religious, or other heresy was regarded as inimical to the welfare of the group, hence could not be tolerated.

Another factor which delayed for several centuries the acceptance of any theory of the importance of the individual was the long-prevalent theory of human nature. Man was assumed to be a "bundle of instincts," and it was believed that these inherent abilities would naturally "unfold" and bring to fruition a civilized man. Moreover, it was assumed that these inherent abilities were similar in nature and in amount in all individuals. The theory of individual differences had not yet been promulgated.

During recent decades, however, experimental psychology has shown the shortcomings of the theory of instincts as a sole or as a major basis of education. It has shown that individuals are not wholly similar in their inborn nature, but are widely different; since the nature and the extent of these differences will be discussed in detail in Chapter 7 (Pupil Differences) of this book, they need not be discussed at this point. These discoveries, suffice it to say, have been responsible for ushering in a new order in education—an order which is posited on the welfare of the individual as well as the welfare of the group.

Education for Both the Individual and the Group. Since neither the group nor the individual is supreme, education cannot have as its aim the glorification of the group alone or of the individual alone. It must glorify both, because they are brothers and neither is king. Without a stable society, the individual would not likely find happiness, if even safety. Without individuals, who were free to think and to create, society would not likely make progress. Both Plato and Rousseau realized the necessity for a certain amount of interaction between the group and the individual, although Plato's sympathies were clearly with the group and those of Rousseau were clearly with the individual. An English educator has given the following appraisal of the views of those two great personages:

But neither Plato nor Rousseau is as one-sided as so sharp an antithesis would suggest, an antithesis better suited to the conflicts of doctrinaire partisans than to the rounded thought of moral philosophers. It is less easy to set these two creative thinkers of the educational tradition of the West in strong opposition when one takes the thought of each in its entirety. There are differences of emphasis, no doubt, due partly to differences of temperament and circumstances. But if we take the thought of each as a whole and extract as well as we can the central meaning it is the identities rather than the differences which strike us. The totalitarian can and does find much in Rousseau, particularly in the doctrine of the Sovereignty of the General Will, which gives plausible support to his own position. And the democrat, especially if he have Fabian inclinations, can derive much comfort from many a passage in the *Laws*. Simply to dub Plato absolutist and Rousseau individualist is to under-estimate what is central and essential in the thought of both.[18]

As usual, therefore, when controversial issues are being debated, the complete views of the extremists may be disregarded, and values sought in each extreme on which a working program can be built. Good practice always seeks to conciliate the poles of theory, though the exigencies of the situation may cause practice to veer farther toward one pole than another. No government and no political or educational philosophy today places supreme emphasis upon the group or upon the individual to the exclusion of the other. Biases, though, toward one or the other are everywhere evident, if we examine the governments of the nations of the world and the educational systems of those nations. It seems fair to say that the governments and the school systems of the totalitarian nations magnify the importance of the group, whereas the governments and the school systems of the democratic nations magnify the importance of the individual.

On this issue the sympathies of the present writer are with the theory of the democratic state rather than with that of the totalitarian state; he is probably more of a Rousseauist than a Platonist. The criticism which he makes of the totalitarian state and of the educational system which it fosters, and which in turn fosters it, is that it makes the production of "the type" the all-important goal; "growth beyond the type" is not provided for, or is not adequately provided for. It cannot be gainsaid that education must—and inevitably will—produce the type, but must also, if society is to advance,

[18] F. Clarke, "The Conflict of Philosophies," *The Year Book of Education*, Evans Brothers, Ltd., 1936, pp. 254–255.

provide for growth beyond the type; it must permit large freedom of personality. The democratic philosophy, which implies free and full participation of all members of the group in the determination and the pursuance of common interests, holds the best promise of accomplishing those aims. The British publication, which has just been referred to, advocates the democratic philosophy for the schools of England. The views of the publication are also applicable to the schools of the United States and for that reason, they are quoted herewith:

> Freedom of Personality to achieve itself, we should maintain is not only a necessary postulate of a democratic society, which rests on the faith that the whole is incomplete and impoverished unless it can count upon the free contribution of each member. It is even more—it is the *raison d'etre* of democratic society itself. That, if anything, is the meaning of Equality, the faith that human personality is so valuable to be beyond valuing, and is to be regarded with the same reverence wherever it is found. With such a tradition as that of England behind us, we shall have to concede freely that Personality, so far as its substance is concerned, is dependent upon the social medium. To that extent, society is authoritative in the making of it. But, in the last resort, the society exists for the sake of the personality, not the personality for the sake of society. A civil society exists and perpetuates itself in the making of fresh generations of personalities in its own type, not for its own ends or to fix a type for all time, but in the discharge of its supreme function in the making of men. In Rousseau's terms, it is not by a preordained and final social pattern that we produce our Emiles; it is the needs of the full growth of an Emile that must determine the structure and adaptations of our social forms.[19]

If society and the individual are to interact for the welfare of each, neither can remain static. Each must maintain sufficient flexibility to permit adjustments to inevitable changes in society. Without this flexibility, there is sure to be stagnation, conflict, and perhaps a breakdown in progress and happiness. Besides serving as an agency for conserving and bringing to the individual the heritage of the past, education must be the means of adding something to that heritage. In brief, education must serve as an agency of progress; it must prepare the individual to be competent and growingly willing to take part in the continuous reconstruction of the patterns of living, in order that he and the remainder of the social group may find greater

[19] *Ibid.*, p. 262.

happiness for themselves. The fundamental aim of education in a democracy is, therefore, the preparation of each individual to participate in the continuous reconstruction, improvement, and enrichment of the patterns of individual and of group living.

Although it is the obligation of teachers in a democracy to operate in the framework of the democratic aim just described, it is not their function to set the "patterns of individual and of group living." The functions of school officials and teachers are to help the pupil to discover any gaps, conflicts, and inefficiencies in the various patterns and to give him the sort of preparation which will enable him to interpret and to reconstruct those patterns. This procedure does not prescribe for the pupil the elements of the good life or the characteristics of the ideal social order; it brings different views of the good life into perspective, in the hope that the pupil will emerge with a wholesome view of his own. It is posited on the belief that the ideal social order is one which best serves the common interests and purposes of man, but it does not prescribe what those interests and those purposes shall be; it permits each individual to have a voice in determining them. We may label this the democratic procedure.

According to the democratic procedure, the school has a two-fold function. In the first place, it must make provision whereby the cultural heritage becomes readily accessible and whereby the discovery and the development of individual capacity are properly promoted. In the second place, it must make provision whereby the individual is made competent and willing to examine and to appraise the goals and the procedures of the social order. These obligations must be met, if the individual is to be prepared to engage in the "continuous reconstruction of experience." It must also be met, if the school is to function as the chief formal agency which society maintains for promoting its continuous improvement, its greatest safety, and its greatest happiness.

The democratic procedure is here firmly favored, in spite of its difficulty and the many problems which it brings. The democratic tree has some thorns as well as much fruit! Its chief thorn is man's egoism, that is, his inclination to forget his social responsibility and to aggrandize himself. This thorn cannot be eradicated in a day, but there is faith that man will somehow and some time eradicate it. There is the further faith that the chief instrument for its eradication will be education—education of a greater amount and of a better type. In the final analysis, therefore, the decision to adopt the democratic philosophy rather than the autocratic philosophy is posited upon faith in the capacity and the desire of the individual to make wise decisions—wise in relation to the interests and the purposes of society as well as to his own.

Since its establishment in 1936 by the National Education Association and the American Association of School Administrators, the Educational Policies Commission has given a large amount of thought to ways and means of making democratic education function. In one of its publications it lists the following hallmarks of democratic education:

1. Democratic education has as its central purpose the welfare of all the people.
2. Democratic education serves each individual with justice, seeking to provide equal educational opportunity for all, regardless of intelligence, race, religion, social status, economic condition, or vocational plans.
3. Democratic education respects the basic civil liberties in practice and clarifies their meaning through study.
4. Democratic education is concerned for the maintenance of those economic, political, and social conditions which are necessary for the enjoyment of liberty.
5. Democratic education guarantees to all members of the community the right to share in determining the purposes and policies of education.
6. Democratic education uses democratic methods, in classroom, administration, and student activities.
7. Democratic education makes efficient use of personnel; teaching respect for competence in positions of responsibility.
8. Democratic education teaches through experience that every privilege entails a corresponding duty, every authority a responsibility, every responsibility an accounting to the group which granted the privilege or authority.
9. Democratic education demonstrates that far-reaching changes of both policies and procedures can be carried out in orderly and peaceful fashion, when the decisions to make the changes have been reached by democratic means.
10. Democratic education liberates and uses the intelligence of all.
11. Democratic education equips citizens with the materials of knowledge needed for democratic efficiency.

12. Democratic education promotes loyalty to democracy by stressing positive understanding and appreciation and by summoning youth to service in a great cause.[20]

Educational Aims

Nature of an Educational Aim. The aims of a teacher constitute the heart of his philosophy. Without a philosophy, the teacher could not have aims, and without aims, he could not have a workable philosophy. The aims of a teacher are his frame of reference or the foundation of his "general scheme of values" regarding education. They are the things which the teacher expects to accomplish; they are the contemplated termini of his teaching methods and his instructional materials. Other terms which are usually used to mean the same as aims are the following: objectives, goals, and purposes.

One group of educators today is concerned only or primarily with finding aims in the educative process itself. According to John Dewey, who was the chief spokesman of that group, "the aim of education is to enable individuals to continue their education—or that the object and reward of learning is continued capacity for growth." [21] That group of educators is opposed to the aim of preparation because it tends "to omit existing powers, and find the aim in some remote accomplishment or responsibility." [22] It regards an aim as a means, a method, a spirit. It accepts the principle of general aims, but rebels at specific aims, especially if they are set up outside the educative process.

That group of educators tries to distinguish between aims and ends. It permits a philosophy of education to have aims, but not ends. As was earlier stated, it sees an aim as a means—a means to an end. It regards an "end" as final, as something set up from without the educative process, and it fears the strictures which finality implies. Dewey said:

> The philosophy of education neither originates nor settles ends. It occupies an intermediate and instrumental or regulative place. Ends actually

[20] Educational Policies Commission, *Learning the Ways of Democracy: A Case Book in Civic Education*, National Education Association, 1940, pp. 35–38. By permission of the National Education Association, publishers.

[21] Dewey, *op. cit.*, p. 117. By permission of The Macmillan Company, publishers.

[22] *Ibid.*, p. 126. By permission of The Macmillan Company, publishers.

reached, consequences that actually accrue, are surveyed, and their values estimated in the light of a general scheme of values.[23]

Another group of educators, on the contrary, is concerned with seeking aims only or primarily outside the educative process. The members of that group accept preparation as an aim of education. They believe that the aim of the first group—"to enable individuals to continue their education"—is too vague and impractical. They seek, therefore, for more specific aims, and they look for these, at least in part, in an analysis of existing society (pupil and adult). Their unstated general objective, according to the interpretation of the Deweyists and in the language of Dewey, "appears to be that education should prepare, by means of blue prints of society and the individual, students to fit efficiently into present life."[24]

As is usually the case, the educational statesman should here avoid adopting *in toto* the extreme views of doctrinaires, and should seek merit in the views of both extremes. Education must find its aims both within and without the educative process. It must keep in mind the interests and the abilities of the pupil as well as the cultural heritage which will contact the mind of the pupil and prepare him to share in democratic living both now and when he becomes an adult.

For anyone to claim that education is not preparation is merely to play on words. Education prepares for something, and that something is better living (in childhood and in adulthood) as well as further education. In spite of his avowed aversion to the aim of preparation, Dewey does not, in this matter, "practice what he preaches," because he states aims which may be regarded as preparation. In his following statement of aims, the aim of preparation is implied both on the psychological and the social side:

On the psychological or individual side, the aim is to secure a progressive development of capacities, having due regard to individual differences, and including a physical basis of vigorous health, refined esthetic taste and power to make a worthwhile use of leisure, ability to think independently and critically, together with command of the tools and processes that give access to the accumulated products of past cul-

[23] John Dewey, *The Sources of a Science of Education*, Liveright, 1929, p. 56. By permission of H. Liveright, publishers.

[24] John Dewey, "The Duties and Responsibilities of the Teaching Profession," *School and Society*, Vol. 32 (August 9, 1930), p. 189.

tures. On the social side, this personal development is to be such as will give desire and power to share in co-operative democratic living, including political citizenship, vocational efficiency and effective social good will. . . .[25]

Importance of Educational Aims. The schools have always been criticized more or less for not having a concept of what they are trying to do, or for attempting to do the wrong things; in other words, they have been criticized for not possessing aims, or for possessing undesirable aims. That this criticism is often valid is demonstrated by the fact that when school officials and teachers are requested to state the aims of the school, they frequently give evidence of not having devoted much thought to the matter. Instead of having ready and clear replies, they often exhibit vagueness, hesitation, and bewilderment. They do not seem to know what they want, and not knowing what they want they cannot act most intelligently.

When the schools are not guided by aims, they are likely to exhibit the happy-go-lucky sentiment of the old saying, "We don't know where we're going, but we're on our way." Without aims, neither an individual nor an institution can realize his or its potentialities. Aims give foresight and suggest planning, all of which are necessary, if the greatest progress is to be made. Desirable aims would be helpful to school officials, parents, school employees, pupils, and the general public in the following ways:

In the first place, such aims would assist school officials in organizing, equipping, and administering the school. If they were guided by such aims, school officials would be better prepared to select teachers and other employees to assist in accomplishing the aims. Moreover, the best kinds and amounts of school buildings, sites, school libraries, textbooks, and other equipment and materials would be obtained which would contribute to the realization of those aims. In brief, good schools require officials with enlightened aims.

In the second place, desirable aims would be helpful to parents and to the general public because they would more surely know what the schools were trying to do and could, therefore, appraise the efforts and the accomplishments of the schools in terms of those aims. Moreover, parents and the general public would have the opportunity of criticizing these school aims and of suggesting other and better

[25] *Ibid.*, pp. 188–189.

ones. At present, it must be admitted that the concept of parents and of the general public of what the schools are trying to do is extremely vague. That condition exists not only because most school officials and teachers possess a hazy concept of educational purposes, but also because they have not taken the time to acquaint parents and the general public with their aims where these are well defined. What is needed, of course, if one adopts the democratic ideal, is a democratic plan for the formulation of aims—a plan in which school officials and teachers, parents, pupils, and the general public, intelligently and unselfishly participate in formulating.

In the third place, desirable aims would give direction and zest to the work of school employees, and especially to the largest group of such employees, namely, the teachers. If all teachers had similar or fairly similar aims, especially general aims, which had been formulated democratically, they would be better qualified to work co-operatively toward their accomplishment. Similarity in specific aims would not permit the teacher to meet the needs of the individual members of his class, and is, therefore, to be frowned upon; in other words, the more specific aims should be formulated by the individual teacher on basis of the interests, the abilities, and the other needs of the pupil.

In the fourth place, desirable aims would assist in giving direction and zest to the work of the pupils. If the aims of the school were made known to the pupils, those precious charges would know for what the school was striving, and they would be more likely to co-operate in trying to accomplish the aims.

Criteria for Educational Aims. For a teacher merely to possess aims is not sufficient; of greater importance is that the aims be desirable. In other words, the teacher must make certain that what he plans to accomplish corresponds with what should be accomplished. Undesirable aims would be worse than none, especially if they were possessed by school officials and teachers who were otherwise intelligent and vigorous, because such officials and teachers would more likely accomplish the undesirable aims. As Mark Hopkins, a great teacher of the preceding generation, once said, "If the ends chosen be folly, the more sagacious the choice of means, the more will the man be a fool." The harm done by undesirable aims often cannot be entirely undone; if it can be undone, it is only at great expense to the school, the pupils, the parents, and the public. Unlike any careless physicians, teachers do not "bury their mistakes"; the results of their mistakes are handed down from generation to generation and are apt to live forever. What, then, are the characteristics of desirable educational aims?

In the first place, educational aims should be inclusive and well balanced. On the psychological and the individual side, the aims should keep in mind the interests and the needs of the individual to be educated to the end that a "progressive development of capacities" in the individual will be obtained. On the social side, the aims should keep in mind the development of the individual, to the end that he will have the "desire and the power to share in democratic living."

Education is a process of growth, and its aim is to enable the individual to continue that growth. Education should facilitate that growth in all phases of the individual's capacities and in all phases of democratic living. If all capacities are not developed, or if certain phases of democratic living are neglected, there is danger of lopsided development both in the individual and in society; there is danger that growth will be hindered rather than facilitated and that the pupil will not be able to share in democratic living with the whole group.

The teacher must, therefore, guard against worshiping one aim of education to the neglect or the exclusion of other aims. There are many desirable aims of education, and the more of such aims the teacher has the better prepared he will be, because, as Dewey said, one statement of aims will emphasize what another omits or slurs over, and "what a plurality of hypotheses does for the scientific investigator, a plurality of stated aims may do for the instructor." [26] On the handicap of narrow aims, the late Professor Boyd H. Bode said:

> The fact that there are so many "ultimate" aims justifies a feeling of misgiving and suspicion. Generally speaking, all these aims are worthy and desirable; it is only when any one is set up as the supreme aim that it becomes objectionable. The reason is that an aim which is accepted as supreme or all-inclusive tends to place an undesirable restriction on growth, by turning it too exclusively in one direction. In some cases, indeed, this restriction is deliberately made a part of the aim. There are, for example, many communities in this country that are eager to transmit

[26] Dewey, *Democracy and Education*, p. 129.

to their children the language, the traditions, the ideals, the creeds, in brief, the general outlook upon life, which the founders of these communities brought with them as immigrants from Europe. The educational system is accordingly organized with this end in view; and to prevent these distinctive traits from becoming immersed and lost, the disposition is sometimes fostered in the community to fence itself off from all unnecessary contact with the outside world. An education of this sort may be fairly extensive and yet disagreeably lopsided. An individual thus trained is in America but not of it; he is unable to share in the national life around about him because of his educational deformity.[27]

In the second place, educational aims must be flexible; that is, they must be capable of change to meet unforeseen conditions. A good aim, according to Dewey, "surveys the present state of experience of pupils, and forming a tentative plan of treatment, keeps the plan constantly in view and yet modifies it as conditions develop." [28] In other words, an aim should be suggestive, experimental, and tentative; it should not be final.

As additional information on the interests and the abilities of the pupil is obtained and as the needs of society change, the aims of education must be accordingly modified. This means that the aims of education must be frequently examined and revised. They must be constantly growing as they are tested in action; they should lead to the development of other and better aims; they should embody the sentiment of James Russell Lowell's quatrain:

New occasions teach new duties;
  Time makes ancient good uncouth.
They must upward then and onward
  Who should keep abreast of truth.

The criterion of flexibility cannot be met when aims, especially detailed ones, are handed down to teachers by school officials or by the community with the expectation that teachers shall impose them upon the pupils. Aims thus handed down place a stricture upon the intelligence of the teacher, because they do not permit the teacher to use his own judgment in making the best contact between the pupil's mind and the subject matter. The result of aims thus imposed is that pupils are constantly confused by the conflict between

[27] Boyd H. Bode, *Fundamentals of Education*, Macmillan, 1921, pp. 9–10. By permission of The Macmillan Company, publishers.

[28] Dewey, *op. cit.*, p. 123.

their own aims and those handed down by superior authorities for their acceptance.

In the third place, whether they be general or more specific aims, all educational aims should be clearly conceived and clearly stated. Many statements of aims, especially of general aims, do not meet the criterion of clarity; on the contrary, many of them are vague platitudes stated in what a wag has dubbed the language of pedagogues, that is, "pedaguese." For example, without the explanations which Herbert Spencer has fortunately provided, his statement of the general aim of education as "preparation for complete living" would not meet the criterion of clarity; it would be too vague and abstract.

SOME DEFINITE STATEMENTS OF EDUCATIONAL AIMS. It was indicated above that the ultimate aim of education may be stated in various ways. Somewhat after Dewey, we have stated the ultimate aim to be the preparation of the individual to participate in the "continuous reconstruction," the improvement, and the enrichment of individual and group living. Like all ultimate aims, the aim is admittedly general; perhaps, it is more of a method or a spirit than an aim.

The primary function of an ultimate aim is to stimulate, to inspire, to guide, and to serve as a general control for the teacher. An ultimate aim is necessary as the spearhead of the teacher's efforts, but it needs to be interpreted in terms of more definite and more immediate aims, if it is to avoid becoming a mere generality. If, as our ultimate aim implies, individuals should be prepared to participate in the "continuous reconstruction," the improvement, and the enrichment of individual and group living, it would seem that serious thought should be directed to the qualifications which the individual should have and the characteristics which society should have, in order that the greatest safety and happiness may be obtained by each member of the group. Happiness and safety can never be obtained, if we do not have a concept of their characteristics; individual and group living cannot be improved and enriched, unless we have a concept of the characteristics of desirable individual and group living. In other words, the ultimate aim of education must be broken down into more immediate and specific aims.

During recent years, the emphasis in statements of more immediate and specific aims has been upon individual efficiency, security and happiness, those aims to be obtained, however, in a democratic frame of reference and with the welfare of society in mind as well as that of the individual. Unquestionably, the most widely known and influential statement of educational aims during this century is that promulgated in 1918 by the Commission on the Reorganization of Secondary Education,[29] which was appointed by the National Education Association. Although that statement of aims was designed especially for the secondary schools, it has become widely accepted for other levels of education as well. The commission affirmed the seven cardinal objectives of secondary education to be:

1. Good health.
2. Command of fundamental processes.
3. Worthy home-membership.
4. Vocational efficiency.
5. Civic efficiency.
6. Worthy use of leisure.
7. Ethical character.

The foregoing aims have been found to be serviceable by hundreds of thousands of teachers and have been patterned after by all succeeding statements of educational aims. In the meantime, though, teachers have been seeking an answer to a prior question; that question concerns the nature of the socio-economic order in which the individual will find greatest happiness and greater efficiency. To attempt to obtain an answer to that question the National Education Association adopted in July, 1931, the following resolution:

Whereas, The widespread economic disturbance thru which the United States, in common with the other nations of the world, is passing, is evidence of serious social-economic maladjustment, and

Whereas, The education of the people of a democracy determines its methods of dealing with those problems, therefore be it

Resolved, That the Board of Directors of the National Education Association recommends to the President of the Association the appointment of a committee of not more than ten to propose to the Association desirable social-economic goals of America and that said committee indicate the materials and methods which the schools of the nation should use to attain these goals.[30]

[29] "Cardinal Principles of Secondary Education," U. S. Bureau of Education, *Bulletin*, 1918, No. 35.

[30] "Social-Economic Goals of America," p. 2. Reprint by the National Education Association. By permission of the National Education Association, publishers. (In its volume titled *The Purposes of Education in American Democracy*, the Educational Policies Commission has patterned its purposes after the goals quoted below, hence they will not be reproduced here.)

Appointed to serve on that committee were John Dewey, Leon C. Marshall, Robert C. Moore, Edward A. Ross, and Fred J. Kelley, Chairman; all were distinguished educators. In December, 1933, the committee issued a report which set forth "the social-economic goals of America in terms of the things we regard as the most desirable for (and presumably as most desired by) the individual American." That report suggested ten goals and briefly discussed the meaning and the importance of each. Those goals might well be called the aims of education. Because the statement of such goals is much needed and is in accord with the democratic ideal of today, it is quoted *in extenso* herewith:

1. Hereditary Strength

The development of rich personalities depends first of all upon the innate strengths and capacities of the individuals. Whether experiences which are socially desirable produce personal satisfactions is often at base a biological question—a question of the level upon which motives make an effective appeal. Furthermore, proposals for social betterment are often limited in practice by the level of innate capacities of those among whom the proposal is to operate. The development, therefore, of individuals capable of the deepest enjoyments, and the building of a culture designed to enrich the personalities of great numbers of individuals are alike conditioned by the biological endowment of the people. . . .

2. Physical Security

To be born with superior innate capacities is but half the picture; to have these capacities conserved and developed is the other half. A strong hereditary base can be ruined by poor medical attention at or before birth, poor nourishment, improper home care, contaminated milk, a speeding automobile, a gangster's bullet, or any one of a thousand other conditions largely outside the control of the individual.

3. Participation in an Evolving Culture

Every new born babe is an intricate bundle of latent potentialities, each ready to develop when touched by the sunlight of experience which culture provides. It follows, then, that if a rich and integrated personality is to be attained, the individual must be able to participate effectively in the cultural life that surrounds him. Society must assure to each individual the fullest possible opportunity to come into fruitful contact with culture. . . .

a. Skills, Technics, and Knowledges.—Every individual must have command of those skills, technics, and knowledges that will enable him, to the limit of his innate capacities, to use and enjoy the culture of the group. Basic to all others are the arts of communication—language, spoken and written, numbers, music, drawing, and the like—with provisions for facilitating intimate and far-flung contacts with men, goods, and ideas. To this end agencies used in accomplishing these far-flung contacts, such as the radio, the newspaper, the cinema, should be trustworthy, not used for purposes subversive of social living. . . .

b. Values, Standards, and Outlooks.—There are values, standards, and outlooks that reflect the experience of the race and—*most important*—regulate the attention of the individual, determine his choices, organize his activities, and shape his personality. The basis of human motivation is found just here—what is right, what is wrong; what is good, what is bad. Responsiveness to motives which harmonize self-interests with social interests will grow by virtue of better appreciation of the values, standards, and outlooks which actuate human conduct. . . .

4. An Active, Flexible Personality

Participation in our cultural resources should promote personalities who are active, not passive and inert; who are motivated by intelligently chosen purposes, not by unguided impulse from within or casual pressure from without; who are not set and rigid but who re-adapt flexibly to social change and to the consequences of their own prior conduct; who express their individual differences, but who do it in ways that are co-operative and socially contributory, not self-centered and egotistic.

In view of the socal maladjustments that work against these ends economic and social goals must be consciously pursued that will foster:

a. Personal Initiative.—At present multitudes are engaged in mechanical and monotonous pursuits that thwart the exercise of initiative. They engage chiefly in carrying out plans made by others with no original activity on their own part. . . . The resulting enfeeblement of personality extends its influence into political life and threatens the success of democratic institutions. Opportunities should be multiplied to share actively in the formation of industrial and social plans and to accept personal active responsibility for their realization.

b. Discriminating Judgment and Choice.—Integrated personality and a coherent social order can be maintained under present conditions only as individuals are trained to think clearly and to the point, and to act in accordance with the outcome of their thinking. This demands that all individuals shall seek for the facts concerned, weigh evidence honestly, and resist prejudice and class interest. . . .

c. Flexibility of Thought and Conduct.—Our society is characterized by rapid pace and constant change, while generally speaking our minds have been attuned to expect that things will remain practically unchanged. The consequence is great friction, with undue disintegration and disorganization. . . . The situation demands more than merely curative measures. Only individuals habituated to adjust to changes and to integrate them into their own personality can meet the necessities of the situation. Society must recognize the difference between stability and the preservation of what has been. They must see that change is normal. Personalities must be habituated in flexibility.

d. Individual Differences.—Traits that are distinctive and unique are not only the sources of one's own keenest satisfactions, but also the ultimate source of all fruitful social change. Present social conditions too often suppress these qualities in the many by enforcing regimentation and conformity, while in the few they are stimulated into one-sided egoistic activity at variance with the needs and rights of others.

e. Co-operativeness.—As a rule, the extent to which people resort to mutual voluntary co-operation is far below the point of maximum advantage. Continually people fail to co-operate when they would greatly benefit by so doing, and abandon co-operative efforts because of petty bickerings, suspicions, jealousy, and bossism. The young should be so educated that as adults they will readily resort to democratic co-operation. In home, classroom, workshop, and on playground, the young should become habituated to smooth, effective, and enjoyable teamwork until co-operation becomes "second nature."

5. Suitable Occupation

A congenial life work is a first requisite of a rich personality. Society can help in three distinct ways to make this possible.

a. Guidance.—Society should provide counsel as to what vocations youths should fit themselves for, taking into account the gifts, aptitudes, and tastes of the individual as well as the prospects of the various callings.

b. Training.—With appropriate regard to what guidance efforts reveal, society should make available to all youths, according to individual liking and social need, the chief skills and technics which underlie current reputable modes of obtaining a living.

c. Placement and Advancement.—The individual worker today is in many cases so far removed from the control of his own occupational fate that society has a stake in connecting him with a fitting job and in seeing to it that progress in his occupation results normally from efficient work.

6. Economic Security

. . . How utterly devastating to personality, and how completely destructive of most of the things we cherish, is a breakdown of our national (and international) economic machinery! . . . Even the many aspects of our ugly plight which seem not to be the result of selfish manipulation point to the need for greatly increased economic planning in the public interest. . . .

7. Mental Security

"What, indeed, may we believe?" Individual personality and public welfare depend upon a satisfactory answer to that question.

Above our heads, giant profit-seeking concerns fight for the privilege of writing on our minds something that will help them make money. Truth-telling organizations abound, but they cannot offer as much for an opportunity to enlighten the people as Mammon will pay for an opportunity to fool them. . . .

. . . Just as society has brought pure drinking water to the houses and the highways, so it ought to bring pure truth within our reach at every point and on every matter where non-social agencies are interested in hoodwinking us.

8. Equality of Opportunity

Our nation had its birth in a struggle for equality as opposed to special privilege. Its birthcry, the Declaration of Independence, began with the statement: "We hold these truths to be self-evident—that all men are created equal: that they are endowed by their Creator with certain inalienable rights; that among these are life, liberty, and the pursuit of happiness."

In the light of modern knowledge of individual differences, we do not construe this to mean equality of powers and abilities or of other innate or acquired personal traits. But equality as a social principle means equality of rights and opportunities, therefore no special privileges; it means the equal chance to attain to one's fullest possible development; it means accepting duties, responsibilities, and service in proportion to abilities; it means compensation in proportion to services rendered; and it means the general diffusion among the people of the knowledge, the ethics, the idealism, and the spirit which as nearly as possible shall make this equality actual and effective. . . .

Education is a function of the state, and certainly the state ought to render its service and extend its benefits equally to all children. But everywhere we find inequalities in the services and benefits of the public schools. . . . The bitter fruits of this inequality of opportunity endure throughout the lives of the generation affected.

Equality of opportunity, the birthright of every American, shall involve for each individual the opportunity to live a healthy, happy, satisfying life, to have a comfortable, sanitary home, to have useful employment that yields a comfortable living for self and dependents, to be surrounded by the beauty and truth that are inspiring and elevating rather than by the ugliness and deceptions that are discouraging and degrading, to enjoy the same rights under the law as are enjoyed by those more powerful or more favored by fortune, and to have the benefits of such educational facilities and other means of proper development as will enable the individual to become the happiest, most efficient, and most useful member of society possible with his natural endowments.

9. Freedom

. . . Self-expression is the source of our keenest satisfactions, and freedom is basic to self-expression.

How to preserve the fullest possible measure of freedom at a time when social living is necessarily surrounding each of us with a network of prohibitions which the welfare of our neighbors imposes upon us, is a very real problem. The deep sense of satisfaction experienced in making one's own decisions, fundamental as it is in preserving self-respect, should be kept in mind by society as it endeavors to assure to every person the widest sphere of freedom compatible with the equal freedom of others and with certain paramount public interests such as safety, health, decency, and quiet. Pains should be taken to assure to all at least freedom of choice of mate, of occupation, of movement, of place of residence, of manner of life, and of industrial, political, religious, and cultural affiliations.

The greatest stress, however, should be laid on what may be termed the *agitative liberties*, i.e., freedom of speech, of the press, of the screen, of broadcasting, of assembling, of demonstrating, of organizing. . . .

10. Fair Play

By fair play as a social virtue, we mean not only the justice defined by the courts but also the good sportsmanship that should be practiced

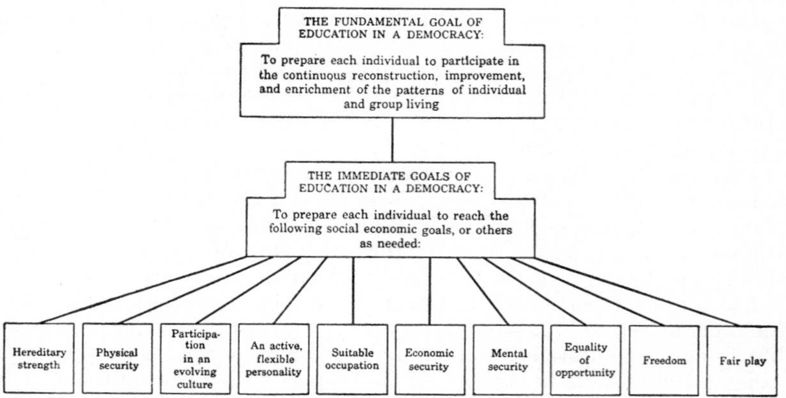

Fig. 12. The goals of education in a democracy. The immediate goals are based upon the "Social-Economic Goals of America," which were formulated by a committee appointed by the National Education Association.

by the individuals constituting our society in all their relations with one another. . . .

Fair play is simply the Golden Rule boiled down to two words. It is the practice by the individual of his duty as a member of society to act in conformity with the highest good of all other members of society. It rests upon mutual respect for the rights of others and must depend for its attainment upon good will more than upon law. . . .

According to the report of that committee, education "must take the lead in spreading among the people an understanding of their national social-economic goals, and in creating an active public opinion for their support. This involves not only the educational system devised for the young, but continued education for adults as well." The committee concludes that the schools cannot progress intelligently with this task, unless education is universal "(1) in its extent and application, (2) in its materials and methods, and (3) in its aims and spirit."

From certain quarters adverse criticisms of this report have come on the ground that it implies that the social-economic goals are to be taught as final values, like the multiplication table. These critics fear that pupils will be indoctrinated in them to the exclusion of other, and possibly better, goals; they fear a crystallization of patterns of living, rather than the realization of the ultimate aim of education, namely, the ability and the desire to reconstruct and to improve patterns of living. It seems, however, that the report has taken every reasonable step to guard against crystallization of patterns. It merely calls attention to what it regards as desirable patterns for present-day democracy. Throughout the report the democratic philosophy seems to obtain and the stated goals are in accord with the following democratic ideal which the committee adopts:

. . . In interpreting this faith and purpose for the life of today we affirm as our most cherished ideal the opportunity for all our people to develop free, co-operative, rich lives, to stand confidently on their own feet, to judge clearly and effectively by means of their own trained intelligence, to act vigorously as occasion requires, to enjoy the highest values that modern life now offers to the most privileged, to engage joyously in the free exchanges of a shared life. This ideal determines the nation's social and economic goals.

Although the above report was written during the severe business depression of the nineteen thirties, it seems to be as sound for the good times of the present writing.

QUESTIONS FOR DISCUSSION

1. What do you believe to be the chief characteristics of a democratic philosophy of education? How would a teacher conduct his classroom democratically?

2. Should we try to indoctrinate our pupils in democracy, or should we acquaint them with other "ways of life" and let them decide which they prefer? Give your reasons. What is an eclectic philosophy, and what are its advantages?

3. What evidences of lack of democracy do you see in the functioning of our life today? What changes would you make?

4. Ignorance and selfishness are usually regarded as the greatest enemies of democracy. To what extent have the schools been successful in thwarting these enemies?

5. Since there are so many philosophies of education in vogue at all times, can the teacher have any assurance that his philosophy is the best? Why or why not? Should persons who are not loyal to democratic principles be employed in the schools? Why or why not?

6. What are a few of the chief tenets of certain eminent educational philosophers, such as Rousseau, Pestalozzi, and Dewey? Do these tenets reconcile with your own? Explain.

7. What are your views with reference to the following questions, all of which have caused, or are now causing, much controversy? Do the views which you hold on these matters square with your democratic philosophy of education? Explain.

   a. Universal education and the universal establishment of public schools.
   b. Universal taxation for public schools.
   c. Compulsory school attendance.
   d. Free education for everyone on every school level.
   e. Separation of church and the public school.
   f. Equality of educational opportunity.
   g. Indoctrination versus letting the pupil decide for himself.
   h. Freedom versus discipline in teaching.
   i. Segregation of the races in the public schools.

8. Do you agree with Bode (see the quotation on page 78 of this book) that educational aims may be a handicap, instead of a help? Why or why not? How may the possible handicaps of educational aims be avoided?

9. As a teacher, supervisor, or school administrator, how would you proceed to formulate aims for your department, school, or school system? To what extent would you confer with other teachers, school officials, pupils, and the general public in formulating your aims?

10. What advantages, if any, would there be in each state formulating a set of educational goals or aims such as the educational leaders of Michigan have formulated and adopted? What dangers, if any, would you see in such a plan? (The plan is quoted on the next page.)

11. From reading the "Social-Economic Goals of America," reproduced in part on pages 81 to 87 of this book, do you see any real danger of indoctrination and crystallization of patterns? Explain.

12. Discuss the following questions which accompany the Michigan set of educational goals and which are calculated to encourage discussion of the goals: [31]

a. Should teachers be obligated to teach that democracy is, or can be made, the best type of government?

b. Does the school devote sufficient time to instruction in social, economic, and political problems of American life?

c. Are there additional qualities of character that should be emphasized in training pupils for a democratic society? Why?

d. Is there a type of discipline that trains the child to direct himself rather than to be dependent on the autocracy of forced obedience?

e. Do children need special training in co-operation?

f. What are some of the activities of a school that afford training in co-operation?

g. Is it better to emphasize that the social world grows, changes, and improves, rather than to teach that "whatever is, is right" in the community or state?

h. Is it possible to have classroom activities that will enable children to discover truths for themselves?

i. Why do some people believe that it would be sufficient to make the following goal the sole purpose of the elementary school: to develop the effective use of the fundamental knowledge and skills required by all?

j. How thorough a mastery of the fundamental skills should be required of all pupils?

k. How much vocational training should be provided in the elementary school? In the junior high school? In the senior high school?

l. Is it likely to be too costly to provide health training for all?

m. How valuable to American civilization are specialized services such as those of the physician, the engineer, the metallurgist, and the scientist?

n. How many persons should be trained for specialized services and how should these persons be selected for training?

o. Is it proper to use public funds for "training for the enrichment of adult life?"

[31] Taken from the *Ninety-Second Annual Report* of the Superintendent of Public Instruction of the State of Michigan, pp. 13–15.

p. How would emphasis on training for the enrichment of adult life tend to decrease crime and unhappiness?

q. Should society re-educate the workers thrown out of employment because of technological changes?

r. Are you convinced that democratic educational training decreases the danger of costly revolutions or dictatorships?

s. Since your experience in school, has the school changed as much as the social and economic conditions have?

SELECTED REFERENCES

Alberty, Harold, *Reorganizing the High School Curriculum,* Revised edition, The Macmillan Co., New York, 1953, pp. 39–57.

Discusses the philosophy and the purposes of the American high school.

Bode, Boyd H., *Democracy as a Way of Life,* The Macmillan Co., New York, 1937, 114 pp.

As here viewed, the school is "peculiarly the institution in which democracy becomes conscious of itself."

Broudy, Harry S., *Building a Philosophy of Education,* Prentice-Hall, New York, 1954, 480 pp.

Examines some of the major problems of education against their philosophical background.

Brubacher, John S., *et al., Modern Philosophies of Education,* Fifty-Fourth Yearbook of the National Society for the Study of Education, Chicago, 1955, 374 pp.

Presents the views of 10 philosophers on education.

Conant, James Bryant, *Education in a Divided World,* Harvard University Press, Cambridge, 1948, 200 pp.

Advocates genuine equality of educational opportunity as an answer to totalitarianism.

Counts, George S., *Education and the Promise of America,* The Macmillan Co., New York, 1945, 157 pp.

A plea for a better type of education.

Dewey, John, *Democracy and Education,* The Macmillan Co., New York, 1916, 424 pp.

A well-rounded statement of a philosophy of education. Chs. 7, 8, and 24 especially pertain to the topics here discussed.

Educational Policies Commission, *Education for All American Children,* National Education Association and the American Association of School Administrators, Washington, 1948, 292 pp.

Describes practices in modern elementary schools.

General Education in a Free Society, Harvard University Press, Cambridge, 1945, Ch. 2.

A brief discussion of the purposes of education, which were made by a Committee of the Harvard University faculty.

Hullfish, H. Gordon, "John Dewey: A Mind Ever Young," *Progressive Education*, Vol. 30 (October, 1952), pp. 16–18.

A tribute to John Dewey by one of his greatest admirers.

Kirkendall, Lester A., *et al.*, *Goals for American Education*, American Federation of Teachers, Chicago, 1948, 130 pp.

An evaluation of the aims of education in the light of world conditions.

Loughery, Sister M. Bernard Francis, *Parental Rights in American Educational Law*, Catholic University of America Press, Washington, 1952, 243 pp.

Legal rights of parents are discussed.

Moral and Spiritual Values in the Public Schools, Educational Policies Commission of the National Education Association, 1951, 100 pp.

States those values which the public schools should teach.

PART TWO

ORGANIZATION AND ADMINISTRATION OF THE SCHOOLS

CHAPTER 3

General Policies of School Organization and Administration

Purposes and Types of School Administration

Necessity for School Administration. The school must be properly organized and administered, if the public and the pupils are not to be cheated. The schools cannot run themsleves, any more than a private business can run itself. School administration exists only to make the schools more efficient. Its purpose is to help to assure that one hundred cents' worth of education is obtained from each dollar expended. It must always be a slave to the pupils' welfare. It must consider both financial and pedagogical efficiency of the schools.

There are hundreds of details pertaining to the administration of a school or of a school system, and for looking after these details someone must be responsible; unless someone is responsible—and he or they well qualified for the responsibility—there is likely to be maladjustment and friction, all of which results in waste. School policies must be formulated, the policies must be placed into operation, and a careful check must be made to ascertain how efficiently the policies are operating. Teachers, principals, janitors, bus drivers, and other school employees must be appointed, paid, supervised, promoted, and a few of them demoted or dismissed. Sites, buildings, equipment, and supplies must be provided. The boundaries for individual schools must be established. A pupil transportation system must be organized, especially in the rural districts. The children must be enrolled in school and kept in regular school attendance; they must be properly classified, instructed, and promoted or demoted. Provision must be made for textbooks, school libraries, and other materials and services. To attend to all these matters requires a large amount of time and effort, and what is more important, properly to attend to them requires special preparation in school administration. Albeit necessary, common sense, which someone has dubbed "the most uncommon thing in the world," will not suffice for the efficient administration of a school or a school system.

Democracy Versus Autocracy in School Administration. In the early days there was little or no democracy in school administration. Teachers were mere "cogs in a machine." They had no part in school-policymaking. Although that autocratic plan is still followed in many schools and school systems, in the more progressive schools and school systems democracy in administration is practiced. In those systems teachers are being given a voice in school administration; their opinions are welcomed and sought. More significant still, much of the work of administering the school or the school system is being placed in the hands of teachers who perform this work as individuals or as members of committees. The teachers serve on special committees, such as those for teachers' meetings, salary schedules, extraclass activities, the curriculum, pupil guidance, public and professional relations, ethics, textbooks, school supplies and equipment, and the school library.

Teachers of today, therefore, must have a quantum of knowledge of school administration. They must know much of how the schools are organized and administered, if they are to co-operate properly with school officials and school administrators and are to make suggestions looking toward the improvement of school administration. Ignorant participants do not beget intelligent co-operation. A large part of the work of modern teachers consists of school administration both inside and outside the classroom.

National Differences in School Control

American Versus Foreign Policies in School Control. In no other country do the schools belong to the people as much as in the United States, and in no other country is the administration of the schools as close to the people. Whereas in most of the other countries of the world, education is a governmental affair concerning which the people do not have much voice, in the United States the people control the schools through such means as the selection of school board members and the voting of school revenues. The administration of the school systems of most foreign countries is much more highly centralized than in the United States. In most of those countries education is a division of the central government, is financed largely or wholly by the central government, and is directed by a minister of education or a secretary of education; moreover, there is complete or large uniformity in education in the various communities of those countries. From the point of view of organization, of financial support, and of administration, therefore, the school systems of most foreign countries may be called national.[1]

In the United States there is a separate school system for each state and each territory; thus, there are forty-eight state school systems and seven territorial school systems. Each of these school systems is sovereign and each controls its own destiny. With the exception of the territorial school systems, there is no Federal control as there is in most foreign countries. There is no American system of education in the sense that there is an English, a French, or a Danish system of education.

Our state and territorial systems of education are, however, more similar than dissimilar. Although they differ much in detail, they are somewhat similar in their fundamentals. They have, for example, somewhat similar forms of organization, somewhat similar means of financial support, and somewhat similar curriculums. Unquestionably, the domination of a common ideal, namely, that every individual shall have a certain quantum of education, and may have almost any amount of education at public expense, has been the chief factor in causing large similarity in our school systems. Guided by that common ideal, our school systems have become increasingly similar through the long-time operation of experimentation and imitation. This experimentation and imitation have come somewhat as follows: a certain state has adopted a given policy, has demonstrated the merit of the policy, and before many years have elapsed, other states—perhaps all of them—have adopted the same policy. It

[1] Since World War II, the school systems of some foreign countries have been patterned somewhat after ours. Japan is a notable example.

is that common educational ideal and that similarity in the more fundamental elements of the American state and territorial school systems which residents of foreign countries and many of our own citizens have in mind when they speak of the "American system of education," of the "school system of the United States," or when they call this system a national system.

Explanations for Our Policy in School Control. There has never been any Federal control of schools in the United States, except that control which follows Federal subsidy. Education was not mentioned in either the Articles of Confederation adopted in 1783 or in the Constitution of the United States adopted in 1787. Apparently those frameworks of government assumed, at least by silence, that the responsibility for education was to be left entirely to the respective states. Moreover, the Tenth Amendment to the United States Constitution, ratified in 1791, affirmed that "the powers not delegated to the United States by the Constitution, nor prohibited by it to the States, are reserved to the States respectively, or to the people." [2] What are the explanations for the failure of our forefathers to make provisions for the Federal organization, financial support, and control of education? The following explanations may be given:

1. The thirteen original colonies which joined hands to form the United States had begun colonial systems of education long before the adoption of the Federal Constitution. Moreover, those colonial systems represented various educational traditions and beliefs which the several colonies were interested in maintaining, and which they were afraid that they could not maintain under Federal control of education.
2. There were many urgent problems of the new Federal Government, without undertaking the problems of education; there were, for example, the problems of national defense, taxation, and national economy. Besides, because society was then less complex than today, education was less necessary; moreover, the home and the church were then much more potent factors in education than today, and their efforts made a formal educational agency, such as the school, less necessary.

[2] In view of this amendment, it is questionable whether, without a change in the Constitution, the Federal Government could legally assume any control of education in the states. Proponents of state and local control argue, however, that it could, through financial subsidies and the control which follows such subsidies, superimpose a Federal system of education upon the state systems.

3. Our forefathers were skeptical of making a central government too strong. They desired to maintain the proper balance of power between the Federal Government and the state governments; that problem is still present. They preferred strong state governments to a strong Federal Government. There was not much feeling of nationalism in those days. There was more rugged individualism than today.

COMPARATIVE MERITS OF STATE AND OF NATIONAL CONTROL OF SCHOOLS. Although education in the United States has historically been under the control of the states and of the local communities, and although there appears to have been general satisfaction with such control, arguments are frequently presented for Federal control of schools. For Federal control such as most foreign countries have, many persons argue that such control would beget greater efficiency for the schools. They affirm that in state and local control, school funds are frequently wasted both through the adoption of poor policies and through the inefficient administration of excellent policies; they maintain that much of this waste would be eliminated through Federal control of schools. They also point out that under Federal control educational opportunities and school-tax burdens would be equalized among the various states, whereas large inequalities in such opportunities and burdens result from state and local control of schools.

The arguments just stated for Federal control of the schools are attacked, however, by the proponents of state and local control. Those proponents affirm that state and local control of the schools enables the states and the local communities to meet their individual needs, whereas Federal control might result in a national uniformity in schools which would neglect the needs of the various states and of the various communities within the states. They argue, too, that state and local control of schools more readily permits educational experimentation, the results of which may become immediately known to, and be adopted by, other states and other communities.

FEDERAL INTEREST IN EDUCATION. Although education was not mentioned in the Articles of Confederation or in the Constitution of the United States, and although there has never been Federal control of education within the states,[3] the Federal Government has always been interested in education. As was indicated in Chapter 1 (America's Historic Faith in Education), the Presidents of the

[3] Except that following Federal subsidy.

United States have universally expressed their faith and their interest in education. For example, George Washington, our first President (1789–1797), said in his Farewell Address on September 17, 1796:

> Promote, then, as an object of primary importance, institutions for the general diffusion of knowledge. In proportion as the structure of a government gives force to public opinion, it is essential that public opinion should be enlightened.

Thomas Jefferson, our third President (1801–1809), recognized the importance of education as few other persons, if any, did. More than any other person of his generation he was responsible for translating and adapting the gospel of the French Revolutionists—the gospel of "liberty, equality, and fraternity"—to American conditions. Jefferson had abiding faith in democracy, and he believed that efficient democracy could not be achieved by an ignorant citizenry. Education was seen by him to be the ferment which was necessary to make democracy work. The faith of Jefferson in education is well seen in the following quotation from him:

> If a nation expects to be ignorant and free in a state of civilization it expects what never was and never will be. The functions of every government have propensities to command at will the liberty and property of their constituents. There is no safe deposit for these but with the people themselves; nor can they be safe with them without information.

It is not with sympathetic sentiments and kind words alone that the Federal Government has shown its interest in education. That interest has been shown in at least two important material ways. In the first place, the Federal Government has granted millions of acres of land and hundreds of millions of dollars to the states for the support of education;[4] further information regarding those land and money grants will be presented in Chapter 6 (Financial Support of the Schools) of this book. In the second place, the interest of the Federal Government in education has been demonstrated through the

[4] This policy was begun as early as 1785, when lot 16 in each "Congressional Township" in the Northwest Territory was set aside for the support of schools. That policy was continued in other sections of the United States, whose states entered the Union later.

creation of many bureaus, offices, and other agencies which are wholly or partly educational.

In certain fields, though, the responsibility of the Federal Government for education is primary and well defined and has been assumed by the Federal Government. According to the Report of the National Advisory Committee on Education (appointed by President Herbert Hoover) there are six fields of educational activity which are outside the jurisdiction of the states. These six fields are:

1. The education of persons resident on special Federal areas, such as government reservations and Federal districts, lying outside the legal jurisdiction of the state and other regional governments.
2. The education of the American Indians and other indigenous peoples within the national jurisdiction.
3. The education of the peoples of the Territories and outlying possessions.
4. The training of persons in the service of the national government.
5. Scientific research and the collection and diffusion of information regarding education.
6. The intellectual and educational co-operation of the United States with other nations.[5]

The chief educational agency of the Federal Government is the *United States Office of Education.* In 1866, the National Association of State and City School Superintendents (now known as the American Association of School Administrators) went on record as favoring the establishment of a Federal bureau of education. That organization was supported in its request by many other organizations and by many private citizens. A bill providing for such a department was introduced in Congress by James A. Garfield, and was enacted into law on March 2, 1867. It read as follows:

Be it enacted, by the Senate and House of Representatives of the United States of America in Congress assembled. That there shall be established, at the city of Washington, a department of education, for the purpose of collecting such statistics and facts as shall show the condition and progress of education in the several States and Territories, and of diffusing such information respecting the organization and management of schools and school systems, and methods of teaching, as shall aid the people of the United States in the establishment and maintenance

[5] *Federal Relations to Education:* Part I, *Committee Findings and Recommendations,* pp. 9–10.

of efficient school systems, and otherwise promote the cause of education throughout the country.—39th Congress, 2nd Session—1867. (14 Stat. L., p. 434.)

In 1869, The Department of Education, which was created by the law of 1867, was replaced by the Office of Education and was made a division of the Department of the Interior. In 1870, the office was renamed the Bureau of Education, and that title was retained until 1929 when the title of Office of Education was restored. In 1939, the Office of Education was transferred from the Department of the Interior to the newly created Federal Security Agency. It is now a division of the Department of Health, Education, and Welfare, and the Secretary of that Department is a member of the President's cabinet. The ranking official of the office has always held the title of Commissioner of Education. Although the Commissioner has sometimes been appointed by the President on a political or a semi-political basis, practically all of them have been outstanding educators. Practically all of the regular employees of the office are under the civil-service laws of the United States government.[6] They are usually regarded as experts in their fields.

The duties of the office as outlined in the statutes of 1867 creating the office have been closely followed. The general duty has been to stimulate the development of education, not to control or to administer it. The main work of the office has been to collect and to disseminate information on education. The office diffuses such information through (1) its many publications consisting of reports of special studies, of the *Biennial Survey of Education*, of a magazine called *School Life*, and of other educational works; (2) conferences of educational and of lay leaders, those conferences being called by the Commissioner of Education or by members of his staff; (3) correspondence; and (4) addresses by the Commissioner of Education and his staff members.

The statistical reports of the office are widely recognized as the best reports on education in the world, in spite of the fact that the office does not have the legal power to require state and local school officials to provide the information on which the reports are based. During recent years, the office has conducted, at the request

[6] The divisions of the U. S. Office of Education and the names of the persons in charge of these divisions may be found in the *Educational Directory*, which is published annually by the U. S. Office of Education.

of local and state governing boards, some surveys or constructive investigations of local and state educational systems and of public colleges and universities. It has also been given the duty of supervising the distribution and the expenditure of public funds for vocational education and for other Federal purposes.

A large part of the service of the Office of Education is provided gratis, and any of that service may be procured at actual cost. Any of the publications of the office may be obtained at actual cost from the Superintendent of Documents, Government Printing Office, Washington, D. C. For the use of its staff and of any citizen, the office maintains the most complete library on education in the world. Among its numerous services the library staff has prepared bibliographies on many educational topics and will, upon request, so far as its time and its other resources permit, prepare other bibliographies; such service is available to any school employee or other citizen, usually free of charge.

In addition to the Office of Education, which is the chief educational agency of the United States Government, there are numerous other Federal agencies which perform educational services. In fact, every department of the Federal Government (Defense, Navy, Commerce, Agriculture, etc.) may be said to be partly educational. Every department has as its reason for existing the giving of service, and one large phase of that service is the providing of educational information to any citizen who may request it.

Many of our citizens believe that the Federal Government has not shown sufficient interest and enough participation in education. Both interest and participation in education for the Federal Government have been advocated from time to time, usually along three lines: (1) a separate Federal Department of Education with a Secretary of Education co-ordinate with the other Federal departments such as the Department of State, the Department of Defense, and the Department of Agriculture; (2) Federal financial aid to general education, as is now given to certain phases of special education, such as vocational (agriculture, home economics, and trades) and distributive[7] education; and (3) the establishment of a national university.

Each of these proposals has had numerous advocates, and many

[7] Distributive education means education for retail selling and other distributive occupations. It is, of course, vocational education.

sessions of Congress have seen bills introduced looking toward placing the proposals into legislation. The proposal for a national university has been made since the days of George Washington, who made provision in his will for such an institution.[8] This recommendation has been repeated by many succeeding Presidents, but no action has been taken and is not likely to be taken now, because of the recent development of many great state and private universities.

Although many earlier proposals had been made for a separate Department of Education and for a Federal subsidy for general education, these two proposals became particularly insistent about the time of the close of World War I (1914–1918). Albeit its results were not always good, that world cataclysm gave one of the greatest stimuli which education has ever received. On the credit side of the educational ledger the war demonstrated that education enabled our soldiers to make greater progress than they could have made without education. For example, it was found that by far the majority of the men who won officers' commissions in the training camps were college graduates. On the debit side of the ledger, the war recorded the fact that one-fourth of the soldiers—and they, it should be noted, were the flower of American manhood, between the ages of twenty and thirty—who responded to the draft were unable to read an English newspaper and to write a letter. The draft also showed that approximately twenty-nine per cent of the men examined could not be accepted for general military service, because of physical incompetency. Moreover, it was found that the men who came from certain states, especially the states which had not developed efficient school systems, had a much larger percentage of illiteracy and of physical disability than the men who came from the other states.[9] These were disconcerting facts and stood out as a hard criticism of some of our state school systems. Then it was that education came to be more and more looked upon as not a state problem alone, but as a problem in which the Federal Government must participate, if the perpetuity and the progress of the nation

[8] In his will, Washington gave fifty shares in the Potomac Company, worth then about $25,000, toward the endowment of such an institution, provided Congress should "incline to extend a fostering hand toward it." The Potomac Company has long since been bankrupt. (For a brief account of the history of these proposals, the interested reader is referred to Paul Monroe's *Cyclopedia of Education*, Vol. IV, Macmillan, 1918, pp. 385–386.)

[9] Similar conditions were found in World War II. Illiteracy, though, was much less common than in World War I.

were to be assured. World War II and later drafts accentuated that belief. Of 18 million men examined for military service during World War II, one in every twelve was found to be illiterate, semi-literate, or mentally deficient.

Since 1918, many sessions of Congress have seen at least one bill introduced for the establishment of a separate Federal Department of Education with a Secretary of Education in the President's cabinet.[10] Most of these bills have also provided for a large subsidy to the states for general education in the elementary and the secondary schools. As yet, none of these bills has been enacted into law, and since the establishment of the Federal Department of Health, Education, and Welfare, the interest in a separate Department of Education has greatly lessened.

The advocates of these proposals believe that education does not have sufficient prestige at present in the Federal Government. They point out that in the Federal Government education does not have a much higher rank that such activities as the dairy industry, the plant industry, and entomology. They affirm that a separate Department of Education headed by a Secretary of Education would make education more articulate. They insist that education vitally affects the welfare and the progress of the whole nation, and that in consequence, the Federal Government should take a larger interest in education. Contrariwise, the opponents of such legislation point out the danger of bureaucracy and autocracy in any Federal subsidy and control of education. They fear an encroachment upon the American ideals of personal liberty and individuality—that a separate Federal department of education and a Federal subsidy for education would tend to remove the control of the schools from the hands of the people and to place it in the hands of Federal officials who would be in a position to regiment the education and the lives of the people. They fear also that placing a separate Secretary of Education in the President's cabinet would throw education into the maelstrom of "politics" on a national scale.

State Control Versus Local Control of Education

Evolution of State Control of Education. An outstanding changing conception of the people of the United States regarding

10 Some recent bills have also provided for a Federal Board of Education.

education has been concerning the relative place of the state and of the local community in education. In the early days the local communities were in complete control of education, and the colonial and the state constitutions and statutes were silent on education. In those days the local communities could provide schools, or not provide them, as they chose, or if they provided schools, they could provide any kind—efficient or inefficient.

To the credit of the faith of the American people in education, it is worth repeating that many communities provided truly public schools before there were state laws requiring their establishment. Schools were often started as soon as the settlers had established their homes. In Massachusetts, for example, the first permanent settlement (Plymouth) was made in 1620, and schools which were truly public were established by certain communities as early as 1635. As has been stated earlier, Massachusetts enacted a colony-wide law requiring a certain amount of education as early as 1642.

Notwithstanding the avid and widespread interest of the early settlers in education, it was soon found that leaving to each community the decision of whether schools should be established resulted in many communities not establishing them. In consequence, the colonial, the territorial, and the state legislatures deemed it necessary or advisable to enact legislation for the establishment, the organization, and the financial support of schools. As was pointed out in Chapter 1, Massachusetts, as early as 1647, enacted a law which required each community having fifty or more families to establish an elementary school, and each community having one hundred or more families to establish a grammar school in addition to an elementary school. It was noted, too, that even before the law of 1647, Massachusetts had enacted in 1642 a law which required parents to see that their children learned to read.

The Massachusetts laws of 1642 and 1647 were the genesis of state control of education. Since that time, hundreds of other laws have been enacted in each of the forty-eight states to provide for the establishment, the organization, the supervision, the control, and the support of schools; in fact, there is today scarcely a feature of the organization and the administration of schools upon which the state laws are silent. Moreover, all of the present state constitutions have a pronouncement of the importance of education and on the responsibility of the state for providing schools.

Education as a State Function.[11] From the earliest days the conviction has been growing that the state must be responsible for seeing that its citizens have a certain kind and a given amount of education. That the state has this responsibility is shown by the state constitutions, by the hundreds of school statutes in each state, and by the scores of decisions of local, state, and federal courts. The assumption of educational control by the state did not come by mere chance. State control has come, because of the early and the ever-growing belief that education is the buttress of a democratic government and that because of its necessity it cannot be left to the whims of any individual, of any church, of any community, of any race, or of any other group.

It is true that in the administration of the schools the state has delegated most administrative functions to counties, parishes, cities, towns, villages, townships, and other local school districts. These powers and duties have been delegated by the state legislatures which are the supreme lawmaking bodies in state government. If a state wishes to increase or to decrease the powers and the duties which it has delegated to local school officials, it may do so through changing its laws. Local school officials and local school employees are, therefore, merely agents of the state for carrying out the educational dictates of the state; if they are also responsible to the people of the local community, it is only because the state has delegated to the people of the local community a certain amount of the responsibility for education.

Desirable Limitations of State Control of Education. From the beginning the tendency has been for the state to assume larger control of education. In brief, as the years have passed, local communities have given back to state government more and more of the control of education. Perhaps, it would be more accurate to say that such responsibility has been taken from local communities by state government, because local communities have not given up willingly their educational prerogatives. States have more and more taken back the educational responsibility, because the local communities could not or would not assume the responsibility satisfactorily. Much as it

[11] Sometimes, the state has delegated to private schools and to parents the function of providing education. The function of providing education is not exclusively a state or public function, as we shall see later when private interest in education is discussed.

has been opposed, the inevitable drift has been toward centralization of school control. As would be expected, there is a larger amount of state control of education in the older states, that is, the Eastern states, than in the newer states of the other sections of the United States.

What are desirable limits of state control? On the one hand, there are many persons who believe that state control of education has already gone far enough in the typical state; in fact, some persons believe that state control has gone too far. These persons maintain that the state control now exercised in certain states is tending to

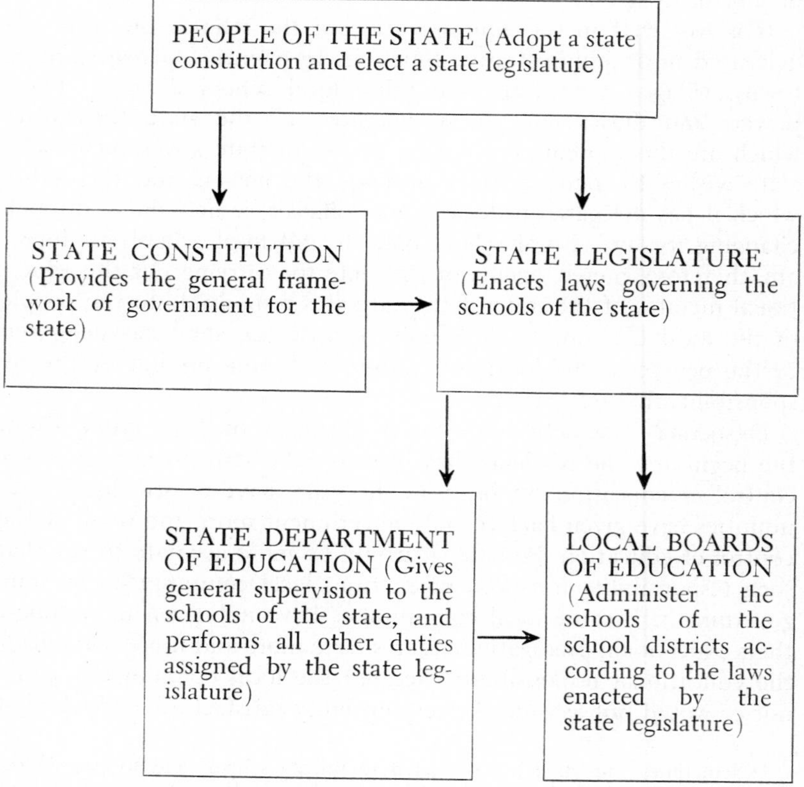

FIG. 13. The flow of authority for the control and the administration of schools in each state of the United States.

stifle community interest and initiative, to standardize education, and to ignore in many ways the educational needs of local communities. They fear that through its power to control education, and especially through its power to determine what shall be taught, the state is likely to try to regiment its citizens by indoctrinating them with only one point of view, namely, the view of those persons in power. These persons worship the god of individuality.

On the other hand, there are many persons who believe that state control of education in the typical state has not gone far enough. These persons contend that schools will be more efficient when the state legislatures have enacted more stringent laws which determine most educational standards, policies, and procedures of local communities. These persons worship the god of social co-operation.

The problem is, therefore, that of reconciling the two American ideals of (1) individuality and (2) social co-operation. That has always been our problem. It is the eternal problem of democratic governments. The two ideals must be kept in proper balance.

Probably the best type of school control—and this is the ideal toward which practice seems to be striving—would be for the state to establish minimum standards, especially in the more fundamental aspects of an educational program, which every community in the state would be expected to meet. When the minimum standards have been established, prudence would dictate that the local community be permitted to exercise its initiative in experimenting with and in exceeding those standards. In any event, since education is so important for the individual and for society, the state should make sure that no pupil, because of his residence, poverty, or other vicissitude of fortune, is denied his educational heritage. To deny such heritage would cheat the child and would harm society.

State Control of Private Effort in Education [12]

Evolution of Private Effort in Education. The first schools established in the United States were private schools, and in many of the colonial and the state governments for several decades

[12] As used here, the term private schools also includes church schools; most private schools are church schools. Parochial schools are the most common type of church schools, but they are not the only kind of church schools.

private-school enrollment exceeded public-school enrollment. Since the universal establishment of public schools and their improvement, the percentage of the total population enrolled in public schools has been increasing, and the percentage enrolled in private schools has been decreasing. This tendency has been noticed, particularly during recent decades, and it has been noticed, especially in the secondary schools and the colleges. It is observed that the percentage of all elementary school pupils enrolled in private schools has decreased from 11.7 in 1890 to approximately 11 today. The percentage of all secondary school pupils enrolled in private schools has decreased from 31.9 in 1890 to approximately 13 today, and the percentage of all college students enrolled to private colleges has decreased from 84.4 in 1890 to approximately 49 today. Private schools have been decreasing, largely because of the difficulty of financing them.

What are the motives which have impelled millions of parents to send their children to private schools where they usually must pay tuition at the same time that they must pay taxes to support the public schools? Two motives stand out: first, there has been the belief on the part of many parents that the private school is better than the public school—at least that it can meet better the needs of their children; second, there has been the desire, especially in the case of the church schools, to give the children instruction in religion, which could not be given legally in a public school.

Amount of State Control of Private Effort in Education. With few exceptions, the historic policy of the state legislatures has been to encourage private effort in education. Private schools, which were not run for profit, have usually been exempt from taxation the same as public schools. Seldom has legislation been enacted which would discourage private schools; neither has there been an undue amount of state control of such schools. In the early days, not only was there an entire absence of state supervision and state control of private schools, but such schools were frequently supported largely by public moneys. Shortly after the opening of the nineteenth century, however, the policy of giving public funds for the support of private schools began to be regarded as unsound, and it was not long until the legislatures of practically all the states enacted statutes prohibiting the use of public funds for such purpose. Moreover, as new constitutions were adopted or as old constitutions were amended, most of the states wrote into their constitutions a section which prohibited the use of public moneys for the support of private schools.[13] Typical of these pronouncements is that of the present constitution of Ohio (Article VI, Section 2) which says:

> The general assembly shall make such provisions, by taxation, or otherwise, as, with the income arising from the school trust fund, will secure a thorough and efficient system of common schools throughout the state; but no religious or other sect, or sects, shall ever have any exclusive right to, or control of, any part of the school funds of this state.

Such pronouncements on the separation of church and state were buttressed on February 10, 1947, by the following decision of the United States Supreme Court (*Everson v. Board of Education,* No. 52, October term, 1946):

> No tax in any amount, large or small, can be levied to support any religious activities or institutions whatever they may be called, or whatever form they may adopt to teach or practice religion.

In the famous Champaign, Illinois, decision of the United States Supreme Court on March 8, 1948, public school property may not be used for religious instruction, and that decision makes the use of public school property for private purposes more doubtful. The decision, however, did not frown on everything connected with the Holy Bible, because the United States Supreme Court also recently ruled legal the New Jersey law which requires the daily reading of at least five verses from the Old Testament in the public schools, and allows any pupil to absent himself, if he does not care to hear that reading.

Coincident with the enactment of legislation prohibiting the use of public funds for the financing of private schools came legislation which established certain state inspection of private schools. At present, such inspection extends from almost nothing in a few states to a large amount in other states. Certain states require the same minimum standards for private schools as are required for public schools; other states have little or no state control for private schools, except

[13] A few states have recently enacted laws which provide health services, textbooks, and transportation for private-school pupils the same as for public-school pupils. The courts have usually declared such aid legal, because it is given to "the pupils and not to the school."

Many public schools now co-operate with private schools by giving free use of such facilities as libraries, shops, laboratories, gymnasia, and athletic fields.

to check the attendance of pupils in these schools. The tendency, however, in both theory and practice is to require the private schools to meet the same minimum standards which are demanded of the public schools.

Although they are easily in the minority, many of our fellow citizens believe that for the state merely to standardize private schools does not go far enough. They would abolish such schools, because of their belief that they are snobbish and do not provide equality of educational opportunity. In brief, they believe that all children, especially in the elementary school, should be required to attend the public schools. This feeling, some years ago (1922), became sufficiently strong in one state (Oregon) to obtain the enactment of a law which would have abolished all private schools for children below the age of sixteen. That law, however, was declared unconstitutional by the United States Supreme Court in 1925; part of that famous decision reads as follows:

> The fundamental theory of liberty upon which all governments in the Union repose excludes any general power of the State to standardize its children by forcing them to accept instruction from public teachers only. The child is not the mere creature of the State; those who nurture him and direct his destiny have the right coupled with the high duty to recognize and prepare him for additional duties.

State Organization for the Control of Education

Earlier in this chapter, it was stated that education has from almost the earliest days been regarded as a state function; this is demonstrated by state statutes, state constitutions, and decisions of the courts. It was not until 1784, however, that any state established a personnel and an organization for the general supervision of the control of education. This first legislation was enacted by the state of New York when it created the so-called "University" with its Board of Regents, and gave this institution and its governing board jurisdiction over the colleges and the academies of the state. In 1787, the law of 1784 was revised, and the Board of Regents was given more definite powers pertaining to the colleges and the academies. The University of the State of New York which was created by the Act of 1784 was not, however, in the commonly accepted sense a university at all; it was rather a state board of education.[14] This was the first state board of education in the nation.

Not only was New York the first state to establish a state board of education, but it was the first state to make provision for a chief state school official. In 1812, the legislature enacted a law which provided for the appointment of a State Superintendent of Common Schools. Gideon Hawley was appointed on January 14, 1813, to this office, and thus became the first chief state school official in the United States. In fact, he was the first superintendent of schools, state or local, in the United States.

How are we to account for the long delay in establishing the offices of state board of education and of chief state school official, which today are considered so necessary that the latter is found in every state and the former in practically every state? At least two retarding influences stand out. First, the early theory of individual and community rights met with popular approval. To our forefathers—practically all of whom were rugged individualists—any centralization of power and authority smacked of autocracy, and to autocracy they were unalterably opposed. Second, the idea of the association of the church and the state, especially in educational matters, was prevalent and was difficult to eradicate from the minds of the people. These two influences made for decentralization in school control and organization down to almost the middle of the nineteenth century and kept even the beginnings of state supervision from appearing until the opening of the nineteenth century. The offices had to wait, therefore, until unmistakable needs brought them into being.

THE EVOLUTION OF THE STATE BOARD OF EDUCATION. The second state to establish a state board of education was Massachusetts in 1837, and one of the first acts of this board was to elect Horace Mann its secretary. Since that date, all states, with the exception of a mere handful, have created such boards with general educational functions. The remaining few states have state boards, but with restricted function, such as administering the vocational-education laws of the United States or administering all or some of the state colleges and universities.

The function of the state boards varies from that of merely advising

14 Contrary to the common impression, New York has a vigorous and elaborate state university organization today; she does not have one state university, however, as do many states.

the chief state school official to large control of the educational system of the state. The Board of Regents, which is the state board of education in the state of New York, has larger powers and duties than the state board of education of any other state. The tendency has been to give the state board of education larger functions, and at present, in most states, it has general supervision over education in the state; this function is exercised with the assistance of the chief state school official and his staff.

In most states there is still a two-headed state organization for education, consisting of a state board of education on the one hand, and a chief state school official on the other hand. The evils inherent in such a two-headed organization have been mitigated in most states by making the chief state school official an *ex officio* officer of the state board; the tendency has been to make him the chief executive officer of the state board. Frequently, however, the state board of education is responsible to a different authority than the chief state school official, and this has often led to friction and duplication of effort.

The number of members on state boards of education now ranges from three to twenty-three, with seven being the modal number. The members are selected in one of the following manners: appointment by the governor, appointment by local boards of education, appointment by the chief state school official, election by popular vote at a regular or a special election, *ex officio* membership, or by a combination of two or more of the plans just mentioned. In most states, the members are selected "at large," that is, to represent the whole state and not a particular section of the state. As a rule, no legal qualifications are prescribed for the members, except residence within the state. In practically all of the states the members serve without salary. The term of office ranges from one year to twelve years; the modal term is six years.

THE EVOLUTION OF THE STATE DEPARTMENT OF EDUCATION. Every state now has a state department of education, which is constituted of the chief state school official and his staff. The title which has been most frequently used in designating the chief state school official is Superintendent of Public Instruction. The next most frequently used title has been Commissioner of Education.[15] The term of office

[15] An up-to-date list of the occupants of this office, together with their official titles, can be found in *Educational Directory*, which is published annually by the U. S. Office of Education.

is now usually prescribed by law at either two or four years, but a few states prescribe an indefinite tenure.

The office of the chief state school official is potentially the most important educational office in a state, the presidency of the state university not excepted. The importance of the office is more fully realized when it is remembered that education is not only the most important business of the state, but by far the largest business of the state. The chief state school official has the responsibility of directing this large and important public enterprise.

Fig. 14. Horace Mann. *(Frontispiece from Ward G. Reeder's* An Introduction to Public-School Relations, *Revised edition. Copyright 1953 by The Macmillan Company.)*

The office should be the head and the heart of the school system of the state. It should encourage, supervise, and direct the development of the whole system of the state from the kindergarten through the university. It should bring every worthy educational endeavor in the state within its vitalizing influence. These aims are not always accomplished, because the legislation pertaining to the office is archaic in many respects. Like Topsy, the office in most states has "just growed." Reforms in most states are sadly needed.

The chief handicap under which the office labors results from the method of selecting the incumbent of the office. Almost two-thirds of the states still elect the chief state school official by popular vote, and practically all of these still elect him on a partisan ticket. The remaining states permit either the governor or the state board of education to select the chief state school official. Popular election of school superintendents may be criticized on the following bases: (1) it establishes residence restrictions for its candidates; (2) it results in a low and a static salary; (3) it begets a short tenure for the holder of the office; (4) and worst of all, it subjects the selection of the person best qualified for the office to the vicissitudes of "politics." The chief state school official should be a technically trained expert in school administration, and the people should delegate the responsibility of selecting him to such a group of their representatives as the state board of education.

There are many other handicaps under which the office still labors. Most of these handicaps are the result of constitutions which were adopted years ago, and which have become petrified and difficult to change. This petrification of the forms of the office has been especially the result of the state constitutions which, as a rule, not only mandate the legislature to create and to maintain the office, but prescribe as well many of the important features of the office. Almost two-thirds of the states now provide for the office in their state constitutions, and most of these constitutions prescribe certain of the features of the office. Thus, it happens that many features of the office have become petrified over a long period of years and have frequently been unable to give way expeditiously to new and better practices. The more modern state departments of education are found, as a whole, in the Eastern states of the United States, which as a rule do not prescribe in their constitutions any of the features of the office, but have left entirely to the legislatures the establishment of such features.

To have the best leadership from the state department of education will require the most favorable conditions pertaining to the office of chief state school official, because that office makes the department largely what it is. These favorable conditions would be somewhat as follows: The chief state school official should be appointed by the state board of education, without regard to his residence, his party politics, or any other extraneous factor. He should be paid a salary commensurate with his ability and with the importance of his office, and such salary should be determined by the state board of education. The term of office should be indefinite, or a sufficient number of years to make possible the development of a constructive educational program. Under the general control, supervision, and direction of the state board of education, the chief state school official should be the executive head of the state school system. For the prompt and efficient performance of its work, the office should be given an adequate and competent staff, and the members of this staff should be selected and paid wholly on the basis of their ability and their accomplishments. School officials and school employees should urge the adoption of state laws which will obtain the practices just mentioned. They should labor ardently for such laws, because the schools can never give full service until they are managed by the most efficient leaders possible.

Local Organization for the Control of Education

School-administrative Units. The state is the legal unit for the control of schools, although most of the actual administration of the schools has been delegated by the state to political subdivisions of the state; these subdivisions are known as school districts. With the exception of a few decades at the beginning of the schools, the school districts have generally been entirely independent from other governmental activities. That separation was decided upon by the legislatures, because of the belief that the schools should have protection from the changing fortunes of partisan "politics" which frequently obtains in the administration of other phases of government. For the reason just given this separation is favored by practically all professional educators, but the separation is vigorously opposed by practically all authorities in political science.

Within the United States there are now approximately 50,000 school districts, and these districts are governed by approximately 230,000 school board members. There are numerous types of school districts; in fact, most states have several types. The districts vary in size from the smallest district, employing only one teacher, to the large city and county school systems, employing thousands of teachers. The districts are known by various names, such as county, parish, city, common school, graded, town, township, consolidated, central, community, joint union graded, union high, township high, and county high. The number of school districts in a state ranges from fifteen in Delaware to more than five thousand each in a few other states. In the New England states the town is usually the school-administrative unit; in the Western states the township, or a modification of it, is usually the school-administrative unit.

The tendency in both theory and practice is toward a larger unit for school administration, especially for the rural schools. Probably, not more than four or five thousand school districts are needed in the whole United States. Every year sees the demise of hundreds of small school districts, through their consolidation or merger with other districts. Every year, moreover, sees powers and duties subtracted from small school-administrative units and given to a larger intermediate unit, which is usually called the county.

Forward-looking educators and laymen are agreed that the largest handicap to rural-school efficiency and progress today is the small units under which the rural schools are organized and administered. Moreover, they are agreed that these small units are a chief explanation for the lag in rural school administration compared with city school administration. In the early days, city schools were organized, financed, and administered by city wards. It was early seen, however, that the whole city was a more practicable administrative unit for schools than the city ward. Gradually, it has come to be recognized that a larger unit for the administration of the rural schools is more practicable than the one-teacher district, the township, or other small school district. Research and experience have not yet demonstrated what the size of the unit for the administration of rural schools should be, although the county is most frequently suggested as the most desirable unit. It is apparent, though, that because of the differences in topography, distance, quality of highways, and population density the county may be too large in certain instances and too small in others. In general, the size of the school district [16] should meet

[16] The "administrative" (school district) unit should not be confused with the "attendance" (individual school) unit. An administrative unit may have more than one school. It is known that small administrative units beget small attendance units and that small attendance units are pedagogically and financially wasteful.

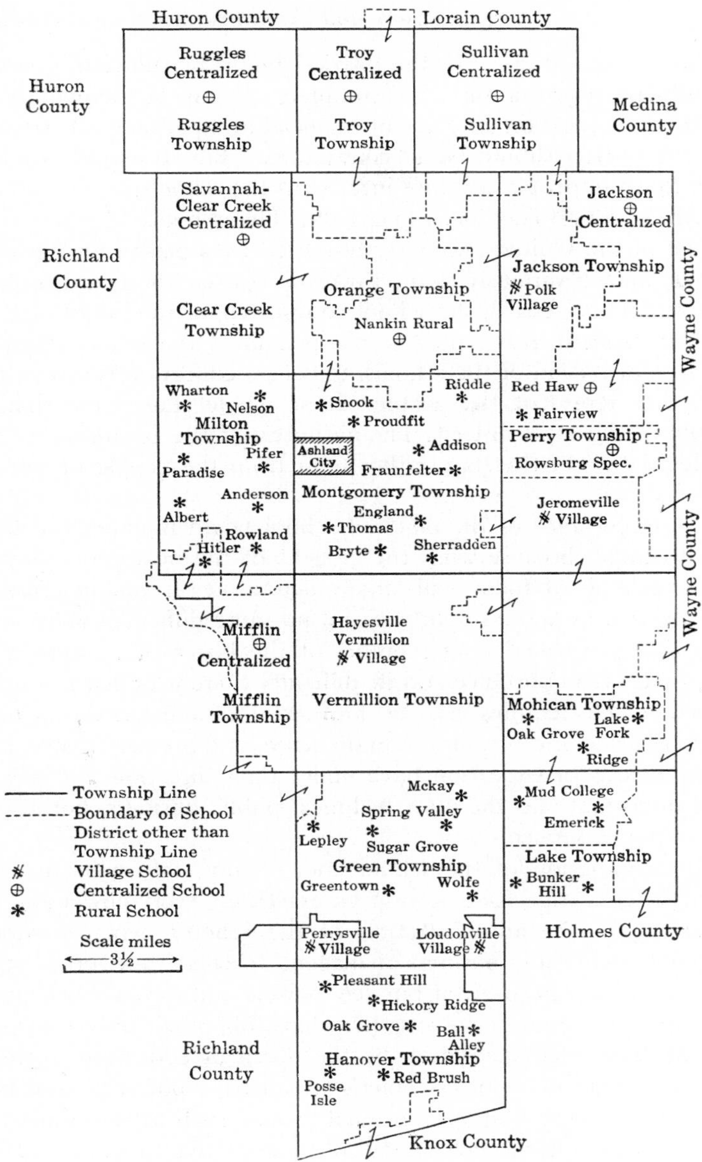

FIG. 15. School districts in a typical county (Ashland) in Ohio, twenty years ago. This county has now no one-room schools and has 11 school districts, several less than 20 years ago when the above map was made.

the following criteria: (1) the district should be sufficiently large to permit the organization of a complete system of elementary and secondary schools on an efficient financial and pedagogical basis, and (2) the district should be a "community," but it should not be so large that the people will lose interest in the schools.

THE LOCAL BOARD OF EDUCATION. The schools of each school district in the United States are governed by a person or a group of persons known variously as the township trustee, the board of education, the school board, the school committee, or the board of school trustees. Such boards represent the people of the school district in the administration of the schools, but since education is a state function, they represent the people of the whole state more than the people of the local district. The authority of the board comes from the legislature of the state rather than from the people of the local school district.

The importance of the office of school board member can hardly be overstated, because what the citizens of the next generation will be the schools of today will largely determine. It can be truly said that there is no more important and no more difficult public service than that performed by a member of the board of education, and because of its importance and its difficulty there is perhaps no public service which requires greater business and educational acumen, more patience and greater common sense, and greater devotion to a cause. Boards of education have under their direction not only the most important and the most technical public business, but also the largest public service.

An examination of the school laws of any state will show that boards of education have been given practically every power and duty pertaining to the administration of the schools, whereas superintendents, principals, business managers, teachers, and other school employees have been given but few powers and duties. Such powers and duties as teachers possess, they have obtained, only because of explicit or implicit delegation by the board of education. Although boards of education possess practically all legal power, a wise board will delegate most to its professional experts such as those just mentioned. In fact, it will delegate all of its executive functions and will reserve to itself the formulation of policies and the inspection and the appraisal of the work of the school system to see how efficiently the policies are operating; on the basis of such inspection and appraisal, the policies will be amended or new policies substituted for the old ones.

The limits set for this chapter will not permit much discussion of the features of the office of school board member. Such information regarding any particular state may be readily found in the school code of that state. As would be expected, the features pertaining to the office are not the same in every state, although there are common veins running through the practices of the various states. The following desirable tendencies are noted: (1) popular election, on a non-partisan ticket, of the holders of the office; (2) a longer term of office, for example, from three to five years; (3) a smaller number of board members, for example, between five and nine; and (4) no salary, except perhaps a small per diem with a limitation on the number of days a year to ten or twelve.

The Superintendent of Schools. Since its beginning in Providence, Rhode Island, in 1836, the local superintendency of schools has become almost universal. Every school system, except the very small ones, employs a superintendent. The small school systems which often do not employ superintendents are almost always rural systems, and these usually have the supervision of a county superintendent. With the exception of county superintendents, who are still elected on a "political" basis in many states, the tendency is to require a school board to elect superintendents on the basis of their administrative and their technical competence.

The superintendent is in many ways, the most important school employee, perhaps the most important public employee, in a community. He determines, more than any other person, the efficiency of the school system. If he is well qualified for his position, he will often be able to cause an efficient school system to emerge from an inefficient school system; he will bring this result by his ability to educate the board of education, the teachers, the other school employees, and the public to his point of view. On the other hand, if he is not qualified, there is danger that the school system which he administers will mark time or even deteriorate. In brief, the superintendent of schools is the educational leader of the community; he makes the school system largely what it is. He recommends new school policies and changes in school policies to the board of education. Acting under the general direction of the board of education, he executes those policies or sees that other members of the administrative personnel execute them. He attempts to co-ordinate all parts of the school system. He tries to eliminate all lost motion and all other waste in the school system. If he is efficient, he can save his salary manyfold, especially if his school system is of any considerable size. In the whole United States the school superintendency provides a career for several thousand persons and at the highest salaries in the teaching profession.

OTHER SCHOOL-ADMINISTRATIVE PERSONNEL. In all school systems,

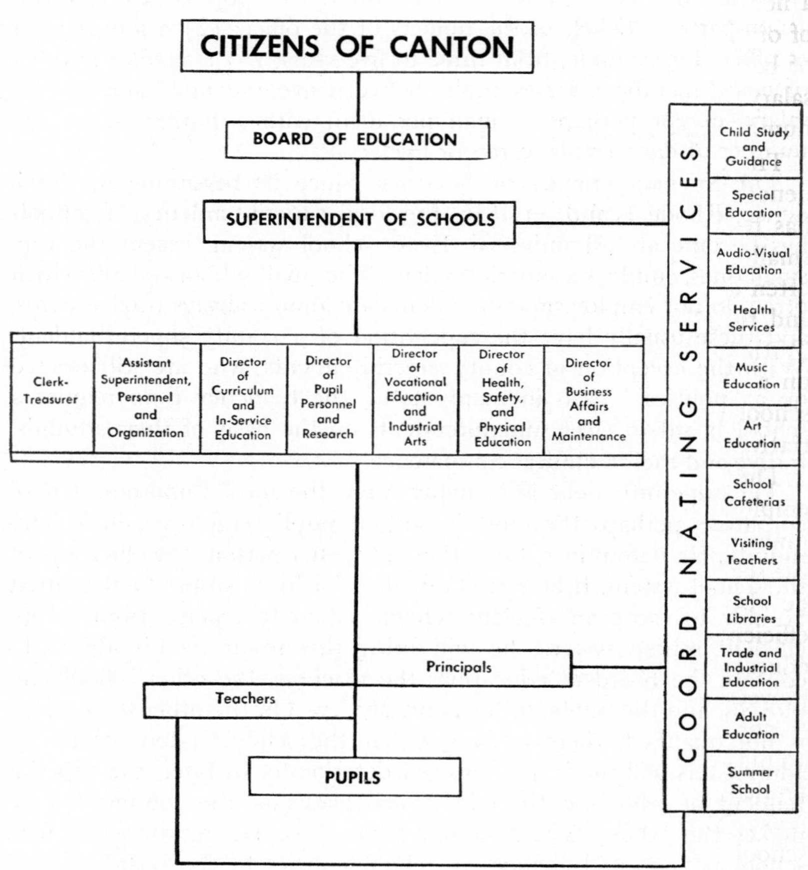

FIG. 16. The administrative organization of a medium-sized city school system. *(Courtesy of the Canton, Ohio, public schools.)*

except the very small ones, other administrative and supervisory employees are usually found. Attached to the office of the superintendent of schools, especially in the larger school systems, are such administrative and supervisory officers as the business manager of schools and his staff, and assistant superintendents in charge of various activities of the school system. In charge of each local school is usually found a principal. Other types of administrative and supervisory positions which are found in the medium-size cities can be seen from an examination of Fig. 16. The opportunities for a career in these positions are discussed in Chapter 17 (Opportunities in the Teaching Profession).

QUESTIONS FOR DISCUSSION

1. What are the functions of school administration? How may, or *must*, the classroom teacher of today co-operate in school administration? Mention some of the frequent opportunities for waste in the administration of the schools.

2. Do you recommend for this country a national system of education such as most foreign countries have? Why or why not?

3. Do you favor a separate Federal Department of Education with a Secretary of Education in the President's cabinet? Why or why not? Do you favor Federal financial support for general education? Why or why not?

4. Do you favor the establishment of a national university supported by the Federal Government? Why or why not? If such a university were established, where should it be located? Why? Should it be a teaching university or one for research only? Explain. What are the advantages of Washington, D. C., as a center for research and other study?

5. How much state control of private schools do you believe there should be? Explain. How much control of such schools is there in your state today? Should private schools have public aid? Why or why not?

6. How do you account for the fact that there is much more state control of education in the Eastern states, especially in New England, than in other sections of the United States?

7. Should there be any differences between the amount of state control of education and the amount of state control of (a) public utilities, (b) highways, and (c) health? Explain.

8. Characterize the chief state school official and his staff of your state as to official title, method of selection, salary, term of office, and powers and duties. What changes, if any, in these characteristics, would you recommend? Why?

9. What type of state board of education, if any, does your state have? Characterize it as to method of selection, number of members, term of office, salary, and powers and duties. What improvements, if any, are needed?

10. How do you account for the historic tendency to centralize educational functions? Point out some evidences of this tendency in your state. Why do the people usually oppose this tendency?

11. What types of school districts are found in your state? How many school districts of each type are there? Is the number becoming larger or smaller, and why? What changes in the number and the type of school districts would you recommend? Why?

12. What criteria should determine the size of school districts? Check the school districts of your state with these criteria and indicate any shortcomings which the districts have. What are the advantages of the county unit over the small district unit for the administration of schools?

13. How do you account for the tenacity with which the older generation holds to the small district system for schools? Would the abolition of small school districts tend to make the people lose interest in their schools? Explain.

14. Characterize the school boards of school districts in your state as to such matters as method of selection, number of members, term of office, salary, and powers and duties. What changes, if any, would you suggest in the present statutes governing these matters? Why? To what extent do these boards determine the efficiency of the schools? Explain.

15. What do you regard as proper functions of school boards? What functions should they delegate to superintendents and to the other professionally prepared employees? Explain.

16. Account for the fact that state and county superintendents of schools are still elected by popular vote in several states. What method of selection would you recommend? Why?

17. Why do most men in teaching positions aspire to school-administration positions?

18. What are recent decisions of the United States Supreme Court on public financing of private schools and on the teaching of religion in public schools? Do you agree with them?

19. What was the famous decision of the U. S. Supreme Court on education, May 17, 1954?

SELECTED REFERENCES

Baker, M. Hindman, "Negro Students Speak on Segregation," *School Executive*, Vol. 74 (November, 1954), pp. 43–45.

A study that revealed the attitude of the youth toward the problem of segregation. Negro youth seem to bear a strong resentment toward racial segregation.

Chamberlain, Leo M., and Kindred, Leslie W., *The Teacher and School Organization,* Second edition, Prentice-Hall, Inc., New York, 1949, 672 pp.

Deals with the teacher's administrative responsibilities and opportunities.

Dawson, Howard A. and Ellena, William J., "School District Reorganization," *School Executive,* Vol. 73 (July, 1954), pp. 39–42.

Shows how the number of school districts has been greatly reduced. Many school districts are still not very large and intermediate units help serve those districts that cannot afford all the modern facilities individually.

Douglass, Harl R., "Leadership or Authority in School Administration," *Educational Administration and Supervision,* Vol. 34 (January, 1948), pp. 25–28.

Advocates democratic leadership.

Fey, John T., "A Legal Authority Analyzes Proposals for Continuation of Separate Schools," *Nation's Schools,* Vol. 54 (August, 1954), pp. 35–37.

Presents some of the problems now facing the public schools as a result of the Supreme Court decision regarding racial segregation in the schools.

Fitzsimmons, Margaret L., "A Teacher Looks at Democratic Administration," *American School Board Journal,* Vol. 115 (December, 1947), pp. 13–14.

Advocates co-operation between teachers and school administrators.

Garber, Lee O., "Issues Involved in Desegregating Public Schools," *Nation's Schools,* Vol. 54 (October, 1954), pp. 87–88.

A discussion of the issues involved in the recent Supreme Court decision.

Haisley, Otto W., "Democratic Procedures Pay," *School Executive,* Vol. 66 (April, 1947), pp. 46–47.

Says that faculty participation gives faculty a greater sense of responsibility.

Hill, David Spence, and Fisher, William Alfred, *Federal Relations to Education,* Report of the National Advisory Committee on Education, Part II, 1931, 477 pp. also Part I, 140 pp.

A history of Federal aid, together with arguments for and against.

Janetos, Peter, "Obstacles to District Reorganization," *School Executive,* Vol. 74 (February, 1955), pp. 54–55.

A listing of what obstacles school-district reorganization attempts have run into.

McIntyre, Kenneth E., "State School Redistricting Continues," *American School Board Journal,* Vol. 138 (February, 1954), pp. 31–33.

Summarizes the progress made in each state in school redistricting.

McKnight, C. A., "The Desegregation Ruling," *School Executive,* Vol. 74 (January, 1955), pp. 82–85.

A discussion of what various states have done with respect to desegregating their schools. Specific examples are cited.

Paton, Alan, "The Negro in America Today" (Part I), *Collier's,* Vol. 134 (October 15, 1954), pp. 52–56, 60, 62, 64, 69.

Discusses the social status of the Negro in the school, church, and the Armed Forces of the United States. It was found that the Negroes were not strictly segregated but, even including the south, were slowly but surely being integrated in these places.

———, "The Negro in America Today" (Part II), *Collier's,* Vol. 134 (October 29, 1954), pp. 70–72, 74–79.

Discusses the racial prejudice that is held against the Negro when he seeks a job or a home. The old practice of discrimination in housing and employment of the Negro has not changed. The Negro is the last to be hired and the first to be fired. He and his family often are badly mistreated, if they buy a home in a white neighborhood. Segregation is very much in evidence in these two phases of the Negro's life.

Reeder, Ward G., *The Fundamentals of Public School Administration,* The Macmillan Co., New York, 1951, pp. 17–40.

Discusses the opportunities and the requirements in school administration; to be revised in 1958.

Your School Districts, National Education Association, Washington, D. C., 1948, 286 pp.

This is the report of the National Commission on School District Reorganization.

CHAPTER 4

Divisions of Our Schools

The Tripartite Organization of Our Schools

A casual glance at the school system of any state of the United States shows clearly that it is divided into three parts. Moreover, a backward glance over the more than three-century history of the school system of any state indicates that it has always possessed this same tripartite organization consisting of (1) the elementary school, (2) the secondary school, and (3) the college and the other institutions of higher learning. According to B. A. Hinsdale, these three divisions were indicated in practice as early as 1641.[1] Although certain changes have taken place from time to time in the organization, the general form of the organization is today essentially the same as it was in the beginning of the schools.

This tripartite organization of our school system was borrowed from European models, which had been in operation for several centuries before our settlers came to America, and the details of the school organization were much affected by the school practices of the particular country from which the colonists came. These foreign models were often aristocratic in character, and sometimes they were followed, without considering whether they would meet the needs of the colonists who had somewhat different ideals and aspirations from those held by the countries from which the colonists came.

[1] B. A. Hinsdale, *Horace Mann and the Common School Revival in the United States*, Scribner's, 1937, pp. 2–5.

Development of the Elementary Schools. Contrary to normal expectations of people today, the elementary school was much slower to develop into an organized system than the secondary school and the college. In the early days, preparation of pupils for the secondary school was usually given by parents or by tutors employed by the parents. In the beginning, the elementary school was conceived, like its foreign model, as a parallel school for the masses, without any intention that they should enter the secondary school. Certain social forces, however, prevented its development in that form and turned it into the foundation part of a single school system, rather than making it one of the parts of a dual school system such as most European countries had, and still have.

Although our early settlers, especially in New England, showed a large interest in education, the rigors of frontier life long militated against the rapid development of a free, a universal, a tax-supported, and a compulsory system of elementary schools, such as every state has today; the people could not afford universal elementary schools in those early days. These democratic characteristics, which are today everywhere associated with the schools, came only by gradual evolution. The idea of free, universal, tax-supported, and compulsory schools developed slowly and was not accepted in every state until about 1850. Outside New England, the early schools were usually either church supported or charity supported, and hundreds of communities, especially in the Middle and the Southern colonies, did not have public schools until later.

Moreover, the elementary school in those early days was very simple compared with the elementary school of today. Like the practice of foreign countries, religion was the chief subject of instruction. Religion was accompanied at first by the subject of reading, and later by the subjects of writing, arithmetic, and spelling. Those subjects constituted the only subjects of instruction in most elementary schools until the opening of the nineteenth century.

In the early days, too, it is worth noting that the elementary school was not organized into school grades as it is today. The present grading system in our schools originated about 1790 and was probably copied from the Prussian *Volksschule* of eight grades. By 1870, the eight-grade elementary school had been generally accepted in all communities of the United States, and it thus remained until the junior high-school movement came upon the scene about the opening of the twentieth century to make it six grades.

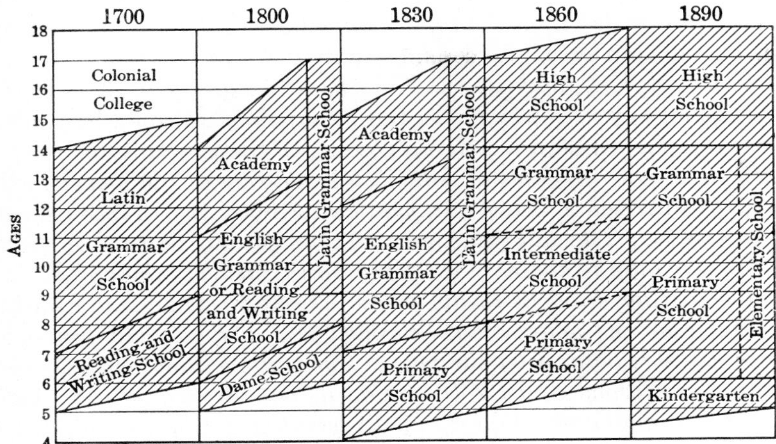

Fig. 17. Evolution of the American school system from 1700 to 1890. *(From Ellwood P. Cubberley,* Public Education in The United States, *Houghton Mifflin, rev. ed., 1934, p. 140.)* The evolution of the system from 1900 to the present is shown in Fig. 20.

With the coming of universal suffrage to our people and the advent of the industrial revolution, there arose shortly after the opening of the nineteenth century the need for a larger amount and a better type of education for the people than before. Following that date, too, the religious motive began to be supplanted by the democracy motive as the driving force for the establishment of schools. Stimulated by such educational leaders as Horace Mann and Henry Barnard, the people began to pressure their legislators and their school officials to give them universal, free, and tax-supported schools. By 1825, several states had made a beginning toward establishing a tax-supported system of elementary schools, and from those beginnings the movement spread into every state and every territory during the next few decades. Moreover, new school subjects were added to the curriculum, better methods of teaching were adopted, and many other improvements in the schools were effected.

Thus, the elementary school has evolved until today it is the most cherished, and probably the most efficient, part of the school system. In every community of every state it is a free, public, and tax-supported institution. It is open gladly to all the people; in fact, attendance in it, or in an equivalent school, is legally compulsory for all children during a certain number of years, the number of years varying [2] in different states. It essays to give a foundation in education to everyone. In giving this foundation, it should be guided by two fundamental principles, according to the Commission on the Articulation of the Units of American Education of the Department of Superintendence (now the American Association of School Administrators). The first fundamental principle is "*to pass on from each generation to the next whatever worthy benefits the civilization of the past has brought to the public welfare.*" [3] The second fundamental principle affirms that "*through the methods and processes by which this heritage of the past is transmitted from generation to generation, formal education must do its best to secure in the individual the development of all those latent and wholesome powers that are essential to the master ability of using that which civilization has transmitted for the promotion of the public welfare.*" [4] In the light of the two foregoing principles the commission suggests the following tentative objectives for the elementary school:

> Any proper respect for the rights of the child and the welfare of the community dictates that during this elementary school period education shall:
>
> 1. Advance the child, although by no means perfect him, in his ability to read, write, and speak correctly the English language, and to know and to use intelligently the elementary processes of arithmetic. . . .
> 2. Advance the child in his ability to know and to observe the laws of physical and mental health and well-being and to appreciate the meaning of life and of nature. . . .
> 3. Advance the child in his ability to know and to appreciate the geography and history of his own community, state, and nation, and of the world at large; to sense his share in the social, civic, and

[2] The number of years varies from fifteen to eighteen. There is a desirable tendency on the part of the states to adopt an educational standard rather than an age standard for compulsory school attendance.

[3] *The Articulation of the Units of American Education, Seventh Yearbook* of the Department of Superintendence, 1929, p. 82. By permission of the National Education Association, publishers.

See footnote 5 on page 131.

[4] *Ibid.*, p. 84. By permission of the National Education Association, publishers.

industrial order of such a democracy as ours, and to meet to the full the obligations which such knowledge and appreciation should engender, to the end that justice, sympathy, and loyalty may characterize his personal and community life. . . .

4. Advance the child in his ability to share intelligently and appreciatively in the fine and the useful arts through the pursuit of music, drawing, and literature; of manual training and the household arts as they are related to the three great universal needs of food, clothing, and shelter. . . .[5]

Development of the Secondary Schools. As is implied in its name, the secondary school is a second school which follows an elementary or a primary school. Secondary schools in the United States have passed through the following three stages: First, the Latin grammar school; second, the academy; and, third, the high school. Those three stages of development will be briefly discussed in the following pages.

1. *The Latin Grammar School.* The first secondary school in the United States was established in 1635 in Boston, and it was known as the Boston Latin Grammar School. Similar schools were soon established in other towns of Massachusetts, and in 1647 the General Court (legislature) of Massachusetts enacted a law which required such a school in every town having one hundred families or more. From Massachusetts, Latin grammar schools spread into all of the colonies, although they had their chief development in New England. They were the dominant types of secondary school in all the colonies until about 1775.

As the name implies, Latin was the chief subject of instruction in the Latin grammar school. The chief purpose of that school was to prepare its pupils for college. Boys only were admitted to the school, because the usefulness of extending school opportunities beyond the rudiments to girls was everywhere questioned in those early days. The curriculum (course of study) of the school was narrowly classical, comprising in the early days only Latin and Greek. The following quotation from Elmer Ellsworth Brown describes the early course of study:

[5] *Ibid.*, pp. 84–85. By permission of the National Education Association, publishers.

Essentially the same objectives were stated in *Education for All American Children*, pp. 2–5. Educational Policies Commission of the National Education Association and the American Association of School Administrators, 1948.

In the Latin school itself, the boys studied Latin from eight o'clock to eleven in the forenoon, and from one in the afternoon till dark. They began with Cheever's Latin Accidence, which was followed by Ward's Lilly's Latin Grammar. The reading consisted of Aesop, with a translation; Eutropius, also with a translation; Corderius, Ovid's *Metamorphoses*, Vergil's *Georgics* and *Aeneid*, Caesar and Cicero. Of these, Caesar and *Georgics* seem to have been less commonly used in grammar schools than the other works mentioned. In the sixth year of the course, the boy was half through Vergil. The master permitted the reading of such translations of Vergil as Trappe's and Dryden's. Composition was begun, apparently, at about the same time with the reading of Aesop or of Eutropius, and Clarke's *Introduction to Writing Latin* was the first textbook used. Near the end of the course, Horace was read, and Latin verses were composed with the help of the *Gradus ad Parnassum*.[6]

During the later years of its existence, the Latin grammar school introduced nonclassical and more practical subjects into its course of study; among these subjects were arithmetic, geometry, trigonometry, algebra, geography, bookkeeping, English grammar, English composition, and navigation. These subjects, though, according to R. F. Seybolt, were more often found in the "English grammar school" than in the Latin grammar school. Seybolt says that it is erroneously believed that the Latin grammar school was the only type of grammar school; but, there was another, namely, the "English grammar school." [7] The latter type of grammar school was established much later than the Latin grammar school. Its course of study was not always determined by college-entrance requirements as was the case in the Latin grammar school. The English grammar school was much more democratic in purpose than the Latin grammar school and thus was a transition from the Latin grammar school to its successor, the academy.

Until about 1800, pupils entered the Latin grammar school at the age of seven or eight, provided they had learned to read; until then, also, the course of study of that school was seven years long. About 1800, the entrance age to the school became ten and the course of study was shortened to four years. Admission to the Latin grammar school did not presuppose the completion of the primary school; admission to that school required only the ability to read.

[6] Elmer Ellsworth Brown, *The Making of Our Middle Schools*, Longmans, 1903, pp. 131–132. By permission of Longmans, Green and Company, publishers.

[7] R. F. Seybolt, *Source Studies in American Colonial Education*, University of Illinois *Bulletin*, Vol. 28, No. 4, p. 99.

In spite of the fact that it was not intended as a school for the masses, but only as a school for the select few who wished to prepare for college, the Latin grammar school was frequently supported, at least in part, by taxation of the people of the community. Other sources of revenue, especially in the early days, were annual gifts, permanent endowments, and tuition of the pupils of the schools.

By 1700, much adverse criticism of the Latin grammar school had begun to appear, and by 1760 that type of secondary school was definitely on the wane. The criticism was that it served only a small percentage of the population, and it provided an aristocratic course of study. It was not in harmony with the growing spirit of democracy which insisted that the needs of the masses be met as well as the needs of the upper classes. By 1800, most Latin grammar schools had been supplanted by the more democratic academies. The influence, though, of the Latin grammar school lingered, and even in the high schools of today the thousands of classical and college-preparatory courses of study are one of their legacies. Institutions change slowly, often too slowly for the needs of the people.

2. *The Academy*. Since the Latin grammar school would not, could not, or at least did not, adapt itself to changing social needs, it died. The institution which emerged and grew up to take its place was the academy, and this latter school dominated secondary school education in the United States for approximately one hundred years. The academy was the dominant secondary school from about 1775 to about 1875. A few academies still exist, especially in the Eastern part of the United States, particularly New England.

Like the Latin grammar school, the academy developed first in Europe, then was imported into this country. Although there are conflicting claims regarding the first academy in the United States, most authorities agree that Franklin's Academy [8] at Philadelphia was the first. Benjamin Franklin, the founder, sketched the plan for such an educational institution as early as 1743, but not until 1749 did he begin to make definite plans for its establishment. In that year he published his "Proposals Relating to the Education of Youth in Pennsylvania." In 1751, his academy began instruction with three schools or departments—the Latin school, the English school, and the Mathematical school. In his "Proposals" for this institution, Franklin said:

[8] This academy later developed into the University of Pennsylvania (a private school).

As to their studies, it would be well if they could be taught *everything* that is useful, and *everything* that is ornamental. But art is long and their time is short. It is therefore proposed, that they learn those things that are likely to be *most useful* and *most ornamental;* regard being had to the several professions for which they are intended. All interested for divinity, should be taught the Latin and Greek; for physic, the Latin, Greek, and French; for Law, the Latin and French; merchants, the French, German, and Spanish; and, though all should not be compelled to learn Latin, Greek, or the modern foreign languages, yet none that have an ardent desire to learn them should be refused; their English, arithmetic and other studies absolutely necessary, being at the same time not neglected.

Following the establishment of Franklin's Academy,[9] the academy movement spread rapidly into other communities in every state. By 1830, according to Cubberley, there were 950 incorporated academies in the United States, and many unincorporated ones; by 1850, when the movement toward the establishment of academies reached its peak, there were "1,007 academies in New England, 1,636 in the Middle Atlantic States, 2,640 in the Southern States, 753 in the Upper Mississippi Valley States, and a total reported for the entire United States of 6,085, with 12,260 teachers employed and 263,096 pupils enrolled." [10] The academy had the following advantages over the Latin grammar schools of earlier days:

1. It provided secondary school education for girls as well as for boys. At first, separate schools for the two sexes were provided, but in time coeducation came to be the mode in the academies.
2. It established practical courses having value aside from mere preparation for college; thus, it made useful education available to larger numbers of students and helped to popularize secondary school education.
3. Although religious exercises were a part of the daily routine of the academy, those exercises were less sectarian than in the Latin grammar school.
4. It built upon, instead of running parallel to, the elementary school courses of study. It stimulated the development of our "one-ladder" system of schools which we still have.

The chief adverse criticism of the academies concerned their financial support and their control. They were essentially private

[9] It should be pointed out that Franklin did not personally operate the academy but delegated that to others.

[10] Ellwood P. Cubberley, *Public Education in the United States,* Houghton Mifflin, rev. ed., 1934, p. 247. By permission of Houghton Mifflin Company, publishers.

Fig. 18. The first secondary school—Boston Latin School, founded in 1635—compared with a modern high school—Frank Cody High School, Detroit, Michigan.

schools, although public funds were frequently used for their support. In the main, they were dependent upon donations, endowments, and student fees for their financial support. Since children of poor parents found it difficult to pay tuition fees, public demand was soon made for a public and a tax-supported institution to provide secondary school education. The high school was established in answer to that demand and has had a huge growth to the present time, as we shall presently see.

3. *The High School.* The first high school in the United States was established at Boston in 1821. Until 1824, the Boston school was called the English Classical School; it was then moved to new quarters and was given the name of the English High School. The name high school seems to be Scotch in origin, having been suggested by the description of the High School at Edinburgh, Scotland, by Professor Griscorn, in an article in the *North American Review*, in January, 1824. The first high school was for boys only, but in 1826 Boston also opened a similar high school for girls. The latter school, though, was abolished in 1828, because it had become so popular that the expense of maintaining it could not be met by the public.

The course of study in the Boston high school was three years long, and the boys admitted were required to be twelve years of age and to "be well acquainted with reading, writing, English grammar in all its branches, and arithmetic as far as simple proportion." The course of study was patterned after that of the typical academy of the day,[11] but was not college preparatory in any sense; it was designed to give the youth an education "that shall fit him for active life, and shall serve as a foundation for eminence in his profession, whether mercantile or mechanical." In its aims and its procedures the school was entirely indigenous, there being no foreign influence to which these matters can be traced. The course of study was practical and was built upon the course of study of the elementary school, instead of paralleling it as was the practice of the earlier Latin grammar school and the earlier academy.

The real beginning, however, of the high school movement in the United States began with the enactment of the Massachusetts law of 1827, a law reminiscent of the Massachusetts law of 1647 which

[11] The chief exception to this was that no other language than English was taught in the Boston school.

required the establishment of a grammar school in every town having at least 100 families (householders). Like the law of 1647, the law of 1827 deeply influenced subsequent legislation in other states as

Fig. 19. The first high school in the United States, established in Boston, Massachusetts, in 1821.

well as in Massachusetts. That law required the establishment of a high school in every town having at least 500 families, and it fixed a heavy penalty for failure to comply with the law. In 1835, the law was amended to permit smaller towns to provide a high school. A few of the main provisions of the law of 1827 are quoted herewith:

> And every city, town, or district, containing five hundred families or householders, shall be provided with such teacher or teachers for such term of time as shall be equivalent to twenty-four months, for one school in each year, and shall also be provided with a master of good morals, competent to instruct, in addition to the branches of learning aforesaid, the history of the United States, bookkeeping by single entry, geometry, surveying, and algebra; and shall employ such master to instruct a school, in such city, town, or district, for the benefit of all the inhabitants thereof, at least ten months in each year, exclusive of vacations, in such convenient place, or alternately at such places in such city, town, or district, as the said inhabitants, at their meeting in March, or April, annually shall determine, and in every city, or town, containing four thousand inhabitants, such master shall be competent in addition to all the foregoing branches, to instruct the Latin and Greek Languages, History, rhetoric, and logic.

The growth of the high school was slow, even in its Massachusetts first home. By 1840, only two dozen high schools had been established in Massachusetts, and only about the same number in all the other states, chiefly New England states. The growth of the high school was slow, primarily because objections were raised to their support through public funds. Another factor retarding the development of high schools was the academy which was already established as a "people's college." Friends of the academy objected to seeing it displaced. The more universal establishment of the public high school must wait until the people could see the need for such an institution and until they were financially able and willing to finance it through universal taxation.

Following 1827, the date of the Massachusetts law requiring the establishment of public high schools, the next historically important date in the development of public high schools was 1874. That date marked the decision of the Supreme Court of Michigan on the now famous *Kalamazoo Case*. In that decision the Michigan Court affirmed the right of school districts to use public funds for the support of secondary schools, "if their voters consent in regular form to bear the expense and raise the taxes for the purpose." [12] Until that historic court decision, the legality of using public funds for secondary schools was questioned; with that decision, however, a precedent was set which has since been followed by the courts of all other states.

Following the Kalamazoo decision and the economic adjustments which were necessary after the Civil War (1861–1865) the growth of the high school was unusually rapid. In 1870, there were about 165 public high schools; in 1880, 800; in 1890, 2,526; in 1900, 6,005; in 1910, 10,213; in 1920, 14,326; and at present more than 23,000.[13] The enrollment in these schools now comprises approximately 8,000,000 boys and girls, and it has approximately doubled each decade since 1890; moreover, more than 75 per cent of the children of high school age are enrolled in high school,[14] and most of the American people are now receiving some high school education.

In every state the high school is today an accepted part of the

[12] Charles E. Stuart, *et al.*, vs. School District No. 1 of the Village of Kalamazoo, 30 Michigan, p. 69.

[13] Many high schools have less than one hundred pupils, and such an enrollment usually results either in a high per pupil cost or an inferior educational program. Since many of these small schools are located from one to five miles of other schools, they should be merged to make larger schools. In practically every state, except those of the South, the number of high schools should be decreased for reasons of financial economy and pedagogical efficiency.

[14] Decreases in enrollment were shown only during World War II, but enrollment has since that time continued upward.

school system and it is supported through universal taxation the same as the elementary school. Practically every state requires every school district either to provide a high school for the pupils of the district or to pay the tuition of the pupils to another school district; moreover, many states require or permit, at public expense, the transportation of all high school pupils who live more than a certain distance (usually from two to four miles) from school.

In 1951, the National Association of Secondary School Principals stated the following goals for secondary schools:

1. All youth need to develop saleable skills and those understandings and attitudes that make the worker an intelligent and productive participant in economic life. To this end, most youth need supervised work experience as well as education in the skills and knowledge of their occupations.
2. All youth need to develop and maintain good health and physical fitness and mental health.
3. All youth need to understand the rights and duties of the citizen of a democratic society, and to be diligent and competent in the performance of their obligations as members of the community and citizens of the state and nation, and to have an understanding of the nations and peoples of the world.
4. All youth need to understand the significance of the family for the individual and society and the conditions conducive to successful family life.
5. All youth need to know how to purchase and use goods and services intelligently, understand both the values received by the consumer and the economic consequences of their acts.
6. All youth need to understand the methods of science, the influence of science on human life, and the main scientific facts concerning the nature of the world and of man.
7. All youth need opportunities to develop their capacities to appreciate beauty, in literature, art, music, and nature.
8. All youth need to be able to use their leisure time well and to budget it wisely, balancing activities that yield satisfactions to the individual with those that are socially useful.
9. All youth need to develop respect for other persons, to grow in their insight into ethical values and principles, to be able to live and work co-operatively with others, and to grow in the moral and spiritual values of life.
10. All youth need to grow in their ability to think rationally, to express their thoughts clearly, and to read and listen with understanding.[15]

[15] *Planning for American Youth,* p. 9. National Association of Secondary School Principals, 1951. Published by the Educational Policies Commission, National Education Association.

Development of Colleges. The early colleges of the United States were patterned after colleges of Europe, especially those of England. Just as the colleges of Europe arose to serve a particular purpose of the people, so did the colleges of the United States. Our first colleges were established for the preparation of ministers, were usually under the control of a particular church, and were expected to propagate the religious dogma of that church. The first college was Harvard, established in 1636, because of "dreading to leave an illiterate ministry to the churches when our present ministry shall lie in the dust." At the close of the colonial period nine colleges had been established in the United States and all of those colleges, excepting Franklin's Academy, which later developed into the University of Pennsylvania, were sectarian. Those first nine colleges, with the dates of their establishment, and the church and the colony founding them, were:

Harvard College	1636	Mass.	Puritan
William and Mary	1693	Va.	Anglican
Yale College	1701	Conn.	Congregational
Princeton	1746	N. J.	Presbyterian
Academy and College	1751–55	Penn.	Nonsectarian
King's College (Columbia)	1754	N. Y.	Anglican
Brown	1764	R. I.	Baptist
Rutgers	1766	N. J.	Reformed Dutch
Dartmouth	1769	N. H.	Congregational

The enrollments in the colonial colleges were small, and the educational services and the plant facilities of them were limited. During the first fifty years of its history, Harvard College seldom enrolled in one year more than twenty students, and the president usually did all the teaching; the course of study was classical and required three years for its completion, until 1654 when a four-year course of study was established. The emphasis in all of the early colleges was upon Hebrew, Greek, Latin, and the Bible, although some attention was given to arithmetic, algebra, geometry, trigonometry, natural science, oratory, general history, ethics, and philosophy.

By 1800, approximately fifteen additional colleges (all private and usually denominational) had been established, but those like the first nine mentioned above were small and struggling institutions. Enrollments were sparse, the faculty was small and poorly prepared, the plant was meager, and the course of study was limited. Cubberley estimated that all of the two dozen colleges then existing did not have more than one hundred faculty members, or more than two thousand students, and property worth not more than $1,000,000.[16] Moreover, none of the early colleges admitted women, it then being generally regarded as a waste of money to provide women with a college education.

A beginning for the college education of women was not made until 1821, when Emma Hart Willard established the Troy Female Seminary at Troy, New York. The next college for women was the Hartford Female Seminary, founded at Hartford, Connecticut, in 1828, by Catherine Esther Beecher. There was no attempt at co-education on the college level until 1833 when Oberlin College, at Oberlin, Ohio, opened its doors to women as well as to men. From those beginnings the movement toward providing college education for women as well as for men has grown by leaps and bounds, and most colleges and universities, especially those which are public, are coeducational; the South is the only section which still follows the male-female pattern to any considerable extent. The public and the private colleges now enroll approximately 3,000,000 students, and of these, more than 936,000 are women.

Following the opening of the nineteenth century, the growth of colleges and universities was rapid; they greatly increased in numbers, in enrollment, and in educational efficiency. This rapid growth was stimulated by various factors, among the more important of which were the rapidly increasing wealth of the nation, the development of new professions, and an awakening public consciousness regarding the value of higher education. The nineteenth century saw the establishment of public-supported colleges in every state, of many public-supported municipal colleges, and of several hundred private and denominational colleges.

Until about 1870, practically all college work was conducted under private and denominational auspices. Following that date, public colleges steadily increased in numbers, enrollment, and influence. The private and the denominational colleges had begun to be criticized for their aristocratic and their sectarian tendencies, and the demand grew for a public-supported and public-controlled institution of collegiate grade which would meet the needs of a larger number of

[16] Cubberley, *op. cit.*, p. 269.

people in various walks of life. The state university developed in answer to this demand.

A large impetus to the establishment of state colleges and universities was given by the Federal Government through its land grants to the states.[17] The first of these land grants for higher education was made in 1787 to The Ohio Company, a New England organization in which Manassah Cutler was the moving spirit. By the terms of that Federal grant The Ohio Company was sold approximately 1,500,000 acres of land in south-central Ohio, and in the grant two "Congressional Townships" (46,080 acres) were given "for the purposes of a university." [18] The second of such grants was made in 1788, when 311,682 acres of land near Cincinnati were sold to John Symmes and his associates. By the terms of that grant, it was provided that one Congressional Township (23,040 acres) was to be used "for the purpose of establishing an academy in the district." The first of those grants formed the endowment from which Ohio University, at Athens, was established by the Ohio legislature in 1809; from the second grant, Miami University, at Oxford, was established by the Ohio legislature in 1824. Ohio University was the first state university in the new West, though the University of North Carolina, which had been founded in 1789, had begun to give instruction in 1795, but was not under full control of the state until 1821. The provisions of those two land grants for institutions of higher learning in Ohio were continued when other states carved from the public domain were admitted to the Union; at least two Congressional Townships were given to each of those states for a "seminary of learning," and those grants formed the basis of the state universities which were established in all the new states.

A second type of land grant by the Federal Government also gave a tremendous impetus to higher education. That was provided by the *Morrill Act* of 1862 which gave each state 30,000 acres of land for each senator and each congressman from that state to endow a college or colleges for the teaching of agriculture, mechanic arts, and military

[17] Another large impetus to the establishment of state colleges and universities was given by the decision of the U. S. Supreme Court on the Dartmouth College case in 1819. That decision made it impossible for the state to take over (without consent) private colleges and to transform them into public institutions.

[18] Both The Ohio Company and the Symmes grants also provided that section 16 of each congressional township should be reserved for common schools and that section 29 should be reserved for religion. A congressional township is illustrated in Fig. 27, page 203 of this book.

science. Every state accepted that gift and soon established a college or colleges of agriculture and mechanic arts.[19] The Southern states, which then required racial segregation, established a college for whites and another for Negroes. Eighteen states added the gift to the endowment of their existing state universities; three states gave it to already existing private institutions; and the remainder of the states established new colleges.

The state universities have grown in public esteem until several of them now enroll more than thirty thousand students annually and have annual budgets of several million dollars. Designed primarily to serve the people of the state, most of them draw their students primarily from the state in which the colleges are located; many of them, though, have become so renowned, especially in certain fields of learning, that students come to them from all over the United States and from many foreign countries. All of them have tended to increase their curriculum offerings to meet the needs of specialization; this has usually led to the creation of several colleges or schools within the university. A typical state university, especially in the larger states, now includes all or most of the following colleges or schools:[20] liberal arts, engineering, agriculture, education, graduate, commerce, law, medicine, pharmacy, dentistry, veterinary medicine, the extension division, and the summer-session division.

Enrollments in the colleges and universities reached unparalleled heights following World War II. These enrollments were stimulated by Federal aid which paid for tuition fees, books, and personal living expenses up to a stated amount for each person in World War II. Of course, college enrollments have not yet reached their peak.

California now has 60 public junior colleges, 10 state colleges, and the giant state university with eight campuses. There are also 57 private four-year colleges and six private junior colleges in California.

Extensions of the Organization of the School System

The preceding section pointed out that the American school system has been tripartite from the beginning and that it grew up in a more or less haphazard fashion without much consideration being given to

[19] Money grants for each of these colleges were begun in 1887 and have been continued annually in increasing amount to the present time.

[20] Other colleges or "schools" less frequently found are: journalism, mining, optometry, forestry, household arts, science, architecture, fine arts, music, and nursing.

articulation of its parts. During recent years, however, attempts have been made to obtain greater unity in the school system; a few of the more significant of these attempts will be described in the following paragraphs.

DOWNWARD EXTENSION IN THE SCHOOLS. The downward extension of the elementary division of the school system began with the inclusion of the kindergarten. The kindergarten had been founded by Frederick Wilhelm Froebel in Germany about 1840 as an attempt to obtain more self-activity in the education of little children. From Germany, the kindergarten idea was carried to the United States by certain well-educated German immigrants who came here to make their homes following the unsuccessful German revolution of 1848. Among those immigrants was Mrs. Carl Schurz, who had been a student of Froebel. She opened the first kindergarten in the United States at her home in Watertown, Wisconsin, in 1855; German was used as the vernacular in this kindergarten. So far as is known, the first English-speaking kindergarten was opened at Boston, in 1860, by Miss Elizabeth Peabody. In 1873, Superintendent William T. Harris of St. Louis opened in the schools of that city the first public school kindergarten in the United States.

From these beginnings the kindergarten idea spread all over the United States, especially in the cities. In the early days most kindergartens were private, but gradually they were accepted as a part of the public school system and were given legal sanction through permissive or mandatory laws enacted by the state legislatures; many states may give state aid for kindergartens. At present more than 1,500,000 children are enrolled in the public and the private kindergartens of the United States.

Started by Froebel to give children an opportunity for self-activity—an opportunity which they did not have in the formal and subject-matter-centered grades of the elementary schools—the kindergarten was originally conducted without relation to the grades of the elementary school. In the twentieth century, however, attempts have been made by the kindergarten and the primary-grade teachers to bridge the gap which formerly existed between the kindergarten and the first grade. In the best schools this gap is being closed by using in the first grade many materials and teaching methods of the kindergarten and by using in the kindergarten many materials and teaching methods of the first grade.

A more recent downward extension of the elementary school is the nursery school. The typical nursery school admits children at the age of two, three, or four, and keeps them until the age of five when they are enrolled in the kindergarten.[21] Although the number of nursery schools has increased, and although the tendency has been toward recognizing the importance of the preschool years, the conclusion is not yet warranted that public education is in the process of being extended below the kindergarten. Nursery schools increased greatly during World War II to provide for the care of children when parents were working in factories and shops.

Many nursery schools have been organized primarily as laboratory schools for the study of the preschool child. They have often been organized in connection with colleges and universities, and at the present time are seldom an integral part of the public school system. Most nursery schools are conducted as private institutions, just as kindergartens were private in their early days. The reason most frequently given for the establishment of nursery schools is the education of young children; a close second reason is the education of parents, especially in child care. Other reasons given are the preparation of teachers and research workers in preschool education and in the care of children during the daytime when parents are at work. The nursery school, like the kindergarten, aims with respect to child education to give motor and sensory control, to provide for social adjustment, to develop interest drives, and to provide for physical development. Of course, the nursery-school pupils are younger and are more immature than the kindergarten pupils; in consequence, they need more emphasis upon motor and sensory control and upon social adjustment than their kindergarten brothers and sisters.

UPWARD EXTENSIONS IN THE SCHOOLS. Although a few collegiate institutions early offered opportunities for obtaining the master's degree, graduate study and research in the modern sense did not begin in the United States until after the Civil War (1861–1865). By 1870, graduate work in the colleges and the universities began to be stimulated by a number of important influences. Chief among these influences was the rapid development of (1) public and private colleges of agriculture and mechanic arts, and (2) public and private uni-

[21] A few kindergartens admit children at four years of age, but most of them require five years of age for admission; this is especially true of public kindergartens.

versities, especially under the leadership of Johns Hopkins University which was established in 1876.

Before 1875, most students who desired to do graduate work of a research character were required to go to European universities, especially to those of Germany. After that date most of the larger American universities established graduate courses leading to advanced degrees, and the trek abroad for graduate work began to wane. At the present time our facilities for graduate work are, in most fields of learning, at least as excellent as can be found in any universities of the world. Moreover, the graduate enrollment in our universities has increased phenomenally, from less than 200 students in 1870 to more than 225,000 today.

In addition to the extension of the school system by means of the addition of the graduate school, some of the professional schools, such as law, medicine, and dentistry, can also be regarded as upward extensions of the college, inasmuch as they require for graduation more than the traditional four-year course of study. In fact, the tendency at present is toward extending the course of study in several professional schools to make it comprise five, six, or seven years, rather than the traditional four-year course of study; medicine, for example, is usually a seven-year course, plus an internship of at least one year.

Internal Changes in the Organization of the School System

Owing to profound changes in a rapidly evolving society many demands for adjustment have been placed upon the tripartite organization of the American school system. In consequence, many changes within the elementary, the secondary, and the collegiate units have been made, and these changes have been especially made to obtain a better articulation among the three units. The need for changes in the original tripartite structure was first recognized at the secondary school level, and the adjustments which were made at that level were forerunners of sweeping changes in the elementary school and the college levels.

Changes Between the Elementary and the Secondary Schools. Since the early part of the present century, large changes have been taking place between the elementary and the secondary divisions of the school system. These changes have usually been characterized by (1) a shortened elementary school and (2) a lengthened secondary school. They have also been characterized by large changes in the curriculum, especially on the secondary school level. Such changes were advocated as early as 1888 by President Charles W. Eliot of Harvard, and in 1893 the Committee of Ten, composed of educators who were appointed by the National Education Association, recommended the reorganization of elementary and secondary school education into two periods of six years each. The Committee of Ten made the following statement which has tremendously affected school practice:

> In the opinion of the committee several subjects now reserved for the high schools, such as algebra, geometry, natural science, and foreign languages, should be begun earlier than now, and therefore within the schools classified as elementary; or as an alternative, the secondary-school period should be made to begin two years earlier than at present, leaving six years instead of eight for the elementary-school period. Under the present organization elementary subjects and elementary methods are, in the judgment of the committee, kept in use too long.[22]

Under the stimulus of such suggestions and recommendations as have just been mentioned, several school systems shortened the elementary school course of study to six years and lengthened the secondary school course of study to six years; usually, though, the secondary school course of study was divided into two units—one known as the junior high school, usually comprising grades seven through nine, and the other as the senior high school, usually comprising grades ten through twelve. Many other variations in grouping came, of course, to be practiced. Developing slowly until 1910, reorganizations such as have just been indicated were made rapidly after that date. While most of the reorganizations are found in the cities, hundreds of them are found in the village and the rural communities. The eight-four school organization is rapidly passing.

Of course, many schools which claim that they have a reorganized school system have not really changed much beyond a shifting of one or two grades from the elementary school to the secondary school.

[22] Quoted from Frank Forest Bunker, "Reorganization of the Public School System," U. S. Bureau of Education, *Bulletin* 1916, No. 8, p. 49.

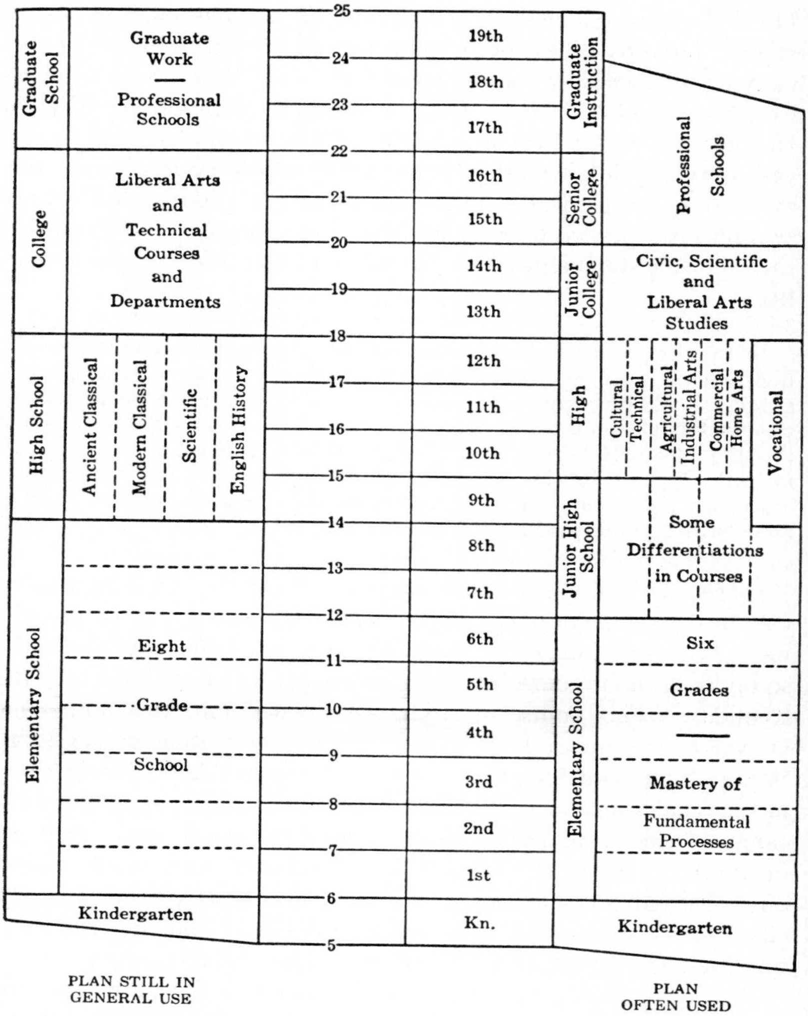

Graduate School
Graduate Work
Professional Schools
College
Liberal Arts and Technical Courses and Departments
High School
Ancient Classical
Modern Classical
Scientific
English History
Elementary School
Eight Grade School
Kindergarten

25
24
23
22
21
20
19
18
17
16
15
14
13
12
11
10
9
8
7
6
5

19th
18th
17th
16th
15th
14th
13th
12th
11th
10th
9th
8th
7th
6th
5th
4th
3rd
2nd
1st
Kn.

Graduate Instruction
Professional Schools
Senior College
Junior College
Civic, Scientific and Liberal Arts Studies
High
Cultural
Technical
Agricultural
Industrial Arts
Commercial
Home Arts
Vocational
Junior High School
Some Differentiations in Courses
Elementary School
Six Grades
Mastery of Fundamental Processes
Kindergarten

PLAN STILL IN GENERAL USE

PLAN OFTEN USED

Fig. 20. The reorganization of American education. (*Adapted from Ellwood P. Cubberley,* Public Education in the United States, *Houghton Mifflin, rev. ed., 1934, p. 559.*)

Such schools are reorganized in name only. A school which is reorganized in fact as well as in name provides for its junior high school pupils such services as the following: differentiated courses with the introduction of electives; more extraclass activities; departmental teaching and promotion by school subjects; a guidance program; flexibility of pupil grouping and other adaptions to individual differences; and better articulation between the elementary school and the junior high school, on one hand, and between the junior high school and the senior high school, on the other hand.

Changes Between the Secondary School and the Colleges. Just as the secondary school has been frequently extended on the lower end, so it is coming to be extended on the upper end to make it include the first year or two of the traditional four-year college course, or a terminal course, made up chiefly of vocational preparation. This latter extension is usually called the junior college. In a survey the junior college was defined as follows:

> A junior college is an educational institution which supplies two years of training beyond the standard high school. Its curriculum thus corresponds to that of the first two years of an accredited college. As it exists today, a junior college may be either the first two years of a fully-organized university, where the course is divided into two units of two years each, or it may be a separate institution. In the latter case it will in all probability be an upward extension of a high school, an independent institution offering two years of collegiate training, or a normal school whose work is closely articulated with the state university.[23]

Since its establishment in 1898 at Decatur, Illinois, the junior college has had a rapid growth. There are now almost six hundred junior colleges in the United States. Approximately one-half of them are publicly financed and publicly controlled. They are distributed over most of the states, but are found most frequently in California, Iowa, Missouri, and Texas; California now has 12 per cent of the junior colleges of the United States. Their value is being discussed in all states. A survey states that the five objectives most frequently mentioned for the junior colleges are:

[23] John Addison Clement and Vivian Thomas Smith, "Public Junior College Legislation in the United States," University of Illinois Bureau of Educational Research, *Bulletin*, No. 51, p. 12.

1. To provide terminal education for those who cannot or should not go on to higher levels of training; (a) to provide vocational or semi-professional courses; (b) to provide cultural training.
2. To take care of the needs of the adolescent student in this transition period, (a) by giving him individual attention, and (b) by offering training which will enable him to orient himself both with reference to vocations and with the whole body of knowledge.
3. To prepare students for the upper two years of college and for professional schools.
4. To enable students to remain at home longer.
5. To bring together in a single institution all secondary work, high school and early college—to complete secondary education.[24]

Other Changes Within the Elementary and the Secondary Schools. Within the elementary schools, probably the greatest change in organization has been along the line of lateral extensions, such as the organization of special school facilities for numerous kinds of deviate pupils. Among the most frequent of these special facilities are those for the mental deviates (both bright and dull) and for physical deviates of various types (blind, deaf, crippled, speech defectives, cardiac, epileptic, and tuberculous). A recent trend in the education of both mental and physical deviates is to integrate their education, so far as practicable, with that of other pupils.

Within the secondary school also, probably the greatest changes have been along the line of lateral extensions. For example, part-time continuation schools, vocational schools, evening schools, graduate courses, and correspondence-study courses have been organized. The establishment of vocational schools and classes has been especially rapid during recent years, and that movement will probably continue, because of public insistence that education be made more practical. The need for skilled workmen for war factories and farms during World War II gave vocational education a tremendous impetus which has continued after that war.

In both the elementary and the secondary schools the greatest developments have come in attempts to provide for individual differences through a changed curriculum, better grouping of pupils, and newer types of teaching procedures. These developments are so sig-

[24] *Seventh Yearbook* of the Department of Superintendence, pp. 302–303. By permission of the National Education Association, publishers. Examine several issues of *The Junior College Journal,* the official publication of the American Association of Junior Colleges.

nificant that Chapter 11 (Pupil Classification and Progress) of this book is devoted to them.

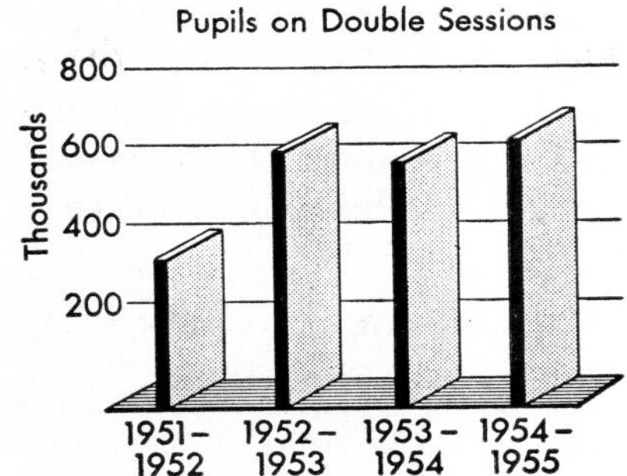

FIG. 21. Number of pupils getting only a part-time schooling. *(From* Teachers for Tomorrow, *p. 31. Courtesy of The Fund for the Advancement of Education.)*

PROBABLE FUTURE TRENDS IN THE ORGANIZATION OF OUR SCHOOLS

This chapter has shown that although the schools of the United States assumed the form which they did, largely through mere chance and imitation rather than by design, the tendency has been to reorganize them consciously and deliberately to make them meet the changing needs of a democratic social order characterized by equality of educational opportunity for all the children of all the people. Although our early school patterns were borrowed from European countries and were more suited to the needs of an autocracy or aristocracy than a democracy, our people have gone far toward developing a school system adapted to a vigorous democracy.

Probably, the reorganization of our school systems has much farther to go. That reorganization can never be complete, because as social, industrial, economic, political, and other changes are made, changes in the school organization will also have to be made. Changes in our school systems in the future will probably continue, as they have in the past, along three major fronts, namely, (1) better articulation of the various divisions and units of the school systems; (2) better adaptation of the subject-matter, the teaching methods, and other phases of educational procedure to the needs of the individual and of society; and (3) larger public support, supervision, and control of school agencies.

The present tendency is toward the use of such a plan as is indicated on the right-hand side of Fig. 20. This plan provides for: (1) an elementary school of six years, this being preceded by a kindergarten; (2) a junior high school of three years; (3) a senior high school of three years; (4) a junior college of two years, this to be closely related to the high school; and (5) a university consisting of a large number of professional schools, beginning with the junior year, or so-called senior college.

QUESTIONS FOR DISCUSSION

1. Do you believe that the elementary school, as many persons claim, is the most efficient division of our school systems? Why or why not?

2. What factors account for the large increase in high school and in college enrollments during recent decades, especially during recent years?

3. What do you predict will be the trend in enrollment in the elementary school, in the high school, and in the college during the next few years? Give reasons for your prediction for each school.

4. What changes, if any, in the organization of our school systems do you predict will be made in the future? Why?

5. What advantages, if any, are there in having in one school building, as a few schools do, all grades from the kindergarten through the junior college? What disadvantages are there in such a plan?

6. Does the large amount of pupil failure in the first year of each of the school levels prove the need for better articulation among these levels? What steps are now being taken to obtain better articulation?

7. Do you believe, as many persons affirm, that the high schools and the colleges are more aristocratic than democratic? Explain. Compare the democracy of the typical high school and college of today with that of earlier days.

8. What effect has tradition had upon the high school curriculum? Is it possible to ignore this tradition in organizing a curriculum for a high school? Why or why not? Is tradition of any value? Explain.

9. With respect to pedagogical efficiency and financial economy, are there too many small high schools in your state? Explain. What should be done to correct the situation? How many students should a high school ideally have? Why?

10. Do you believe that it is good policy to offer at public expense to anyone who desires it, complete schooling from the kindergarten through the university? What advantages, if any, would there be in making secondary and college education selective as do the foreign countries? What disadvantages would there be in such a practice?

11. Is there as much equality of educational opportunity on the college level as there is on the elementary and the secondary school levels? Give evidence. Do you believe that there should be as much equality on the higher levels as on the lower? Why or why not? Are high schools entirely free? Show how or how not.

12. Do you believe that college education justifies its cost to the public? Cite evidence to support your belief.

13. What rules and regulations does your state have regarding the standards which elementary, secondary, and higher schools shall meet? Criticize these standards as to their general adequacy.

14. Do the colleges, through their entrance requirements, dominate too much the secondary school curriculum? Why or why not? What domination of the elementary school curriculum is there on the part of the secondary school?

15. What factors should determine whether or not a community should start a junior college?

16. What is meant by vocational education? Do you believe it is good policy to spend public funds to provide vocational education? Why or why not? In what school year should vocational education begin? Why?

17. Should we organize specialized secondary schools, or comprehensive secondary schools which would give all or most types of secondary education under one roof? Give reasons?

18. What legal provision, if any, is made for kindergartens in your state? For junior colleges? For nursery schools?

19. Do you believe that the kindergarten should be required by law in every community and be supported by taxation the same as the elementary school and the secondary school? Why or why not? Answer the same questions with reference to the nursery school.

SELECTED REFERENCES

Aiken, Wilford M., and Aiken, Marjorie, "The Eight-Year Study of the Progressive Education Association: The Thirty Schools Have Some Evidence," *Educational Method*, Vol. 20 (March, 1941), pp. 307–311.

Presents data bearing on articulation between high school and college.

Brown, John Franklin, *The American High School*, The Macmillan Co., New York, 1909, Ch. I.

This chapter gives a history of the Latin grammar school, the academy, and the high school.

Bunker, Frank Forest, *Reorganization of the Public School System*, U. S. Bureau of Education, *Bulletin*, 1916, No. 8, Ch. 1.

Gives a brief history of the elementary school, the secondary school, and the college.

"Cardinal Principles of Secondary Education," U. S. Bureau of Education, *Bulletin,* 1918, No. 35, 32 pp.

A statement which has tremendously influenced secondary school education; the statement was made by the Commission on the Reorganization of Secondary Education, appointed by the National Education Association.

Committee of Ten, Report, Published for the National Education Association by the American Book Company, New York, 1894, 249 pp.

Report has had a large effect on school practices.

Essex, Martin W., and Spayde, Paul E., "Junior High School Is Here to Stay," *Nation's Schools,* Vol. 54 (August, 1954), pp. 31–34.

A study of the first forty years of the junior high school movement. It shows that the junior high school appears to be firmly established as a part of the American plan of education.

Good, H. G., *A History of Western Education,* The Macmillan Co., New York, 1947, Chs. 16, 18, 19, 20.

Ch. 16 discusses "American Beginnings";
Ch. 18, "The American System";
Ch. 19, "Transforming the Elementary School"; and
Ch. 20, "Creating the High School."

Jacobsen, Paul B., "Fifty Years of Secondary Education," *Nation's Schools,* Vol. 49 (January, 1952), pp. 38–41.

Johnson, Clifton, *Old-Time Schools and School Books,* The Macmillan Co., New York, 1904, 381 pp.

An interesting account of old-time schools and school books, especially on the elementary school level.

Kearney, Nolan C., *Elementary School Objectives,* Russell Sage Foundation, 1953, 189 pp.

Noustakas, Clark E., and Berson, Minnie Perrin, *The Nursery School and Child Care Center,* Whiteside, Inc. and Wm. Morrow and Co., New York, 1955.

A description of nursery schools in the United States.

CHAPTER 5

School Facilities

The school site, the school building, the school equipment, and the school supplies affect for good or for ill the general welfare and the progress of the pupils, and teachers have many responsibilities for the use, the protection, and the improvement of these facilities. A "well-qualified teacher at one end of a log and a pupil at the other end," as Mark Hopkins said, will not alone make the most efficient school. Instruction can be best given in or on attractive, hygienic, safe, commodious, and well-equipped classrooms, libraries, laboratories, shops, playgrounds, gymnasiums, and studios. Moreover, for their best work the pupils must have stationery, pencils, pens, ink, chalk, crayons, and other supplies. A log will not suffice as the altar of instruction.

Expenditures for the School Plant

The school plant includes the site, the building, and the equipment. The expenditures made for obtaining these relatively permanent possessions of the school are known in school financial accounting as capital outlays. Next to teachers' salaries, which require in the average community more than fifty per cent of the school budget, the largest expenditure is for new school plants. During World War II and the years immediately following it, the construction of school buildings almost ceased. These factors plus the large crop of war babies have created a huge shortage of school buildings. That shortage now amounts to many thousand classrooms—in fact, almost everyone is concerned today about the shortage of classrooms. The shortage is found in almost every state and in thousands of school systems, but it is much more severe in certain communities than in others. In the whole United States, the land, buildings, and equipment of the public and the private schools and the colleges are now valued at approximately twenty billion dollars, but to meet the present shortage in classrooms an expenditure of several billion dollars more will be necessary.

Although it is gigantic, the original expenditure is not the only expenditure which must be made for the school plant. After school buildings have been erected, they must be kept in repair, they must be operated, and they must be insured; and expenditures for those purposes must be made as long as the buildings are used. In the average school system of the United States, slightly more than nine per cent of the school budget is expended for the operation of the school plant, and slightly less than five per cent of the budget is expended for school-plant maintenance. Operation of school plant is a term used in school-financial accounting to include expenditures for school-janitorial employees and for operation supplies, such as fuel, electric current, water, and cleaning materials. Maintenance of school plant is a term used to include school expenditures for repairs and upkeep of school sites, school buildings, and school equipment.

The Trend Toward a Better School Plant

It is a far cry from yesterday's "little red schoolhouses" with their small sites, their one room, and their simple equipment to today's palatial school buildings with their commodious sites, their many rooms, and their modern equipment. In the early days a knowledge of carpentry was believed to qualify a person to plan and to construct a school building, but the modern school building is necessarily the combined product of an educator, of various types of engineers, of an artist, of a hygienist, and of an economist. Although the developments in school housing have not been as rapid as the developments in many other phases of life, it cannot be gainsaid that large improvement has been made in all phases of the school plant. In the main, though with a slight tendency to lag, the development of the school plant has paralleled the development of the curriculum, of teaching procedures, and of other phases of the work of the school. As the purposes and the procedures of the school have changed, the school plant has had to be modified to meet the work of the school. Some of the ways in which the school plant has been improved, and some of the ways in which it needs still further improvement, will be discussed in the following paragraphs. Teachers should know something of school-plant standards and school-plant procedures, because they are often in a position to make constructive suggestions on those matters that can be adopted by school officials.

THE SCHOOL SITE. In spite of the abundance and the comparative cheapness of land in the early days when we were primarily a rural people, the schools of those days were usually located on small sites—sites too small for playgrounds, for school gardening, and for landscaping. Moreover, the school sites did not always meet other exacting standards. During recent years, however, there has been a tendency toward the selection of school sites which are more desirable in every way. In fact, many states have enacted laws which establish various standards that school sites must meet, especially regarding size and environment. The following are the chief standards that a school site should meet as fully as possible:

1. Be located within easy, or feasible, walking distance of the pupils whom it is designed to serve. In rural communities, of course, pupil transportation is often necessary, and making arrangements for it must not be forgotten when a school site is being selected.
2. Serve a natural community center, that is, be reasonably close to churches, markets, lodges, etc.
3. Be located in an environment which is wholesome for a school.
4. Possess proper size, shape, and topography.
5. Have a soil which is quick-drying and free from decaying organic matter and artificial construction.
6. Possess natural drainage, or the possibility of constructing an artificial drainage system at not too large cost.
7. Have an ample supply of good water, especially drinking water.
8. Receive sunlight during the entire school day.
9. Be available at a reasonable cost.

THE SCHOOL BUILDING. During recent decades, a tremendous improvement has been made in the planning and in the construction of school buildings. Casual observation shows that the school building of today is often the largest, the most beautiful, and the most expensive building in the community; these characteristics are found especially in secondary school buildings. From the beginning of schools, there has been a tendency toward making the school building more useful, more safe, more healthful, more enduring, more economical, and more beautiful. Perfection along these lines has not, however, been reached, because in many school buildings which have been erected, there is much waste—waste resulting from many factors, but usually stemming from lack of foresight in planning the buildings. Numerous school buildings have not been erected in the proper location, or they have been made too large, too small, or ill-adapted to the needs of their community in some other way. The classrooms, in many instances, have not been adapted to the curriculum needs of the pupils. In numerous communities, also, the school buildings are architectural monstrosities.

In planning school buildings, modern school officials and architects are keeping in mind desirable objectives for school buildings. They are keeping in mind especially the excellent objectives listed many years ago in the *Report of the Committee on School-House Planning* (pp. 14–19), of the National Education Association. Since these objectives are also applicable to present times, they are quoted herewith in abbreviated form:

1. *Adaptation to educational needs.* The plan should conform to the schedule of rooms already adopted.
2. *Safety.* The corridors and the stairways should permit the building to be vacated in three minutes even if one stairway is made useless by smoke.
3. *Healthfulness.* Every room should have abundant natural light.
   The toilets should be distributed conveniently on each floor and should have windows opening directly to the open air.
   There should be a sufficient number of bubblers for drinking purposes, so located that they will not block traffic.
   Washbowls should be adequate in number.
   To avoid damp, insanitary, or poorly ventilated rooms there should be no basement as this term is usually understood, with the possible exception of space for the heating plant. This plant should, when possible, be located entirely without the confines of the building.
   In rural communities the one-story type is often desirable, as it is a reasonable guarantee of safety in case of fire.
   To avoid excessive climbing of stairs, the building should not contain more than three stories and a basement, except in congested cities where land is very expensive.
4. *Convenience.* The location of rooms with reference to one another should be carefully studied.
5. *Expansiveness.* The building should be so planned that it can be enlarged as much as may be needed without unnecessary cost and without cutting off natural light and ventilation of any of the existing rooms.

6. *Flexibility.* Since it is not possible to foresee all the requirements of the future, every school building should be so planned and constructed that changes can be made if necessary in the lengths of the room.
7. *Aesthetic fitness.* The skill of the architect as a designer is shown by his ability to clothe the building with a pleasing exterior, without doing violence to the interior.
   The interior should likewise produce attractive and pleasing effects. The decorations should be modest and cheerful.
8. *Economy.* Economy in the plan is secured by
   (a) Accurate determination of the size needed for each room.
   (b) Duplicate uses of rooms.
   (c) Elimination of waste areas.

The School Equipment. Although there has been much improvement in school equipment, it has not kept pace with developments in school buildings. Compared with the furnishings of cultured homes and with the equipment of well-managed private businesses, the equipment of the typical school of today is decidedly out of date. Much school equipment, in fact, must be classed as antique, and it is probable that, as is the case with antique furniture in homes, the less comfortable and the less useful items have survived, while the more comfortable and the more useful items have been worn out. In many instances the equipment of a school building is older than the building.

In thousands of classrooms the pupils must occupy the same uncomfortable and dilapidated seats, use the same out-of-date globes and maps, read the same library books, gaze upon the same pictures and other wall decorations, and use other types of equipment which served their grandparents and their parents. In hundreds of classrooms the equipment is limited to an ancient desk for each pupil and for each teacher; there are no libraries, no maps, no globes, no filing facilities, no bulletin boards, no wall pictures, no shades for the windows, no radios, and no televisions. Those sad conditions are found especially in the rural schools.

The explanation for the historic failure properly to equip our school buildings is difficult to seek. The most plausible explanation for the failure is lack of appreciation on the part of the general public and of school employees of the importance of school equipment. Education has been too long and too much associated with book learning and recitations—types of activities for which the pupils need only a place to sit or to stand. The lack of funds to purchase new school equipment is not always the explanation; poor school equipment is found in good times as well as in times of economic stress, and it often obtains, even in the palatial school buildings of wealthy communities.

The tendency to spend too little on school equipment has had the unfortunate result of making it impossible for the schools to carry on their educational program with adequate vigor. Only a small expenditure for school equipment would often make a large contribution to educational results. For example, only a few dollars spent on modern globes, on good reference books, and on up-to-date maps would greatly improve pupil results in a geography class; in fact, investigation might show that a few dollars spent on school equipment would enable the teacher to instruct a larger number of pupils, thus reducing the per pupil cost by several dollars. Pupils and teachers cannot do their best work, without proper tools, any more than can the laborer or the artisan; moreover, to require pupils and teachers to use some of the tools which they must now use is injurious to their health, their safety, their comfort, and their happiness.

When prospective teachers are in college and are engaged in preparing for their profession, they should become acquainted with modern types of school equipment which their future work requires; and they should learn how to use this equipment. Since new inventions are constantly making old equipment obsolete, teachers have the obligation of maintaining this acquaintance with modern school equipment throughout their professional careers. They have the further obligation of requesting school officials to provide them with the most up-to-date equipment which the school district can afford; and they should not feel too embarrassed or irritated, if they have to repeat the request, or if they have to repeat it again and again.

Care and Use of the School Plant

Teachers can contribute much toward prolonging the life of the school plant, and toward reducing the annual expenditures necessary for repairs, for replacements, and for janitorial services. They should realize that any unnecessary expenditure made for the school plant will tend to reduce the amount of money available for their salaries, for school libraries, for instructional supplies, for textbooks, and for other requisites for good schools. The contributions which teachers can make toward a better use of the school plant are discussed in the following paragraphs.

RESPONSIBILITY FOR THE PROTECTION OF THE SCHOOL PLANT. Casual observation shows that school plants wear out, decay, and become obsolescent the same as all other tangible possessions. Although the depreciation of school plants cannot be entirely prevented, it can be greatly retarded. The amount and the kind of use which a school plant receives are the chief factors in determining the annual depreciation and the life of the plant.

Teachers supervise the pupils' use of the school plant and in that supervision they have definite responsibility for instilling in the pupils a wholesome respect for property. Instilling that respect will not only protect school property from damage, but will inevitably carry over into life situations and protect all other forms of property, public and private, from unnecessary damage caused by careless use.

Pupils do not always treat school property with adequate respect. In some schools the desks and other furniture have been almost whittled away by pupils' knives; paper wads and finger marks mar the walls; pencil, ink, and crayon marks are found everywhere; and window glass is frequently broken. These are only a few of the examples of misuse, and occasionally of downright vandalism, on the part of pupils and other persons who use the school plant. Such depredations not only make the school plant unsightly and less useful, but they greatly shorten its life. They result in the loss of millions of dollars annually in the school plants of the nation. This loss can be largely prevented through the watchful efforts of teachers, and none of these efforts need be unduly burdensome to teachers.

Many boards of education have placed in their rules and regulations a requirement that teachers shall report to their school principal any pupil who has been deemed guilty of careless or of wanton destruction of school property. A lesser number of boards stipulate that pupils shall pay a fine for any willful damage which they may inflict upon school property. In any attempts which they may make to fine guilty pupils, teachers should know that the courts have usually decided that school officials and school employees "may not require pupils to pay for injury to school property where the injury grows out of acts of neglect or carelessness."[1] In buttressing their

[1] Newton Edwards, *The Courts and the Public Schools,* The University of Chicago Press, 1933, pp. 532–533. By permission of The University of Chicago Press, publishers.

decision on the question, the courts have argued that pupils do not have money with which to pay fines, and that so-called acts of carelessness are sometimes unintentional. Teachers may extend reasonable punishment to pupils for proven acts of willful destruction of property, but there is serious doubt about the legality of fines as a punishment for pupils who are minors.

If they are given a small amount of supervision by their teachers, pupils will co-operate in keeping the school plant in excellent repair and spick and span in every way. Pupils are not vandals born and bred; and, contrary to common belief, pupils cherish beautiful surroundings in the school.

The first step in obtaining proper treatment for the school plant is to place all parts of the plant in a respectable condition. By calling the attention of their immediate administrative supervisors to the need for repairs, teachers may often be the means of obtaining improvements. Under ideal conditions, of course, these repairs would be made, without the teachers being compelled to request them, and in most schools they are being made in this ideal manner. The school site should be landscaped; the classrooms, corridors, foyers, and other parts of the school building should be decorated; the floors should be refinished; the furniture should be revarnished, stained or painted; broken window glass should be replaced; and damaged furniture and other equipment should be repaired. When these and other decorations and repairs have been made, it is an easy matter to win the co-operation of pupils in keeping the school plant in a respectable condition. On the contrary, one pencil mark on the walls may suggest another mark; one paper wad is apt to call for another paper wad. In brief, any act of seemingly condoned vandalism will likely suggest similar depredations upon not only school property, but upon other property, public and private, in the community. Schools that are in good repair do not invite vandalism.

Under the title of Safety Education a section of Chapter 12 of this book discusses the large damage to life and to school property which school property fires and school accidents entail annually. The steps which teachers may take in preventing fires and in assuring safety to pupils are also suggested in that chapter. In view of that discussion it will not be necessary to treat the problem at this point.

Responsibility for School-janitorial Services. In one-room schools, and many of these schools are still found, the teacher is usually entirely responsible for the janitorial services of his school. In schools of more than one room, which usually provide at least part-time janitorial services, the teacher is partly responsible for the cleanliness and the tidiness of his classroom, shop, laboratory, studio, or other work place. If the school has a janitor, the teacher does not have any obligation to do the janitor's work; however, the teacher is in a position to lighten the janitor's load in numerous ways. He can especially help to lighten that load by seeing that his pupils give adequate co-operation to the school janitor in his attempts to make the school plant meet high standards of housekeeping.

The teacher has a responsibility for seeing that his pupils do not enter the school building with unclean shoes, for assuring that they do not scatter waste paper about or otherwise litter the school building or the school grounds, and for seeing that they are not guilty of other acts of carelessness which would make the school plant unclean, untidy, or which in some other manner would increase unnecessarily the work of the school janitor. It is not unreasonable for the teacher to expect his pupils to sweep up any litter which accrues from an industrial-arts class or from any other laboratory period, or is it unreasonable to expect the teacher to request his pupils to lift their school seats at the close of the school day. Giving pupils these lessons is a desirable part of preparing them for life; if the pupils learn habits of co-operation and good housekeeping in school, they are likely to carry the habits into their homes and into all other activities of their lives.

Contrary to the thoughtless belief of many teachers, the janitor is an important school employee. He does, or should do, much more than build fires and sweep out. The school janitor performs, or should perform, the following services:

1. More than any other person, the school janitor sets the housekeeping standards of the school. He keeps, or should keep, the school building and the school grounds spick and span. Since the housekeeping standards of the janitor are likely to determine the housekeeping standards of the pupils and to carry over into the after-school life of the pupils, they should be kept on a high plane.
2. The school janitor has custody of a building, equipment, and grounds which cost a large amount of money. He makes many repairs. He keeps the building locked when it is not in use, and he protects the grounds, building, and equipment from unnecessary injury.

3. The school janitor uses annually hundreds or thousands of dollars' worth of supplies in cleaning, in heating, in lighting, and in other servicing of the building. In a large school building it is possible for him to waste or to save his salary in the use of school supplies.
4. With the exception of the school principal, the school janitor has more to do with the health, the safety, and the comfort of the occupants of the school building than any other school employee. He sees that the building is properly heated and ventilated, that it is clean, and that it is fumigated after an epidemic of contagious disease. He sees that the fire escapes and the sidewalks are in good repair, and are cleared of snow and ice. He removes all fire hazards such as often accumulate in the basement, under the stairways, and in other parts of the building.
5. The school janitor has an important educational and public-relations influence in the school and in the community. The pupils hobnob with him at recess and at other school intermissions. Unless he is intelligent and is clean in mind and body, his influence upon the pupils is not likely to be the best. Moreover, the school janitor hears much, sees much, and often says much regarding the school, and all of this makes him an important public-relations agent for the school.

The teacher should realize, of course, that well-qualified school janitors are scarce—more scarce even than good teachers—and that he will have to make the most of the quality of the janitorial service with which he is provided by school officials. Not all janitors can or will perform the five types of services just mentioned. The teacher will often have to make the most of a bad bargain—a bargain which he was not a participant in making. Something, though, can usually be salvaged from bad bargains, and even the worst janitorial service can be improved, if the teacher knows what constitutes efficient janitorial service and how to procure it. Above all, the teacher must know how to deal with the janitor.

In dealing with the janitor the teacher should remember that the janitor is a human being, and that his co-operation cannot be obtained, if he is treated as a menial. To greet him regularly with a cordial "Good day" or a similar greeting is a mark of neighborliness and is bound to be reflected in a more co-operative spirit on his part. A school janitor who is treated as a human being is more likely to co-operate in performing the many small services which teachers frequently find it necessary to request of school janitors.

If the janitorial work is not being performed properly, the teacher is obliged to try to obtain a more efficient performance of it. The typical school janitor will not take offense, if the teacher calls his attention to needed janitorial services, provided, of course, that tact and reasonableness are employed in making the request. In some instances it will be necessary for the teacher to inform the school principal of the untidy condition of his classroom, and to leave to the principal the responsibility of informing the janitor of the need for correcting the situation. The regulations of many schools and school systems require that teachers who desire any special services from the janitor shall make the request through the school principal. When the regulations of the school or the school system do not require teachers to make these requests through the principal, the requests should normally be made directly to the janitor; use of this plan will tend to refute any inference that the janitor is being reported to the principal. A sincere "Thank you" from the teacher to the janitor for performing any special services is bound to pay dividends upon future requests which the teacher may find it necessary to make.

RESPONSIBILITY FOR THE SUPERVISION OF SCHOOL EQUIPMENT. Many teachers, especially those of shop and laboratory courses, have several thousand dollars' worth of equipment under their care, and all teachers have some equipment. Unless proper supervision is given to this equipment, it may be damaged, misplaced, stolen, or lost. When pupils use equipment, they should be expected to use it carefully, and to return it to its proper place, when they have finished using it; this practice should be regarded as an important part of the education of pupils. If cases or cupboards are provided, the equipment should be found in them, when it is not in use, and these receptacles should be locked. Likewise, when school is not in session, the doors to the classroom and to the buildings should be locked to lessen the danger of theft and of vandalism.

In the more progressive schools and school systems, another phase of the supervision of school equipment is the taking of an annual inventory of the equipment. The inventory is usually taken at the close of the school year, and includes a listing or a checking of all movable items such as desks, chairs, bookcases, maps, globes, filing equipment, and portable blackboards. Special forms are usually provided for this procedure by the board of education, and teachers are called upon to list or to check each item of equipment under their supervision. The taking of an equipment inventory serves the following purposes:

1. It helps to prevent the loss or the misplacement of school equipment.
2. It aids in determining the amount of school insurance to carry, and in adjusting any insurance claims.
3. It aids in replacing school equipment.
4. It helps to prevent the purchase of any unnecessary school equipment.
5. It aids in calculating school costs.

Community Use of the School Plant. Within recent years, the historic tendency toward making the school the center of community life has been much accelerated. Thus today, school buildings are being opened for the use of the general public during the evenings, and at other times when the work of the regular pupils will not be hindered. Everywhere today, adult education is being emphasized, because it is being more and more realized that only a beginning in education can be obtained in eight, twelve, or any other number of years of the institutional school. Many states now give financial aid to school districts for the establishment of adult evening schools and classes, and in the whole United States millions of adults are enrolled in these schools and classes. Some school districts have more students enrolled in adult-evening classes than they have pupils in day classes. Regular day-school teachers are sometimes asked to teach one or more classes in the adult-evening school, and usually teachers are paid extra for those services.

In addition to being used as a meeting place for adult classes, the school plant is being used by a large number of associations, clubs, societies, and other organizations. Some of the organizations which make frequent use of the school plant are Parent-Teacher Associations, mother's clubs, Red Cross, community clubs, people's forums, social-service federations, welfare associations, health organizations, farm bureaus, farmers' institutes, granges, Boy Scouts, Girl Scouts, Chambers of Commerce, labor organizations, Americanization clubs, and lyceums. The modern school is trying in many ways to co-operate with community organizations, especially those organizations interested in educational and welfare activities; this co-operation helps to vitalize the work of the day-school pupils and contributes also to the improvement of the whole community, and it makes the public more willing to pay taxes for school support. Teachers should give this co-operation, so long as it does not interfere with the first aim of the school, namely, the education of all the children of all the people of the community; the first duty in education of a community is to look after the education of its children.

Classroom Seating

During the school day, pupils spend most of their time in sitting. A large part of after-school life is thus utilized also. Since habits of sitting are largely acquired in school, and since *good* habits of sitting contribute to comfort, to good posture, and to general efficiency, the school should give much more attention to the proper seating of pupils and to good sitting habits than it has in the past. Many investigations have found that the seating equipment of most schools is far from ideal and that when ideal seating equipment is found, it is not always properly used. Teachers have the responsibility of seeing that the seating equipment with which their classrooms are provided is properly used; if they know what constitutes good seating equipment, they can sometimes obtain replacement of archaic types of seating equipment with modern types.

As is well known, most pupils are right-handed, but a small percentage of pupils are left-handed. Desks for left-handed pupils are being manufactured now, and teachers should ask for them for all left-handed pupils.

Adjustment of Classroom Seats to the Pupils' Sizes. In most classrooms, provision is made for at least some adjustment of seating to pupils in one of the following ways: (1) through having nonadjustable seats and desks of two or more sizes, and (2) through having seating and desks adjustable as to height and as to spacing between desk and seat. Many classrooms, of course, have seating of only one and nonadjustable size. What is more tragic is to find, as is frequently the case, adjustable seating which has never been adjusted. The results of such educational malpractice are likely to be discomfort and bad posture for the pupils through life.

The teacher must accept the chief responsibility for making needed seating adjustments in his classroom. When the seats and desks are adjustable, or when they are provided in more than one size, the solution of the problem is largely in the teacher's own hands. When the seating does not meet or cannot be made to meet proper standards, the teacher should request the school principal to consider the

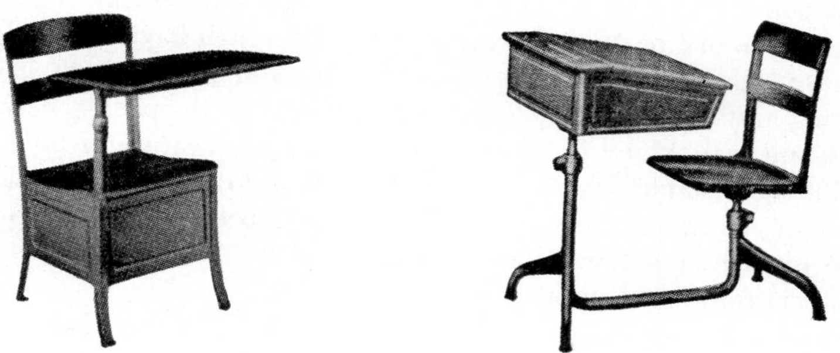

Fig. 22. The evolution of the classroom seat. The top picture illustrates types of seats in use from about 1635 to 1850; the middle shows types in use from about 1850 to 1920; and the bottom exhibits two types being manufactured since about 1920. Many teachers of today prefer tables and chairs for pupils.

need for other school equipment; of course, lack of school funds will often prevent the board of education from purchasing new equipment for the school.

In his treatise on *School Posture and Seating,* Henry Eastman Bennett makes many helpful suggestions for the better adjustment of classroom seating to the pupils. The more important of these suggestions are epitomized herewith.

1. Lower seats are needed in most classrooms. The seat should not be high enough to exert any pressure under the thighs at or near the edge of the seat when the feet are resting on the floor.
2. A clearance of approximately three inches should be found between the edge of the seat and the knee angle of the occupant.
3. The writing surface has proper height if it provides an easy rest for the arms of the pupil when he is seated in a correct position for writing. Lower writing surfaces are needed in most classrooms.
4. When a plumbline dropped from the edge of the desk strikes the seat approximately two inches from its edge, the seat and desk have proper spacing.[2]

ARRANGEMENT OF CLASSROOM SEATS FOR THE PUPILS. Desirable objectives to be attained by the arrangement of classroom seats have been stated by Henry Eastman Bennett as follows: "(1) Best direction of light on every desk; (2) writing focus of the class, so that for ordinary recitation purposes all will face toward a common point; (3) pupils facing toward well-lighted blackboards and away from windows; (4) favorable arrangement for supervision by teacher; (5) economy of floor space; (6) aisles convenient for travel to and from door; (7) pupils not to be in such proximity to each other as to obstruct the view of some; (8) or so placed as to be tempted to mischief or too much communication; (9) adequate and well-shaped space for class activities at the front of the room." [3]

To obtain the objectives just mentioned, Bennett [4] developed a quadrant seating arrangement. Such an arrangement permits the light to come over the left side of the pupil, and thus reduces the glare often found in classrooms in which the seats are arranged in straight lines parallel to the windows.

[2] *School Posture and Seating,* 1928, p. 246. Ginn and Company, publishers.
[3] These suggestions are found on practically every page of the book. Ginn and Company, publishers.
[4] *Ibid.,* pp. 251–254.

Teachers who have tried the quadrant arrangement of seats are enthusiastic in their praise of it. The quadrant arrangement of seats may be immediately and easily made in classrooms having movable seating. In classrooms which have seats and desks fastened to the floor, the quadrant arrangement could not be effected, without obtaining permission from the school principal to fasten the desks in small units to two strips of wood so that they could be arranged at any angle desired.

Many teachers, particularly in the elementary school, prefer to group pupils by ability, and have a seating arrangement such as is shown in Figure 23.

FIG. 23. Informal seating of pupils. *(Courtesy of the Cincinnati, Ohio, public schools.)*

SEATING OF PHYSICALLY-HANDICAPPED PUPILS. In school systems which do not have special classes for the physically-handicapped pupils, these pupils must usually attend regular classes and special provisions must be made for the seating of such pupils. These provisions must be made especially for pupils who are crippled and for those who are deficient in sight or in hearing. They should be made for each handicapped pupil according to the advice of a physician or other specialist when such advice is available. Many school administrators and teachers believe that pupils who are blind or nearly blind, those who are deaf or nearly deaf, and those who are unable to walk should be taught in special classes, whenever possible. Many workers in special education do not accept that view. For example, they point out that a totally blind child can be taught, and accepted by other pupils, in a regular elementary school class, provided the teacher is competent and that there is some special help available, e.g., to teach Braille outside the regular class.

Physically-handicapped pupils will sometimes need special types of desks or other work stations, and they will usually need to have their desks or other work stations placed in the part of the classroom most advantageous to them. The pupil, for example, who can't walk, or who walks with much difficulty, should be placed near the entrance and exit of the room.

Pupils with myopic eyes, and pupils with astigmatic eyes, should be placed near the front of the classroom and near the windows. Pupils with hypermetropic eyes should be located toward the rear of the room and near the windows.

Pupils with limited hearing should be placed toward the front of the classroom and in a position that will enable them to supplement their hearing by lip-reading. The hearing of an occasional pupil will be so limited that he will need a hearing aid; if this device cannot be provided by his family, funds for it may often be procured from the public or from welfare agencies. In fact, pupils who need spectacles, crutches, canes, wheel chairs, or any other aids or services to enable them to attend school will almost always have a sympathetic public or a private agency to help them if their families are unable to assist them.

Classroom Illumination

Amount and Quality of Illumination Needed. Illuminating engineers and ophthalmologists agree that the illumination of classrooms should meet two standards: it should be in the proper amount, and it should possess the proper quality. Unless those standards are met, pupil and teacher fatigue is likely to occur, vision permanently may be impaired, and teaching and learning efficiency is apt to be handicapped.

The amount of illumination is measured in foot-candles. A foot-candle may be defined as the amount of light shed by a standard candle at a distance of one foot. The number of foot-candles in any part of a room may be quickly measured by means of an instrument known as a light meter; because of the utility and the inexpensiveness of a light meter, every school should own such an instrument. Teachers do not need any technical instructions to enable them to use the instrument.

Although much research has been done by various persons and committees seeking to ascertain the minimum and the most desirable numbers of foot-candles for different parts of the school building, a final answer to the question has not yet been obtained. The Illuminating Engineering Society and the American Institute of Architects have recommended the following minimum number of foot-candles for classrooms and for other parts of school buildings:[5]

PART OF BUILDING	MINIMUM NUMBER OF FOOT-CANDLES RECOMMENDED
Classrooms, study halls, gymnasiums, shops, laboratories, lecture rooms, offices, and libraries	15
Sewing rooms, drafting rooms, art rooms, and other rooms where fine detail work is to be done	25
Auditoriums, cafeterias, and other rooms in which people congregate for an extended period, but not for study	6
Locker rooms, stairs, corridors, and toilets	4
Sight-saving rooms	30

Other authorities on classroom illumination have recommended a minimum number of twelve to twenty-five foot-candles for classrooms.[6] It is agreed, of course, that the most desirable number of

[5] Reported in *Proceedings of the Fifteenth Annual Meeting of the National Council on Schoolhouse Construction*, p. 18.

[6] John O. Kraehenbuehl, *Problems in Building Illumination*, p. 13, Engineering Experiment Station, Circular No. 29, University of Illinois, 1937. See also "Recommended Practices for Lighting California Schools" (mimeographed), California State Department of Education, 1943.

foot-candles would be slightly larger than the minimum number above recommended.

During many days of the school year, the brightness of the sun reaches in the out-of-doors as high as ten thousand foot-candles, compared on those days with one hundred foot-candles at a window inside a classroom. From the windows to the opposite side of the room, the number of foot-candles decreases rapidly, often necessitating some lighting adjustment by the teacher. When the illumination in any part of the room does not meet the minimum standards above recommended, the artificial lights may be used or the window shades may be adjusted to admit more natural light. Because nature's light is free and is more hygienic than artificial light, it should be utilized, during the day, so long as it is adequate.

The light in classrooms should have the proper quality as well as be in the proper amount. The greatest handicap in most classrooms to the quality of light is glare. According to the Illuminating Engineering Society, glare is "any brightness within the field of vision, of such a character as to cause discomfort, annoyance, interference with vision, or eye fatigue." Glare is the greatest source of ocular discomfort, and teachers have the responsibility of doing everything possible to eliminate it from their classrooms; some of the things which they can do, or can urge school officials to have done, are mentioned in the following paragraph.

Glare may be either direct or reflected. Direct glare is experienced when a person looks at an incandescent lamp that is unshielded or when he looks at the sun on a bright day. Reflected glare is experienced when light is reflected into the eyes from glossy surfaces such as blackboards, desks, walls, glass, and mirrors. Glare may be reduced by the proper use of window shades, by seating the pupils so that none faces a window, by covering naked light bulbs, and by eliminating glossy surfaces. The bureau of plant operation and maintenance of the New York City schools suggests that the following additional factors be kept in mind in connection with the control of glare and the increase of illumination in classrooms: [7]

1. Framed pictures and other glossy-surfaced objects should not be placed between windows; they should be hung on other walls to avoid reflected glare.

[7] Harold D. Hynds, *Paint Colors,* pp. 11–12. The Board of Education, New York City, 1944.

2. Plants, flower pots, etc., should not be placed on window sills where they obstruct light.
3. Unused blackboard areas may be covered with white paper to increase the illumination in classrooms.
4. Glass areas of closets, bookcases, etc., may be covered with curtains.
5. Window glass should not be covered with pictures, curtains, papers, etc.
6. Glass-top tables are particularly objectionable.

There is a widespread use in new buildings of natural lighting from an overhead source and of broad-glass expanses, with curtains where needed.

Standards for Windows for Classroom Illumination. Unless the school building has been erected within recent years, the teacher is not likely to find ideal conditions, especially of a structural nature, pertaining to the windows of his classroom. If he knows what constitutes ideal conditions, however, he can often make adjustments which will help to achieve the ideal. Among the more important of those ideal conditions are the following:

1. All windows are on one side of the room. That side should be the left side of the pupils, since practically all pupils are right-handed.
2. The glass area is not less than eighteen per cent of the floor area of rooms in which the windows begin three feet above the floor. The area is not less than sixteen per cent when the windows begin four feet above the floor.
3. The distance from the floor to the top of the window opening is at least one-half the width of the room.
4. The window area begins as near the rear wall of the classroom as possible, and stops within four feet of the front wall of the classroom.
5. The windows are so placed that light is not admitted below the eye level of the pupils at their work stations.
6. The windows have clear glass which is kept clean.

Control of Light from Windows. Windows should be equipped with shades, blinds, shutters, or some other type of light-control device to distribute the daylight throughout the room. The color of the light-control device should blend with the color of the walls.

The teacher has full responsibility for adjusting the window coverings, so that the direct sunlight will be properly diffused throughout the room, and so that glare from exterior sources will be minimized. Before beginning the work of a class period the teacher should see that the shades or other window coverings are best adjusted to obtain the objectives just mentioned, and he should not fail to make any further adjustments which may become necessary during the class period. In order that he may not obscure light, the teacher should avoid standing in front of an unshaded window.

Since each classroom has its own problem of light control, the teacher should carefully study the room to obtain for varying conditions of sunlight the best results from shade adjustments. Because of the larger amount of direct sunlight and the greater likelihood of glare, classrooms having a southern exposure usually require the most frequent as well as the most careful adjustment of shades. Classrooms with a northern exposure usually require the least adjustment of shades, but they demand the greatest use of artificial lighting. Rooms with eastern or western exposures usually have shade-adjustment problems that are not nearly as great as those of rooms with a southern exposure but much greater than those of rooms with a northern exposure.

Since light which comes through the top of the window is more likely to reach the opposite side of the room, the entrance of the light should not be handicapped by shades hung from the top of the window. Shades hung from the center of the window, and which are adjustable both up and down, will afford the best distribution of light and will also control uncomfortable brightness and reduce or eliminate glare. The criterion, of course, for the best quantity and the best quality of light is the eye level of the pupil at the proper position at his work station, not the eye level of the teacher.

Artificial Lighting of Classrooms. With the possible exception of some one-room schools, practically all schools are now equipped with electric lights. These should be available in every classroom to be used when daylight does not afford sufficient illumination to meet the standards mentioned previously in this chapter. Since teachers are often able to obtain improvements in the artificial lighting system of their classroom, they should be aware of the chief standards which such a system should meet. Those standards are listed herewith:

1. The outlets should come from the ceiling, rather than from the walls. There should be a minimum of six outlets in a classroom. The outlets should be so connected with switches that the units next to the inner wall of the classroom may be lighted independently of the units next to the windows.
2. Indirect lighting should be preferred to direct lighting. In indirect lighting, the light is sent to the ceiling and is reflected downward. In direct lighting, the light comes immediately downward.

3. All light bulbs should be covered to prevent glare.
4. The lighting units should be cleaned every three to six months. Dirty units lose much of their illuminating efficiency.

Classroom Temperature, Ventilation, and Humidity

Temperature and Ventilation of Classrooms. The usually accepted standard for the temperature of classrooms is sixty-eight degrees. This amount contributes to comfort and good working conditions, especially if the relative humidity is approximately twenty per cent; what constitutes relative humidity and how to control it will be discussed in succeeding paragraphs of this chapter.

The usually accepted standard for the ventilation of classrooms is from ten to thirty cubic feet of air per pupil per minute. The statutes of several states require thirty cubic feet of air per pupil per minute.

Most school buildings are now equipped with mechanical systems of heating and ventilation, and these systems are designed to obtain automatically the standards for temperature and ventilation just mentioned. Since the operation and the regulation of these systems require considerable technical knowledge, teachers should not attempt to correct a difficulty in the systems, but rather should report the difficulty to the engineer in charge of the building or to the school principal who in turn will report the difficulty to the engineer. Only a small amount of unintelligent tinkering with the heating and ventilating system is apt to injure the functioning of the system all over the building; for example, opening the windows or the doors of a classroom, when the system is in operation, is likely to bring this injury.

On mild or warm days when the mechanical system of heating and ventilating is not likely to be in operation, teachers must look after the ventilation of their classrooms through proper window adjustment. Moreover, many schools, especially the smaller ones, still have gravity systems of ventilation, and in these schools the teachers are partly responsible at all times for the rate of air change through proper window adjustment. Any tendency, though, to admit too much or too little air from the outside, or to admit it in such manner that pupils must sit in a draft, is likely to make the pupils uncomfortable and to cause colds and other respiratory illnesses among the pupils and the teachers.

HUMIDITY OF CLASSROOMS. The amount of moisture in the air, that is, the humidity, partly determines whether the temperature at any time of a room or of the outdoors is comfortable, too hot, or too cold. If the relative humidity is low, even though the temperature is normal (approximately sixty-eight degrees), the occupants may complain of feeling cold; if it is high, they may complain of feeling hot. Relative humidity may be defined as the ratio of the quantity of moisture actually present to the greatest amount possible at the given temperature; this ratio is usually expressed as a percentage.

For a normal temperature of approximately sixty-eight degrees in a classroom, a relative humidity of approximately twenty per cent is recommended. When the relative humidity is less than twenty per cent, the air more rapidly absorbs moisture from the persons in the classroom, tending to make them feel cold. When the relative humidity is higher than twenty per cent, the air will not so rapidly absorb moisture from the persons, tending to make them feel warm.

Most school buildings now have heating systems which regulate the relative humidity of classrooms as well as the temperature of the classrooms. On warm days, of course, when there is no need for operating these systems, the humidity and the temperature of the classrooms are determined by the humidity and the temperature of the outside air. A small but increasing percentage of school buildings have air-conditioning units which cool and properly humidify the air.

AESTHETIC QUALITIES OF THE SCHOOL PLANT

The school plant should be made like the best homes in landscaping, in repairs, in decorations, and in furnishings. The effort and the expense given by school officials and teachers to such attempt would not need to be large, but the results in better education and in greater happiness for the pupils would be large indeed. Albeit silent, the tuition of beauty is potent.

The corridors, the foyers, and the classrooms of school buildings should be made veritable art galleries for good pictures, beautiful statuary, and other works of art. Many persons believe that the art gallery may not be the best way to develop art appreciation. They affirm that a child who passes the same picture for six or eight years does not necessarily come to love it. In an elementary school the corridors, foyers, and classrooms are often used to display children's work, art work included. In many school buildings, however, there is not one specimen of art; the walls are barren of these evidences of high civilization, and worst of all the walls are marred with pencil marks, paper wads, and other symbols of carelessness and sometimes of vandalism.

Teachers can do much toward the beautification of the school plant, particularly their own classrooms. Teachers in the elementary school are in a favored position to do this, because they usually occupy the same classroom through the school day; teachers in the secondary school have less opportunity, because their classes usually meet in more than one room. Teachers can call the attention of the principal and other supervisory and administrative employees to the bareness of the classrooms and possibly obtain thereby a small amount of money for the beautification of the classrooms. Even though the teachers may not receive co-operation from school officials, by their own efforts they can obtain some growing plants, pictures, bulletin boards, or other objects of usefulness and beauty. The Parent-Teacher Association or other community agencies will often be able to help obtain these improvements. Whenever teachers have the will, a way will be found by them to improve the aesthetic qualities of their classrooms. Some of the more important contributions which can be made to those qualities will be discussed in the next following paragraph.

PICTURES IN CLASSROOMS. Every classroom should have one or more good pictures. These should be appropriate to the grade of the pupils and to the subject or subjects taught in the classroom. They should not, as is often the case, be limited to the traditional portraits of authors, of generals, or of graduating classes of the school, but should include such subjects as copies of famous paintings, such as the search for the Grail and portraits of eminent scientists or of beautiful buildings. If the pictures are hung on the walls, as they usually will be, they should be hung in the proper place. They should be hung straight and at the average eye level. Because of the danger of reflected glare, they should not be hung between windows.

Since pupils are likely to become tired of looking at the same pictures day after day and year after year, the teacher should change the pictures in his classroom from time to time, if at all possible. It will help merely to change now and then the position in the room of the pictures. In school buildings which have several teachers, exchanges with the other teachers may often be made at appropriate times during the year. The changing of pictures may be facilitated through the use of frames which hold several pictures.

Good posters may be used to make the classroom more attractive and to motivate instruction. These may be made by the pupils or they may be purchased or obtained gratis from commercial firms. Many industrial firms provide free educational posters for schools, and these may be used when they are in good taste and when they do not propagandize for the product or the service of the firms distributing them. Since even the best posters are of transitory interest, posters should not be kept on the walls for too long a time. When a classroom has too much blackboard area, as is often the case, the ugliness and the glare of the unused part may appropriately be covered with attractive and significant posters. Bulletin boards should be generously used.

Fig. 24. Posters made by pupils. *(Courtesy of the Cincinnati, Ohio, public schools.)*

Flowers and Growing Plants in Classrooms. All pupils, whether young or old, are fond of flowers; indeed, a single flower in an attractive container can add much to classroom atmosphere. From flowers in the classroom, pupils not only receive the silent tuition of beauty, but they can also become acquainted with the names and the characteristics of various types of flowers. Pupils, especially the younger ones, like to bring flowers from their homes to the teacher, and their gifts will often keep the classroom supplied throughout the school year. Bulbs and pots of flowering plants may be used during the winter months. In fact, during the winter months any type of growing plant, whether flowering or not, adds much to the atmosphere of a room. It goes without saying that dead plants and faded flowers should soon be removed. Flowers and plants should not be placed on window sills when they obscure too much light.

Ornaments in Classrooms. Ornaments that are beautiful and otherwise significant can contribute to a wholesome classroom environment, hence an appropriate number of them should be welcomed by the teacher. To be avoided, however, are numerous types of relics, antiques, and similar items which are neither beautiful nor otherwise significant and which serve only to collect dust and to give the classroom the appearance of a junk shop. To be avoided also are too many ornaments, because they tend to give the room a crowded and cluttered appearance. Ornaments are most significant, when they have definite relation to the educational program of the classroom; there can be no standard list for a school class or a community.

Color Scheme for Classrooms. Teachers are being more and more invited by school officials to suggest the colors in which they like to have their classrooms decorated, and this tendency makes it necessary for teachers to have a quantum of knowledge of the suitability of various color schemes for different types of classrooms. In selecting the color scheme for a decorating program in a classroom, the following aims should be kept in mind:

1. Obtaining the most artistic and cheerful environment.
2. Providing the highest visual efficiency and comfort.
3. Obtaining the most desirable reflecting characteristics for lighting. White is the greatest reflector of light, and black is the poorest reflector.

Educators, illuminating engineers, ophthalmologists, psychiatrists, and psychologists are agreed that the following advantages accrue when school interiors are painted in bright, harmonious colors:

1. The pupils have a better mental attitude toward their school and their school work. They are more attentive and more orderly, hence they accomplish more.
2. Visual acuity is improved.
3. Electricity is conserved, because less natural light is absorbed.
4. Pupils and school employees tend to make a greater effort to keep the building clean and otherwise in good repair.

In selecting or recommending the color scheme for a classroom the teacher should keep in mind first of all the welfare of the pupils who use the room. The educational program of the room and the age of the pupils will be factors in determining the colors. Other factors that should be kept in mind in selecting the colors are the orientation of the room, shading from adjoining buildings or other objects, furniture, window area, blackboard area, size of room, height of ceiling, and color of floor.

The bureau of plant operation and maintenance of the New York City schools has engaged in a large amount of experimentation on the reflecting characteristics of various colors and on the best types of color combinations for various types of classrooms. That bureau recommends that rooms with northern and with eastern exposures have warm colors (red, yellow, orange, buff, and certain colors of gray) and that rooms with southern and with western exposures have cool colors (green, blue, and certain colors of gray). The bureau recommends the following five color combinations as being the most harmonious and as having the most desirable reflecting qualities for classroom walls and dados:

COMBINATION	WALL COLOR	REFLECTION VALUE OF WALL COLOR	DADO COLOR	REFLECTION VALUE OF DADO COLOR
1	Blue Green	52.7%	Green Gray	25.2%
2	Yellow	66.6%	Blue	23.2%
3	Silver Gray	56.4%	Dark Silver Gray	29.3%
4	Warm Green	61.3%	Copper Rose	23.2%
5	Light Green	61.6%	Gray Green	34.2%

In very dark rooms in which the above color schemes are used, it is recommended that ceilings be painted with an off-white color. A light-cream ceiling is recommended for other rooms.[8]

[8] *Ibid.*, The Board of Education, New York City.

Because it aids in glare control, a flat finish should be used on the ceiling and on the walls above the dado line. Since the dado is subject to more wear and will need to be washed frequently, a semi-gloss satin finish may be used on it.

Care and Use of School Supplies

School-supply Practices. Every phase of the work of a modern school requires the use of appropriate supplies, and in the typical school system of today it is estimated that approximately five per cent of the current funds goes annually for this purpose. There are, of course, dozens of types of school supplies, some of the chief ones being fuel, electric current, gas, water, stationery, laboratory materials, and shop supplies. Supplies are used only once. Textbooks are not here regarded as supplies, because they are used several years.

As public funds have become progressively available and as the principle of equality of educational opportunity has been additionally accepted by the public, the tendency has grown for the school to provide all of the supplies needed for the school's operation. In the early schools, pupils were required to furnish all school supplies, even to the wood for heating the stove. That practice, however, soon gave way to the practice of using public funds to provide not only fuel but all other supplies needed in the operation of the school plant.

For the school to provide instructional supplies is a more recent development. Some schools now provide all instructional supplies, whereas other schools supply few of these. The tendency everywhere, however, is toward furnishing free instructional supplies to all pupils; this practice is followed, especially in the elementary school. Since teachers, school buildings, pupil transportation, school fuel, janitors, and all other school services and facilities are furnished free, it would seem logical to furnish free pencils, free paper, free workbooks, and all other school supplies. When the condition of the school budget does not permit furnishing free supplies to all pupils, they are usually furnished to indigent pupils first; and they are usually furnished to pupils in the elementary school before those in the secondary school.

In modern school systems teachers are being given many responsibilities in the administration of school supplies. For example, teachers are expected to serve on committees for determining the kind and the amount of school supplies to be purchased for each school purpose; and they are called upon to look after the storage of, the accounting for, and the supervision of pupil use of the supplies. Above all, teachers are called upon to see that the school supplies are used economically.

Proper regard for good taste and good ethics prevents professionally-minded school officials and school employees from having any pecuniary interest in any school supplies or other materials which they may recommend for purchase by their schools. The statutes of many states specifically prohibit such practices on the part of school officials and school employees; in fact, the practices are illegal by common law, even in states which do not have specific statutes prohibiting them. Any school official or school employee who violates these laws is subject to dismissal from his post and to a fine besides.

Economical Use of School Supplies. Since extravagance in the use of school supplies is unfair to the school system and to the public which must pay for the supplies, and since any such practice breeds wasteful habits in the pupils, teachers should take steps to see that school supplies under their jurisdiction are used without waste. If the pupils are given adequate leadership and direction, they will co-operate in an economy program; they will become careful about wasting school stationery, pencils, shop materials, laboratory supplies, and other materials which are provided at public expense. Teachers should as wholeheartedly accept responsibility for providing this supervision, when any of the school supplies are provided at the expense of the pupils or of their parents.

Teachers can also help to obtain an economical use of school supplies which are used in the operation of the school plant. For example, they can see that the artificial lights are turned off, when they are not needed and they can give similar care to the use of other public utilities; and they can co-operate with the school janitor in his reasonable attempts to save fuel.

QUESTIONS FOR DISCUSSION

1. Compared with the expenditures for other school items, is too much money being expended on the school plant? Explain. Is the practice of spending much more for the secondary school plant than for the elementary school plant justified? Discuss.

2. What control should the state exercise over school-plant standards? Explain.

3. Would you recommend that school buildings be erected for longer life or for shorter life? Why?

4. What are some of the more common wastes in the erection and in the use of school buildings?

5. To what extent, if any, should public money be expended for architectural beauty in school buildings? Explain.

6. Are you satisfied with the comfort and the attractiveness of the typical classroom? If not, what suggestions would you make looking toward improvement? What can the teacher reasonably do to accomplish this end?

7. Outline a plan which you would use in teaching pupils respect for school property and the desire to co-operate with school officials and teachers in keeping the school plant as attractive as possible.

8. Account for the large amount of vandalism against school property. How may the teacher co-operate in reducing this destruction? Should pupils be fined for any willful damage to school property?

9. By what means may the teacher co-operate with the school janitor? Account for the friction so often found between school janitors and teachers. How may this friction be avoided?

10. To what extent and under what conditions should the school building be used by the general community? Explain.

11. Should schools be run on a year-round basis in order that the school plants could be used more? Why or why not?

12. What are some of the more important matters to watch in the seating of pupils?

13. List the items of school equipment needed for conducting the work of the grade or the major subject which you expect to teach.

14. When public funds or family funds are not available, for hearing aids, eye glasses, and other aids and services needed by handicapped pupils, how may the teacher procure them?

SELECTED REFERENCES

American School Buildings, American Association of School Administrators, Washington, 1949, 525 pp.

Presents designs, construction, furniture, and equipment for school buildings.

Clark, William F., "The Parasite Classroom Building," *Journal of Education,* Vol. 137 (January, 1955), pp. 20-22, 24.

Newton, Massachusetts, is putting into use completely movable classrooms that can be moved from school to school as enrollment changes occur.

Collins, M. D., "Can State Building Agencies Solve the Classroom Shortage?" *Nation's Schools,* Vol. 55 (April, 1955), pp. 49–51, 92.

A discussion of the question by schoolmen from Georgia, Indiana, Maine, and Pennsylvania.

Combs, Jane, *et al.,* "The School with Built-In Ideas," NEA *Journal,* Vol. 44 (February, 1955), pp. 73–75.

Teachers, children, and parents made many suggestions for changes and new incorporations for a proposed new school. The results were highly satisfactory for all concerned.

Garber, Lee O., "Courts Disagree on Use of School Buildings for Religious Purposes," *Nation's Schools,* Vol. 55 (May, 1955), pp. 53–54.

Discusses several recent court decisions.

Harmon, D. B., "Lighting and Child Development," *Illuminating Engineer,* Vol. 40 (April, 1945), p. 228.

Shows that lighting influences child development and child health.

Moore, Hollis A., and Caudill, William W., "Schoolhouse Planning for the Early Teenager," *Nation's Schools,* Vol. 55 (January, 1955), pp. 56–64.

The article presents many of the factors taken into consideration in the planning of a new junior high school building.

Reeder, Ward G., *The Fundamentals of Public School Administration.* The Macmillan Company, New York, 1951, pp. 239–331.

The four chapters included in these pages discuss the planning, constructing, and financing of school buildings; the use of school buildings; the school janitor and his work; and maintenance and insurance of school property; revised in 1958.

Van Winkle, Harold, "Busiest Building in the Town," *Nation's Schools,* Vol. 54 (October, 1954), pp. 44–48.

Describes how Huron, Ohio, utilizes its school buildings for the whole year. The program provides recreational and cultural activities not only for the children but also for the adults in the community. This plan helps to build good public relations.

CHAPTER 6

Financial Support of the Schools

Need for Adequate School Funds

The efficiency of the schools is determined largely by the amount of financial support which is given the schools and by the wisdom with which the money is expended. The size of classes, the adequacy of the school plant, the merit of the curriculum, the quality of textbooks and of all other instructional materials, the qualifications and the salaries of teachers and of all other school employees—in fact, all phases of the school program—are affected by the amount of money which is spent for the program and by the efficiency with which the money is expended. If there were no financial support, there would be no schools, or if the funds were inadequate or were unwisely expended, the schools would not realize their potentialities.

For any complete perspective of the schools, a view must be taken of school finance. This chapter is designed to give that view, emphasizing outstanding movements and problems in school finance with the hope that the prospective teacher will be better qualified to evaluate the movements in school finance and to make his contribution toward the solution of the school-finance problems. Teachers cannot justly claim that school finance is the responsibility of school officials alone and that teachers are not in any way concerned with it. Teachers must have a quantum of information on school finance, because they are being required more and more to take part in the financial deliberations and practices of the school and to assume a responsibility in informing the public regarding these matters. When teachers have received that information, the schools will be more efficiently managed and will be better supported by the public, and teachers will receive higher salaries and have better working conditions in general.

Changing Conceptions of School Financing

In evolving a plan for financing the schools, the conceptions of the public regarding school support have undergone many changes. Two of these changes are so significant that they will be briefly discussed herewith.

From Private Support to Public Support of the Schools. The first change in the public's conception of the financial support of the schools is that the public has gradually abandoned the belief that making provision for schools is a private concern, which should be privately supported, and has adopted the belief that education is a public function and should be supported through universal taxation. Many years elapsed before the latter belief was widely accepted; as was logical, it was accepted first for the elementary school, then for the secondary school, and finally for the college and the university. The belief was not accepted, without much controversy and conflict; in fact, the battle over the acceptance or the rejection of the idea of universal taxation for school support was one of the longest and one of the most severe of any battle in the history of American schools. The battle, though, was long ago won in every American state and territory, and at present there is universal taxation for schools. Persons who do not have children in school are required to pay school taxes the same as persons who have children in school, and it has been many years since the argument has been heard that "it is as wrong to take my money to educate my neighbor's children as it would be to take my oxen to plow my neighbor's field." Taxes for schools and for other public purposes have long been regarded as part of every person's contribution to good citizenship; moreover, the principle has been established that each person shall pay those taxes according to his financial ability. In this country the ideal has long been to give every pupil who desires it, and is competent to obtain it, an education extending from the elementary school to and through the university. Our people have not only wanted free schools, but they have wanted those schools to be good enough for all the children of all the people.

America's practice of requiring universal taxation for school support from the elementary school through the secondary school and the college and the university is unusual among the nations of the world. Although in foreign countries public support of elementary schools is almost universal, in none of those countries is secondary school education or college and university education financed entirely through public funds obtained by universal taxation. In brief, the United States has the only truly public secondary schools and colleges and universities in the world. She adopted that policy, because of her belief that the welfare and the progress of the nation and of each person comprising it could best be assured through universal education. She has concluded that equality of economic, political, and social opportunity could best be obtained for her citizens through equality in educational opportunity. She has regarded equality of educational opportunity as a birthright of every person. Foreign countries, as a rule, on the contrary, have believed that after providing elementary school education for everyone, secondary school education and college education at public expense should be provided for only a select few persons—those few to be chosen on the basis of prospective leadership. Those countries have regarded as wasteful America's ideal of providing free secondary school and free collegiate education to everyone who desires it. They have apparently adopted the philosophy of Froude who says, in *Short Studies on Great Subjects*, that "Men are made by nature unequal," and "It is vain, therefore, to treat them as if they were equal." Although equal educational opportunities may not make all men equal, nothing will achieve that aim as much as education.

From Local Support to State Support of the Schools. The second outstanding changing conception in the financing of the schools of the United States has been regarding the relative place of the local community and of the state in school support; perhaps, it would be more accurate to say that this conception is in the process of changing, because it has not entirely changed. In the early days, the state placed upon the local community the entire responsibility of financing the schools. In those days, local financing of the schools did not result in an unequal burden to the people, because we were then an agricultural people, and wealth was not concentrated in the urban communities as it often is in the present industrial and commercial age. As state educational standards for the people were raised and as wealth became more and more concentrated in certain communities, inequalities in educational opportunities and in taxation burdens among various communities became pronounced. In an attempt to decrease or to eliminate these inequalities, the states soon began to give financial aid, especially to communities which lacked a sufficient tax base to support their schools. During recent years, the belief that the state has the obligation of assisting all communities to maintain their schools up to the minimum standards established by the state has become almost universal. Every state now gives a certain amount of state aid for schools, and the tendency everywhere has been to increase that amount. The late Professor Henry C. Morrison said:

> It is bootless to raise money to support schools in a prosperous and intelligent community if the graduates of its excellent schools are to drift away to other communities and their places are to be taken by undisciplined semi-illiterates who are the products of the financially inadequate schools of the taxed out farming township. . . . The state legislature, moreover, is as much the representative of the latter class of communities as of the former. Further, equality of individuals before the law and equality in economic opportunity are the fundamentals of our conception of political society. We know that neither one can be fully attained by the statutory enactment or constitutional declaration. The only equality we know anything about is freedom from the handicaps of ignorance, which is the parent of individual incapacity and the opportunity of the exploiter. Such equality can assuredly not be generated in a state in which gross inequalities of school opportunity among its several communities must be the rule.[1]

No objection can be raised to the practice of the state assisting local school districts in meeting the educational standards which the state has prescribed; according to that practice, all school districts are taxed to help the poor school districts. It would appear to be but elemental justice for the state to pursue such a policy of financing the schools. The state must, in fact, pursue such a policy for its own perpetuity and its own progress. It should be recognized, however, that in the giving of state aid to local school districts two dangers are ever lurking and those dangers must be minimized.

In the first place, there is danger that local communities will be pauperized—that they will say, "There is slight excuse for our working to support our schools, because the state will look after them for

[1] Henry C. Morrison, *School Revenue*, 1930, pp. 165–166. The University of Chicago Press, publishers.

us." There is danger that the state will help those communities who do not help themselves, as much as it helps those who do help themselves. When such danger is not thwarted, local communities tend to lose interest in their schools, because they do not have the responsibility of supporting them; in such circumstances, mediocrity throughout the state is placed at a premium. In the second place, the giving of state aid for schools, without establishing proper checks upon school expenditures, entails the danger of continuing, if not of increasing, the waste of school funds. Regarding waste of school funds, all that needs to be said is that it is bad to have local school funds wasted, without pouring state funds into the same "rat hole." Waste of school funds is always regrettable, because the public is robbed thereby, and the pupils are cheated of some of their educational heritage.

Most states have not established sufficient safeguards against the two dangers just stated, and especially against the second; in fact, the dangers have never been generally recognized by school officials, school employees, and the general public. Too often, the states give money to local communities, without making sure that the money will be spent in an efficient manner; too often, the states implicitly trust local school officials and school employees to spend those funds, without much state inspection and state supervision. Too often, local communities insist upon obtaining state funds, but they strenuously object to any attempt of the state to supervise the expenditure of those funds; local communities want the money, but they usually want it, without any strings. It is unfortunate that educational organizations composed chiefly of school employees do little or nothing to correct this tendency.

Although the state cannot go too far in presenting regulations which local school districts must meet, it is doubtful whether the typical state has gone far enough in establishing those standards. On one hand, the state should not go so far in its control and supervision of the schools as to stifle community initiative. On the other hand, since education is so important, and since the money of all of the people is being utilized more and more for the support of schools, the state should make certain that its money is efficiently expended. In brief, a certain amount of state supervision and state control is a necessary corollary of state aid. Indeed, a certain amount of such supervision and control has always followed state aid.

It is reasonable to urge that the state see that small and unnecessary schools be closed and merged with neighboring schools, that small and unnecessary school districts be abolished and merged with adjoining school districts, that pupil transportation routes be reorganized where reorganization will permit the elimination of one or more school buses. It is within the responsibility of the state to insist that pupil-teacher ratios be changed when they are too large or too small, that co-operative purchasing of school supplies be required when it will eliminate waste, that the curriculum be revised to provide for individual development and social improvement. The state should demand that all graft in school administration be eliminated and that any other change be made which will obtain a better type, or a larger amount, of education for the money expended. The state has those responsibilities, especially where the expenditure of state funds for schools is concerned, and it cannot shirk the responsibilities, even where local funds are concerned. It cannot risk having the pupils of any community cheated, since the pupils are wards of the state more than of the local community.

The Mounting Expenditures for Schools

Total Expenditures for Schools. With the exception of the few periods of severe economic depression in the nation, the expenditures for schools have constantly mounted from the time of the founding of the first schools in the United States. As was stated in Chapter 1 on America's Historic Faith in Education, these increases may be regarded as another evidence of the increasing faith of the American people in education. The total expenditures in the United States for public elementary and secondary schools have increased from $63,396,666 in 1870 to more than $8,000,000,000 today. For all types of public and private schools and colleges, more than $9,000,000,000 is annually expended. The United States Office of Education collects financial and other school statistics every two years, and those statistics may be consulted by anyone desiring the most recent data for the whole nation, for any state, or for any large city. The reports are published by the United States Government Printing Office, in a volume titled *Biennial Survey of Education in the United States*.

It cannot be denied that the increases in school expenditures have been large, and that the increases have been particularly large during the last three or four decades. In fact, the expenditures have increased so rapidly that many of the staunch friends of the schools have become somewhat perplexed, because they do not know how

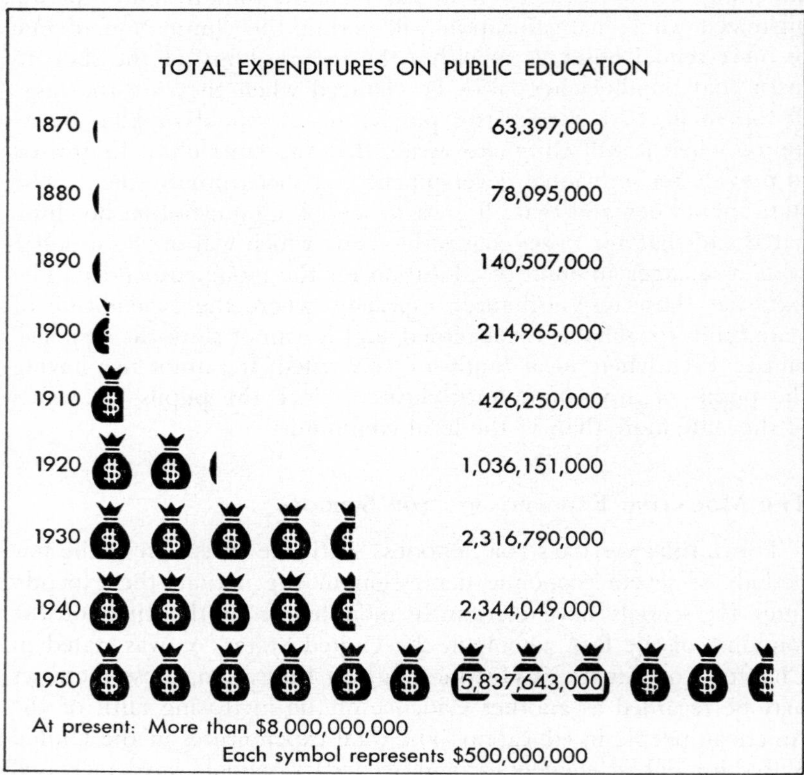

Fig. 25. Expenditures for public elementary and secondary-school education, each decade, 1870 to the present.

much longer the public will be willing to finance the constantly expanding school program, especially since the public will have to bear for many years the staggering debt of World War I and World War II, and it must be prepared for any future wars. As would be expected, persons who are lukewarm toward the schools, and the proponents of low tax rates, have viewed with alarm the mounting school costs; they have criticized school officials and school employees for engaging in what they have called an "orgy of expenditures," and for making larger expenditures than they believed to be justified by the purposes of the schools and by the financial ability of the people. An appraisal of those criticisms will be reserved for a later section of the chapter.

Per Capita Expenditures for Schools. Not only have the total expenditures for schools increased by leaps and bounds, but the per capita expenditures for those purposes have similarly increased. The total annual expenditures per capita of population for public elementary and secondary schools have increased from $1.64 in 1870 to approximately $50 today. We are now spending annually approximately thirty times as much for schools per inhabitant as we spent in 1870; in other words, total expenditures have increased approximately thirty times as rapidly as total population.

The total annual expenditures per pupil in average daily attendance in the public elementary and secondary schools have increased from $15.25 in 1870 to more than $270 today. When the per pupil expenditures in the various states are examined, wide variations are found. A few states spend less than $100 annually per pupil, while a few others spend approximately $400 per pupil.

These large differences in expenditures result in large inequalities in educational opportunities among the states, and they have called forth the suggestion that Federal funds for schools be granted to the states, especially to the states which have low financial ability and therefore make small expenditures for schools. Inequalities in expenditures for schools are due primarily to inequalities in wealth and income among the states. They are also due to (1) differences in the desire of the people for good schools, and (2) differences in the size and the difficulty of the educational problem occasioned by differences in such environmental factors as climate, cost of living, and density of population.

Explanations for the Mounting Expenditures for Schools

The data of the preceding section make clear that school expenditures have increased by leaps and bounds; they indicate that since 1870 the total annual expenditures for public elementary and secondary schools in the United States have increased more than one hundred fold. During the same period, the total population of the nation has increased approximately three-fold, or approximately one-thirtieth as rapidly as school costs. The people's faith in education is abundantly proved by the increasing expenditures for schools.

The increases in school costs have been gigantic, but merely to point out those mounting costs, without attempting to explain them, is likely to place the schools, at least with any unthinking persons, in a vulnerable position. That mistake has been made many times in the past by persons who were unfriendly toward the schools. Whatever explanations for the mounting school costs are made will probably have to be made by the faithful friends of the schools. It is the obligation, therefore, of school officials and school employees to know the explanations of the mounting school costs and to offer those explanations when occasion demands. In the following paragraphs the explanations for the mounting school costs will be briefly discussed.

Increase in School Attendance as a Factor in School Costs. The increase in school attendance is the first explanation for the increase in school expenditures. This increase is one of the most significant facts in the history of education in this or in any other country. Whereas in the early days, formal education, especially above the elementary school, was provided for only a favored few of the children—that is, for those who were able to pay tuition—it has within recent years become universal. At the present time, almost one-fourth of the people of the United States are regularly enrolled in school. This increase in school enrollment has been particularly rapid during the latest three or four decades. The increase has been especially rapid in the secondary schools, where the per pupil expenditure, justly or unjustly, is almost twice the per pupil expenditure in the elementary schools. The crop of World War II babies has also greatly increased school attendance.

The percentage of children five to seventeen years of age (inclusive) enrolled in school has gone from 57 in 1870 to approximately 85 today. The percentage of pupils enrolled in the secondary school has showed a phenomenal increase; it has increased from 1.2 in 1870 to approximately 28 today. Most of the people of today have received some secondary school education.

Not only have the schools attracted a larger percentage of children of school age, but they are keeping a larger percentage of them in regular school attendance; this factor, also, has required increased school funds. The percentage of children enrolled in and attending public school each day, that is, the percentage of pupils in average daily attendance, has gone from 59.3 in 1870 to approximately 85 today. Still more, the number of days the public schools were in session has greatly increased, going from 132.3 in 1870 to more than 178 today.

THE PURCHASING POWER OF THE DOLLAR AS A FACTOR IN SCHOOL COSTS. During the period between 1914 and 1929, school costs increased especially rapidly, and one of the chief explanations of the increase was the decrease in the purchasing power of the dollar which occurred during that period. From the latter part of 1929 to the latter part of 1932 and the earlier part of 1933, deflation continued apace, and the purchasing power of the 1932 and 1933 dollar became approximately equal to that of the 1914 dollar. Since the middle of 1933 to the present time, the purchasing power of the dollar has been decreasing during most years, and this has caused the expenditure of more money to maintain the schools.[2] It greatly decreased during and following World War II, but is somewhat stable at the present writing. There is, however, a tendency for the purchasing power of the dollar to decrease at present.

IMPROVEMENT IN THE QUALITY AND THE AMOUNT OF EDUCATION AS A FACTOR IN SCHOOL COSTS. From 1914 to the present, approximately one-fourth of the increase in school expenditures can be explained by the increase in school attendance, and approximately one-fourth of the increase can be explained by the decrease in the purchasing power of the dollar. The remainder of the increase, which amounts to approximately one-half of the total increase, may be charged to the larger amount and the better quality of education provided the pupils. From the time of the establishment of the first schools in the United States, the schools have been improved, and that improvement has come, because the public has demanded it and has been willing to pay for it. To say, as a few persons have said, that school officials and school employees are "parasitic tax spenders" and are taking the people's money, without the people's approval, is a canard. The people have approved the mounting school expenditures,

[2] Data on the purchasing power of the dollar are based upon indexes of the cost of living which are published in the *Monthly Labor Review* by the U. S. Bureau of Labor Statistics.

and they have approved them because they have deemed the expenditures necessary. When complaints are heard over high taxes for schools, they are usually found to come from large property owners and from persons without children in school.

It is a tradition of America that every parent shall desire for his children a better education than he received, and that he shall be willing to make great sacrifices, if necessary, in order to realize that ambition for his children. School terms have been lengthened from only a few weeks each year to thirty-two, thirty-six, or forty weeks each year. Better-qualified teachers, school administrators, and school supervisors have been employed; better and more adequate school plants and school supplies have been provided; better-qualified school janitors have been employed; more enriched courses of study have been offered; evening classes for adults have been established; and numerous school conveniences and services, such as pupil transportation, school libraries, school cafeterias, free lunches (especially to indigents), free textbooks, free supplies, playgrounds, and health service have been provided. In fact, it would be difficult to mention one feature of the schools which has not been improved. In brief, the data show that more people are receiving a quantum of education than ever before, and what is of greater significance, they are receiving a much larger amount and a much better quality of education than ever before. To provide those improved services and better facilities has required the expenditure of increasing amounts of money for the schools.

Ability to Support Schools

In interpreting the mounting school costs, not only should the explanations of those costs be remembered, but the trend of the ability of the people to support the costs should also be kept in mind. There are two measures of ability to acquire and to maintain anything. Those measures are (1) wealth and (2) income. In addition to those two measures, there should be considered the relative value of schools compared with the value of other activities and other enterprises. Perhaps, the latter is not a measure of ability, but it should always be kept in mind in both public and private finance. It should be kept in mind, because the people have only a certain amount of money to spend on various services, activities, and enterprises, and they must properly apportion that income; they must, like the tailor, "cut the garment to suit the cloth." Above all, the people must place "first things first" and not handicap a vital function of government for the sake of financing a less important function; they must not be "penny wise and pound foolish." The people will, of course, make the final decisions on these matters; they will decide how they wish to spend their wealth and their income.

WEALTH. In terms of its wealth, the nation has tended to finance its schools better and better as the years have rolled by. Although the wealth of the nation has rapidly increased, school expenditures have increased more rapidly. In 1870, $2.89 was expended for public elementary and secondary school education per $1,000 of wealth; at present, it is estimated that approximately $15 per $1,000 of wealth is expended.[3]

It should be kept in mind that the figures which have just been given are based upon actual wealth and not upon wealth reported for taxation; actual wealth is here used, because it is a much more accurate measure of ability than taxable wealth. Taxable wealth is not an accurate measure of ability, because it is well known that much property, particularly personal property (stocks, bonds, money, commodities, etc.), entirely escapes taxation; moreover, it is common knowledge that both real estate and personal property tend to be taxed at much less than their true value. It seems safe to conclude that if all property were on the tax duplicate at its true value, the rate of taxation for schools and for other public functions could be greatly reduced in most communities. If we estimate our national wealth today at approximately $800,000,000,000, it is seen that an annual tax of approximately one cent on each dollar of wealth would be sufficient to support the public schools and the public colleges at their present level of expenditure.

INCOME. In other countries, if a person is asked how much he is worth, he usually replies that he is worth an income of so many pounds, francs, marks, guilders, pesos, yen, or other units of money per annum. In the United States, on the other hand, the financial ability of the individual is usually stated in terms of dollars of wealth,

[3] Data on the nation's wealth may be obtained from *Wealth, Public Debt, and Taxation*, a publication of the U. S. Bureau of the Census. Similar data may also be obtained from the National Industrial Conference Board, Washington, D. C.

rather than in terms of dollars of income. In the long run, the amount of income must be the measure of ability to pay for anything, whether in private affairs or in public affairs. This is the reason for the widespread agitation for an income tax to take the place of the property tax. If wealth does not produce an income, or if it does not afford a comfort or a psychic value, it is a dead weight and hardly worth retaining. The wealth of a Croesus would not last forever, if it did not produce an income.

It is known that the annual income of the people of the United States has increased at a rapid rate. It is unfortunate, though, that official data on annual income are not available, except for recent years.[4] In 1929, the nation's income reached a total of $83,000,000,000, then gradually receded to $39,400,000,000 in 1932. Following 1932, the income gradually increased and soon exceeded the 1929 total. In each year in which the nation was a combatant in World War II, the income exceeded $100,000,000,000. Following World War II, it exceeded $200,000,000,000 each year for several years, and at present it is more than $300,000,000,000.

Anyone is certain to be impressed with the huge size of the annual income of the people of the United States and with the tremendous power residing in that income. That income, of course, belongs to the people, and since the people are sovereign, they can spend the income in any way that they choose. They can spend it on schools or on something less important.

Unfortunately, official data showing how the people of the United States spend their income are not available. It is estimated, though, that approximately one-fourth of the nation's annual income is used in maintaining government—Federal, state, and local. Admittedly, that is a large percentage, but it is a much smaller percentage than is devoted to government by any other major country of the world. Although government now costs annually a large amount, probably no expenditure which the typical citizen makes obtains greater benefits for him than his expenditure for government. From the taxes which he pays for government, a parent obtains schools for his children, the construction and the maintenance of highways and streets, health protection, fire protection, police protection, playgrounds and parks, hospitals, libraries, welfare agencies, national defense, and scores of

[4] During recent years, annual data on income have been published by the U. S. Department of Commerce and by the U. S. Department of Agriculture.

similar services and conveniences. Although it cannot be claimed that taxes are a blessing, they are certainly not an unmixed evil.[5]

The amount which is spent for schools is rather definitely known; the annual amount which is spent for all types of public and private schools and colleges is now approximately two per cent of the total national income. When we compare the amount spent for certain other public or private enterprises, the emphasis on schools does not seem to be too large, if indeed it is large enough. It is a provocative thesis that if we increased the amount and improved the quality of education, the amount of crime would be decreased. Most crimes are committed by persons who have had little or no schooling. Persons who do not know right conduct can hardly be expected to engage in right conduct.

From the reports of the U. S. Bureau of Internal Revenue it can be estimated that the expenditures per annum for tobacco amount to more than two and one-half billion dollars. Thus, the nation annually sends up in smoke and chews up approximately one-third as much as it spends for all types of schools and colleges (public and private). Its liquor bill per annum is as much as its expenditures for schools, and its bill for soft drinks, ice cream, candy, and chewing gum is approximately one-half its expenditures for schools. World Wars I and II have already cost the nation several times as much as has been spent on all types of schools since the founding of the first permanent English settlement at Jamestown, Virginia, in 1607, and the end of expenditures for those wars is not in sight.

As has already been stated, the revenue for financing the schools cannot be obtained from thin air, nor on the good wishes of the friends of the school; it must be obtained from the income of the people. If more money is to be obtained for the schools, it will have to be obtained from certain of the other activities which are now being financed by the public. "Peter cannot be paid without taking something from Paul." Relative values must always be considered. If education is so vitally necessary to the welfare of the nation, the public can afford, if necessary, to decrease the expenditures for certain other purposes and to give that extra amount to the schools.

[5] Because of the huge Federal debt, created largely to finance World War II, Federal taxes are certain to be heavy for many years. This will probably result in large demands to decrease state and local taxes for schools and other public institutions and agencies. These demands are certain to come in times of business recession or depression.

If the amount of education possessed by the individual increases his productivity and his other contributions to society, then the expenditures for schools are justified on a purely economic basis. Likewise, if the amount of education possessed by the individual increases his desire and his ability to consume more and better goods, expenditures for education are also justified. Both of these assumptions seem to be well founded. Without an educated citizenry, it is difficult to see how publishing houses and newspapers could exist, or how manufacturers of innumerable modern conveniences and services, such as bathtubs, radios, televisions, air conditioners, merchanical refrigerators, vacuum cleaners, airplanes, and automobiles could survive. The savage may be content with simple food and with meager protection from the elements, but educated people are certain to demand better and more comforts and luxuries; it is tragic, however, to have to report that civilized man still insists upon going to war the same as savage man, and that many of his resources are still devoted to the destructive pursuit of war.

Sources of School Revenue

From what has been said in preceding paragraphs, it is obvious that the efficiency of a school or a school system is determined largely by the adequacy of financial support which is given the schools. There is an old saying that "money makes the mare go"; likewise it may be said that money makes the school go. If a school department, a school, or a school system is not giving the type of school service needed or desired, one of the first matters which should be examined is whether the financial support is adequate. To have an efficient school or school system requires the presence of personnel, materials, conveniences, and services, such as adequate school sites, buildings, and equipment, ample and proper school supplies, and well-qualified school employees. None of those employees, materials, conveniences, and services can be obtained gratis. They can only be obtained by paying for them with the coin of the realm; and that coin must come from the pockets of the people.

The schools have always been criticized for possessing certain shortcomings, and they are being criticized today for having many shortcomings. For example, it is being pointed out that a large percentage of the teachers are inadequately trained and are inexperienced;

that school buildings and equipment are archaic and inadequate; that school terms are too short; that school libraries, textbooks, and school supplies are not what they should be; and that many other characteristics of the schools are far from perfection. The truth of those criticisms will be readily admitted; the schools are far from being perfect; in fact, probably no characteristic of them even approaches perfection. It cannot be gainsaid, however, that those deficiences are being gradually corrected, and when they are corrected, more school revenues are usually necessary. More money will continue to be needed, but it will probably become more and more difficult to obtain, because of the sharply increased Federal taxes required to pay for World Wars I and II, to provide for national defense, and to pay for social security of the aged and the infirm.

By far the largest percentage of school revenue comes from taxation—taxation of property, income, sales, natural resources, inheritances, and other things. According to the *Biennial Survey of Education in the United States,* which is made regularly by the United States Office of Education, the public elementary and secondary schools of the United States now obtain their revenue from the following sources: appropriations and taxation, approximately 95 per cent; federal aid, approximately 2 per cent; permanent funds, approximately, 1 per cent; and all other revenue receipts, approximately, 2.5 per cent.

By and large, there are three units of support for the public elementary and secondary schools: (1) Federal, (2) state, and (3) local. The approximate percentages of the total revenue receipts now furnished by each of these units are as follows: local, 59.7; state, 37.9; and Federal, 2.4. All of these percentages for the three units of school support are shown in Figure 26. Of course, those percentages vary from state to state; in Delaware, for example, the state furnishes more than 85 per cent of all school funds; in Maryland, the county (here included in local) provides more than 36 per cent of all school revenues; in Iowa and New Hampshire the local units provide more than 86 per cent of all school revenues. Those percentages vary from year to year.

FEDERAL SOURCES FOR SCHOOL SUPPORT. There are two regular types of Federal aid for the public elementary and secondary schools. The first is the income from the early grants of Federal lands to most of the states for schools and colleges, and the second is the annual subsidy for vocational and distributive education, and to school districts which are burdened by federal activities that have greatly increased the number of pupils.

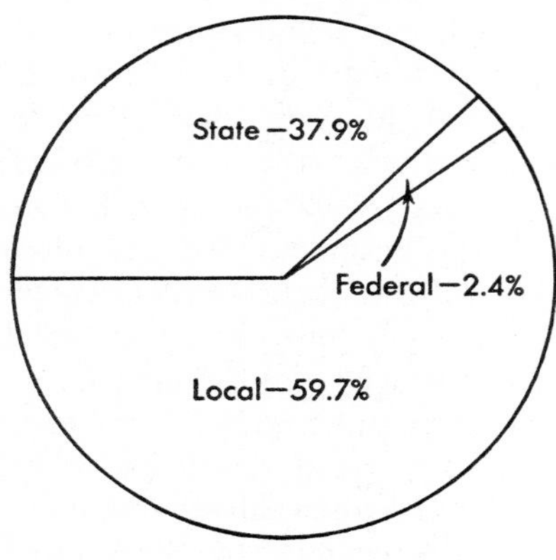

FIG. 26. The units of school support in the United States and the approximate percentage of revenue provided by each school unit. These percentages vary, of course, in different states.

By the provisions of the ordinance of 1785, "an ordinance for ascertaining the mode of disposing of lands in the Western Territory," the lands in the Western Territory were to be surveyed into "townships of six miles square" with each township having thirty-six "lots" of one mile square, or 640 acres; the ordinance said further that "There shall be reserved the lot No. 16 of every township, for the maintenance of public schools, within the said township." Figure 27 shows a "Congressional Township" provided by the ordinance of 1785. Remember that this was the ordinance of 1785, and not of 1787, as many persons erroneously believe.

The ordinance of 1785 must be regarded as one of the most momentous educational acts in the history of the nation, because it instituted a Federal policy of supporting schools. In 1802, the provisions of this ordinance were applied to other territories seeking admission into the Union. All the states, with the exception of the thirteen original colonies, Texas, Vermont, West Virginia, Kentucky, and Maine have received at least one "lot" of each township for the support of public schools;[6] twelve states have received one "lot" of each township. The states which have been more recently admitted to

[6] Texas owned its own land when admitted, and West Virginia and Maine were carved from original states. Vermont and Kentucky had been admitted to the Union before 1785.

the Union have received two or four "lots" of each township; Arizona, New Mexico, and Utah have received four "lots" of each township. All the states, including Alaska Territory, have received a total of 98,519,946 acres from those grants for the maintenance of public schools. The number of acres received by each state, together with the number of "lots" of each township received by each state, is shown in Table 3.

6	5	4	3	2	1
7	8	9	10	11	12
18	17	**16**	15	14	13
19	20	21	22	23	24
30	29	28	27	26	25
31	32	33	34	35	36

FIG. 27. A "Congressional Township," provided by the Ordinance of 1785. Section 16 was given for the endowment of public schools.

In addition to the land grants just mentioned, other grants of land and money have been given to many of the states for public schools. Among the more important of the money grants were the so-called "Surplus Revenue Distribution" of 1837, and the "Five Percentum Fund" started in 1803. The grants mentioned in this paragraph were not specifically made for public schools, but many of the states have dedicated them to that purpose.

The total amount of permanent school funds in the various states is now approximately $1,000,000,000, and practically all of this has come from the sale of lands which were given to the states by the Federal Government. In addition to this amount, the states own approximately 40,000,000 acres of unsold school land with an estimated value of approximately $200,000,000. The states which lead in the amount of permanent school funds are Minnesota and Texas. Only the income from the permanent school funds and from the unsold school lands may be utilized in supporting the schools. The capital cannot be used. The receipts from these permanent funds and the leases of school lands now amount to approximately $50,000,000 annually. Although the percentage of the total school budget provided by the income from these funds is now very small, the income in the early days, when total school expenditures were not nearly so

TABLE 3. LANDS GRANTED BY THE FEDERAL GOVERNMENT TO STATES AND TERRITORIES FOR PUBLIC SCHOOLS

STATE	*Sections of Each Congressional Township*	*Number of Acres*
Alabama	16	911,627
Alaska Territory	16 and 36 reserved (estimated)	21,009,209
Arizona	2 and 32, 16 and 36	8,093,156
Arkansas	16	933,778
California	16 and 36	5,534,293
Colorado	16 and 36	3,685,618
Florida	16	975,307
Idaho	16 and 36	2,963,698
Illinois	16	996,320
Indiana	16	668,578
Iowa	16	988,196
Kansas	16 and 36	2,907,520
Louisiana	16	807,271
Michigan	16	1,021,867
Minnesota	16 and 36	2,874,951
Mississippi	16	824,213
Missouri	16	1,221,813
Montana	16 and 36	5,198,258
Nebraska	16 and 36	2,730,951
Nevada	16 and 36, and lieu lands, act June 16, 1880	2,061,967
New Mexico	16 and 36, act June 21, 1898	4,355,662
	2 and 32, act June 20, 1910	4,355,662
North Dakota	16 and 36	2,495,396
Ohio	16	724,266
Oklahoma	16 and 36	1,375,000
Oregon	16 and 36	3,399,360
South Dakota	16 and 36	2,733,084
Utah	2, 16, 32, and 36	5,844,196
Washington	16 and 36	2,376,391
Wisconsin	16	982,329
Wyoming	16 and 36	3,470,009
TOTAL		98,519,946

large, was considerable. The establishment of these funds in the latter part of the eighteenth century, and in the early part of the nineteenth century provided a stimulus to the public schools which was sorely needed in those early days.

The second type of regular Federal support for public schools is found in the Smith-Hughes Act of 1917; this is the Federal vocational-education act, and has been amended several times.[7] This act provided for the Federal subvention of vocational education in agriculture, home economics, and industrial and trade education. It also provided for the preparation of teachers of those school subjects. According to the provisions of the act, the subvention was to amount to $1,860,000 in 1917–18, and was to increase annually until a maximum of $7,367,000 was reached in 1925–26. This money is apportioned to the several states on the basis of population, and in order to be eligible to receive it, "the state or local community, or both, shall spend an equal amount" for this work; each state and each local school district that participates must also meet certain other standards prescribed by the act. Departments of agriculture, home economics, industrial education, and distributive education, are now found in thousands of schools, especially secondary schools, and thousands of new teachers are required annually by the departments. Salaries paid these teachers are higher than the average salary for teachers of the nation; these must, however, work 11 months of the year.

In 1933–34, the Federal Government started the policy of granting emergency funds for various educational purposes (FERA, WPA, CCC, NYA, etc.). The chief aim of those grants was to relieve the unemployed, and secondarily they aimed to stimulate education. Since there was little or no unemployment during and following World War II, no appropriations for those emergency purposes were made.

The Federal Government has never given money grants for the general support of elementary and secondary schools, but the need

[7] The George-Deen legislation, enacted in 1937, provides an annual Federal subsidy for preparing workers for retail selling and other distributive occupations. Departments for the training of workers for these distributive occupations are already found in hundreds of secondary schools, and hundreds of new teachers are needed annually for the departments.

The George-Barden Act of 1946 continued the general provision of the Smith-Hughes and George-Deen Acts and greatly increased the appropriations for vocational education.

for such aid, especially by the less wealthy states, has been pointed out constantly. For many years, bills have been introduced into Congress providing for such aid; in fact, since World War I there has not been a session of Congress that has not had at least one such bill before it. As yet, however, none of the bills has been enacted into law, although one of them passed the Senate in 1948 and again in 1949. The prospects for such Federal aid seem, however, to be constantly improving, at least for the less wealthy states. The White House Conference on Education in 1955 recommended Federal aid for school buildings in financially poor school districts. The Conference recommended this by a vote of 2 to 1, but Congress did not act.

STATE SOURCES FOR SCHOOL SUPPORT. During recent years, the state as a unit has furnished larger and larger amounts of funds for the support of schools. These funds usually come from taxation upon income, sales, corporations, inheritances, and other sources. California, New York, Ohio, Pennsylvania, and Texas, for example, each furnishes more than $200,000,000 annually, and each of the smaller states provides several million dollars annually. At present, approximately forty-two per cent of all school revenue is furnished by the state as a unit. In many states, more than fifty per cent of all school funds is furnished by the state, and Delaware provides more than eighty-five per cent. Three objectives have been progressively realized by this tendency: first, educational opportunity for all pupils in a state has been made more equal; second, the taxation burden among the various school districts has been made more equal; and third, the tax on real estate has been lowered.

In some states, aid from the state is given to every school district, whereas in other states, aid is given only to the school districts which need it most; in still other states, a combination of those practices is found. All states provide both general aid and special aid. General aid may be used by the school district for any educational purposes not prohibited by state law. Most state funds are granted for this type of aid. Special aid may be used by the school district only for the special purpose prescribed in the laws of the state, and to receive it most states stipulate that the local school district must match the state grant. The more common school projects for which the states have provided special aid are the following: school libraries, pupil transportation, county school supervision, vocational education, and the education of handicapped children. Many authorities in school finance are opposed to special aid, because the tendency is for school districts to receive it which are most able to match the Federal or state subsidy. They affirm that the stimulation principle works against the equalization principle.

County and Local Sources for School Support. In most states the schools are financed primarily by the county and the local community. At present, those two units furnish more than one-half of all school revenue. During recent years, larger and larger amounts of state aid have been given, and this tendency has increased the percentage provided by the state and decreased the percentage provided by the county and local sources. In some states (especially in the South where the county is the school-administrative unit), the county has a large part in the financing of the schools, but in most states the local school district furnishes the bulk of the school revenues.

By far the chief source of county and local school revenue is still the property tax, but the tendency in theory and in practice is to use that tax less. Minor sources of local revenue which are commonly utilized are the following: poll taxes, license fees of various sorts, tuition fees of nonresident pupils, interest on school funds deposited in banks, rentals and fees on school property, and private endowments.

Practically all authorities on taxation have dwelt upon the shortcomings of the property tax. These authorities are agreed that the property tax is a failure as a main source of revenue and that it will have to be largely supplanted by other forms of tax. In the early days, when most wealth reposed in lands and buildings, the property tax was more equitable and more productive of revenue; it is not suited, however, to the present industrial and commercial era. Much of the wealth of the nation today is of an intangible sort (stocks, bonds, commodities, goods, etc.), and it is this intangible property which the property tax cannot reach. Real estate, therefore, must bear the brunt of the tax burden, and this causes much complaint from real estate owners.

The Elimination of Waste in School Management

The Many Opportunities for Waste in School Management. Probably no business, public or private, presents as many opportunities for waste as does school management. What is the origin of these opportunities? In the first place, they grow out of the huge size of the school enterprise. With the exception of the activities of the Federal Government, school management is by far the largest public business; more money is spent on it, more people are engaged in it, either as pupils or employees, and more people are affected by it than is true of any other public enterprise, except that of the Federal Government. There are, indeed, few private businesses as large as school management. In the whole United States more than eight billion dollars is now expended annually on public elementary and secondary schools, and in the typical community approximately one-half of all local public revenue goes for schools.

In the second place, innumerable opportunities for waste grow from the technical and complex nature of school management. Contrary to common belief, education is one of the most complex and technical enterprises. Education is concerned with the development of the human mind and body, and very little is yet known, compared with what should be known, concerning the best methods of meeting those important responsibilities. Moreover, it should be kept in mind that each pupil is a law unto himself, for no two pupils learn in exactly the same way, and no two pupils' interests, needs, and capacities are exactly the same.

NECESSITY FOR THE ELIMINATION OF WASTE IN SCHOOL MANAGEMENT. Because of the technical and complex nature of education, it is too much to expect that all waste in school management can be easily eliminated. That, however, is the ideal to be kept in mind by all school officials and school employees. Waste in education is unfortunate for two reasons: in the first place, the pupil is cheated of part of his educational heritage; in the second place, public funds are wasted and the taxpaying public is treated unjustly.

School economies may be roughly classified as (1) financial, and (2) pedagogical. These two types of school economies, though, are not mutually exclusive, because a real financial economy results in a pedagogical economy and a real pedagogical economy results in a financial economy. In attempting to effect school economies, false economies should not be mistaken for true ones. When money is saved and the efficiency of the school is not injured or is increased, that is a true economy; or, when the same amount of money is expended, and the efficiency of the school is increased, that is a true economy. On the other hand, when money is saved and the efficiency of the school is injured, that is a false economy; or, when the expenditure of an additional amount of money could be made, which would obtain educational results for pupils clearly beyond the cost, but is not made, that is a false economy.

The prime test, therefore, of whether a given school practice or procedure is a true or a false economy must be determined by its effect upon the educational welfare and the progress of the pupils. Manifestly, a given school practice or procedure may result in a true economy in one situation, but in a false economy in another situation; for example, the elimination of a certain school subject in one school, and the saving of the expense or the allotting of the same amount to other school subjects, may be a true economy, whereas in another school that decision would result in a false economy.

There are literally thousands of opportunities for waste in school management, and conversely, there are literally thousands of opportunities to effect economies. As a rule, the opportunities to waste, or to effect economies, are presented primarily to boards of education, superintendents of schools, business managers, principals, and other school administrators, but teachers have innumerable opportunities to waste or to effect economies. For example, teachers may effect economies in the use of general school supplies, home-economics supplies, and industrial-arts supplies; they may effect economies by seeing that the school plant is carefully used; and above all, they can effect economies in not requesting more days for disability leave than necessary, and in making more efficient their classroom organization, management, and instruction. When school employees have taken all such steps, the public will have more confidence in the management of the schools and will more gladly pay additional taxes for school support when they are needed.

QUESTIONS FOR DISCUSSION

1. State pro and con the arguments on charging some or all tuition of secondary school and college students. If tuition must be charged, should it be first charged to secondary school or to college students? Why? What would be the effect upon enrollment of charging tuition in (a) the secondary school, and (b) the college and university? If tuition is charged, should scholarships or loans be provided for financially poor students? From what sources?

2. What is the annual per student cost in your state in (a) the public elementary schools, (b) the public secondary schools, and (c) the public colleges and universities? Why do secondary schools and colleges and universities cost much more than elementary schools? Are we justified in spending much more per pupil in the secondary school and in the colleges and universities than in the elementary school? Explain.

3. Do you prophesy a decrease or an increase in our total expenditures for schools? Why?

4. Do you regard our present expenditures for schools as (a) beyond our ability to pay, or (b) beyond our need? Explain. Discuss the relation between education and the economic and cultural development of a state or the nation.

5. Should persons who send their children to private schools be required to pay taxes for the support of public schools? Why, or why not? Should private schools receive public support? Why or why not?

6. What are the present sources of school revenue in your state? What changes, if any, would you suggest in those sources? Why?

7. To what extent do inequalities in educational opportunity exist among the states? What are the causes of these inequalities? To what extent do you believe that they should be eliminated? By what means? Should Federal support of education in the states entail Federal control, and how much control? Explain.

8. To what extent do inequalities in educational opportunities exist in your state? What are the causes of these inequalities? What are the social results of the inequalities? Would you favor complete state support of education? Should state support of education imply a larger amount of state control of education? Would you favor complete equality in educational opportunity? Why or why not?

9. To what extent do you believe that there is waste in the administration of the schools? Compare the amount of this waste with that in (a) private business, and (b) other public businesses. Mention a few examples of waste in the management of the schools. In what ways may the teacher co-operate in the elimination of school waste?

10. What is meant by a unit cost in education? What are some examples of unit costs? What uses may be made of unit cost data? Are we justified in spending more on certain school subjects and departments than on others? Why or why not? Why do certain school subjects and departments cost more than others? Would it be possible for a school system which spends only $150 per pupil annually to give as much education as a school which spends $200 or $300 per pupil? Explain.

11. To what extent, if any, would the elimination of music, art, and other so-called "fads and frills" result in financial savings to the schools? Explain. Is the cost of a school determined primarily by the number of school subjects offered or by the number of pupils enrolled? Explain.

12. Should public funds be used for vocational education? Or should vocational education be supported by private funds? Explain.

SELECTED REFERENCES

Burke, Arvid J., *Financing Public Education in United States,* Revised edition, Harper and Brothers, New York, 1957, 679 pp.

A textbook on school finance.

Harris, Seymour E., *How Shall We Pay for Education?* Harper and Brothers, New York, 1948, 214 pp.

Advocates the expenditure of more money for schools; recommends Federal aid and higher salaries for teachers.

Mort, Paul R., and Reusser, Walter C., *Public School Finance,* Revised edition, McGraw-Hill Book Company, New York, 1951, 600 pp.

A textbook on public school finance.

Report of the Advisory Committee on Education, U. S. Government Printing Office, Washington, 1938, 243 pp.

Discusses the importance of education and recommends Federal aid for schools.

Federal Funds for Education, U. S. Government Printing Office, Washington, 1955, 130 pp.

History of federal grants for schools down to 1954.

Financing Public Education in the Decade Ahead, National Citizens Commission for the Public Schools, 2 West 45th Street, New York, 1954, 62 pp.

Predicts a large increase in population, in school enrollment, and in school expenditures.

How Do We Pay For Our Public Schools? National Citizens Commission for the Public Schools, 2 West 45th Street, New York, 1954, 76 pp.

Written in simple language for public understanding of school finance.

Public School Finance Programs of the United States, U. S. Government Printing Office, 1955, 130 pp.

Presents state and local procedures for financing schools in each state down to 1953–1954.

Rosenstengel, William E., and Eastmont, Jefferson N., *School Finance,* The Ronald Press, New York, 1957, 442 pp.

A textbook on school finance.

"School Finance Goals," *Research Bulletin* of the National Education Association, Vol. 24 (October, 1946), pp. 87–127.

Presents 77 goals, some of which are of doubtful value.

"Statutory Bases of State Foundation Programs for Schools," *Research Bulletin* of the National Education Association, Vol. 26 (April, 1948), pp. 43–99.

Describes and evaluates the bases used in each state.

Swift, Fletcher Harper, *A History of Permanent Common-School Funds in the United States*, H. Holt and Company, New York, 1911, 493 pp.
The best history of these funds.

Trends in Significant Facts on School Finance, 1929–30—1953–54, U. S. Government Printing Office, 1957, 77 pp.
Data and graphs show trends through the 28-year period.

PART THREE

THE PUPILS AND THE EDUCATIVE PROCESS

CHAPTER 7

Pupil Differences

The Challenge of Individual Differences Among Pupils

In the early days of schools, teachers believed that all pupils should be "run through the same mold." If the pupils did not "fit the mold," attempts were made to remodel the pupils rather than change the "mold." All pupils were required to pursue the same course of study, and the pupils were taught by the same methods. Only a small amount of attention was devoted to individual differences among the pupils and to ways of meeting those differences. The nature, the extent, and the significance of individual differences, especially in intelligence, were only vaguely recognized by the teachers of those times, and means for measuring the differences had not yet been devised.

During recent years, however, teachers have, in increasing numbers, tended to discard their uniform "mold" and to construct a separate "mold" for each pupil; in other words, teachers have attempted to adapt the school to the needs of the individual pupil. Many large schools and school systems have established special classes for pupils who deviate widely from the average. Identical subject matter and uniform methods of teaching have largely given way to attempts to ascertain the needs of the individual pupil and to meet those needs with different types of subject matter and different teaching methods. Moreover, pupil needs beyond the purely intellectual needs are being more and more considered today by teachers and by school administrators.

The movement toward attempting to meet the needs of the individual pupil has been largely an outgrowth of investigations of individual differences among pupils. Those investigations have made available a large body of knowledge on the nature, the extent, the causes, and the significance of individual differences. Since a quantum of knowledge of those differences should be early known by every prospective teacher, in order that he may begin his classroom observations, this chapter will essay to give an orientation in that knowledge. The present discussion will, of course, have to be of an introductory and an elementary nature, and the student who is preparing to teach will need to supplement it in numerous ways in later courses, especially in such courses as psychology, biology, and sociology.

Extent of Individual Differences Among Pupils

Universality of Individual Differences. Of the billions of fishes in the sea, of the thousands of leaves upon a tree, of the countless snowflakes in a snowstorm, of the billions of pebbles along the beach, and of the millions of people in the world, any careful and detailed examination will show that no two specimens are exactly alike. Even casual observation will show that individual differences are universal.

Individual differences, especially among people, have been recognized for centuries. They were portrayed in the characters of ancient and of medieval literature, of history, of sculpture, and of painting. They were observed when the eye was the only measuring instrument, which was centuries before the invention and the use of objective measuring instruments such as the yardstick, the micrometer caliper, the microscope, the intelligence test, and the aptitude test. Their recognition long antedated the pioneer work of Sir Francis Galton, Charles Darwin, and Gregor Mendel who did so much to stimulate the study of individual differences, especially in the field of genetics; brief comments on the contributions of each of those men to our knowledge of individual differences will be made in later paragraphs of this chapter.

To find even two pupils with many similar characteristics is exceedingly difficult. Likeness may be found in a few anatomical characteristics, such as weight, height, cephalic index (relation of length of head to width of head), chest measure, and blood pressure, but it is almost certain not to be found in intelligence, in emotional nature, in general appearance, and in any of the thousands of other characteristics which every person possesses. Fingerprints, for example, are sufficiently different to have long been used for the detection of criminals. So-called "identical" twins are far from being identical, and even the famed Dionne quintuplets, who were sometimes called "identical," were known, at the age of one, to possess innumerable characteristics which differentiated them; and as they have grown older, other differentiating characteristics have appeared also. In brief, the chance of finding two individuals with exactly similar traits or characteristics is so small as to be practically negligible.

AMOUNT AND DISTRIBUTION OF INDIVIDUAL DIFFERENCES AMONG PUPILS. In even the best-graded class, large differences among the pupils will be found. These differences will be observed in physiological and anatomical development, in social maturity, in emotional stability, in general intelligence, in ability to do the work of the class, and in numerous other traits.

The chief individual difference among pupils of which the school must take account and attempt to serve is the difference in general intelligence. General intelligence is sometimes called general ability of the pupil—that is, his ability to achieve; during recent years, intelligence tests have come to be widely used for determining the general intelligence, or general ability, of pupils. In the typical class as organized in the schools of today, the general intelligence of the pupils is widely different. In an investigation of the intelligence quotients of several hundred representative children between the ages of 2 and 18, L. M. Terman and Maude A. Merrill found that the following I.Q.'s had the accompanying percentages:

I. Q.'s of 140–169 .... 1.33 per cent of the children.
I. Q.'s of 120–139 .... 11.30 per cent of the children.
I. Q.'s of 110–119 .... 18.10 per cent of the children.
I. Q.'s of 90–109 .... 46.50 per cent of the children.
I. Q.'s of 80– 89 .... 14.50 per cent of the children.
I. Q.'s of 70– 79 .... 5.60 per cent of the children.
I. Q.'s of 30– 69 .... 2.63 per cent of the children.[1]

In any large number of measurements of any trait, it has been found that the differences among individuals possessing the trait are distributed in a continuous gradation. Each group of individual

[1] L. M. Terman and Maude A. Merrill, *Measuring Intelligence*, Houghton Mifflin, 1937. Copyright by Houghton Mifflin Company.

differences merges imperceptibly into the next group; there are no gaps or sharp lines of demarcation at any point in the gradation. Although in everyday discussion, such terms as subnormal, normal or supernormal, short or tall, narrow or wide, soft or hard, etc. are used, those terms cannot be used in scientific work, since they do not have a sufficiently explicit meaning. There is no definite point in the measurement of intelligence, for example, where subnormality ends and where normality begins, nor is there a definite point where normality ends and where supernormality begins. If he is to be definitely understood, therefore, the scientist must describe the results of measurements in such accurate terms as inches, pounds, and ounces, percentiles, intelligence quotients, etc.

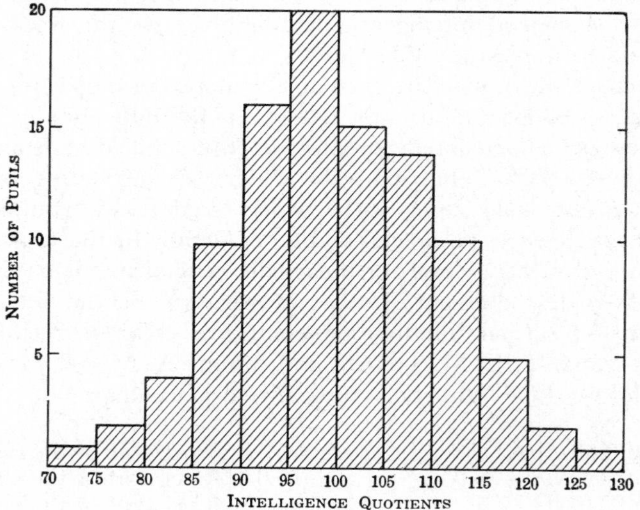

Fig. 28. Histogram or column diagram showing the distribution of the I.Q.'s of 100 random-selected fifth-grade pupils.

When any large group of measurments of any trait of a biological specimen is plotted out into a graph, the result is a bell-shaped curve. This curve is variously known as the normal curve, normal-frequency curve, normal-frequency polygon, probability curve, normal-probability curve, or normal-distribution curve.[2] This tendency for quanti-

[2] See Fig. 29 for a curve which approximates the normal curve.

tative differences to be distributed over a surface approximating a bell-shaped curve is found in differences due to environment and education as well as to differences due to heredity.

The phenomenon just mentioned can be readily checked by measuring any trait of a biological specimen, provided a sufficiently large number of random-selected cases is included. Gather at random a few hundred leaves from a tree. Then measure the length of each leaf, and it will be found that a few leaves are very long and that about the same number of leaves are very short; next to these extremes will be found a larger number of leaves that approach the average in length; finally most of the leaves can be grouped between these extremes. When the measurements are plotted out into a graph, the bell-shaped curve will result with its high middle and sloping off on the two sides toward the extremes. Repeat the measurements on the width of the leaves and the same phenomenon will be observed.

Let us check the principle just mentioned by measuring the general intelligence of one hundred fifth-grade pupils who are random-selected, then plot the results into a graph. We shall measure the intelligence of each pupil by means of a standardized intelligence test and shall report the results for each pupil in terms of an intelligence quotient or I.Q. The I.Q. or intelligence quotient expresses the ratio between the "mental age" and the chronological age of the pupil. By a given mental age is meant that degree of mental ability which is possessed by the average child of corresponding chronological age. It is obtained by dividing the pupil's "mental age" by his chronological age, then multiplying the quotient by one hundred. Thus, the formula for expressing the I.Q. of a pupil is as follows:

$$\frac{\text{Mental Age}}{\text{Chronological Age}} \times 100 = \text{Intelligence Quotient}$$

The I.Q.'s of the 100 fifth-grade pupils were found to range from 70 to 126. Beginning with the lowest I.Q., the record went as follows: 70, 75, 77, 80, 81, 82, 84, . . . 126. Of course, a few pupils had the same I.Q., and there were a few gaps in the series; however, there were forty-four different I.Q.'s in a possible total of fifty-six different I.Q.'s. These forty-four different I.Q.'s could, of course, be plotted into a graph, but a grouping of fairly similar I.Q.'s into one measure will make the data more convenient to handle and to interpret. If groupings of five units each are made, the distribution found in Table 4 results. Such an arrangement of data is called a frequency distribution, and it constitutes the first step toward the organization, the summarization, and the interpretation of any series of data.

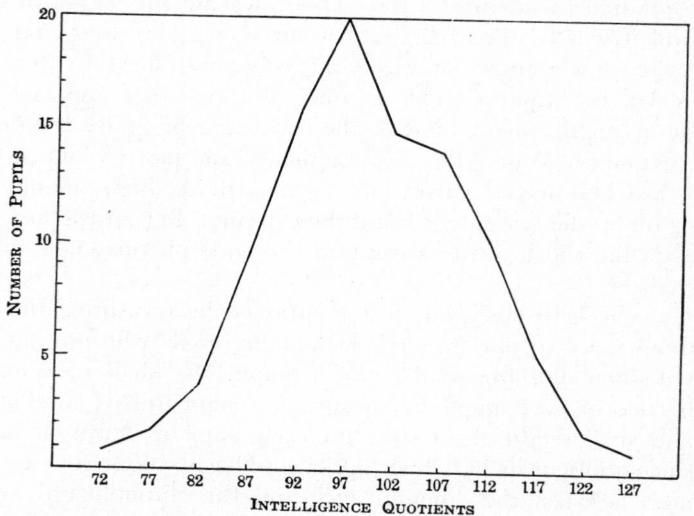

FIG. 29. Frequency polygon or normal curve showing the distribution of the I.Q.'s of 100 random-selected fifth-grade pupils.

The making of a frequency distribution is, therefore, the first step in the statistical treatment of groups of data. That first step should be followed by two other steps, if the data are to be summarized so that they may be thoroughly understood. In the first of these two steps, the data of the frequency distribution are condensed into "averages," and in the second step the data are condensed into a measure or measures of "variability." The chief measures of "averages" are the mean and the median, while the chief measure of "variability" is known as the standard deviation. The page limits set for this chapter preclude a discussion of the uses of those measures and of the mathematical processes necessary to obtain the measures. Such discussion can well wait until a later course or subject in the student's

TABLE 4. FREQUENCY DISTRIBUTION OF THE I.Q.'S OF 100 FIFTH-GRADE PUPILS

Group Range or Interval	*Frequency or Number of Cases*
125–129	1
120–124	2
115–119	5
110–114	10
105–109	14
100–104	15
95–99	20
90–94	16
85–89	10
80–84	4
75–79	2
70–74	1

program, and fortunately most teacher-preparing institutions make provision for such discussion in a part of the course in psychology, in mental tests, in educational tests and measurements, or in mathematics.

One of the greatest aids to a clear interpretation of statistical data comes from the graphic presentation of the data. By plotting the data of the frequency distribution shown in Table 4, the data can be more easily comprehended and interpreted. We shall first plot the data into a histogram or column diagram. Such a graph may be constructed by plotting the I.Q.'s along the base line of the graph and by plotting the frequencies with which the I.Q.'s are found on the vertical lines of the graph. There results from this plotting a series of rectangles in which the widths of the rectangles represent the class ranges or class intervals, and the heights represent the number of frequencies or cases found to fall in the respective class ranges or class intervals. The completed histogram is shown in Fig. 28.

A more common type of graph which may be used in presenting the data of a frequency distribution is the frequency polygon, which was mentioned in a preceding paragraph. Such a curve is made by plotting a series of points corresponding to the mid-points of the class ranges, then connecting these points by straight lines; using the same data as were used in Fig. 28, we have the curve shown in Fig. 29, which approaches a normal curve.

Types of Individual Differences

For the purposes of studying individual differences, it is helpful to classify the differences into types. It would be possible to take any group of persons—say, women as a class, five-year-old children as a class, Negroes as a class, the members of the same family as a class, individuals of the same amount of formal education as a class—and examine the group to ascertain whether or not differences were peculiar to the group as a "group." Hundreds of such investigations have, of course, been made, and the results have been recorded in the literature of biology, of sociology, and of psychology. From the results of those investigations it is possible to classify individual differences into hundreds of types. The types of differences which are most frequently discussed are the following: (1) age differences, (2) family differences, (3) race differences, and (4) sex differences.

Age Differences Among Pupils. Differences in maturity of individuals have always been observed. The world early learned not to expect intellectual, physical, and other types of maturity in children; it soon learned that "old heads cannot be expected on young shoulders." Individuals have long been classified into such periods as infancy, childhood, youth, middle age, old age, etc. The tendency has been toward the development of more accurate measuring instruments and measuring techniques and toward the formulation of terms which would express more accurately the maturity differences that the more scientific measurements are constantly revealing. One series of terms which has been developed to express some of these outstanding differences is known as "ages." The "ages" most frequently used by modern teachers of today are:

1. Chronological age
2. Mental age
3. Subject age
4. Anatomical-physiological age
5. Social age
6. Emotional age
7. Educational age

Most of the terms just mentioned have been created by students of psychology, and especially by students of genetic psychology, because genetic psychology uses largely as its materials the progressive changes in mental processes which occur with increasing chronological age. As may have been inferred, all of these new "ages" are based upon the chronological age which, of course, has been used for centuries. By a given "mental age," for example, is meant that degree of general mental ability which is possessed by the average child of corresponding chronological age. The other "ages" (subject age, anatomical-physiological age, social age, emotional age, etc.) may be defined according to the same general formula; to give another example, "arithmetic age" (which is one of the many "subject ages") may be defined as the degree or arithmetical ability or accomplishment which is possessed by the average child of corresponding chronological age.

Although practically all investigations of the matter have indicated a tendency for the child's development in all his "ages" to proceed at approximately the same pace, exceptions to the rule are fairly frequent. A pupil of a chronological age of twelve years, for example, may be usually expected to have a "mental age," a "subject age," an "anatomical-physiological age," a "social age," an "emotional age," etc., of twelve years also; in such instance the problem of classifying the pupil for instructional purposes is relatively simple. If, however, a pupil has a "mental age" of fifteen years and a "social age" of ten years, the problem of classifying him becomes much more complicated. If the pupil is placed in a group of pupils fifteen years old "socially," he may develop an inferiority complex or suffer in some other manner, or if he is placed in a group of pupils ten years old "mentally," he is not likely to be stimulated to put forth his best efforts; in any event, he will become a special problem for his teacher.

Although there are obvious difficulties in meeting the needs of the various "ages" of the individual pupil, teachers are now working assiduously toward that goal; thus, teachers are now giving attention to the physical, the social, and the emotional development of pupils as well as to the strictly intellectual growth. In brief, their goal for every pupil is a well-rounded development which takes account of every aspect of the pupil's nature. In striving for this goal teachers have learned that the old-fashioned types of pupil classification and instruction, which often handicaps the pupil, must give way to an educational program that is based on the many-sided needs of the individual pupil. This movement toward attempting to meet the many-sided needs of the individual pupil is so important that Chapter 11 of this book will be devoted to a brief description of the movement.

Sex Differences Among Pupils. Whether one sex is superior to the other in ability or in accomplishment, and the nature and the amount of the superiority, if any, have long been moot questions. The arguments over the question have frequently been characterized by claims that one sex has large superiority over the other in ability and in accomplishment, but as is often the case, the more vociferous and the more persistent the claims, the less the evidence to support them. During recent years, especially in scholarly circles, the emphasis has been less on making claims, which were supported by opinion only, and more on obtaining evidence to show the nature and the extent of any differences which might exist; thus, during recent years, there have been dozens of investigations of these differences and the results of the investigations have been reported. Most textbooks on psychology discuss the differences.

In the main, the investigations of intellectual ability have shown that sex differences, when found, are not large. Also, one sex does not do consistently better than the other. The investigations have pointed to the probability that many of the differences, which were originally claimed to be hereditary, are really due to education, to environment, and to general social conditions. The chief conclusions of the many investigations are summarized herewith:

1. Girls, on the average, mature physically earlier than boys, but they are not as tall, heavy, or strong as boys, except that girls are taller and heavier for about two years during the junior high school period.
2. No significant difference in the general intelligence of the two sexes has been found.
3. In aptitudes for special types of school work, such as spelling, reading, and arithmetic the evidence shows that the sexes do not differ greatly from one another.
4. Although it is commonly assumed that boys are more self-asserting and more pugnacious than girls, and that girls have greater sympathy than boys, no information is yet available which would suggest such emotional differences of the amount frequently reported.
5. There is some, but no conclusive, evidence that boys are more variable than girls in tests of different abilities.

What bearing have these findings on the amount and the type of education to be offered the two sexes? Especially, shall a different amount and a different type of education be given the two sexes? Since the intellectual abilities of the two sexes are relatively equal, the two sexes must be educated equally well; any other practice would be contrary to the democratic ideal of America which desires and prescribes an equal opportunity for everyone. That there should be equality in the amount of education does not necessarily mean that the same type of education should be given, because it is likely that the type of education needed by one sex will differ in many respects from that needed by the other sex. Men marry women, and women marry men; and the life needs of men and of women are very similar.

Race Differences Among Pupils. Although as much research has been done on race differences as on sex differences, the conclusions to be drawn from that research are more tentative and more uncertain than in the case of the research on sex differences. Of the research on race differences, that on anatomical differences has provided a more solid basis of fact than any other because these differences are fairly easily measured. Anthropologists have generally made use of the following criteria in their classification of races: (1) color, (2) stature, (3) hairiness of the body, (4) texture of the hair, (5) cephalic index, (6) cranial capacity, (7) prognathism (protrusion of the lower jaw), and (8) nasal index.

The question of race differences has, however, not been limited to the anatomical differences, which can be readily measured by the criteria just mentioned. Rather the question has usually turned upon the superiority of one race compared with the other races. By superiority in such arguments, mental superiority is usually meant.

In the United States, since the two most populous races are the white race and the Negro race, the question of racial superiority has usually narrowed down to the white race versus the Negro race; hence, as would be expected, most of the research on racial differences has been made on those two races. The first conclusion which might be drawn from the data of these investigations is that the white race has much more native intelligence, on the average, than the Negro race. Such a conclusion, however, must be tempered by a consideration of the probability that the white race has much better environmental opportunities than the Negro race. Indeed, it has been found that the northern Negroes make higher school marks than the southern Negroes and that the higher school marks are in direct proportion to the number of years which they have lived in the North; however, it is possible that the more capable Negroes have migrated to the North. When such possibilities are considered, the first conclusion to the effect that the white race has much more native intelligence than the Negro race cannot be considered final.

Many investigations comparing the general intelligence of whites with Indians and of whites with orientals have also been made. Without exception, these investigations have found that the whites made better scores on general intelligence tests, on the average, than the Indians and the orientals. Any conclusions from these results, however, must be qualified by the same comments which were made above regarding the comparison of the whites and the Negroes. The results do not give conclusive evidence that the better scores of the whites are the result of better native intelligence; they leave the possibility that the better scores of the whites may be partly the result of better environmental conditions for the whites, or of the fact that the general intelligence test which was used was built upon white culture and was standardized upon white children. Conclusions must be held in abeyance until means are devised, if ever, to measure native intelligence separately and distinctly from the many selective forces of environment, such as climate, educational opportunities, home conditions, and general social and economic conditions.

Until the evidence is more conclusive that one race has greater native superiority than other races, the schools are not justified in giving better educational opportunity to one race than to another; in fact, the schools would not be justified in making a difference, even then. The schools might, of course, be justified in giving a different type of education to the various races, but such differentiation would have to be justified on the basis of economic, social, or other type of need rather than on the basis of a difference in native ability. Moreover, the members of the various races should be treated as individuals, not as members of a group to be treated alike; in fact, the members of all groups should be treated as individuals. That again is based upon a belief in "the fatherhood of God, and the brotherhood of man."

Family Differences Among Pupils. Of all the types of individual differences, those differences pertaining to families have been observed longest and have been investigated most extensively. It has long been known that members of the same family are much more similar than the members of different families, and that many family traits, such as hair color, eye color, weight, stature, and general intelligence, are inheritable.

Several of these studies on family intelligence and family accomplishment have become almost classic, especially a study by Sir Francis Galton.[3] Galton found that the offspring of eminent parents was much more likely to become eminent than was the offspring of obscure parents. He found, for example, that the son of an eminent British judge had approximately one chance in four of becoming eminent, whereas the son of a man selected at random from the general population had approximately one chance in a thousand of becoming eminent.

In the United States a study similar to that of Galton found that only one person in 500 had a chance of being a near relative of one of the 3,500 eminent persons of the United States. This study also revealed that these 3,500 eminent persons were related in the ratio of 1 to 5 rather than in the ratio of 1 to 500 as was characteristic of the general population.[4]

The evidence on family resemblance is even more striking in the case of studies of families of inferior strains. Probably, the most famous of these studies was that by the late Professor H. H. Goddard on the family of Martin Kallikak, a soldier of the Revolutionary War.[5] Kallikak gave rise to two lines of descendants, one by a union with a more or less talented mother and the other by a union with a feeble-minded mother. Goddard traced those two lines of descendants and found that feeble-mindedness, crime, pauperism, and other inferior and antisocial traits were frequent in the line of the feeble-minded mother; on the contrary, he found that the descendants of the more or less talented mother were not afflicted with feeble-mindedness and forms of antisocial behavior.

The above studies of family differences, though, have come in recently for criticisms of their shortcomings.[6]

[3] Sir Francis Galton, *Hereditary Genius,* Macmillan, 1869.

[4] F. A. Woods, "Heredity and the Hall of Fame," *Popular Science Monthly,* Vol. 82 (1913), pp. 445–452.

[5] H. H. Goddard, *The Kallikak Family,* Macmillan, 1912.

[6] For a summary of these studies, see Anne Anastasi, and J. P. Foley, *Differential Psychology,* Revised Edition, Macmillan, 1949, Chapter 10.

Causes and Significance of Individual Differences

Two groups of factors operate to cause individual differences in the biological world. These are: (1) heredity (stock or nature), and (2) environment (culture or nurture). The first group of factors may be classified as "internal," and the second group may be classified as "external." Which of these groups of factors is more important has always been a moot question, and attempts to answer the question have led to warm arguments, to extravagant claims, and to temptations to assign a percentage value to the influence of each factor. For example, one writer has stated that "heredity is twice as important as environment," whereas another writer has affirmed that "environment is fifty per cent more important than heredity." Such arguments and claims were especially frequent before the development of instruments and techniques of measurement and before the study of the question had been placed upon a scientific basis.

Recent investigations have shown that there is no factual basis for either of the percentage estimates just mentioned. Both heredity and environment affect the individual, and any argument over which is more important is likely to be as fruitless as an argument over the relative importance of air and of water. As Roger de Coverley has stated, "Much might be said on either side." Without a place to grow, a seed could never grow, and without a seed, the best environment could never produce anything. Since a knowledge of the interplay of heredity and of environment and of the potential limits of each factor should assist prospective teachers in observing and in teaching pupils, some of the high points of that knowledge will be presented in the next succeeding pages.

Hereditary Factors in Pupil Differences. That many of the differences among individuals are due to heredity has long been known. Casual observation has long shown that an animal or a plant has the capacity to produce specimens of a kind similar to itself. Thus, similarities among the same race, and especially among the same family, were observed long before the epoch-making researches of Sir Francis Galton (1822–1911) and of Gregor Mendel (1822–1884); in fact, such similarities were doubtless noticed by Neanderthal man who lived between fifty thousand and a hundred thousand years ago.

Research has shown that heredity proceeds according to certain principles or laws. Since one of the most important obligations of society is to promote the production of a better stock of human beings, knowledge of the laws of heredity should be a part of the equipment of every teacher. Many institutions for the preparation of teachers consider this knowledge to be so important that they require every prospective teacher to pursue a course either in biology or in genetics; and most teacher-preparing institutions provide this knowledge in the required courses in psychology. All that the present discussion is designed to do is to emphasize the significance of the problem and to encourage further study of the problem by the prospective teacher.

Every individual is the result of the fusion of two cells, one from each parent. The female cell is known as the ovum, and the male cell as spermatozoon. All the cells which give rise to the reproduction elements are known as germ plasm. There are two theories regarding the continuity of the germ plasm. One of these theories (known usually as the Weissmann theory) holds that the germ plasm is continuous and passes unchanged from one generation to the next. According to this theory, the only way in which a tainted stock can be improved is through its union with a superior stock.

The other theory holds that characteristics which are acquired may affect the germ plasm in such a way that the germ plasm will transmit the acquired characteristics to succeeding generations. This is known as the Lamarck theory. Later statements of this theory (the Neo-Lamarckian theory) grant that all or practically all which is inherited exists in the germ plasm, but they claim that the body cells, which recent experimentation shows are influenced by environment, may also influence the germ plasm. Scientists are still at work on these theories.

The first theories and laws of heredity were formulated by Sir Francis Galton who made the first scientific investigations of heredity. His investigations were made especially on families, with particular emphasis on such family traits as genius, disease, stature, and eye color. The first law which Galton proposed is known as the law of ancestral inheritance, which says that the contribution of the immediate ancestors to the progeny exceeds the contribution of any other ancestors and equals that of all other ancestors. According to this law, therefore, each parent contributes, on the average, one-fourth to each trait of inheritance, and both of them contribute, on the average, one-half; the four grandparents contribute, on the average, one-fourth, and each grandparent contributes, on the average, one-sixteenth. The infinite series continues until the total heritage of the individual is included according to the following formula:

$$\tfrac{1}{2} + \tfrac{1}{4} + 1/8 + 1/16 + 1/32 \ldots = 1.$$

According to this formula, each term equals the sum of all the terms which follow; $\tfrac{1}{2} = \tfrac{1}{4} + 1/8 + 1/16 + \ldots$ Fig. 30 shows pictorially Galton's law of ancestral inheritance.

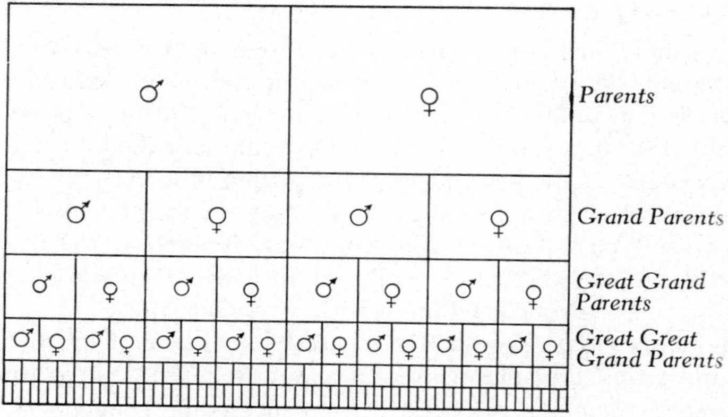

Fig. 30. Galton's law of ancestral inheritance. *(After H. Thompson.)* The whole heritage of an individual is represented by the entire rectangle; the heritage derived from each progenitor is represented by the smaller rectangles; and the number of the latter rectangles doubles in each ascending generation while its area is halved.

The second law which Galton formulated is known as the law of filial regression. According to this law, nature tends to maintain the type or the average of its stock. This law came from Galton's observations that extremes in traits of parents are not so likely to result in extremes in traits of their children. For example, extremely tall parents are likely to beget children who are taller than the average, but not as tall as the parents; and children of very short parents are likely to be shorter than the average, but not so short as the parents. On the mental side, children of very talented parents are likely to be more talented than the average, but not as talented as the parents, and children of mentally subnormal parents are likely to be less subnormal than their parents, but more subnormal than the average.

Although the work of Galton is still accepted as epoch-making, succeeding investigations have shown that some of his conclusions were extravagant. His laws, especially the law of ancestral inheritance, appear to be valid only when applied to large numbers of individuals; they are apt to be invalidated when applied to only one, or a few, families. In this latter application the laws of chance must be considered. G. E. Conklin has affirmed that although we inherit approximately equally from our parents, we usually inherit unequally from our grandparents and our other ancestors. Moreover, he affirms that in stating his law of filial regression Galton did not always distinguish between hereditary and environmental influences:

> . . . Inheritance from the four grandparents is usually unequal, and the farther back we go, the more ancestors we find who have contributed nothing to our inheritance. Of all the thousands or even millions of ancestors that each of us has had, only a relatively small number have contributed anything to our inheritance; although we are descended from all the others, we are not related to them biologically and have received none of their traits. Those who have contributed to our inheritance may be called "contributing ancestors" or merely "contributors," to distinguish them from non-contributing ones, and the fact that ancestors do not equally contribute to heredity disproves Galton's "law of ancestral inheritance."
>
> The second principle also cannot be taken as Galton originally interpreted it, for he did not always distinguish between heredity and environmental characters.[7]

Gregor Mendel, an Austrian monk, and a contemporary of Sir Francis Galton, also formulated some well-known laws of heredity. These laws were the result of Mendel's observations and experiments on mice, bees, and garden plants, and especially on garden peas. Mendel had observed that some of his peas were tall, and that others were short; that some had white flowers, and that others had colored flowers; and that some had green seeds, and that others had yellow seeds. From these casual observations he was made to wonder what caused the differences in the peas—in brief, whether a law of heredity

[7] G. E. Conklin, *Heredity and Environment in the Development of Men*, Princeton University Press, 1922, p. 80. By permission of Princeton University Press, publishers.

was operating. He organized certain experiments to attempt to answer this question.

To describe Mendel's experiments and to enumerate all of his discoveries would lead us too far afield. We shall have to be content with a brief statement of two of Mendel's well-known laws. The first law is known as the law of unit characters. According to this law, the total inheritance of a plant or of an animal is composed of unit characters or traits and these behave as units in heredity, each unit being inherited somewhat independently of the remainder of the other units; for example, if one parent has light eyes and the other has dark eyes, their child will have either light eyes or dark eyes, and both eyes of the child will be the same color. Eye color behaves as a unit.

Mendel's second law determines, for example, whether the child's eyes will be light or dark. This law is known as the law of dominant and recessive characters. According to this law, if one parent has only the characters for dark eyes and the other parent has only the characters for light eyes, only dark eyes will appear in their offspring. If, however, one parent has characters for both light and dark eyes and the other parent has characters for only light eyes, both color of eyes may appear in their offspring. The trait which thus appears is said to be dominant. The trait which is latent and which only occasionally appears is said to be recessive. As long as the dominant factor is operative, the recessive factor cannot produce any noticeable effect, except in cases where blending takes place.

Mendel formulated estimates regarding the probable frequency of occurrence of the various types of offspring from different combinations of these dominant and these recessive traits, and he showed that no estimate regarding the proportions of various types of offspring could be made until it was known whether a trait was dominant or recessive in each parent.

Environmental Factors in Pupil Differences. Previous discussion has shown that the development of an individual is determined by a lifelong interplay of heredity and environment on the individual. The school cannot change heredity; it cannot make a superior heredity; it cannot make even a normal child from a child of inferior heredity. In brief, the potential value of the tutelage of the school is determined in part by the quality of the child's ancestry, just as the potential growth of a seed is determined in part by the quality of the seed's stock.

The school must, therefore, regard the child's heredity as the foundation on which to build, and it must realize that the hereditary foundations of children differ widely in quality. All that the school can do is to modify, to control, and to direct the environmental factors in such a way that the potentialities of the hereditary factors will be most fully realized. A child endowed with superior heredity will not reach full physical and intellectual stature in an inferior environment any more than a healthy seed will thrive in barren soil. That "genius will out" despite all environmental handicaps is as likely not to be true as it is to be true. In spite of what the Declaration of Independence says, all individuals are not "created equal," nor can they be made equal. All that can be done toward making individuals equal is to provide them with the best environmental and educational opportunities to realize most fully their potentialities. Here, then, is the big opportunity for the school. Grasping the opportunity will tend to prevent the result which Thomas Gray deplored in his famous "Elegy Written in a Country Churchyard":

> Full many a gem of purest ray serene
> The dark unfathomed caves of ocean bear;
> Full many a flower is born to blush unseen,
> And waste its sweetness on the desert air.

What are the environmental factors that affect the pupil? These may be classified as prenatal, natal, and post-natal. They include all the experiences, helpful or harmful, which the pupil has had before birth, during birth, and after birth. They comprise all the experiences which the pupil has acquired in the home, in the school, and in other formal educational institutions, and in the community.

Since the school has the pupil under its tutelage only a few years, only seven, eight, nine, or ten months during the year, only five days in the week, and only five, six, or seven hours during the day it is obvious that the school controls only a small portion of the experiences of the pupil. During this short span, however, teachers can almost work miracles. They can partly or largely see that the school plant is safe and sanitary, that the emotional and the physical health of the pupils is carefully supervised, and that the pupils are properly nourished when they are in school. They can make sure that the subject matter and the teaching methods are adapted to the needs of the pupils, and that the pupils are properly classified and promoted. In brief, they can make sure that every feature of the school is such that every pupil will receive the sort of instruction which his heredity demands.

Over the experiences of the home and of the community the school does not have any direct control. The school can, however, indirectly exert a large influence over these experiences through its tutelage of the pupils; it can instruct the pupils regarding the best principles of living and can instill in them a desire to abide by those principles. That is the birthright of every child of every race, of both sexes and of every family. Indirectly through the pupils, and directly through the school nurse, through the visiting teacher, through the parent-teacher association, through adult-education programs, and through the newspapers and other public-relations agencies, the school can improve home and community conditions and thus enhance the opportunities for the development of the individual pupil. Through these agencies teachers can work for balanced diets in the meals of the home, for proper conditions for sleep, and for hygienic clothing; they can encourage the removal of community conditions which are hazardous to the health, the safety, and the morals of the people.

If teachers are to meet more fully the needs of their pupils, they must know what those needs are. This will demand that teachers become greater observers of their pupils, and of the culture in which the pupils live.

QUESTIONS FOR DISCUSSION

1. Should pupils be grouped for instructional purposes on the basis of one "age" alone? Discuss. If one "age" were selected for such grouping, which "age" should be selected? Why? Do you favor special classes for deviate pupils? Why or why not?

2. Do you believe that the grouping of pupils on the basis of general intelligence is undemocratic? Why or why not?

3. The Declaration of Independence affirms: "We hold these truths to be self-evident, that all men are created equal. . . ." Discuss this statement from the viewpoint of heredity.

4. Can you suggest why the hereditary basis for mental traits has been more difficult to establish than the hereditary basis for physical traits?

5. Does heredity explain all the differences between men and women? If not, what other explanations are there?

6. List several human traits which might be easily influenced by changes in environment and suggest the environmental changes that might be expected to influence each trait. Likewise, list some human traits which would not be easily influenced by changes in environment.

7. Is there any evidence that various growth processes and environmental factors are interrelated? Describe.

8. What are the possible interactions of heredity and environment on such a trait as baseball ability?

9. Give your answer to the following questions: Is deafness hereditary? Is insanity hereditary? How could this question be better asked?

10. Does your state have a sterilization law for chronic criminals? If so, what are its provisions, and how does it function? Do you favor such a law? Why or why not?

11. Should the normal left-handedness of a child be interfered with? Why or why not? What provisions for left-handedness should the schools make?

SELECTED REFERENCES

Anastasi, Anne, and Foley, J. P., *Differential Psychology*, Revised edition, The Macmillan Co., New York, 1949, 894 pp.

Carmichael, Leonard, ed., *Manual of Child Psychology*, John Wiley and Sons, New York, 1946, 1068 pp.

A comprehensive review of all the major research studies on child development. Contains 19 chapters, each prepared by a specialist.

Galton, Francis, *Hereditary Genius*, The Macmillan Co., New York, 1869, 180 pp.

A study of the relation between heredity and genius.

Gesell, Arnold, *et al.*, *The First Five Years of Life*, Harper and Brothers, New York, 1940, 393 pp.

Presents a comprehensive analysis of child development from the age of four weeks through the age of five years.

Gesell, Arnold, *et al.*, *The Child From Five to Ten*, Harper and Brothers, New York, 1946, 475 pp.

Presents a comprehensive analysis of child development from the age of five years to the age of ten years.

Gesell, Arnold, *et al.*, *Youth: The Years From Ten to Sixteen*, Harper and Brothers, New York, 1956, 505 pp.

The theme of this book is the adolescent's mind and personality; of interest particularly to elementary school teachers.

Goddard, H. H., *The Kallikak Family*, The Macmillan Co., New York, 1912.

A study of the two lines of descendants of Martin Kallikak.

Helping Teachers Understand Children, American Council on Education, Commission on Teacher Education, Washington, 1945, 151 pp.

Recommends that children be observed more by teachers.

Mendel, Gregor, "Experiments in Plant-Hybridization," Berh. naturf Ver in Brunn, Abhandlunger IV (1865). (English translation published by Harvard University Press, Cambridge, 1925).

Reports some of the experiments from which Mendel's laws grew.

"Mental and Physical Development," *Review of Educational Research.*

Every third year a number of this magazine is devoted to a review of the research on "mental and physical development."

Stoddard, George D., *The Meaning of Intelligence*, The Macmillan Co., New York, 1943, 504 pp.

Discusses the nature and the significance of intelligence.

Terman, Lewis M., and Merrill, Maud A., *Measuring Intelligence*, Houghton Mifflin Co., Boston, 1937, 461 pp.

Presents a revision of the Binet-Simon intelligence scale.

Warner, W. Lloyd, Havighurst, Robert J., and Loeb, Martin B., *Who Shall Be Educated?* Harper and Brothers, New York, 1944, 190 pp.

Shows that class distinctions are reflected throughout the public school systems of the country.

CHAPTER 8

Pupil Learning

Definition and Significance of Learning

The school exists primarily (1) to facilitate the best quality and the largest quantity of learning on the part of the pupils, and (2) to prepare the pupils for further learning. The merit of any teacher, therefore, must be determined largely by the degree to which the teacher contributes to the accomplishment of those purposes. What facts and principles does the teacher need to know, in order best to facilitate pupil learning, and how may he obtain knowledge of those facts and those principles? This chapter is designed to give only a tentative and an introductory answer to this question and to prepare the prospective teacher to begin immediately his observation and his study of the learning activities of children and adults. A more complete answer to the question will be given in the student's later courses, especially in the courses in psychology.

Definitions of Learning. Because of the universality of its use, learning is a term for which people have become accustomed to believe that they do not need a definition; everyone speaks almost daily of having learned something new, or of having learned something better. As if in agreement with that belief, many of the treatises on psychology and on teaching do not bother to submit a definition of learning. In the treatises which include definitions of learning, many different expressions are used, but when they are stripped of their verbiage and "pedaguese" and stated in the American language, the definitions are seen to mean essentially the same.

When differences in the definitions are found, they usually stem from a different emphasis of the authors. Some of the definitions emphasize learning as a product or result, whereas other definitions emphasize learning as a process or event. Following are some of the definitions which are found in treatises on psychology and teaching: "Learning is the act of acquiring habits and knowledge"; "Learning is profiting from experience"; "Learning is the establishment of responses to stimuli"; "Learning is the general term for the changes or process of change induced directly by experience whereby the organism is able to respond more adequately to a given situation"; "Learning consists of changes in the nature and the behavior of human beings"; "Learning is the process by which we become able to do something which we previously could not do." Because of its clarity, its simplicity, and its adequacy, the last definition appeals to most students of education; it should suffice at least for beginning students of education, for whom this book has been primarily written. In fact, the definition will be accepted by experienced teachers.

In the definitions just quoted, and in many others which might be quoted, there is implicit agreement that learning is identified with growth—growth in thoughts, in feelings, and in actions. In this chapter that view of learning will be accepted; moreover, learning will be used as synonymous with education. In his well-known and widely-quoted definition of education, the late Professor John Dewey has conceived of education as growth, just as this chapter will regard learning as growth. Dewey defined education as "that reconstruction or reorganization of experience which adds to the meaning of experience, and which increases ability to direct the course of subsequent experience." [1]

Most teachers of former years interpreted learning in a too narrow sense. They assumed that the only mental traits which people possessed were traits that dealt with the purely intellectual functions. Teachers assumed, moreover, that their only task was to teach the pupils to learn the things which had been discovered, invented, and described by the pupils' elders. Thus, the learning activities which were fostered by the old-time school were directed wholly or largely toward the developing of skills and amassing of information, or toward the development of a simple thinking process which made

[1] John Dewey, *Democracy and Education*, Macmillan, 1916, pp. 89–90. By permission of The Macmillan Company, publishers.

use only of information. The interpretation and the use of information were neglected.

Modern teachers, on the contrary, are more and more recognizing that people possess many mental traits which are not of a purely intellectual nature. Some of these other traits, which are usually called emotional traits, are morale, sentiment, mood, appreciation, and ambition. Modern teachers are more and more recognizing the driving force of these emotional traits and are trying to stimulate or to control them. Of still greater significance, modern teachers have discovered that emotional traits can be modified through education, especially if the education is provided in childhood.

Another erroneous assumption which is widespread concerning learning is that it is limited to the years of school attendance. Many persons believe that learning does not take place before the child enters school and that it ceases when the days of schooling are finished. Although casual observation had long indicated the falsity of the foregoing assumption, it was not until recent years that the problem was attacked experimentally and the assumption proved to be false by objective data.

Regarding the presence or the absence of learning during the preschool years, there is abundant evidence to show that learning does take place during those early years. In fact, there is no period of equal duration in which the individual learns as much as in the years from birth until the age of six or seven. At the age of six or seven when the pupil starts to school, he has already learned an unbelievable amount. The amount of knowledge or of skills which he has acquired determines his "readiness" for instruction in the various school subjects; of course, his "readiness" for each school subject is not the same when he enters school. He has acquired the rudiments of a language, has learned to care for the elemental needs of his body, and has acquired thousands of other facts, habits, and attitudes which have started him on the way to becoming a civilized creature. Although the world is still somewhat bewildering to the child when he enters school, it is not, as William James said, the "big blooming' buzzing confusion" which it was to the child as an infant.

Those early years have gradually come to be recognized by psychologists, teachers, churchmen, and others of the more enlightened members of the general public as unquestionably the most important years in life so far as education is concerned. During those years the child is building his foundation for life; he is acquiring information, habits, attitudes, and ideals which are likely to remain with him throughout life and to affect for good or for ill his whole life. In brief, those years are the most important part of the "tide" of his affairs—a tide, according to William Shakespeare, "which, taken at the floods, leads on to fortune."

The tendency in progressive families and progressive communities has been toward trying to obtain a more intelligent direction and better guidance of those early years. For example, nursery schools and kindergartens—schools which enroll the child at three, four, or five years of age—have been established in hundreds of communities, especially in the cities. It should be mentioned, though, that only approximately twenty per cent of the preschool-age children of the United States are now receiving the advantages of nursery or of kindergarten education, but that percentage is increasing all the time. Another movement designed to increase the educational opportunity of the preschool child has been directed toward the education of parents in child care. That movement should be much more accelerated. The modern school is becoming more and more aware of the fact that the parents have a large responsibility for the education of their children, and that until the children enter school, the parents almost wholly bear the responsibility for the education of their children.

Regarding the education of adults, it was long assumed that "the old dog could not be taught new tricks," or if he could be taught "new tricks," it would be only by the expenditure of an inordinate amount of time and effort. Contrary to this belief, experimentation has shown that perhaps the "old dog" is slow in learning many of the tricks which are taught to puppies—tricks often useless, but it has shown that the "old dog" can learn the things which he desires to learn. The late Professor Edward L. Thorndike, who probably did more experimentation on adult learning than any other person, had the following to say of the ability of adults to learn:

> The assumption was shown to be false by the experience of everyday life and of schools for adults. In an earlier volume *(Adult Learning)* we confirmed this by experimental evidence and also measured roughly the changes in the ability to learn up to age forty-five. We showed that the

ability to learn increased from early childhood to about age twenty-five and decreased gradually and slowly thereafter, about one per cent per year. Childhood was found to be emphatically *not* the best age for learning in the sense of the age when the greatest returns per unit of time are received. The age for learning that is best in that sense is in the twenties, and any age below forty-five is better than ages ten to fourteen.

Later investigations by Miles, Jones, and others make it probable that the decline in ability to learn from age forty-five on to seventy is not much more rapid than this, so that a man of sixty-five may expect to learn at best half as much per hour as he could at twenty-five and more than he could at eight or ten.[2]

In the belief that the individual will never grow too old to be able to learn, modern schools are placing more and more emphasis upon the sources and the tools of knowledge, in order that each individual may desire and be made competent to continue his education throughout life. For example, those sources and those tools are making the pupils acquainted with the importance and the proper use of books, magazines, newspapers, the radio, the cinema, television, and other sources of information which are available throughout life. Moreover, thousands of school systems now have programs of adult education, and millions of adults are extending their education through such programs; in fact, a few school systems have more adults in school than they have children in school. The need for adult education is increasing, because people are living longer all the time.

Significance of Learning. Although there is much difference of opinion regarding how learning takes place, regarding the best means of promoting learning, and regarding many other matters pertaining to learning, there is no difference of opinion on whether learning does take place. That learning does take place is universally and unanimously agreed. Learning occurs in school and out of school during all waking hours, and it continues from birth until death. In fact, as the preceding chapter has indicated, learning probably starts even before the birth of the child.

Man differs from other animals in many ways, but it is his ability to learn, and especially his ability to solve problems, which primarily distinguish man from other animals. Learning is man's greatest and most distinctive accomplishment. Learning has enabled man not

[2] Edward L. Thorndike, *Adult Interest*, Macmillan, 1935, pp. 1–2. By permission of The Macmillan Company, publishers.

only to adapt himself to his environment but to modify his environment to make it give him greater comfort and greater happiness. It has enabled man to improve his standards of living as regards food, clothing, shelter, recreation, and all other aspects of living. Through learning, man has developed the many sciences and the many arts which increase his happiness, his comfort, and his security in thousands of ways. Above all, it has enabled him to build civilizations.

As Lord Kelvin, eminent British physicist, once said, "Behind all known forces and above all known laws there is an intelligent mind." Minds which stimulate progress have become intelligent through learning. Our whole civilization has been made possible only by the fact that man could and did learn. Our civilization will continue to advance in the degree to which man augments his learning and puts that learning to an altruistic use. If man does not put his learning to an altruistic use—if he uses it for socially destructive pursuits—civilization will not advance. The social value of the learning is as important as the amount of the learning. The fruits of any vicious learning are certain to be evil.

From the beginning of the human race, man has been learning. Adam, the Bible's first man, learned, and some of the things which he learned were vicious. In his learning man has not been satisfied with maintaining only the *status quo*, but has constantly pushed back the "frontiers of knowledge." Each generation has added something to the social heritage and has tried to hand down all that heritage to succeeding generations. The result is that each generation lives in a much more complex civilization than the preceding generation, and that each generation needs more education. In an address at Cornell University, Edward L. Thorndike stated the significance of learning in the following words:

> Civilization is, indeed, the chief product of human learning. Homes and tools, language and art, customs and laws, science and religion are all created by changes in the minds of men. Their maintenance and use also depend on human modifiability—the ability of man to learn. If that were reduced by half, in the sense that the next generation could learn only things half as hard to learn as those which man now can learn, most of human civilization would be unusable by the next generation and would soon vanish off the face of the earth. For example, most if not all, that is taught in this (Cornell) university nobody could then learn. The contents of drugstores would poison us. Ships and trains and automobiles, if

they moved at all, would go in somewhat the disorder of the toy boats and trains of children.[3]

To summarize, learning, especially learning to help the individual to make a living, has ever been the chief activity of man. Each succeeding generation has seen the learning activity of man become larger and more important, because the cultural heritage of man grows by leaps and bounds; that heritage is the substance of learning. For several centuries that heritage has been so large and so important that society has given primarily to the school the task of selecting, of organizing, and of presenting to the children the most valuable learning situations possible. To perform well the task becomes increasingly difficult and increasingly important. The importance of the task is more fully seen, when it is realized that the life pattern of an individual is largely determined by the early years of life. A person's attitudes, habits, and his mental, moral, and physical well-being in adulthood will largely reflect the forces which were prevalent in childhood. Alexander Pope's couplet says:

> 'Tis education forms the common mind;
> Just as the twig is bent the tree's inclined.

"Setting the Stage" for Pupil Learning

The preceding section of the chapter indicated that the school exists primarily for the purpose of facilitating the largest amount and the best quality of learning on the part of the pupils. The school has the task of "setting the stage for learning"; that is, it must provide the best conditions under which the pupils may learn. In setting the stage for learning, innumerable details must be kept in mind, and all of this book is fundamentally an attempt to describe the larger details of that stage, both regarding the *status quo* and regarding any changes which should be made in the stage.

On that stage the pupil is, of course, the main attraction; he is the "Hamlet." Every other detail of "the stage"—the curriculum, school officials and school employees, the school plant, the school library, textbooks, supplies, and the like—exists only to serve the main "actor." To serve adequately the pupil, it is necessary that

[3] Edward L. Thorndike, *Human Learning*, Appleton-Century, 1931, p. 3. By permission of D. Appleton-Century Company, publishers.

educational employees, and especially the teacher, have an extensive knowledge of the nature of the pupil. Contributing to that knowledge are many sciences, among the more important of which are psychology, anatomy, sociology, anthropology, and physiology. Making probably the largest contribution of any of the sciences is psychology, because a large part of the knowledge of the learning process must be based upon the science of psychology. The present section of the chapter will, therefore, discuss a few of the outstanding contributions of psychology to the learning process.

Proper Psychological Background for Teachers. Every school employee who has anything to do with directing pupil learning should have extensive knowledge of psychology, and especially of the psychology of the type of pupil with which the school employee deals. Such knowledge is especially necessary on the part of the teacher, because he has the prime responsibility for setting the learning stage for the pupil; he cannot set that stage without knowing the pupil.

Psychology may be defined as the science which seeks to ascertain and to organize the facts of human behavior and to interpret and to use those facts in directing and in controlling human behavior. Behavior to the psychologist includes all types of expression—thoughts, feelings, and actions of the individual; it is the response which the individual makes to the situations which confront him. Responses are continually being made by the individual, and the responses become more and more complex and more and more intelligent from birth until deterioration in old age.

For convenience in studying it, psychology is divided into several fields. One of the more common of the numerous bases on which the division is made is that of chronological age of the individual; according to this classification, there are the psychologies of infancy, of childhood, of adolescence, of adulthood, and of senility. Another common basis of classification is regarding the use or application of the psychological facts; thus, there are several types of applied psychologies, such as medical psychology, social psychology, advertising psychology, and educational psychology.

Of the so-called "age" psychologies, the elementary and the secondary school teachers are most concerned with the psychologies of childhood and of adolescence. In view of the fact, though, that learning is a continuing process from birth until death the teacher cannot be oblivious to the facts and the laws of the psychologies of the other ages. Of the applied psychologies, the teacher is most concerned with educational psychology, which treats of the use or application of psychological facts in such a way that the educational growth of the pupil will be efficiently directed and efficiently controlled.

Colleges and universities which have departments for the preparation of teachers have gradually come to see the value of a knowledge of psychology for the teacher and more and more they have introduced courses for providing that knowledge. More and more, too, they have tried to make those courses function in meeting the needs of teachers of the various age and grade levels, of the various school subjects, and of exceptional children such as the bright and the dull. All of them require at least one course in psychology, and most of them, especially those which have four-year curricula, require several of such courses.

The course in psychology which is most frequently required is that usually labeled "General Psychology," [4] which most psychologists believe should be a prerequisite to all other courses in psychology. The next course most frequently required is "Educational Psychology" with special emphasis upon the ages and the types of pupils with which the teacher will work. These two courses in psychology are regarded as the minimum essentials for teachers, and they are usually required of all prospective teachers, irrespective of the type of educational service which the teacher expects to enter. To supplement and follow the courses just mentioned, most teacher-preparing colleges offer other psychology courses, especially in particular fields. Among those other courses are "Psychology of the Preschool Child," "Psychology of Adolescence," "Abnormal Psychology," "Clinical Psychology," and courses in the teaching of reading, handwriting, arithmetic, language, and other school subjects, which often include psychological principles. These extra courses are being more and more organized for special educational employees, among the more common of which are the following: Psychological examiner of a school or a school system, guidance counselor, visiting teacher, and teacher of atypical children such as blind, deaf, speech

[4] "General Psychology" deals with the normal adult human. The theory back of this requirement is that the prospective teacher should have a knowledge of the psychology of himself before he attempts to study the psychology of children.

defective, and mentally abnormal (bright or dull); these special educational employees are found fairly frequently in the larger school systems, and the salaries paid such employees are slightly higher than the salaries paid to regular teachers.

Knowledge of Individual Differences Among Pupils. Psychologists have directed their energies largely toward the discovery and the formulation of psychological laws and principles. This effect has been predicated on the assumption that people are naturally much alike, hence they should be dealt with somewhat similarly. The result has been that psychologists and teachers have tended to regard the problems of teaching in terms of groups of students, rather than in terms of individual students. Moreover, the emphasis has been placed upon the group, rather than upon the individual, because many people have believed that it was undemocratic to deal with any pupil in a manner different from all other pupils.

Recently, however, studies of individual differences have proceeded apace, and everywhere it has been found that the differences among people are large in every trait which all human beings possess; it has been found that there are large differences in general traits or general abilities and in special traits and special abilities. Moreover, modern teachers have come to believe that it is not undemocratic to deal with the individual in a different manner from other individuals, provided that the needs of the individual are met. In other words, educators have ceased to believe that equal opportunity means same opportunity.

In consonance with the view just stated, teachers have attempted more and more to meet the needs of each pupil rather than the needs of only the average pupil of the group. In fact, the emphasis upon individual differences has become so large and so fruitful that Chapters 7 and 11 of this book are largely devoted to an introductory discussion of that topic. The extent of differences within a random-selected group of thirty-four fifth-grade pupils is indicated in the following quotation from S. L. Pressey and F. P. Robinson.

> The children in this class varied in age from 9 to 13 years, in height from 47 to 60 inches, and in weight from 55 to 103 pounds. Of the 34 youngsters, 7 had appreciable defects of vision, 1 was slightly deaf, 4 had impacted teeth, 3 had adenoids, 1 was crippled, 8 were malnourished, and 5 had at some time suffered a serious illness. Two girls had already begun to menstruate.

The I.Q.'s of the class varied from 68 to 147; 2 children had distinct musical ability, 1 drew unusually well, and 4 had exceptional mechanical skill. Tests in school subjects showed reading rate to range from second-to-ninth-grade level, and ability in other subjects to vary about as much.

As would be expected from the last statement, several children showed great interest in reading, but others none. Most of the boys liked baseball, but one spent all his spare time in his basement carpenter shop, and another was an electrical "wizard" whose skill with radios and other appliances was a matter of neighborhood comment. One girl wanted to be an actress, another a nurse; one was already so boy-crazy that she presented a conduct problem, and one boy had been in juvenile court for petty thieving.

Three of the children were leaders; one was an isolate who seemed completely apart from the others. Five girls who came from the better side of the school district constituted a little clique; they tended to reflect home attitudes and to look down on the girls from the factory-worker area. Four boys from this latter district were members of a gang. The only son of the social leader of the community was considered a sissy by the other boys. But the teacher favored him because of his mother's prominence, and he made a special effort to obtain the teacher's regard because the children disliked him—with the result that the other children disliked him still more.[5]

All of these individual differences must be kept in mind by the teacher, if the needs of the individual pupil are to be met. Moreover, it should be remembered that physical and emotional differences must be met as well as intellectual differences. The total condition and the attitude of the pupil are so obviously a part of the total learning situation that to mention them is almost trite, but the fact that they are so often disregarded demands that they be mentioned in a chapter on pupil learning. The pupil must be ready to learn before he will learn, at least all that he might. The more important elements for a favorable learning situation are as follows:

1. The health of the pupil should be at its best. If the pupil is malnourished, ill, or otherwise physically handicapped, he cannot fully realize his potentialities as a learner.
2. The emotional tone of the pupil should be at its best. A pupil who is unhappy, discouraged, or otherwise does not possess the proper emotional tone is certain to be handicapped in his learning attempts.
3. The learning tasks, that is, the subject matter of the curriculum, must be adapted to the ability and the interest of the pupil, and must help

[5] S. L. Pressey and F. P. Robinson, *Psychology and the New Education*, Harper, 1944, p. 320. By permission of Harper and Bros., publishers.

the pupil to solve the problem that he faces. A pupil cannot learn at his best rate, if the grade or the school subject is not appropriate to his intelligence, to his preparation for the grade or the school subject, or to his interest.

4. The "total situation" must be favorable for learning. This total situation includes the three elements just mentioned. It includes also a good school and a good home environment and effective methods of teaching.

Teachers must keep in mind the foregoing elements of good learning situations even though the acquiring of them will usually be difficult. Teachers, parents, and the whole community must work together if the ideal conditions for pupil learning are to be acquired.

Methods of Studying The Learning Process

The preceding section affirmed that the task of the teacher is fundamentally to analyze, to explain, to direct, and to control the behavior of his pupils. It also pointed out the necessity for the teacher's having a knowledge of psychology, because psychology is the science which deals with human behavior. That discussion, though, may have left the impression that a knowledge of behavior can be obtained only from textbooks and other literature, or only from courses in psychology. Such an impression would be unfortunate, because knowledge of behavior may be obtained during every day of life. Anyone may obtain such knowledge by observing the persons with whom he comes into contact. The teacher may obtain it especially by studying his pupils, and the prospective teacher may also obtain it by studying prospective pupils. The three chief methods of obtaining knowledge of behavior are through (1) controlled experimentation, (2) observation, and (3) introspection. These methods will be explained briefly in the next following paragraphs.

Controlled Experimentation by Teachers. The most scientific way of studying behavior is through controlled experimentation, and during recent years the tendency among psychologists has been toward the use of that method. That method has the advantage over introspection and observation, which are later discussed, of being more objective, hence of being more exact and more trustworthy.

To organize a controlled experiment in learning is, however, one of the most difficult tasks imaginable. In a controlled experiment all variable factors are controlled, and the experiment is conducted upon constant factors. Thus, if we were organizing an experiment to ascertain whether the whole or the part method of memorizing a piece of poetry was the more efficient, among the steps which would have to be taken in controlling the experiment are the following: The piece of poetry memorized by each method would have to be of the same difficulty, the same interest, and similar characteristics; the intelligence, the educational preparation, the physical condition, and the interest of the two groups of learners would have to be the same; the teaching of the two groups would have to be of the same quality and of the same amount; and the environmental conditions of the two groups of learners would have to be the same. When all variable factors had been controlled, the two groups of learners could be placed under the stop watch, and their accomplishment in memorizing measured and studied further.

During recent years, hundreds of experiments on learning have been performed and reported in the literature of psychology and of education. The student's courses in psychology and in methods of teaching will bring acquaintance with some of the more significant of these experiments. It is sufficient to say here that the teacher must be concerned with the results of the work of other investigators; moreover, the wide-awake teacher will have many opportunities to perform many simple learning experiments of his own. The ability to organize a controlled experiment should be demanded of every prospective teacher. Interest in these matters should go far toward helping the teacher to develop a scientific attitude toward the learning process.

Observation of Pupils by Teachers. If the teacher does not have the time, the equipment, or other resources to do controlled experimentation on pupil behavior, he can always do something which is closely akin to it—namely, he can be a close observer of pupil behavior. The greater the care with which the teacher conducts his observations the more scientific he will become; that is, the closer he will approximate the characteristics of a controlled experiment. The teacher can, and should, always be sensitive to the conditions which make each pupil learn best; he can do this by carefully observing the responses of each pupil, then trying to improve the learning situation so as to call forth better responses. Chapter 24 of this book is entirely devoted to a discussion of school and class observations, especially for beginning students of teaching.

Fig. 31. A kindergarten market. *(Courtesy of the St. Louis, Missouri, public schools.)* Real life experiences are integrated by such projects.

Introspection by Teachers. Introspection is an attempt of the individual to analyze his own mental processes. It means to look inward. Such introspection will help the teacher to interpret the mental processes of his pupils. It will be especially valuable, if the teacher will reminisce and try to re-interpret the experiences of his own childhood.

In introspection, however, the teacher should guard against inferring that the child's mental processes are the same as those of an adult. Until there is evidence supporting that conclusion, the teacher cannot conclude that pupils of all grades, or the same ages, or of similar intelligence, learn in the same way.

The Laws of Learning

The effort of the scientist has always been directed toward reducing related facts to laws. This effort has also guided the student of the learning process, because he has ever attempted to discover the conditions under which learning may best take place, at least for the typical person. In spite, however, of the zeal with which the students of the learning process have worked and notwithstanding the large amount of experimental work, it must be concluded that the laws of learning are still in the process of being formulated. The laws are not yet final—in fact, most of them are as yet only hypotheses or working principles.

Most of the so-called "laws" of learning bear strongly the earmarks of a systematic bias of the student who formulated them. They are more theory than fact. The person, therefore, who uses psychology as an aid to teaching should be warned to distinguish between what is known and what is not known about learning. An hypothesis or working principle should not be mistaken for a demonstrated law.

In the main, the laws of learning have originated in one or more of the types of learning, for example, rote learning, trial and error learning, and associative learning. Thus, it was early observed that in rote learning a piece of prose or poetry could be memorized by reading and by repeating the piece over and over. From that observation it was concluded that, other things being equal, "practice makes perfect," and that the necessity for repetition should be formulated into a law. This law is known as the law of exercise; it was formulated by the late Professor Edward L. Thorndike in 1913, and at the same time he formulated the laws of readiness and of effect.[6]

Law of Readiness in Learning. According to the law of readiness in learning, the individual must be ready to learn before he can learn—at least all that he might. The learning tasks must be satisfying to him, not annoying to him; the health and the emotional tone of the individual must be at their best; and the school environment and the methods of teaching must be appropriate. Of all the laws of

[6] For a complete exposition of these laws, the interested reader may consult Edward L. Thorndike, *Educational Psychology*, Columbia University, 1913, Vol. II, pp. 1–5. These laws have, however, been under attack by many other psychologists.

learning, most students of the learning process regard the law of readiness as the most important and as most applicable to the various types of learning.

Law of Exercise in Learning. The law of exercise says that, other things being equal, the performance of an act tends to make subsequent performance of that act easier, more fluent, and less likely to error and to forgetting.

Two corollaries of the law of exercise are often recognized by psychologists. The first of these is known as the law of frequency. It says that "learning is proportional to the frequency with which the learning factors are made operative."

The second corollary is known as the law of recency. It affirms that "other things being equal, whatever it is that makes for learning is more effective when recent." This corollary makes provision for the phenomena of forgetting which is an inevitable characteristic of all learning.

In spite of the many facts which seem to validate the law of exercise and its corollaries, and notwithstanding that the law and its corollaries play a large part in modern methods of teaching, there are certain considerations which create doubts regarding the complete validity of the law. For example, there are many data which suggest that "continued use of some functions is a sure way to destroy the functions and so to bring about quick forgetfulness." [7] Practice, therefore, to obtain perfection must be of the proper kind and in the proper amount. Only intelligent practice makes perfect.

Law of Effect in Learning. Protagonists of the law of exercise soon formulated the law of effect to supplement the law of exercise and to lessen the criticisms of that law. The law of effect affirms that "one learns quickly those reactions which are accompanied or followed by a satisfying state of affairs; one does not learn quickly those which result in an annoying state of affairs or learns not to make such reactions." [8]

Other Laws of Learning. As with the law of exercise, so with

[7] For a detailed criticism of the law of exercise the interested reader is referred to Coleman R. Griffith, *An Introduction to Educational Psychology*, Farrar, 1935, pp. 411–413.

[8] The definition is from Horace B. English, *A Student's Dictionary of Psychological Terms*, Harper, 1935, p. 43. By permission of Harper and Bros., publishers.

the laws of readiness and of effect there are many data which must temper any wholehearted acceptance of the laws. For example, even a casual inspection of our recollections will show that we remember many unpleasant events; moreover, all of us have spent many unhappy practice periods in acquiring a skill. It must be concluded that there are other factors in learning than readiness and exercise and effect, and that uncritical acceptance of the laws just mentioned make too simple a matter of the most baffling thing in the world—the learning process. The following laws must be followed if learning is to occur without waste of effort and without unnecessary fatigue and discouragement:

1. The desire to improve.
2. A clear understanding of the task. Illustration: It would not be practical for a person to attempt to build a house if he had studied only how to lay a floor.
3. Appropriate repetition. "Practice makes perfect" only when repetition of the subject being learned is accompanied by other factors, such as the desire to learn.
4. A measure of progress. Rewards as well as punishment aid the satisfaction which arises from learning, but both are secondary to mere knowledge of success: A golfer's best score is greater incentive for improvement than any money reward.[9]

QUESTIONS FOR DISCUSSION

1. What is meant by the experimental attitude? Of how much importance do you regard the experimental attitude on the part of the teacher? Discuss.

2. What is a controlled experiment? Compare the difficulty of setting up such an experiment in, say, physics or chemistry with one in learning. Outline a controlled experiment on learning.

3. When it has been found through experimentation that the pupils of a certain grade and in a certain school subject learn best by means of a given method of instruction, could it be concluded that pupils in other grades and other school subjects would also learn best by means of the same method? Why, or why not?

4. To what extent are a teacher's observations of the behavior of his pupils subjective? Do such observations have any of the characteristics of objectivity? Explain. What is objectivity? What is subjectivity?

[9] Summarized here from Ernest R. Hilgard's *Theories of Learning,* Revised edition, Appleton-Century-Crofts, 1956.

5. Many persons believe that psychology is not, and can never be, a science, because behavior cannot be accurately measured. Do you agree with that view? Why, or why not?

6. Many persons hold the view that the laws or principles of learning are practically worthless, because each individual is a law to himself and that other laws or principles cannot be applied to him. Do you agree with that view? Why, or why not?

7. That the pupil should have a desire to learn has been stated as a foremost principle of learning. Should this be interpreted to mean that the pupil should not be requested or be required to engage in tasks which do not interest him? Would it be possible for the teacher to create pupil interest in every task assigned? Discuss. If a pupil could not be interested in learning the multiplication table, for example, should he be excused from that task? Why, or why not? When is a pupil ready to learn?

8. Compare in potential significance for teachers the first six or seven years of life with later periods of similar duration. What steps are now being taken, and what further steps might be taken, to realize the potentialities of these early years for learning?

9. What steps should the school take to prepare the pupil to continue his education to the fullest after he leaves school? What are the chief agencies through which the pupil may continue his learning after he leaves school? Evaluate each agency.

10. In the directing of learning activities should the emphasis be placed upon the acquisition of information or upon the interpretation and use of information? Explain.

11. Discuss the significance of the emotions in learning and in life. Should the teacher attempt to educate the emotions? Why, or why not? Is there any danger in trying to stifle the emotions? Discuss.

12. Discuss the significance of problem solving in the learning process.

SELECTED REFERENCES

Blair, Glenn M., *et al.*, *Educational Psychology*, The Macmillan Co., New York, 1954, 601 pp.

A treatise on educational psychology, but with emphasis on learning.

Burton, William H., *The Guidance of Learning Activities*, Second edition, Appleton-Century-Crofts, Inc., New York, 1952, 737 pp.

Bases principles of teaching on the principles of learning.

Deese, James E., *The Psychology of Learning*, McGraw-Hill Book Co., 1954, 384 pp.

Presents the psychology of learning in terms of its basic concepts.

English, Horace B., A *Student's Dictionary of Psychological Terms*, Harper and Bros., New York, 1935, 131 pp.

A list of definitions of several thousand terms used in psychology.

Flugel, J. C., *One Hundred Years of Psychology,* The Macmillan Co., New York, 1933, 384 pp.

An interesting discussion of the history of psychology.

Hilgard, Ernest R., *Theories of Learning,* Revised edition, Appleton-Century-Crofts, Inc., New York, 1956, 409 pp.

An outstanding discussion of various theories of learning and the psychologies behind them.

Kingsley, Howard L., *The Nature and Conditions of Learning,* Prentice-Hall, Inc., 1946, 579 pp.

Discusses learning as a process that is controlled by certain tendencies.

Monroe, Walter S., ed., *Encyclopedia of Educational Research,* Revised edition, The Macmillan Co., New York, 1950, pp. 668–690.

This is an article on learning by Arthur W. Melton.

Pressey, Sidney L., and Robinson, Francis P., *Psychology and the New Education,* Harper and Bros., New York, 1944, 654 pp.

An excellent treatment of educational psychology, based on experiments of pupil learning.

The Psychology of Learning, Part II of the *Forty-first Yearbook* of the National Society for the Study of Education, Public School Publishing Co., Bloomington, Ill., 1942, 140 pp.

Presents the different psychologies of learning.

Thorndike, Edward L., *Human Learning,* D. Appleton-Century Co., New York, 1931, 206 pp.

A series of lectures which discuss the significance of learning and the types of learning.

Trow, William Clark, "When Are Children Ready to Learn?" NEA *Journal,* Vol. 44 (February, 1955), pp. 78–79.

Determining the reason for a child's disinterest or inability to learn at school is often not as simple as some teachers try to make it. Degree of readiness and proper guidance are important factors the author discusses.

Wheat, Harry Grove, *Foundations of School Learning,* Alfred A. Knopf, Inc., New York, 1955, 395 pp.

Discusses the development of the individual as to physical, mental, and social growth. It stresses the importance of balance and implies that the forces that condition development are continuous and ever-present. Development is not a process that confines to any single place or time.

CHAPTER 9
Teaching Procedures

Teaching as a Science and as an Art

Because of the almost universal use of the term, *teaching* is another term for which a definition is almost trite. If a definition of teaching is needed, the following would seem to suffice: Teaching is the art of helping someone to learn, that is, of helping him to acquire knowledge, skills, attitudes, ideals, habits, or some other type of learning which he did not previously possess. With the exception of hermits and of the feebleminded, all persons are at least teachers every day throughout life; all persons answer questions, for example, and that make all persons teachers in a sense. Teaching is the stimulus, and learning is the response to the stimulus. The function of teaching, therefore, is to provide the best stimuli in order that the best learning may take place.

Society has established and at large expense maintains the school, in order that teaching and learning may be conducted in the most effective manner possible. When the teaching of the school is not effective—and that condition often obtains—learning does not result or the type of learning which the school desires to obtain does not result. The test of effective teaching is effective learning.

Much teaching is not effective, because the conditions which make for effective learning are not present. Often the learning is not effective because the teacher's aims are not clear, because the materials of instruction are not adapted to the pupils' interests and to the pupils' needs, because the school environment is not conducive to learning, and because the pupils are not in the best physical and the best emotional condition to receive the instruction offered. The preceding chapter showed that the pupils must be ready to learn before they will learn, at least all that they might.

Teaching as a Science. Since it possesses much organized knowledge, which is the chief criterion for a science, teaching is, at its basis, a science. Teaching as a profession already possesses thousands of facts and hundreds of principles, and new facts and new principles are being constantly added, and old principles are being constantly revised and constantly improved. To be most successful, teaching must proceed according to those facts and those principles. It cannot be conducted on the basis of mere opinion or by "meeny-miney-mo" methods. Nor will common sense—facetiously called "that most uncommon thing in the world"—suffice. Furthermore, the best common sense in any field of learning is predicated on sound knowledge of that field, and on successful experience in the field; as the Bible says, "A wise man is strong, yea, a man of knowledge increaseth strength."

The more a teacher knows about the teaching process the more effective his tutelage will be. He must know the responses which are desired from each pupil and he must also know the type and the amount of stimuli which must be applied to call forth those responses. Without that knowledge, the teacher is likely to follow rule-of-thumb procedures in the formulation of aims, in the selection and the organization of the materials of instruction, in the choice and use of teaching procedures, and in the selection of school supplies, equipment, and other materials; without knowledge, a teacher is apt to drift and to degenerate into a quack in his profession.

Teaching as an Art. Ralph Waldo Emerson said, "There is no knowledge that is not power." Although knowledge is always necessary for accomplishment in any endeavor, it alone will not beget the greatest accomplishment. When applied to teaching, therefore, Emerson's statement needs qualifying, because mere knowledge of the facts and the principles of teaching does not guarantee that a person will be an excellent teacher. Whether he be teacher, musician, painter, butcher, baker, or candle-stick-maker, the great "artist" is a master of performance in his field as well as a master of knowledge; he not only has knowledge, but he is able to draw proper conclusions from it and otherwise to make the best use of it. In brief, if it is to possess the greatest power, knowledge must be applied; more than that, it must be correctly applied. The artist is skilled in his field.

A teacher will have arrived at the state of artist when he is able to attend to all or to most of the details which insure mastery over the means of execution, but it is likely that no teacher will ever completely arrive there. The test of the execution of the teaching act—the test for the artist teacher—is whether the pupil learns as much as his ability indicates that he should learn. The obtaining and the organizing of knowledge are the function of science. The applying of knowledge is the function of art. The successful teacher must possess all of these commands over knowledge. Jesus of Nazareth was the most skilled teacher of all time, and he paid a price—a price for preparation—for acquiring that eminent skill. Jesus was an artist teacher.

Requisites for Effective Teaching

The primary purpose of the school is to facilitate learning on the part of the pupils. In order that learning may be the most effective, the teaching procedures must be the best. If those procedures are not the best, there will, of course, be waste—waste of the pupils' time and of public funds. Indeed, it is probable that the largest wastes in education occur in the selection and the use of teaching procedures. Those wastes occur primarily because of ignorance on the part of teachers of what constitutes the best teaching procedures, but wastes occur also because of failure to apply the principles and the procedures of teaching which experience and research have demonstrated to be the most effective. In other words, the wastes occur because of ignorance of and neglect of both the science and the art of teaching.

All that can feasibly be attempted in this chapter is to mention and to discuss briefly some of the more important requisites for effective teaching. But, the information of the prospective teacher on these important requisites need not be limited to these few pages, because for most of the requisites here mentioned other chapters of this book are devoted; moreover, most colleges and universities which are engaged in the preparation of teachers offer courses in each of these outstanding requisites. A brief discussion of the outstanding requisites for teaching is given herewith.

KNOWLEDGE OF DESIRABLE EDUCATIONAL AIMS FOR TEACHERS. Chapter 2 of this book stated that the effectiveness of the tutelage of any teacher is determined largely by the presence or the absence, and by the merit, of the educational aims of the teacher. It is difficult to arrive anywhere, by any means, if the destination is not known, and if the destination is wrong, all effort expended in trying to reach it will have been wasted. Aims give direction and zest to the teacher's efforts. Worth-while aims are always a necessity, but poor aims are worse than none because they will likely lead to the inculcation of knowledge, skills, attitudes, and ideals which are injurious to both the pupils and society. When they are possessed by a vigorous and skilled teacher, poor aims are especially dangerous because such a teacher is almost certain to accomplish the aims quickly and effectively; when poor aims are accomplished by the pupils, they must be "unlearned" at some future time, and the "unlearning" process is often more difficult than the learning process.

The educational aims of the teacher will largely determine the teaching method that is used. If the teacher conceives the fundamental aim of the school to be to maintain society as it is, he will try to perpetuate a fixed pattern of habits, beliefs, and attitudes in the individual, and the method of teaching which he will employ is likely to stress habit formation and unquestioning obedience to the established order. If, on the other hand, the teacher conceives the fundamental aim of the school to be to help society reconstruct itself, he will try to prepare his pupils to choose and to reconstruct their own habits, beliefs, and attitudes, and the method of teaching which he will employ is likely to emphasize the development of thinking on the part of his pupils.

KNOWLEDGE OF DESIRABLE SUBJECT-MATTER FOR THE PUPILS. If method may be called the vehicle of instruction, subject-matter—that is, the materials of instruction—may be labeled the cargo of the vehicle. To load an efficient vehicle with worthless cargo would, of course, be absurd. To use efficient methods in the teaching of worthless subject-matter would be equally absurd. Another of the necessary requisites, therefore, for effective teaching is for the teacher to use desirable subject-matter—subject-matter which will meet the needs of pupils and of adults in a complex and a rapidly changing civilization.

The teacher must know the materials which he is expected to

teach; he cannot teach something which he does not know. He may try, but his efforts are sure to be bungling and his results are certain to be puny. The recent slogan, "Teach children rather than subject-matter," is almost as absurd as was the earlier and the opposite slogan, "Teach subject-matter rather than children." Both subject-matter and children must be taught. But children must be taught subject-matter which is on the level of their interest, their understanding, and their needs; to know each of these levels pupils need guidance.

To select and to organize the subject-matter of instruction, or to guide the pupils in the selection and the organization of it, is one of the most difficult and one of the most important responsibilities of the school. The modern teacher is expected to shoulder this responsibility *in toto* or in part. If he is to be able to shoulder this responsibility, the teacher must be a persistent and an intelligent student of the complex and the constantly changing panorama of society. On one hand, he must ever be eliminating from the curriculum the old activities and old experiences which no longer meet social needs; on the other hand, he must ever be introducing new activities and new experiences which meet social needs. In brief, the teacher who would be most effective must be well informed on the curriculum. To give the prospective teacher an orientation in the curriculum, Chapter 13 (The Curriculum and Social Trends) of this book has been included.

Just as the method of teaching which is used will be determined by the teacher's concept of the purpose of the school, so the selection of subject-matter will be determined by that same concept. If the purpose of the school is believed to be to develop a fixed pattern of habits, of beliefs, and of attitudes, subject-matter will be selected to develop those habits, beliefs, and attitudes, and methods of teaching which will most effectively accomplish that purpose will be used by the teacher.

If the primary aim of the teacher is to give his pupils mental discipline, methods of teaching which purport to accomplish that aim will be employed, and subject-matter will be selected which will meet the same purpose. In earlier chapters, however, it was stated that mental discipline (especially when narrowly conceived) as an aim of education is rapidly passing into the limbo of forgotten things; and it was also stated that teaching methods and subject-matter are being more and more selected because of their content value rather than because of the belief that they provide mental discipline. Whereas such school subjects as mathematics and foreign languages formerly constituted the core of the secondary school curriculum because it was believed that they provided mental discipline, such subjects as the social-studies, the natural sciences, and the vocational subjects are being given larger prominence, and whereas subject-matter was formerly "drilled" into the pupils irrespective of whether the pupils liked drill methods, today more interesting and more effective teaching methods such as the project method are being more and more employed. This shift of emphasis is predicated on the belief that the pupils should be prepared for taking their place in a constantly changing social order.

Knowledge of Desirable Psychological and Biological Laws for Teachers. The preceding chapter has tried to show that the learning process is very complex—that it is one of the most baffling things in the world. Although experimentation has provided much information regarding the way in which the human mind works, even the Solomons of the teaching profession are still far from knowing the exact way in which the mind works and the stimuli which make it work best.

The most valuable discovery of psychological investigations has been concerning the nature and the extent of individual differences. These investigations have shown that any two individuals are far from being alike in their interests and in their abilities. Since effective teaching procedures are dependent on adequate knowledge of the learning process, the successful teacher must have a large knowledge of psychological principles. He must know the interests and the capacities of each pupil in his class. As well as knowing the response desired from each pupil and that this response must be determined in part by the pupil's interests and capacities, the teacher must know the stimuli in kind and in amount to apply to each pupil in order that the desired response may be obtained. The teacher must know the stimuli which will most effectively interest each pupil and he must cause each pupil to desire to work at his maximum capacity; and the teacher must realize that the stimuli which are effective with one pupil in his class will not necessarily be effective with another pupil. In brief, the teacher must know how to motivate each pupil to his best efforts, and he should know that a pupil who is not made *ready* to learn is not likely to learn much.

All colleges and universities which are engaged in the preparation of teachers offer, as has been earlier noted, several psychology courses and they require at least one of these courses of all prospective teachers. Such courses, however excellent they may be, can only give the teacher the foundation knowledge which he needs of the learning process. To this foundation the artist teacher can add much through classroom experience, because the classroom is the best laboratory in the world for the observation and the study of children.

In his classroom the teacher has human beings for his subjects and he has them under natural conditions—conditions which do not obtain in the psychological laboratories of the colleges and universities. Moreover, his subjects never grow old. Pupils come to him in constant procession year after year; they come with different problems and different challenges—differences in ages (chronological, mental, social, etc.), interests, attitudes, and ideals. To obtain value from his experience the teacher must be wide awake. Experience which uncritically repeats another experience—which follows the "cow-path of tradition"—is of little or no value to teachers, even though salary schedules often reward teaching experience.

In addition to knowing and to following the best psychological laws, the teacher must also know and must follow the best biological laws. He must know how the whole human organism works. He must realize that the whole child comes to school, and not merely the child's mind. He should know that anything which affects one part of the human organism also affects every other part of the organism; mind and body are an entity. Knowledge of those biological laws is usually provided by a course or courses in health and physical education which most colleges and universities offer and which teachers are required to pursue. Chapter 12 of this book will discuss health and physical-education; hence any further discussion of the subject is unnecessary at this place.

Knowledge of Desirable Pupil Environment for Teachers. The most effective learning can take place only when the environmental setting for the pupils is best. This means, among other things, that the school site, the school-building, and the school equipment must be adequate, safe, sanitary, comfortable, and attractive. Over most of those details, school officials rather than teachers have control. Teachers, on the other hand, often have the power to correct or to improve poor environmental conditions in the school; they can request school officials to correct such conditions, and often it is a case of asking, "and ye shall receive." For example, teachers can suggest that shades be obtained for the windows, that pupils' desks be placed so that each pupil will have proper light, and that pupils' desks be obtained which fit or are adjustable to the size of the pupils. They can request that the school equipment be made adequate and that it be kept in a proper state of repair, that the school-building be properly cleaned and properly heated, that the school-building and site be landscaped and be decorated so that they will be attractive, and that unnecessary noise be eliminated. They can ask that attention be given to every other detail which would make the school-plant more adequate, safe, comfortable, sanitary, and otherwise conducive to learning.

Fig. 32. A well-equipped school department office-machine class in Timken Vocational High School. *(Courtesy of the Canton, Ohio, public schools.)*

Knowledge of Desirable Classroom Management for Teachers. Closely related to proper school and proper classroom environment is proper classroom management. For the details of proper classroom management the teacher is almost wholly responsible. Among the more important details of proper classroom management for which the teacher is wholly or largely responsible are the following: providing for the proper seating of pupils; arranging for the pupils to pass to and from the classroom and to and from the schoolbuilding at noon, recess, and other school intermissions; checking of pupil attendance; providing for the distribution, the administration, and the supervision of educational supplies and equipment; arranging for fire drills; and in general, making certain that everything in the classroom proceeds without confusion, friction, and other waste. In brief, the function of the teacher in classroom management is to assure, as James Whitcomb Riley said, that the pupils are

> Humpin' on to somethin' fair,
> Bumpin' no one gettin' there.

In establishing a routine of proper classroom management the dangers of over-routinization as well as those of under-routinization should be avoided. There must be organization and pupil-discipline, of course, but that organization and that discipline should not be repressive. In order that they may become self-reliant the pupils should be taught and permitted to exercise their initiative as often as possible; however, the pupils should know that there are certain rules of conduct which they must obey, if they are to avoid injuring themselves and interfering with the rights of their fellows. Somewhere between the "heel-clicking" type of discipline and the ultra-freedom type which permits each pupil to "run riot" is the desideratum.[1] For teachers to have proper classroom management is considered so important that most colleges and universities which are engaged in the preparation of teachers offer a course in or devote part of another course to classroom management.

Lessons for Teachers from Wartime Training

During World War II the armed services of the United States operated one of the largest and most intensive educational programs

[1] Many beginning teachers fail because of "poor discipline." Such discipline is usually the result of lack of understanding of children and of poor teaching in general. Well-prepared teachers need have little fear of pupil-discipline problems.

of all time. Millions of men and women were trained for both military and civilian purposes. One of the largest accomplishments of that program was to bring 400,000 illiterate inductees up to the fourth-grade standard of literacy in from two to three months.

Since the end of the war, educators have wondered whether some or many of the training efforts of the armed forces might not be used by the civilian schools. To answer such questions the American Council on Education appointed a commission to study the training program of the armed forces. A report of the Commission states that the GI way of teaching had the following chief characteristics:

1. It was knowledge stripped for action.
2. The end was always more important than the means to the end.
3. Traditional methods were abandoned with ease in order to produce results.
4. Clear and specific objectives characterized each integral part of the learning program.
5. Learning by doing and realism in the learning situation generally were provided.
6. Constant supervision of teaching and learning prevailed.
7. Aids to teaching and to learning were developed on a huge scale.
8. Human talent was identified and every attempt was made to have the right person in the right place at the right time.
9. Constant evaluation of results was regarded as essential.
10. Classes in general were kept small.[2]

Thinking as the Aim of Teaching Procedures

Importance and Definition of Thinking. A main thesis of this book is that society should not permit itself to become petrified, but should ever be trying to improve itself. Another thesis of the book is that the school should accept the obligation of fostering a type of education which would energize and qualify its pupils constantly to help in the continuous reconstruction of society. For its teaching creed the school should accept the doctrine of flexible habits which means that our habits should not be permitted to become petrified but should be always in process of change to meet new demands. The mental instrument or the mental procedure which may be used

[2] Alonzo G. Grace and others, *Educational Lessons from Wartime Training*, 1948, p. 247. By permission of American Council on Education, publishers.

Fig. 33. Experiences as a part of good teaching. *(Courtesy of the Euclid, Ohio, public schools.)*

to keep our habits—our patterns or ways of living—flexible is thinking. Only through thinking can intelligence be liberated, and can social and individual progress be assured.

What, then, is thinking? It may be briefly defined as the reorganization or the reconstruction of habits with the purpose in view of solving a problem. John Dewey defined thinking as "that operation in which present facts suggest other facts (or truths) in such a way as to induce belief in what is suggested on the ground of real relation in the things themselves, a relation between what suggests and what is suggested." [3] H. Gordon Hullfish defines thinking as "a special type of adjustment—and adjustment that is used by man in solving problematic situations." [4] Both of the foregoing definitions agree that thinking is used to solve problems and that it requires the use of the constructive faculties of the intellect. Thinking is the highest type of mental effort.

To give his pupils their first lessons in thinking will not be necessary on the part of the teacher, because every pupil will already possess this ability to a certain degree. When he enters school, the pupil has already met hundreds of thousand of problematic situations on which he has used his thinking powers. Moreover, the desire to think is possessed to a certain degree by every pupil. The task of the teacher is to develop this ability and this desire, and the task well done is the largest contribution which the teacher can make to his pupils.

If the teacher fails to make this contribution to pupil thinking, his educational efforts and products will be characterized by narrow training—training which in future days may bind the pupil to the galleys of tradition and of routine. Narrow training may catch the pupil in the "trap of his habits" and make it difficult for him to adjust himself to the constantly changing social order; moreover, it may disqualify him for making good suggestions regarding changes which should be made in the social order.

If life is at all full, as it is sure to be with all normal persons, there is not a day when the individual is not called upon to solve many problems. Every normal person is confronted every day by situa-

[3] John Dewey, *How We Think*, Heath, rev. ed., 1933, p. 12. By permission of D. C. Heath and Company, publishers.

[4] H. Gordon Hullfish, "Training in Thinking," *Journal of the Ohio State Teachers Association*, Vol. 2 (August, 1924), p. 31.

tions which must be thought through and a logical conclusion reached; he must reconstruct or reorganize his habits to meet new situations; his old habits won't suffice him. In the main, and with most persons, these problems are relatively easy and involve choosing among two or more simple alternatives. On the relatively easy level, they involve such questions as the following: "Which automobile shall be driven today?" "What color shall the house be painted?" "What kind of meat, if any, shall be served for dinner today?" "What ensemble shall be worn today?" "Shall wheat or oats be planted this spring?" At the other extreme, the problems become very complex, if not baffling, and involve "creative work" of the highest type. The more complex problems involve, for example, the formulation of a plan for a desirable social order, the control of war, the elimination of disease, the improvement of the money system of the nation, the liquidation of the Federal debt, the elimination of unemployment, the perfection of television, the obtaining of more competent public officials, financial aid to foreign countries, and the use of atomic energy in war or in peace.

Phases of Thinking. In its most highly developed form, the thinking process possesses the following phases:

1. The individual becomes aware of the problem, and he develops a desire to solve the problem.
2. He sets up hypotheses, guesses, hunches, or tentative answers regarding the solution of the problem. (Unfortunately, the thinking of many people never advances beyond this step, hence the large amount of credulity and intolerance. Many people jump at conclusions; their hypotheses, guesses, or hunches become the final answers.)
3. He collects and organizes all pertinent data which bear upon the hypotheses, guesses, hunches, or answers mentioned in phase 2.
4. The data are interpreted, and conclusions, either tentative or final, are formulated.

Dewey and Hullfish recognize two phases of thinking; those two phases, though, include the four steps just mentioned. Hullfish includes the first two phases just mentioned under the heading of "finding meanings" and the last two steps under the heading of "testing meanings." [5] We shall quote briefly from each of these discussions; we turn first to Dewey:

[5] A meaning may be defined as an answer or a fact in a certain relationship. Hullfish gives credit to his teacher, Boyd H. Bode, for this formulation.

> . . . the origin of thinking is some perplexity, confusion, or doubt. Thinking is not a case of spontaneous combustion; it does not occur just on "general principles." There is something that occasions and evokes it. General appeals to a child (or to a grown-up) to think, irrespective of the existence of his own experience of some difficulty that troubles him and disturbs his equilibrium, are as futile as advice to lift himself by his bootstraps.
>
> Given a difficulty, the next step is suggestion of some way out—the formation of some tentative plan or project, the entertaining of some theory that will account for the peculiarities in question, the consideration of some solution for the problem. The data at hand cannot supply the solution; they can only suggest it. What, then, are the sources of the suggestion? Clearly, past experience and a fund of relevant knowledge at one's command. If the person has had some acquaintance with similar situations . . . , suggestions more or less apt and helpful will arise. But unless there has been some analogous experience, confusion remains mere confusion. Even when a child (or a grown-up) has a problem, it is wholly futile to urge him to think when he has no prior experiences that involve some of the same conditions.[6]

Hullfish affirms that the initial step in thinking is the "finding of meanings," but he says further that the most important and the most difficult step in thinking is the "testing of meanings." He says:

> . . . We may see at once, therefore, that thinking is more than the finding of a meaning; it is, in addition, a matter of testing that meaning. And the greatest of these is testing! . . .
>
> Man is not slow in finding meanings, but his very readiness in finding them is also a barrier to his advancement. We have no more striking example of this than in current superstition—striking because it flourishes in an age known as a scientific one. . . . Finding meanings is natural, as natural to man as breathing. Testing meanings, however, is a matter of training, and though some may do this more readily than others, all may be helped by the development of the critical attitude. Thinking, then, is essentially a matter of clues, of meanings; but it becomes thinking only as these clues, or meanings, are tested. . . .
>
> Man is, as we have said, a ready guesser. This fact gives a clue to classroom procedure. When a meaning is offered, thinking has started; when this meaning has been tested, thinking has been completed. It is the failure to test which makes for credulity.[7]

By what methods may meanings be tested? Two methods are available. One of these is known as the inductive method and the

[6] Dewey, *op. cit.*, pp. 12–13. By permission of D. C. Heath and Company, publishers.

[7] Hullfish, *op. cit.*, p. 32.

other as the deductive method. In the inductive method the facts are first found, then the facts are explained and conclusions drawn from them. In the deductive method the existence of certain facts is deduced or predicted, then the facts are searched for. Both methods are necessary in the best type of thinking, because some facts would never be found except by the process of deduction, and some conclusions would never be drawn if certain facts had not been observed.

When has a meaning been tested sufficiently to justify a conclusion? The answer is—when all facts or all evidence have been accounted for, and there is no room for a competing hypothesis. If certain facts or evidence do not fit into the hypothesis, doubt is cast over the validity of the hypothesis, and only a tentative conclusion, if any, can be drawn. The desideratum of the school is, therefore, to develop pupils who will want to test every reasonable hypothesis and who will not "jump at conclusions." This disposition to inquire and to test is the essence of the scientific attitude, and this attitude should be regarded as the supreme goal of education and as the heart of any method of teaching.

Means of Stimulating Thinking Among Pupils. The discussion thus far has pointed out the importance and the nature of thinking and the obligation of the teacher to stimulate thinking. How may the teacher stimulate the desire and increase among his pupils the ability to think? The first suggestion is that pupils be given an opportunity to think, especially upon problems of social significance which are on their level of ability and their interest. Like all abilities, the ability to think increases with the proper kind and the proper amount of exercise. To give this preparation the teacher has myriad opportunities throughout the school day—in fact, during every class meeting. The first obligation of the teacher is, therefore, to see that the "thinking stage" is kept laden with desirable problems—problems of social significance which are on the level of interest and ability of the pupils. This obligation cannot be met by the teacher merely by asking questions and the pupils reciting the ready-made answers of the textbooks.

A second suggestion is that the teacher give the pupils guidance in their efforts at thinking. In giving this guidance, an excellent teacher will be interested, of course, in helping his pupils to find a solution of a problem, but he will be more interested in developing the ability to arrive at a correct solution and to test that solution. He has the obligation of tentatively accepting the answer (right or wrong) of a pupil, then of demanding proof from the pupil for the answer which he has given. Without this proof—without this "testing of meanings"—the act of thinking is not complete, and the pupil has missed one of the most valuable parts of his preparation in thinking. According to John Adams, the pupil's wrong guess is "golden," if the teacher will utilize the opportunity to "bore in" for the purpose of finding any element of truth in the wrong answer. Adams says:

> It is the teacher's business to discover what element of truth underlies each of the false answers his pupils supply. Every time that she succeeds in getting at the true reason for the false answer, she should give herself a good mark; every time she cannot, she should give herself a bad one. For it is her business to know just this sort of thing. . . . It was not a guess, but a confused explanation, that resulted in the exposition of an inquest: "When you have died unexpectedly you are cross-examined by a coroner." Every time a pupil has a rational explanation for his answer, however far-fetched the explanation may be, he must be exonerated from the charge of illegitimate guessing.[8]

In the "game of thinking," to summarize, it is the business of the teacher to guide in the selection of problems and in the solution of the problems. The goal of the game is a thinking pupil. In conducting the game, a democratic method of teaching rather than an autocratic method should be used. The teacher should be a participant in the game as well as the referee. He should work with the pupils on the selection and the solution of problems. He should not hand down, Jove-like, the problems to be attacked or the solution of them. He should give information and clues when he deems them necessary, and he should withhold them when that is advisable. Always the teacher should be a leader and a guide to his pupils.

Language as a Tool for Thinking. Man's most distinctive and most important trait is his ability to think, that is, to find and to test meanings. This ability has enabled him to discover, to invent, or otherwise to make changes in society. Many of these discoveries or inventions have become magnificent tools for learning, as the mere mention of such discoveries or inventions as the fountain pen,

[8] John Adams, "The Golden Guess," *Educational Review*, Vol. 67 (May, 1924), p. 258.

the printing press, the typewriter, the camera, the moving picture, the phonograph, the radio, television, the telephone and telegraph, measuring instruments, and language will show.

Probably the greatest of these contributions is the invention and the improvement of language, so that it can be used accurately and quickly to express meanings. Without the invention and the development of language, the invention and the development of the fountain pen, the printing press, the typewriter, the telephone, the radio, television, and other means of communication would have been useless. Without a symbolism, such as language provides, learning would be immeasurably handicapped. In fact, without language, there is doubt whether the highest type of learning, namely, thinking, could exist.

The lower animals seem to be able to find meanings, but they are unable to detach these meanings from an object. Man, on the contrary, is endowed with the ability not only to find meanings, but to detach those meanings from an object, that is, to form an abstraction. In forming an abstraction language is necessary. Language is constituted of symbols. Man makes use of a symbol or a combination of symbols for each meaning which he obtains, and through the ages man has attempted to improve his system of symbols for each meaning which he obtains, in order that it might better serve him in expressing his ideas and his thoughts. Although man has developed and makes use of many other types of symbols, words are unquestionably the best system of symbols which man has developed. Through the use of one word, man can express an idea, that is, a simple meaning, and through the combination of words he can express various shades of meanings and more complex meanings. What a marvelous invention is language!

But language is a two-edged tool. It can be used to advance and to clarify thinking, or it can be utilized to obstruct and to obscure thinking. It can be used to elucidate thinking, or to gloss over the absence of thinking. It can be used to express accurate meanings or inaccurate meanings. It is the ready tool of the ignorant and of the demagogue, just as it is the faithful servant of the intelligent and the honest. Another task of the prospective teacher, therefore, is to develop his own language habits (both written and oral) and to prepare himself to do all he can to assist his pupils to make conscious use of this tool as an aid to thinking—as an aid to the finding, the testing, and the expressing of meanings. John Dewey had the following to say of the importance of this task and of steps which may be taken to accomplish it:

> . . . That problem is to *direct pupils' oral and written speech, used primarily for practical and social ends, so that gradually it shall become a conscious tool of conveying knowledge and assisting thought.* How without checking the spontaneous, natural motives—motives to which language owes its vitality, force, vividness, and variety—are we to modify speech habits so as to render them accurate and flexible *intellectual* instruments? It is comparatively easy to encourage the original spontaneous flow and not make language over into a servant of reflective thought, it is comparatively easy to check and almost destroy (so far as the school room is concerned) native aim and interest and to set up artificial and formal modes of expression in some isolated and technical matters. The difficulty lies in making over habits that have to do with "ordinary affairs and conveniences" into habits concerned with "precise notions." The successful accomplishing of the transformation requires (a) enlarging the pupil's vocabulary, (b) rendering its terms more precise and accurate, and (c) forming habits of consecutive discourse.[9]

QUESTIONS FOR DISCUSSION

1. Distinguish between a child-centered school and a subject-centered school. Which do you prefer? Why? Can an efficient school be totally child-centered or totally subject-centered? Why? What should be the proper balance?
2. Distinguish between logical presentation of subject matter and psychological presentation. Illustrate. Discuss the relative merits of these two types of presentation.
3. What has been the traditional purpose of the recitation? What do you regard as the limitations of this traditional purpose?
4. How do you explain the fact that many accomplished athletes make inefficient coaches and that many average or inferior athletes make excellent coaches?
5. Someone has said that "the best government is one that governs least" and that "the best teacher is one who teaches least." Do you agree or disagree with these statements? Explain.
6. This chapter has tried to defend the thesis that the development of thinking should be the heart of teaching method. Do you agree with this view? Why or why not? Do you believe that the emphasis in teaching

[9] Dewey, *op. cit.*, pp. 239–240. By permission of D. C. Heath and Company, publishers.

has been too much upon fact acquisition and too little on thinking? Explain. Discuss the relation between information and thinking. Is it possible for a person to think without having appropriate information on the problem? Why?

7. Discuss the importance of language and of the necessity for all teachers to co-operate with the English teachers.

8. Discuss the importance of measuring learning as a test of teaching procedures. Can one teaching procedure be adjudged superior to another until such measurement has taken place? Explain. What is the difference between evaluation and measurement?

SELECTED REFERENCES

Aiken, Wilford M., *The Story of the Eight-Year Study,* Harper and Bros., New York, 1942, 157 pp.

Compares the efficiency of thirty progressive schools with that of traditional schools.

Burton, William H., *The Guidance of Learning Activities,* Second edition, Appleton-Century-Crofts, Inc., 1952, 737 pp.

Relates teaching procedures to the principles of learning.

Dale, Edgar, *Audio-Visual Methods in Teaching,* Revised edition, Dryden Press, New York, 1954, 534 pp.

Comprehensive treatment of audio-visual materials and methods.

Dewey, John, *How We Think,* Revised edition, D. C. Heath and Co., Boston, 1933, 301 pp.

Discusses the relation of reflective thinking to the educative process.

Grace, Alonzo G., *Educational Lessons from Wartime Training,* American Council on Education, Washington, 1948, 264 pp.

Discusses essentials which made the GI way of teaching a notable success.

Grambs, Jean D., and Iverson, William J., *Modern Methods in Secondary Education,* Dryden Press, New York, 1952, 562 pp.

Discusses newer methods in secondary-school teaching.

Herrick, Virgil E., "Approaches to Helping Teachers Improve Their Instructional Practices," *School Review,* Vol. 62 (December, 1954), pp. 527–534.

The teacher should set definite educational goals based on sound objectives. Development of subject areas too often forget to recognize other subject areas necessary to complete understanding. The child-study method is growing, although it is more used in elementary schools than secondary schools.

Hirschi, L. Edwin, "A Student Evaluation of Classroom Procedures," *School Review,* Vol. 62 (September, 1954), pp. 354–356.

Answers to a questionnaire indicated that the group tested wanted individuality, flexibility, self-direction, all which would tend to build better adults.

Monroe, Walter S., ed., *Encyclopedia of Educational Research,* Revised edition, The Macmillan Co., New York, 1950, pp. 316, 745–753, 1446–1454, 1488.

Reviews several important investigations on methods of teaching.

Morrison, Henry C., *The Practice of Teaching in the Secondary School,* Revised edition, University of Chicago Press, Chicago, 1931, 688 pp.

The discussion is built around the unit plan of teaching.

Mursell, James F., *Successful Teaching,* McGraw-Hill Book Co., Inc., New York, 1955, 321 pp.

Based on an eclectic psychology of learning.

Review of Educational Research.

This publication reviews every few years the research on teaching procedures in the elementary school, the secondary school, and the college.

Richard, J. A., "Teaching Shut-In Children by Telephones," American *School Board Journal,* Vol. 129 (October, 1954), pp. 25–27.

Discusses the use of the telephone in teaching children that are confined at home. It is not to replace the teacher but to be the link between the home and the school for the handicapped child that cannot attend school.

Smith, Henry P., *Psychology in Teaching,* Prentice-Hall, Inc., New York, 1955, 466 pp.

Based on original research and classroom difficulties of both experienced and inexperienced teachers.

Thorpe, Louis, *Child Psychology and Development,* The Ronald Press Co., New York, 1955, 700 pp.

Describes both the recent and classic studies of physical, mental, and psychological growth of children.

Umstattd, J. G., *Secondary School Teaching,* Revised edition, Ginn and Co., Boston, 1954, pp. 176–195.

These pages discuss objectives and assignments of the teacher.

CHAPTER 10

Pupil Guidance

In modern schools, teachers and all other educational employees are expected to help with the pupil guidance and other phases of the pupil-personnel program of the school. All educational employees are expected to help with the guidance program, in spite of the fact that in many of the larger schools special-guidance and personnel functionaries, such as deans of boys and of girls, counselors, and visiting teachers, are employed. This chapter will give an overview of the responsibilities of the school and of each educational employee for pupil-guidance, and will indicate the opportunities and the requirements in pupil-guidance as a profession.

Evolution of the Pupil-Guidance Movement

Although pupil-guidance has, in the broad sense, always been an activity of the schools, as an organized activity it is a product of the present century. As an organized activity, it dates back to 1908 when the Boston Vocation Bureau was established. The purpose of that bureau was to give assistance to men and to women in selecting a vocation and in obtaining a position. The work of the bureau was so successful with adults that in 1910 the Boston School Committee ordered the appointment of a vocational counselor in every high school of Boston.

The good leaven of those beginnings soon spread to other communities, for in the period between 1910 and 1915 such cities as Chicago, Cincinnati, Grand Rapids, Hartford, New York, and Philadelphia provided for organized vocational-guidance work in the schools. In the succeeding years the movement spread rapidly, embracing practically every large school system, especially those possessing secondary schools. In 1913, the National Vocational Guidance Association was formed at a meeting in Grand Rapids, and in 1915 *The Vocational Guidance Magazine* was founded. These ventures gave the guidance movement a decided impetus which has continued with constantly accelerating pace until the present time.

In the beginning, as has probably been inferred from the preceding paragraphs, the guidance movement in the schools was limited to vocational-guidance—to attempts at assisting the student in choosing a vocation and in obtaining employment in the vocation. Realization soon came, however, that the student needed guidance in many ways. It was soon seen that the vocational needs of the pupil were inextricably related to his school needs, his health needs, his leisure-time needs, his moral needs, and his numerous other needs. During recent years, therefore, other phases of pupil-guidance have come into prominence, and everywhere the tendency is to emphasize "whole-child" guidance rather than only one part of the pupil's needs. The development of an integrated, a well-rounded, a happy, and a wholesome personality for every pupil has become an important aim of the school; and it should always be an aim of every teacher.

As was noted above, organized guidance began outside the schools; it began as a venture to give assistance to adults in selecting a vocation and in obtaining a position. As was noted, too, guidance soon found its way into the schools. In the schools guidance was started in the secondary schools, and it has obtained by far its largest impetus there. Following its introduction into the secondary-schools, it was introduced into the colleges, then into the elementary-schools. During recent years there has been a renewed interest in adult guidance. This renewed interest has been evidenced in such ways as the establishment of hundreds of local, state, and Federal vocational bureaus and employment agencies, and by the large emphasis upon adult-education in the schools; these movements have often been stimulated by the use of Federal and state funds for those purposes.

Meaning, Kinds, and Functions of Pupil-Guidance

Meaning of Pupil-Guidance. A survey of the literature on guidance and of the organized programs of guidance shows that there is a difference of opinion on what the field of guidance really is or should be. A few authors have treated guidance as synonymous with education. Among the authors who adopted this broad conception of guidance was one of the pioneers in the guidance movement, Professor John M. Brewer of Harvard University.[1]

Other authorities, on the other hand, have expressed the belief that such a broad concept of guidance as that held by Brewer is likely to "direct attention away from guidance proper and therefore endanger the performance of the guidance function."[2] While these other authorities have no quarrel with Brewer's affirmation that guidance is as broad as education, they believe that for practical reasons certain aspects of education, that is, of guidance, must be "signaled out for special consideration and definite organization." The aspects which these other authorities say should be singled out are concerned generally with crises in the life of the individual. The view that guidance is concerned with life crises has been well stated by Professor Arthur J. Jones of the University of Pennsylvania in the following words:

> . . . Guidance, as organized, is, then, concerned with crises, with times of choice, times when the ways diverge, with times of needed adjustment.
>
> . . . it is clear that the help given may be direct or indirect, the one guided may be conscious of the help given or may be entirely unconscious of it. The guidance may be given at the time of a crisis or long before it occurs. Indeed, the best guidance is usually that given long before the need for choice arises. It consists in assisting the individual in the gradual *accumulation* of facts and experiences that will, when the time comes, enable him to decide wisely. Guidance is thus seen to be an essential and a fundamental aspect of education. It is inherent in all education but certain aspects of it are singled out for special consideration and definite organization.[3]

Careful inspection of the two views expressed above indicates that there is no fundamental disagreement on what guidance really is. When the smoke of battle over the two views has cleared, the combatants find that they have been contending for the same thing,

[1] John M. Brewer, *Education as Guidance*, Macmillan, 1932, pp. 2–3.

[2] This view is taken, for example, by Koos and Kefauver in their *Guidance in Secondary Schools*, Macmillan, 1932, pp. 15–17.

[3] Arthur J. Jones, *Principles of Guidance*, McGraw-Hill, 1930, pp. 28–29. By permission of McGraw-Hill Book Company, publishers.

namely, a well-rounded education for each individual; they have had a battle of words, not of ideas. If one examines the criteria which the various authorities say that guidance should meet, he finds large agreement. Running throughout all of the statements of criteria is a common vein, namely, that guidance and arbitrary compulsion are incompatible, and guidance is best when it helps the individual pupil to obtain the proper information on which he will make his own decisions; in other words, in all of the statements of criteria there is seen at work the spirit of guidance and of democracy. Among the statements of the criteria of guidance, the statement by John M. Brewer breathes especially the spirit of democracy, and for that reason it is quoted herewith.

1. The person being guided is solving a problem, performing a task or moving toward some objective.
2. The person being guided usually takes the initiative and asks for guidance.
3. The guide has sympathy, friendliness, and understanding.
4. The guide is a guide because of superior experience, knowledge, and wisdom.
5. The method of guidance is by way of offering opportunities for new experiences and enlightenment.
6. The person guided progressively consents to receive guidance, reserves the right to refuse the guidance offered, and makes his own decisions.
7. The guidance offered makes him better able to guide himself.[4]

KINDS OF PUPIL-GUIDANCE. In its broadest sense, guidance is concerned with every phase of the life of the individual. Life is broad, complex, and largely unpredictable, and guidance must consider the whole sweep of life. Guidance must, therefore, be as broad as education. Guidance must keep in mind that society is always in a process of change, and it must prepare the individual to adjust himself to those changes; moreover, it must have a philosophy of what society should be, and must qualify the individual to help to obtain that ideal society.

Since life is a unit, the guidance of every individual should be a unitary process. For practical purposes, however, and especially for closer study, we commonly recognize various aspects of life which need particular guidance; to differentiate these aspects will be help-

[4] Brewer, *op. cit.*, p. 22. By permission of The Macmillan Company, publishers.

ful, provided we do not forget to integrate each aspect with all other aspects. Since, in its more limited sense, guidance is concerned with crises in the life of the individual, it will be helpful to indicate herewith some of the more important of those crises concerning which decisions must be made by the individual and concerning which guidance in making those decisions is needed: [5]

1. *School guidance.* This is sometimes called educational guidance and is concerned with such matters as the selection of schools, the choice of courses of study, and the making of proper adjustments to the educational program.
2. *Vocational guidance.* This is concerned with giving assistance in choosing an occupation, in preparing for it, in obtaining a position in it, and in making progress in it.
3. *Leisure-time guidance.* This is concerned with giving the individual assistance in utilizing more worthily his leisure time. Because of the decrease in the number of working hours, this type of guidance is receiving more and more attention by the school.
4. *Health guidance.* This is concerned with assisting the individual to develop and to maintain the best health, physical and mental, of which he is capable.
5. *Character guidance.* This is concerned with the development of ethical character and the moral sense. It develops knowledge of what is right and the will to do the right.
6. *Home-membership guidance.* This is concerned with the development of those qualities which make the individual an efficient member of his family.
7. *Civic guidance.* This is concerned with developing the individual to be an efficient factor in the government of the community, of the state, of the nation, and of the world.

People differ in their evaluation of how well the schools are meeting the above needs or areas of pupil guidance, but there is general agreement that perfection in none of the fields has yet been attained, nor will that perfection probably ever be attained.

Many of our most forward-looking citizens believe that the schools are now weakest in the following fields of pupil guidance.

1. Health guidance.
2. Character guidance.
3. Civic guidance.

[5] The reader will immediately notice the similarity between these crises and the "seven cardinal principles of education" listed on page 81 of this book.

In 1946 the New York State Institute research staff worked out a detailed "Job Analysis of a Good Citizen" in conference with city and state officials, general and vocational educators, industrial and business employers, labor representatives, and other citizens. Knowledge of this job analysis should be helpful to all guidance workers, and the analysis is reproduced herewith, although it may sound too ideal.

A *Good Citizen:*

A. Plans carefully
   1. Sets up clear constructive goals.
   2. Plans in co-operation with his family for the interests and needs of all its members—for education, work, recreation, religion, health.
   3. Keeps goals constantly in sight.
   4. Lives within his budget.
   5. Pays bills promptly.
   6. Buys goods and services wisely.
   7. Discriminates in distribution of energies.

B. Is approachable and interested in other people
   1. Converses easily with other people.
   2. Asks intelligent and interested questions when he needs to.
   3. Visits with other people in their homes and his.
   4. Keeps confidences.
   5. Listens well.
   6. Advises other people only when asked and knows himself competent to do so.
   7. Maintains sense of humor.

C. Is identified constructively with one or more active social groups—recreational, service, political, religious
   1. Expresses himself in group planning.
   2. Supports and participates in the activity of the group.
   3. Takes initiative and assumes responsibility.
   4. Keeps sense of proportion about importance of his organizations.

D. Commands respect as a worker
   1. Works efficiently.
   2. Is conscientious and accurate.
   3. Is resourceful.
   4. Places all of his abilities at employer's disposal without stint.
   5. Takes upgrading education.
   6. Welcomes supervision.
   7. Sees his job as part of the whole industry.
   8. Sees his job in relation to employer-employee problems.
   9. Commands respect for his opinions through his status as a worker.

E. Keeps abreast of current ideas in science, society, politics, and art
   1. Uses authentic sources for information about such area.
   2. Uses various kinds of literature and art as indications of current trends.
   3. Identifies trends in scientific development, social thought, political action, and artistic creation; relates these trends as dynamics of modern society.
   4. Expresses judgment on governmental policy through voting and participation in community organizations.

F. Carries his own weight in personal and social contacts
   1. Recognizes the validity of his own ideas.
   2. Shares in discussion of current issues.
   3. Presents views in politic manner.
   4. Backs up ideas with fact or application.[6]

FUNCTIONS OF PUPIL-GUIDANCE. In organizing and in conducting a guidance program the following functions of pupil-guidance should be kept in mind by school officials and school-employees:

1. *Obtaining information.* This information must possess a wide scope; ideally, it should include every aspect of life. It should encompass especially the chief life crises such as those mentioned under the heading of "kinds of pupil guidance" in preceding paragraphs. Guidance which is not based on truthful information is sheer quackery and is likely to be positively harmful to the pupils.
2. *Co-operating with other community agencies.* The guidance program of the school must co-operate with the other interested and qualified agencies of the community. Among the more frequently found of these agencies are farm, business, and industrial organizations, labor organizations, other educational institutions, civic organizations, welfare organizations, parent-teacher associations, mothers' clubs, and churches.
3. *Placing and following up pupils.* The guidance program of the school must help to place each pupil in the proper position, school, or course of study. It may do this through organizing a placement service which will work in co-operation with employers and with other schools.
4. *Counseling of pupils.* Such counseling by the school may be given in part through group instruction in try-out courses or in life-career classes. It may be given also through individual counseling by means of home visits and a study of the needs of the individual pupil. All pupil guidance must reach the individual pupil and meet his special needs; in other words, each pupil must be regarded as a "case problem" and must be treated individually.

[6] *Wanted: 30,000 Instructors for Community Colleges*, pp. 34–35, American Council on Education, Washington, 1949. By permission of American Council on Education, publishers.

Many schools, especially the smaller ones, are performing these guidance functions without the assistance of a counselor. The tendency, however, especially among the larger secondary schools, is to supplement the regular teachers of the school with a pupil-guidance specialist, usually known as counselor; in fact, many of the larger secondary-schools employ several counselors. The counselor becomes a member of the faculty of the school and performs special functions which cannot reasonably be expected from the other members of the faculty.

FIG. 34. A guidance counsellor advising a student. *(From Cremin and Borrowman's* Public Schools in our Democracy, *p. 30. Copyright 1956 by The Macmillan Company.)*

SCHOOL ORGANIZATION FOR PUPIL-GUIDANCE SERVICE

GENERAL POLICIES OF ORGANIZATION FOR PUPIL-GUIDANCE SERVICE. Since the facilities and the problems of schools vary widely, it is impossible to suggest a pupil-guidance organization which will meet the needs of every pupil in every school; there can be no such thing as an ideal guidance organization for every pupil in every school. All that shall be attempted here, therefore, is to suggest certain principles which school officials and school-employees should keep in mind in forming a guidance organization for a given size of school.

In planning a guidance organization it should be recognized that guidance is an integral part of every activity of the school and that every educational employee has a part to play in the guidance program. In order that there may be the proper co-ordination of effort, and that none of the guidance functions will be neglected, it is necessary that the program be definitely organized. In planning the organization it is worth repeating that guidance should be regarded as a unitary process in which every part of child life shall be guided and integrated.

Organization for Pupil-Guidance Service in a Small School. Because of the lack of school resources, and the relative simplicity of the guidance problem, the guidance organization for the small school will necessarily be relatively simple. Except in unusual cases, the small school will have to get along without the aid of a pupil-guidance specialist.

In a small school, the principal of the school is looked upon as the director of the pupil-guidance activities of the school. He should appoint from among the faculty a pupil-guidance committee to have general direction and supervision of the pupil-guidance program. The members of this committee should work with the teachers of the school in "selling the guidance idea" and in co-ordinating all of the guidance activities of the school.

Many small schools have pupil advisers for the various grades. One adviser is suggested for grades one to six; another, for grades seven and eight; and other advisers for each grade of the secondary school. The suggested organization also should make provision for using community agencies in the guidance program. In brief, through such an organization all of the four guidance functions mentioned in previous paragraphs could be performed.

Organization for a Pupil-Guidance Service in a Large School. Because of the larger number of employees, a larger curricular offering, and better facilities generally, the guidance organization for a large school will necessarily be more complex than that for a small school. Although the guidance functions to be performed by the large school will be essentially the same as those to be performed by the small school, the large school will usually have more guidance functionaries to help with the guidance program. Incidentally, the larger school will often be able to employ special-guidance functionaries, such as counselors, deans of girls, deans of boys, and personnel directors, which the small schools cannot employ.

FIG. 35. Students taking tests to discover interests, abilities, and achievements. *(Courtesy of the Syracuse, New York, public schools.)*

Opportunities and Requirements of School Employees in Guidance Service

EVOLUTION OF GUIDANCE SERVICE. Whereas in the early days of the pupil-guidance movement in the schools, organized guidance was provided for only the problem pupils, that is, those who failed, left school, or were handicapped in some way, the ideal of the schools today is to provide organized guidance service for every pupil. In trying to realize this ideal, guidance service has passed through several stages.

OPPORTUNITIES FOR EMPLOYMENT IN GUIDANCE WORK. As the need for organized guidance has come to be realized, the need for the school to have employees who are qualified to perform the guidance functions has also come to be more fully realized. So widespread has the interest in organized guidance become that educational employees who have special preparation and other qualifications for doing guidance work have a better chance to obtain positions than employees without those special qualifications. In addition to the school principal and the classroom teacher who possess better employment opportunities if they are qualified to assist in a guidance program, several other types of educational positions in the area of pupil guidance have recently been created which provide excellent opportunities for employment in the schools. Among the more frequent of these positions are those of dean of girls, dean of boys, pupil-personnel director, pupil counselor, and visiting teacher.

During recent years, more and more schools, especially the larger secondary schools, have created guidance positions, and persons with the proper qualifications have not had much difficulty in obtaining appointment to these positions. The demand has been especially strong for pupil counselors.

It should be pointed out, however, that guidance positions are infrequently available to anyone who has not had teaching experience. The entrance to a guidance position is usually through a regular teaching position in a school. For example, the teacher of social sciences, of English, of industrial arts, of business education, or of another subject sees the need for pupil-guidance services and obtains permission from the school principal to start the work; he makes the guidance program successful, and gradually he is released from his regular teaching duties to become a part-time or a full-time guidance functionary with the title of counselor, adviser, personnel director, or such.

Requirements for Employment in Guidance Work. As is true in every other endeavor, the efficiency of a guidance program cannot rise higher than the efficiency of the persons who organize and conduct the program. Since all educational employees, from the superintendent of schools to the classroom teacher, have responsibilities for the guidance program, all educational employees should have a vision of the functions of guidance, of its importance, and of the methods of conducting it.

Realizing the need for special preparation in guidance, many colleges for the preparation of teachers, especially of secondary-school teachers, have introduced guidance courses. The most frequent of such courses is a general course which is designed to serve as an introduction to the field of guidance; it is usually offered under such a title as "An Introduction to Guidance," "Principles of Guidance," "Fundamentals of Guidance," "Guidance in the Schools," or "Guidance." Such a course has been found to be useful to classroom teachers, principals, and superintendents as well as counselors and other specialists in guidance.

In addition to the general course in guidance, several of the larger institutions for the preparation of teachers have introduced many specialized courses for the preparation of guidance specialists in school and in industry. Among the more frequent of such courses are the following: "Counseling," "Occupations," "Tests and Measurements," and "Pupil Personnel." Other courses which are occasionally offered, and which have considerable bearing on guidance are the following: "The Visiting Teacher," "Social Case Work," and "Methods of Interviewing." Many of the most valuable courses may be found in fields other than that of guidance; among the college departments which frequently offer helpful courses for the guidance specialists are those of sociology, psychology, commerce, and industrial arts.

During recent years several states have made compulsory certification requirements for various types of guidance specialists. Thus, the teacher who has charge of the course in guidance or in occupations is usually required to have a teaching certificate in that field. Likewise, a certificate is being more and more required of the guidance counselor, even though he may not have the responsibility of teaching a class.

Since it states many of the qualifications which counselors should have and many of the duties which they should perform, a code of ethics for counselors is reproduced herewith:

A Code of Ethics for Counselors

The Child

1. To guard the confidential information secured in interviews and otherwise as scrupulously as do members of other long-established professions.
2. To view the child as the center of all school effort and favor no plan or practice which is known to be of no benefit to the best interests of boys and girls.

3. To employ tests, interviews, and every other possible means to secure a scientific conception of the pupil's health, mental ability, personality, and rate of improvement.
4. To revere unfolding personality and surround pupils with such a school program as shall tend to stimulate fullest individual development through active participation in a number of varied activities.
5. To testify frankly, candidly, and confidentially on the qualifications of the child.
6. To secure for the child such employment as is in keeping with his or her abilities, at a wage commensurate with the child's training.

THE COMMUNITY

1. To recommend students to positions they are qualified to hold as proved by their record in school.
2. To keep the community informed as to the needs and achievements of the schools and to promote constructive co-operation in the proper training of the youth.
3. To assume such obligations and responsibilities in the community as shall encourage citizens to display an active interest in counseling.

PARENTS

1. To seek intelligent co-operation between the school and the home in matters relating to the development of the child for entrance in society.
2. To respect wishes of parents where scientific procedure confirms the opinion of the parents in the selection of a course or vocation for the child.

THE PROFESSION

1. To seek the largest possible vision for the profession as a worthy life's work and to maintain an open mind and sympathetic attitude toward the advance of counseling.
2. To promote the profession by personal affiliation with professional organizations and by striving to raise its standards and increase public confidence in its standards and increase public confidence in its program of service.

THE SCHOOL

1. To assist the administration in carrying out the policies of the school where the success of the policies hinges on a duty recognized as in the routine of a counselor.
2. To co-operate with teachers in an effort to adjust difficulties arising in the classroom so that an attitude of interest will enable both student and teacher to work at the highest efficiency.

SELF

1. To exalt sterling character above success and cultivate all personal qualities essential to high ethical conduct.
2. To improve in professional knowledge and grow continually in efficiency and service, always manifesting a true professional spirit.[7]

QUESTIONS FOR DISCUSSION

1. What wrong decisions have you made, or what talents have you largely wasted, which better guidance would have enabled you to avoid? Cite examples of how guidance has helped you.

2. Make a list of common "crises" in the lives of boys or of girls, which a program of guidance could help them to meet.

3. Compare the need for pupil guidance today with the need several decades ago. What factors have caused the changes in the need?

4. To what extent does the view of "education as guidance" magnify the importance of the teacher? Show that the excellent teacher is a "guide."

5. Do you believe that the best guidance which can be given is to place the individual in contact with all pertinent information on his problem or problems, then to insist that he make his own decisions? Explain. Can young children be trusted to make their own decisions? Explain.

6. When, if ever, should compulsory guidance be used? Explain. Would the use of compulsory guidance be contrary to the spirit of democracy? Why or why not?

7. Discuss the relative importance of guidance on each of the following school levels: the elementary school, the junior high school, the senior high school, the college, and the university. What kinds of guidance should be emphasized on each of those school levels?

8. Discuss the dependence of vocational guidance upon the other kinds of guidance. What is meant by saying that guidance should be a unitary process?

9. Do you believe that the schools are now doing enough toward placing and following up their graduates? Why? How long should vocational guidance "follow" the worker? How long should other types of guidance follow him?

10. In what ways, if any, does counseling differ from teaching?

11. Do you believe that the typical teacher is too much addicted to "giving advice" to make a good counselor? Explain.

[7] John F. Reinel, "A Code of Ethics for Counselors," *Vocational Guidance Magazine*, Vol. 8 (March, 1930), pp. 263–264.

12. What are the dangers of placing all counseling in the hands of special counselors?

13. What requirements, if any, for the certification of pupil guidance specialists does your state have? What requirements should it have?

SELECTED REFERENCES

American Youth Commission, *Youth and the Future*, American Council on Education, Washington, 1942, 296 pp.

A general report of the American Youth Commission.

Anderson, Bert D., "Obstacles Encountered in Organizing Community Counseling and Placement Services for Youth," *School Review*, Vol. 62 (November, 1954), pp. 465–468.

Discusses some obstacles to community-sponsored counseling and placement services for young people.

Cassidy, Rosalind, and Kozman, Hilda C., *Counseling Girls in a Changing Society*, McGraw-Hill Book Co., New York, 1947, 441 pp.

Addressed to persons who counsel girls.

Coleman, William, "Some Criteria for Evaluating Elementary-School Guidance Services," *Elementary School Journal*, Vol. 55 (January, 1955), pp. 274–278.

Submits a list of questions as a possible guide for evaluation of elementary-school guidance.

Detyen, Ervin Winfred, and Detyen, Mary Ford, *Elementary-School Guidance*, McGraw-Hill Book Co., Inc., New York, 1955, 270 pp.

Designed to help elementary school teachers understand children, and to interpret and deal with symptoms of maladjustment.

Erickson, Clifford E., ed., *A Basic Text for Guidance Workers*, Prentice-Hall, Inc., New York, 1947, 547 pp.

An overview of guidance presented by twenty different authors.

Foster, Charles R., and Stripling, Robert O., "Strengthening School-Community Relations Through Vocational Guidance," *American School Board Journal*, Vol. 129 (August, 1954), pp. 27–28.

Discusses the value of vocational guidance to the school and its pupils, also to the community. A career-day program is just one of the various types of vocational guidance activities which can be very beneficial.

Greenleaf, Walter J., *Occupations and Careers*, McGraw-Hill Book Co., Inc., 1954, 579 pp.

Discusses the individual and occupations available to him.

Kaplan, Oscar J., ed., *Encyclopedia of Vocational Guidance*, Philosophical Library, New York, 1948, 1422 pp.

A two-volume work by nearly three hundred contributors.

Leonard, Edith M., *et al.*, *Counselling With Parents in Early Childhood Education*, The Macmillan Co., New York, 1954, 330 pp.

Discusses the means of executing a guidance program with parents of kindergarten and elementary school children.

Low, Camilla M., "What Principles of Learning Imply for Guidance," N.E.A. *Journal*, Vol. 44 (January, 1955), pp. 18–20.

Discusses means by which the teacher may incorporate guidance in the classroom teaching.

Personnel and Guidance Journal, published September through May by the American Personnel and Guidance Association, 1534 "O" Street, N. W., Washington, D. C.

Roemer, Joseph, and Hoover, Oliver, *The Dean of Boys in High School: His Qualifications and Functions*, American Book Co., New York, 1939, 94 pp.

Discusses the work of this relatively new employee of the schools.

Smith, Glenn E., *Counseling in the Secondary School*, The Macmillan Co., New York, 1955, 364 pp.

Discusses counseling as the central service of the guidance program.

Traxler, Arthur E., *Techniques of Guidance*, Harper and Brothers, New York, 1952, 288 pp.

Techniques of guidance in the secondary school are emphasized.

Wright, Barbara H., *Practical Handbook for Group Guidance*, Science Research Associates, Chicago, 1948, 225 pp.

Discusses the place of group guidance in the over-all guidance program.

CHAPTER 11

Pupil Classification and Progress

Individual Instruction Versus Group Instruction

Importance of Proper Classification and Progress of Pupils. Chapter 7 of this book pointed out that in their interests, abilities, accomplishments, and needs, pupils differ widely. Even in what is usually considered to be a well-grouped class in any school subject, large differences among the pupils will be found. In an arithmetic class, for example, some pupils will be found who add, subtract, multiply, divide, or perform other operations several times as quickly, many times as accurately, or both, as the average pupils of the class, or as the slowest pupils of the class.

These differences among pupils are coming to be recognized more and more by educational employees and by the general public, and attempts are being made everywhere to meet them. In fact, no recent movement in education has been more prominent than the attempt to break up the traditional lock step in the school and to meet, as far as possible, the interests, the abilities, and the needs of the individual pupil. The modern school is trying to adjust itself to the pupil rather than trying to require the pupil to adjust himself to it. This movement is commendatory, because any failure of the school to make needed adjustments to pupil differences is likely to result in dire consequences to the pupil and to society.

Although most schools should go much farther in adjusting themselves to the interests of their pupils, schools could, of course, go too far in making these adjustments. The interests of a pupil should not be worshipped to the extent of promoting a lopsided development in him. For the welfare of the pupil and of society the school often has the obligation of trying to make the pupil more like his fellows, and to do this it will occasionally be called upon to stifle interests. Many interests are worthless, some are even vicious, and all such should be eliminated, or more worthy ones substituted for them.

In attempting to meet the varying interests and the varying abilities of pupils and to enable each pupil to progress at the rate which his ability dictates, numerous teaching procedures and types of pupil classification and promotion have been used by the schools. Dozens of those procedures and plans are in extensive use today, and all of them have as their fundamental objective the meeting of the needs of the individual pupil as far as possible. Probably the best procedures and the best plans—best for every situation—have not yet been developed. Most of the earlier procedures and plans were designed primarily to help the duller pupils, and practically all of them neglected the brighter pupils. During recent years, however, special provision has been made for the brighter pupils as well as for the duller.

To neglect to meet the needs of any group of pupils would be unfortunate, but to neglect to meet the needs of the brighter pupils would be particularly unfortunate, because society must look to those pupils, when they become adults, for the greatest contributions. Nearly all slower pupils can be taught to make a considerable contribution to society, but the brighter pupils will provide society with its distinguished statesmen, its eminent artists, its great educators, its famous inventors, and its leaders in other worthy activities of life.

EVOLUTION OF GROUP INSTRUCTION OF PUPILS. The earliest schools used individual instruction, not group instruction. Although the pupils of the early schools were generally classified into groups according to their ability, especially ability in reading, each pupil recited individually and was given an individual assignment. This method of instruction had been copied from the home, where with meager equipment each child was taught as an individual. The late Professor Samuel Chester Parker said of this early method of individual instruction:

They (the pupils) were generally roughly classified into three groups according to their reading ability, but each pupil in a group was taught in the same way as if he had been alone. In the lowest class were those who were just learning their letters and syllables and could puzzle out a few words by spelling them; in the second class, those who could read somewhat without spelling the words, using the primer; and in the highest class, the more expert who read in the Bible. Very little of the teacher's activity was actual instruction; it was simply hearing recitations. Giving of information by the teacher or inductive discussions with groups of children were almost unheard of.[1]

The practice just described continued until the end of the eighteenth century. About the latter date the giving of instruction to a whole class of children, that is, group instruction, came into

FIG. 36. Old-time method of individual instruction. The bunch of switches on the table indicates that the old-time schools did not "spare the rod." (*From Samuel Chester Parker,* A Textbook in the History of Modern Elementary Education, *p. 101.*)

vogue and has been since used. Although Comenius in his work titled the *Great Didactic* (published in Latin in 1657) had recommended the substitution of group instruction for individual instruction, Jean Baptiste de La Salle, a French nobleman, must receive

[1] Samuel Chester Parker, *A Textbook in the History of Modern Elementary Education,* Ginn, 1912, p. 90. By permission of Ginn and Company, publishers.

special credit for the introduction of group instruction into the schools on a large scale. La Salle accomplished his work primarily through an organization known as the Brethren of the Christian Schools, which was an association of Catholic laymen organized by him in 1684 to instruct poor children in the elementary schools.[2]

Both types of instruction—group and individual—have always had their proponents, and these proponents have caused the pendulum of practice to swing from one direction to the opposite. The pendulum is now swinging back toward individual instruction as a means of breaking up the lock step which came with group instruction. Just where school practice should try to bring the pendulum to rest between the two extremes is still a controversial question. Most educators agree, however, that instruction should be partly group and partly individual. The usual advantages claimed for each plan of instruction have been well summarized by Clapp, Chase, and Merriman in the following words:

A. *Advantages of Individual Instruction*
   1. It permits the slow child to go at his own rate and thus get better and more thorough results.
   2. It prevents the child from overestimating his progress.
   3. It concentrates the attention upon the work of individuals rather than upon the average work of the class.
   4. It allows the more gifted to go ahead and use his extra power upon the work of his own choice. It thus prevents him from falling into habits of idleness.
   5. It permits the teacher to catch little glimpses of the child's interests and possible vocational tendencies.
   6. It gives the teacher an opportunity to develop diagnostic skill in ascertaining just how a child's mind works as it finds its way through a problem.

B. *Advantages of Group Instruction*
   1. It makes better provision for the social aspects of education, because there is opportunity for co-operation, speech, social, and political participation.
   2. It assists in motivation, because it appeals to the desire for the good opinion of others, and to the interest in group-discovered problems.
   3. It is economical, because it saves duplicate preparation and explanation.
   4. It permits the slow learner to get something from the more rapid learner.

[2] J. W. Adamson, *Pioneers of Modern Education*, 1600–1700, Cambridge University Press, 1905, Ch. 12.

5. It also enables the fast learner to learn his material better through the experience of explaining it to the slower pupil.
6. It reduces the amount of preparation that the teacher must make for her daily work and simplifies the problem of management and discipline.[3]

New Plans for Pupil Classification and Pupil Progress

Some of the new plans of attempting to meet the needs of the individual pupil involve school-administrative adjustments, such as breaking up the traditional class organization to permit individual work with the pupils. Other plans are based upon changes in the teaching procedures, such as differentiated assignments. In a nation-wide survey, several years ago, of the plans used in the secondary schools to meet individual differences, Roy O. Billett found that all such plans then in use "may be classified under seven categories, namely, (1) homogeneous grouping, (2) special classes, (3) plans characterized by the unit assignment, (4) scientific study of problem cases, (5) variation in pupil load, (6) out-of-school projects and studies, and (7) advisory or guidance programs." [4] Although Billett's survey did not include the elementary school, casual observation indicated that most, if not all, teachers' plans of the elementary school could have been classified also under the seven categories just named; those conditions still largely exist.

Since, according to Billett, the first three plans, that is, (1) homogeneous grouping, (2) special classes, and (3) the unit assignment, then were used most frequently and "have been found to be core elements in a typically successful program to provide for individual differences," [5] those three plans will be emphasized in the discussion which follows, since they are still frequently used in the elementary and secondary schools. Billett characterized these plans as "a kind of trinity, a sort of three-in-one answer of the nation's outstanding schools to the problem of providing for individual differences." [6] He said further that the plans should be regarded as complementary rather than as alternative procedures.

[3] Clapp, Chase, and Merriman, *Introduction to Education*, Ginn, 1929, pp. 466–467. By permission of Ginn and Company, publishers.
[4] Roy O. Billett, in *National Survey of Secondary Education*, Vol. 13, p. 415.
[5] *Ibid.*, p. 11.
[6] *Ibid.*

Before describing a few of the most widely used of these new plans for the classification and the promotion of pupils, attention will be directed to the criteria which such a plan should meet. The following criteria should be kept in mind in selecting a plan for a particular school:

1. As far as possible, the plan should meet the needs of all pupils from the highest to the lowest level of intelligence found in the school. It should adapt the teaching procedures and the curriculum to each pupil, and should, as far as possible, enable each pupil to progress at his own rate and to be promoted when he is ready for promotion.
2. The plan should be financially practicable. It must meet that criterion because the public has only a limited amount of money which must be spent to meet the needs of the largest number of pupils possible. Although educators might dream that it would be ideal to have a teacher for each pupil, instead of giving twenty-five, thirty, or another large number of pupils to each teacher, a pupil-teacher ratio of one to one would be utterly unattainable because of the large expense to the public which such a ratio would entail.
3. The plan should be administratively and pedagogically feasible. It should not require an undue amount of school machinery for its operation. It should not be a "teacher killer."

Homogeneous and Ability Grouping of Pupils. The practice of grouping pupils for instructional purposes is almost as old as the school, and usually the basis for grouping has been pupil ability. The tendency has always been toward more refined methods of classifying pupils for instructional purposes, that is, toward greater homogeneity of grouping. Of course, complete homogeneity in pupil classification would be impossible to attain because of the wide differences which exist even between any two pupils; the only really homogeneous group would consist of but one pupil. In the strict sense of the term, therefore, homogeneous grouping can only mean reduced heterogeneous grouping.

Contrary to common belief, homogeneous grouping and ability grouping are not synonymous, because homogeneous grouping may be effected on many other bases than pupil ability, and it is their synonymous use which often leads to confusion. Schools are using one or more of the following criteria or bases, or a combination of them, to group pupils on ability:

1. Mental age of pupil.
2. Intelligence quotient or intelligence percentile of pupil.
3. Average scholarship marks of pupil in all school subjects combined.

4. Average scholarship marks of pupil in one school subject or in several related school subjects.
5. Score of pupil on an achievement test.
6. Achievement quotient of pupil.
7. Teacher's rating of pupil's ability.
8. Average of several teachers' ratings of pupil's ability.
9. Score of pupil on a prognostic test.
10. Health and physical maturity of pupil.
11. Social maturity of pupil.

Experimentation has not yet determined what basis or what combination of bases is the most satisfactory for the grouping of pupils. There is a general belief, though, that a combination of bases is better than one basis, and that the bases used in the combination should be determined by varying conditions, such as the age of the pupil, the grade, and the school subject. Although the tendency is toward more ability grouping of pupils, there is much difference of opinion over the merit of the tendency.

FIG. 37. Ability grouping by a teacher. *(Courtesy of the South Glens Falls, New York, public schools.)*

The chief criticism which is made of ability grouping is that it is undemocratic to recognize and to provide for individual differences through such grouping. Many persons claim that to recognize superiority complexes, will give the dull pupils inferiority complexes, and will beget social cleavages in a democratic society. In answer to this criticism, the proponents of ability grouping affirm that the plan is democratic, because it attempts to meet the needs, the interests, and the abilities of the individual pupil; any other practice, they claim, would not be democratic. It should also be pointed out that some of the argument against ability grouping stems from a confusion of equal opportunity and same opportunity. To be equal, opportunities need not be the same.

Ability grouping can, of course, be more readily used in schools which have enough pupils in each school subject or each grade to organize two or more sections. The organization of more than one section for a grade or a school subject in a small school, say, of fifteen or twenty pupils only in the grade or school subject, would usually be impossible, because of the large expense of maintaining small classes. If a school has enough pupils in a grade or school subject to organize two or more sections, ability grouping may be readily effected. Thus, if thirty pupils were the average size of the classes, sixty pupils in a grade or a school subject would permit the organization of two sections. Of course, the number of sections which could be feasibly organized would be determined by the total number of pupils in a grade or a school subject.

In grouping pupils on an ability basis most schools have limited the number of groups to three—bright, average, and dull. A few of the larger secondary schools, however, have organized as many as ten groups. A certain school comes to mind, for example, which has three hundred pupils enrolled in ninth-grade English; these 300 pupils are instructed in ten groups of approximately thirty pupils each. In determining the group into which each pupil shall be placed the school gives standardized English tests to the pupils. The thirty pupils who make the best scores on these tests are placed in section one; the thirty pupils who make the next best scores are placed in section two; and the pupils for the remaining eight sections are grouped on a similar basis. This school classifies its pupils on the basis of special abilities and special accomplishments in the various school subjects; it uses subject-matter tests to ascertain those accomplishments and those abilities in each school subject.

Although the school in which he is teaching may not be able or may not be inclined to practice ability grouping as described above, the teacher can do his own grouping, if the rules of the school do not prevent, which they usually do not. In fact, he could regroup his pupils on a more ability basis, even though they had been sent to him on an approximate ability basis. Although he may have received the thirty brightest pupils in any grade or school subject, they will have varying abilities, and for instructional purposes they might be divided into two or more groups. Elementary school classes often are subdivided by the teacher for reading instruction, on the basis of reading ability, and may be separately subdivided for arithmetic instruction, on the basis of arithmetic ability. All classes in any subject, and in any division of the school may be thus subdivided. Many teachers have regrouped their pupils, and all of them report excellent results for the pupils. They admit that to have two or more groups, instead of one group, results in more work for the teacher, but they insist that the benefits to the pupils clearly outweigh the extra time and the extra energy required of the teacher.

Differentiation of teaching procedures for pupil groups of varying abilities has occurred more frequently than differentiation of subject matter for those groups. Both types of differentiation should be practiced, if the needs of the pupils are to be met. On the curriculum side this will mean variations in the kind and the amount of subject matter to meet the needs of each group; better still, it will mean meeting in every feasible manner the subject-matter needs of each pupil in the group.

Special Classes for Pupils. Many schools and school systems, especially the larger ones, have organized special classes into which exceptional or atypical pupils are placed. Three large groups of exceptional or atypical children are recognized; those groups are (1) the mentally exceptional (bright and dull), (2) the physically handicapped (defective in sight, hearing or speech, crippled, tuberculous, etc.), and (3) the socially handicapped (truants, delinquents, etc.).

Since such classes are more expensive than classes for normal pupils, many states give special financial aid to school systems that provide those special classes. For such classes, teachers of special preparation are required, and persons who desire to obtain that preparation will usually find opportunities for employment at salaries above the average; such teachers are more scarce, hence higher salaries are paid to obtain them.

The largest number of special classes has been organized for the mentally exceptional pupils. As a rule, special classes have been organized for the duller pupils only, but a few schools and school systems have also organized them for the brighter pupils. In such classes, pupils of various grades are found, and a large amount of individual teaching is given the pupils in these classes.

Pupils who have failed, or who are in danger of failing, are sent to these special classes with the hope that individual instruction will enable them to return to their regular classes within a short time. In the case of the brighter pupils, the hope is that individual attention will make it possible to promote them to the next grade as soon as possible, or that they will be given work which is better suited to their interests and their abilities.

As with most of the newer plans of pupil classification and promotion which are in use today, as with special classes better—at least differently—qualified teachers are necessary than in schools which use traditional plans of pupil classification and promotion. In special classes, the teacher may have pupils enrolled in each of the grades from the first to the eighth; moreover, he will be responsible for teaching all of the subjects in these grades. The teacher of such a class frequently has almost the replica of the one-teacher school in which one teacher must instruct pupils in all grades and all school subjects; in fact, the teacher of the special class has an even more difficult task than the teacher in the one-room rural school, because all his pupils are atypical and each pupil presents an unusual problem for the teacher.

Units and Unit-assignment Plans for Pupils. There are several teaching plans, procedures, or techniques which have as their chief characteristic the use of the unit and the unit assignment. These plans, procedures, or techniques are known variously as the project method, problem method, individualized instruction, contract plan, laboratory plan, differentiated assignments, Winnetka plan, Dalton plan, Morrison plan, subject-matter unit, and experience unit.

The earliest used of these terms was the project method which was first applied to agricultural teaching. It was next applied to home economics and to industrial arts, and in many cases, attempts have been made to make the term include all phases of the curriculum. Many teachers believe that the term project method lacks sufficient comprehensiveness, and they recommend the use of the term unit, because of its greater comprehensiveness.

Since the terms unit and unit assignment are so frequently used in pedagogical literature to express a variety of meanings, it seems worth while to define the terms. Billett's definitions are as follows:

> The unit is regarded in this study as a concept, attitude, appreciation, knowledge, or skill to be acquired by the pupil, which, if acquired, will produce a desirable modification of his thinking or other forms of his behavior. The unit assignment consists of those activities and experiences planned by the teacher to enable the pupil to master the unit.[7]

Billett's definitions, however, do not represent current thought as to "unit of work," at least for the elementary school. The traditional assign-study-recite-test formula has been superseded in modern schools by (1) subject units and (2) experience units. Burton gives the following definitions of those units:

> A subject-matter unit is a selection of subject-matter materials, and of educative experiences centering upon subject-matter materials, which are arranged around a central core found within the subject matter itself. The core may be a generalization, a topic, or a theme. The unit is to be studied by pupils for the purpose of achieving learning outcomes derivable from experiences with subject matter.
>
> An experience unit is a series of educative experiences organized around a pupil purpose, problem or need, utilizing socially useful subject matter and materials, and resulting in the achievement of the purpose (solution of the problem or satisfaction of the need) and in the achievement of learning outcomes inherent in the process.[8]

MORE FREQUENT PROMOTIONS FOR PUPILS. In the early schools, promotions were always made only annually. It was found, however, that annual promotions frequently handicapped the pupil by not permitting him to advance at his own rate, so more frequent promotions were used in the large school systems. The trend at present, however, is toward annual promotions or to a flexible, irregular plan, wherever changes are made.[9]

A shorter promotion interval assists the pupil who fails a school subject or a grade, because failure is often the result of not taking an examination, of missing school for a few days or a few weeks, or of not doing the work of a small portion of the school year. Under

[7] Billett, *loc. cit.*

[8] William H. Burton, *The Guidance of Learning Activities,* Second edition, pp. 390–391. Copyright 1952 by Appleton-Century-Crofts.

[9] Henry J. Otto, *Elementary School Organization and Administration,* Third edition, p. 271.

annual promotions a failed pupil is often required to repeat the work of the whole school year, even though practically all of the work has been successfully completed. Under more frequent promotions, on the other hand, the pupil is required to repeat only six weeks, the quarter, or the semester in which his school deficiency is found. Small schools have always found it difficult not to use annual promotions because of their inability to organize classes for more than one section in a grade or a school subject.

Double and Special Promotions for Pupils. In order that the needs of the especially bright pupils may be more readily met, many schools permit such pupils to skip a certain grade. For example, if a pupil is unusually proficient in the work of the fifth grade, he is permitted to skip the sixth grade; that is, he is promoted at the end of the fifth grade to the seventh grade. Most schools which permit double promotions require evidence, of course, that the pupil is competent in the subject matter of the grade or school subject which is skipped.

Other schools do not wait until the close of the semester, the school year, or other promotion period to promote the especially competent pupils. They promote such pupils as soon as the pupils are qualified to do the work of the next grade. For example, if after a few days of school a pupil shows that the work of his present grade is too easy for him, he is promoted immediately to the next grade. In such instances, though, as in double promotions, most schools require evidence that the specially-promoted pupils will not miss any of the vital work of the grade for which they are to be promoted.

Trial Promotions for Pupils. Many schools promote on trial, or they "condition" the pupils who have failed. If these pupils make good in the work of the next grade or school subject, they are retained. If they do not make good, they are returned to the school subject or grade from which they came, or some other arrangement is made for them. That trial promotions for pupils who have failed are efficacious is seen from the fact that most of such pupils successfully perform the work of the grade or school subject to which they are promoted. In pupil progress, "nothing succeeds like success."

Most schools have used trial promotions chiefly with pupils who have failed. Such a plan, though, could be provided for the especially competent pupils as well as for the failures. The especially competent pupils could be promoted at any time, with the proviso that if they made good, they would remain in the work of the school subject or grade, but if they did not do the work successfully, they would be returned to their previous classification in the school.

Subject Promotions for Pupils. Pupils frequently fail in one school subject, but pass their other school subjects. Pupils are often deficient in one or more of their school subjects, but they are average, or above average, in their other school subjects. Although psychologists have found that pupils who rate high in one special ability usually rate high in all other abilities, they have found that there are many exceptions to that rule. In consequence, teachers should keep in mind special abilities as well as general abilities when they are classifying pupils. Pupils who have passed one school subject, but have failed every other school subject, should not have to repeat the school subject passed. Promotion by school subjects makes possible the carrying out of the recommendation just made.

Most of the city schools now promote by school subjects, especially in the upper grades of the elementary school and in all the grades of the secondary school. Promotion by school subjects is, however, possible in the smaller schools; in fact, it is possible even in the one-teacher school. Many educators, however, oppose promotion by school subjects because it involves departmental teaching which makes it difficult for the teacher to become acquainted with the large number of pupils which he has.

Summer School for Pupils. Many schools, especially those of the cities, provide classes during the summer months for pupils who desire to spend their vacation in school. Such classes usually run for only a portion of the summer vacation, for example, from three to six weeks. They enable pupils who have failed or have been "conditioned" in a grade or school subject to remove the failure or the "condition" and to enter school at the beginning of the regular term with their particular class. Moreover, they make it possible for the normal or the bright pupils to complete the regular school course of study in less than the usual amount of time.

Decreasing Pupil Failure and Stimulating Scholarship

Results of Failure for Pupils and for Society. Failure results in a loss both to the pupil and to society. The largest loss from failure comes to the pupil. Failure usually means that the pupil must repeat the work of the school subject or of the grade failed. It means that the pupil becomes retarded, usually resulting in his becoming a member of a class of pupils younger than he; this causes a form of maladjustment in the pupil's school life. Worst of all, failure results in the pupil being branded as a failure by his schoolmates, his relatives, and his friends. Failure incurs the risk that the pupil will develop an inferiority complex and will acquire a grudge against the school and against society. When a pupil fails school, there is danger that he is being prepared for failure in later life.

A loss to society also results from pupil failure. A part of this loss may be measured in financial terms. It cannot be concluded, however, that when a pupil fails, the money which was spent on him is entirely wasted. Persons who affirm that the money is entirely wasted assume that the pupil who has failed will repeat the work of the school subject or the grade failed, thus requiring a double expenditure for him. Regarded from another point of view, it is cheaper to fail pupils than to promote them, because when a pupil is promoted, he enters a subject or a grade which is more expensive than the preceding subject or grade; thus, secondary school education is more expensive than elementary school education, and the upper grades of the elementary school are more expensive than the lower grades of the elementary school. Failure does cause a real waste in preventing pupils from completing their schooling in the normal number of years, but if the compulsory school-attendance laws require all pupils to remain in school until the ages of fourteen, fifteen, sixteen, or some other number of years, failure has no effect on the school budget.

Amount and Incidence of Failure of Pupils. The amount of pupil failure varies from school subject to school subject, from teacher to teacher, from grade to grade, from school to school, and from school system to school system. The first year of the elementary school, the first year of the secondary school, and the first year of the college show a much larger percentage of failure than any other school year. Certain school subjects show a much larger percentage of pupil mortality than others. Certain teachers consistently fail a much larger percentage of pupils than other teachers. Certain schools and school systems fail a much larger percentage of pupils than other schools and school systems.

Reducing and Controlling Failure of Pupils. The school should do everything possible to prevent pupil failure. In attempting to prevent failure, the first step to take is to ascertain the cause or the causes of failure. The cause or causes which operate in one pupil's case may be entirely different from the cause or causes operating in another pupil's case; these causes follow no pattern. Hundreds of possible factors operate to cause pupils to fail. Among the more frequent and the more potent of these factors are the following: lack of interest or of ability on the part of the pupil, poor teaching methods, too much home work, or too many outside activities on the part of the pupil, his poor health, his absence from school, and educational programs inadequate for modern living. Most of these causes need to be further analyzed by the teacher, if failure is to be dealt with intelligently. Further analysis might show that irregular school attendance was causing a pupil to fail, but that such attendance might be the result of one or more factors, such as too great distance of the pupil from school, poor health of the pupil, and his being required to remain at home to work.

In attempting to reduce the amount of or to eliminate pupil failure, the teacher should become a student of the individual pupil. When a pupil starts to fall behind in his school work, the teacher should do something about it then and there. The teacher is in a key position to ascertain the reason or the reasons for the pupil not doing his school work. He should make a case study of the pupil; in such study, a conference or conferences with the pupil and his parents may be found necessary or advisable. Through this procedure, many pupils who would otherwise have failed may be kept from failing. Such attention to failing pupils will, of course, require extra time and extra thought on the part of the teacher, but awareness of its contributions to the life happiness and the life accomplishment of the pupil should be sufficient reward to the teacher for his extra time and extra thought.

As was reported in an earlier section of this chapter, many schools are promoting pupils to the next school subject or the next grade on trial, instead of failing them outright. According to this arrangement, pupils who have failed are given a few weeks, usually from two to six weeks, to attempt to do the work of the subject or the grade to which they would normally be promoted. If the pupil does the work satisfactorily enough to justify his remaining, he is retained. If he does not do the work, he is returned to the school subject or the grade from which he came. Giving pupils another chance usually brings out the best in them, because most of the pupils who are promoted on trial make good in the work of the next school subject or the next grade. Giving the failing pupil the benefit of the doubt and an opportunity to make good brings out the best in him, but requiring him to repeat the work of a school subject or a grade has the opposite result, because many studies have shown that a large proportion of the pupils who are required to repeat a school subject or a grade do not do better work than the first time that they were enrolled in the school subject or grade. In fact, many repeaters do even poorer work the second time than the first time.

Some teachers fail a much larger percentage of their pupils than other teachers. They seem to consider that it is their prerogative, if not their duty, to fail one-fourth, one-third, one-half, or another large proportion of their pupils. Probably many of these teachers have never reflected upon the losses resulting from pupil failure, or they believe that the only way by which they can maintain their standards is through proscribing a large percentage of their pupils; to some teachers a high percentage of pupil mortality is the best evidence of high standards of scholarship on the part of those teachers.

Many teachers use the normal probability curve as a check upon the percentage of pupil failures and the quality of the marks given to pupils. According to the theory underlying the normal probability curve, in a nonselected group of one hundred or more pupils it would be expected that approximately five per cent of the pupils would receive the grade of E or failure; about twenty per cent, D; about fifty per cent, C; about twenty per cent, B; and about five per cent, A. These are arbitrary percentages, and it is not recommended that the normal probability curve be ever followed slavishly, but only as a check on marking practice. If a teacher finds that year after year he has been failing ten, fifteen, twenty, or a larger percentage of his pupils, he should raise for himself the question of whether his marking system is too rigid. On the other hand, if he finds that year after year he has been giving ten, fifteen, twenty, or a larger percentage of A's, he might appropriately raise for himself the question of whether he has been too charitable in giving pupil marks. Many schools request each teacher to make a percentage distribution of his pupil marks at the close of each reporting period. In many schools

FIG. 38. Teachers are not expandable. (*Courtesy of* Better Schools.) The teacher sometimes believes that he is expected to be expandable and turn out graduates in assembly-line fashion, but he doesn't really believe that such procedures are best for the student.

the principal of the school reports to the various teachers the percentages of marks of each kind given by each teacher. In such a report, the names of the teachers are not indicated, so that any embarrassment to the teachers will be avoided.

STIMULATING SCHOLARSHIP OF PUPILS. To reduce or to eliminate pupil failure is only one of the tasks of the teacher, so far as maintaining scholarship, that is, a high quality of learning, is concerned. Many pupils do not do all that they could do and should do. One of the most important aims of the teacher should be to stimulate a high standard of scholarship on the part of the pupils. Such standards are particularly important in the secondary school, the college, and the university, but they cannot be neglected in the foundation period of the pupil's school career; this foundation period is, of course, the elementary school years. Pupils should be stimulated to do the best work of which they are capable, and they should be encouraged to have respect for scholarship in every field of learning; they should be aided by their teachers in developing an abiding interest in scholarship.

The best way in which scholarship may be stimulated among the pupils is for the teacher to be scholarly. The example of the teacher is always potent. If the teacher has careless habits of scholarship—in brief, if he is unscholarly—the pupils are not likely to advance beyond his level. On the other hand, if the teacher has high standards of scholarship—if he "lives and breathes" scholarship—the pupils are likely to be raised to his level. Scholarship is contagious, and for that reason all teachers should live and breathe it.

Another important way of stimulating scholarship among his pupils is for the teacher to recognize and to reward it. When a pupil does his school work especially well, the teacher should congratulate him upon his accomplishment. On the other hand, when the pupil turns in "sloppy" work, the teacher should show his displeasure, particularly if the student is competent to do much better work. The present writer recalls his teaching experience with pupils in all school grades from the elementary school through the graduate school of the university, and he also recalls that pupils can do better work, if it is required of them. The following statements describe other means which various schools have successfully used in encouraging a higher standard of scholarship on the part of pupils:

1. By sending letters or notices to parents or guardians informing them of a very low quality or of a very high quality of work of their children.
2. By publishing the names of pupils having high marks in the school paper, magazine, handbook, yearbook, or public newspaper.
3. By mentioning at the graduation, or similar school exercises, the names of those pupils who have done a high quality of work.
4. By posting the names of honor pupils on the bulletin board of the school.
5. By awarding scholarship pins or other insignia, and by granting prizes for high scholarship.
6. By awarding scholarships in higher institutions of learning to pupils with excellent scholastic records.
7. By awarding the valedictory and the salutatory orations to the two pupils respectively who have the highest scholarship.
8. By organizing and fostering honor societies, such as the Phi Beta Sigma Society, the Pro Merito Society, the Cum Laude Society, and the National Honor Society for Secondary Schools. All of these are secondary school societies, and their general aims are to stimulate

scholarship and a desire to render service, to promote leadership, and to develop character in the students. And there is the renowned Phi Beta Kappa for college students.

9. By organizing city, county, district, or state scholarship contests.
10. By giving extra credit for a high quality of school work and less credit for a poor quality of school work.
11. By permitting pupils who have excellent marks to take extra school work and thus to cut down the time required for graduation.
12. By exempting from examinations those pupils who maintain a high standard of scholarship.
13. By requiring certain scholastic standards for eligibility to compete in interschool athletic contests and in other extraclass activities.

Of course, many teachers oppose such stimuli, because they claim that they are artificial; they believe that the only stimulus needed for learning is the interest of the pupil in his school work. They affirm that competition is not the only sound motivation for learning, if indeed it is the most important motivation; perhaps, it is not.

The Holding Power of the School

Amount of Pupil Elimination from the School. The measure of the "holding power" of a school is the extent to which the school retains its pupils until they have finished the course of study, or until the pupils are transferred to another school, have died, or have become physically incapacitated further to attend school. Thus, if a given school keeps all its pupils until they have met the conditions just mentioned, whereas another school keeps only fifty per cent of its pupils, the former school has twice the holding power of the latter school. The holding power of schools and school systems varies widely; it varies from teacher to teacher, from school to school, from school system to school system, and from state to state. A glance again at Table 2, page 24, will show how the states differ in their holding power. No state failed to increase its holding power between the U. S. Censuses of 1940 and 1950, and it is here predicted that the same record will be found for every state in the U. S. Census of 1960.

One of the most significant educational facts of recent years has been the large increase in the holding power of the schools. As the years have gone by, the people of the United States have more and more believed that education is the greatest single lever to opportunity and an open-sesame through which the individual may best realize his potentialities. In 1870, only 57 per cent of the children between the ages of five and seventeen years of age, inclusive, were enrolled in school; at present, that percentage is approximately 85. The holding power of the secondary school has increased especially rapidly. In 1870, only 1.2 per cent of the pupils enrolled in the elementary and the secondary schools were enrolled in the secondary schools; at present, the percentage of secondary-school pupils is more than 28. A large part of these increases has been due to the enactment of more rigid compulsory school-attendance laws, and to a more efficient enforcement of those laws, but a large part of the increase has been the result of the advent of better schools and the desire of pupils to attend those schools. The typical resident of the United States now receives some secondary school education, and that amount is constantly increasing.

Increasing the Holding Power of the School. To keep all the pupils in school until the compulsory school-attendance laws are satisfied is, of course, a legal necessity in all states. In most states, though, the mere satisfying of the requirements of the compulsory school-attendance laws does not provide much more than the rudiments of an education. The extent to which pupils remain in school after those legal requirements have been met is another excellent measure of the holding power of a school, because when the state law no longer requires the pupil to be in school, the pupil decides whether he shall remain in or leave school. Pupils who leave school as soon as the compulsory school-attendance laws permit are called dropouts. Two factors usually determine whether the pupil will remain in or leave school. The first of these factors is the interest which the pupil has in school, and the second is the economic status of the pupil and his parents.

Over the second of these factors school officials and school employees can exert little or no immediate influence. Over the first factor, though, they can exert considerable influence. They can maintain a school which will challenge the interest of the pupils. They can take steps to show the pupils the advantages of an education and the opportunities afforded by the local school or school system. In brief, as was stated in Chapter 10, the school can provide proper educational guidance for the pupils, and it is generally agreed that the best educational guidance which can be given most pupils is to encourage them, through providing school activities which they enjoy and respect, to remain in school as long as practicable. The amount of time which should be spent in school beyond the limits of the compulsory school-attendance laws will depend on the individual pupil and will be determined by such factors as the economic conditions of the pupil and his parents, the pupil's opportunities for employment, and the intelligence and the age of the pupil. The school cannot expect to keep its pupils forever, but it must try to increase its present holding power.

The Age-Grade Progress of Pupils

Making and Using an Age-Grade-Progress Table for a School. An age-grade-progress table shows the progress of pupils through the school. Figure 39 is an example of an age-grade-progress report. This particular report was made by the teacher at the beginning of the school year in September for his 2-B grade. Of the twenty-nine pupils in this grade, eighteen had made normal progress; that is, they had completed the school work of the first grade in normal time, namely, one school year; seven pupils, on the other hand, had been in the first grade one and a half school years, and four members of the grade had been in school two school years. Those pupils who have not done the work of the previous grade in a normal amount of time are said to be retarded; thus, eleven pupils in this particular grade were retarded; seven of them were retarded one-half school year, and four were retarded one school year. A pupil who does the work of a semester or a school year in less than the normal amount of time is said to be accelerated; it so happens that in this particular grade no pupil was accelerated.

Such a form as is exhibited in Figure 39 shows the number of school years which the pupils have spent in school, and it also shows the ages of the various pupils. Such a table requires only a few minutes of time to make, and its value is large in giving the teacher further acquaintance with his pupils. Moreover, when such data have been collected by principals, superintendents, or other school employees and have been summarized, a bird's eye-view may be had of the progress of pupils through a given grade, a given school, or the school system.

Retardation Versus Acceleration of Pupils. Definitions of retarded and of accelerated pupils have been given in a preceding

DISTRIBUTION OF PUPILS BY AGE AND BY NUMBER OF YEARS IN SCHOOL

School ____Garfield____ Grade __2B__ Date __Sept. 12, 1956__

Ages	Years in School																			Total
	0	½	1	1½	2	2½	3	3½	4	4½	5	5½	6	6½	7	7½		15	15½	
4																				
4½ 5																				
5½ 6			1																	1
6½ 7			15	4																19
7½ 8				3																3
8½ 9			2		4															6
9½ 10																				
10½ 11																				
11½ 20																				
20½ 21																				
Total			18	7	4															29

The above report is correct to the best of my knowledge.

(Signed) ____Florence J. Bode____
Teacher

FIG. 39. A teacher's sample age-grade-progress report.

paragraph. Warning should here be given, lest retardation be confused with overageness, and lest acceleration be confused with underageness; the terms are not synonymous, nor are the causes the same. The cause of retardation is always pupil failure, whereas the cause of overageness may be either pupil failure or late entrance into school or both. An overage pupil is not necessarily a retarded pupil; an overage pupil may not have entered school until the age of eight, nine, or later, but he may have made normal or even accelerated progress after entering. Likewise, the only cause of acceleration is double promotions, or the operation of other factors, which have enabled the pupil to complete the work of a given grade or grades in less than the normal amount of time. The chief cause of acceleration is double promotions.

Just as there are many times as much overageness as underageness, so there are many times as much retardation as acceleration. An ideal distribution curve for all children of school age would show a normal distribution. Hence, one would expect to find as many cases of acceleration as of retardation. The existing conditions in the schools do not follow this normal distribution.

The conclusions which have just been stated indicate that the schools are not meeting sufficiently the needs of the brighter pupils. Pupils who do not do the school work are failed; thus, they automatically become retarded. On the other hand, pupils who would be able to do the school work of one school year in a half year, or the work of two school years in one year, are not being provided with such opportunity.

The Age-Grade Status of Pupils

Making and Using an Age-Grade Table for the Pupils. An age-grade table shows the number of pupils of each of the various grades of a school or a school system. Such a table shows, for example, how many pupils of each of the various ages are in the kindergarten, in the first grade, and in each of the other grades of a school or a school system. Table 5 is an age-grade table for a certain school system. From that table, it is observed that of the three pupils who are four and one-half years of age, one is in section B of the kindergarten, one is in section A of the kindergarten, and the third is in section B of the first grade. Of the ten pupils who are five years of age, three are in section B of the kindergarten, two are in section A of the kindergarten, four are in section B of the first grade, and one is in section A of the first grade. In the column showing the twelve-year-olds, it is observed that there is one pupil in section B of the second grade, one is in section A of the third grade, two are in section A of the fourth grade, two are in section B of the fifth grade, three are in section A of the fifth grade, five are in section B of the sixth grade, ten are in section A of the sixth grade, six are in section B of the seventh grade, and one is in section A of the seventh grade.

TABLE 5. AGE-GRADE TABLE OF A SYSTEM OF SCHOOLS OF A CERTAIN CITY, DECEMBER 31, 1956. AGES COMPUTED AS OF SEPTEMBER 1, 1956.

GRADE:	KG.		1ST		2ND		3RD		4TH		5TH		6TH		7TH		8TH		9TH		10TH		11TH		12TH		
SEC.:	(B	A)	(B	A)	(B	A)	(B	A)	(B	A)	(B	A)	(B	A)	(B	A)	(B	A)	(B	A)	(B	A)	(B	A)	(B	A)	Total
Ages[a]																											
4½	1	1	1																								3
5	3	2	4	1																							10
5½	6	4	5	3																							18
6	3	3	15	6	1	1																					29
6½	.	3	17	12	3	2	1																				38
7	1	1	9	12	8	3	1	1																			36
7½			3	6	12	9	4	3	1																		38
8			2	6	9	11	12	2	3	1																	46
8½			1	5	2	5	10	7	3	2																	35
9				3	3	4	5	12	8	3	3	1															42
9½				1	2	2	5	3	14	8	3	1															39
10				1	2	1	3	5	6	13	4	3	1														39
10½						2	1	3	2	5	12	7	2			1											35
11						2		4	3	3	7	10	7	2	1												39
11½						1			1	3	3	5	8	6	2												29
12					1			1		2	2	3	5	10	6	1											31
12½									1	1	1	3	3	3	6	5	3	1									27
13												1	1	4	3	7	7	1	2								26
13½										1		1	1	3	1	3	5	3	3								21
14											1				1	1	4	7	3	2	1						20
14½												1				2	1	5	4	5	2						20
15														1		2	2	1	3	4	4	2	1				20
15½																		1	1	4	3	4	1	1			15
16																		3	1	1	2	3	4		1		15
16½															1						2	2	2	2			9
17																			1	1	1	2	3	4	1	1	14
17½																				1	.	1	1	4	3	1	11
18																						1		1	2	3	7
18½																											2
19																							2		2	1	5
Total	14	14	57	56	43	43	42	41	42	42	36	36	28	29	21	22	22	22	18	18	15	15	14	12	9	8	720

[a] Four years runs from 3 years and 9 months to 4 years and 3 months.

A glance at that table shows that a large number of the pupils of this school system are overage, that is, they are older than they should be for the grades in which they are found. An age-grade table, therefore, enables the teacher, the principal, the superintendent, or other school employee to obtain a view of the age-grade status of the pupils of a classroom, department, school, or school system. Such a table does not indicate the reasons for overageness; it merely points out any overageness and suggests that further investigation be undertaken to ascertain whether the age-grade status of the pupils is what it should be. Within the last two or three decades, such tables have been made in thousands of schools and school systems, with the result that educational employees are much better acquainted with the age-grade status of pupils than ever before. In a few hours of time such a table can be made by a teacher for his own pupils, by a principal for his school, or even by a superintendent for his school system.

In interpreting the age-grade status of the pupils of a grade, school, or school system, it is helpful to compare various grades, schools, and school systems. In order that comparisons may be more meaningful, they should be made on the same basis; in other words, the technique for making age-grade tables should be standardized. Some of the details which should be standardized are the following: the date on which pupils' ages are figured; the procedure for determining the ages; and the number of semesters or school years during which a pupil is considered to be of normal age. In making age-grade tables, one of the most perplexing problems has been that of determining pupils' ages. The usual, and probably the best, practice is to figure pupils' ages as of September 1st, which is the approximate date on which the school term begins, and to define age as the age at the nearest birthday of the pupil.

Overageness Versus Underageness of Pupils. According to their age-grade status, the pupils of a grade, department, school, or school system may be divided into three groups; first, those who are normal age; second, those who are underage; and third, those who are overage. The normal-age pupils are those who are neither younger nor older than the ages which have been agreed upon as normal for the grade in which the pupils are found. A glance at Table 5 shows that for section B of the kindergarten, ages five and five and one-half are regarded as normal ages; for section A of the kindergarten, ages five and one-half and six are regarded as normal; for section B of the first grade, ages six and six and one-half are regarded as normal. The normal ages for the pupils of each of the grades are found between the two diagonal lines shown in Table 5.

Underage pupils are those who are younger than normal for the grades in which they are found. In the age-grade table exhibited in Table 5 the pupils above the two diagonal lines are underage. In section B of the first grade, for example, there are ten pupils who are underage. In section B of the first grade the ages of six and six and one-half are normal, but one pupil is only four and one-half years of age, four are only five years of age, and five are only five and one-half years of age. The five pupils who are only five and one-half years of age are underage one-half year; the four who are only five years of age are underage one year; and the one who is only four and one-half years of age is underage by the amount of one and a half years.

Overage pupils are those who are older than normal for the grades in which they are found. In Table 5 the pupils who are found below the two diagonal lines are overage. In section B of the first grade, for example, there are fifteen overage pupils. Of these fifteen pupils, nine are seven years of age, or overage one-half year; three are seven and one-half years of age, or overage one year; two are eight years of age, or overage one and a half years; and one is eight and one-half years of age, or overage two years.

A final glance at Table 5 makes evident that the number of overage pupils in this school system is several times the number of underage pupils. Such a situation is common in schools and school systems; in practically all schools and school systems there is a much larger percentage of overageness than of underageness. Under more ideal conditions these percentages would be somewhat similar.

The causes of overageness are (1) late entrance to school and (2) pupil failure. The causes of underageness are (1) early entrance to school and (2) extra promotions. If a pupil did not enter the first grade until the age of seven, he would be one-half year overage when he entered school. On the other hand, if the pupil entered school at the age of five and a half years, he would be one-half year underage when he entered school.

Class Size

Evolution of Class Size in the Schools. The first schools used individual instruction, and the grouping of pupils by classes was then unknown. The grouping of pupils into classes came largely as an economy measure and as the result of a demand for the education of more children. The break from individual instruction soon went to the opposite extreme of placing an unusually large number of pupils under each teacher; this happened especially under the system of "monitorial" schools.

In the monitorial schools, which originated about the opening of the nineteenth century, as many as five hundred pupils were frequently placed under the direction of one teacher. These large numbers of pupils were usually divided into smaller groups to be instructed by the brighter, the larger, and the older pupils who were known as "monitors." It was soon seen, however, that pupils possessed many handicaps as instructors for other pupils, and consequently teachers were asked to assume all teaching responsibilities, but with smaller classes. From the time of the demise of the monitorial schools, therefore, the tendency has been for the pupil-teacher ratio to become smaller.

The pupil-teacher ratio varies from school to school, from school system to school system, and from state to state. As a rule, it is larger in required courses than in elective courses, larger in the elementary school than in the secondary school, larger in the cities than in the rural districts, and larger in the thickly settled regions than in the sparsely settled regions. Some school systems have regulations which set both the minimum and the maximum sizes of classes. Most school systems try to keep the size of classes between twenty-five and thirty-five pupils.

Class Size Versus Per Pupil Cost in the Schools. The two largest factors which determine the per pupil cost of instruction in a given school subject or grade are (1) the number of pupils in the subject or grade, and (2) the salary of the teacher. Of these two factors, the first is the most potent. If the teacher's salary and all other costs of the class are kept the same, decreasing the size of a class by fifty per cent increases the per pupil cost by fifty per cent. On the contrary, increasing the size of the class by fifty per cent decreases the per pupil cost of instruction by the same amount. In the school system of a large city, increasing the pupil-teacher ratio by only one pupil would result in decreasing greatly the number of teachers needed; on the contrary, decreasing the pupil-teacher ratio by only one pupil would make necessary the employing of several additional teachers.

Class Size Versus Pupil Progress in the Schools. It has just been stated that small classes are much more expensive than large ones. Cost is, however, only one consideration to keep in mind in setting the size of classes. The other considerations are pupil efficiency and pupil progress. How does the pupil efficiency of small classes compare with the pupil efficiency of large ones?

During recent years, this question has been much discussed, and many investigations have been conducted seeking to obtain information on the question. Practically all of the investigations have pointed to the same conclusion, namely, that small classes are only slightly more efficient than large ones. These investigations have been conducted on all the school levels from the first grade of the elementary school through the college and the university. Moreover, they have been conducted with various school subjects and various teachers.

Such results are contrary to expectations, and perhaps a sad commentary on teaching methods today. In any event, the results show merely what is, not necessarily what ought to be. Perhaps small classes are little more efficient than large, because present teaching methods are not adapted any better to small groups than to large ones. Perhaps teachers are instructing groups of pupils, rather than individuals. If teachers really employed the opportunity which small classes afford to meet the needs of the individuals, perhaps small classes would show a much larger percentage of efficiency over large classes than investigations have indicated. Perhaps, also, the objectives of the school have been such that the larger classes have proved just as efficient as the small classes. If, for example, the objective is to have the pupils amass large quantities of factual information, it appears that large classes should be as efficient or more efficient than small ones. If, on the other hand, the objective is to have pupils develop the ability to solve problems in a manner consistent with democratic principles, the small classes might prove more efficient.

Further investigation needs to be undertaken on the efficacy of classes of different sizes. These investigations should have as their chief objective the determination of the most desirable size of class under varying conditions. Such investigation might show that the size of a class should be determined by various factors, such as the intelligence of the pupils, the subject of instruction, the qualifications of the teacher, the number of classes for which the teacher is responsible and the amount of extraclass and other duties which he must perform, and the amount and the quality of school supplies and equipment with which the teacher and the pupils have to work. To summarize, the best size of class for all conditions has not yet been determined.

QUESTIONS FOR DISCUSSION

1. Trace the evolution of group instruction. Why did the transition from individual instruction to group instruction come at the same time that school enrollment began to increase rapidly?

2. What are the theoretical advantages of individual instruction? Of group instruction? Should one type of instruction be used entirely to the exclusion of the other? Discuss.

3. Ability grouping of pupils has frequently caused friction with the home. How may this friction be avoided or lessened? Is ability grouping undemocratic? Discuss.

4. Do you favor departmental teaching and promotion by school subjects? Are the advantages of such practices as large in the lower grades as in the upper ones? Explain.

5. What plans for meeting individual needs can you propose other than the plans that are mentioned in this chapter?

6. Account for the fact that the first year of the elementary school, of the secondary school, and of the college shows more pupil failure than any other year. What steps might be taken to reduce pupil failure in the first year of each of these levels?

7. What steps should the school take to obtain the co-operation of the home in reducing pupil failure?

8. What, if any, legitimate causes of pupil failure are there? Under ideal conditions would there by any pupil failure? Discuss.

9. Account for the fact that several times as many pupils are retarded as are accelerated. Account for the fact also that several times as many pupils are overage as are underage.

10. Account for the larger percentage of elimination from school of boys than of girls. How may the percentage of pupil elimination from school be reduced?

11. Do you believe, as many persons have charged, that commencement exercises at the close of the elementary school cause many pupils to believe that their educational careers are finished?

12. How do you explain the fact that small classes accomplish only slightly more than large classes?

13. Why do small classes cost much more than large ones? Is the slight advantage in pedagogical efficiency which small classes have worth the extra cost? Discuss.

14. Should a teacher who can instruct more than the average number of pupils be paid accordingly? Why or why not?

15. Do you predict that the pupil-teacher ratio will become larger or smaller? Why? What is the present tendency regarding that ratio?

16. Could classes be made larger, if pupils and teachers were provided with more and better equipment and materials? Discuss.

SELECTED REFERENCES

Aiken, Wilford M., *The Story of the Eight-Year Study*, Harper and Bros., New York, 1942, 157 pp.

Summarizes the findings of the eight-year study of thirty progressive schools.

Billett, Roy O., *Provisions for Individual Differences, Marking, and Promotion, National Survey of Secondary Education*, Vol. 13, U. S. Office of Education, *Bulletin*, 1932, No. 17, 472 pp.

A report of a nation-wide survey in secondary schools.

Caswell, H. L., and Foshay, A. W., *Education in the Elementary School*, Third edition, American Book Company, 1957, New York, 430 pp.

Discusses limitations of grade standards and many other school practices.

Cook, Edward S., "How I. Q. Figures in the Drop-out Problem," *School Executive*, Vol. 74 (September, 1954), pp. 56–57.

Discusses a study of the dropouts in the S. M. Inman School in Atlanta, Georgia and what the school can do to cut down the number of dropouts.

Davis, Frank G., "High School Report Cards Can Be Modernized," *American School Board Journal*, Vol. 128 (March, 1954), pp. 59–60, 100.

Discusses the problem of reporting to parents in the secondary school field, and also lists some suggestions to improve report cards. Gives an example of the report card developed by the principals, teachers, counselors, parents and central-office staff members in St. Paul, Minnesota.

Davis, Frank G., ed., *Pupil Personnel Services*, International Textbook Co., Scranton, 1948, 638 pp.

Eight authors discuss various phases of the pupil personnel program of the school.

Gaumnitz, W. H., "High School Retention: How Does Your State Rate?" *School Life*, Vol. 35 (February, 1953), pp. 69–71.

Shows the holding power of the high schools of each state.

Otto, Henry J., *Elementary-school Organization and Administration*, Third edition, Appleton-Century-Crofts, Inc., New York, 1954, 719 pp.

Considers basic problems in the organization and administration of elementary education.

Review of Educational Research.

These reviews summarize every few years the research on pupil personnel, guidance, and counseling.

Shibler, Herman L., "Attacking the Drop-out Problem," NEA *Journal*, Vol. 44 (January, 1955), pp. 24–26.

A secondary school that offers such courses as barbering, shoe repair, beauty culture, and auto-body repair helps keep many students in school that would otherwise quit much earlier to go to work.

Sumption, M. R., *Three Hundred Gifted Children*, World Book Co., Yonkers-on-Hudson, New York, 1941, 233 pp.

A report of a study of these children.

"Symposium on Current Theory and Practice in the Grouping of Pupils in Secondary Schools," *California Journal of Secondary Education*, Vol. 30 (January, 1955), pp. 22–28.

Discusses a system of elementary school organization which eliminates the conventional grade levels.

The Grouping of Pupils, Part I of the *Thirty-Fifth Yearbook* of the National Society for the Study of Education, Bloomington, Ill., 1936, 220 pp.

Discusses various problems of pupil classification and progress.

Westcott, Regina H., "The Problem of Report Cards," NEA *Journal*, Vol. 44 (January, 1955), pp. 34–36.

Teachers must often help parents and children alike to get a proper perspective on the meaning and importance of report cards.

Yeager, William A., *Administration and the Pupil*, Harper and Brothers, New York, 1949, 483 pp.

Discusses many phases of relationships of school administration, and pupils with chapters on classification and grouping of pupils and promotion policy.

CHAPTER 12

Health and Safety Education

Need for, Aims, and Scope of Health Education

Need for Health Education in the Schools. Next to high intelligence, good health is the most valuable asset which any person can possess. A Croesus with poor health would gladly exchange all his worldly possessions for the blessings of good health. Who would not! Without good health, and especially when there is no chance of obtaining it, a person is poor indeed—poor in opportunity for happiness and for success in life. Without good health, a child is not likely to realize his potentialities in school, nor is he likely to realize his potentialities when he leaves school and takes his place in the workaday world as an adult.

The annual loss which is caused by sickness and premature death is colossal, yet health authorities are agreed that most sickness is preventable and that life may be greatly prolonged. In fact, the length of life is being constantly prolonged. The Committee on Waste in Industry reported a few years ago that the annual loss in the United States from preventable sickness was $1,800,000,000. During World War I, 50,385 United States soldiers were killed in battle; that number was tragically large, but a much larger number of civilians are "killed" annually by tuberculosis, cancer, polio, and other mainly preventable diseases. Health authorities are widely predicting that the discoveries of Dr. Jonas Salk in 1955 will do much toward the elimination of polio. There are, of course, other afflictions which take their toll in the hundreds of thousands, and all these causes, large and small, operate year after year.

Where physical examinations have been given, either to adults or to school children, a startling number of physical defects has been discovered. Approximately thirty per cent of our men examined for military service during World War I were found to have physical defects which prevented them from doing a soldier's full duty; the men examined, it should be noted, were the "flower" of American manhood, being between the ages of twenty and thirty. Data from the draft for World War II and for the Korean War showed that physical defects were almost as numerous as during World War I; disqualifying defects of the teeth, eyes, ears, and feet were particularly numerous; yet a large percentage of the defects could have been eliminated through efficient programs of health education in the schools.

Examinations of hundreds of thousands of school children in numerous and widely different communities of the United States indicate that practically all children have one or more physical defects which are actually or potentially detrimental to health. Moreover, contrary to common belief, a larger percentage of rural children have physical defects than city children; rural children have more defects primarily because of lack of physical examinations and of medical attention.

Illness and physical defects among school children result annually in a tremendous loss to the children and to society. The most obvious loss comes from the large amount of non-attendance at school. Approximately one-sixth of the pupils are absent daily, and by far the largest cause of this absence is pupil illness. To the hundreds of thousands of pupils who are absent daily, and who in consequence cannot profit from the tutelage of the school, must be added the several million more pupils who come to school with illness and with physical defects which handicap their happiness and retard their educational progress. There is a close relation between physical well-being and mental efficiency. The mind can do its work only through that precious "machine" known as the human body; in fact, mind and body are an entity.

To summarize, it may be said that the need for a health program in the schools becomes articulate from the following facts: first, the importance of excellent health to the individual and to society; second, the large amount of illness and of physical defects, most of which could be cured, improved, or corrected through a thoroughgoing program of health education; third, the tremendous loss of money which is spent annually for education that illness prevents children from receiving.

Aims of Health Education in the Schools. In any ranking on importance of the aims of education, good health should head the list. A "balanced person" should be the aim of the school, or as Juvenal says in his *Satires: "mens sana in corpore sano"*—"sound mind in a sound body." Stated in general terms, the aim of health education in the schools is the protection and the improvement of the physical and the emotional health of the child. That general aim has been stated more specifically in the following words by two specialists in health education:

1. To understand the school child thoroughly; and to help him to realize the best health and development of which he is capable.
2. To protect the pupil against contracting disease from any other child during this period; and to prevent his conveying disease to any other pupil.
3. To discover and call to the parent's attention any existing health defects, more especially those of a remediable nature, and to inspire and assist the parent to provide suitable remedial treatment.
4. To enlist co-operation of all existing agencies and all available influences for the correction of defects of school children and teachers.
5. To provide special and optimum conditions for certain handicapped children who would be at a disadvantage otherwise and to furnish exceptionally satisfactory supervision for them.
6. To provide suitable and healthful surroundings and conditions for the child in school.
7. To teach the pupil how to lead a life of health always, and if defective, to teach him also as far as possible how to escape the handicap of infirmity.
8. To furnish technical information and guidance for all those who contribute in any way to school health service.[1]

One of the most complete and authoritative statements of the "rights" of every child regarding "child health and protection" was made by President Hoover's "White House Conference on Child Health and Protection." Since that statement—called "The Children's

[1] T. D. Wood and H. G. Rowell, *Health Supervision and Medical Inspection of Schools*, Saunders, 1927, p. 7. By permission of W. B. Saunders Company, publishers.

Charter"—deals largely with the aims of health education it is quoted herewith:

1. For every child spiritual and moral training to help him to stand firm under the pressure of life.
2. For every child understanding and the guarding of his personality as his most precious right.
3. For every child a home and that love and security which a home provides; and for that child who must receive foster care, the nearest substitute for his own home.
4. For every child full preparation for his birth, his mother receiving prenatal, natal, and postnatal care; and the establishment of such protective measures as will make child-bearing safer.
5. For every child health protection from birth through adolescence, including: periodical health examinations and, where needed, care of specialists and hospital treatment; regular dental examination and care of the teeth; protective and preventive measures against communicable diseases; the insuring of pure food, pure milk, and pure water.
6. For every child from birth through adolescence, promotion of health, including health instruction and a health program, wholesome physical and mental recreation, with teachers and leaders adequately trained.
7. For every child a dwelling place, safe, sanitary, and wholesome, with reasonable provisions for privacy, free from conditions which tend to thwart his development; and a home environment harmonious and enriching.
8. For every child a school which is safe from hazards, sanitary, properly equipped, lighted, and ventilated. For younger children nursery schools and kindergartens to supplement home care.
9. For every child a community which recognizes and plans for his needs, protects him against physical dangers, moral hazards, and disease; provides him with safe and wholesome places for play and recreation; and makes provision for his cultural and social needs.
10. For every child an education which, through the discovery and development of his individual abilities, prepares him for life; and through training and vocational guidance prepares him for a living which will yield him the maximum of satisfaction.
11. For every child such teaching and training as will prepare him for successful parenthood, homemaking, and the rights of citizenship; and, for parents, supplementary training to fit them to deal wisely with the problems of parenthood.
12. For every child education for safety and protection against accidents to which modern conditions subject him—those to which he is directly exposed and those which, through loss or maiming of his parents, affect him directly.
13. For every child who is blind, deaf, crippled, or otherwise physically

handicapped, and for the child who is mentally handicapped, such measures as will early discover and diagnose his handicap, provide care and treatment, and so train him that he may become an asset to society rather than a liability. Expenses of these services should be borne publicly where they cannot be privately met.

14. For every child who is in conflict with society the right to be dealt with intelligently as society's charge, not society's outcast; with the home, the school, the church, the court and the institution when needed, shaped to return him whenever possible to the normal stream of life.
15. For every child the right to grow up in a family with an adequate standard of living and the security of a stable income as the surest safeguard against social handicaps.
16. For every child protection against labor that stunts growth, either physical or mental, that limits education, that deprives children of the right of comradeship, of play, and of joy.
17. For every rural child as satisfactory schooling and health services as for the city child, and an extension to rural families of social, recreational, and cultural facilities.
18. To supplement the home and the school in the training of youth, and to return to them those interests of which modern life tends to cheat children, every stimulation and encouragement should be given to the extension and development of the voluntary youth organizations.
19. To make everywhere available those minimum protections of the health and welfare of children, there should be a district, county, or community organization for health, education, and welfare, with full-time officials, co-ordinating with a state-wide program which will be responsive to a nation-wide service of general information, statistics, and scientific research. This should include:
    (a) Trained, full-time public health officials, with public health nurses, sanitary inspection, and laboratory workers.
    (b) Available hospital beds.
    (c) Full-time public welfare service for the relief, aid, and guidance of children in special need due to poverty, misfortune, or behavior difficulties, and for the protection of children from abuse, neglect, exploitation, or moral hazard.

    For EVERY *child these rights, regardless of race, or color, or situation, wherever he may live under the protection of the American flag.*[2]

[2] *White House Conference*, pp. 44–46, The Century Co., 1930. By permission of the Century Co., publishers.

The Midcentury White House Conference on Children and Youth called by President Truman in 1950 extended the provisions of the "Charter" in a "Pledge to Children." The "Pledge to Children" contained seventeen items and dealt mainly with emotional development and mental hygiene.

Scope of Health Education in the Schools. In its evolution the health program of the schools has passed through three stages. The first stage was that of health protection—protection of pupils and of school employees from an unsanitary school environment, from communicable diseases, and from a school program unsuited to the pupils' physical and mental health. The second stage was that of remedial work—work designed to correct the defects which physical and mental examinations had found. The third stage was that of health promotion—promotion through such means as courses of study in health and physical education, the provision of school lunches, and a hygienic school program.

The progress which has been made in carrying out the three-fold program just mentioned varies from school to school and from school system to school system. Some schools and some school systems have hardly reached the first stage; others have progressed as far as the second stage; still others have progressed through the third stage and thus have a complete school-health program. A complete school-health program—which, because of lack of finances, will probably not be immediately attainable in all school systems—would provide for the three phases just described.

It is an unfortunate commentary that hundreds of school systems are doing almost nothing in health supervision; hundreds of them do not have the services of nurses, of physicians, or of other special health employees; they do not spend one cent on a school-health program. They spend annually $100, $200, or $300 per pupil on the teaching of the school subjects and on the remainder of the school program—all of eminent importance, it is admitted—but they fail to spend one cent on the most important aim of education and the most important thing in life, namely, good health.

The tendency, though, is in the right direction, for in theory and in practice the importance of a school-health program is being more and more recognized by the general public and by school officials and school employees. This movement was given a tremendous impetus by World War I and World War II. Practically all states have enacted certain legislation designed to protect and to promote the health and the safety of school children and of school employees. The first of these laws were permissive in character and were designed for health protection—protection against such hazards as an unsafe and an unsanitary school plant and against contagious diseases. Many of the laws are still permissive. Recent years, however, have seen the enactment of mandatory laws which govern many health practices, such as school sanitation, medical inspection of the pupils, the employment of school nurses, courses of study in health education, and courses of study in physical education.

School Employees in the School-Health Program

How School Employees May Assist in the School-Health Program. Although the school or school system may provide nurses, physicians, dentists, nutritionists, psychiatrists, clinics, and other health employees and conveniences, the value of these will be largely lost without the sympathetic and the intelligent co-operation of the classroom teacher and all other educational employees. In schools and school systems which do not provide special health employees—and most schools and school systems unfortunately do not provide them—the school-health program, if any, is left entirely to the teachers and to the other educational employees. In any program of school health, the teacher is the most important school employee.

There are numerous ways in which the teacher may assist in carrying out the school-health program. The teacher should prepare himself for that service. He can keep himself in excellent physical, mental, and emotional health and thus be a good example to his pupils; he can help to see that the pupils work in sanitary school surroundings, and under hygienic conditions; he can help to interpret the school-health program to the pupils and to their parents; he can make suggestions to pupils and to parents looking toward the improvement of the pupils' health; he can co-operate with physicians and with nurses in the health and physical examinations of pupils; he can assist in the control of communicable diseases; he can supervise the play and recreation of pupils; and he can give instruction in health and hygiene and take all reasonable steps to see that such instruction functions with the pupils.

As has been stated in preceding paragraphs, protection should be the first step taken in a school-health program. This means that the health of the pupils should be protected from any hazards inherent in the school plant or in the intermingling of children. Contagious disease among the pupils is one of the chief hazards against which the teacher must guard, and he should inform himself concerning the symptoms of such diseases and concerning other matters which would enable him to control the diseases among the pupils of the school.

Co-operating with Other Health Agents and Agencies. In the school-health program of most communities, teachers and other educational employees will find various other agents and other agencies interested to a greater or less extent in the health of school children. Some of these agents—for example, school nurses, school physicians, school dentists, and similar school employees—have as their only function the protection and the promotion of the health of pupils and of school employees. Other of the agents—for example, the officials and the employees of city or of county boards of health, of welfare societies, of civic clubs, and of Parent-Teacher Associations—are often interested in the health of school children either as an official duty or as a free-will public service. Thousands of Parent-Teacher Associations are co-operating with the school in providing free lunches for indigent pupils and in arranging for health examinations of all pupils. Other community agencies are also giving free assistance in health promotion.

The health service of the agents and agencies—whether they be school or non-school—can realize its potentialities only with the co-operation of the teacher and the other educational employees. With school officials and other public officials and employees, the teacher has the duty of co-operating in health protection and health improvement; with the non-public agents and agencies he should likewise co-operate when this co-operation would serve the interests of the pupil, the school, and the public. He can co-operate with such agents and agencies by such means as reporting to them any pupils in need of health service and by carrying out the health directions of the agents.

The health agent with whom the teacher and the other educational employees have the greatest opportunity to co-operate is the school nurse. This opportunity is greatest because the school nurse is not only the most frequently found health employee but is probably the most important health employee which the school can have. More and more school systems are employing nurses, and no school system should be without such health service. Authorities are agreed that for the most effective results not more than one thousand pupils should be supervised by one nurse. Persons who have prepared themselves for school nursing find ready employment at approximately the same salary as teachers.[3] The chief duties of a school nurse are the following:

1. To assist the teacher in the program of health instruction in the school.
2. To hold conferences with, and to make addresses to, teachers and parents on health.
3. To help the teacher in making health inspections of the pupils.
4. To assist the school physician in health examinations of the pupils.
5. To make health examinations, and to refer to a physician those cases requiring his attention.
6. To care for minor dressings of wounds, and to arrange for the care of other emergencies.
7. To call upon parents for the purpose of obtaining their co-operation in obtaining as good health conditions for their children as finances permit.
8. To serve as attendance employee for the school or school system.
9. To co-operate with all agencies of the community to obtain the best possible health standards for the pupils.

Preparation Needed for Health Supervision in the School-health Program. In terms of importance no phase of education is more neglected than health education. Much of this neglect arises from the fact that school officials and school employees do not always sense the pre-eminent importance of health education, but a much greater part of the neglect is the result of a lack of knowledge of what constitutes a desirable school-health program and of the procedures for realizing such a program.

The deficiencies just mentioned can best be corrected by educational employees qualifying themselves in health supervision. They cannot obtain ample preparation by the perusal of a short treatise, such as the present chapter must necessarily be. They must do a much larger amount of reading[4] and of observation, and preferably such reading and observation should be obtained in a college course on school-health education. Most colleges now provide such courses, and

[3] Students who are considering entering school nursing as a career would do well to consult the book entitled *Manual of Public Health Nursing*, published by The Macmillan Company. The book was prepared by The National Organization for Public Health Nursing and discusses opportunities and requirements in all areas of public health nursing.

[4] A list of references from which such reading may be chosen is given in the Selected References at the close of this chapter.

in many states fortunately such a course or courses must be pursued as one of the conditions for teacher certification. Among the topics which are usually discussed in such courses are the following: the relation between health and personal efficiency; school sanitation; the features to be observed in giving physical examinations, for example, posture, nutrition, methods of weighing and measuring, and the use of height and weight tables; the correction of physical defects; the common diseases of the skin, the scalp, and the hair; the anatomy, physiology, and diseases of the eye and the methods of ascertaining eye defects; the anatomy, physiology, and diseases of the ear, the nose, and the throat; the development, the eruption, and the care of the teeth; the common defects of the back, the chest, and the extremities; the common contagious and infectious diseases, with particular reference to their method of transmission and their early symptoms; the supervision of play; safety education; and health records of the pupils.

The preparation just outlined should be regarded as the minimum needed by every educational employee of the school. Persons who expect to enter the teaching or the supervision of health and physical education should plan, of course, to go much beyond that minimum. More than half of the states have laws which establish certain requirements for obtaining physical-education certificates, and most teacher-preparing institutions have physical-education programs which enable all interested candidates to meet those requirements. During recent years, teachers and supervisors of health and physical education have been finding employment opportunities above the average. Most secondary school beginners, however, since they begin in the small schools, must be prepared to teach one or two other subjects as well as health and physical education.

THE SCHOOL EMPLOYEE'S HEALTH IN THE SCHOOL-HEALTH PROGRAM. The school employee should have a high standard of health for at least three reasons. In the first place, good health is necessary for the employee's happiness, his economic welfare, and his efficiency; without it the school employee might not possess the strength, the ambition, the alertness, and the emotional tone demanded of him.

In the second place, the health of a school employee, especially of the teacher, is important because it affects not only his own welfare, but the welfare of his pupils. Ill health prevents the teacher from accomplishing all that he might with his pupils, and not infrequently it becomes a positive menace to his pupils. If the teacher is nervous and irritable, as many a teacher is, there is danger of transmitting such characteristics to the pupils, or if the teacher possesses a communicable disease, such as tuberculosis, there is danger that the pupils may contract the disease.

In the third place, the school employee's health is important, because poor health means an immediate financial loss to the board of education when the employee is absent and a substitute must be employed for him. Such a loss is incurred only when the board provides a certain amount of pay for disability leave—a practice which has become common, especially in the city school systems. Several states have laws which give all school employees a certain number of days of full pay each school year for sickness. There is also a loss of pupil interest in certain phases of school work when a substitute must be employed, and time is lost in making adjustments and in getting adjusted to the new situation by both the teacher and the pupil.

There was a time when teachers were employed largely on a basis of charity, and when the ill, "the lame, the halt, and the blind" stood as good a chance of obtaining teaching positions as the well and the able-bodied. Those were the days when it was commonly believed that "anyone could teach school," and that physical imperfection or illness was no handicap to the teacher. Fortunately, though, that belief has largely passed, and boards of education are more and more demanding that teachers possess high qualifications in health as well as in professional ability; many boards require a physical examination of all school employees. The goal toward which enlightened boards of education are striving has been stated as a series of suggestions to all boards of education. These suggestions were prepared by Thomas D. Wood, J. W. Brister, Olive Jones, and Juliet O. Bell and have been published by the Metropolitan Life Insurance Company in a monograph entitled *The Teacher's Health*. Their suggestions follow:

1. Provide thorough health examinations for all teachers in service. These examinations should include a thorough survey of the teacher's physical condition, consideration of her mental health, inquiry into her hygienic daily program, and instruction of the teacher regarding her health needs and how to maintain positive health, the examinations to be made by a school physician or by one approved by the school authorities. . . .
2. Require health qualifications for the employment of teachers, the

acceptance of the teacher to be based on the results of a thorough examination given by the school physician or by one approved by him.

3. Employ periodic examinations for promoting the teachers' health and not as a means for disqualifying them. It is of paramount importance that school boards respect in all cases the confidential nature of these examinations.
4. Follow up examinations and stimulate the correction of defects. Provide probationary period for the correction of defects.
5. Gain the early confidence of teachers in the development of a health-supervision program for teachers. This for the purpose of dispelling fear that may be aroused through misunderstanding or inadequate preliminary publicity. Moreover, it assures the full co-operation and participation of the teachers.
6. Provide a sanitary and healthful teaching environment, including proper ventilation, temperature, and lighting, adequate janitorial service, rest rooms, and lunch rooms. . . .
7. Improve the living conditions of teachers by means of adequate salaries, by provision of teachers' homes, or by securing a selective list of available living accommodations in the community. . . .
8. Require the withdrawal of the teacher from the classroom when she is suffering from certain minor health handicaps which are not necessarily severe illnesses. This provision is particularly important in the case of colds.
9. Consider teachers' yearly attendance upon summer school and university courses during school year in relation to their health.
10. Provide leaves with some remuneration for recuperation and rest whenever the condition of the teacher warrants this. . . .
11. Make provision for insuring teachers against loss of salary during illness.
12. Analyze the absences of teachers for the purpose of determining methods of safeguarding the positive health of teachers. A required health examination by the school physician after absence due to illness is advantageous to both teachers and pupils.
13. Furnish salaries to teachers sufficient for study, recreation, and an adequate standard of living.
14. Provide some doctor's, nurse's, or hospital care for sick teachers. This promotes the mental as well as physical health of teachers by reducing causes of worry.
15. Furnish some recreational facilities and encourage outdoor recreational pursuits among teachers.
16. Make provision for courses or other means of instructing teachers relative to personal and community health.
17. Reduce cause of worry by providing adequate retirement allowance.
18. Adopt a plan for tenure of office which will properly secure teachers in their positions.

Carrying out the above suggestions will not avail much if teachers do not co-operate with school officials and do nothing toward protecting and improving their health. To keep in good health and good physical condition is, in the last analysis, the responsibility of the teacher. The same monograph mentioned above suggests the following steps which teachers should take to improve their health:

1. Avail themselves of all the facilities provided by the community and the school board for the promotion of their health.
2. Adopt a hygienic program of living, giving sufficient attention to recreation, sleep, eating, rest, and exercise. Protection against certain specific diseases, such as smallpox and typhoid fever, by vaccination is also a wise and social procedure. Adequate social life and recreation are imperative needs.
3. Avoid worry and anxiety in regard to health.
4. Prepare themselves in the use of modern methods of teaching, since these are conducive to more effective teaching and to a better understanding of children, and thereby to greater social and emotional health on the part of the teacher.
5. Develop sympathy, tact, and understanding in dealing with children, parents, fellow teachers, and supervisors, thus lessening the strain of teaching.
6. Foster a wholesome respect for the profession to which they belong and seek to make their work a contribution to that profession.
7. Withdrawal from the teaching profession if its demands and conditions are at variance with health and temperament.

Provisions for Physically-Handicapped Children

Scope of Such Provisions in the School-health Program. School systems are more and more making provisions for special programs for the physically-handicapped children. Since such programs are much more expensive than programs for normal children, many states give special subsidies to local school systems that organize such programs. Most states have established state schools for the deaf and for the blind, and a few states have provided similar schools for epileptics. The chief types of physically-handicapped children for which hundreds of local systems now make special provision are the following: blind and partially sighted, deaf and hard of hearing, epileptic, crippled, cardiac (heart), tuberculous, and speech defective.

Opportunities and Requirements in Teaching Physically-handicapped Children. In the United States hundreds of classes for

Fig. 40. A speech correction class in the Pittsburgh, Pennsylvania, public schools. Classes for physically-exceptional children of many types are now found in hundreds of school systems.

physically-handicapped children of the various types mentioned above are found, and these provide hundreds of employment opportunities each year for teachers at salaries above the average. Each type of such a special class demands, of course, a teacher with special preparation, and only a few colleges and universities make provision for giving such preparation. Students interested in preparing for a career in one or more of these types of special education should write to the following societies for the names of colleges and universities which provide such preparation and for the other services of the societies: American Heart Association, 44 East 23rd Street, New York, N. Y.; American Medical Association,[5] 535 North Dearborn Street, Chicago,

[5] Students interested in preparing to become a physio-therapist or an occupational therapist should write the American Medical Association for information on these professions and on the colleges and universities which prepare students for them. The demand for these workers is already greater than the supply.

Ill.; American Society for the Hard of Hearing, 1535 35th Street, N. W., Washington, D. C.; American Society to Promote the Teaching of Speech to the Deaf, 1537 35th Street, N. W., Washington, D. C.; American Speech Correction Association, 419 Boylston Street, Boston, Mass.; National Foundation for Infantile Paralysis, 120 Broadway, New York, N. Y.; National Society for the Prevention of Blindness, 1790 Broadway, New York, N. Y.; National Foundation for the Blind, 105 East 22nd Street, New York, N. Y.; and National Tuberculosis Association, 1790 Broadway, New York, N. Y. If students want further information on addresses of these societies, they should consult *National Associations of the United States*, published by U. S. Department of Commerce; addresses sometimes change.

Provisions for School Lunches

During recent years, the tendency everywhere has been toward the school's providing lunch facilities for its pupils and its employees; and for indigent pupils the tendency has been to provide free lunches. These provisions have been made especially by the larger schools, but many of the smaller ones have also made them; in fact, many of the one-room schools now provide at least one warm dish daily for the lunch of each pupil. Since these facilities make a direct contribution to pupil health, and since school employees must prepare themselves to manage the school-lunch facilities, they will be briefly discussed herewith.

Management of School-lunch Facilities. In addition to having the responsibility of providing the proper equipment for the lunch period, the school must make provisions for the proper management of the lunch facilities. Making these provisions will include the selection and the supervision of the lunchroom personnel, and the prescription of certain business practices to be followed. The aim in lunchroom management should be to provide appropriate food at the lowest cost possible. Since pupils and school employees are expected to pay for the operation of school lunchrooms, the school should establish purchasing, accounting, auditing, and other business practices which will guarantee that the pupils and the school employees will always receive "their money's worth." Likewise the public must be protected against mismanagement and graft.

Since teachers of home economics are almost always given the

Fig. 41. Another of the many classes for physically-handicapped children. *(Courtesy of the Syracuse, New York, public schools.)*

duty of supervising the school-lunch facilities, those teachers should not neglect this phase of their college preparation. They should learn how to manage or to supervise the management of the school lunchroom which will sometimes have excellent and adequate equipment, but which will more often have, especially in the smaller schools, much inferior and inadequate equipment. Many of the schools are, of course, sufficiently large to require full-time lunchroom managers, and these positions provide another excellent employment opportunity for the graduates of college departments of home economics.

The more progressive schools are trying to make the school-lunch period more than merely an "eating interlude"; they are making it a vital part of the educational experience of the pupils. They have abolished the cafeteria style of meal and have substituted for it a well-planned meal for every pupil. Committees of pupils help the lunchroom manager to plan the meals, and the menus are changed each day. Pupils rotate in serving the meals and in being hosts and hostesses at the various dining tables. In brief, attempt is made to teach high standards of dining etiquette and to make in every way the school-lunch period an enjoyable, a health-contributing, and a socializing experience for the pupils.

Lunches for Indigent Pupils. Thousands of pupils are malnourished because of parental ignorance of the principles of nutrition, and thousands of others are malnourished because of poverty in their homes. All these underprivileged pupils should be a special concern of the school, because malnourishment is sure to affect the educational accomplishment of the pupil, his emotional tone, his health, his conduct, and his happiness.

In all states public funds may be legally used to provide food for indigent pupils, and in thousands of communities public funds are being used for this purpose. For many years state funds for this purpose have been supplemented by Federal funds. In most communities, however, public funds for the purpose are insufficient and must be supplemented by private funds. In most communities private funds may be readily obtained from Parent-Teacher Associations, from welfare agencies, from other community organizations, and from individuals; in fact, private funds for this humanitarian purpose may be so easily obtained that school officials and school employees who do not take steps to obtain them when and if they are needed are deserving of universal condemnation.

The School's Responsibility for Safety Education

The Toll Taken by Accidents in the United States. The toll taken annually by accidents is colossal. In the whole United States, according to the National Safety Council, accident fatalities increased from 91,087 in 1933 to approximately 92,000 annually in 1955. Approximately 9,200,000 persons suffer nonfatal injuries, and approximately 350,000 of these persons are permanently injured. These deaths and these injuries cause untold distress and suffering. They blast the opportunities of hundreds of thousands of persons, and since life and limb have value, accidents, in the whole nation, result in a loss of billions of dollars annually. In addition to the losses resulting from death and from nonfatal injury—which cannot be measured adequately in dollars and cents—accidents also result annually in the destruction or the damage of hundreds of millions of dollars' worth of property.

These accidents result from innumerable causes or instruments, the chief ones being automobiles, falls, railroads, drownings, explosions, burns, poisonous gases, and firearms. These instruments or causes are, of course, part and parcel of the civilization of the times, and they change as the work, the habits, and the customs of the people change. Many inventions, which come to be widely adopted, result annually in thousands of deaths and of injuries, as witness the automobile. Motor vehicle accidents cause approximately one-third of the fatalities; home accidents another one-third; occupational accidents, one-seventh; and miscellaneous accidents, the remainder.

Accidents are not limited to any particular age, although the available data show that certain ages are afflicted with more accidents than other ages. According to the National Safety Council, approximately 600,000 pupils annually suffer accidents and more than 11,000 of these were fatal in 1954. Drab though it is, the picture of pupil accidents is not entirely unlovely, because during recent years the number of accidents and of fatalities among pupils has been greatly reduced. Those reductions have been made through programs of safety education in the schools and through better school and community co-operation in accident prevention. They have been made in spite of the increasing hazards and notwithstanding the increasing number of accidents among the adult population of the nation.

Fig. 42. Learning to be safe. The upper picture shows proper protective equipment for future scientists, and the lower picture shows student safety engineers learning while serving. *(Courtesy of the National Safety Council.)*

Reducing the Number of Accidents. All, or practically all, accidents are preventable. "Accidents do not happen; they are caused." They are not acts of God, but of man. They may be prevented through the universal education of the people in the causes of accidents and in the ways and means of eliminating those causes. The attainment of this goal, though possible, will not be easy; it will require universal instruction in safety education and universal following of that instruction. Every teacher should be prepared to co-operate in giving that instruction.

In any program for reducing the number of accidents, the school has as its first responsibility the protection of the pupils from injury, particularly while they are on the school premises or are on the way to or from school. Although the courts have declared with near unanimity that school corporations cannot be held legally responsible for injuries suffered by school employees, pupils, or other persons, nevertheless, it is not too much to expect that the school shall be morally responsible for the safety of pupils. The moral responsibility to make the school premises as safe as possible is always present, whatever the legal responsibility may be.

Since most pupil accidents occur on the playground, in the gymnasium, in the laboratories and shops, and on the streets, school officials and teachers should, first of all, take steps to try to prevent such accidents. After steps have been taken to eliminate school accidents, steps should next be taken to assist in the prevention of non-school accidents. The latter steps are urged because pupils soon leave the watchful care of the school and take their places in the workaday world in which the danger of accidents lurks everywhere. To teach the child to become a careful adult should be a chief aim of the school in safety education.

In most schools and school systems the battle for the prevention of accidents is now being fought along the four following fronts: first, the making of school sites, school buildings, and school equipment more safe for the work and the play of pupils and school employees; second, the closer supervision of the pupils while they are on the school premises and when they are on their way to and from school; third, the provision of instruction in safety; and fourth, the obtaining of co-operation between the school and other public and private agencies for the reduction of accidents, particularly traffic accidents.

Teachers and other educational employees have many opportuni-

FIG. 43. Schoolboy safety patrol. (*Courtesy of the St. Louis, Missouri, public schools.*) Thousands of schools have organized these patrols to protect pupils from injury. Automobile clubs often provide raincoats for the patrols.

ties to co-operate in carrying out the safety programs just mentioned. They can assist by calling the attention of school officials to hazards around the school plant; for example, they can call attention to any school machinery which needs guards or to any playground equipment which is unsafe for the age and the size of the pupils. They can give their pupils instruction in the use of dangerous school machinery and of other school equipment, in the performing of certain experiments which have possibilities of being dangerous, and in the traffic laws of the community and of the state; they can also provide ample supervision to make more certain than the instructions are followed by the pupils.

The most significant phase of the program for accident prevention during recent years has been the introduction of safety education into the schools as a subject of instruction. In some schools, instruction in safety education is provided in a separate course of study, and in other schools the instruction is correlated with the subject matter of other courses. Driver education has become a frequent subject, especially in the secondary schools. The officials and the employees of schools and school systems which have provided safety instruction are unanimous in the view that such instruction has proved its efficacy. They affirm that during and following such instruction the number of accidents is greatly reduced. St. Louis, which was one of the first cities to introduce safety instruction into the schools, reports that within a period of three years following the introduction of a program of safety instruction the number of accidents among pupils was reduced to nearly zero.

Fire Prevention and Fire Drills in Schools. The National Safety Council stated that the fire loss in 1955 in the United States amounted to $850,000,000. To this huge loss, approximately 4,000 school-building fires contributed more than $10,000,000 annually. Scores of lives are lost, and hundreds of nonfatal injuries are suffered in these fires; and deaths and injuries frequently occur in school-building fires, although fortunately not nearly as frequently as in fires in other buildings.

When it is considered that the annual fire loss of the United States amounts to a large percentage of the expenditure for schools—and when it is known that practically all fires are preventable—the opportunity which the schools have to teach fire prevention and fire control is brought into clear perspective. Someone has pointed out that the schools could partly pay their way by teaching methods of waste prevention—prevention of fires, of unnecessary illness, of accidents, and of premature death; of course, there are many other

Fig. 44. Some practices of the Erie, Pennsylvania, public schools in safety education. *(Courtesy of the Erie, Pennsylvania, public schools.)*

wastes. Wastes are preventable, and education can reduce all of them, although it may not be able to eliminate all of them.

In their campaign to eliminate fires and fire injuries, school officials and school employees have as their first responsibility the elimination of school-building fires and the prevention of injury to pupils. Such steps as the following should be taken:

1. *Fire hazards should be removed from schools.* Fire hazards may be due to faulty construction of the plant or to careless usage of the plant. Most states now have laws which prescribe certain standards which the construction of school buildings shall meet, and the tendency has been to make such laws more rigid.

Beyond the obligation of calling the attention of school officials to construction hazards, teachers cannot do much toward the removing of such hazards. The other type of hazards—those resulting from the use of the school plant—they can, however, do much to eliminate. They can see, for example, that rubbish and similar fire menaces are not allowed to accumulate in their classrooms or in other parts of the plant over which they are responsible; they can see that any highly combustible materials used in laboratories, industrial-arts shops, and domestic-science rooms are properly stored or carefully used; they can teach pupils safety habits in the use of matches, of chemicals, and of similar materials; they can see that fire escapes, classroom aisles, and exits from the building are not obstructed; and they can make certain that they know how to use the fire extinguishers of the building and that those extinguishers are ready for instant and effective use.

2. *Regular fire drills should be conducted in every school.* The purpose of the school fire drill is to get all occupants out of the building in as short a period of time as possible. To accomplish this purpose every pupil must know exactly what he is to do when the fire alarm is sounded, and he must know this for every hour of the school day and for every condition under which he may be working or playing. These results cannot be accomplished with halfhearted or with perfunctory compliance with the state law or with the rules and regulations of the local school or school system.

Most states now require every school, public or private, to hold a fire drill at least once each month. Such legislation had its beginning immediately following certain school-building fires in which pupils and school employees lost their lives. The most horrible of these catastrophes happened in the Collinwood school in Cleveland, Ohio, in 1908; in that fire, 173 pupils and 2 teachers died. Following that holocaust, legislation was soon enacted which demanded safer construction of school buildings, provisions for fire escapes and for fire-fighting apparatus, and frequent fire drills.

FIG. 45. Driver education. *(Courtesy of the Canton, Ohio, public schools.)* Driver education is now taught in thousands of secondary schools.

The organization of the fire drill should receive special thought on the part of school officials and school employees. Superintendents, principals, and other school administrators are expected to take the lead in organizing and co-ordinating fire drills for each school, but the efficacy of any fire drill is largely determined by the sympathetic and the intelligent co-operation of the teachers. Teachers have the responsibility of getting their pupils out of their rooms, of seeing that the pupils properly join the line of march, and of maintaining strict discipline. Moreover, the fire drill affords teachers another excellent opportunity to impress upon pupils the value of carefulness and the possible tragedy of carelessness; if such a lesson is taught, fewer pupils will regard the fire drill as nonsense or as an abbreviated lark.

Protection against bombing. Although no part of the United States has ever undergone a bombing by a foreign country, and it is hoped that it never will, many of the school systems, especially in the large cities, have already begun to prepare the pupils on how to act in case of a bombing attack. The lessons of Hiroshima have not been lost here.

QUESTIONS FOR DISCUSSION

1. Discuss good health as an aim of education. Compare it in importance with the other aims of education.

2. Compare the purposes of health and physical education today with its purposes a few years ago.

3. How do you account for the historic neglect of health education in the school?

4. What provisions do the laws of your state make for health, safety, and sanitary control of the schools? What changes, if any, would you suggest in the laws on those school matters?

5. Would you favor compulsory medical inspection, compulsory physical examinations, and compulsory remedial treatment of school children? Why or why not? Would you favor compulsory physical examinations, and compulsory remedial treatment of school children? Why or why not? Would you favor compulsory vaccination of pupils? Discuss. What are the laws of your state on these matters?

6. Do you believe that the control of school-health work should be in the hands of school officials or in the hands of the public-health authorities? Discuss. What co-operation should there be?

7. How do you account for the larger percentage of physical defects among the rural children than among the city children?

8. Do you agree with the view that if a school system can have only one health employee, that one should be a school nurse? Explain.

9. What provisions should the school make for pupil play? Should school playgrounds be kept open during the summer months? Explain.

10. What provision do you believe the school should make for a noon lunch for pupils and school employees? Why? What special provision should be made for indigent children? Explain.

11. What are some steps which the teacher can take to reduce school accidents?

12. What is the legal responsibility of school officials and school employees for school accidents in your state?

SELECTED REFERENCES

1. *Health Education*

Blundell, W. Irvin, "Health and Physical Fitness," *Nation's Schools*, Vol. 54 (November, 1954), pp. 57–59.

Lists and discusses the kind of facilities needed in the school plant besides the gymnasium and the health unit that will contribute to every student's health and physical fitness.

Ford, Marie, "School Health Services in England and the United States," *Elementary School Journal*, Vol. 55 (January, 1955), pp. 279–287.

This is a comparative study of the English and United States health services, both through schools and non-school-connected.

Lamers, William M., "School Health Program Grows," *Nation's Schools*, Vol. 39 (January, 1947), pp. 31–32.

A report on the school-health program of Milwaukee, Wisconsin.

Malt, Pauline, "Relationships of Physique and Temperament," *School Review*, Vol. 61 (May, 1953), pp. 267–276.

Describes the research conducted by W. H. Sheldon concerning the relationship of physique and temperament. Three components resulted from the study. Through factor analysis, Sheldon determined three so-called clusters. Each cluster described one type of temperament.

Nereau, Robert J. and Sweeney, Aryln G., "We Used Food to Improve Group Relation," *School Executive*, Vol. 74 (February, 1955), pp. 135–136.

Points out a new slant in the improvement of human relations, the importance of food.

Sparks, Richard K., *et al.*, "Why Should Education Take Time Out for Lunch," *School Executive*, Vol. 72 (November, 1952), pp. 103–104, 106, 108, 110.

Importance of the school-lunch program, and need for carefully planning it.

Walker, Herbert, *Health in the Elementary School*, The Ronald Press Co., New York, 1955, 228 pp.

Written primarily for the college student preparing for an elementary school teaching career.

2. *Safety Education*

Abramoski, E. R., "Safety Education," *Nation's Schools*, Vol. 54 (September, 1954), pp. 54–56.

Discusses the ways in which an entire community taught safety and provided a safe environment for its children. The business of safety was everybody's responsibility. There were safety lessons taught regularly in school.

National Bureau of Casualty and Surety Underwriters, 1 Park Avenue, New York City.

Publishes much material on safety education.

Safety Education.

A magazine published monthly, except June, July, and August, in two sections; published under the auspices of the National Safety Council, at 425 N. Michigan Avenue, Chicago, Illinois.

Safety Education in Schools, D. Appleton-Century Co., New York, 1932, 61 pp.

This is the report of the subcommittee on safety education of the White House Conference on Child Health and Protection; contains helpful suggestions on the organization of a program of safety education.

PART FOUR

THE MATERIALS OF INSTRUCTION

CHAPTER 13

The Curriculum and Social Trends

Definitions and Scope of the Curriculum

Definitions of the Curriculum. Definitions of the curriculum have undergone large changes during recent years. In the early days the curriculum was regarded as a list of subject matter—that is, a course of study [1]—which pupils were expected to read, to memorize, and to recite. Since this subject matter was usually found in and limited to the school subjects—reading, writing, arithmetic, and others—the school subjects usually determined the curriculum. In those days it was believed that book learning was the only type of learning—at least, the only type worth pursuing; hence, the textbook determined largely or wholly the curriculum. Pupil experiences obtained outside the classroom were not regarded as a part of the curriculum; in fact, many school officials and school employees tried to insulate the pupils from such experiences because they were considered to possess little or no value in education.

During recent years, however, definitions of the curriculum have become much more inclusive. Those definitions now include not only the school subjects, but all other pupil activities and pupil experiences which the school may direct. They include all the so-called "extracurricular" activities, various home and community activities—in brief, all pupil activities and all pupil experiences which the school

[1] This subject matter is usually called a course of study. That part of the curriculum which is organized for classroom use constitutes the course of study. Secondary schools and colleges usually have more than one course of study; this is especially true of the larger schools and colleges.

may direct, wherever and whenever they may be found. Some of these activities and experiences are admittedly vitiating in their influence, but they are nevertheless a part of the total learning situation and cannot be ignored by the school because the pupils cannot be insulated from them; educational agencies which have been under severe scrutiny and frequent attack during recent years are comic books, motion pictures, radio, television, and recreation, but not all parts of them or of their program have been under attack. According to this view, which is the view taken in this book, the curriculum may be defined as "all the activities and all the experiences in which pupils engage under the direction of the school to achieve the objectives of the school." The curriculum is the means by which the objectives of the school may be accomplished; it is all of the learning experiences directed by the school.

SCOPE OF THE CURRICULUM. The potential curriculum is, of course, all of the social heritage; it is as broad as life—life in the past and at present. From this huge potential curriculum school officials and school employees have the herculean task of selecting, organizing, and presenting the actual curriculum for the pupils. The proper performance of this task presents the greatest challenge which school officials and school employees ever face; it is worthy of the time and the best thought of all of them.

In the United States the school subjects have traditionally constituted the heart of the curriculum; hence, an excellent view of the growth of the curriculum may be had from observing the historical development of those subjects. Regarding this development it will suffice to say that the school subjects have become more and more numerous as society has grown more and more complex and as the increasing congestion of home duties has caused the responsibility for the education of children to be shifted more and more from the home to the school. Facility in reading and in writing and a knowledge of the Bible, which were the curricular requirements of the earliest schools, did not long suffice to meet entirely the needs of the people. Changing social conditions—always in the direction of greater complexity—constantly made necessary the introduction of new school subjects into the curriculum. The tabulation on page 356 of this book summarizes the development of the school subjects of the elementary-school curriculum in the United States from the first schools to the present.

The subjects of the secondary school have had an even more phenomenal development than the subjects of the elementary school. Whereas the Latin grammar school, which was the progenitor of the academy, as the latter was the progenitor of the high school, limited its curriculum to such school subjects as Latin, Greek, and higher arithmetic, the secondary school of today offers dozens of school subjects. Because of the development of the automobile and the large increase in automobile accidents, driver education has become a very prominent offering in the secondary school during recent years. In fact, in many of the secondary schools of the large cities it would be possible for a pupil to attend school for a large portion of his lifetime, pursue a normal program of study, and not have to repeat a school subject.

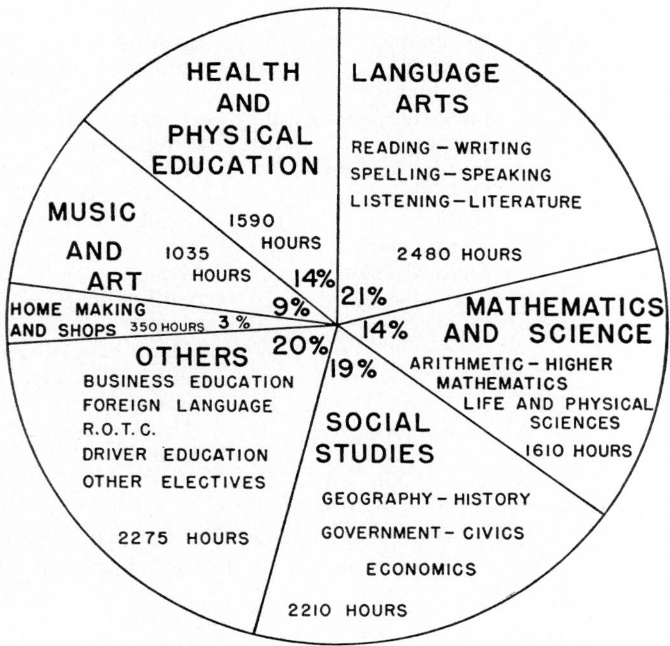

FIG. 46. Distribution of pupils' time to the various school subjects. A pupil attending school from kindergarten through twelfth grade will spend approximately 11,550 hours in school. (*From* Oakland Public Schools, *Vol.* 2, *p.* 1.) Of course, this distribution will not be the same in all school systems.

During recent years, attempt has been more and more made to introduce vocational subjects into the secondary school and to take other steps to make the secondary school more utilitarian. The large amount of employment preceding, during, and following World War II and the crying need during that war for skilled workers to build war machines and war supplies have given vocational preparation a great impetus which is almost certain to continue in peacetime. It is to be hoped, however, that this vocational training will always be related to preparation of the students for good citizenship.

The evolution of the subjects in the elementary school is shown in the following tabulation:

1642	1775	1875	At Present
Reading	Reading	Reading	Reading
Writing	Writing	Writing	Writing
Bible	Arithmetic	Arithmetic	Spelling
	Spelling	Spelling	Language and grammar (often called language arts)
	Bible	Conduct	Geography
		Language and grammar	History, civics, and current events (often called social studies)
		Geography	Art
		History and civics	Music
		Drawing	Arithmetic
		Music	Science
		Nature study	Health education
		Physical exercises	Safety education
			Industrial arts
			Home economics
			Agriculture

The approximate amount of pupils' time now devoted to the various school subjects, from kindergarten through the secondary school (twelfth grade), is shown in Figure 46 for a large city (Oakland, California).

The Historic Lag of the Curriculum

The Lag of the Curriculum Behind Social Changes. The chief criticism which has been made of the curriculum is its lag behind social conditions and social needs. The "changing curriculum" has not changed enough to meet the needs of a changing society. The curriculum has not taken sufficiently into account the problems which pupils face and which they will likely face when they become adults; it has not sufficiently prepared the pupils for living in a rapidly changing society. That criticism of the curriculum is being made today; in fact, it has always been made. It was made by Comenius (1592–1671), Froebel (1782–1852), Harris (1835–1909), Parker (1837–1902), and scores of other master teachers of former generations. During more recent years it has been made by John Dewey and his legion of disciples. What to do, if anything, about this lag has always constituted the chief problem for school officials and school employees.

In his great essay entitled, "What Knowledge Is of Most Worth," published first in 1859, Herbert Spencer (1820–1903), eminent English philosopher, made a devastating attack upon the schools of England of his time for their failure to prepare the pupils for "complete living." [2] In one place in his essay he says, "Had there been no teaching but such as is given in our public schools, England would now (1859) be what it was in feudal times"; in another place he described the curriculum of the schools of his time as one suitable only for celibates.[3] In brief, the schools then spent most of their time in preparing the pupils for reading the books of extinct nations, for appreciating the "grandeur that was Greece and the glory that was Rome." As Spencer said, the schools of his time gave little attention to preparation for "complete living"; that is, to preparation for engaging in a vocation, for maintaining good health, for performing one's duties of citizenship, for becoming parents, and for participating in worthy leisure-time activities.[4] They reveled in the classics and other contributions, especially those of the past, and were largely oblivious to the problems of the present and of the probable problems of the future.

This lag of the curriculum behind life has always been large, except in the earliest days of the school. It has been large, although the highest educational statesmanship has always been conscious of the lag and has worked diligently toward its correction. In the early

[2] Herbert Spencer, *Education: Intellectual, Moral, and Physical,* Appleton, 1860, p. 54.

[3] *Ibid.*, p. 55.

[4] *Ibid.*, p. 34.

days of the United States, life was much more simple than it is today, and preparation for life was then given primarily by the home, the church, the guild, or some other appropriate group; in those days the role of the school in the educational program of society was relatively small. Preparation for life was largely obtained by the boy or the girl through imitating the work and the play—the life—of their parents and their other elders. Moreover, the curriculum of the simple school of those days was made up of life activities. School subjects and courses of study had not yet made their appearance, and textbooks and other reading materials, except the Bible, were then unknown.

A certain amount of lag of the curriculum is inevitable because of the nature of education. Since the school, like all other institutions, is the result of experience, it will by its very nature be essentially conservative; it must be built on experience. It is everywhere agreed that the prime purpose of the school is to transmit to the pupil the heritage of the race—the accumulated knowledge, techniques, discoveries, and art. Since only a small part of this heritage can be transmitted in the brief time during which the school has the pupil under its tutelage, school officials and school employees will always have the task of deciding what knowledge is of most worth, and since this question must be answered largely by opinion—and mere opinion is ever fallible—there will always be the danger that the most valuable heritage of the race will not be selected for the curriculum. Since it is "human to err," any lag in the curriculum which is caused by the fallibility of judgment may perhaps be forgiven.

There are other causes of the lag of the curriculum behind social needs. Those causes also make the lag somewhat inevitable, but not always forgivable. Those causes stem from the human trait of conservatism and the closely related trait of inertia. Many people resist change, especially change which does not meet their own desires; they prefer to go the easiest way—to follow the "cowpath of tradition." These people sometimes sloganize their desires by saying, "What was good enough for our parents is good enough for us." This becomes their slogan, especially when they see that a proposed public service would tax them more heavily. These people sometimes avow that we already live in a perfect or a nigh perfect civilization and that the school should do nothing beyond attempting to adjust the pupils to that civilization.

The traits of conservatism and inertia should not be regarded as altogether bad, in spite of the fact that they cause the delay of institutional changes which are often sadly needed. They frequently serve the purpose of causing the rejection of philosophies, theories, proposals, opinions, and "isms" which at first blush seem excellent, but which upon closer inspection are seen to be worthless. They serve as checks upon "crackpots," as bulwarks against self-appointed "voices of America" and would-be messiahs who promise abundant manna for every human need if the people will but follow their leadership. Conservatism and inertia act as governors against undesirable and too rapid change; they require all would-be reformers to prove the merit of their proposed reforms. In a democracy persons with those traits have a voice which must be heard the same as the voice of the apostles of change.

What has been the effect of this conservatism and this inertia upon the curriculum? These traits have been too much in dominance.

FIG. 47. Arousing neighborhood interest in cleanness. *(Courtesy of the Detroit, Michigan, public schools.)*

They have resulted in a conservative curriculum for the schools of today. Although social change may have long suggested the need for a new type of material for the curriculum, this material has not been introduced until many years later—until perhaps a serious business depression, a war, or other cataclysm has forced action. Although he constantly needs reforming, it is axiomatic that "the devil can be more easily reformed when he is sick." And the devil, although he is bad, is always worth reforming.

Strange as it may seem, conservatism and inertia are not found among laymen alone; those traits also obtain among a large body of school officials and school employees, and such motives always retard changes in the curriculum. Many of these officials and employees are opposed to curricular innovations because they see in them a threat to the continuance of their vested interests. They fear that if changes in the curriculum are made, they will be thrown out of employment or be required to teach subjects which they don't want to teach; they see that textbooks and similar materials which they have prepared will no longer be used. It is a sad commentary that new subjects have usually come into the curriculum upon the demand of lay groups and not from the leadership of educators. The vocational subjects were introduced into the curriculum, for example, upon the insistence of the industrial, the agricultural, and the commercial interests, and without the support of the educators as a group.[5]

On the other hand, after a subject has obtained a place in the curriculum, it has been like pulling teeth to eliminate it or any part of it. Scores of new subjects and hundreds of parts of subjects have come into the curriculum of the elementary school, the secondary school, and the college, but only a few of them have been eliminated. Many of these subjects or parts of them are retained long after the need for them has passed away. They are kept intact by conservatism, worship of tradition, and vested interests, and often these vested interests are vigorously active. The "essentialists" of modern education were the "progressives" of yesteryear, and the liberals of today will probably be the reactionaries of tomorrow. When reformers

[5] Many educators have always opposed the use of public funds for the teaching of strictly vocational subjects on the grounds that such education serves a private purpose primarily rather than a citizenship purpose. It is strange, too, that the great teachers' organizations of the nation did not advocate desegregation in the public schools until the U. S. Supreme Court decision on May 17, 1954; neither did the present writer.

have revamped or reformed an institution, they usually set about to "protect" it from new reformers; the reformers of yesterday are usually the vested interests of today.

One view of the relation which should exist between the curriculum and social change has just been presented. To summarize, that view holds that society is now perfect or nearly so, and that the function of the school is to help to perpetuate society unchanged; if it concedes, as it occasionally does, that new factors are introduced into the social order, it denies that these new factors require a new type of school program. Most school officials and school employees and most of the general public have held that view.

The other view holds that society is not perfect and that the school should assiduously and constantly prepare its pupils to seek improvement in society. It holds that the patterns of living—that is, the social heritage—must always be under close scrutiny, in order that they may be improved wherever possible. It relates the social heritage to the problems which pupils face and which they will likely face when they become adults. It attempts to use the experiences of the race to help pupils to construct a more glorious present and future. This view is coming more and more to be held by educators, and it was given a tremendous impetus by World War II. That war has made us more anxious about our future than ever before.

Almost before a new curriculum is finished, although its planning may have been attended with profound thinking and great care, it will have become archaic in many parts. This out-of-dateness happens because social conditions and social needs change from year to year. With Heraclitus we can well say that, "There is nothing permanent; everything flows." Society changes whether the school does or not; often it changes in spite of the school. Fortunately, society has many other educational agencies, besides the school, which help it in its onward march.

It should not be inferred from the foregoing remarks that there is a revolution in social needs every change of the moon. Social needs change usually by gradual evolution, rather than by revolution. In his long struggle for a better life man has developed certain verities, or what he regards as verities, and he is not likely to throw these verities into the garbage heap of civilization overnight. When, however, institutions such as the school, the church, capital, organized labor, and government are notoriously tardy in adjusting themselves

Fig. 48. Making the curriculum more real. *(Courtesy of Euclid, Ohio, public schools.)* High school students act as city council for one day.

to social needs, the public is likely to lose patience with them and to change them by revolution—not necessarily a revolution accompanied by bloodshed but one characterized by violent changes in the institutions to bring them in line with social needs. Society changes gradually, but the adaptations of institutions to these changes must sometimes be made by revolution. Revolution must sometimes be used because institutions come to be controlled by conservative, careless, and selfish interests, and these interests always insist upon perpetuating themselves. That society progresses gradually, although the curve of advancement has many ups and downs and that the momentum of progress through the years is not uniform, will be seen by a study of progress in any field of human endeavor.

To summarize, the curriculum must be under constant revision; it must be kept up to date. In brief, it must be constantly adapted to the needs of a continuously changing—and, let us hope, constantly improving—society. If the needed revisions in it are not made, the curriculum cannot meet the needs of a dynamic society, and there is danger that it will lag many years behind social progress and become an excrescence upon society rather than a nourishment. This lag will result in a loss of money, time, and energy for school purposes; pupils will become attracted to progressing activities outside the school and will want to leave the school; and the public is likely to lose faith in the school and to regard the school's budget as obese. The lag can best be corrected by an informed body of educational employees—employees who are constant and intelligent students of the never-ending and turbulently flowing stream of civilization. These employees should regard the school as the chief source and as probably the greatest purifying agent of the stream of civilization; they should not permit that stream to become stagnant.

THE LAG OF THE CURRICULUM BEHIND THE LEARNER. Another chief criticism which has been made of the curriculum is that it is not always adapted to the needs of the learner, especially that it does not sufficiently consider the interests and the abilities of the pupil. This criticism has been made, especially by leaders in psychology and in education; less frequently has it come from laymen. It was made by educational reformers of centuries ago before experimental psychology was born; it was made by Rousseau (1712–1778), Pestalozzi (1746–1827), Herbart (1776–1841), and many other educational pioneers. The criticism has become particularly frequent and cogent during recent years as a result of the development of an experimental psychology and of a science of education. As a result of this development, no longer must educators entirely theorize or guess regarding "how the mind works" and how learning takes place. Educators now have many facts on such problems, although they are far from having—probably they will never have—final knowledge about them.

The old-time school was run on a philosophy of life which emphasized the importance of group solidarity and placed little or no emphasis upon developing the potentialities of the individual members of the group. Moreover, the conceptions of mind held by old-time educators worked hand in glove with that philosophy which emphasized the group and neglected the individual—perhaps they germinated that philosophy. Those conceptions and that philosophy held that individuals were alike in natural endowment or that they could be made alike through education; the way in which they were to be made alike was through similar subject matter presented in the same manner. With those views in vogue, it is easy to see how the old-time school came to be subject-matter-centered and how the individual pupil came to be "the forgotten man." Pupils were regarded as "funnels" into which the same kind and the same amount of subject matter were to be "poured," and at the same rate for each pupil.

In the early days one large group of educators assumed with John Locke (1632–1704) that the mind was a *tabula rasa*—a "clean slate" upon which anything might be written. That group discounted theories of differences in innate abilities and in potentialities among individuals; it believed that one slate was as clean, and could be written upon as easily, as another slate. The mind was a "slate," and subject matter was the material to be written upon the slate. That was, indeed, an engagingly simple theory of the mind and of how the educative process was to be conducted. Long ago, however, the theory was everywhere discarded by educators, and other theories supplanted it.

Another group of educators, which was closely related to and soon succeeded the *tabula rasa* group, believed that the mind was composed of a series of distinct and separate faculties—thinking, feeling, willing, etc.—and that each of these faculties could be trained through exercise just as a muscle may be thus trained; by inference that group regarded the mind as composed of several "slates" rather than of one slate. In psychology the members of the group came to be known as the faculty psychologists, and in education they came to be called the formal disciplinists. Those educators believed that the chief purpose of education was to "train the mind," and that such school subjects as arithmetic, algebra, geometry, and Latin were subjects par excellence for giving that "training." They believed, moreover, that the training received in a given field would automatically "transfer" to other fields. Method of instruction was pre-eminent with them, and pupil interest and instructional content were of slight concern. The faculty psychologists and the formal disciplinists have been rapidly decreasing in number and in influence, and it is no longer believed that transfer of training will automatically take place.[6]

[6] The questions of the amount of transfer of training and of how that transfer takes place are still controversial. For a critical summarization of the several theories and several investigations on these questions, the interested reader is referred to Pedro T. Orata, *The Theory of Identical Elements*, 1928, The Ohio State University.

Also see Walter S. Monroe, ed., *Encyclopedia of Educational Research*,

During recent decades another group of educators has come to the fore, and it is easily the largest group today. This group denies that the mind is made up of separate and distinct faculties functioning separately. It believes that the mind is an entity—an entity with itself and with the whole human body. It emphasizes the unitary character and the coherence of mental processes. It no longer worships the disciplinary and the knowledge-is-power processes and aims of education, but it emphasizes the harmonious development of all capacities of the pupil and the preparation of the pupil for economic, home, civic, and social usefulness in a democracy. With this group, method of instruction, of course, is not neglected, but method no longer dictates what shall be taught; method has become instead the vehicle for carrying the precious cargo of instruction, namely, the content, and for helping the pupil to evaluate and to use that content.

This group of educators believes that the interests and the needs of the educational consumer—that is, the pupil—should be kept in mind as well as the needs of society. It realizes that unless the interests and the needs of the pupil are kept in mind the consumer will not consume—at least all that he might, and it knows that if the pupil does not consume he will not be prepared to take his proper place in society when he becomes an adult. The modern educator is, therefore, studying and catering to the learner; he is attempting "to psychologize instruction," as Pestalozzi did many years ago, but he is using different procedures than Pestalozzi used. He realizes that there are large differences in the interests and the abilities of pupils, that the pupil learns best when he is gripped with a vital and a worthwhile purpose, and that self-activity is a *sine qua non* for the most effective learning. He believes that under the guidance of the teacher, the pupil should be permitted to have a voice in determining the content of the curriculum, and that without this voice the content is not so likely to be adapted to the pupil's interests, purposes, and abilities. He believes, moreover, that giving the pupil a voice in determining the content of the curriculum helps to prepare the pupil for participation in the democratic way of life. The school is the cradle of democracy, and that cradle should not be rocked by school officials and school employees who are dictators.

Often, though, subject matter has become both the means and the

---

article by T. G. Andrews, L. J. Cronbach, and P. Sandiford, The Macmillan Co., 1950, pp. 1483–1489.

end with certain members of this modern group of educators. Perhaps as frequently the pupil has become both the means and the end with other members of the group. Somehow both factors—subject matter and the pupil—must be united in proper relationship; without this marriage education cannot take place, and it is the obligation of the teacher to see that the proper marriage between subject matter and the pupil takes place. The school should not be wholly "child-centered" or wholly "subject-matter-centered"; rather it should be "teacher-centered." A school without an excellent teacher to serve as a "midwife at the birth of ideas" would not likely produce many worth-while ideas. Although the pupils' opinions on what they would like to study should always be considered, the teacher should always make the final decision on what the pupils shall study. But the teacher should try to convince the pupils of the merit of his decision on what should be studied.

The Technique and the Personnel for Curriculum-making

In an earlier paragraph of this chapter the curriculum was defined as "all the activities and all the experiences in which the pupils engage under the direction of the school to achieve the objectives of the school." From this definition it is correctly inferred that the curriculum is the most vital part of school instruction; therefore, the manner in which the curriculum is used determines largely the value of instruction, hence the value of the school. If the objectives of the curriculum are not the best, if the pupil activities and the experiences which make up the curriculum do not meet psychological and sociological needs, there will be waste—waste to the pupil and waste of public funds. If the teachers of the nation spend as much as ten per cent of their time on nonessential or "dead" materials in the curriculum—and they probably spend much more than that—more than $800,000,000 of the taxpayers' money is wasted annually. The opportunities for waste in the use of the curriculum are stupendous; they lurk everywhere.

The preceding statement emphasizes the large amount of waste of public funds in the curriculum. There are other wastes resulting from a poor curriculum, and those cannot be measured in dollars and cents; if they could be measured, the ten per cent waste mentioned in the preceding paragraph would seem small in comparison. The cost of these unmeasurable wastes falls heaviest upon helpless sufferers—the pupils. A poor curriculum often causes pupils to be bored, to become discouraged, and—what is more to be deplored—to fail of promotion and to quit school as soon as the school-attendance laws permit. Lack of interest in the school is one of the largest causes of nonattendance and of pupils quitting school, and it is one of the largest causes of poor discipline, which is the most frequent bugaboo of teachers, particularly of beginning teachers.

THE OLD-FASHIONED TECHNIQUE OF CURRICULUM CONSTRUCTION. The old-fashioned technique of curriculum-making may be illustrated from an inglorious chapter in our professional biography. This has its setting in a small city many years ago. We had just been graduated from college and elected superintendent of schools in the city in question. We were young and ambitious to do something "big and startling"; therefore, one of our first official acts was to start a revision of the curriculum. We did not seriously consider whether a revision was necessary, or whether we were competent to make the revision. Quixotically we plunged into the task. An experienced school board member once defined the curriculum to a new school board member in these words: "The curriculum is that thing which every new superintendent finds it necessary to revise immediately upon taking up his work."

The technique which we used in making a curriculum for the school system in question was almost universally used at that time and is employed, even today, by many old-fashioned school officials and school employees. As an example of a technique which should be avoided, it invites further description. The first step taken was to write to the superintendents of a few of the larger school systems, such as New York City, Chicago, and Philadelphia, requesting copies of their curricula. Those in hand, our work and malpractice began in earnest. Our technique of curriculum construction was the "scissors-and-paste" technique; it might also be labeled the tinkering technique. Work was begun on spelling, because we had read or had been told that spelling was one of the most mechanical and the easiest of the school subjects, and we desired to tackle the easiest subject first. We would read what seemed to be an excellent paragraph in the Chicago spelling curriculum and would transfer it by scissors and paste, without any attempt at adaptation, to our curriculum;

another paragraph would be transferred from the New York City curriculum, another from that of Philadelphia, and still others from the curricula of other school systems. In a few hours the subject of spelling was finished and we proudly surveyed our handiwork. To us the making of a curriculum required but to say "presto change," and the whole task was finished.

It is likely that the curriculum which we constructed was worse than none. The chief mistakes which we made were the following: we assumed that curriculum-making was a one-man job rather than a co-operative undertaking of the superintendent, the principals, the supervisors, and the teachers; we did not have a well-formulated philosophy of life and of education, hence no fundamental objectives which the curriculum should be expected to realize and the method by which they should be accomplished; we did not keep in mind the social conditions and the educational needs of our community; we were oblivious to the abilities, the interests, and the other psychological needs of the pupils, no provision being made for individual differences; no suggestions were made to teachers regarding the topics which were of most importance and the sequence in which the topics should be taught; no suggestions were made regarding the most efficient methods of instruction which teachers might use; no reference books, bulletins, or other materials were listed; no criteria were given for judging the results of teaching; and the curriculum was regarded as an inviolable instrument with no provision for variation from it by the different teachers or for keeping it up to date. What a nightmare that curriculum must have been to teachers and to pupils!

THE MODERN TECHNIQUE OF CURRICULUM-MAKING. The modern technique of curriculum-making is vastly different from the old-fashioned technique just described.[7] More and more this modern technique is being used; consequently, valuable curricula are much more frequently found than formerly. What is of greater significance, an attempt is being constantly made to improve the technique. In fact, during recent years, the improvement of the curricula of the American schools has probably received more thought and attention of school officials and school employees than any other phase of

[7] This modern technique is briefly described herewith. It is more completely described in several of the references listed in the Selected References at the close of this chapter.

school work. The lag of the curriculum, described in the preceding section, is being rapidly reduced through these ubiquitous efforts. There is scarcely a school system which is not questioning the merit of the present curriculum and which is not attempting to improve it. The world-wide upheaval during recent years has greatly stimulated this attempt by calling attention forcefully to the lag of the curriculum behind socio-economic needs, both national and international.

In constructing a curriculum certain steps must be taken, and defensible principles must be followed in taking those steps; in other words, there must be an underlying philosophy for all steps. The central aim of all the steps should be to obtain a curriculum which will meet the needs of pupils and adults in a constantly changing civilization; moreover, the materials of the curriculum should be selected, organized, and presented to the pupils in such a way as to contribute to the realization of the central aim of good teaching, namely, creative thinking. If adult needs monopolize the school's time, and if pupil abilities and interests are neglected, the instruction is not likely to "get across" to the pupil; on the contrary, if pupil interests and abilities monopolize the school's time and if adult needs are neglected, the pupils are not likely to be prepared to take their proper place in an adult society. The curriculum must be both "child-centered" and "adult-centered"; it must be adapted to the stage of development of the individual pupil, but it must look ahead also to the time when the pupil has grown into adulthood. To reconcile these two poles is a perplexing problem for educational statesmanship, and the problem is faced by every teacher.

What are the steps which should be followed in curriculum construction? A perusal of the literature evinces that there is general agreement among the authorities regarding the steps in curriculum construction. All the authorities agree that the determination of worth-while objectives for the curriculum should be the first step in curriculum construction. All of them also agree that there is need for a study of child life at its various stages, for a study of social and economic conditions and trends, and for a highly critical selection of subject matter which will meet these stages, conditions, and trends. When disagreement among the authorities is found, it is usually concerned with the relative emphasis which should be given to psychological and to sociological needs. To summarize, the authorities agree that the following steps are necessary in curriculum construction:

1. Desirable objectives for the curriculum must be formulated, and all succeeding steps should be taken in the light of these objectives. To formulate those objectives requires consideration of (a) the kind of world we believe in and the kind that we should live in and (b) the kind of philosophy of the educative process that we should have.
2. Materials of instruction, that is, subject matter, must be selected, organized, and presented to meet the objectives formulated in step 1.
3. The preceding steps must be experimented with and the results evaluated. A questioning attitude on values attained must always be maintained by school officials and school employees.
4. Revisions of subject matter and of teaching methods must be made in the light of the experimentation and the evaluation mentioned in step 3.
5. The procedure must be continued. Curriculum-making is a never-ending task. It proceeds as society changes and as greater knowledge of the needs of pupils and of adults is obtained.

Co-operation of Science and of Philosophy in Curriculum-making. Until about 1910, curriculum-making was largely in the hands of subject-matter specialists who were dominated by a philosophy of formal discipline, by a belief in the sacredness of subject matter, and by a worship of the past and of the *status quo*. Moreover, in those earlier days mere opinion determined school procedures, and that opinion was largely unsupported by objective data. The science of education, as we know it today, had not yet been born.

About 1910, however, a group of educators led by such pioneers as J. M. Rice, Edward L. Thorndike, and Charles H. Judd began to use objective methods of research upon educational problems. The members of this group—and the group soon came to number hundreds—were no longer satisfied with guessing at the aims, the processes, and the procedures of education; they demanded facts. Thus the science of education, as we know it today, came into being; it has grown by leaps and bounds, but it is far from being full grown.

These educators set about to study society, subject matter, and the learner—all necessary factors to be kept in mind by curriculum-makers. They raised questions regarding each of these factors, and they organized investigations using objective techniques to try to find the answers to the questions. They undertook to ascertain social needs through such procedures as tabulating the vocabularies of pupils and of adults, the problems of mathematics which pupils and adults meet in actual life, and the language which pupils and adults use and sometimes use incorrectly. By means of case studies and job analyses they tabulated the activities of people in various walks of life. They tabulated and compared the content of various textbooks and various courses of study. They constructed standardized tests which were designed to ascertain the ability of pupils to learn and to measure how much the pupils had learned. They investigated pupil reactions to various types of subject matter and to different methods of teaching each type of subject matter. They studied the nature of the individual learner—his intelligence, his eye-movements, fatigue factors, etc. They made public-opinion polls of what the people believe and of what they want and don't want. These are only a few of the fields which the science of education has been exploring and evaluating.

Unquestionably, this movement—the "scientific movement in education"—has been of incalculable benefit to the curriculum-makers. Although it has done scarcely more than scratch the surface of its potentialities, it has provided much helpful information of social conditions and trends, and on the nature of the learner; it has accomplished much toward showing school officials and school employees what is regarding these matters. Without the help of the science of education the teaching profession would still be guided by hunches, guesses, and "isms." It was soon discovered, however, that the science of education could not solve all school problems; it was seen that it could only make school officials and school employees familiar with the present conditions and with the past, but that it could not suggest the line of march for the future.

Science is one of the two handmaids of social progress. The other handmaid is a sound philosophy. If there is to be a desirable curriculum, science and philosophy must work together in experimenting for its formulation. Science has the function of obtaining data which will show what has been and what is; for example, it will point out—in fact, it has already pointed out—that the writing vocabulary of the average person has been, and is, limited to a few words, and it will name those words. A sound philosophy has the function of suggesting what ought to be; for example, it will suggest that the writing vocabulary of the average person be enlarged rather than kept as it is. It is the function of philosophy to establish values and to set large goals; but, those values and those goals cannot be formulated by "armchair" philosophers who have no interest in, or respect for, present and past conditions. A good philosophy has its roots in the experience of the past and the present.

"Fads and Frills" in the Curriculum. The schools have frequently been criticized for harboring "fads and frills," for engaging in "boon-doggling." When these terms are used, the criticism is implied that a nonessential is being harbored by the schools. Practically every new school subject has been compelled to run this gauntlet of criticism—a criticism which has come especially from conservative persons. Even the "three R's" did not escape. For many years after their introduction into the curriculum the criticism was made against older school subjects such as language and grammar, geography, and history and civics. The charge is now frequently made against the more recently introduced school subjects such as fine arts, music, health education, industrial arts, home economics, agriculture, driver education, and commercial education. When economy waves strike the school, as they always do in times of severe business depression, these newer school subjects are usually the first to feel the axe, in spite of the fact that they may be more valuable to the pupil and to society than some of the older school subjects. In consonance with the primitive ethic, the young school subjects are "thrown to the wolves" before the old ones; but, they usually survive.

These new school subjects—the so-called "fads and frills"—are also frequently criticized on the ground that they are more expensive than the traditional school subjects and therefore cannot be afforded. Although some of the newer school subjects require more equipment, smaller classes, and more expensive teachers than the traditional school subjects, it has been discovered that many of the newer school subjects are not more expensive than the traditional school subjects. When pupils come to school, they expect to enter, or are required to enter, a certain number of classes, and it is often as cheap to provide classes in the newer school subjects such as art, music, agriculture, and commerce as it is to provide classes in the traditional school subjects such as English, history, mathematics, science, and foreign languages.

Teachers and school administrators, therefore, must ever be students of educational values, especially of the relative values of the school subjects and of all parts of those subjects. They must keep in mind relative values because only a small portion of what might be taught can be taught. They must put first things first because "art is long and time is fleeting." Herbert Spencer's memorable book tells in catchy rhyme the necessity for the curriculum-maker to keep in mind our short-life span and to be guided by relative values; the rhyme (Spencer calls it a "song") goes:

Could a man be secure
That his days would endure
As of old, for a thousand long years,
What things might he know!
What deeds might he do!
And all without hurry or care.[8]

On one hand, teachers and school administrators must not be guilty of harboring useless fads and frills. On the other hand, they must be able and willing to defend new subject matter and new teaching procedures when such are an improvement over, or a supplement to, the old; in fact, they should be on the lookout for that type of subject matter and of teaching methods. They should remember that the "fad and frill" of yesterday often become the necessity of today. The locomotive, the automobile, and the airplane were fads of yesterday, but they are necessities of today. An old couplet admonishes:

Be not the first by whom the new is tried,
Nor yet the last to lay the old aside.

The Personnel for Curriculum-making. Whereas in former years the curriculum was made or revised by one "master mind," usually the superintendent of schools, a supervisor, or some other person appointed by the superintendent, the modern curriulum is made or revised through the co-operation of the superintendent, the supervisors, the principals, the teachers, and all other educational employees; moreover, persons from other fields, especially parents, are frequently requested to give their views, especially regarding objectives and subject matter. In all progressive school systems, the practice of having one person make or revise the curriculum has passed into limbo; this is fortunate, because the performance of this task is too time-consuming and too technical for one person, however omnipotent and energetic he may be. Since it is difficult for any

[8] Spencer, *op. cit.*, p. 29.

person to see "wholes," and since the curriculum should take account of wholes—society as a whole and the whole nature of the pupil—it is advisable to have a conclave of the best minds in various fields working on the curriculum. In this conclave both scientists and philosophers should be represented, both students of sociology and of psychology—in fact, all points of view should be represented and integrated.

The tendency, therefore, is for the superintendent of schools to appoint committees and to delegate to them the task of making or revising the curriculum, and since it is necessary to keep the curriculum in pace with a constantly changing society and with new knowledge of the nature of the pupil, there are advantages in making these committees somewhat permanent. In small school systems, for example, those having less than eight or ten teachers, the usual practice is to have the whole teaching corps work on one subject or a group of subjects at a time under the immediate direction of the superintendent of schools; the whole personnel also works cooperatively on curriculum objectives. In the larger school systems the usual practice is to appoint various committees to be responsible for each of the several subjects or groups of subjects. Over these committees is often placed an executive or supervisory committee which sees that the whole curriculum is balanced, without gaps, and in line with the formulated objectives of the curriculum and the school.

The making of the curriculum should not, however, be entirely a committee function. The suggestions of all members of the teaching corps, whether they happen to be members of the committee or not, should be sought; to obtain these suggestions should lead to improvements in the curriculum and should be stimulating to the teachers who make the suggestions. Every teacher must use the curriculum, and he should therefore be familiar with how the curriculum was made and how it may be adapted to the needs of his pupils; only by the watchful solicitude of every teacher can the curriculum be made to function as it should.

The implications of the foregoing remarks on committee revision of the curriculum are obvious. If the teacher is to revise or to help revise the curriculum—and more and more he is being called upon to shoulder his responsibility—he must be informed on the technique of curriculum construction and administration. For the teacher to obtain this information after he has been catapulted into a teaching position is discouraging to him and wasteful to the pupils; it is wasteful of the time and energy of the teacher, and of the pupils. Therefore, while he is in college obtaining his preparation, the prospective teacher should make certain that he obtains as large an acquaintance with the curriculum as possible. It is especially necessary that he obtain this acquaintance with the curriculum of his department or of his school subjects, and he should also see the relation between his area of teaching and other teaching areas, if he is to avoid a lopsided development of his pupils. Fortunately, most colleges which are engaged in the preparation of teachers now offer one or more courses which include units on the curriculum and require all prospective teachers to pursue this instruction. Many of the large school systems now employ curriculum specialists, and these positions provide well-paying opportunities to persons of educational experience and excellent collegiate preparation; many of the smaller school systems are also employing curriculum specialists.

The Use of the Curriculum. The old-fashioned curriculum was a stereotyped affair with, as has already been said, its emphasis on the mere acquisition of facts. All schools were expected to teach the same facts, and all pupils—dull, bright, interested, and uninterested—were expected to learn and to "recite" those same facts. Only a small amount of attention was devoted to problem-solving, particularly to the solving of problems which were interesting to the pupils, and were socially valuable. The "project curriculum" or the "activity curriculum," that is, a curriculum whose activities and experiences arise from the natural activities and the widening interests of the pupils, either was unheard of, or was considered shallow pedagogy. The old-fashioned curriculum was perhaps more suited to lethargic apes than to the restless, the thinking, and otherwise dynamic representatives of the human species who only have attended school.

Modern school officials and school administrators, on the contrary, make it possible for the curriculum to be used by teachers in a more sensible manner than formerly. They do not insist that the curriculum in use, whether it be state, city, or county, be followed slavishly; rather they permit—even insist—that the curriculum be adapted to the needs of the local school and of the individual pupils of the school. Moreover, the modern curriculum is so constructed that it may be readily adapted to varying situations. For example, although it may establish certain minimal essentials or constants, which it is expected shall become a part of the experience of all normal children, it reduces these essentials to bedrock; it suggests certain alternatives in subject matter from which teachers and pupils may choose; it is rich in suggestions on optional subject matter—which may be presented or omitted as the teacher deems best; and suggestions on excellent teaching methods are given in the modern curriculum.

In every way possible, therefore, the modern school is encouraging its teachers not to regard the curriculum as an inviolable instrument, but as a growing, dynamic affair. It encourages the teachers to adapt the curriculum to the needs of the individual pupil, and gives them many suggestions on how to make this adaptation. It encourages the teachers to experiment with new curricular materials and with new teaching methods.

Teaching Controversial Subject Matter

To Include or to Exclude Controversial Material. Problems innumerable and baffling have always faced society and probably will face it until the millennium. These problems concern every phase of human affairs, and many of them have existed since the beginning of man. They concern religion, temperance and prohibition, racism, evolution, marriage and divorce, war and pacifism, collectivism versus "rugged individualism," immigration, democracy versus other types of government, the constitution, crime, delinquency, capital and labor, strikes, natural resources, electric power, the railroads, taxation, relief and unemployment, the tariff, racial segregation, and the money and banking system. The list could be continued *ad infinitum*. Even the question of whether schools should be supported by taxation has always been and still is controversial. Shall such problems be included in, or excluded from, the curriculum? If they are included, how shall they be presented? These questions are faced sooner or later by every member of the teaching profession. They are faced especially by teachers in the secondary schools and the colleges.

Wars have been fought, political campaigns have been waged, strikes have been called, religious crusades have been conducted, and communities, states, and nations have divided over these issues. Whatever the attitude taken by the school regarding the discussion of these problems of human affairs, the discussion of them goes on in all spare time by persons in every walk of life. The problems vie with health and with the weather as the chief topics of conversation, and unlike health and the weather they are debated vigorously. Innumerable school administrators and teachers have become embroiled in bitter fights over their attempts to deal with these issues; many have become the objects of investigations which have sometimes caused them to lose their positions. Sometimes these employees have been martyrs to worthy causes, but at other times they have been guilty of undemocratic and tactless acts in their efforts to deal with these issues; in dealing with controversial issues they are like the angel described in Addison's "Campaign," who "rides on the whirlwind and directs the storm."

Either of two positions may be taken with respect to the teaching of controversial issues in the school. First, such issues may be ignored and excluded; second, they may be included and discussed. A considerable portion of the public believes that the school should not deal with any controversial problems or topics. This portion believes that the proper function of the school is to maintain the social order as it is and that there are enough facts to teach without spending time on controversial questions; it believes that such questions cannot be answered by the school anyway and that if they are let alone, they "will answer themselves." Certain of the more liberal members of this group would normally favor the discussion of controversial questions, especially the less controversial and the less baffling ones, but they believe that most teachers are not qualified to direct the discussion of them, or they feel that inflamed differences of opinion, "set ways," and prejudices on the part of the adult community would prevent free and scientific discussion.

The other position affirms that it is the obligation of the school to deal with life in all of its important aspects, and since controversial issues are a prominent part of the drama of life, they cannot be conscientiously ignored by the school. This position is defensible. The school should not concern itself with facts, known truths, and settled problems alone, but should bring that knowledge to bear upon the problems which present society faces. Knowledge of the past is of little value unless it is brought to bear upon the understanding of the present and the predicting and the controlling of the future. "Knowledge is power" only when it is used. The school must decide whether it will qualify its pupils to take an intelligent part in the discussion of controversial issues, or whether it will ignore the issues and leave these future citizens to be the easy victims of vicious propaganda which is sometimes sponsored by newspapers, magazines, books, radio or television orators, the newsreel, the movies, "politicians," and other agents and agencies. It must decide whether it will qualify pupils to think for themselves and to choose intelligently, or whether it will leave them in the hapless position of making it easy for other people to think for them and perhaps to dupe them.

THE METHODS OF PRESENTING CONTROVERSIAL MATERIAL. If controversial issues are to be discussed in the school, which ones shall be discussed, and how shall they be discussed, if at all? Regarding the first part of the question, it is manifest that all controversial issues cannot be discussed in the school because of lack of school time; there are millions of controversial issues. Those few must be selected, therefore, which have the largest and the most urgent social bearing and which are best adapted to the needs of the learner; moreover, those chosen must be in conformity with and must contribute to the realization of the objectives of the curriculum. In the upper school grades, the old-time debate on such subjects as whether fire is more destructive than water should give way to such questions as whether the government should provide a job for everyone; in the lower school grades—and at least a beginning in discussing controversial questions should be made in these grades—such questions as whether marbles should be played "for keeps" would be more appropriate to discuss than the tariff question. Moreover, many issues will have to be banned from discussion, at least temporarily, because of inflamed public opinion, or because of state laws and local regulations opposed to such discussion; still other issues will have to be discussed with special tact, if discussed at all.

According to an investigation of the Commission on the Social Studies Curriculum of the Department of Superintendence, most school principals reported that they believe that public opinion does not require the school to avoid the discussion of controversial issues; this belief was held especially at the secondary school levels.[9] The issues which the principals believed had to be avoided or handled with special tact (but these were never mentioned in more than

[9] *The Social Studies Curriculum, Fourteenth Yearbook* of the Department of Superintendence, Table 27, p. 303. The Department of Superintendence is now the American Association of School Administrators.

fifteen per cent of the replies) were, in order of frequency of mention: (1) local and state politics, (2) religion, (3) labor-capital problems, (4) politics, (5) communism, (6) "New Deal," (7) temperance and prohibition, (8) racial problems, (9) public ownership of utilities, (10) evolution, and (11) socialism. Practically all communities will permit a discussion of controversial questions in the school, provided the questions are tactfully selected and handled in a scholarly manner; excellent school officials and school employees will seldom suffer repression on this score. The public does not want "spineless" teachers. It wants intelligent and fair teachers to handle those questions.

We come next to the final and the most important problem: How shall controversial questions be discussed? There are two groups of thought with reference to this problem. One group is unwilling to have all sides of a question presented; it believes in indoctrinating in—in propagandizing for—only one point of view; it would tell the pupils what to believe and would insist upon their believing it; it would indoctrinate opinions as well as facts. This view frequently finds expression in the resolutions of various organizations—political, religious, economic, fraternal, etc.—which ask that certain beliefs be taught in the schools and that competing beliefs be banned; these organizations are occasionally successful in having their views written into state laws or into the rules and regulations of boards of education. Many textbooks also present only one view of controversial questions, and that view, of course, is the most frequently accepted view in the state or in the community in which the textbook is used. Many teachers teach only one side of controversial questions and insist upon their pupils believing as they do; often the pupil's mark or his promotion becomes a Damoclean sword to enforce this expectation. The usual arguments for indoctrination—that is, one-sided indoctrination—have been well summarized by Carleton Washburne as follows, although it should be stated that Washburne is opposed to indoctrination on the ground that its methods and its aims are opposed to the methods and the aims of true education:

(1) We must rebuild our social order, or, if we are on the other side of the fence, we must maintain the status quo. . . .
. . . the State needs trained citizens. It needs a certain like-mindedness among them in order that there may be cohesiveness. It needs certain common ideals. . . .
(2) Education to be realistic and to count in the life of the child must

have the same zeal and emotional drive which is called for by the necessity of changing—or preserving—the social order. Schools in which there is no indoctrination tend to be cloisteral, to be out of touch with the live world outside. . . .

(3) Indoctrination is inevitable. . . . A teacher, by his very nature as a teacher, imposes his views and attitudes on children. . . . A failure to indoctrinate, moreover, is in itself an indoctrination for the status quo or for the point of view held by parents of the community.[10]

The other group of thought, while admitting that a certain amount of indoctrination is inevitable because of "the frame of reference" of the teacher or of the school, rejects any theory of teaching which attempts to close a person's mind on controversial issues, or which attempts to prohibit a person from the exercise of his inherent right "to believe and to act as he pleases." It believes that the welfare of a democracy rests upon the free interchange of opinions. It realizes that free interchange of opinions is the keystone of democracy, and it indoctrinates, of course, for the preservation of that keystone. Washburne gives the following arguments against indoctrination:

(1) Indoctrination is unfair to the child. . . . He has a right to see each side clearly and fairly presented. . . . But, if he cannot count on his teacher's objectivity and honesty, where shall he turn?

(2) Indoctrination is the antithesis of education. . . . Education should lead toward growth. Indoctrination stultifies growth.

(3) Anyone who supposes that he has the one and final solution to any problem is inexcusably bigoted and is, therefore, unfit to educate children. . . . The growth of society depends upon our free exploration of all possible avenues of escape, of all possible avenues toward our ultimate ideals. Indoctrination shuts off all avenues but one.

(4) . . . If one group can use the schools to indoctrinate the children toward its particular answers to controversial questions, so can another group. . . .[11]

On any controversial question this latter group would bring out the facts and the arguments on all sides of a question. It would permit—in fact, insist—that the pupil state his own opinions and formulate his own conclusions; complete impartiality would be its goal. In other words, it would practice the scientific attitude, that is, the inclination to find the truth, and by precept and example it

[10] "Indoctrination versus Education," *The Social Frontier*, Vol. 2 (April, 1936), pp. 212–213.

[11] *Ibid.*, p. 213.

would try to instill this attitude into the pupils. This admittedly would be indoctrination—but, it would be only indoctrination in the scientific attitude and in the spirit of democracy. It would teach pupils to distinguish between facts and mere opinions. It would realize that views which cannot be verified, and that is true of most views, are opinions, and that when they are verified, they become facts and are no longer opinions. It would indoctrinate facts when they have been incontrovertibly demonstrated to be facts, but it would be certain that facts were present before they were given only one interpretation—before pupils were indoctrinated in them. It would realize that "truth is an elusive goddess"—elusive because of new discoveries and differences in interpretations of what the truth is.

Academic Freedom and Social Responsibility. The recommended place of the teacher in the handling of controversial issues has been given in broad outline in the preceding paragraphs. That place demands that the teacher—a well-prepared and democratic teacher is, of course, meant—not be shackled in his attempts to lead his pupils to the fountain of truth. In other words, the teacher should have academic freedom, and he should have it so long as he is seeking the truth and is using fair means in his quest for the truth.

Like all rights, the right to academic freedom is, however, a relative matter; it does not give the individual a license to say and to do anything that he pleases. The right does not permit careless handling of the truth; it does not permit libel and similar practices. As former Justice Holmes of the United States Supreme Court once said, "It does not permit any one to yell 'fire' in a crowded theater." Whereas the teacher has the right in the classroom to state his own views on any issue which is being discussed, he has the obligation to present all sides of the issue and of placing his pupils in a position of being able to formulate their own patterns of belief. The right to academic freedom does not give the teacher the right to be an eternal propagandist for any doctrine, creed, or dogma; if he must propagandize, he should "hire a hall" or "publish a tract." His obligation is fundamentally to teach, rather than to advocate. When he states his views, he should state them calmly and judiciously, and always with the stipulation that they are his opinion only, which need not be accepted by his pupils; he should speak more in the tone of opinion and less in the tone of certainty. This is the only sort of academic freedom to which the teacher has a right; for him to expect or to exact more than this is undemocratic and is likely to make him the fair quest of heretic seekers.

The right to academic freedom places upon the teacher the responsibility of being well informed on the many sides of all important controversial questions to be discussed in his classroom. Without this erudition the teacher is not likely to be able to bring out all sides of a question and to guide the search for the solution of the question; without it, too, there is greater danger that he will try to substitute his mere opinion for knowledge, and this is the worst form of pedagogical quackery.

The Organization of the Curriculum

The Types of Curriculum Organization. Many types of curriculum organization are in use in the schools today. These types are distributed between two extremes. In one of these extremes, the curriculum is organized by separate and isolated subjects—reading, spelling, algebra, botany, history, etc. This is the traditional type of curriculum organization and is found in most schools today. In the other extreme, subject lines in closely related subjects are eliminated, and the subject matter is merged into what is usually known as a fused, integrated, core, or unified curriculum. This type of organization, or a variation of it, is coming to be widely used, especially in the language arts and the social studies.

Merits of the Various Types of Curriculum Organization. Which type of curriculum organization is best? Shall the curriculum be organized on a separate subject basis, or shall all subjects be abolished and a "fused," "integrated," "core," or "unified" curriculum substituted? If neither of these extremes is deemed best, where is the optimum position between them? These questions have been widely discussed, since Herbart (1776–1841) advocated the correlation [12] of the various subjects of the curriculum. Under the leadership of the "Progressive-education" group, which vigorously advocated "activity" organization, fusion, integration,[13] and unification, the questions have become very live during the two or three latest decades.

[12] In correlation, the subjects are retained, but the materials in each subject are related to the materials in other subjects. In fusion, integration, core, or unification all school subject lines are obliterated, and a problem or topic becomes the controlling factor in the organization of material.

[13] Wilford M. Aiken, *The Story of the Eight-Year Study*, Harper, 1942.

Although there has been much experimentation with the various types of curriculum organization, and although each type has many advocates, there are as yet no conclusive data which indicate superiority for any type. The Eight-Year Study has, however, reported certain advantages of the "activity" type of curriculum organization over the old-fashioned subject-matter type of organization.[14] The Commission on the Social Studies Curriculum suggested that the following instructional and administrative factors be kept in mind when selecting the type of curriculum organization; although these suggestions were made especially for the social-studies curriculum, they would seem to be pertinent to the whole curriculum.

(1) Are the teachers familiar with the adopted plan and adequately prepared to give it a fair trial?
(2) Are the patrons of the school and the public in general likely to assume a sympathetic attitude toward the proposed innovations?
(3) Are the principals and supervisors thoroughly familiar with the changes and competent to direct the new program?
(4) Are appropriate building facilities and proper equipment and furnishings provided?
(5) Are suitable textbooks and adequate instructional supplies available?
(6) Can the proposed plan be administered in a departmental school, platoon school, or any other type of school organization now in operation in the local school system?
(7) Does the proposed plan provide a comprehensive study of the social studies as a whole and at the same time insure a proper emphasis of each aspect of the social studies?
(8) Does the plan present human relationships in the most natural and realistic manner?
(9) Does the plan promote horizontal articulation of experiences in the different subjects at each grade level?
(10) Does the plan demand constant reorganization of materials by the pupils and insure the consideration of all elements or aspects of the topic of instruction mentioned above?
(11) Does the plan afford the teacher the greatest possible freedom in adapting the made-in-advance curriculum to the needs and interests of pupils in a particular classroom situation? [15]

The difference in views of those who favor subject organization and of those who favor the fused, integrated, or unified organizations is occasioned primarily by a difference in philosophy of education.

[14] *Ibid.*

[15] *The Social Studies Curriculum*, 1936, p. 179. By permission of the National Education Association, publishers.

The advocates of the subject-matter plan of curriculum organization hold the view that the school subject contains the necessary knowledge and that this subject matter has been obtained from the best experience of the people. The advocates of the fused, integrated, or unified plans of curriculum organization hold the view that curriculum-making should start with socially significant problems, issues, or topics, and should organize all material around such problems, issues, or topics.

In the final analysis, therefore, the question becomes: Shall the subject-matter organization of the curriculum be used, or shall the activity [16] organization be employed? Since objective data are not available to answer the question, we shall have to be content with a summarization of the arguments in favor of each plan.[17] The usual arguments advanced for the school-subject organization are as follows:

1. The school subject—at least when it is well organized—contains the subject matter which pupils need and which they should, therefore, be expected to study. The activity curriculum, on the contrary, is child-determined and likely to be whimsical. Pupils are not competent to decide what they shall study.
2. The school subject gives assurance that knowledge, attitudes, and skills which are needed by the pupils will not be missed. The child-determined curriculum, on the contrary, is likely to fail to meet many pupil needs.
3. The school subject is likely to be logically organized, and pupils are brought to see the structure of knowledge on a subject.

The usual arguments in favor of the activity curriculum are as follows:

1. It is organized in terms of problems, issues, and topics of interest to the pupils. In the belief that pupil purposes are necessary learning stimuli, it keeps in mind such purposes. It stimulates pupil thinking.
2. Provided proper pupil guidance is given by the teacher, it may be made to include all subject matter which is really necessary. The

[16] There are many views of what the activity program or curriculum really is. Some persons see it as a plan which gives full play to the spontaneous interests, the likes and dislikes, of the pupil. The best authorities, however, see it as an opportunity for the pupils and the teachers to work together in choosing and in attacking problems of social import adapted to the interest and understanding of the pupils.

[17] Some data which tend to favor the activity organization are presented in Aiken, *op. cit.*

school-subject curriculum, on the contrary, is likely to contain much subject matter which is not socially valuable and which is adult centered.

3. It leads to individual growth by teaching the pupil to see relationships, without which learning is not very profound. The school-subject curriculum, on the contrary, emphasizes isolated facts which are not necessarily related to the problems of life.

"The Good Citizen"

The making of good citizens should be the fundamental aim of the schools, and the curriculum of the school should have in mind that aim and try to accomplish it. The 1953 Yearbook of the American Association of School Administrators, on the *American School Curriculum,* pages 24–27, states the following requirements for good citizens:

1. Civic competence.
2. Educational flexibility.
3. Social understanding.
4. Occupational efficiency.
5. Home loyalty.
6. Religious consciousness.
7. Leisure-time opportunities.

Not all of our people meet those requirements to perfection; perhaps, they never will. As a nation, we are perhaps more deficient in Civic competence, in Religious consciousness, and in Social understanding than in any of the other categories requisite for "the good citizen." We are also deficient in our understanding of economics—personal, community, and social. The school can help to eliminate these deficiencies.

QUESTIONS FOR DISCUSSION

1. What are the differences between courses of study and the curriculum?

2. What subjects do the laws of your state require to be taught in (a) the elementary school and (b) the secondary school? Is the amount of time to be devoted to each subject also prescribed? Mention the usual arguments for and against such prescription.

3. What are the advantages and the disadvantages of state courses of study? Will the present tendency toward socio-economic planning on the part of the states and the Federal Government result in greater or less prescription of courses of study? Explain. Is the present tendency toward such planning to be encouraged? Why or why not?

4. How closely should teachers be expected to follow the official course of study? Would your views be different if teachers were better prepared to determine the course of study? Explain. How may teachers become better informed about the curriculum?

5. What has been the effect of college-entrance requirements on the secondary school curriculum? Should the colleges have entrance requirements or should they permit the secondary schools to determine their curricula without reference to college-entrance requirements? Explain.

6. Many educators believe that an examination of the course or courses of study gives the best single measure of the merit of the school or school system. Do you agree with this claim? Why or why not?

7. What are the relative contributions of research and of philosophy in curriculum construction? What would be the limitations of one without the other?

8. How would you justify to a doubting school board member or other citizen the value of the so-called "fads and frills," for example, home economics, industrial arts, and gardening? Why must the curricular offerings of the school always keep in mind relative values of subject matter?

9. What objection, if any, would you make to a course of study which was based upon pages in textbooks?

10. In deciding upon what to teach, how much emphasis should be placed upon sociological needs, and how much upon psychological needs?

11. It has been said that social needs vary (1) historically, (2) geographically, and (3) individually. Give illustrations of these variations.

12. Mention a few items of "dead wood" which you believe should be eliminated from the curriculum. Justify your views. What are the influences which keep this "dead wood" in the curriculum?

13. What opportunity, if any, would you give the elementary school pupil to elect subjects? The junior high school pupil? The senior high school pupil? The college or university student? Explain your views. To what extent should the pupil decide what he shall study?

14. Under what limitations do the small secondary schools operate with respect to their curricular offerings? Explain. What feasible steps might these schools take to increase their curricular offerings?

15. The schools have been recently criticized for emphasizing too much the "bread and butter" aim of education and for neglecting the citizenship aim. Do you believe that this criticism is just? Explain. Do you agree with certain educators that public funds should not be used for providing vocational education? Why or why not?

16. Do you believe that the requirements for a good citizen, p. 385 of this book, include all of those requirements? How would you modify the statement?

SELECTED REFERENCES

Aiken, Wilford M., *The Story of the Eight-Year Study,* Harper and Bros., New York, 1942, 157 pp.

Compares the work of thirty Progressive schools with that of traditional schools.

Alberty, Harold, *Reorganizing the High School Curriculum,* Revised edition, The Macmillan Co., 1953, New York, 560 pp.

Believes that there are no sharp divisions between subject matter and method, the curriculum and the extracurriculum, education and guidance, philosophy and practice. Presents much material on the "core" curriculum.

American Education and International Tensions, Educational Policies Commission of the National Education Association, Washington, 1949, 50 pp.

Recommends that only those who believe in democracy should be permitted to teach.

"American School Curriculum," pp. 5–358, *Thirty-First Yearbook of the American Association of School Administrators,* 1953.

Discusses developments in the elementary and the secondary schools.

Blackman, Mildred Russell, "Let's Not Bridge the Gap," *Educational Administration and Supervision,* Vol. 40 (May, 1954), pp. 313–318.

"Bridging the gap" refers to the gap between educational theory and practice. The author suggests that the gap be not bridged, but filled in with better knowledge and practices to eliminate the great gap that exists at present.

"Controversial Issues," *Educational Leadership,* Vol. 8 (March, 1951), pp. 326–387.

The whole issue is devoted to this topic.

Education for All American Youth—A Further Look, Educational Policies Commission of the National Education Association, Washington, 1952, 402 pp.

Contains much material on the changing curriculum.

Education for All American Youth, Educational Policies Commission of the American Association of School Administrators, Washington, 1952, 402 pp.

States an ideal education for American youth.

Exton, Elaine, "Controversies Affecting Public Education," *American School Board Journal*, Vol. 129 (September, 1954), pp. 50–51.

With the system, one must first determine the motive of the attacking person or party. Then a positive, constructive approach in answering the attacks would usually settle the controversy.

Fordyce, W. G., "We Wrote Our Curriculums," *Nation's Schools*, Vol. 54 (November, 1954), pp. 78–81.

Reports how teachers' guides for all grades and departments were developed by teachers, school administrators, and parents' committees.

Gavian, Ruth Wood, and Nanassy, Louis C., "Economic Competence as a Goal of Elementary-School Education," *Elementary School Journal*, Vol. 55 (January, 1955), pp. 270–273.

High school curriculums increasingly contain general economics or personal economics, but there is also a place for the subject in the elementary school as well. The authors give some of the desirable goals of elementary school economics.

General Education in a Free Society, Harvard University Press, Cambridge, 1945, 280 pp.

Discusses the place of general and of vocational education in the secondary school and in the college.

Gwynn, J. Minor, *Curriculum Principles and Social Trends*, Revised edition, The Macmillan Co., New York, 1950, 768 pp.

A splendid source for such principles and trends.

Murray, Ruth, and True, Helen M., "Team Up for Greater Learning," *NEA Journal*, Vol. 43 (October, 1954), pp. 439.

Two secondary school teachers, one in American literature and one history, found many benefits from combining units studied and formed a sort of two-class core curriculum of their own.

Organizing the Elementary School for Living and Learning, 1947 Yearbook of the Association of Supervision and Curriculum Development of the National Education Association, Washington, 1947, 209 pp.

Discusses new and desirable practices in the elementary school curriculum.

Ragan, William B., *Modern Elementary Curriculum*, The Dryden Press, New York, 1954, 400 pp.

Analyzes the extreme points of view in education and relates them to the elementary school curriculum.

Russell, Harris E., and Lake, Earnest G., "Curriculum Development from Kindergarten to Grade Twelve," *Journal of Education*, Vol. 137 (December, 1954), pp. 2–3, 30–32.

Racine, Wisconsin has a continuous program of curriculum improvement. A teacher from each school building meets monthly to consider problems and methods of handling them. The program has succeeded in getting a program that moves from kindergarten to 12th grade. Classroom teachers and parents are given every chance to contribute all they can.

Saylor, J. Galen, and Alexander, William M., *Curriculum Planning*, Rinehart and Co., New York, 1954, 637 pp.

The book is organized around several major questions concerning curriculum planning and is useful for elementary and secondary school personnel.

Sennett, T. B., "Reorienting the English Curriculum Toward Communication," *School Review*, Vol. 62 (November, 1954), pp. 474–479.

English teachers place too much emphasis on literature and little or none on such other means of modern communication as radio, motion pictures, magazines, newspapers.

Toward a New Curriculum, Forty-Fourth Yearbook of the Department of Supervision and Curriculum Development of the National Education Association, Washington, 1944, 200 pp.

Emphasizes the secondary school curriculum.

Toy, Henry, Jr., "Planning Curriculum With Citizens," *School Executive*, Vol. 74 (November, 1954), pp. 19–20.

Discusses the responsibility of the citizens for the welfare of their schools, and their co-operation with the school program.

Williams, Catherine M., "Sources of Teaching Materials," *Educational Research Bulletin*, Vol. 34 (May 11, 1955), pp. 113–140.

An excellent bibliography of sources.

CHAPTER 14

The Contributions of Extracurricular Activities

Extracurricular Activities and the Curriculum

Definition and Scope of Extracurricular Activities. Although the term is hardly appropriate, in common parlance extracurricular activities refer to all pupil activities which are not a part of the regular studies of the school. Among the more frequently found of these activities today are athletics, debates, dramatics, clubs, and school publications. Many of the activities are almost as old as the school, but the term extracurricular is of fairly recent coinage and usage.

During recent years, these activities have had a phenomenal development in number and in prestige. They have developed in response to the demand for a type of educational experience which the home, the church, the regular curriculum of the school, and other educational agencies of the community were not providing or were not sufficiently providing. They came in to supplement the regular curriculum and to make it more interesting and more practical.

The extracurricular activities have had their largest development in the college and in the secondary school, but they have also become prominent in the elementary school, especially in the upper grades. Today it is not uncommon to find several of the extracurricular activities in one school. In a large school system, which has many secondary schools, hundreds of types of those activities are likely to be in operation. They may be roughly classified under the same headings as the subjects and departments of the school. Most of them may be subsumed under the following headings: literary, journalistic, forensic and declamatory, scientific, musical, foreign language, historical, geographical, mathematical, industrial, home economics, agricultural, commercial, arts and crafts, civic, social, and physical. The most frequently found extracurricular activity is athletics, it being almost universal, especially in the secondary schools.

VALUES OF EXTRACURRICULAR ACTIVITIES. In the early days extracurricular activities were considered to be outside the curriculum, hence the name extracurricular. In those days school officials and school employees took little or no interest in the extracurricular activities and in many instances condemned them as parasites of time and energy which should be devoted to the school subjects, and by the general public those activities were regarded as wholly wasteful of time, energy, and money.

During recent years, however, forward-looking educators and laymen have come to see that such activities, if properly directed and supervised by the school, have distinct educational value. Whereas they were formerly considered to be extracurricular, today they are coming more and more to be regarded as curricular. They are coming to be looked upon as an integral part of the curriculum, because they possess educational value, and as was stated in the preceding chapter, any experience or any activity which has educational value and which is directed by the school is really a part of the curriculum. Since these activities are in fact curricular, they should not continue to be called extracurricular; it would seem more appropriate to call them extraclass, and in the remainder of this chapter that term will be used in referring to them.

There is agreement among modern educators that extraclass activities have potential value and are worthy of a prominent place in the school program. Indeed, it is agreed that, if they are properly directed, many of them have greater value than some of the school subjects. They stem from a dynamic present rather than from a cadaverous past. They have the especial merit of arising spontaneously from the interests of the pupils; pupils like to participate in them, even without school credit.[1] Many of the school subjects, on

[1] Some schools now give pupils a small amount of credit toward graduation for participating in extraclass activities.

the contrary, are formal and uninteresting and give rise to what Shakespeare describes, "the whining schoolboy with his satchel . . . creeping like a snail unwillingly to school." It is the obligation of the school to supervise the pupils in doing these things which they are going to do willy-nilly, and to use these interests, provided, of course, they are not vicious, in developing higher types of interests. In brief, these interests may be regarded as springboards from which pupils may be helped to jump to more worthy interests. Under proper guidance the interests may be integrated with and used to motivate the school subjects and thus to become a part of the class activity. They may be used as aids for keeping the pupils, especially the older ones, in school and for stimulating the pupils to work more arduously on their school subjects. They are good medicine for the school organism, but like all good medicine they must be prescribed in proper kind, in proper amount, and at the proper time.

If any extraclass activity is to realize its potentialities, the purposes of the activity must be kept clearly in mind by school officials and teachers, and the proper steps must be taken to accomplish those purposes. Purposes are seldom achieved unless they are clearly seen and unless assiduous and intelligent efforts are made to accomplish them. Above all, these purposes must be worthy. They will be worthy only in so far as they help to meet pupil needs. The purposes of extraclass activities should be the same as the purposes of the regular class activities. They should prepare the pupils for participation in the democratic way of life. They should teach the pupils social co-operation through providing experiences in group living. They should develop in the pupils higher standards of ethics, better sportsmanship, more self-discipline, and better school and community spirit. They should make pupils more aware of both their individual rights and their social responsibilities. They should prepare pupils for better leadership and for better followership, for more worthy home membership, for better recreational and aesthetic participation, for good health, for vocational efficiency, and for the highest type of citizenship in a democracy. "The good citizen" should be their goal.

Necessity for Teacher Assistance in Extraclass Activities. In accordance with the increasing appreciation of the values of the extraclass activities, the more progressive schools and school systems today are encouraging and supervising the extraclass activities; they are making them an official and an integrated part of the school pro-

Fig. 49. Electing officers by the student council. (*Courtesy of the Pittsburgh, Pennsylvania, public schools.*) Such extraclass activities can be rich in educational experience.

gram. For example, teacher sponsors are being assigned to them and public funds are being utilized for their encouragement; furthermore, in many schools and many school systems a special period in the school day or the school week is set aside for the extraclass activities and credit toward graduation is given to the pupils who engage in the activities.

The success of any program of extraclass activities depends upon the willing and the intelligent co-operation in that program of the teachers of the school. Although school superintendents and school principals are responsible for the general administration and the supervision of the program, they cannot be expected to give the multifarious and the diverse activities the close supervision which is needed; in consequence, the responsibility for such supervision is being delegated more and more to the teachers of the school, and the work is regarded as a regular and an important part of the teachers' duties. The typical teacher of today, especially in the secondary school, is called upon to supervise at least one extraclass activity, and often he is called upon to supervise several of them. He should, therefore, keep this fact in mind when he is obtaining his preparation for teaching. Indeed, ability and willingness to supervise one or more of these activities have almost become a *sine qua non* for obtaining a teaching position, especially in the secondary school; moreover, ability to supervise one or more extraclass activities, especially to coach an athletic team, will often enable the teacher to command a higher salary. Many school systems have adopted salary schedules which pay extra amounts for coaching extraclass activities. Other systems do not give extra pay but lighten the regular teaching load for teachers who supervise extraclass activities. Extraclass activities have become so prominent that many of the larger secondary schools now employ someone who gives his entire time to their supervision.

If the teacher is to give intelligent direction and supervision to extraclass activities, he needs preparation for the work the same as he needs preparation for the teaching of reading, history, industrial arts, science, or any other school subject. Probably the best means by which he can obtain this preparation is through participation in extraclass activities in college or university. Thus, the person who would become the most successful coach of athletics or debates should receive large benefit from becoming a member of the appropriate team or squad while he is a student in college or university. The same suggestion is pertinent for coaches, directors, or sponsors of orchestras, glee clubs, choruses, bands, student publications, or other extraclass activities. In employing new teachers one of the questions most frequently asked of candidates by school officials or school administrators is, "In what extraclass activities did you participate when you were a college or university student?" A candidate who must answer, "None," to that question often indicts himself as an unsocial creature and incompetent to perform the task of advancing the socialization of pupils. "All work and no play makes Jack a dull boy," and is likely to handicap him in obtaining a teaching position when he grows into adulthood.

A second means which teachers might profitably use in qualifying themselves more fully for the supervision of extraclass activities is to pursue a college or university course in such activities, and in some of these departments all prospective teachers, especially in the secondary school, are required to receive this instruction. If such a course is not available to the student, he can, as a partial substitute for it, read one or more of the excellent books on the subject, the names of several of which are listed in the Selected References at the close of this chapter. Or under the guidance of his professors he can study the problem through selected magazine articles; during recent years, hundreds of such articles have appeared, and these articles may be readily located through the card catalogues, indexes, and other facilities of good school and good college libraries.

Principles for Directing Extraclass Activities

In the preceding section of this chapter the aims and values of extraclass activities were emphasized. In the present section will be discussed briefly some of the more important principles of organization, administration, and supervision which school officials and school employees and college students should keep in mind in accomplishing the desired aims and values. College students will find that all or practically all of these principles apply to college extraclass activities as well as to similar activities in the elementary and the secondary schools. The principles follow:

1. *All extraclass activities of the pupils should be supervised by the school and the activities should be subject to school control and school discipline.* In the first place, school supervision of the activities is recommended because it is necessary if any activity is to accomplish all that it might. Of course, too much or the wrong kind of supervision would be as bad as none, because it might kill or stifle spontaneity and make it difficult for the pupils to develop initiative and other desirable attitudes and ideals. The amount of school supervision to be extended to these activities will depend on several factors, such as the type and the age of the organizations, or the activity and the maturity of the students participating. As a rule, a larger amount of supervision will be needed by new organizations or activities than by old ones; more by athletics, dramatics, and similar activities than by chess clubs and similar organization; and more by elementary and junior high school pupils than by senior high school pupils.

In the second place, school supervision is recommended because it will protect the reputation of the organization, of the individual members of the organization, and of the school. Whenever any activity is conducted under the name of the school, or whenever any school organization holds a meeting, school officials and school employees must assume a certain responsibility for supervising the activity; this responsibility comes whether the activity or the meeting is held on the school premises or is held elsewhere. The reputations of the organization and of the school must be jealously guarded, for, justly or unjustly, the public usually associates with the school any misconduct of the pupils and often blames the school for such behavior. By a strange irony a pupil who commits a misdemeanor receives more unfavorable publicity than an outsider receives for a similar, or even a more heinous, offense. Any aberrant behavior of the school personnel, whether pupil or school employee, is likely to be news, apparently because it is unusual.

2. *Before a new activity is launched it should be approved by the principal, by the general supervisor of extraclass activities, or by another central authority of the school.* Before a new activity is approved, there should be assurance that the activity will meet a need of the school, that it will not duplicate some other school activity, that the pupils are sufficiently interested in it to support it, and that there is a teacher in the school who is qualified, has the time, and is willing to direct the activity.

3. *Every activity should beget civic-social-moral and other worthwhile values for the pupils participating in it.* Some of the chief values of extraclass activities were mentioned earlier in this chapter. Activities which do not have a purpose beyond the harmless enjoyment of leisure time or the creation of an outlet for superabundant energies should be reduced to a minimum particularly in view of the fact that the realization of this purpose is usually a by-product of activities which have more worthy purposes.

4. *Since the principal and the teachers of a school are responsible for the administration of their school, they should have the power to veto any proposal of any extraclass organization.* It should not often be necessary for them to exercise this power, but in view of the fact that they are in charge of the school, they must be privileged and expected to exercise it when necessary. Of course, their decisions on any matter should always be open to review by the superintendent of schools, and the decisions of the superintendent should in turn be open to review by the board of education which sits as a court of final authority and which represents the people of the community. The board of education should be open to review by the people of the community.

5. *The number and the type of extraclass activities to be developed in any school should be determined by the size of the enrollment of the school and by the needs of the school.* The advantage of having a large number of activities is that students are given a leeway for meeting their individual needs and their interests. The danger of having a large number is that the school will be "overorganized" and that the students will become mere "joiners." Between these two extremes the happy medium must be sought.

That many schools have too many extraclass activities, there is little doubt. Several of these activities do not meet a useful purpose, and the students would be better served if some of the activities were permitted to sink into innocuous desuetude and limbo. Although "overorganization" is frequently found in the large schools, it more frequently exists in the small schools which often believe that their prestige demands that they have as many organizations and activities as the large schools. Overambition can be as harmful as underambition.

6. *The introduction of a program of extraclass activities in a school should be gradual.* The pace of introduction should be dictated by

the needs of the school and by the rapidity with which the school can establish proper supervision of the activities. Any new extraclass activity should usually arise from a regular curricular activity of the school and should be developed in close connection with that curricular activity; for example, the History Club would arise from and be developed in connection with the work of the history department of the school.

7. *The number of organizations in which a student is permitted to have membership, or the number of activities in which he is permitted to participate during a semester or a school year, should be limited by the school.* A limitation on participation in extraclass activities is recommended for two reasons: first, it will prevent the overambitious, the brilliant, the versatile, and the popular students from overloading with activities to the possible detriment of their health and their regular school studies; second, it will distribute participation in the activities among a larger number of students.

Although it is generally agreed that the number of school organizations and activities in which pupils are permitted to participate should be limited, there is no formula for indicating with mathematical precision where the delimiting line should be drawn. In attempting to solve the problem just mentioned, some schools have listed their extraclass activities as "majors" and "minors" and have indicated the number of majors and minors which a student shall be permitted to "carry" during a semester or a school year. Other schools have established a "point" system for regulating these matters; according to this system each activity of the school is rated according to the time and the energy that it requires, and students are limited in the number of points which they may "carry" each semester or each school year.

8. *In order that each student shall have a well-rounded development in both the regular curricular and the extraclass activities, the plan of educational guidance of the school should consider both types of activities in advising the pupil regarding his school program.* Such guidance is particularly helpful in the elementary and in the junior high schools. In a school which has a well-organized program of extraclass activities and an efficient system of student guidance, there would be few, if any, students who would not participate in at least one extraclass activity. Shy pupils are frequently reluctant to enter

extraclass activities, yet they are the pupils who most need the socializing experiences which such activities afford. Schools have heretofore placed too much emphasis, especially in athletics, on the development of "champions" and have neglected the average pupils. To win is a laudable ambition, but there are other important values that come from playing a game.

9. *Since it is desired that as many students as possible shall participate in each activity, there should be democracy in the activity.* Democracy can be obtained by making participation in each activity equally open to all pupils. This would not, of course, be interpreted to preclude the organization of separate activities for boys and for girls, nor the establishing of reasonable standards for achievement for eligibility to participate in certain activities. Whatever may be their merits in the colleges and universities, school officials and school employees are agreed that secret organizations should not be permitted in the elementary and the secondary schools; in fact, most states either have state laws, or rules of the state department of education, which prohibit secret organizations in the elementary and the secondary schools. It is a sad commentary that in some states these laws are poorly enforced by local school officials and school employees. The laws should be enforced or repealed, and it is the belief of the writer that they should be enforced. Secret organizations in the elementary and the secondary schools should be banned.

10. *Only active members of the school, that is, students and school employees, should be permitted to enroll as members of school organizations.* Since they are not amenable to school control and school discipline, outside members frequently cause trouble for both the organization and the school. Pupils who have severed their connection with the school should not be members of extraclass organizations.

11. *Whenever possible, the school building or school grounds should be the place of meeting for all school functions.* School functions which are not held on the school premises are usually more difficult to supervise, and they are usually more costly to hold.

12. *In order to avoid conflicts in dates and in order to obtain better administration in general, the meetings of all organizations and all school activities should be definitely scheduled as far ahead as possible.* Many schools have found it desirable to devote a certain period of the school day to such activities. For most organizations and most

activities, day meetings are preferable to evening meetings. If evening meetings are necessary, they should usually be held on an evening which is not followed by a school day.

13. *To obtain large participation by the students and at a small cost to them, the necessary expense incident to all organizations and activities should be kept as low as possible.* Not only should the fees, the dues, and the admission charges be kept low, but employment provisions should somehow be made for the few pupils who cannot meet even the lowest expense. The extraclass activities are not free, and perhaps that is better if school officials and school employees will take steps to assure that no pupil is unable to participate in any activity because he does not have the fees, the dues, or the admission charges for participating.

14. *There should be supervision by the school of all extraclass funds.* Most extraclass organizations have certain expenses to meet, and therefore, they require revenue. The amount of money which they annually take in and pay out varies from a few dollars in the small schools to several thousand dollars in the large schools, especially the secondary schools. In most schools athletic contests are the chief source of revenue. Whether the amount of money be large or small, the school must exercise supervision of it. Many progressive boards of education have adopted rules and regulations requiring every school to provide this supervision. No organization of the school can justly claim that since it has earned its own money, it should be permitted to expend it as it chooses.

School supervision of the finances of all extraclass activities is recommended for two reasons. In the first place, supervision obtains more economical expenditure of the funds. Under complete student control, there is the ever-lurking danger that the funds will be wasted. To permit the waste of funds is not fair to the members of the group which furnishes the funds, nor does waste inculcate desirable habits in the students who are responsible for the waste. In the second place, supervision guarantees the financial integrity, and protects the reputation, of the persons who handle the funds. Without a proper system of audits and of public reports of funds, defalcation on the part of persons who administer the funds is risked; morever, the reputations of honest persons are likely to be besmirched. Even school officials and school employees, who often assume control of these funds, must take heed lest "whispering campaigns" be launched against their integrity. All accounts should be so kept that no one, at any time, or at any place, could legitimately question the fidelity to their trust of the persons who keep the accounts. To summarize, the following recommendations are made for supervising the extraclass funds: (1) they should not be under the control of the students alone; (2) they should not be under the control of the principal, of a teacher, or of any other person alone; and (3) they should always be open to inspection, be regularly audited, and itemized reports of their status should be publicly made every year. The board of education should have general supervision of the extraclass funds the same as it does of the public funds.

It is an excellent plan to have the financial affairs of the extraclass activities directed by a committee composed of both students and faculty members. Under ideal conditions this committee would represent the financial affairs of all extraclass organizations and activities of the school and not merely the affairs of one or a few. Such a committee is particularly advisable in schools which have centralized financing of all extraclass activities. Its general functions are to prepare budgets for the activities, or to assist in preparing them; to assist in obtaining ample revenue for each activity; to aid in obtaining an economical expenditure of all extraclass activity revenues; and, in general, to serve as a clearing house for all financial phases of the extraclass activities.

QUESTIONS FOR DISCUSSION

1. Do you agree with the frequently stated criticism that the schools are spending too much time on extraclass activities to the neglect of the school subjects? Why or why not?

2. Do you disagree with any of the "principles for directing extraclass activities" mentioned in this chapter? Why? What other principles, if any, would you add to the list? Why?

3. Do you believe that there is too much of a tendency to emphasize extraclass activities of the athletics type and to neglect those of a more intellectual type? Explain.

4. How should extraclass activities be financed? Should they be financed by public funds? Why or why not? What provisions should be made for pupils who are financially poor?

5. What facilities does your college or university have which you may

utilize in preparing yourself for supervising one or more extraclass activities? What should it have?

6. Should the emphasis in sports and in other school contests be upon interschool competition or upon competition within classes or among other groups of the school? Explain.

7. Statistics show that coaches of athletic teams are paid higher salaries than other faculty members. Do you favor this practice? Why or why not? Should they have release from other school duties and not be paid extra amounts? Why or why not?

8. How large an enrollment should a secondary school have before it should have a full-time supervisor of extraclass activities?

9. How may better sportsmanship in competitive activities in the school be obtained?

SELECTED REFERENCES

Chisholm, Leslie L., *The Work of the Modern High School,* New York, The Macmillan Co., 1953, Chapter 15.

Discusses the extraclass program of the modern high school.

Elicker, Paul E., ed., "Vitalizing Student Activities in the Secondary School, "*Bulletin of the National Association of Secondary-School Principals,* 36 (February, 1952), pp. 1–229.

Principles and practices of the extraclass program in the secondary school; problems discussed.

Hughes, Pat, "Wanted: An Extracurricular Specialist," *School Executive,* Vol. 74 (November, 1954), pp. 52–53.

Discusses the employing of a leader for all extracurricular activities in the school. If a full-time specialist were hired, instead of tired school teachers, the club programs could be integrated to a certain degree with each other and also with the curriculum. No more money would need to be spent in hiring a specialist than to pay a teacher extra for such duties.

Hughes, William Leonard, and Williams, Jesse Feiring, *Sports, Their Organization and Administration,* A. S. Barnes and Co., New York, 1944, 414 pp.

Of special interest to the school administrator.

McKown, H. C., *Extracurricular Activities,* Third edition, The Macmillan Co., New York, 1952, 666 pp.

Presents various types of programs of extraclass activities.

McKown, H. C., *School Clubs,* The Macmillan Co., New York, 1929, 498 pp.

Discusses the organization and administration of school clubs.

Trump, Lloyd J., *High School Extracurricular Activities,* The University of Chicago Press, Chicago, 1944, 210 pp.

A survey of the status of these activities in a group of high schools of the North Central Association.

Walsh, J. Hartt, and Johnson, Lowell, "Courts Favor Student Activities," *Nation's Schools,* Vol. 40 (December, 1947), pp. 30–31.

Discusses the responsibility of school officials and school employees for supervision of the extraclass activities.

CHAPTER 15
The Place of School Textbooks

Importance of Textbooks

European Practice Versus American Practice. In the schools of most European countries the lecture method of instruction is used and only a small amount of emphasis is placed upon textbooks. The lecture method is used in these countries, after the first grade, to and through the university. The teacher completely fills the instructional stage, and he presents all new material as if it were original with him.

In the schools of the United States the emphasis in instruction is placed on textbooks. This emphasis is found especially in the elementary and the secondary schools; in fact, in a large percentage of the schools what the pupil learns from the school is determined chiefly by the textbook. The textbook has always been a sort of "educational bible" to be devoutly followed by pupil and teacher. Even at this late date, in thousands of schools the teacher begins the term's work by assigning page one of the textbook, then continues his assignments page by page and day by day until the whole book has been assigned, learned and "recited"; this plan is especially followed by the inadequately prepared teachers. Under this method of instruction the teacher regards his function to be to make assignments in the textbook and to ascertain, after the pupils have been given the scheduled amount of time to "learn their lessons," how well they have mastered them. Perhaps it would be more accurate to say that, under complete use of the textbook method, teachers do not instruct, but merely "hear recitations."

In brief, the textbook has always been the chief vehicle of instruction in the schools of the United States; it has largely determined both the content and the method of instruction. The emphasis on the textbook is due in part to the historic desire of the people to read. This desire of the people to read and to have their children taught to read is evidenced first in the Massachusetts Law of 1647, known as the "Old Deluder Satan Act," a portion of which was quoted in Chapter 1 of this book.

Another explanation for the emphasis on the textbook method of teaching has been the meager preparation of the teachers of the United States compared with the teachers of some of the European countries. Since the teachers of some European countries have a larger amount of college preparation than the teachers of the United States, they are better qualified to use the lecture method; conversely, they are not so dependent on textbooks or on any other "ready-made" method of instruction.

What are the comparative merits of instruction by the lecture method and by the textbook method? Unfortunately, there are no objective data bearing on this question, and all that this discussion can do is to summarize oft-quoted opinion. For the lecture method, it is argued, in the first place, that it enables the teacher to meet the needs of his pupils better than the needs could be met by a textbook. In the second place, it is claimed that the lecture method teaches pupils to be good listeners—that it makes them "ear-minded." In the third place, in the European schools the pupils are frequently or usually called upon at the close of a lecture to summarize the chief points of the lecture, and it is argued that this practice teaches the pupils to express themselves. In the fourth place, it is claimed that the lecture method does not limit the pupils' knowledge to the textbook; the merit of this argument, of course, would depend upon the knowledge possessed by the teacher and upon his teaching skill. In the fifth place, the lecture method requires much preparation on the part of teachers, and this tends to keep them professionally alive and growing.

For the textbook method of teaching the following arguments are advanced, especially when the textbooks in use are of excellent quality. In the first place, it is claimed that the textbook presents the most pertinent information on the school subject and presents the information in a clear, interesting, and well-organized manner. The author of an excellent textbook has probably spent thousands of hours in selecting, in organizing, in experimenting with, and in presenting clearly his material. In the spirit of a true artist he has written and rewritten his material. On the contrary, the teacher is able to spend only a few minutes or a few hours in preparing for a lesson and in organizing his subject matter; in brief, the textbook is a timesaver to the teacher. In the second place, it is argued that the textbook method of teaching makes pupils better readers; in fact, it is a provocative thesis that this method has been largely responsible for making the people of the United States the most facile and avid readers in the world. Through the emphasis upon textbooks the American people have been better taught to read and they have been further given an abiding interest in reading; of course, they read much trashy material, and that part of their reading proclivity is unfortunate and should be redirected in some manner by the school. When the people possess this ability and this interest in reading, their information is not limited to lectures or to what is contained between the covers of a textbook; instead the whole world of literature becomes their inheritance as long as they live.

Quality of Textbooks in the United States. The emphasis on textbooks has resulted in the schools of the United States developing the best textbooks in the world. These textbooks are the premier product of the book world. It should be noted, however, that it was not until the latter part of the nineteenth century that these books showed much improvement in quality. After that date the development of textbook editing and textbook manufacturing was phenomenal. Frank A. Jensen says that there were three chief influences in the development of modern textbooks:

> First, a study of the child, resulting in the development of a more scientific educational method; second, the establishment of the textbook business as a specialized industry rather than a subordinate branch of a general printing or publishing business; and third, the revival of interest in printing, which had been a decadent art for over two hundred years.[1]

[1] Frank A. Jensen, *Current Procedure in Selecting Textbooks,* Lippincott, 1931, p. 5. By permission of J. B. Lippincott Company, publishers.

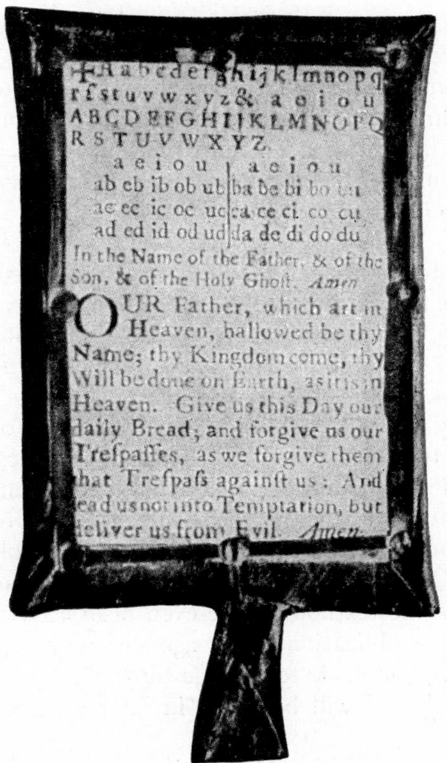

Fig. 50. A hornbook. The first *Hornbook* was published in Europe in 1450. It was first printed in Latin, then in English. It was the first "textbook" in Europe and in America, and from it children learned the alphabet and began to read. It was really not a book, but a thin paddle-shaped board, on which was pasted a sheet of paper containing the alphabet, a list of syllables, and the Lord's Prayer; the paper was covered with a sheet of transparent horn to protect it from becoming soiled. Of course, there were many types of hornbooks.

It is known that more than one hundred forty million dollars are now spent each year for textbooks in the public and the private schools of the United States. Numerous publishing companies have been organized to cater to this business. Competition has always been keen, and it has required publishers to attempt to produce the best books; in fact, the publishers have been compelled to pursue such a policy or be forced from business because of failure to receive purchase orders. Stimulated by increasingly higher standards of the members of the teaching profession and driven by keen competition, textbook publishers have progressed from the *Hornbook*, the *Battledoor*, and *The New England Primer*,[2] which were used in colonial days, to the splendid specimens of textbook artistry which are almost universal today.

Although the textbooks of the schools of the United States are unquestionably the best in the world, and although they are being constantly improved, there are still many mediocre and inferior textbooks. The schools will continue to have many mediocre and inferior textbooks as long as school officials and teachers persist in using such books, especially when better ones are available. For most of the school subjects, there are several textbooks, and for each of the universally required school subjects such as spelling, reading, arithmetic, and language, there are at least a dozen recently published textbooks. All, of course, are vigorously promoted by their publishers. Not all textbooks are of the same quality; none are perfect, and some are distinctly inferior; some textbooks have even been accused of being un-American. It is the obligation of the agencies which select textbooks to select the best ones. A few suggestions on how the best textbooks may be selected will be made in later sections of this chapter.

Cost of Textbooks. Although certain mountebankish and rabble-rousing "politicians" question the cost of textbooks, that cost is surprisingly low when it is considered in relation to the educational contributions of textbooks, in relation to the quality of textbooks, and in relation to the total cost of the school. These persons glibly claim that "millions of dollars" could be saved each year through state publication of books. They promise to save "millions" notwithstanding the fact that the total textbook bill per annum in any state does not amount to as much as "they would save" annually.

The annual per pupil cost of textbooks in the elementary and the secondary schools is approximately four dollars; it is less than three cents per day of schooling for each pupil. Of course, the per pupil cost is higher in the upper grades than in the lower grades. Less than two per cent of all money spent for schools is devoted to textbooks.

[2] The *Hornbook*, the *Battledoor*, and *The New England Primer* are illustrated and described in Figs. 50, 51, and 52 of this book.

When textbooks are properly used, the contributions of good ones are so large that increased expenditures for them should be made if at all possible.

It should be pointed out that the cost data just given are from school systems which provide public-owned textbooks. Regarding the cost of textbooks, under the practice of requiring the pupils to purchase them, it is known that the average expenditures per pupil are less than in school systems which provide free textbooks.

FIG. 51. A battledoor. The *Battledoor* was a sort of advanced Hornbook and succeeded the *Hornbook* in later Colonial times. It was widely used in the schools of England and in the northern colonies of the United States. It consisted of a sheet of cardboard folded once, with a little flap like a pocketbook. It included alphabets, syllables, and religious materials such as prayers.

Ownership and Publication of Textbooks

Public-owned Textbooks. The practice of providing public-owned or so-called free textbooks for all public-school children originated in Philadelphia in 1818. Similar provisions were made by many other cities, especially in the East, in the course of the next half-century. The first state to enact a state-wide free-textbook law was Massachusetts in 1884; that law required all school districts to provide, at public expense, textbooks for all public-school children. Maine made similar provisions in 1889. From these beginnings the movement for free textbooks gained rapid momentum which has continued to this day.

At present more than half of the states require free textbooks, and practically all of the other states permit local boards of education to provide them. Only a few states have not enacted legislation which requires or which permits local school boards to provide free textbooks, but in those few states many local school boards have long provided free textbooks, notwithstanding the fact that the statutes of the states are silent on the matter. Gratuity of textbooks and of other instructional materials has come to be regarded by the public as the natural and the inevitable sequel to gratuity of tuition. It is known that all other things in the school are free, so why not textbooks.

The legislation pertaining to free textbooks was first applied to the elementary school, then to the secondary school. As a rule, the first laws permitted local boards of education to provide free textbooks; the next laws required these boards to provide them. A more recent step—a step which has already been taken by approximately one-fourth of the states—requires the state to provide textbooks, these to be paid for by the state and to be furnished every pupil in the public elementary and secondary schools of the state; [3] this is another evidence of the tendency toward equalization of educational opportunity throughout the state. More than half of the states now require boards of education to furnish free textbooks, and practically all of the remaining states permit boards of education to furnish them. In several states, especially in the South and the Southwest, free textbooks are provided with state funds, but in most states they are provided with local funds. The tendency everywhere is toward the

[3] A few states also provide free textbooks to private-school pupils.

furnishing of free textbooks for both the elementary and the secondary school; this tendency should continue.

Most educators have come to believe that free textbooks should be provided in all public schools, and a few believe that they should be provided in all private schools as well. The arguments which are usually advanced in favor of free textbooks in the public schools are summarized herewith. The reader is reminded, however, that most of these arguments, as well as most of the arguments for pupil-owned textbooks, are opinions only; the determination of their validity awaits the collection of further data and further thinking about the problem.

1. All other school services and facilities are free, and free textbooks would require only a small additional expenditure. In a free-textbook practice all pupils are placed on the same plane, and indigent pupils are not embarrassed or otherwise handicapped because of having to go without textbooks or because of having them provided by public funds.
2. The cost to the community is less. Under careful usage, a public-owned textbook will last from three to five years, thus permitting the same book to be used by more than one pupil; under the pupil-owned-textbook plan, the textbook is often used by only one pupil.
3. The criticism of many parents over the cost of textbooks is eliminated. In spite of the fact that the annual cost of public-owned textbooks is approximately four dollars per pupil, even that amount is difficult for many parents to provide; moreover, the expenditure for pupil-owned textbooks must be made at the same time that expenditures must be made for new clothing and for other necessities for the pupils preparatory to the start of school.
4. Public-owned textbooks may be more easily changed when the need for changing them is imminent; thus, the pupils are not as likely to be handicapped by being compelled to use out-of-date textbooks.
5. Uniformity of textbooks in each school-administrative unit is more easily procured than under the pupil-owned-textbook plan. Under the pupil-owned-textbook plan, many parents are content for their children to use out-of-date textbooks.
6. On the first day of school each pupil is provided with his textbooks by the school and is prepared to begin his school work immediately. Under the pupil-owned-textbook plan, there are many delays in obtaining the textbooks, and such delays handicap both pupils and teachers.

Pupil-owned Textbooks. There are at least two sides to every question, and many arguments have been advanced in favor of pupil-owned textbooks; among the more frequently mentioned of these arguments are the following:

He that ne'er learns his A, B, C,
For ever will a Blockhead be :

Praiſe to GOD for learning to Read.

THE Praiſes of my Tongue
  I offer to the LORD,
That I was taught and learnt ſo young
  To read his holy Word.

2 That I was brought to know
  The Danger I was in,
By Nature and by Practice too
  A wretched ſlave to Sin.

3 That I was led to ſee
  I can do nothing well ;
And whether ſhall a Sinner flee
  To ſave himſelf from Hell.

Fig. 52. Two specimen pages from *The New England Primer*. *The New England Primer* was the first textbook written and published in America. It was written by Benjamin Harris of Boston, and was first printed in 1690. It soon superseded the *Hornbook* and the *Battledoor* as the beginning reading text in the schools of the colonies; it also had a large sale in England and Scotland. It has been said of this book of about eighty pages of 3½ by 4¼ inches in size, that it "taught millions to read, and not one to sin." On the left side above is a page of the illustrated alphabet, and on the right side is a page of the reading matter.

1. The cost of providing free textbooks is too large a burden for the public to bear; it increases taxes.
2. For the public to do too much for the pupil is likely to pauperize him; if the pupil is required to provide his textbooks, he is apt to be more appreciative of what society is doing for him through its many other educational expenditures.
3. Free textbooks are apt to be unhygienic, and the danger of the spread of disease is inherent in the plan. Of course, this argument applies only to used textbooks, not to new ones.
4. Pupil-owned textbooks encourage pupils to build up home libraries, whereas the free-textbook plan does not give that encouragement.
5. When pupils own their textbooks, they have access to them during school vacations, whereas they do not have access to public-owned ones during vacations.

6. Pupils take better care of their own textbooks than they do of public-owned ones. Carelessness of pupils toward public-owned textbooks involves a large and an unnecessary waste of public funds, and teaches pupils disrespect for property.
7. The custodial care of free textbooks places an extra burden on school officials and teachers, and such burden can be avoided through having pupil-owned textbooks.

TEXTBOOKS FOR INDIGENT PUPILS. In those states which do not require boards of education or the state to provide free textbooks, the laws usually stipulate that local boards of education shall provide indigent pupils with free textbooks; few persons object to this policy. The laws usually stipulate also that clothing shall be provided to indigent children of school age. These laws are another practical application of the educational creed of America which says that no pupil shall have his education handicapped because of family poverty.

In school systems which do not provide free textbooks to all pupils, teachers have the duty of ascertaining why pupils have not procured their textbooks and the further duty of reporting such information to the school principal, the superintendent, or other appropriate school administrators. In obtaining and in using such information, tact must be exercised; if certain pupils are not provided with books, because their parents or their guardians are too poor to purchase them, this information should not be permitted to become public lest it result in the embarrassment of the pupils. The board of education will usually be able and willing to provide public funds for the books of such pupils. If the board is not able or willing to provide the books, they may usually be obtained through welfare organizations or through public-spirited citizens of the community.

STATE PRINTING OF TEXTBOOKS. In two states (California and Kansas) elementary school textbooks are printed by the state. In California all basic elementary school textbooks are printed by the state printing office, and in Kansas most of the elementary school textbooks are printed by the state printing office. In the other states all textbooks are purchased from private publishers. Several states have considered the state-printing plan, but all of them with the exception of California and Kansas, have decided against it, because of the belief that it is uneconomical and pedagogically unsound.

Selection of Textbooks

Unit of Selection. Every state has long had laws affecting the selection of textbooks. Approximately one-half of the states now provide for state selection and limited state uniformity. The remainder provide for local (that is, county or local school-district) selection and local uniformity. In some of the states which provide for state selection and state uniformity, provisions for local selection are made for a few of the large cities. In some of the states, also, which provide for state selection and state uniformity, provision has been made for a multiple list of textbooks from which local school districts may select. This provision for a multiple list is made especially for the secondary schools of the state.

In spite of the fact that most school officials and most school employees, as well as most publishing companies, prefer local adoption of textbooks, the states which provide for local adoption are slightly in the minority; moreover, changes in state laws to permit local adoption are made slowly and grudgingly by state legislatures. The arguments which are usually advanced against uniformity of textbooks, particularly state uniformity, are as follows:

1. Uniformity of textbooks, particularly state uniformity, does not permit the use of books which are adapted to local needs. In the same school system, the educational needs of the pupils in one school will often vary widely from the educational needs of the pupils in another school. These varying needs are due to a diversity of social customs, occupations, and interests of the community.
2. It is argued further against state uniformity, that the adopting authorities are not always competent to perform this function. Members of state boards of education and of other state adopting bodies are sometimes "politically" appointed, "politically" minded, and are susceptible to "pull" and other unethical influences. Often, the members of these adopting agencies are not engaged in school work, or if they are engaged in school work, they are engaged in the administration of colleges and universities, or similar educational endeavors which are far removed from the elementary and the secondary school pupils. Infrequently is a teacher—the person who must use the textbook and consequently the person most vitally concerned with obtaining the best textbook—a member of the adopting agency.

Uniformity of textbooks, however, has many proponents, and many arguments are advanced in favor of that plan. Among the more frequently mentioned of these arguments are the following:

1. Uniformity is advantageous to the pupil who moves from one school district to another, or who is transferred from one school to another. If he finds the same textbooks used in the new school as in the old, the pupil is not as likely to be handicapped educationally in making the transfer; moreover, the pupil does not need to go to the expense of purchasing another textbook, nor does the board of education have to incur that expense.
2. Uniformity is advantageous to the teacher who transfers from one school system to another, because he does not have to spend time in getting acquainted with new textbooks.
3. Uniformity makes it possible to effect economies in the purchase of textbooks. These economies grow out of the fact that a publisher who obtains a state adoption for a period of one or more years is enabled to manufacture and to sell in large quantities.
4. Uniform selection obtains a better quality of textbook than does local adoption. In elaboration of this argument it is stated that state adopting agencies are more competent to perform this service and that they have more time to devote to the service than local school officials.
5. Finally, uniformity gives greater assurance that the minimum essentials of the curriculum will be taught in all schools.

Term of Selection. Practically all states have enacted legislation setting a certain term for which textbooks shall be selected. Most states prescribe a term of three, four, five, six or seven years, with five years being the most frequent term prescribed. A few states leave to the state board of education, or other adopting agency, the task of prescribing the term of selection.

Laws which prescribe the term of selection for textbooks have in mind the financial protection of the public from too frequent changes in textbooks. Such laws effectively accomplish the purpose just mentioned. Most of the laws, however, may be criticized because they do not make provision whereby an inferior textbook may be changed before the period of adoption is concluded; under most of the laws a change in a textbook cannot be effected before the close of the prescribed term even though the book is found to be wholly unsatisfactory, and even though another book has appeared which would be eminently more satisfactory. When the proper agencies have been established for the selection of textbooks, it would seem that those agencies should be given the decision as to how long textbooks should remain in use. Most authorities recommend, therefore, that the adopting agency be the local school officials, and that these officials be permitted to change textbooks, just as they are permitted to change superintendents, principals, teachers, or other school services and school facilities when the need for a change is demonstrated.

STANDARDS FOR SELECTION. Since textbooks frequently determine what is taught, since they are usually selected for a fairly long term, and since a considerable amount of public or of private funds is expended for them, fine discrimination must be used in their selection. An unhappy choice of a textbok means that the teacher will be handicapped in his work, and that the pupils will not receive all the instruction which they might. As was stated in an earlier paragraph of this chapter, there are many textbooks available for each subject, and the best of these should be selected, but the best cannot be selected by "meeny-miney-mo" methods. Knowledge of the characteristics of an excellent textbook and the will to choose the best are the chief requisites for effectiveness in selection.

Another requisite for obtaining superior textbooks is for the best-qualified agency to be given the task of selecting them. According to the present state laws, county or state textbook commissions, or county or local boards of education, have this responsibility, but since the members of these commissions or boards are usually laymen, and since the selection of textbooks is a professional and a technical function, textbook commissions and boards of education should not select textbooks without the assistance, or without the recommendation, of superintendents, principals, supervisors, teachers, or other professionally-prepared employees in education. One of the best contributions to desirable methods of textbook selection has been made by the American Textbook Publishers Institute in a six-page booklet titled *Desirable Methods for Selecting Textbooks*.

As the years go by, teachers are being given larger and larger responsibilities in the selection of textbooks. In local school systems which are permitted to select their own textbooks, and in states which provide for county adoption of textbooks, teachers are frequently required to serve as members of textbook committees; in fact, many school systems permit each teacher, particularly the secondary school teacher, to select his own textbooks. This tendency presupposes that teachers should be familiar with the criteria which textbooks should meet and with the methods of selecting textbooks. All prospective teachers should obtain this acquaintance while they are students in teacher-preparing institutions.

The tendency toward teacher co-operation in the selection of textbooks is meritorious; teachers are peculiarly qualified to perform this service, because they use textbooks every day in the school year and are in a position to know the comparative merits and shortcomings of various textbooks. Moreover, teachers—like all other workers—prefer to have something to say about the tools with which they work; they do not relish having their tools foisted upon them. Teachers, however, should not expect to contribute to textbook selection until they have prepared themselves for the task. They should become acquainted with textbook score cards and standards and with the best textbooks for the subjects which they expect to teach. A code of ethics for the selection of textbooks is reproduced herewith:

1. The selection of textbooks is an important educational undertaking to be carried out in a professional manner. The responsibility and the authority should rest with the educational administration of a school system, rather than with a board of education or a group of laymen.
2. The purpose should be always the selection of the best textbooks for the use of the pupils. Hence, it is not ethical to make any effort to distribute the business among several competing firms or to give weight to personal likes and dislikes toward publishers' representatives.
3. It is unethical, in general, for representatives to interfere with the relationship obtaining between superintendent and board of education; thus they should not appeal to boards of education to reverse the superintendent's recommendations, nor, if the superintendent is required to recommend textbooks, should they furnish samples of such books to school board members.
4. It is not ethical for a superintendent or a member of a selecting committee to receive from a publisher any reward for services in the selection of textbooks.
5. Representatives should not foment dissatisfaction or circulate petitions calling for changes in textbooks. Neither should they circulate criticism of superintendents who have made decisions adverse to their companies.
6. It is not ethical for a representative to try to secure the appointment of administrators or teachers to their regular positions or on textbook committees for the purpose of influencing the selection of textbooks in his favor, or to try to influence the election of members of schoolboards.
7. It is not ethical to interview teachers without the prior consent of their superiors or to try to secure information about secret committees.
8. It is not ethical to utilize the influence of organizations of laymen to secure adoptions or to appeal to sectarian prejudices in meeting competition.

9. It is in general an undignified practice for an author to use his professional position to try to secure adoptions of his textbook thru field work, professional addresses, or classroom instruction.
10. While it is not unethical to make use of secret committees in the selection of textbooks, there is considerable sentiment against such committees and evidence to show genuine secrecy is not often attained; and it is charged that frequently the intent of the secrecy is to conceal an unethical selection.
11. The superintendent is justified in taking drastic measures if the conduct of publishers' representatives falls below high standards of practices of transacting public business.
12. It is unethical to give opportunity to some representatives to present the merits of their books and not to give this opportunity to others. Similarly, it is unethical to give confidentially to some representatives information which is withheld from others.
13. It is not ethical to favor local authors unless their textbooks are as good as other competing textbooks.
14. It is neither legal nor ethical to reproduce, whether by printing or by mimeographing, any material covered by copyright unless expressly permitted by the holder of the copyright. This applies to books adopted as well as to books not adopted.
15. It should be considered ethical for a publisher's representative to bring to the attention of the superintendent any unethical practices of a textbook committee.[4]

Use of Textbooks

After textbooks have been selected and purchased, school officials and teachers have two further responsibilities. In the first place, they have the responsibility of doing everything possible to protect the textbooks from damage; in the second place, they have the responsibility of seeing that textbooks are properly used in the giving of instruction.

Increasing the Life of Textbooks. As with all other possessions, the life of a textbook is determined largely by the care with which it is used. Under normal usage a textbook which has a durable binding and other excellent qualities of manufacture should last at least three years. Teachers can assist in prolonging the life of textbooks and in seeing that pupils are given proper instructions on the care of textbooks, and in seeing that those instructions are followed. Special precautions should be taken against pupils losing their textbooks, and

[4] *Thirtieth Yearbook* of the National Society for the Study of Education, Part II, 1931, pp. 218–220.

Fig. 53. A group of children listening to a broadcast designed especially for them. Modern teachers use such experiences to supplement textbooks. *(Courtesy of the Cleveland, Ohio, public schools.)* Television also is now available, and is being used in many schools.

against depreciating their value through unnecessary marking, tearing, and soiling. These precautions should especially be taken in school systems which provide free textbooks. One of the lessons which pupils should learn is to respect property, whether public or private.

Use of the Textbook in Instruction. The materials of instruction for any group of pupils should be determined by the needs of the pupils. These needs vary from school system to school system, and from school to school; even in the same school the needs of the pupils in one fifth-grade history class, for example, will vary more or less from the needs of another class in the same grade and school subject. It is difficult, if not impossible, to select a textbook which will entirely meet the needs of a particular group of pupils. Even the best textbook is likely to possess the limitations of presenting too much or too little material, of being colored with the author's views to the neglect of other views, of being out of step with recent social changes, and of lacking adaptation to the needs of the individual pupil. The textbook should not determine the curriculum of the school; rather the needs of the pupils should determine the curriculum. Many teachers prefer not to use textbooks, but to direct their pupils to other sources of information and to experience obtained in and outside the community.

In using a textbook, the teacher should take steps to adapt the textbook to the needs of his pupils. He should supplement the material of the textbook with material found in other textbooks, in reference books, in newspapers, in magazines, in other curriculums, in cinema, on the radio, on television, in the life of the community, and in other appropriate sources. The textbook should not be "king" over all other sources, but should be "brother" to all of them. The teacher will often find it advisable to omit certain parts of the textbook. It would be extremely unfortunate for him to follow a textbook so slavishly that his pupils would receive no instruction, except that contained between the covers of the textbook. The objectives of a course should be determined by the teacher or by the local curriculum rather than by the author of the textbook. The needs of the pupils must, of course, determine what should be taught. The chief objective of the school is to develop pupils who can think and plan, and this objective cannot be accomplished by any method of teaching which limits its material to a single textbook or which emphasizes textbook memorization.

The old-fashioned recitation is rapidly passing, and fortunately so. Prospective teachers must prepare themselves to use textbooks more intelligently than they have been used in the past. Good textbooks can be valuable servants, but no servant should be overworked.

QUESTIONS FOR DISCUSSION

1. Would you favor state publication of textbooks, such as two states now practice, and as is sometimes suggested in the legislatures of other states? Why or why not?

2. What should be the unit for the adoption of textbooks? Should it be the classroom, the school department, the school, the school district, or the state? Why?

3. Assuming that the laws of your state permit local adoption of textbooks, by what persons do you believe that textbooks should be

selected? What should be the place of the teacher in that selection? Discuss. What preparation should he have for this?

4. What criteria should be kept in mind in deciding whether to change textbooks? Should the term of selection be set by the state?

5. If a school system can provide free textbooks for only the elementary school pupils or for only the secondary school pupils, which group should be provided for? Why? Do you favor free books for both groups? Why?

6. What tendencies regarding the use of textbooks in classroom instruction have you discerned since you were a pupil in the elementary and the secondary schools? Do you regard those tendencies as progressive or as retrogressive? Why?

7. As a college student, do you prefer to use or not to use textbooks? Why? In what ways, if any, do you like to see a textbook supplemented?

8. As a teacher, would you prefer to use or not to use textbooks? Why? In what ways, if any, would you supplement them?

9. How do you account for the fact that the expenditures for textbooks are frequently criticized, in spite of the fact that those expenditures are small compared with the total cost of public education? Should the schools spend more money for textbooks? Why or why not? Should public funds be used to provide workbooks? Why or why not?

10. Assuming that the board of education which is employing you does not provide free textbooks or make provision even for furnishing textbooks to indigent pupils, how might you as a teacher provide textbooks for your indigent pupils?

11. Do you believe that the schools should use workbooks? Why or why not?

SELECTED REFERENCES

Cronbach, Lee J., ed., *Text Materials in Modern Education*, University of Illinois Press, 1955, 216 pp.

Discusses who writes the texts, how they are produced and distributed, and how they function in actual use.

Desirable Procedures for Selecting Textbooks, The American Textbook Publishers Institute, New York, 1953, 6 pp.

Recommends desirable policies for textbook selection.

Jensen, Frank A., *Current Procedure in Selecting Textbooks*, J. B. Lippincott Co., Philadelphia, Pa., 1931, 157 pp.

Describes the evolution of different methods of textbook selection and appraises these methods.

Otis, E. M., "A Textbook Score Card," *Journal of Educational Research*, Vol. 7 (February, 1923), pp. 132–136.

The author made a score card by which textbooks could be judged upon six different bases.

Rogers, Virgil M., "Textbooks Under Fire," *The Atlantic* (February, 1955).

Exposes some of the recent attacks on textbooks, and suggests some standards that parents can use in judging textbooks.

The Textbook in American Education, Part II of the *Thirtieth Yearbook* of the National Society for the Study of Education, Public School Publishing Co., Bloomington, Ill., 1931, 364 pp.

One of the most complete single references on the subject of textbooks; contains a complete bibliography, but chiefly of historical interest.

Underwood, Willis O., "A Guide for Textbook Analysis," *American School Board Journal*, Vol. 103 (March, 1941), pp. 23–24.

Outlines a score card for selecting textbooks, based on a questionnaire study in seven states.

"What are Textbooks For," *Phi Delta Kappan*, Vol. 33 (January, 1952), pp. 341–346.

A symposium on textbooks.

CHAPTER 16

The Contributions of the School Library

Importance of the Library

The preceding chapter on "The Place of School Textbooks" stated that the tendency in modern schools is away from the traditional practice of limiting instruction to the materials found in a single textbook. The tendency is toward supplementing the textbook with the many other sources of information which also have contributions to make to the education of the pupil; in fact, many teachers do not use textbooks, but use other sources entirely. Among the more important of these other sources are the radio, cinema, television, the adult and child life of the community in all aspects, and other books, magazines and other printed materials. Probably, most important among these other sources is "the printed word" as it is found in books, magazines, newspapers, and similar materials.

Since the function of the library is to make available as many of the more valuable of these learning sources as possible, this chapter will discuss the place of the library in education, various ways and means of improving the facilities of the library, and the possibility of increasing the use of these facilities. The discussion will be concerned primarily with the school library, but it will not forget the place of the public library, especially as an instrument in lifelong education.

Importance of the Public Library. Public libraries have traditionally been known as preservers of the social heritage. During the last few decades, however, they have come to be known as more than "preservers" of that knowledge; they have come to be regarded as outstanding agencies of public education, and their development during this period has been amazing. The recent increase in the number and in the use of libraries has been caused by the increasing demand for adult education and by the expanding interest of the people in recreational and cultural reading. Although they read much trash, the people of the United States are probably the most avid readers in the world, and the development of public libraries has been a potent factor in stimulating the people to read. It is, however, a sad fact that approximately four million of the adult population of the nation can't read, and thousands of these are native-born. Practically all of our illiteracy is found among our older people.

Although the development of public libraries in the United States has been phenomenal, and although the United States leads all other countries in library facilities, there are still thousands of communities and millions of our people wholly without library service. The areas without any or without adequate local library facilities are usually found in the open country, but the majority of the small villages are also without such service. County libraries and their traveling units (usually called bookmobiles) are rapidly being developed to serve the library needs of the villages and rural districts. A bookmobile is shown in Figure 54.

Importance of the School Library. During recent years, the teacher's concept of the place of the school library in the educational program has changed greatly. It has changed from the belief that the library is of small importance or is unnecessary to the belief that the library is one of the most important, if not indispensable, features of the school. There is an unmistakable tendency away from the traditional emphasis on the textbook to a larger emphasis upon the library. Indeed, in all progressive schools, the library is regarded, next to the teacher, as the most important feature of the school, and steps are everywhere being taken to expand its facilities and to increase its use.[1] In the modern school firmament the library is recognized as the master planet, whereas textbooks are regarded as mere satellites of the master planet.

One of the chief evidences of the growing importance of the school library is seen in the tendency of the state legislatures to make the establishment of school libraries mandatory, to set standards which

[1] Many elementary schools now have a library in each classroom.

the libraries must meet, and to provide for their financial support. Practically all of the states have enacted laws which require or permit boards of education to establish and to finance school libraries. More than one-third of the states are attempting to stimulate the establishment and the improvement of school libraries through the policy of granting state aid to them. Several states have also created state library commissions and have delegated to those commissions the work of stimulating the establishment and the use of public and school libraries.

Thousands of schools, however, do not have a library, or if they have one, the reading materials in it have not been well selected, or are not being used. Not to have a library is unfortunate, but to have a library and not to use it is worse still, because of the waste of funds which have gone into establishing and equipping it. All libraries are designed for use, and not merely to serve as ornamentation. Carlyle has said that "a true university of these days is a collection of books." It would, however, be more accurate to say that a used collection of books is a true university. The merit of a library must be determined in the final analysis by the extent to which the library is used. Although it may be true in a few instances, as a wag has said, "A librarian is happiest when all the books and other materials are securely on the shelves," it is certain that such an attitude does not characterize most librarians of the present. The attitude expressed years ago in the *Old Librarian's Almanac* is rapidly passing into limbo:

> Keep your Books behind stout Gratings and in no wise let any Person come at them to take them from the Shelf except yourself. Have in Mind the Counsel of Master Enoch Sneed (that most Worthy Librarian) who says: "It were better that no Person enter the Library (save the Librarian Himself) and that the Books be kept in Safety, than that one Book be lost, or others Misplaced." Guard well your Books—that is always your foremost Duty. . . . So far as your Authority will permit of it, exercise great Discrimination as to which Persons shall be admitted to the use of the Library. For the Treasure House of Literature is no more to be thrown open to the Ravages of the unreasoning Mob, than a fair Garden to be laid unprotected at the Mercy of a Swarm of Beasts.

School officials and teachers are rapidly changing their belief and their practice that the textbook is the only source of knowledge, and

Courtesy of Staten Island Advance

FIG. 54. A mobile unit of the type that brings library facilities to rural communities are striving to make the pupils acquainted with other books and with other sources of information. Among the more progressive teachers of today the textbook is no longer regarded as an educational bible which does not need supplementation and which must be accepted without question by its readers. If, as is now generally agreed among educators, one of the chief purposes of the school is to make pupils acquainted with the sources of information, then the recent emphasis on the school library is commendable. Acquaintance with the sources of knowledge will help the pupil to obtain the greatest benefit from his schooling and will prepare him to continue his education throughout life. One of the most valuable lessons which pupils can learn is that education is a lifelong process and that it does not cease when the pupils leave school; modern teachers are expected to instill those views in their pupils.

The pupil in the modern school is reading many times as much as the pupil in the old-time schools. Moreover, owing to the decreasing emphasis on oral reading and the increasing emphasis on silent reading, the pupil is being taught to read much more rapidly. He is no longer required to memorize his textbooks in order to participate properly in the recitation; in fact, the old-fashioned recitation is rapidly becoming extinct, and its death will be attended by few intelligent mourners. The pupil is being given the opportunity to read more through the establishment of an excellent library and through his being encouraged and required to use its resources. In brief, an increasing number of school officials, teachers, and school librarians are trying to realize the objectives of the school library as stated by the American Library Association; those objectives are as follows:

1. All pupils in both elementary and secondary schools should have ready access to books to the end that they may be trained:
   a. To love to read that which is worthwhile.
   b. To supplement their school studies by the use of books other than textbooks.
   c. To use reference books easily and effectively.
   d. To use intelligently both the school library and the public library.
2. Every secondary school should have a trained librarian, and every elementary school should have trained library service.
3. Trained librarians should have the same status as teachers or heads of departments of equal training and experience.
4. Every school that provides training for teachers should require a course in the use of books and libraries, and a course on best literature for children.

5. Every state should provide for the supervision of school libraries and for the certification of school librarians.
6. The public library should be recognized as a necessary part of public instruction and should be as liberally supported by tax as are public schools, and for the same reason.
7. The school system that does not make liberal provision for training in the use of libraries fails to do its full duty in the way of revealing to all future citizens the opportunity to know and to use the resources of the public library as a means of education.

Types of School-library Control

There are three types of school-library control in the various communities of the United States. They are, in the inverse order of their contributions to school efficiency, as follows: first, control by the public library; second, joint control by the school district and by the public library; and third, control by the school district.

The tendency in both theory and practice is toward having the school library controlled and administered entirely by the school district; indeed, in many communities the school district has the responsibility of administering public libraries as well as school libraries. Control of the school library by the school district gives greater assurance that the needs of the pupils will be met than would be the case in joint control or in public-library control. Under school control the responsibility for administering the library is centered in the public agency which has as its only function the education of the children. Although control of the school library by the public library gives library service which is infinitely better than none, that type of library control has certain limitations. Among its limitations are the following:

1. Under public-library control there is danger that friction will develop between school officials and school employees and public library officials and employees.
2. The officials and employees of a public library are not always conversant with the needs of the school, nor are they always familiar with the ways and means of meeting those needs. Under public-library control, the needs of both the general public and the school must be met, and often it is difficult to meet the needs of one clientele without neglecting the needs of the other.
3. Under public-library control the school library is usually made a branch of the public library, is located in the school building, and must be used by both the pupils and the general public. When the

school library is used by the general public, there is no way of controlling who shall come to the school premises; this means, therefore, that undesirable persons in the community will sometimes mingle with pupils.

Using the School Library

It should be repeated that a library is established for use and not merely for ornamentation. It is of small avail to have excellent library quarters, a carefully chosen collection of reading materials, and the services of a well-qualified librarian, if the library is not used. In most schools and most school systems steps need to be taken to increase the use of the library by both teachers and pupils. Teachers are in the best position to stimulate the use of the library on the part of pupils, because they make the assignments to pupils, and if they make frequent assignments to the library, pupils will learn to use it. Moreover, this enforced and day-by-day acquaintance with the library is likely to stimulate pupils to use the library of their own free will and accord; and what is of even greater importance, any habit of using the library—public as well as school—is likely to persist throughout life. The first obligation of the school is to teach the pupils the tools of knowledge—reading, writing, speaking, calculating, spelling, and others; the second obligation is to make the pupils acquainted with the best sources of knowledge—good books, good magazines, good newspapers, good pictures, good recordings, and others. Pupils cannot be best taught to think, to plan, and to choose, if they lack knowledge of these tools and these sources. In the following paragraphs suggestions are made which look toward stimulating a larger and a more discriminating use of the school library.

Library Instructions.[2] Millions of adults do not use libraries, because they do not know how to use them. Whereas libraries should be as "enchanted isles" to everyone, to millions of people they are "domains of mystery." Millions of pupils must also be included in this unfortunate category. The best way by which this deficiency may be corrected is for every school to teach the never-ending nature of education, the importance of libraries in education, and efficient methods of using libraries. Prospective teachers should learn how to

[2] Several of the books in the list of Selected References at the close of this chapter are devoted entirely to the giving of library instructions.

inculcate such lessons when they are obtaining their college preparation for teaching; they cannot teach their pupils to use the library if they have never learned how to use it. Teachers should be expected to begin the library instruction of their pupils in the early years of the elementary school and to continue it in the secondary school. In the elementary school, instruction should be given on such topics as the following: how to use dictionaries and encyclopedias; how to use the table of contents and the index of a book; how to withdraw, to take care of, and to return books; where to look for certain books in the library; and characteristics of excellent books and of poor books, also of excellent magazines and of poor magazines.

In the secondary school the following topics should be discussed, and the topics suggested above for discussion with elementary school pupils should be reviewed as needed: the values to be obtained from using a library; getting acquainted with the library; how to use a book; the use of general reference books; the use of special reference books; how to evaluate books, magazines, and newspapers; the use of magazines; the card catalogue as an index to the library; the better known periodical indexes and how to use them; library rules; library facilities in the community, other than school libraries; services provided by the state library, if there is one, and by other libraries; the library as an adjunct to the classroom; how to prepare a bibliography; how to take notes; selection of books for the home library; visual material and its use; and books from which vocational and other types of guidance information may be obtained.[3]

Special Library Day in the School. Numerous schools are setting aside a special day, known as school-library day, on which a program is given on the purposes of the school library and on proper ways and means of using the library. Many schools are using the school-library day also to increase the facilities of the school library; on this day they encourage pupils, school officials and school employees, and the general public to make suitable gifts to the library of books, magazines, pictures, and other appropriate material. If a school-library day is sponsored, it is obvious that the largest benefit from it would be obtained by having it as early in the school year as possible.

[3] Acknowledgments for most of this list are made to Hannah Logasa, *The High School Library*, Appleton-Century, 1928, p. 175.

Bulletin Boards for the Library. On library and classroom bulletin boards may be posted such materials as well-chosen newspaper and magazine clippings, reading lists for the various school subjects, jackets of new books, and other interesting material. Such material possesses educational value and leads to a larger and more discriminating use of the library. Many schools are making the library a clearing-house for such material and are obtaining the co-operation of pupils and of teachers in carrying out the project.

Book Exhibits of the Library. Attention may be called to new books and to other new reading materials by placing such materials on a "New Book Shelf" in the library. Special attention may be called to particularly excellent books and to other reading materials by placing such materials on a "Have You Read This Book?" shelf; such materials may, of course, be old or new.

Special Reading Lists of the Library. The use of the library may be stimulated by the preparation of reading lists on various school subjects and topics. For example, reading lists may be prepared on the various types of guidance, economics, fiction, biography, science, and other especially alive subjects. Teachers are in especially favorable positions to prepare or to supervise the preparation of such lists. Pupils can often be asked to help prepare the lists. To give the lists proper publicity, they may be mimeographed and handed to the students; the lists may be posted on the bulletin boards of the school; they may be published in the school paper or magazine; or attention may be called to them in appropriate class discussions. These lists may also be circulated among the parents in order that they may see what the school is doing. They will often encourage parents to read.

Personal Interest of the Librarian in Library Service. The use of the library may be stimulated and improved by the librarian taking a personal interest in the requests and the needs of every user of the library. If the librarian is an "old grouch," is lazy, or does not co-operate with the people who use the library, the library can never realize its potentialities; such a librarian will drive pupils and all other persons away from the library, instead of attracting them to it.

Book Reviews. Attention may be called to new books in the library by having reviews of these books written and published in the school newspaper or magazine. If a review cannot be obtained for every new book, merely publishing the name of the book or posting the name, or the jacket, of the book on the bulletin board of the library will help to call attention to the book. Usually, such reviews can be written appropriately by the older pupils; for example, secondary school pupils in the science department could review new books on science, and pupils in the commercial department could review new books on commercial subjects.

In addition to written reviews of books, oral reviews may be presented. These reviews may be made in brief talks about books and may be presented by the librarian, by the teachers, or by the pupils. They may be given in school assemblies, in home-rooms, or in regular classes.

FIG. 55. A corner of a library which serves as the heart of the school. This library is found in the University High School, The Ohio State University. *(Courtesy of Roy Wenger and Hazel Gibbony.)* The chairs of this library would be more usable, however, if their arms permitted the chairs to be pulled closer to the table.

LIBRARY CONVENIENCES. The use of the library may be stimulated by providing it with the conveniences and the comforts which every good library should have. In the first place, the shelves of the library should be marked to show the contents of each shelf. In the second place, the library should have an accurate card catalogue which lists every reference contained in the library and indicates where the reference may be immediately found. In the third place, the library should be an attractive and a comfortable place to visit. This means, among other things, that the library should be provided with comfortable chairs and tables, good pictures and other works of art.

STUDENT AND TEACHER LIBRARY BOARDS. Many schools have found that the library and its use can be improved by organizing a library board constituted of pupils or of teachers or both. It is the function of such a board to co-operate with the librarian and with school officials and school employees in selecting materials for, in administering, and in promoting the use of, the library.

THE LIBRARIAN AND HIS WORK [4]

IMPORTANCE OF THE LIBRARIAN. Just as the teacher makes the classroom, the shop, or the laboratory largely what it is, so the librarian makes the library largely what it is. An excellent school librarian constantly seeks information on the needs of every department of the school, tries to meet those needs, and attempts to promote the use of the library in every school department. The librarian is in a strategic position to see the results of teaching and to improve those results. He manages the school's "storehouse of information and ideas," and he is ever present to make mental notes of the pupils and the teachers who avail themselves of the resources of that storehouse. He knows those who come to "scoff" as well as those who come and "remain to pray," and he knows those who never come to that altar of knowledge.

Under ideal conditions every school library would have a librarian, either part-time or full-time. Such conditions, however, do not, and because of financial limitations probably cannot, obtain in the smaller schools. As a rule, full-time librarians are found only in the large secondary schools. The smaller secondary schools and the elementary

[4] Throughout this book the masculine gender is used in referring to all school officials and school employees; for consistency it is here used in referring to the librarian, in spite of the fact that four-fifths of the school librarians of the United States are women.

schools are usually not provided with the services of a librarian. In the smaller secondary schools, however, one or more of the teachers are frequently asked to devote one or more of the class periods each day to the school library; in such schools, moreover, some of the students are frequently called upon to assist in the school library.

Fig. 56. A corner of another school library. *(Courtesy of the Cincinnati, Ohio, public schools.)*

Qualifications for the Position. The higher the grade level of the school, the more important the school library and the school librarian become; that is to say, these school facilities and school services are probably more important in the secondary schools than in the elementary schools, and they are probably more important in the colleges and universities than in the secondary schools. If it is true that "a library is a school," and if it is true that "the librarian makes the library largely what it is," the necessity that the librarian have high qualifications is obvious. In personality, in college preparation, and in other qualifications, the school librarian should be among the best qualified employees of the school, and he should be certicated under state law in the same manner that teachers and other educational employees are certificated.[5] If his qualifications are as

[5] The Council of the American Library Association has recommended the certification of all librarians.

high as those of other school employees, justice dictates that his salary and other rewards should compare favorably with the salaries and other rewards of other school employees.

In fact, there is much argument for requiring the school librarian to possess even higher qualifications than teachers. He should have considerable acquaintance with all school subjects taught in the school. Without this acquaintance with science, mathematics, English, history, commerce, and the other subjects taught in the school, he is certain to have difficulty in meeting the peculiar needs of each school department. In view of these facts, therefore, it would not seem unreasonable to urge that the school librarian possess the same amount of undergraduate preparation as the typical teacher, and in addition, that he possess at least one year of postgraduate preparation in school-library science. In schools which are not large enough or which are unable to afford the services of a full-time librarian, it would be well if one of the teachers possessed some of the qualifications just recommended in order that he might give part-time supervision to the library. All of the regional accrediting agencies (New England, North Central, Southern, Western, etc.) now have certain standards which secondary school libraries must meet; these standards are fairly similar. The North Central Association of Colleges and Secondary Schools has the following typical standards for the librarians of its secondary school members:

Personnel. (a) Schools of 1,000 or more pupils, at least one full-time librarian who is professionally trained and who holds a bachelor's degree or its equivalent.
(b) Schools of less than 1,000 pupils, part-time teacher-librarian with technical library training.

Since the school librarian is essentially a teacher, many schools give him the title of "teacher-librarian." Emma J. Brock has well summarized in the following words the qualifications which a school librarian should possess:

The work demands not only careful but broad scholarship. A mere high school education plus even the most technical training is not enough. We must have not only a librarian, able to buy and to catalogue, to issue, and to keep a record of books lent, but the teacher-librarian, with an intelligent knowledge of all sources of information desired, competent, if necessary, to supervise the preparation of reports and special studies, cultured enough to make her library a place of refinement and inspiration. Moreover, she must have a strong yet winning personality, be able to command respect and therefore to keep the library a laboratory for work; at the same time she must be one who attracts students to her and what she has to offer by her sympathy, encouragement, and power to interest and inspire. No other position in the school offers such possibilities for universal service; no other makes greater demands upon her who fills it. . . .[6]

Co-operation Between the Teachers and the School Librarian. It was stated above that in function the school librarian is largely a teacher. Perhaps, it would be more accurate to say that he is a co-operating teacher, because his chief obligation is to co-operate with the teachers of the various departments in instructing the pupils. If the librarian does not co-operate with the teachers, they cannot accomplish all that they might. If the teachers do not co-operate with the librarian, he cannot accomplish all that he might. There are many ways in which teachers may co-operate with the librarian. Among the more important of these ways are the following: by making definite rather than vague assignments to pupils; by responding immediately to requests of the librarian for reading lists for various school subjects; by requesting pupils to return materials to the library as soon as their use has been finished; by being on the lookout for excellent new references for the library, and by notifying the librarian of those new references; by reducing to a minimum the requests for duplicate copies to be purchased by the library.

Opportunities in School-library Work.[7] School-library work presents another employment opportunity for persons who possess the requisite qualifications. The amount of salary, pension and tenure regulations, and other opportunities in the school librarianship compare favorably with those pertaining to the members of the teaching profession; moreover, the opportunities for obtaining a position as a school librarian, especially in the secondary schools, are easily as good as those for obtaining a teaching position. All colleges now employ one or more librarians, and practically all of the large and the medium-sized secondary schools also employ one or more, and every year sees hundreds of the smaller secondary schools start the practice of employing a full-time or a part-time librarian. Beginning teachers,

[6] "The Efficient High-School Library," *English Journal*, Vol. 5 (January, 1916), pp. 16–17.

[7] Chapter 17 of this book is devoted to opportunities in the teaching profession, and most of that discussion will be found to be pertinent to the school librarianship.

especially of the secondary school, who can show that they have had at least one college course on the school library will find that preparation an excellent selling point when they come to look for a school position; moreover, that special preparation will often enable them to command a slightly higher salary than classroom teachers.

The Materials of the School Library

Importance of Proper Selection of the Materials. The type of reading materials in the library determines largely the merit of the library. There are, of course, millions of books, thousands of bulletins, and hundreds of periodicals which might be obtained for the library; however, because of budgetary limitations no school library can expect to obtain more than a small percentage of any of these. School officials and school employees must, therefore, select all materials from the point of view of relative values; their obligation will be to procure first of all the absolutely necessary books, periodicals, and other materials. Unless such discrimination is used in selecting the materials for the library, the library may become loaded with "junk" which will never or seldom be used; moreover, unless care is exercised, improper materials may be placed in the library, and these will be read and have a deleterious influence on the pupils and on school and home relations.

In selecting materials for the library, school officials and school employees should keep in mind that there cannot be a standardized school library. Standardization may be obtained in a few materials, such as dictionaries, encyclopedias, and indexes, but beyond these standard references each library must be a law unto itself. The materials in the library must meet the needs of the community and of the curriculum of the school. For example, if science has a prominent place in the curriculum of the school, there should be more materials on science than would be necessary if science were not taught or did not have a prominent place in the curriculum. Moreover, the collection of materials should be properly proportioned among the various departments of the school; it should not be constituted too much of science, history, mathematics, fiction, or any other school subject. The school library should be given a "balanced diet" the same as the human body.

During recent years many libraries have improved their services through including films, filmstrips, pictures, charts, maps, globes, recorders, projectors, records, slides, and similar audio-visual aids.

Selection of Books for the Library. It has already been said that millions of books are now on the publishers' trade list; moreover, several thousand new books are published annually in the United States alone. Confronted with this dilemma, school officials and school employees should keep in mind quality, instead of quantity, when they are selecting books; they should realize that one excellent book may be of greater value than hundreds of worthless or mediocre books.

As has been stated above, the reading materials for the library should take into account the needs of the school. Materials should be selected only after conferring with the teachers of the various departments regarding the needs of the various school departments. Prospective teachers should become familiar with those needs when they are obtaining their college preparation. In selecting materials for the school library, many suggestions may be obtained from various book lists. Most of the states as well as the school standardizing agencies (New England, North Central, Southern, Western, etc.) have established regulations governing the minimum number and the kind of books to be found in schools of various types and sizes; these regulations apply more often to the secondary schools than to the elementary schools.

In addition to the minimum standards which most of the states have established for school libraries, particularly secondary school libraries, many of the states have prepared lists of books suitable for school libraries. As a rule, these lists may be obtained gratis from their publishers, namely, the state departments of education. Book lists for school libraries are now being published by practically all state departments of education, by a few library commissions, and by a few state libraries. Frequently, these lists are published for various sizes and types of schools. In addition to the lists just mentioned, there are various other excellent lists for various grades and school subjects, and persons who are preparing for teaching should become acquainted with the lists appropriate to their chosen fields of service.

Selection of Magazines for the Library. Since the United States is primarily a nation of periodical readers, and secondarily a nation of book readers, teachers should become acquainted with the best magazines appropriate for the pupils of the grades and classes which they teach. They should strive to obtain those magazines for the school library and to make the pupils acquainted with them.[8] The fact that millions of copies of trashy magazines are read annually by pupils and by adults may indicate a failure of the teaching profession to develop a high standard of reading interest among pupils, past and present. Some of the magazines of the school library should be primarily for recreational reading, while others should be primarily for use in connection with the study of various school subjects. Some of the comic magazines have come under serious attack during recent years and their selection should come under careful scrutiny.

To make the magazine material more useful, a good periodical index should be provided the library. Although there are many other indexes, the *Reader's Guide to Periodical Literature* is one of the best. Prospective teachers should become acquainted with these indexes when they are students in college; this acquaintance will not only help their college work, but will also make them competent to help their pupils to become acquainted with the indexes.

QUESTIONS FOR DISCUSSION

1. Do you agree with the statement that "reading is the greatest intellectualizing agency in the world today?" Is reading more important than the radio or television? Why or why not? Do you agree with the statement that "the library is, next to the teacher, the most important feature of a good school?" Why or why not?

2. What obligation does the teacher have to teach his pupils to use the library and to stimulate them to use it? Why? By what means may this preparation and this stimulation be given? What supervision should the teacher give to the type of library materials which his pupils read? What attitude should the teacher take toward the sale of trashy periodicals and books in a community? What can he do to decrease or to eliminate the sale?

3. What attention should the teacher give to the development of good habits of magazine and newspaper reading on the part of his pupils? Why? How may the teacher develop those habits in his pupils?

4. What co-operation should there be between the teacher and the librarian in selecting materials for the library? In what other ways may

[8] Every school library should also have at least one good daily newspaper (such as *The New York Times*, or *The Christian Science Monitor*), and pupils should be taught to read such newspapers.

the teacher co-operate with the librarian in increasing the usefulness of the library? What resources in addition to books and magazines should a good school library have? Explain.

5. Assuming that your community has neither a school library nor a community library, and assuming further that there are no public funds for a school library, how might you as a teacher proceed to build up a library for your pupils?

6. Would you favor keeping school libraries open during the summer vacation? On Saturdays and Sundays? Why or why not?

7. How do you explain the fact that so many secondary school and college graduates do not read books? By what steps would you suggest that this situation be corrected?

8. As a teacher, would you use the library to supplant or to supplement the textbook? Why?

9. What are the laws of your state pertaining to the establishment and the support of school libraries? What changes, if any, do you believe should be made in the laws? Why? Should school officials control both school and public libraries? Why?

10. Should each room of the elementary school have its own library? Why or why not?

SELECTED REFERENCES

Alexander, Carter, and Burke, Arvid J., *How to Locate Educational Information and Data,* Revised edition, Teachers College, Columbia University, New York, 1950, 441 pp.

A guide to research tools and techniques for workers in education.

Burke, John Emmett, "What School Board Members Should Know About the School Library," *American School Board Journal,* Vol. 129 (September, 1954), pp. 37–40.

Discusses the important place a library should hold in building an educational program in any school today. A school library should be the center of all instructional material and should be adequate in size and number of books and magazines. Says that the schools often are negligent in building up their libraries, and that few school libraries really provide material for all the various class needs.

Dawson, Dorotha, *et al.,* A *Basic Book Collection for High Schools,* American Library Association, Chicago, 1950, 204 pp.

Lists, classifies, and evaluates 1700 titles.

Dyke, Elwood E., and Merow, Lloyd G., "Public Library Bookmobile," *Nation's Schools,* Vol. 55 (March, 1955), pp. 60–61.

Describes the bookmobile at Kenosha, Wisconsin; illustrated.

Fargo, Lucile F., *The Library in the School*, American Library Association, Chicago, 1947, 405 pp.

This is a survey of present practice among school libraries in the United States, covering both elementary and secondary schools; bibliographies.

Henne, Frances, *et al.*, *A Planning Guide for the High School Library Program*, American Library Association, Chicago, 1951, 160 pp.

Lists in nine sections the basic services and facilities that a good high school library should have.

Johnson, B. Lamar, *The Librarian and the Teacher in General Education*, American Library Association, Chicago, 1948, 69 pp.

The liaison between the library and the teaching staffs greatly increases student reading.

Snow, Mirian, *et al.*, *A Basic Book Collection for Elementary Grades*, American Library Association, Chicago, 1951, 136 pp.

Describes more than 1,000 books. Presents graded lists on all school subjects.

Topping, Elizabeth R., *Periodicals for Small and Medium-Sized Libraries*, American Library Association, Chicago, 1948, 106 pp.

Prepared by a special committee. Describes and evaluates some 300 magazines in all fields.

Walraven, Margaret K., and Hall-Quest, Alfred, *Teaching Through the Elementary School Library*, H. W. Wilson Co., New York, 1948, 183 pp.

Discusses how to make full use of the school library in teaching the younger children.

Wilson Bulletin for Librarians, Editorial Office, 950–972 University Ave., New York City, 1914 to date.

This magazine is published monthly and contains many helpful articles and suggestions for school librarians. Each issue contains a selected list of the best new books which have appeared during the previous month.

Wilson, Martha, *School Library Management*, Sixth Edition, Revised by Althea M. Currin, H. W. Wilson Co., New York, 1939, 169 pp.

A general treatment of school-library organization, administration, and use.

PART FIVE

EDUCATION AS A PROFESSION

CHAPTER 17

Opportunities in the Teaching Profession

Necessity of Choice of a Vocation

When a person begins to face the problems of earning a living, the necessity of choosing and preparing for a vocation comes immediately to the fore. That problem must be faced by everyone, except those few persons who are born rich, and it must usually be faced early in life. In choosing and in preparing for a vocation the following factors should be kept in mind: first, the opportunities afforded by the vocation, and, second, the requirements for entering, and for achieving success in, the vocation. In this chapter the opportunities in the teaching profession will be discussed. In the next chapter the requirements for entering, and for achieving success in, the teaching profession will be discussed. Of course, earlier chapters have discussed the opportunities and the requirements in a few special areas of educational service, such as pupil personnel and guidance, school attendance, the school librarianship, school nurse, physical education, teaching the handicapped and other types of atypical children, and school-lunchroom management.

Importance of the Teacher

"As is priest, so is parish," is believed to be an old Russian proverb. This proverb may be paraphrased and applied to the person in charge of any activity, because the person in charge makes an activity largely what it is. If he is well qualified for his task, the person will overcome all obstacles and make the activity function to the fullest; as Napoleon said of himself, he will "specialize in doing the impossible." If the person is not well qualified, the activity will not realize its potentialities, although all other conditions for such realization may be favorable.

In school affairs the teacher primarily determines whether the school will be efficient or inefficient. "As is the teacher, so is the school." Or, in the words of Henry Adams, "A teacher affects eternity. He can never tell where his influence stops." Although they can never be neglected in an educational program, such facilities as school buildings, school equipment, and school supplies are of secondary importance compared with teachers. Granted that hovels were safe and sanitary, it would be better for children to attend school in them, there to be instructed by excellent teachers than to attend school in palaces, there to be under the tutelage of inferior teachers. James A. Garfield once defined an ideal school as "Mark Hopkins at one end of a log and a student at the other end." In that definition Garfield was no doubt attempting to call attention to the indispensability of an excellent teacher, of which Mark Hopkins was a splendid example. He probably did not believe that a mere "log"—at least not *any* kind of a log—would suffice as the altar of instruction. He did believe, though, that school personnel was much more important than school matériel.

Garfield's remark applies to all levels of schooling—elementary, secondary, and college. It applies with particular cogency to the lower grades of the school, because the younger the pupil, the more he must depend upon his teacher. In the lower grades of the school it is expected that the tools of learning will be taught, that desirable habits and high ideals will be developed, and all in all that an enduring foundation will be laid for future learning and for life. As the pupil ascends the educational ladder, his teacher becomes less necessary to him, but a good teacher never becomes dispensable, even at the top of the ladder. In brief, when we realize the importance of education to society and to the individual, and when we realize the rôle of the teacher in providing that education, we become more aware of the importance of the teacher. Good schools and qualified teachers are expensive, but ignorance and selfishness among a people are much more expensive. Wars, unemployment, crime, waste, graft, disease, and other social handicaps will continue as long as ignorance and selfishness exist. When the light of education is snuffed out, if it ever is snuffed out, the dark ages will return, and civilization will have committed suicide. In inimitable style Henry van Dyke has stated the contributions of the teacher to his pupils and to society:

> I sing the praise of the unknown teacher. Great generals win campaigns, but it is the unknown soldier who wins the war. Famous educators plan new systems of pedagogy, but it is the unknown teacher who directs and guides the young. He lives in obscurity and contends with hardship. For him no trumpets blare, no chariots wait, no golden decorations are decreed. He keeps the watch along the borders of darkness and makes the attack on the trenches of ignorance and folly. Patient in his daily duty, he strives to conquer the evil powers which are the enemies of youth. He awakens sleeping spirits. He quickens the indolent, encourages the eager, and steadies the unstable. He communicates his own joy in learning and shares with boys and girls the best treasures of his mind. He lights many candles which, in later years, will shine back to cheer him. This is his reward. Knowledge may be gained from books; but the love of knowledge is transmitted only by personal contact. No one has ever deserved better of the republic than the unknown teacher. No one is more worthy to be enrolled in a democratic aristocracy, "King of himself and servant of mankind." [1]

Supply and Demand in the Various Types of School Positions

The Total Number of School Positions. Because the answer to the question is one of the best measures of the opportunities for employment in the vocation, one of the first questions which should be asked by the person who is faced with the problem of selecting a vocation is: "How many positions are there in the vocation under consideration?" On this score, education as a vocation ranks high. According to the most recent census of the United States, only a few vocations, such as agriculture, construction, manufacturing, the railroads, other public services, and textiles employ more people than the schools. In the public and in the private schools and colleges of the United States there are more than a million teaching, administrative, and supervisory positions. Making up this large army of school employees are more than 1,100,000 public elementary and secondary school teachers, approximately 125,000 nonpublic elementary and

[1] Henry van Dyke, "A Tribute to the Unknown Teacher," *The Mathematics Teacher*, Vol. 25 (May, 1932), p. 302.

secondary-school teachers, more than 210,000 teachers in public and private collegiate departments, approximately 16,000 teachers in other types of teaching activities, and approximately 50,000 school administrators and supervisors.[2] Those numbers are increasing annually because of the increase in the population.

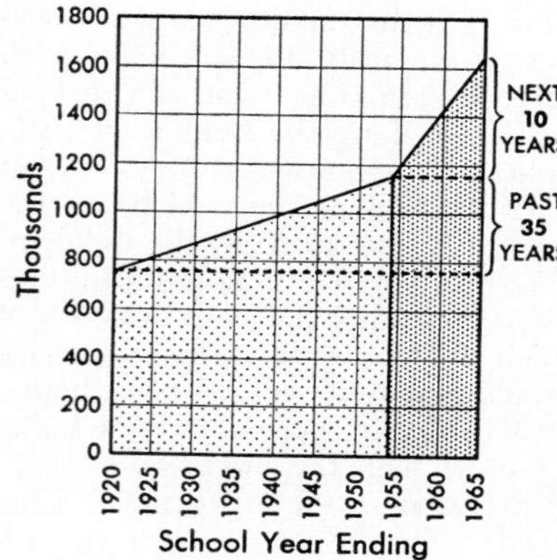

Fig. 57. The present and near-future demand for teachers. (*From* Teachers for Tomorrow, *p. 18. Courtesy of The Fund for the Advancement of Education.*)

Types of School Positions Available. The preceding paragraph has indicated that in relation to the total number of its employees education is a gigantic business, employing more than one million persons. That paragraph has also shown the approximate number of positions in each large field of school service. More than two-thirds of all school employees are classified as teachers in the public and the private elementary schools, and most of the remaining one-third are classified as teachers in the public and private secondary schools and colleges. Although they are helpful in giving a general picture, the data of the preceding paragraph do not provide sufficient detail concerning the types of school positions. We need to seek elsewhere, therefore, for more detailed information on the types of school positions.

A study by Miss Marjorie Rankin, who made an examination of the waxing and waning occupations in the public school systems of certain cities in the United States, will be found helpful in seeing the

[2] For the exact number of school employees for any year and in any state, the student may consult *Statistics of State School Systems,* which is published biennally by the U. S. Office of Education.

types of school positions available.[3] Although that study was made several years ago, and there is no more recent study, the types of school positions are approximately the same today as then, though they are probably more numerous today. In the fourteen cities (ten large and four small) which she investigated, Miss Rankin found almost four hundred different types of school positions. She classified these positions into six "lists." In the first four of the "lists," 239 different positions of a nonteaching type were found. Sample positions from each of her four "lists" are herewith reported:

In "List 1," which is captioned "Personnel of Maintenance," 37 different positions are mentioned. These positions are concerned primarily with the business phases of school administration. Among the 37 positions mentioned are the following: accountant, auditor, cafeteria manager, clerk, purchasing clerk, draftsman, and storekeeper.

In "List 2," which is captioned "Personnel of Professional Services," 29 different positions are mentioned. Among them are the following: architect, director of educational research, engineer, director of medical inspection, landscape gardener, school psychologist, and statistician.

In "List 3," which is captioned "Personnel of Personal Service," 44 different positions are mentioned. Among them are the following: attendance officer, nurse, coach, dentist, librarian, optometrist, nutritionist, physician, placement officer, and visiting teacher.

In "List 4," which is captioned "Administration and Supervision," 129 different positions are mentioned. Among them are the following: superintendent, assistant or associate superintendent, business manager, principal, dean of boys, dean of girls, and directors and supervisors of various departments or fields such as home economics, industrial arts, commercial education, music, art, special education, health, visual education, and citizenship.[4]

The remaining positions of Miss Rankin's study were classroom-teaching positions, and these comprised 72.12 per cent of all school positions. She discovered, however, that there were several hundred types of teaching positions, if the different subjects of instruction were considered. In the secondary schools, for example, she found that nineteen different kinds of English were being taught, fourteen kinds of music, thirty-one kinds of art, and eighty-three different trades.

It is unfortunate that such a study as that of Miss Rankin's is not

[3] Marjorie Rankin, *Trends in Educational Occupations*, Teachers College, Columbia University, 1930.

[4] *Ibid.*, pp. 8–13.

available for the rural and the village schools—schools in which many educational employees must begin their careers. Casual observation, though, indicates that the rural and the village schools do not have nearly the diversification of services that the city schools possess. In those smaller school systems few educational positions beyond those of teacher, principal, and superintendent of schools are found. Casual observation also indicates that the typical educational employee must begin his career in classroom teaching or in one of the school activities which Miss Rankin has classified as "personnel of personal service" (school nurse, attendance officer, school librarian, visiting teacher, etc.).

Number of School Vacancies. Another question which is asked by the person who is contemplating entrance into a particular vocation is: "How many vacancies are there each year in the vocation under consideration?" The answer to this question will give another view of the opportunities for obtaining a position in the vocation. Compared with other professions the tenure of position of the teaching personnel of the schools of the United States is perhaps unstable. That instability provides annually, especially during recent years, an unusually large number of vacancies in the teaching profession. Because of the large amount of turnover in it, a wag has dubbed the teaching profession "the teaching procession." The teachers of many European countries usually remain several years—often their whole career—in the same position, but the teachers in many American communities, especially in the smaller communities, are almost professional "tramps." Although some turnover may be an evidence of vitality, the unusual amount of turnover in the members of the teaching profession sometimes indicates a lack of professional consciousness and prestige. In brief, vacancies in the teaching profession are perhaps too plentiful for the best interests of the general public, of the pupils, and of the profession; but, a teaching position is now available for any person who is qualified.

The *National Survey of the Education of Teachers*, which was a nation-wide survey conducted and financed by the United States Office of Education, reported that approximately 11.5 per cent "new additional" [5] elementary school teachers were employed; "new addi-

[5] "New additional" teachers includes those employed to take the place of those leaving the profession, plus those employed to fill newly created positions. See footnote 7.

tional" teachers employed for the junior high school and for the senior high school were 8.7 per cent and 11.8 per cent respectively.[6] In the fall of 1955, there were 1,136,000 teachers—729,000 in the public elementary schools and 407,000 in the public secondary schools. The number of elementary school teachers increased 39,000, or 5.6 per cent, and the number of secondary school teachers increased 30,000, or 8.1 per cent over 1954.[7] It should be kept in mind that the data just given are limited to the public elementary and secondary schools. The figures do not include the several thousand "new additional" teachers required in the public and the private colleges and in the private elementary and secondary schools, nor do they include the several thousand "new additional" administrative and supervisory officers needed in the public and the private schools and colleges.

To summarize, many thousand "new additional" employees are needed in the public and the private schools and colleges of the United States each year (1) to take the place of employees leaving the teaching profession, and (2) to fill new school positions. In addition to these "new additional" employees, several thousand employees change from one educational position to another each year. The *National Survey of the Education of Teachers* found that approximately one-fifth of the elementary school teachers were "new" to their positions each year, that approximately one-seventh of the junior high school teachers were "new," and that approximately one-fifth of the senior high school teachers were "new." [8] This means that approximately 200,000 teachers were "new" to their positions each year. The survey found also that the amount of teacher mobility was much larger in the rural districts than in city districts, and that it was much larger in certain states than in others. The city school districts pay the highest salaries, and when teachers arrive there, they have no other place to go. The above conditions still are found.

There were in 1955 more than 700,000 public elementary school

[6] E. S. Evenden, *National Survey of the Education of Teachers*, U. S. Office of Education, 1933, Vol. 6, p. 222. See also footnote 8.

[7] These figures are for emergency years following World War 2; an unparalleled shortage of teachers has happened during this period, largely because of the huge increase in the birth rate. That emergency still continues.

[8] Evenden, *op. cit.*, Vol. 6, p. 201. (As used here, new means new to the position, not necessarily a beginning teacher.)

In a study made by the National Education Association for the school year of 1955–56 these conditions are verified. See *Research Bulletin of the National Education Association*, Vol. 35 (February, 1957), pp. 3–63.

teachers in the United States, and about 200,000 more will be needed by 1960 to meet the needs of about 7,000,000 more children that it is predicted will enter the elementary school by then. After a few years, those elementary school pupils will enter the secondary school, and then the colleges. Many thousand more teachers will then be needed by the secondary schools and finally by the colleges and the universities.

It is tragic that the colleges are not now preparing nearly enough teachers to meet the present and the future demands for teachers. The present and the probable future shortage of teachers is now one of the most serious problems facing the public.

What are the factors that create demand for teachers? And what are the sources of supply of teachers? The *National Survey of the Education of Teachers* also provided answers to those questions. From one of the reports of the survey, it is observed that the three chief factors creating demand for teachers were the following: (1) "predecessor left to teach somewhere else in state"; (2) "predecessor married"; and (3) "predecessor holds newly created position." During recent years, the creation of new positions to meet the increasing deluge of pupils has been the chief factor in creating the increasing demand for teachers. The same national study indicated also that the three chief sources of teacher supply were the following: (1) "another school system in the same state"; (2) "college or university in same state"; and (3) "teacher-training class, normal school, or teachers college in same state"; and they are believed to be the same today.

THE CHANGING SUPPLY AND DEMAND FOR TEACHERS. Although several thousand new teachers are now needed annually in the whole United States, it should be pointed out that this condition has not always obtained. Except during and immediately following World War II, practically every state has had an oversupply, and in some of the more populous states the oversupply has amounted to several thousand teachers. Of course, during recent years there has been an unprecedented undersupply of teachers, due probably to the increasing birth rate and to the unprecedented prosperity of the nation.

It might be argued with much logic that no state has ever had an oversupply of "blue-ribbon" teachers, but only an oversupply of persons who had been certificated and thus made eligible for employment as teachers. The tragedy of oversupply in earlier years came from the fact that the "mine-run" teachers handicapped the "blue ribbon" ones in obtaining positions; inferior teachers cheapen the whole profession, just as fiat money has cheapened the best currency. It has long been observed that prosperous times beget an undersupply of teachers, whereas depression or recession times bring an oversupply.

Many of the states have neglected to maintain a balance between the supply and the demand of teachers; not enough evidence of foresight and planning with respect to this problem is observed on the part of school officials, school employees, and the public. A policy of *laissez faire* has been sometimes pursued. The large disparity between supply and demand for teachers, especially of certain secondary school subjects, has been unfortunate for the schools; it has given many prospective teachers the impression that teaching has little promise as a desirable career.

Teachers should assume the lead in trying to raise standards, just as physicians have taken the lead in advocating higher standards for the members of their profession. If the problem is attacked vigorously and with statesmanship, large and immediate improvement can be made. In attacking the problem the public must be further educated to see the need for improving the opportunities and the working conditions in the teaching profession as well as the need for increasing the level of teacher qualifications. Looking toward increasing the level of qualifications for teachers, the following program is suggested:

1. A more critical selection of the candidates entering teacher-preparing institutions.
2. A lengthened period of college and university preparation for teachers.
3. An improvement in the facilities and in the services of teacher-preparing institutions.
4. More rigid state supervision over matters pertaining to the selection, the preparation, and the certification of teachers.
5. Higher salaries, better pensions, and better conditions of work in general for teachers. This factor is probably foremost.

At present, though, many teachers have substandard credentials. In the fall of 1954, seven per cent of the public elementary and secondary school teachers of the nation had substandard credentials, but in the fall of 1955 that percentage had dropped to 6.8.

Any scarcity of employees in a given field usually results in higher salaries being paid in that field. Whether we agree or disagree with its operation, the law of supply and demand has always applied to school employees and other workers as well as to commodities; according to that law, underproduction results in higher prices, and overproduction brings lower prices. In a free system of economics and in the absence of government price ceilings, services as well as commodities are always seeking higher prices. When prospective teachers discern a scarcity of teachers in a given field, they tend and should tend to decide to enter that field. The result of their decision, as a rule, is that supply and demand are soon balanced; in fact, it often happens that supply soon exceeds demand, and this results in many teachers being unable to obtain positions and in a tendency toward lower salaries for teachers.

What fields in teaching have an oversupply of teachers, and what fields have an undersupply? Many studies of this question have been made for various states and localities. As a whole, those studies report a present tendency toward an undersupply of teachers in agricultural education, commercial education, Spanish, nursing education, home economics, industrial arts, mathematics, physics, chemistry, general science, and music. The same studies have reported a present tendency toward an oversupply in the social studies, English, French, German, physical education, and biology. As has been earlier stated, there has been a large shortage of elementary school teachers following World War II, but there has been some shortage also of secondary school teachers.

In considering any data on supply and demand, the prospective teacher should remember that changes in supply and demand are likely to make the picture of tomorrow different from the picture of today. Opportunities for employment in a certain field may be plentiful today, but tomorrow the opportunities may be few or nil. If he desires or must have a position, the prospective teacher should keep himself informed concerning these changes; his best source of information on the changes will probably be the placement office of the college in which he is studying, and he will often save himself much grief by keeping in close touch with that office. Placement offices cannot fill vacancies which do not exist.

In selecting a field of endeavor, the prospective school employee is entitled to helpful guidance, and every teacher-preparing institution has the obligation of giving that guidance. Although prospective school employees should be permitted—in fact, required—to select their fields of endeavor, they should be provided with up-to-date information which will assist them in making an intelligent choice. The "sink or swim" policy, which some teacher-preparing institutions have pursued, has resulted in entirely too many of the graduates of those institutions "sinking." Practically every teacher-preparing institution, at present, is organized to give all necessary guidance, provided the students will seek it; only short-sighted and careless students will fail to take advantage of all such services.

Important though that consideration is, the opportunity for employment should not dictate entirely, if even chiefly, the field for which the candidate should prepare; never to be neglected in choosing a life work are other considerations. Especially important among these are the candidate's abilities, his desires, and his aptitudes. Those factors may weigh so heavily that the student should prepare for a certain endeavor, in spite of the fact that his opportunity for obtaining employment in that field is certain to be limited. Possibly a wait of one or more years until the candidate is able to obtain a position is not too high a price to pay for the privilege of working in a field where his abilities, his desires, and his aptitudes lie. In the end, such a wait is sure to bring greater happiness and greater and greater professional progress than a life-time spent as "a square peg in a round hole."

Subject Combinations for Teachers. The prospective teacher should keep in mind that he will probably be required to begin his career in a rural, a village, or a small city school system. On the assumption that every beginning teacher is a "gamble" until he has been tested in the crucible of experience, the school systems of the large cities sometimes demand successful experience of one to three years of all new appointees. Since the city school systems usually pay higher salaries than the rural and the village school systems, and, since they provide many other advantages, they do not have much difficulty in enforcing that requirement; however, during the recent teacher shortage, many school systems have abandoned this rule. Of course, the requirement can be questioned, because it prevents the employment of all beginners, although some of them may be outstanding prospects.

In brief, the rural, the village, and the small city school systems have usually been the preparing ground for the teaching personnel of the large cities, and this in spite of the fact that the city systems provide more adequate supervision. Since the typical beginning teacher must look forward to a few years of service in the smaller school systems, he should keep this fact in mind when he is obtaining his preparation for teaching. For example, if he is planning to teach in a secondary school or in a departmentalized elementary school, he should consider the advisability of equipping himself to teach two or three different school subjects. Although he would probably prefer to teach only in the field of his major interests, he is not likely to find many opportunities for such employment; in fact, investigations show that he stands almost a fifty-fifty chance of having to teach more than one school subject, even when in later years he is employed by a larger school. Experience indicates that teachers of industrial arts, music, fine arts, physical education, agriculture, commercial subjects, distributive education, and home economics have the best chance of teaching in one field alone.

Although the basis or the justification for the combination is not always clear, the beginning teacher should keep in mind also that in practice certain subjects tend to go together. For example, mathematics goes with physical and biological sciences, and physical sciences and biological sciences go together. There is some demand for an art and a music combination; Latin goes more often with English than it does with other languages; industrial arts and athletics frequently go together.

Data concerning the combination of school subjects of elementary school teachers, who are doing departmental teaching, are not plentiful. It is known, though, that only few schools and school systems use departmental teaching in the elementary school. When it is used, it is usually found in the upper grades only of the elementary school. This means, therefore, that the typical elementary school teacher will have to be prepared to teach all school subjects which are offered in the grade or grades that he teaches. The teacher in the one-room rural school is usually called upon to teach all grades and all school subjects of the elementary school curriculum. In the larger elementary schools the typical teacher has only one grade.

Opportunities for Men and for Women in Teaching. Until about the beginning of the nineteenth century, practically all teachers in the United States were men. At about that time the movement for the college education of women gained momentum and women began to enter the professions, especially the teaching profession; that movement increased the supply of women teachers and it decreased the demand for men teachers. About the same time also, a period of large industrial expansion started, and that provided many new business opportunities, especially for men. With the exception of the years of severe business depression, the percentage of men teachers has dropped during recent decades. The percentage of men teachers in the public elementary and secondary schools fell from 38.7 in 1870 to 17.7 in 1932, but has increased since 1932 to approximately 31 today. Whether the recent increase in the percentage of men teachers indicates a reversal of the major trend of the last century, or is merely an intermediate upswing, cannot be foretold.

A few states report the number of teachers of each sex in the various types of teaching positions in the public elementary and the secondary schools. An examination of those data shows that the percentage of men teachers in each state varies widely and that the percentage of men teachers varies also with the type of school and with the school subject. This percentage is highest in the traditional four-year high school, next highest in the reorganized types of high schools, and lowest in the elementary school and kindergarten. In the public elementary schools only one teacher in every eight is a man, whereas in the public secondary schools approximately five teachers in every ten are men. In the college and university, except those for women, by far the majority of the teachers are men.

Unfortunately, nation-wide data showing the sex of school administrators are not available, but a perusal of the latest *Educational Directory* of the United States Office of Education will show that by far the majority of the 50,000 school administrators of the nation are men. In the colleges and universities men hold practically all of the administrative positions; in the elementary and the secondary schools men hold practically all of the school superintendencies and most of the principalships; and in most of the other types of administrative positions men are in the majority. Men have sought the school-administrative positions, because of the higher salaries and the greater prestige which those positions give, and they have not had much difficulty in obtaining them, because of the widespread belief, justified or unjustified, that men are better school administrators than women. Although a few women are found in every type of school-administrative position, it is only in the elementary school principalship that their number even approximates the number of men.

Many of our fellow citizens believe that more and better qualified men are needed in the teaching profession, and they have concluded that to obtain them larger salaries will have to be paid men. Many efforts at augmenting the number of men teachers have been directed, therefore, at increasing the pay of men to a point where it would compare more favorably with that of men in the other vocations. In attacking the problem of pay, many boards of education have concluded that it is necessary to pay men teachers more than women teachers of equal qualifications. Recent studies show that many school systems pay higher salaries, at least in certain positions, to men than to women of equal preparation and equal experience; but, the trend is toward equal pay.

The practice of paying men more than women has been strenuously opposed by many persons, especially by the women teachers. In many communities the women have organized to eliminate this practice—a practice which appears to them to be "rank discrimination and patent injustice." The women have adopted as their slogan, "Equal pay for equal work." They attack in the following manner the two chief arguments for a pay differential for men:

Regarding the first argument, namely, that men teachers have dependents, whereas women teachers do not, the women affirm that women teachers, as well as men teachers, frequently have dependents. As evidence they point to such investigations as that by Theresa P. Pyle. In that study Miss Pyle obtained questionnaire returns from 775 widely scattered teachers regarding their dependency load. The mean dependency load (including the teacher himself) was as follows: single women, 1.6; single men, 1.4; married women, 1.9; married men, 3.4. She found that all the married men supported dependents as compared with sixty-three per cent of the married women, fifty-two per cent of the single women, and thirty-three per cent of the single men.[9] A recent bulletin of the National Education Association confirms those data for the present.

The women point out that there are many men teachers without any dependents, just as there are many women teachers without any. They are unable, therefore, to see any justice in paying all members of a group an additional salary, because the majority, or a few, of

[9] Theresa P. Pyle, *The Teachers' Dependency Load*, Teachers College, Columbia University, 1939, p. 100. See also *Research Bulletin of the National Education Association*, Vol. 35 (February, 1957), pp. 23–24.

the members of the group have dependents. They conclude that if an additional salary is to be paid for dependents, it should be paid only those who really have them.

Regarding the second argument, which is to the effect that the influence of the masculine personality is needed in the schools, particularly in the upper grades, the women point out that this is entirely a matter of opinion. They affirm that there is no objective evidence showing that the influence of the masculine personality is a *sine qua non* for a well-rounded development of the pupil. They conclude that teaching ability is an individual matter, and that it is fallacious to attribute certain invariable traits or abilities to a given sex.

Pecuniary Rewards and Opportunities

Amount of Salary for Teachers. If the welfare and progress of society and of the individual are or can be determined largely by the teacher—and this is admitted by all intelligent and altruistic persons—then it is the responsibility of educational statesmanship to see that the teacher is the best qualified person possible. In undertaking to obtain teachers of high qualifications the salary paid them is one of the first matters which should be examined, because there is almost sure to be a relationship between the salary and the qualifications. A salary of $4,000 will usually purchase a much higher type of qualification than a salary of $3,000. Teachers are like other persons in their desire to earn as much as possible, and they consciously and inevitably drift toward the communities and the positions which pay high salaries. Teachers require the same necessities, and they desire the same comforts and luxuries as other persons. They want to provide for their families and for their own old age. They are normal human beings, and they are not ascetics.

In the first place, a sufficiently high standard of pay is needed to attract the best young people into teaching. A low standard of pay will not attract such persons. The joy of service, albeit potent, is not a sufficient magnet. Although Moses affirms in Deuteronomy, vii. 3, that "man doth not live by bread alone," he did not imply that man could live without any bread; bread continues to be the "staff of life," and to purchase it the coin of the realm is necessary. In the second place, the schedule of pay must be high enough to keep the choicest spirits in the profession and to enable them to be progressive and happy in their work. Teaching must constantly compete with other vocations; if its standards of pay are low compared with other vocations, there is danger that the best members of the teaching profession will be lost to other vocations, especially in prosperous times. In the third place, the salary must be high enough to enable the teacher to take his proper place in community life, to give him a feeling of security, and for him to maintain a standard of living equal to or approximating that of the most cultured people of the community.

Teachers, therefore, are justified—in fact, they are obligated—to demand adequate pay; they should assume that obligation, not because of their own selfish interests, but because society will suffer if they do not assume it. Of course, the members of a profession, which is worthy of the name of profession, do not work for salary alone; with them service is primary and pecuniary reward is secondary. In the following words John Ruskin has stated the sentiment which should guide the members of a profession in their pecuniary relationships:

> If your fee is first with you and your work is second, then fee is your master and the lord of all fees, who is the devil; but if your work is first with you and your fee is second, then work is your master and the lord of all work, who is God.

In campaigns to increase the salaries of teachers, hundreds of local, state-wide, and nation-wide studies of teachers' salaries have been made during recent years. Those studies have shown not only the salaries of teachers in the several types of school service, but some of the studies have indicated also the economic position of teachers compared with workers in other fields of endeavor. The high points of a few of the more important of those studies are reviewed herewith.

Since its establishment in 1923, the Research Division of the National Education Association has been the most prolific agency in collecting and in disseminating data on teachers' salaries and in showing the usually unfavorable economic position of teachers compared with other workers. Similar data have been collected and disseminated regularly by most of the state education associations, by many of the state departments of education, by the United States Office of Education, and by many local education associations. These studies can, therefore, always be consulted for the most recent data, and all of them may usually be found in school, college, and public libraries.

Studies made by those organizations show that, although the tendency is toward greater uniformity in the salaries of teachers when qualifications are equal, teachers' salaries still vary widely; they vary from state to state, from school system to school system in the same state, from secondary school to elementary school, and from school subject to school subject. Teachers in the one-room schools receive the smallest salaries, and teachers in the secondary schools receive the largest ones. Salaries are lowest in the rural, the village, and the small city school systems, and highest in the large city school systems. Those disparities result in a large turnover annually in the lower-paid positions and in a constant and inevitable drift of the teachers in those positions toward the higher-paid positions. Practically all teachers in the cities started their careers in the rural and the village school systems, and they migrated from there in to the better-paying positions of the cities.

Thousands of public school teachers receive less than $2,000 annually—in fact, in a few states the average annual pay is not much more than $2,000. By far the lowest salaries are found in the Southern states, largely because of the lack of sufficient taxable wealth, and because the cost of living is lower there. In only a few states is the average annual salary more than $3,000 and in only a few other states is it more than $4,500. The overwhelming majority of the teachers now receive salaries ranging between $2,500 and $5,000, but many teachers receive less and many receive more. The average salary in the nation is approximately $4,000 annually. The wealth of any state or any school district is the chief determinant of teachers' salaries in that state or that school district, and teachers who work in the less wealthy states and school districts must expect to receive salaries smaller than those paid in the more wealthy states and school districts.

Any worth while study of teachers' salaries should compare those salaries with the wages of other workers in the community in which the study is being made. Such comparison should be made because the incomes of the people of a community largely determine the standard of living of the people of the community—a standard which teachers are expected to meet, or to approximate. "When in Rome we are expected to live as Romans." The "have nots" cannot be expected to live in happiness with the "haves," if, indeed, they can live at all. If wearing patched clothing is fashionable, and if the simple life is the mode of the people of a community, then teachers will not need such a large salary to maintain a respectable standard of living compared with other people. If, however, most of the people have many luxuries, then teachers must possess comforts at least, and for obtaining them larger salaries will be necessary.

Although the economic position of the teacher, compared with other workers, has been improving, it is not yet what it should be. The remark has often been made, and it has never been contradicted, that the teacher's work constitutes the bulwark of the nation. The cruel fact is, however, that this well-founded theory has been disregarded by society in making its salary awards, because the pay of the teacher is much less than that of other workers who have equal standards of preparation. Of course, there will probably continue to be some differential between the pay of teachers and the pay of workers in many other vocations because of such advantages of teaching as its short hours, frequent holidays, vacations, healthfulness, tenure, and social service. As has been previously stated, the members of a profession worthy of the name do not work for salary alone; they want to give much more than they receive.

In comparing the salaries of teachers with the salaries of other workers, the disparity of teachers' salaries cannot be justified by the argument that teachers work only eight, nine, or ten months, whereas workers in other vocations must labor twelve months. Persons who offer that argument tend to forget that the teacher must live twelve months, although he is paid for a less number of months; expenses continue whether income does or not. They forget also that many teachers spend their vacation months in attending the summer sessions of colleges and universities, or in taking other steps to improve themselves for their work. They further forget that to improve one's competence usually requires the expenditure of money for college tuition, books, periodicals, and other services. Most teachers who are worth their "salt" really "work" during the twelve months of the year; they are constantly engaged either in teaching or in improving themselves for teaching.

Salaries of Beginning Teachers. The salaries of beginning teachers compare favorably with the salaries of beginning physicians, dentists, lawyers, engineers, or other workers who are just starting to "build up a practice." Over a period of years, however, the salaries of teachers do not increase nearly as much as the earnings of members of many other professions. Teachers seldom become wealthy, and they never become wealthy on only their salary. The author was a teacher for 44 years, retiring in 1956.

The large shortage of teachers, during recent years, has impelled the legislatures of several states to set minimum salaries for beginning teachers. For beginning teachers with college degrees, the large cities (above 100,000 population) pay on the average approximately $3,900 at present, while the smaller cities and the rural districts, where most teachers begin their careers, pay much less; but, some school systems pay much more.

SALARY SCHEDULES FOR TEACHERS. Of almost equal importance with the amount of salary is the manner in which the salary is determined. As an aid in determining the amount of salary, most school systems, especially the city systems, have devised salary schedules. A few states require every school system to have a salary schedule. A large percentage of the small school systems—systems in which teachers must usually begin their careers—do not yet have salary schedules; in these systems each salary is determined each year by the board of education. A salary schedule is advantageous both to the administration and to the teachers. To the administration it is a salary plan and helps in school-budget making. Salary schedules set the minimum salaries for teachers with various amounts of college preparation, and they also provide steps for salary increases based on teaching experience and additional college preparation.

A salary schedule is advantageous to the teachers because it tends to assure that at least approximate justice will be given the teachers. When a salary schedule is in operation, the teacher knows what his normal expectancy in salary will be in two, five, ten, or some other number of years. When there is no salary schedule, it often happens that the teacher is left to obtain as much as he can, and the school officials are left to pay no more than they must; there is no normal expectancy in salary under such an arrangement.

At first glance the lack of a salary schedule would seem to be advantageous, because the salary could then be determined on basis of merit. The difficulty, though, is to measure merit. When the Solomons of the profession do not agree on what a good teacher is—on what constitutes merit—imagine the difficulty which the well-intentioned "school officials up the creek" must have in distributing salary awards on basis of merit. Without a salary plan, "politics," "pull," and other evidences of partiality are likely to be potent considerations in determining salaries. There is danger that those teachers who are aggressive, nervy, and perhaps unethical, will be paid too much, whereas those who are modest, though efficient, will be cheated.

It is unfortunate that practically all salary schedules in operation today tend to give the salary awards wholly on the bases of (1) the number of years of college preparation, and (2) the number of years of experience in teaching. Thus, after the minimum amount of college preparation, say, two, three, four, or five years, has been obtained, an increase in salary of $75, $100, or some other amount for each additional one-third or one-half year of preparation is paid. Likewise, $200, $250, or some other amount is paid for each year of teaching experience. A schedule of this type is shown in Table 6. "Single" schedules, which are coming to be rapidly adopted, pay all teachers having equal qualifications the same amount; thus, elementary-school teachers are paid as much as secondary-school teachers, provided their qualifications are equal. Table 6 shows a "single" salary schedule.

Strange to say, many of the automatically operating schedules have been called "merit" schedules by their designers. Obviously, such schedules are not merit schedules, because college preparation and teaching experience are not necessarily measures of merit. Many doctors of philosophy are inferior teachers, and many excellent teachers have had only one, two, or three years of professional preparation. Likewise, some of the most inefficient teachers are those of long experience, and some of the most efficient are those of short experience. If age and experience were a sure index of accomplishment, Methuselah would be the most eminent man in history, but Scripture records that all that good man did was to live for more than 900 years. A schedule which gives its reward entirely for college preparation and teaching experience will please the "time-serving" type of teachers, but will not please the more ambitious and capable teachers.

It is an unfortunate commentary that many teachers' organizations, especially in the large cities, insist upon retaining the automatic type of schedule and are not willing even to explore the possibilities of rewarding merit. Some of those organizations will not concede that some teachers are more efficient than others; other organizations will concede the possibility or the probability of a difference, but they insist that nothing can or should be done about it. Such actions of teachers' organizations damage the profession and often keep choice spirits from entering and from remaining in the profession.

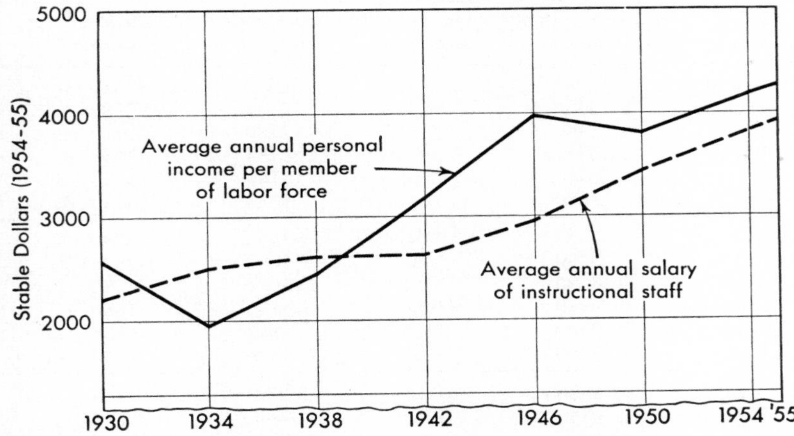

Fig. 58. Salaries of teachers from 1930 to 1955. (*Courtesy of* School Life, *Vol. 38 (March, 1956), p. 10.)*

Requisite to the operation of a merit type of salary schedule is a plan for the evaluation of teaching efficiency. Most school systems which use such a schedule, rate teachers at least twice a year according to categories similar to the following: A, excellent; B, superior; C, good; D, fair; E, poor. The annual salary increments usually provided for the various categories are the following: A, $100; B, $75; C, $50; teachers rated D or E usually receive no increment. When such a plan of distributing salaries is used, the percentages of teachers placed in the five different categories are usually made to approximate the normal probability curve; that is, approximately five per cent receive the mark of A; approximately twenty per cent, B; approximately fifty per cent, C; approximately twenty per cent, D; and approximately five per cent, E. It should be mentioned, though, that few school systems undertake to rate their teachers for salary awards. Teacher-rating is a "hot potato" which few school officials, school administrators, or teachers have the courage to attempt "to handle."

TABLE 6. A SINGLE-SALARY SCHEDULE FOR TEACHERS *
(USED IN THE MADISON, WISCONSIN, PUBLIC SCHOOLS,
EFFECTIVE 1956–57)

Year on Schedule	Group 1 60 sem. hours 2 year normal graduates	Group 2 90 sem. hours 3 year normal graduates	Group 3 Bachelor's Degree	Group 4 Master's Degree	
0–1	$2080	$2180	$2380	$2580	
1–2	2280	2380	2580	2780	
2–3	2480	2580	2780	2980	
3–4	2680	2780	2980	3180	
4–5	2880	2980	3180	3380	
5–6	3080	3180	3380	3580	Barrier †
6–7	3280	3380	3580	3780	
7–8	3480	3580	3780	3980	
8–9	3680	3780	3980	4180	
9–10	3880	3980	4180	4380	
10–11	4080	4180	4380	4580	
11–12	4280	4380	4580	4780	Barrier †
12–13	4480	4580	4780	4980	
13–14	4580	4680	4980	5180	
14–15			5180	5380	

* Basic schedule only; cost-of-living adjustment in addition, $1318.20 beginning January 1, 1956.

Teachers in any group classification shall receive in excess of their scheduled maximum for their service in the Madison school system, a longevity service increment of 2% at the beginning of their 18th year of service; 4% at the beginning of their 22nd year of service and 6% at the beginning of their 26th year of service, all such service to be in the Madison schools; or 2% starting the beginning of the 4th year at the maximum for their classification, 4% starting the beginning of the 8th year at the maximum and 6% starting the beginning of the 12th year at the maximum, provided they present additional evidence of further study, travel or other professional growth, or unusual value to the Madison school system.

† These barriers may be crossed by presenting evidence of the completion of twelve college or university credits, or six college or university credits plus six credits earned by travel.

During recent years, a few school systems have adopted types of salary schedules—usually called super-level schedules—which provide extra compensation for teachers, principals, and supervisors who give outstanding service. These awards are in addition to the pay provided by the automatic schedule; to receive them, evidence of superior service must be presented. When it is properly administered, such a plan of recognition does much to break up the "lock step" found in most salary schedules. It postpones contact with the inevitable stone wall, which in practically all schedules is reached in a few years, and over which even the artist teacher is unable to climb to a higher salary.

Summary of Principles for Teachers' Salaries. In the following paragraphs the chief principles which should be followed in paying teachers are summarized, although not all school systems of today follow those principles:

1. On the theory that the larger the salary, the better will be the qualifications of those who receive it, attempt should be made to make that percentage of the school budget which is devoted to teachers' salaries as large as possible, without, of course, crippling another vital school facility or service.
2. When a salary schedule is instituted, it should be known whether there will be ample funds within the next one, five, ten, or fifteen years to finance it. The cloth must always be cut to suit the garment. Breaking faith with teachers regarding salary promises should not be countenanced by school officials; moreover, teachers should have no part in the formulation of salary schedules which communities are unable or unwilling to finance.
3. The beginning salary should be sufficiently high to cause the better secondary-school students to desire to spend the necessary time and money in preparing for teaching.
4. The standards of pay should be at least as high as those of other vocations which require equal qualifications. This applies both to the beginning salary and to the salary of succeeding years. Moreover, if funds permit, the pay should approximate in amount that of other school systems, provided of course that equal qualifications are demanded.
5. Since maximum teaching efficiency is not reached early in experience —at least with thoroughly live and ambitious teachers—salary increases should be made as long as there is evidence of increased efficiency. This means that some teachers will receive salary increases for thirty, forty, or more years. Lack of school revenue is the only justification of ceasing salary increases at the close of ten or fifteen years of experience, as many salary schedules do.
6. It should be made possible to employ experienced teachers from other school systems and to start them at the same salary which local teachers having equal experience and qualifications are receiving.
7. Equal pay should be given for equal qualifications and equal services. Granted that they have equal qualifications and give equal services, elementary school teachers should have as much pay as secondary school teachers. In other words, the single-salary schedule, that is,

equal pay for equal qualifications and equal services, should be placed in operation. That type of schedule will permit the assignment of the teacher to that type of service for which he is best qualified and which he desires to enter.

8. A general increase in salary to all teachers can seldom, if ever, be justified, except for an increase in the cost of living. Such a policy assumes that all teachers are entitled to an increase, and of the same amount, which is seldom, if ever, true. The same remark is also germane to a general decrease in salaries, except for a decrease in the cost of living.
9. Provision should be made for adjusting the salary schedule to meet changes in the cost of living. This includes downward as well as upward revisions.
10. No salary schedule can be rightly made to operate automatically. All that a schedule can rightly do is to serve as a general plan. Teachers should be paid on the basis of merit, and this requires that some means of ascertaining merit be instituted. In working out this plan of ascertaining merit the help of the teachers should be elicited, and also their help should be invited in designing the salary schedule. Teachers are more and more being called upon to help in these matters.

Pay for Disability of Teachers. Although teaching presents fewer hazards to life, health, and limb than most vocations, sickness and accidents occasionally overtake teachers and render them incapable of performing their regular duties. To be disabled is a handicap, but to have one's income cut off at the same time that one is disabled is apt to be a tragedy. Boards of education have long been aware of that problem, and they are coming more and more to realize the advisability of providing financial assistance for teachers who are disabled; in fact, several states now require that such provision be made. Most city boards of education provide such assistance, but most rural boards still do nothing in this regard. In providing such assistance, boards are confronted, on the one hand, with the problem of seeing that teachers are properly protected against worry and other inconveniences which often come when one's regular income is cut off; boards are faced, on the other hand, with the problem of seeing that the public is properly protected against the small fringe of "chiselers," because there is in the teaching profession, as in all other vocations, a small group of teachers who would take unfair advantage of provisions for pay for disability. Attempts of school systems to provide pay for disabled teachers have usually taken the four following directions, and most teachers can expect to be covered by one of the plans: [10]

1. A *certain number of days of full pay or part pay each year for disability*. This is by far the most frequently used plan, and is required by law in several states. The number of days of pay given each year varies from school system to school system. Some school systems give full pay for a certain number of days and follow those days with part pay for a certain number of days; other school systems stipulate that the disabled teacher shall pay the salary of the substitute and that any part of the regular salary which remains shall go to the disabled teacher.
2. *Cumulative pay*. A few school systems provide a certain number of days of pay for disability each year and permit such days to accumulate from year to year. For example, if the school system provides ten days of disability pay each year and the teacher does not use any of his disability leave for a certain year, he would have twenty days' pay for disability leave coming during the next year. If the teacher left the school system, he would be paid for the number of days of disability leave which he had not utilized, or the next employer would assume that responsibility.
3. *Bonus for nondisability*. At the end of the school year many school systems pay their teachers a bonus for regular attendance upon their work; that is, a certain number of days of full pay or part pay is added to the teacher's salary, if he has not been absent during the school year. If, for example, a bonus of $5 per day for ten days is provided, a teacher who has not been absent a day would have a bonus of $50 coming to him at the close of the school year. For each day that the teacher is absent, $5 would be deducted; thus, if he were absent two days, his bonus would be $40; and if he were absent ten days, his bonus would be nothing.
4. *Group-disability insurance*. Instead of establishing their own system of paying for disability, many boards of education are co-operating with their teachers in obtaining group-disability insurance with old-line companies. A few boards of education are paying the whole premium for such insurance, but most boards of education are contributing part of the premium and teachers are contributing the remainder. Many boards of education believe that old-line insurance companies can give their teachers protection against disability at less cost to the community than could the board of education by establishing its own system. The advantage of group-disability insurance over individual insurance comes from the fact that it is much cheaper.

[10] In addition to these local practices, several states have workmen's compensation laws which protect all workers, including school employees, against occupational accidents.

Pensions or Old-age Annuities for Teachers. During recent years, one of the large public questions has revolved around the advisability of providing economic security for all workers through a system of pensions. The public has apparently accepted the theory of pensions for all groups of workers, and much Federal and state legislation has already been enacted to that end. Most teachers of the United States are now included under the provisions of this legislation.

Pensions or old-age annuities for teachers in the United States are a fairly recent development, dating back only a few decades. The first pension systems for teachers were local, and, as a rule, teachers were not required to join them; the systems appealed primarily only to the older teachers. During recent years, however, the tendency has been toward the establishment of state-wide pension systems, New York taking the lead in this movement in 1894. All states now have state-wide and compulsory pension systems for teachers. The tendency is to require every new teacher to join the pension system and to make the system more sound actuarially. Although pension systems have been established primarily to assure a better type of teaching service for the public, they keep in mind also the welfare and the rights of the teacher; they protect both the teacher and the pupils. The arguments in favor of a pension system for teachers—an excellent system, of course, is meant—may be summarized as follows:

1. A pension system protects the pupils from the incompetency of senile teachers. When a pension system is not in operation, boards of education hesitate to retire such teachers, because they are aware that the retired teachers would perhaps not have means of support and might become paupers. Such a system permits the retirement with justice of old teachers, and it has the further merit of giving young teachers greater opportunities for employment.
2. A pension system helps to attract desirable people into the teaching profession and to keep them there until the age for retirement is reached. It reduces turnover in the profession.
3. A pension system reduces or removes the teacher's anxiety and worry over old age and thus enables the teacher to give a better type of service. It gives a greater feeling of economic security.
4. A pension should not be regarded as "charity," but as "deferred pay." A pension system forces the teacher to start saving early in life and thus to provide for his old age; statistics on the amount of pauperism and near-pauperism in old age demonstrate that most persons need

such a stimulus to saving. Moreover, since the teacher's as well as the public's contributions are required to be invested in high-grade bonds (usually local, state, or Federal) there should be small doubt of the security of the investment.

Not all of the states, which have adopted a teachers' pension system, have systems which are actuarially sound. Teachers must, therefore, continue their pension campaigns until none of their number is without proper pension protection. The excellent pension systems of such states as Louisiana, Maryland, Ohio, Pennsylvania, Texas, and Wisconsin should be imitated and improved upon by all the states. In one of its recent reports the Carnegie Foundation for the Advancement of Teaching lists the fundamental principles upon which it deems that a teachers' pension system for a state should be based. Since these principles have had wide acceptance by teachers and by the public, they are being epitomized herewith in order that the pension system, present or proposed, of any state may be evaluated by them:

1. Membership in the system should be optional for those persons who were teaching prior to the going into operation of the pension law. Membership should be compulsory, however, for all teachers accepting appointment after the enactment of the law.
2. The rules of the system should provide for the retirement of any teacher when old age or disability makes satisfactory service no longer possible. The retirement allowance should be sufficient to enable the teacher to live in comfort.
3. The contributions of the teacher and of the public should be approximately equal, and in no case should the teacher or the public provide the contribution without the help of the other. The amounts to be paid by the teacher and by the public should be stated in the law creating the pension system.
4. The teacher's and the state's contributions should be made regularly and concurrently during the period of service of the teacher.
5. An individual account for each teacher should be kept.
6. The system should be on a sound reserve basis and periodic actuarial investigations of the system should be made.
7. A retirement allowance should be made for disability after a reasonable period of service.
8. The teacher's cumulative deposits should be returnable upon withdrawal from teaching, from the state, or upon death prior to retirement. Interest at an established rate, as well as the principal, should also be returnable.
9. The teacher should be permitted to select the manner in which he will receive his retirement allowance.

10. Credit should be allowed for all service prior to the enactment of the retirement legislation. Moreover, credit for such service should be allowed for service in the local state or in other states.
11. The retirement board should be representative and its personnel should be prescribed so as to assure a high type of representation both for the public and the teacher.[11]

All pension systems are of the "joint-contributory" type. Teachers pay a certain percentage of their salary each month, and that amount is matched by the school district that employs them, or by the state. The amount of the pension is determined by the number of years of teaching service and by the salary of the teacher, especially during the latter years of his service. Compulsory retirement ages of 65 or 70 are usually set by the act, but voluntary retirement at an earlier age, though with partial-pension benefits, is usually permitted.

Miscellaneous Pecuniary Opportunities for Teachers. In addition to the pecuniary rewards and opportunities for teachers which have been indicated in preceding paragraphs, a few other pecuniary rewards and opportunities should be kept in mind. Many teachers are today supplementing their salary incomes by means of those other opportunities which are open to every teacher, although few take advantage of them. Of course, if more teachers should take advantage of the opportunities, the "market would be glutted," and the opportunities would not be as large as they are today.

In the first place, many teachers have prepared textbooks, workbooks, or other instructional materials which are published and marketed and from which they receive royalties. Likewise, some teachers write for magazines and receive compensation for their productions; it should be mentioned, though, that most of the writing of teachers is designed for pedagogical magazines and that only a few of those pay their contributors. When the teacher can engage in those literary activities without injuring his health, his emotional tone, and above all, without neglecting his regular school work, the activities would seem to be entirely commendable; such work, if well done, enhances the prestige of the teacher, his profession, and his school system.

In the second place, teachers have opportunity to add to their

[11] "Pension Systems and Pension Legislation," *Twenty-Third Annual Report of the President and of the Treasurer*, Carnegie Foundation, pp. 73–100.

incomes through occasional lectures. Many teachers, even in the elementary and the secondary schools, have acquired such renown for doing certain things well that they are in demand to give lectures before lay and professional groups, especially before groups of teachers; some of them are invited by colleges and universities to offer courses in the summer sessions of those institutions. Other teachers do consulting work for pay. In fairness, though, it should be stated that such opportunities come, as a rule, only to school administrators and to college and university professors; moreover, the honorarium for such work is seldom large, and frequently such services are expected to be given gratis.

Nonfinancial Rewards and Opportunities

Important though they are, financial rewards and opportunities are not the only criteria to keep in mind in choosing a life's work. Every vocation, especially every profession, has rewards and opportunities of a nonfinancial nature. Although some of these are admittedly intangible, they are worth keeping in mind by anyone who is considering a career. The chief nonfinancial rewards and opportunities of teachers are briefly discussed herewith.

Opportunity of Teachers for Service. At the risk of appearing trite, it is repeated that the welfare and the progress of civilization depend upon the proper education of all the people. Universal education is especially necessary in a democracy such as ours, because in such a government and democratic way of life the people make the laws and are otherwise sovereign. Education must always be the good leaven of a democracy. Those beliefs, which a European visitor once dubbed the "American religion," have been accepted from the time of the first settlements in the United States and they have been an American tradition for more than three centuries. The school was born from those beliefs, and from small beginnings has grown to be America's most cherished public institution.

It is universally agreed that the teacher makes the school largely what it is, and what is more important, that he has a vital and a lasting influence upon the lives of his pupils. He helps his pupils to lay their foundation for life, and each of his ministrations becomes an enduring stone in that foundation. He—an excellent teacher, of course, is meant—assists his pupils to acquire the tools of knowledge and instills in them an abiding desire to use those tools; he stimulates them to think for themselves; he inculcates in them high ideals for self and for society, and he points the way to the realization of those ideals; he teaches his pupils to discipline themselves.

In his pupil relationships the teacher stands in *loco parentis;* indeed, he frequently shapes his pupils' lives more than the pupils' parents. In helping to shape their lives he can have assurance that they will in turn help to shape the destinies of civilization. In after years his tutelage will shine back from their lives to bless him or to curse him; it can never be blotted out. In a democracy the teacher is, or can be, a real maker of history; he is, or can be, an architect of civilization.

In every sense the teacher is a servant of mankind, and no worker possesses a greater opportunity for service. If he possesses this passion for service, and if the passion is accompanied by a burning love for teaching, his life is certain to be full of valuable accomplishment and profound happiness. Without these attributes, no one can be a true teacher.

Opportunity of Teachers to Learn. Every person has an inherent desire to learn, and no person has a greater opportunity to learn than the teacher. The whole teaching situation is conducive to learning on the part of the teacher. The teacher has an even greater opportunity to learn than his pupils. He has the opportunity to observe his pupils, and those precious charges come to him in constant procession; they never grow old, and they are never alike. He has the opportunity to study all civilization—past and present. Try as diligently as he may, the teacher can never exhaust his learning opportunities.

At the same time that the opportunity which the teacher has to learn is being mentioned, a possible danger of his calling should be pointed out. That danger comes from the fact that the teacher, especially in the lower grades, associates with immature minds, and if he is not on his guard—if he is not driven by an insatiable desire to learn—he may develop an immature mind. Just as Ernest, through association and through imitation, became like the Great Stone Face, so the teacher may become like his pupils. Although the teacher must be able to descend to the level of understanding of his pupils, he must guard against forever remaining on that level, if he is to be a real leader in the school and in the community. In a sense, then, the teacher must have a dual existence.

Pleasantness of Professional Associations of Teachers. The professional associations of the teacher, especially if he is well qualified, are among the more pleasant of those of any worker. The level of education on which the teacher works keeps him informed with a large degree of accuracy and completeness of the problems and the conditions facing persons engaged in other fields of endeavor. With that large body of knowledge the teacher is able to make pleasant associations with the members of a diversified number of vocations. Moreover, the teacher works and plays with other teachers —persons who have high ideals, pleasing personalities, excellent education, and a desire to make a contribution to society,[12] and because of the increasing requirements for teachers, the teacher's professional associations are constantly growing more pleasant. Many teachers are helping to make their associations increasingly more pleasant by trying to stimulate desirable young people to enter the teaching profession, and by trying to discourage undesirable persons from entering the profession; this should be a challenge to every teacher.

Opportunity of Teachers for Recreation. Although teaching is far from being an easy work, it does not require the confinement of most positions. With its summer vacations of two, three, or four months and its vacations at Christmas, Easter, and other times, it provides greater opportunities for study, travel, and other types of recreational and cultural advancement than most vocations. The minimum amount of time which must be given by the typical teacher in meeting his pupils is six or seven hours per day, five days a week, and eight, nine, or ten months a year; the remainder of his time can be spent largely as he desires.

Contrary to the belief of many persons, the work of a teacher who is worthy of the name of teacher cannot be limited to the mere meeting of his classes. After the school day and during weekends and other vacations, the teacher must spend a large amount of time in preparing to meet his classes; he must plan his work for the next school year, semester, week, or day; he must mark examination papers, reports, themes, and similar work of his pupils; he must have conferences with pupils and their parents; he must make reports to and have conferences with school administrators and supervisors; he must coach an athletic team or sponsor a school club; he must be a member

12 All teachers, of course, do not meet these high standards. Some teachers are mentally ill, even to the point of being psychopathic. Others are unethical. And still others are lazy or possess some other shortcoming.

of one or more school committees; he must attend meetings of the faculty and of the Parent-Teacher Association; he is expected to take part in many community activities. During the summer months, the typical teacher is not idle, for as a rule he will be found enrolled in a college or university, or to be engaged in another activity calculated better to qualify him for his work during the following school year.

Relatively Assured Tenure of Teachers. Although there have been many instances of unceremonious dismissal of teachers, compared with workers in most other vocations, teachers have greater assurance of tenure. In practically all school systems teachers are given a contract for a year, and their services cannot be terminated within the period of the contract except for good cause such as gross neglect of duty or immorality. The tendency in practice is to retain the teacher year after year, provided his services are satisfactory; in fact, most states have enacted statutes which are calculated to protect the tenure of all teachers who are giving satisfactory service, and hundreds of boards of education, especially in city school districts, have adopted rules and regulations usually providing for a probationary period of three years before a teacher can be placed under tenure; after the teacher has satisfactorily completed his probationary period, he serves under a continuing contract and cannot be dismissed except for good reason, which is usually defined in the law as gross neglect of duty or immorality.

The theory underlying those tendencies is that the teacher needs freedom from worry, if he is to do the best work. The teacher cannot do his best work, if he is constantly haunted by the possibility of losing his position, especially for a specious reason. Teachers should continue their campaigns for tenure laws which protect competent and worthy members of the profession, and they should oppose laws which protect the incompetent and the unworthy. It must be sorrowfully reported, however, that some organizations of teachers have insisted upon protecting incompetent teachers as well as the competent; and it must also be sorrowfully reported that under some tenure laws, school administrators are "on trial" to prove incompetency, while teachers are assumed to be competent.

Increasing Respect and Prestige of Teachers In the early days the teacher did not have a large amount of prestige. He was a common subject for caricature and was frequently the butt of jokes.

He was pictured and described as a "queer" person—queer in dress, in language, and in action. In those days the humorist could convulse with laughter his audience by starting his address with Mark Twain's salutation, "Ladies, gentlemen, and school teachers"; the cartoonist could obtain the same response by portraying the pedagogue as a longhaired, a bespectacled, and an absent-minded individual. There was a widespread belief—perhaps not unjustified—that the teacher was a less intelligent, a less practical, and a less ambitious person than was found in other professions; that belief was perhaps summarized by George Bernard Shaw when he said, "He who can, does; he who cannot, teaches."

Even today the teaching profession is criticized, questioned, and heckled more than any other profession. It is not *lese majeste* to criticize the teaching profession, and such criticism is frequently indulged in by members of other professions as well as by artisans, unskilled workers, and businessmen. Practically every person claims to know how the schools should be run, what school subjects should be taught, and how they should be taught. The physician, the architect, the veterinarian, or the member of any other profession is seldom advised or "told" how to perform his work, but almost everyone feels competent to advise or to "tell" teachers how to conduct the complex and important work of education. Since they are public servants, teachers can probably never escape a critical attitude on the part of their employers, namely, the public. All that teachers can hope for is that the criticism directed at them will become more intelligent and more constructive—in fact, teachers should always desire criticism of that sort.

Fortunately, the situation just described is rapidly improving. More and more the public is coming to regard the profession of teaching as one of the most important professions and is coming to accord greater respect to its members. More and more the members of the teaching profession are being called upon to give advice to the government, to industry, and to other activities; more and more, in every way, they are asked to assume positions of leadership in society. This greater respect and prestige is being accorded for two reasons: In the first place, the public has seen that other agencies and the institutions which have been accorded a prominent place in the life of society have failed to produce the best type of social order for a country such as ours, and it has concluded that it is in the proper education of the youth that the solution to this problem lies; more and more the public is turning to the teachers for that education. In the second place, the members of the teaching profession are rapidly increasing their qualifications, and in consequence are deserving of greater respect and greater prestige. A recent study shows that most teachers would enter the teaching profession again.[13]

Notwithstanding numerous exceptions to the rule, society is disposed to give its rewards on the basis of merit and of accomplishment. Society prefers to applaud and to reward its servants rather than to frown upon and to penalize them. When the teacher possesses as much college preparation, personality, and ability as the physician, lawyer, architect, dentist, or the member of any other profession, he is accorded as much respect and prestige, even though he may not be highly paid. When he does not possess such traits in equal amount—and that is often the unfortunate situation—he does not command equal respect and prestige. A "full-blooded" teacher will not ask for more than this. He will remember Cassius' reply to Brutus, "The fault, dear Brutus, is not in our stars, but in ourselves, that we are underlings."

QUESTIONS FOR DISCUSSION

1. In its importance to society, how does teaching compare with such professions as medicine, law, engineering, and the ministry?

2. In contemplating entrance into a certain vocation, what emphasis should a person place upon the opportunity for obtaining a position, and what emphasis should he give to his desire and aptitudes? Compare the opportunity for obtaining a teaching position with that in other vocations; compare also the opportunities for promotion. Compare the opportunity of obtaining a position in your major subject or department with that in other subjects and departments. Why do salary trends of public employees lag behind those of other workers?

3. What are the chief advantages of teaching as a vocation? What are the chief disadvantages?

4. Does teaching present as many opportunities to men as to women? Explain. Do you believe that the teaching profession needs more men in it? Why or why not? If more men are needed, how would you suggest that they be obtained?

[13] *Research Bulletin of the National Education Association*, Vol. 35 (February, 1957), pp. 38–40.

5. What bearing, if any, does each of the following factors have upon the salary of the teacher: supply and demand, sex, college preparation, experience, marital status, the level of teaching, and results obtained with the pupils? Do you believe that teachers today are usually paid on basis of merit? Why or why not? Account for the fact that teachers frequently object to having their services evaluated and rewarded on basis of that evaluation.

6. Do you favor a retirement system for teachers? Discuss from the point of view of both the teacher and the public. Are teachers more entitled to pensions than other workers? Explain. Should all teachers be required to retire at a given age? Why or why not? Does your state have a teachers' retirement system, and if so, what are its provisions, merits, and limitations? Should a pension system be state or national?

7. Account for the fact that teachers of former generations were so often made the butt of jokes. Do you see any evidence of such lack of respect today, and to what extent, if any, is such practice today excusable?

8. How does the prestige of the typical teacher today compare with that of the typical member of other professions? Account for any differences which you may discern.

9. Do you believe that working with minds of pupils tends to make the teacher similar to his pupils? Explain.

10. Do teachers and pupils need more time for recreation and vacation than other people? Explain. Do you regard teaching as easy work? Why or why not?

11. What type of tenure law, if any, do you favor for teachers? What are the advantages and the dangers of tenure laws for teachers?

12. What are the causes of the large amount of turnover in the teaching profession? What waste, if any, results from such turnover?

13. What provisions does your college make for the guidance of its students in obtaining a position?

SELECTED REFERENCES

Ashley, L. W., "Issue of Added Compensation for Extra Responsibility or Extra Work," *Bulletin of the National Association of Secondary School Principals,* Vol. 35 (March, 1951), pp. 167–172.

Discusses the extent to which teachers should be paid for extra work.

Bowes, Erna Hoffman, "A New Approach to the Teacher Shortage," *American School Board Journal,* Vol. 129 (October, 1954), pp. 23–24.

Discusses some of the assets in the teaching profession. Also compares the salaries of teachers with other professionally trained people working in Syracuse, New York.

Caldwell, Sarah, "Teaching is Hard Work," *The Atlantic* (November, 1954).

Aunt Sarah tells her niece, Karen, that although the teaching profession can be frustrating at times, she never once thought of quitting.

Davis, Hazel, "Factors Determining Teachers' Salaries," *School Executive*, Vol. 66 (April, 1947), pp. 58–59.

Discusses the standards that are used and those that should be used in determining teachers' salaries.

Erskine, John, *My Life as a Teacher*, J. B. Lippincott Co., Philadelphia, 1948, 249 pp.

Tells in delightful style Erskine's experiences as a teacher.

Garber, Lee O., "What Constitutes a Private Hearing," *Nation's Schools*, Vol. 55 (February, 1955), p. 72.

A report on the latest court action concerning the right of a teacher to request a private hearing upon being discharged.

MacVittie, Robert William, "Professional Program for the Substitute Teacher," *Nation's Schools*, Vol. 55 (March, 1955), pp. 83–85.

Suggests practices for recruitment, orientation and assignment, and evaluation of service of substitute teachers which are basic to a planned program of administration.

Maul, Ray C., "Teacher Shortage is Reversed," *Nation's Schools*, Vol. 57 (May, 1956), pp. 51–53.

Presents the total number of college graduates and the number prepared to teach during recent years.

Maul, Ray C., "What Becomes of Teacher Candidates?" *School Executive*, Vol. 74 (November, 1954), pp. 46–48.

Discusses a study, that was carried on in thirteen states and in Hawaii, to determine the number of college graduates that took the professional courses required for the teaching certificate, but did not enter the profession. One out of every three college graduates trained to become teachers did not become teachers.

Maul, Ray C., "High School Teacher Shortage Impends," *American School Board Journal*, Vol. 128 (February, 1954), pp. 37–38.

Predicts a shortage of qualified secondary-school teachers.

Maul, Ray C., "Current Salary Practices in Higher Education," *NEA Journal*, Vol. 43 (January, 1954), pp. 43–44.

Discusses salaries of teachers in the colleges and universities.

National Education Association, Washington.

This Association publishes each year, especially through its Research Division, studies of teachers' salaries, etc. in each state.

Oliva, Peter F., "Certification Laws Restrict Mobility of Teacher Supply," *Nation's Schools*, Vol. 54 (December, 1954), pp. 44–46.

Discusses variations in certification laws in the states; recommends reciprocal agreements for interchange of teachers; a large map showing the certification requirements of each state is shown.

Pritchett, Henry S., *The Social Philosophy of Pensions, Bulletin* No. 25 of the Carnegie Foundation for the Advancement of Teaching, 1930, 85 pp.

Reviews existing pension systems for professional groups.

"Public-School Retirement at the Half Century," *Research Bulletin* of the National Education Association, Vol. 28 (December, 1950), pp. 143–144.

Discusses state and local retirement systems for teachers.

Research Bulletin of the National Education Association, Vol. 35 (February, 1957), pp. 3–63.

A recent discussion of the status of the American public-school teacher.

Roach, Stephen F., "Alteration of Teacher Contracts," *American School Board Journal*, Vol. 130 (February, 1955), pp. 5, 96.

Reports recent court rulings on alteration of contracts by teachers or school boards.

"Salaries of School Employees," *Research Division* of the National Education Association.

Such data are collected and published every year by the Research Division of the National Education Association.

Teachers for Tomorrow, The Fund for the Advancement of Education, New York, 1955, 73 pp.

Presents data on increasing enrollments and teacher shortages.

Shull, Martha A., "I Love to Watch Them Grow," NEA *Journal*, Vol. 40 (January, 1951), pp. 38–39.

Describes some of the satisfactions that come to successful teachers.

Siggelkow, Richard A., "Meaningful Interviews with Beginning Teachers," *Nation's Schools*, Vol. 53 (June, 1954), pp. 43–46.

A study carried on by the University of Wisconsin Teacher Placement Bureau to gain insight into what information was usually sought by school administrators and what information the interviewee wanted to know about the school and the community.

Simpson, Alfred D., and McLeary, Ralph D., "The Professional Improvement Salary Schedule," *American School Board Journal*, Vol. 116 (February, 1948), pp. 27–29.

Discusses eight basic requirements for a good schedule.

Smith, May C., "A New Salary Schedule for New Jersey," *NEA Journal*, Vol. 44 (February, 1955), pp. 94–95.

By persistent effort and sound backing of state education association and state citizens, New Jersey obtained a state minimum salary schedule, including yearly increment minimum of $150.

State Education Associations.

Several of the state education associations have a research division which publishes each year the average salaries of the teachers in each school district of the state.

Statistics of State School Systems, U. S. Office of Education, *Bulletin.*

This bulletin, which is published biennially by the U. S. Office of Education, contains data on salaries by states.

"The 1956 Teacher Supply and Demand Report," *Teacher Education,* Vol. 7 (March, 1956), pp. 33–88.

Presents national and state data on teacher supply and demand.

Thorne, Edmund H., "Career Salary Plan," *Nation's Schools,* Vol. 55 (March, 1955), pp. 51–52.

Describes how and why one school system selects and rewards outstanding teachers who have reached the maximum salary (of regular salary schedule) with additional financial reward.

Trent, W. W., "Single Salary Schedule," *Nation's Schools,* Vol. 54 (November, 1954), pp. 63–64.

Reports the success of single salary schedule for teachers of a state and of a single-salary schedule for principals of that state; how these schedules came about and how they work is described.

Weber, C. A., "Basic Rights and Obligations of Teachers," *American School Board Journal,* Vol. 130 (February, 1955), pp. 32–33.

Discusses minimum salaries, working conditions, leaves of absence and growth in service. Recommends techniques for producing growth of teachers.

Whitman, Howard, "A New Way to Pay Teachers," *Collier's,* Vol. 136 (September 30, 1955), pp. 102–105.

Urges merit salary schedules for teachers.

Wilson, Margery, "Honor Our Teachers," *Ladies' Home Journal,* Vol. 71 (October, 1954), p. 56.

Discusses the need to raise the prestige of the teaching profession. Says that the people can help teachers gain prestige through: social recognition (providing social contacts for them), honoring them publicly (arranging special courtesies and privileges) and moral backing (never criticizing a teacher before a pupil).

CHAPTER 18

Requirements in the Teaching Profession

Importance of Knowing the Requirements for Teaching

Before anyone decides to enter the teaching profession, he should know as much as possible regarding the demands which the profession will make upon his abilities, his energies, and his happiness. A person needs such information to help him decide whether he desires to prepare for teaching, and to guide his preparation for it. Without such information, there is danger that he will enter the teaching profession and then find that he does not like the work, or that his abilities are not suited to it. The chief requirements for a happy and fruitful life for any person are that he be working in the vocation for which he is best qualified and to believe firmly that he is working in that vocation. If he meets those requirements, the worker is apt to develop into an artist rather than remain on the level of a drudge and of a time server.

Changing Beliefs Regarding the Qualifications for Teaching

During the first two centuries of the history of schools in the United States, only a small amount of attention was given to the improvement of the teaching personnel. Although public schools had been in operation in certain communities of Massachusetts as early as 1635, not until 1823, when Samuel R. Hall established his private normal school in Concord, Vermont, was there available an institution, especially designed for the preparation of teachers. Not until 1839, at Lexington, Massachusetts, was the first state-supported institution for the preparation of teachers established in any state. In those early days the teaching "vocation" was not accorded much respect by the public, and almost anyone was permitted to teach school. Teaching, then, was merely a vocation and had not yet assumed any of the characteristics of a profession. About the only qualification necessary for a person who aspired to the position of teacher was to possess sufficient energy and "pull" to find a school board or community that would "hire" him. All teachers were then regarded as having essentially the same merit, and the position of teacher was usually given to the lowest bidder; bidding for the position was frequently conducted at public auction. The schools of those days were conducted in "little red" schoolhouses and were taught by "little-read" teachers. In his *Lectures on School Keeping,* published in 1829, Samuel R. Hall quotes a writer in the *Journal of Education* who scathingly criticized the low standards for teachers in those times:

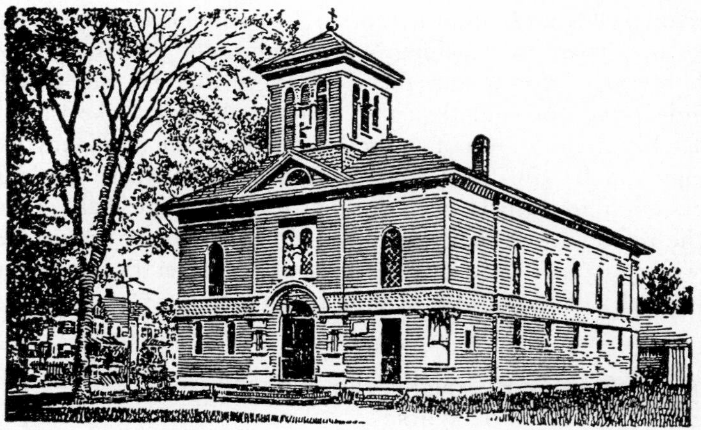

FIG. 59. The first state normal school in America, opened at Lexington, Massachusetts, in 1839. During recent years, the name normal school has been rapidly changing to teachers college or college of education.

Every stripling who has passed four years within the walls of a college, every dissatisfied clerk who has not ability enough to manage the trifling concerns of a retail shop, every young farmer who obtains in the winter a short vacation from the toils of summer—in short, every person who is conscious of his imbecility in other business, esteems himself fully competent to train the ignorance and weakness of infancy into all the virtue and power and wisdom of maturer years—to form a creature, the frailest and feeblest that heaven has made, into the intelligent and fearless sovereign of the whole animated creation, the interpreter and adorer, and almost the representative of divinity.

Although some of the conditions of earlier days still remain in some communities of a few of the states, large changes have come almost everywhere in the public's concept of what the teacher should be. The public has come to recognize more and more that the teacher makes the school largely what it is and that a good school makes a vital contribution to the pupils and to the welfare of society. With the growing recognition of the importance of the teacher to the pupils and to society has come an ever-increasing demand that the schools have teachers of better qualifications.

Teaching has at last become a profession. There is, to be sure, still considerable disparity between the amount of preparation of teachers, and the amount of preparation of physicians, dentists, veterinary surgeons, lawyers, and members of many other professions. Nonetheless, the time is probably approaching when society will insist upon as much preparation of its teachers as it demands of the members of any other profession. Teaching is at last getting the recognition from society that it has long deserved. It may be predicted that sometime in the future every new teacher will be required to have five, six, or seven years of college preparation; moreover, the quality of the college preparation will be improved; at least that is hoped devoutly. Teachers can and should hasten that day by voluntarily acquiring more formal education and by conducting a campaign for other teachers, especially new teachers, to meet the same high standards of formal education. In attempting to obtain a better qualified teaching personnel, the beliefs of the public regarding teacher preparation have undergone and are undergoing many changes. Some of the more prominent of these changing beliefs are discussed in the following paragraphs.

"BORN" TEACHERS VERSUS "MADE" TEACHERS. In the early days the belief that good teachers were "born" and not "made" was almost universal. In fact, this belief is frequently held even today, particularly by laymen. Such a belief implies that formal preparation for teaching is of little or no importance and that inherent qualities of the teacher are the all-important factors making for the teacher's success. That belief, however, is rapidly passing because it is evident that the teacher, like the physician and the members of other professions, needs many qualifications which he cannot inherit. The teacher needs, for example, knowledge of the principles of learning, of the nature and the extent of individual differences, of social and economic changes, of the principles of hygiene and health, and of effective methods of presenting valuable subject matter to groups and to individuals. Knowledge of these and of hundreds of other matters requisite to a teacher's success cannot be inherited; they must be learned, and to learn them requires years of effort both in the college classroom and in the crucible of teaching experience. Knowledge of many of these matters can, of course, be obtained by the teacher through experience in the schoolroom, but it can be thus obtained by the teacher only through long travail and endless discouragement for the teacher and at the risk of much malpractice being inflicted upon the unsuspecting and helpless pupils. The teaching process is admitted by all persons who have long studied it to be unusually technical and complex. Persons who have studied the process longest and most ardently readily admit that the more they study the process the more baffling it becomes. "A little learning is a dangerous thing," said Alexander Pope, and that statement would seem to be especially applicable to the work of the teacher. Democracy's schools must have teachers who possess profound and broad learning.

KNOWLEDGE OF SUBJECT MATTER AS THE ONLY SINE QUA NON FOR TEACHERS. Many well-educated persons (and, strange to say, some of these persons are teachers) affirm that knowledge of subject matter is the only qualification needed by the teacher. They affirm that "if the teacher knows his subject he can teach it." They imply that knowledge of the principles of learning, of social needs, and of methods of presenting subject matter are of little or no importance in ability to teach. While a teacher cannot teach a subject if he doesn't know it, mere knowledge of subject matter will not assure that the subject matter will "get across" to the pupils, and, of course, if the subject matter doesn't "get across" to the pupils, the teacher's tutelage will have been in vain. In order that his tutelage will be most effective, the teacher must be informed on the interests, the abilities, and the needs of his pupils as well as know his subject matter. His obligation is to teach pupils as well as to dispense subject matter. Pupils soon discover that knowledge of subject matter is not the only requisite for a teacher. It is a frequent happening to hear a pupil say that his teacher "knows his subject but is not able to present it." Pupils always characterize such teachers as failures.

AMOUNT OF PREPARATION FOR TEACHING IN THE VARIOUS GRADES. In the early days, school administrators followed the policy of assigning the "blue-ribbon" teachers to the upper grades of the school and of giving to the lower grades the "scrub" teachers. The belief underlying this practice was that the chief tasks of a teacher were to keep the pupils busy and well-disciplined, and that almost anyone, especially if he had a dictatorial mien, could accomplish those tasks with young children. Although that practice is still followed in some schools and school systems, it is rapidly being abandoned in all enlightened communities. School administrators and the general public are coming to realize more and more that teachers of the lower grades need as much preparation as teachers of the upper grades; in fact, they are gradually coming to realize that there are valid reasons for requiring an even larger amount of preparation for teachers of the lower grades. They are coming to realize that the pupils in the lower grades need much more personal guidance from their teachers than the pupils in the upper grades. The pupils in the lower grades must acquire the tools of learning, and those tools cannot be acquired without the tutelage of a teacher. In the upper grades, on the other hand, pupils already possess an acquaintance with the tools of learning and in consequence those pupils are able to work somewhat independently. Those older pupils learn much through their own initiative, and they often learn in spite of poor teaching, provided they have learned in the lower grades the tools for acquiring knowledge.

It may be properly contended, therefore, that the elementary school, and especially the first grades of the elementary school, are of greatest importance among the school levels, because it lays the foundation for the pupil's educational career and for his whole life. It should have "prior rating", so far as the resources of the public are concerned; it is democracy's school *par excellence*. In those early years the pupils acquire the tools of knowledge and form habits and ideals which will remain with them throughout life. Unless the proper foundation is laid in the lower grades, the best superstructure for future educational accomplishment cannot be erected. Moreover, because they must start early to earn their living, or because secondary schools are not readily available to them, some pupils are unable to obtain more formal education than that provided by the elementary school, and that is another potent reason for making the elementary school as thorough and as practical as possible. When these facts have become generally known by school officials and by the public, teachers in the lower grades will be required to have as much education as, if not more education than, teachers in the upper grades. Let not the teachers of the secondary schools and the colleges forget the same facts, because where importance of work is concerned, they must humbly bow before the teachers of the elementary schools.

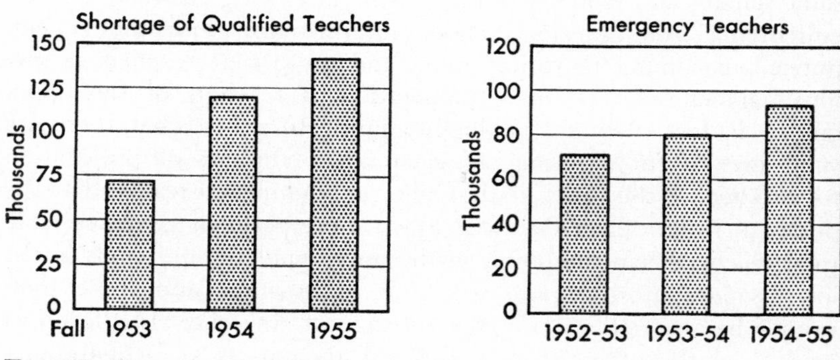

Fig. 60. Shortage of qualified teachers, and the number of emergency teachers in the United States. (*From* Teachers for Tomorrow, *p.* 29. *Courtesy of The Fund for the Advancement of Education.*)

From the foregoing remarks on the amount of preparation needed by teachers, it should not be inferred that the type of preparation for teachers in the lower and the upper grades should be the same. The preparation for all levels of teaching service will require many identical elements which are different in kind and in amount. Most institutions for the preparation of teachers are aware of these varying needs, and they have organized different curricula for teachers of the various grades. The larger institutions, for example, have organized separate curricula for the kindergarten and for the primary grades, the intermediate grades, the junior high school, and the senior high school. Many of the institutions have developed separate curricula for the education of principals, superintendents, general supervisors, teachers and supervisors of special subjects, and other types of school specialists.[1] This is a day of specialization, and the teaching profession is coming more and more to be constituted of fields of specialization. The teacher can no more expect to perform efficiently all types of educational service than can a general practitioner in medicine expect to be an expert in all branches of surgery and medicine.

The single-salary schedule, which school systems are gradually adopting, has been a tremendous influence for increasing the preparation of elementary school teachers. That type of salary schedule pays elementary school teachers as much as secondary school teachers, provided their qualifications are equal. When such a schedule is in operation, the elementary school teacher feels justified in undergoing a longer regimen of preparation because he will receive as much salary for the extra preparation as will the teacher in the secondary school. No other factor has been so potent in decreasing the disparity between the preparation of the elementary school teacher and the secondary-school teacher as has the widespread movement toward the adoption of the single-salary schedule. All members of the profession should support movements for the universal adoption of such a schedule.

Education of Teachers in America and in Europe

Educational Status of American Teachers. Ideally, any measure of the preparation of teachers would take into consideration the quality, the effectiveness, and the appropriateness of their schooling as well as the amount of their schooling. Unfortunately, though, measures of these components of preparation are difficult to obtain, with the exception of the amount of schooling. The

[1] Several states, which have more than one teacher-preparing institution, have delegated to each institution the task of preparing employees for a certain specialty. Each institution is thus enabled to do well its task rather than to dissipate its energies and its resources in trying to prepare employees for all or several types of educational positions.

amount of schooling is tangible and can be measured by ascertaining the amount of "time spent" in educational institutions by the teachers of the United States. Unfortunately, however, there is no Federal agency such as the United States Office of Education which regularly collects information on the amount of schooling of teachers; moreover, few of the state departments of education regularly collect such information.

Independent surveys of the amount of schooling are occasionally made, and these surveys indicate a gradual increase in the amount of college preparation among all types of teachers found in every state. These surveys show that approximately four-fifths of the secondary-school teachers of the nation have had at least four years of college preparation and that approximately one-third of the secondary-school teachers have completed at least one year of graduate work; the majority of states require the bachelor's degree, and some states require 5 years of college work. Almost one-half of the elementary school teachers have had less than two years of college preparation. Most of the underprepared teachers are found in the rural and village communities; they are employed there primarily because of the low salaries and in spite of the fact that their positions are the most difficult of any in the teaching profession. Because of low salaries the Southern states usually have a larger percentage of underprepared teachers than the states of other sections. In the whole nation there are now several thousand teachers with substandard preparation.

Educational Status of European Teachers. Although America's penchant for education has been called her "national religion," and in spite of the fact that her people more firmly believe in universal education than the people of any other country, her teachers are perhaps not as well prepared and are perhaps not held in as high esteem as the teachers of some of the European countries, notably France and Germany. After an intensive study, a few years ago, of teacher qualifications in England, France, Germany, and Sweden, compared with teacher qualifications in the United States, the *National Survey of the Education of Teachers* came to the following conclusions:

1. With the exception of Sweden, the elementary teachers in the four European countries mentioned are now expected to have as much preservice education as is required in the states of the United States

in which the standards are highest and more than is generally accepted as necessary in the majority of the states.
2. With the exception of England, the secondary teachers of those countries have a much larger amount of training than our secondary teachers. In fact, the secondary teachers of France, Germany, and Sweden "possess such thorough and extensive educational preparation that they may well be compared on that item with the faculties of our better staffed colleges and universities."
3. During recent years there has been a tendency for some of the European countries to decrease the disparity in the amount of training required of elementary and secondary teachers by increasing the amount for elementary teachers.
4. Explanations for the larger amount of preservice training in these European countries are the following: (1) a larger amount of competition in those countries for desirable positions, this competition resulting from overpopulation and increased numbers of university graduates; (2) in those countries "teaching has been made more attractive to capable persons by means of very secure tenure, economic security at a level which permits a standard of living comparable with other professional groups, high social prestige, and a consciousness of performing a patriotic service"; (3) teaching standards there have been influenced by the secondary schools, whereas here they have been influenced by the elementary schools.[2]

The above quotation, however, is from a 1933 publication. Since then, teacher education has been steadily upgraded in the United States.[2]

Qualifications Needed by the Teacher

If a person is to obtain and retain a position as a teacher, if he is to accomplish all that he might with his pupils, and if he is to acquire advancement and happiness in his profession, he must be adequately prepared for his work. The day when "anyone can teach school" has passed. The teacher who expects to succeed must have at least the following qualifications, and it should be the responsibility of the state and of the teacher-preparing institutions to demand these qualifications.

[2] Epitomized from the *National Survey of the Education of Teachers,* Vol. 6, pp. 64–65.

For the preparation of teachers in the United States for the school year of 1955–56, see *Research Bulletin of the National Education Association,* Vol. 35 (February, 1957), pp. 13–15.

High Intelligence as a Qualification for the Teacher. The first requisite for a successful teacher is high native ability or high intelligence. In accordance with this belief many teacher-preparing institutions require all prospective students to give evidence of above-average native ability before they will be admitted to the college. They obtain that evidence through requiring all students to take an intelligence test. Teaching is primarily a scholarly vocation, and for the successful pursuit of such a vocation a high degree of intelligence is required. Although there have been cursory investigations of the amount of intelligence needed by the teacher, these investigations have not pointed to any final conclusions. They have indicated, however, that persons of below-average intelligence cannot succeed as teachers; on the other hand, they have shown that intelligence of an unusually high type may often be a handicap to the teacher because persons with such intelligence are frequently unwilling or unable to give attention to the large amount of routine and detail which successful teaching requires. Many persons believe that a higher degree of intelligence is needed for teaching in the upper grades than in the lower grades; while such a belief seems to have a certain amount of plausibility, there are as yet no objective data to support it.

Good Health as a Qualification for the Teacher. Next to high intelligence, good physical and emotional health and freedom from physical defects are the greatest assets which anyone can have. "A sound mind in a sound body" is the foundation for the fullest success in any activity. Contrary to widespread belief, teaching is not easy work. It is not a vocation for "the lame, the halt, and the blind." It demands regular habits, constant application, a good emotional tone, and abundant energy.

If the teacher does not possess good physical and emotional health, he is likely to find the work of the schoolroom unusually wearing; for example, if he is nervous or has defective sight or poor hearing, he is apt to find the discipline problem more difficult than it would otherwise be. All of this, of course, is likely to interfere with the teacher's success with his pupils, to worry the teacher, and to injure his health still further. Worst of all, there is danger that the poor health of the teacher will injure the health of his pupils; this is even more true of emotional or mental health. If the teacher is afflicted with tuberculosis or with any other malignant disease, the disease may be transmitted to his pupils. So, too, if the teacher is nervous and grouchy, the pupils are likely to become nervous and grouchy also. A speech defect or a speech difficulty is apt to be imitated by the teacher's pupils, especially in the elementary school, and to fasten itself upon them throughout life.

Realizing the importance of good health for teachers, many teacher-preparing institutions require health examinations as one of the entrance requirements of the institutions, and the tendency is to make these examinations more rigid. In addition, practically all of these institutions have organized recreational programs and maintain departments of health and physical education which are calculated to improve the health of their students. Still more, most school systems require a high standard of health as a condition of appointment and retention of position by the teacher; many require a health certificate of all teachers who are appointed and many also require periodic health examinations after appointment. School systems are making these requirements as a guarantee that the health of the pupils will be protected and improved, and that the educational advancement of the pupils will be more certain. Figure 61 shows a typical form used by school systems in making physical examinations of teachers.

To summarize, a person with poor health, or with an uncorrectable physical defect which is likely to interfere with teaching success, should steer clear of the teaching profession, because such a person is not likely to be the most successful teacher, or to have complete happiness in his work. The person who possesses sufficiently good health to enter the teaching profession should so order his habits that good health will continue to bless him.

ETHICAL CHARACTER AS A QUALIFICATION FOR THE TEACHER. One of the foremost aims of the school should be the development of ethical character in the pupils. The pupils must be taught standards of conduct which will enable them to distinguish between right and wrong, and they must have instilled in them the desire to do the right. These elements in the education of children must not be neglected by the home, the church, the school, and other educational agencies, because any neglect of them is likely to breed criminality and to sabotage democracy.

In the development of ethical character in the pupils the example of the teacher is potent, and any person unwilling to try to be a

PITTSBURGH PUBLIC SCHOOLS

Educational Personnel Medical Examination

Form S H S 62 394

Number............*New Applicant* ☐ *Reinstatement* ☐ *Disability* ☐ *Promotion* ☐ *Sabbatical* ☐ *Date*..............*19*........

Full Name...*Date of Birth*..................................

Residence...*Sex*.................... M☐ S☐ W☐

Position....................*Habits*....................*Vaccination*..................................

Family History..

Previous Illnesses...

Injuries and Operations..

Height:..........*ft*..........*in.* *Weight:*..........*lbs*..........*oz.* *Nutrition*..........................

Pulse..........*Temperature*..........*Respiration*..........*Skin*..........................

Blood Presure: Systolic..........*Diastolic*..........*Remarks*..........................

Eyes { *Without glasses: Right—20/*.......... *Left—20/*.......... } *Ophthalmoscope*..........
{ *With glasses: Right—20/*.......... *Left—20/*.......... } *Remarks*..........

Ears { *Whispered Voice—R.E.*..........*ft.* *L.E.*..........*ft.* } *Otoscope*..........
{ *Audiometer—R.E.*.......... *L.E.*.......... } *Approximate Hearing*..........

Teeth..........*Oral Hygiene*..........*Nasal Passages*..........

Tonsils: Enlarged..........*Imbedded*..........*Diseased*..........*Remarks*..........

Mastoids, Sinuses, Antra..........*Anemia*..........

Nervous Symptoms..........*Reflexes*..........

Gastro Intestinal..........*Hernia*..........

Orthopedic Defect..........*Gynecological* / *Urological* }..........

Heart { *Organic*.......... } *Remarks*..........
{ *Functional*.......... }..........

Lung { *Resonance*.......... } *Remarks*..........
{ *Pathology*..........*Cough*.......... }..........

Urine { *Gross Appearance*..........*Reaction*..........*Sp. Gr.*..........
{ *Albumin*..........*Sugar*..........*Microscope*..........

Endocrine Glands..........*B. M. R.*..........

Laboratory Tests..........*X-ray*..........

**Rating: 1—2—3—4—F. Physical*..........*Personality*..........

Remarks:..

....

....

....

....*M.D.*

Board of Public Education Examiner

Remarks:.. ....

Director of School Health Service

**Key: Rating 1—Excellent, 2—Good, 3—Fair, 4—Poor, F—Failure.*

FIG. 61. A typical form used for recording the results of physical examination for teachers. This particular form is used in the Pittsburgh, Pennsylvania, public schools. *(Courtesy of the Pittsburgh, Pennsylvania, public schools.)*

good example of ethical character should not enter the teaching profession. A high regard for ethics is so important for the teacher that all of Chapter 21 of this book is devoted to that topic. Pupils acquire many habits and ideals through imitation, and no person, next to the pupil's parents, is more imitated by pupils than the teacher; indeed, pupils usually accept the teacher as a model. The teacher sets standards, and he forms tastes. This tendency of pupils to imitate their teacher, especially in the early school years, makes it necessary for the teacher to possess the highest type of character. What the teacher is in moral character speaks more loudly than what the teacher says about moral character; the hypocrite is soon discovered and is thereafter despised. If the teacher possesses low ideals of life or vicious habits of any sort, there is danger that those traits will be transmitted to the pupils through precept or example. If, on the other hand, the teacher possesses high ideals and has exemplary habits, those are likely to be transmitted to the pupils, and such is the desideratum. The impression which the teacher's character and related traits are likely to make on the pupil is indicated by the following quotation:

> In my memory chest there is stored away a picture of the teacher who made the greatest impression on my life, when I was a child of ten. I do not recall any particular subject that she taught me, but my picture shows her standing before the class, perfectly groomed, glowing with health, always ready with a smile and a bit of encouragement for the child who had tried and was never allowed to feel that he had entirely failed. She could be stern when occasion demanded, but there were few problems of discipline in that room. Children learned from example as well as precept the joy of right living, and the value of order, personal neatness, and cleanliness. The good-morning and good-by, as the lines filed in and out, carried a personal message to each child. In an age when sarcasm and ridicule were frequently used on children, I believe her influence showed me the great opportunity afforded by teaching and led to my choice of the profession.[3]

The teacher should believe in the brotherhood of man and the fatherhood of God. He needs to be a decent person himself before he is to be trusted with the guidance of the young.

PLEASING AND WELL-ROUNDED PERSONALITY AS A QUALIFICATION FOR THE TEACHER. Personality may be defined as the habits and the physical characteristics which differentiate an individual from other individuals. It is the whole person in action. It is the sum total of the traits of an individual. There are thousands of personality traits of any individual, and many of those traits slowly but constantly

[3] *Character Education, Tenth Yearbook* of the Department of Superintendence, 1932, p. 289.

change under the impact of environment and of education. Although the total bundle of habits and of physical characteristics can be slowly modified, it cannot be rapidly or completely changed; certain central tendencies remain from birth till death. Some of the personality traits are inborn, while others are acquired.

Although every individual has a personality, not every individual has a pleasing and well-rounded personality. A person has a pleasing personality when he possesses traits which attract people to him. He has a displeasing personality when he possesses traits which offend and repulse people.

Many persons believe that knowledge of the details of one's vocation, plenty of ambition, and hard work are the only ingredients of success. Although it cannot be gainsaid that these ingredients are of significant importance in bringing success and happiness to the individual, it is affirmed that a pleasing and well-rounded personality is of as great importance as any of them. Note, of course, that a pleasing and a well-rounded personality is more important in some vocations than in others. It is of little or no importance to a hermit or other recluse. It is particularly important in vocations in which the employee is required to have many personal contacts. It is of especial importance to the teacher, because he must constantly associate with people—with his pupils, the parents of his pupils, his colleagues, and the general public—and these persons should be attracted to and have confidence in him. Only by having the confidence of these persons can the teacher gain that self-confidence which is necessary for his happiness and his success.

Not only should the teacher attempt to develop pleasing and well-rounded personality traits in himself, but he should have as one of his chief teaching aims the development of such traits in his pupils. In fact, it would not be far wrong to say that the aim of education is to develop a pleasing and a well-rounded personality. If the pupil develops a pleasing and a well-rounded personality, he will be able to make the necessary social adjustments in life. The period when the pupil's mind is plastic and he is forming life habits is the time *par excellence* to develop such traits. Without a pleasing and a well-rounded personality, the teacher is not apt to realize his potentialities for success with his pupils, for his own professional advancement, and for his own happiness. The pupils are not likely to be attracted to him, and if they are not attracted to him, they are not apt to co-operate with him in discipline and in learning. Moreover, without a pleasing personality, the teacher is apt to displease or to offend school officials, parents, or members of the community, and such displeasure or offense will surely handicap the teacher—in fact, such a handicap may cause him to lose his position and make it difficult for him to obtain another one. Many investigations have shown that more teachers fail because of a weak or a missing link in personality than fail because of poor scholarship. Even the genius is likely to fail as a teacher if he has an overbearing manner, is cynical, uses incorrect language, possesses slovenly habits of dress, or has some other displeasing or objectionable trait. It should not be forgotten that only one displeasing or obnoxious trait may cause the teacher to fail, although all of his other traits may be pleasing.

The teacher should not be content to develop a personality which is characterized by a cheap veneer for fooling the people. He should strive to acquire a personality which will be pleasing to the most discerning persons who may care to penetrate the veneer. He should remember that intelligent persons know that "a skunk has beautiful fur and that a parrot can talk."

A fortunate aspect of personality is that it is largely acquired and can be changed. Practically every trait which any person possesses is within his individual control, and thereby hangs hope for all of us. Just as we have "made" ourselves, so we can "remake" ourselves. One does not inherit a selfish or a cynical disposition; that is acquired. One does not inherit slovenly habits of dress; those are acquired. Since such traits and habits are acquired, they can be modified. Every teacher should, therefore, introspect (look inward) occasionally to attempt to ascertain any displeasing traits which he may possess, and yet he should not neglect those traits already pleasing. The traits which are displeasing should be made over, while those that are pleasing should be consciously cultivated and improved. In attempting to improve his personality the teacher should not only study his own traits but he should associate with and learn from persons of pleasing and well-rounded personality as much as possible; pleasing personality is contagious, and it is free.

During recent years, many tests for analyzing and measuring personality have been devised. Some of these tests are designed for self-rating; others are designed for rating a person by other persons; and still others may be used in either procedure.[4] As a part of their student-personnel work, many departments and colleges of education now require all students to take one or more of these tests and to use the results in an attempt to improve their personality. Many of these departments and colleges have established personality-guidance clinics, and require all students to make use of the services of these clinics in developing a well-rounded personality. The following traits are among those which are most frequently analyzed and measured by personality tests:

1. Introvert, or extrovert
2. Ascendant, or submissive
3. Unsocial, or social
4. Shy, or bold
5. Quiet, or talkative
6. Even-tempered, or hot-tempered
7. Calm, or excitable
8. Cautious, or impulsive
9. Sluggish, or overactive
10. Carefree, or worrying
11. Dependent, or independent
12. Careful, or careless
13. Fearful, or fearless
14. Lazy, or industrious
15. Unreliable, or reliable
16. Dishonest, or honest
17. Non-co-operative, or co-operative
18. Trustful, or suspicious
19. Rude, or courteous
20. Cold, or affectionate
21. Slovenly, or neat
22. Unhappy, or happy.[5]

The person who would develop a pleasing and a well-rounded personality might well emulate the practice of Benjamin Franklin as described in his autobiography. At the end of each day, Franklin was wont to analyze himself for the purpose of discovering any deficiencies which he had exhibited during the day. When he ascertained a deficiency, as he often did, he promised himself to correct or to start correcting it at once. No doubt this self-analysis stimulated self-improvement and helped to make Benjamin Franklin the great person that he became; probably it helped to earn for him the sobriquet, "the first educated American." Franklin was his own severe critic.

[4] For a classified list of these tests, together with the names of the authors and publishers, see Gertrude H. Hildreth, *A Bibliography of Mental Tests and Rating Studies,* Psychological Corporation, 1939. See also O. K. Buros, *The Fourth Mental Measurements Yearbook,* Gryphon Press, 1953.

[5] Walter S. Monroe, ed., *Encyclopedia of Educational Research,* Revised edition, Macmillan, 1950, p. 809. By permission of The Macmillan Company, publishers.

What are the personality traits which persons who expect to enter the teaching profession should possess, or should try to develop? A complete list of such traits cannot be given within the limits of this chapter because such a list would include thousands of items. Moreover, as would be expected, there is no unanimity of opinion on what constitutes even the most important traits. In his book on *School Discipline,* the late Professor W. C. Bagley reported the composite judgment of one hundred experienced school officials and school employees on the most important elements entering into teaching personality; the first ten of those elements were the following:

1. Sympathy
2. Personal appearance
3. Address
4. Sincerity
5. Optimism
6. Enthusiasm
7. Scholarship
8. Physical vitality
9. Fairness
10. Reserve and dignity

In a nation-wide investigation, the late Professor W. W. Charters and Douglas Waples found that the kind of traits needed by teachers varied in certain instances with the type of educational service in which the teachers were engaged. Breadth of interest, leadership, and scholarship, for example, were found to be more important for teachers in the senior high school than for teachers in the junior high school, and in the elementary school. As a rule, though, they found that the various traits needed in the various grades ranked fairly closely, as will be observed from Table 7. In making this investigation they requested several hundred educational leaders to indicate the most important traits which they believed that teachers should possess. The twenty-five traits most frequently mentioned, together with the ranking in importance for the various grades of the school, are indicated in the table just mentioned. The teacher or the prospective teacher should find this list helpful in analyzing himself. Since all of us would be helped by seeking and knowing the answer to the prayer of Robert Burns,

> O wad some power the giftie gie us,
> To see oursel's as ithers see us!

the teacher or prospective teacher might desire to have one or more of his colleagues, supervisors, or administrative superiors measure him by means of the list. Only by criticism—criticism by one's self or by

TABLE 7. RANK-LIST OF TEACHERS' TRAITS *

TRAITS	RANK FOR TEACHERS OF: Grades 10–12 Senior High School	Grades 7–9 Junior High School	Grades 3–6 Inter-mediate	Grades Kdg. 2 Kdg. Primary	Rural School
1. Adaptability	8	10	8	6	1
2. Attractiveness, personal appearance	17	14	9	10	15
3. Breadth of interest (interest in community, interest in profession, interest in pupils)	1	10	11	15	2
4. Carefulness (accuracy, definiteness, thoroughness)	11	13	9	14	12
5. Considerateness (appreciativeness, courtesy, kindliness, sympathy, tact, unselfishness)	17	3	1	1	3
6. Co-operation (helpfulness, loyalty)	11	9	14	16	3
7. Dependability (consistency)	14	19	16	17	15
8. Enthusiasm (alertness, animation, inspiration, spontaneity)	9	4	5	2	11
9. Fluency	23	24	25	23	25
10. Forcefulness (courage, decisiveness, firmness, independence, purposefulness)	5	4	18	19	13
11. Good judgment (discretion, foresight, insight, intelligence)	2	1	3	4	3
12. Health	16	16	12	10	9
13. Honesty	7	12	7	9	6
14. Industry (patience, perseverance)	19	8	14	13	17
15. Leadership (initiative, self-confidence)	4	17	19	21	8
16. Magnetism (approachability, cheerfulness, optimism, pleasantness, sense of humor, sociability, pleasing voice, wittiness)	11	4	5	3	9
17. Neatness (cleanliness)	20	16	13	4	18
18. Openmindedness	9	20	23	24	22
19. Originality (imaginativeness, resourcefulness)	22	22	16	12	19
20. Progressiveness (ambition)	23	23	22	20	22
21. Promptness (dispatch, punctuality)	21	14	20	18	21
22. Refinement (conventionality, good taste, modesty, morality, simplicity)	14	20	2	8	13
23. Scholarship (intellectual curiosity)	5	16	21	21	20
24. Self-control (calmness, dignity, poise, reserve, sobriety)	2	2	3	6	6
25. Thrift	25	25	24	25	24

* W. W. Charters and Douglas Waples, *The Commonwealth Teacher-Training Study*, University of Chicago Press, 1929, p. 18. By permission of the University of Chicago Press, publishers.

other competent persons—can the individual bring out the best in himself. Only the angels are perfect, and they do not inhabit this world.

In seeking to see himself as others see him, probably no one is in a better position to help the teacher than the teacher's pupils; such an appraisal by the teacher's more mature pupils would seem to be especially helpful to the teacher. Although it may be claimed that pupils, especially younger pupils, lack maturity of judgment and sometimes thoughtlessly place their wishes above their needs, these inclinations are not associated with youth alone. Regarding the ability of high school seniors to appraise their teachers Frank W. Hart says:

> . . . They (high school seniors) are in a better position than anyone else. They are with us day in and day out, for weeks, months, and years on end. They see, hear, and know us at our best, at our worst, on good days and on bad days, in high spirit and low. Furthermore, they have had experience with many teachers of many different ways of teachings; thus they have standards of comparison. They are in a position to judge.[6]

In a nation-wide investigation Hart asked all seniors in sixty-six high schools of various sizes and types to give certain information regarding their high school teachers. The seniors were requested first to consider all of the teachers which they had had, then "to think of the one *you have liked best*" and to write down "your *reasons for liking this teacher best;* not necessarily the best teacher." The reasons which the pupils gave for liking best the teacher which they selected are shown in Table 8.[7]

As a second part of the inquiry the same seniors were requested to "think of the one *you have liked least of all,*" and to write down "your reasons for *not liking this teacher.*" On this assignment the responses of the pupils are shown in Table 9.[8]

A third question which was asked the same seniors was the following: "Was the teacher *you liked best* also the *best teacher,* that is, the one who taught you most effectively?" They were also asked whether the teacher they liked least was the best teacher. Eighty per cent of the seniors stated that the best-liked teacher was also the best teacher, that is, the one who taught them most effectively; and

[6] Frank W. Hart, *Teachers and Teaching,* Macmillan, 1934, p. 6. By permission of The Macmillan Company, publishers.

[7] *Ibid.,* pp. 131–132.

[8] *Ibid.,* pp. 250–251.

TABLE 8. REASONS FOR LIKING "TEACHER A" BEST ARRANGED IN ORDER OF FREQUENCY OF MENTION, AS REPORTED BY 3,725 HIGH SCHOOL SENIORS

REASONS FOR LIKING "TEACHER A" BEST	FREQUENCY OF MENTION	RANK
Is helpful with school work, explains lesson assignments clearly and thoroughly, and uses examples in teaching	1950	1
Cheerful, happy, good-natured, jolly, has a sense of humor, and can take a joke	1429	2
Human, friendly, companionable, "one of us"	1024	3
Interested in and understands pupils	937	4
Makes work interesting, creates a desire to work, makes class work a pleasure	805	5
Strict, has control of the class, commands respect	753	6
Impartial, shows no favoritism, has no "pets"	695	7
Not cross, crabby, grouchy, nagging, or sarcastic	613	8
"We learned the subject"	538	9
A pleasing personality	504	10
Patient, kindly, sympathetic	485	11
Fair in marking and grading, fair in giving examinations and tests	475	12
Fair and square in dealing with pupils, has good discipline	366	13
Requires that work be done properly and promptly, makes you work	364	14
Considerate of pupils' feelings in the presence of the class, courteous, makes you feel at ease	362	15
Knows the subject and knows how to put it over	357	16
Respects pupils' opinions, invites discussion in class	267	17
Not superior, aloof, "high hat," does not pretend to know everything	216	18
Assignments reasonable	199	19
Is reasonable, not too strict or "hard-boiled"	191	20.5
Helpful with students' personal problems, including matters outside of class work	191	20.5
Dresses attractively, appropriately, neatly, and in good taste	146	22
Young	121	23
Work well planned, knows what class is to do	110	24
Enthusiastically interested in teaching	108	25
Gives students a fair chance to make up work	97	26
Home-work assignments reasonable	96	27
Recognizes individual differences in ability	86	28
Frank, "straight from the shoulder," a straight shooter	78	29.5
Personally attractive, good-looking	78	29.5
Teaches more than the subject	74	31
Interested in school activities	68	32
Sticks to subject	53	33
Modern	52	34
Sweet and gentle	50	35.5

REASONS FOR LIKING "TEACHER A" BEST	FREQUENCY OF MENTION	RANK
Pleasing voice	50	35.5
Intelligent	42	37
Prompt and businesslike	41	38
Sincere	36	39
Knows more than the subject	32	40
Has pep	31	41
Uses good judgment	22	42
Cultured and refined	20	43

approximately one-half of one per cent reported that the least-liked teacher was the best teacher when judged by teaching effectiveness.[9]

Finally, the seniors were requested to indicate how the best teacher which they had selected differed from the best-liked teacher. Table 10 shows the comments of the seniors on this request.[10]

BROAD EDUCATION AS A QUALIFICATION FOR THE TEACHER. More and more the tendency in educational theory and practice is away from the "compartmentalization" of knowledge and toward the integration of knowledge in a given field with knowledge in other, especially related fields. If he is to participate in this movement, the teacher must have an excellent general education. He must be informed not only on the subjects which he teaches but also on as many other fields, especially related fields, of learning as possible. He should feel "at home in many lands." He should be familiar with past and present happenings in economics, science, invention, international relations, politics, literature, religion, music, art, and other fields of learning. When he possesses such knowledge, the teacher is more likely to have confidence in himself, to be expert in instructing his pupils, and to be highly regarded by his pupils and by the community; with such erudition he is likely to be regarded as a broadly educated and cultured person rather than as a narrow, cloistered "pedagogue." In the days ahead teachers must have a greater knowledge of world geography and of history than ever before. Teachers must more and more realize that America is an important part of one world.

An excellent beginning toward obtaining this general education should have been made in the secondary school, and this should be continued in college courses. As a college student, therefore, the

[9] *Ibid.*, p. 256.
[10] *Ibid.*, p. 278–279.

TABLE 9. REASONS FOR LIKING "TEACHER Z" LEAST, ARRANGED IN ORDER OF MENTION, AS REPORTED BY 3,725 HIGH SCHOOL SENIORS

REASONS FOR LIKING "TEACHER Z" LEAST	FREQUENCY OF MENTION	RANK
Too cross, crabby, grouchy, never smiles, nagging, sarcastic, loses temper, "flies off the handle"	1708	1
Not helpful with school work, does not explain lessons and assignments, not clear, work not planned	1025	2
Partial, has "pets" or favored students, and "picks on certain pupils"	859	3
Superior, aloof, haughty, "snooty," overbearing, does not know you out of class	775	4
Mean, unreasonable, "hard-boiled," intolerant, ill mannered, too strict, makes life miserable	652	5
Unfair in marking and grading, unfair in tests and examinations	614	6
Inconsiderate of pupils' feelings, bawls out pupils in the presence of classmates, pupils are afraid and ill at ease and dread class	551	7
Not interested in pupils and does not understand them	442	8
Unreasonable assignments and homework	350	9
Too loose in discipline, no control of class, does not command respect	313	10
Does not stick to the subject, brings in too many irrelevant personal matters, talks too much	301	11
"We did not learn what we were supposed to"	275	12.5
Dull, stupid, and uninteresting	275	12.5
Too old-fashioned, too old to be teaching	224	14
Not "fair and square" in dealing with pupils	203	15
Knows the subject but "can't put it over"	193	16
Does not hold to standards, is careless and slipshod in her work	190	17
Too exacting, too hard, gives no chance to make up work	183	18
Does not know the subject	170	19
Does not respect pupils' judgments or opinions	133	20
Too changeable, inconsistent, unreliable	122	21
Lazy, not interested in teaching	115	22
Not friendly, not companionable	98	23
Shows boy or girl favoritism	95	24
Dresses unattractively or in bad taste	92	25
Weak personality	85	26
Insincere	75	27
Personally unattractive	65	28
Does not recognize individual differences in pupils	64	29
Voice not pleasant	63	30

prospective teacher should not neglect to elect those courses which acquaint him with many fields of activity in which truly educated persons should be conversant. At best, however, because of the time

TABLE 10. DIFFERENCES BETWEEN BEST TEACHER AND BEST-LIKED TEACHER, ARRANGED IN ORDER OF FREQUENCY, AS REPORTED BY 763 HIGH SCHOOL SENIORS

BEST TEACHER DIFFERENT FROM BEST-LIKED TEACHER AS FOLLOWS	FREQUENCY OF MENTION	RANK
More exacting in standards of work, stricter in marking, "we learned more"	267	1
Better at explaining lessons and assignments, work is better planned	155	2
Knows the subject better and can "put it over" better	95	3
Stricter, more rigid discipline	85	4
Makes the work more interesting	46	5
Is less friendly	39	6
More serious, more businesslike, keeps closer to the subject, more conscientious	38	7
Less understanding of pupils, less interested in pupils	13	8
More sarcastic	12	9
Less attractive	10	10.5
More cross and crabby	10	10.5
More aloof	6	12

that must be given to the entire program of studies, a college course can give the prospective teacher only a taste of these various fields. This necessitates that the teacher supplement his knowledge after he is through college; especially he must keep his knowledge up to date. He can accomplish this through reading good books, magazines, and newspapers, through hearing public lectures, through travel, and through listening to the radio, or watching television. The "school of experience" will always be the great school, and a teacher will have that school as long as he lives; he will have it twenty-four hours a day, year in and year out, and usually its tuition is free.

KNOWLEDGE OF SUBJECTS TO BE TAUGHT AS A QUALIFICATION FOR THE TEACHER. A person cannot teach something which he does not know; he may make the attempt, but the result is sure to be a bluffing, stumbling, and bungling effort. Therefore, another requisite for the teacher is an excellent command of the subjects which he will teach. Arithmetic cannot be taught unless the teacher knows arithmetic, and grammar cannot be taught unless the teacher knows grammar. The same remark is true for all subjects. In their knowledge of subject matter the best teachers are always more than a day or a week ahead of their pupils; the pupils of such teachers, as Thomas Arnold said, "drink from a running stream rather than from a stagnant pool."

Colleges which prepare teachers for the elementary schools usually expect every graduate to show competence to teach all of the school subjects required in the elementary school curriculum.[11] The elementary school subjects which are usually required in one or more grades of the school are reading, writing, arithmetic, spelling, language, science, geography, history and civics, and health education. Many states also require other school subjects to be taught in one or more grades of the elementary school; among these school subjects are art, music, safety education, physical education, and practical arts.

Colleges which prepare teachers for the secondary schools usually require every graduate to have at least one major field and one or more minor fields of work; in fact, the laws of many states make such a requirement for secondary-school teachers. Many states, moreover, now certificate secondary-school teachers by subjects, and prohibit schools from employing teachers to teach subjects in which they have not been certificated.

Desire to Teach as a Qualification for the Teacher. "Will I like better to teach than to do any other work?" is a fundamental question to be asked and intelligently and frankly answered by everyone who is considering preparing for the teaching profession. "Am I interested in other people, particularly in young people?" "Will I like to work with children, both when I am young and when I have grown old?" "Will I desire to stand *in loco parentis* to a constantly changing group of dynamic children who come or are assigned to me for tutelage?" "Will I want to serve as guide to those children, to teach them, to have patience with them, and to get along with them?" "Will I find the problem of discipline not too wearing and tearing?" "Will I be happy in work which constantly demands service to others?" "Will I like to study and to keep pace with all aspects of a changing world?" Anyone who can give an unhesitating and a sincere "Yes" in answer to these questions has met another test for entering the teaching profession. Anyone who cannot give that answer should avoid the teaching profession as he would a scourge. A person who does not like to teach will never become a great teacher; he will be caught in "the trap" of his decision, and his life is certain to be full of disappointment and misery.

[11] This requirement is especially important today, because of the growing practice in the elementary school of having the teacher advance to the next grade with the pupils; thus, the teacher of a fifth grade this year would teach the same pupils in the sixth grade next year.

Knowledge of Professional Education as a Qualification for the Teacher. During recent decades professional education has made unusually rapid strides, and an excellent beginning has been made toward the development of a science of education. Thousands of investigations have been conducted on the learning process, on the curriculum, on pupil classification and pupil progress, and on myriad other educational problems. Probably, no field of learning during recent years has made greater progress toward obtaining a scientific basis than has teaching. During recent years, also, more attention than ever before has been devoted to the formulation of proper educational aims and to other phases of a sound philosophy of education. The successful teacher must be informed concerning as many of these matters as possible. Without attempting to mention the specific college courses which should be pursued, the outstanding types of knowledge in professional education with which the teacher should be familiar are indicated herewith:

In the first place, the teacher needs a sound philosophy of life and of the educative process. He must have such a philosophy in order that his own life and his teaching efforts will be properly directed. As a part of his educational philosophy he must develop good aims and high ideals for education in American democracy, and he must ever be improving those aims and those ideals. In fact, a sound philosophy of life and of education is deemed so necessary to the teacher that Chapter 2 of this book has been devoted to a detailed discussion of that topic.

In the second place, the teacher needs to be a student of social forces and of social changes, and he especially needs such information for the community in which he expects to teach. Atomic energy has recently come upon the scene and may tremendously affect our mode of living and our very lives. Such knowledge is particularly important for the modern teacher because of recent and present social and economic problems and the many diverse solutions which have been proposed for those problems. He should possess this knowledge in order that he may adjust the curriculum to meet those social and economic changes and in order that he may keep his educational aims in proper focus. Many colleges which prepare teachers offer at least one course in educational sociology, and such a course should give the teacher a start in obtaining the necessary knowledge of social forces and social changes. Such a course, though, can give only a start, and in order that he may keep up to date the teacher must ever be a student of the changing panorama of society; in fact, the chief obligation of the teacher is, through the instrumentality of the school, to cause improvement in the changing panorama of society.

In the third place, the teacher needs a knowledge of the psychological and biological laws affecting the pupils. He needs to know as much as possible concerning the "mysteries" of how the pupils' minds function, and he should immediately become aware of the fact that no two minds function in an exactly similar manner. To obtain information on how the mind functions he will need to pursue various courses in psychology, and to study the various individuals with whom he works. He should become aware also that health education is as important as, and is closely related to, mental education, and he must become proficient in directing it. He must be informed on the physical defects among children and on ways of preventing and correcting them. Chapters 7, 8, and 12 of this book have given an introductory discussion of these problems.

In the fourth place, the teacher must acquire knowledge of, and skill in, proper methods of presenting his subject matter. He must be able to present his subject matter in the most effective manner to individuals who differ widely in interests, in desire to learn, and in capacity to learn. The wide-awake teacher, of course, will discover many effective methods of teaching through trial and error and through experimentation, but during such procedures the pupils may suffer. To protect the pupils, all teacher-preparing institutions offer courses in methods of teaching and require their students to enroll in them. These college courses are usually of two types: first, general methods of teaching, and second, special methods of teaching a certain school subject or school area.

Most teacher-preparing institutions provide one or more courses in each of the four areas just mentioned, and these courses are usually required of all prospective teachers. In addition, and in the fifth place, most teacher-preparing institutions require a certain number of school and classroom observations. Since the tendency is to begin these observations in the first course in education, Chapter 24 of this book is devoted to that topic. Following those courses and those observations, and toward the close of his college course, the prospective teacher is inducted into practice teaching and is expected to conduct classes under typical school conditions. Practice teaching is deemed so valuable that the American Association of Colleges for Teacher Education has recommended a minimum standard of ninety clock hours of it. Many teacher-preparing institutions have established internship or apprentice teaching for all teacher candidates; this is usually done off the campus, comprises at least one semester, and sometimes the student is paid a small amount for it. Such courses, observations, and practice teaching are expected to give the student a good start in gaining familiarity with the science and the philosophy of education. This regimen of preparation will qualify the student to receive the first two letters of the alphabet (A.B.) and open the door to the school of educational experience wherein he will receive as many other letters as he may earn.

Special Requirements for Certification and Appointment of Teachers

State Requirements for Certification and Appointment. Every state has enacted statutes which govern the certification of teachers. Such statutes apply universally to elementary and to secondary teachers in the public schools, and in most states they also apply to those teachers in the private schools. From the beginning of teacher certification the tendency has been for the states to assume the leading role in the control of it. In the early days the laws usually permitted local school agencies to grant certificates for teachers. During recent years, however, the tendency has been for the state to take from the local communities all power of granting teaching certificates. The belief underlying this tendency is that the state is obligated to assure the highest type of teaching personnel possible throughout the state, and that when local officials have the power to certificate teachers, there is danger that the standards demanded by the state will not always be met.

At present, practically all of the states grant either temporary or provisional certificates to all graduates of standard teacher-preparing institutions of the states. This policy almost always applies to the public teacher-training institutions, and it frequently applies also to the private colleges and universities which have been authorized to prepare teachers. Most of the states also make provision for the exchange of certificates with states which have equal and similar standards. Most of them grant the graduates of their standard teacher-preparing institutions a temporary or provisional certificate of one to four years in length; at the end of that trial period, provided the teacher's experience has been satisfactory, a more permanent type of certificate is granted.

A few states also make provision for certificating teachers by examination. Such provisions are made for persons who are not graduates of standard teacher-preparing institutions and who are therefore unable to qualify automatically for teaching certificates. These states

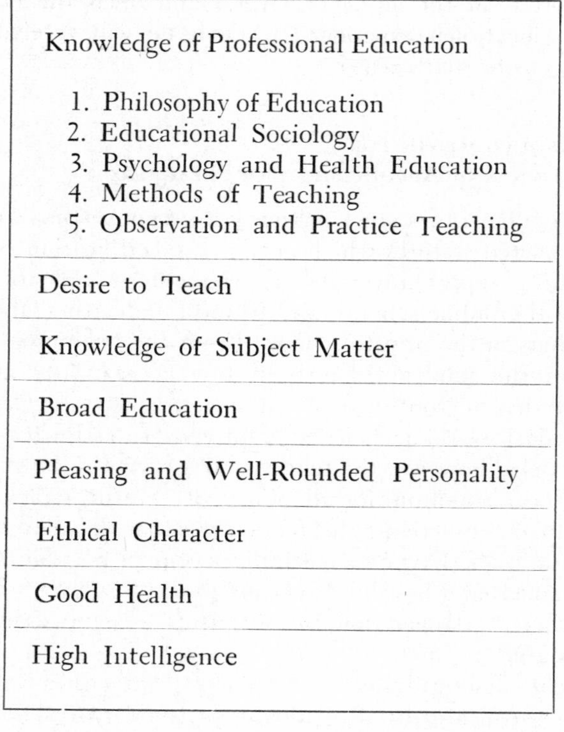

FIG. 62. The foundation equipment for the teacher.

make provision for such examinations several times during the year at various places in the state; the questions for the examinations are usually prepared and the answers marked by state officials.

Of course, the requirements of the various states vary for obtaining teaching certificates, and the prospective teacher should early become acquainted with the requirements of the state in which he expects to seek employment. He will be able to obtain this information from the school code of the state, from correspondence with or from bulletins of the state department of education, or from the college in which he is obtaining his preparation to teach. Attention to this matter will often save the prospective teacher disappointment and loss of time. Practically all states now require at least two years of college preparation for new teachers in the elementary school and at least four years of college preparation for new teachers in the secondary school; of course, a few states require more, and a few others permit less. It is here predicted that when the present shortage of teachers passes, the states will increase the number of years of college preparation for new teachers; and the states should.

Local Requirements for Certification and Appointment. In no phase of educational endeavor does any state prohibit the local community from establishing higher standards than those which the state provides. The state establishes minimum standards, not maximum ones. Many communities therefore require higher standards for the certification of teachers than do the laws of the state. Perhaps, some of these local requirements may be more accurately described as different rather than higher. The chief local requirements are listed herewith:

1. Approximately five per cent of the school systems (practically all of these being city systems) require all candidates for teaching positions to pass a written examination. Since 1940, written examinations have been given a stimulus through the National Teacher Examinations. These examinations are given and scored under the sponsorship of the American Council on Education. They are given annually in several cities of the United States. A teacher's score on the examination is released only to himself or to school officials designated by him. Information for any year regarding the dates on which and the cities in which the National Teacher Examinations will be given may be obtained by writing the American Council on Education, Washington, D. C.

2. One or more years of teaching experience is often listed as a prerequisite for appointment in some of the city school systems. Such experience, though, is almost never required by the rural and village school systems. Although the tendency in theory and practice is away from requiring such experience, many city school systems still believe that their higher salaries justify them in requiring it.

3. A few of the city school systems have a minimum age limit

(usually twenty-one years) for the appointment of teachers, and a few also have a maximum age limit (usually forty years) for new appointees. Such age limits are seldom found in the rural and village school systems.

4. Although the tendency in theory and practice is away from such rules and regulations, a few of the city school systems still will not employ married women as teachers. Such rules and regulations are also found in a few of the rural and village school systems, although they are not found there nearly as frequently as in the city systems. Owing to the undersupply of teachers during and following World War II, practically all school systems have abolished such restrictions, and it is here hoped that they have permanently abolished them. Many thousands of married women are teaching in the public schools today.

5. Only a small percentage of boards of education have rules and regulations against the appointment of nonresidents as teachers, but most boards of education give local residents preference over nonresidents if qualifications are equal. A few boards of education have rules against the employment of local residents until they have had one or more years of teaching experience elsewhere.

In addition to the local requirements which have just been mentioned, many school systems require special professional qualifications on the part of their teachers. For example, they frequently require ability to coach an athletic team or to sponsor one or more other extraclass activities; also many schools require some of their teachers to be able to teach special subjects such as music, art, or physical education. These requirements are found especially in the smaller school systems in which many teachers begin their professional careers. While he is enrolled in a teacher-preparing institution, therefore, the prospective teacher should keep in mind these special requirements and attempt to obtain the preparation which will enable him to meet them. Attention to this matter will often mean the difference between obtaining a position and not obtaining one. Attention to it may also mean a larger salary for the teacher.

Requirements of Standardizing Agencies for Teachers. The laws of the various states have always been calculated to bring the schools to a higher and higher standard, and hundreds of laws in every state have been enacted for that purpose. The state laws, therefore, may be regarded as the chief standardizing agencies of the schools. In addition to these laws, which may be regarded as public standardizing agencies, there are many private or quasi-public standardizing agencies, and these have performed a noteworthy service in raising school standards. Every section of the United States now has one of these private or quasi-public standardizing agencies. As a rule, the agencies operate in the secondary schools and the colleges and are infrequently found in the elementary schools. The better known of the agencies are the North Central Association of Colleges and Secondary Schools, the New England Association of Colleges and Secondary Schools, the Middle States Association of Colleges and Secondary Schools, the Southern Association of Colleges and Secondary Schools, the Western Association of Colleges and Secondary Schools, and the Northwest Association of Secondary and Higher Schools. The chief function of the agencies is to raise school standards to a higher and higher plane. The associations have formulated certain standards which schools seeking and retaining membership in the associations must meet; for example, they have established standards for graduation, length of school year, size of teaching staff, program of studies, size of classes, school library, preparation of teachers, and teaching load.

The schools invited to membership in these associations are regarded as the better types of schools, and teachers usually aspire to obtain employment in them. Teachers aspiring, therefore, to obtain employment in one of those schools should know the requirements for teachers of the standardizing agencies. For example, if the teacher expects to obtain employment in a school which is a member of the North Central Association of Colleges and Secondary Schools, he should know the requirements for teachers in the schools of that association; likewise, if he desires employment in a school which is affiliated with the New England Association of Colleges and Secondary Schools he should become aware of the requirements for teachers in those schools. Failure to meet those requirements would, of course, prevent the teacher from obtaining employment in those schools. The requirements for teachers of the North Central Association of Colleges and Secondary Schools may be regarded as somewhat typical and are quoted herewith. That association requires of its secondary-school teachers graduation from a college having membership in the North Central Association of Colleges and Secondary Schools, or graduation from a college having equivalent standards; it requires also that academic teachers and the superintendent of schools and the secondary-school principal shall have at least fifteen semester hours of credit in education, and that all secondary-school teachers shall teach only school subjects in which they majored or minored in college.

Summary of Principles of Teacher Education

In this chapter attempt has been made to give a view of the status of the education of the teachers of the United States and to point the way to improvement. As a summary of this discussion, the "principles of teacher education" which were formulated by the *National Survey of the Education of Teachers*, and which seem to be applicable today, will be quoted *in extenso:*

A. It is the responsibility of the state to establish standards for the preparation of its public school teachers, to insure an adequate supply of teachers meeting those standards, and to protect its standards and the services rendered by the teachers by maintaining a balance between the supply of teachers and the demand for teachers. This control should be exercised primarily by means of certification and the enforcement of adequate regulations of state departments of education.

B. The importance of the work of the teacher, particularly in a democracy, justifies securing the strongest recruits possible for the teachers' curricula. This end will be assisted by:
   1. Admission requirements aimed to select the most capable of the applicants as shown by all known prognostic measures including health and personality.
   2. Programs of "selective recruiting" to interest exceptionally capable high-school graduates in teaching.
   3. Systems of student personnel and guidance service which will start at admission to a teacher's curriculum and continue through a period of adjustment following graduation.
   4. A rigid system of elimination of students who, during their preparation, show themselves to be unsuited or unfit for teaching.

C. The preparation of teachers and other educational workers should be determined by the demands which will be made upon them in the different types of positions and not be arbitrarily or traditionally set requirements for majors or minors. This implies that:
   1. Competence in the total work of the teacher should be the criterion for determining curriculum content and arrangement.
   2. Graduates should be aware of the desirable elements in present

educational practice and also sensitive to needed changes in educational procedures.

3. Graduation from curricula for teachers should depend upon mastery of the content and skills demanded by the work to be performed and not by time spent nor courses passed.

D. In order to assume their appropriate positions of leadership in the communities in which they work, teachers should have sufficient general education to compare favorably with that of members of the "learned professions" and with that of the better educated citizens of representative communities. This education should include:
   1. Survey contacts, preferably on the college level, with the major established fields of knowledge—English, social sciences, mathematics, music, fine arts, and philosophy.
   2. A scholarly mastery of the subject or subjects to be taught and of the subjects most closely related to them.
   3. A familiarity with the social, political, industrial, and aesthetic developments in this and other countries.
   4. The development of one or more fields of intellectual avocation.
   5. The development of a growing and integrated philosophy of living.

E. Teachers should have the distinctly professional knowledge and skills required in the type of position for which they are preparing. These distinctly professional elements include:
   1. Professional orientation with respect to education and teaching.
   2. Mastery of essential educational tools—psychology, measurements, and statistics.
   3. Knowledge of the individuals to be taught—in most cases, children.
   4. Essential teaching methods and techniques for the subjects taught and the groups taught. These may be presented in four or more different ways.
   5. Knowledge of class organization and class instruction.
   6. Observation of and participation and practice in teaching.
   7. Professional integration and the development of a working philosophy of education.

F. In order to protect the learners from the effects of inexperienced teaching all initial practice teaching should be closely supervised. . . .
   1. The period required to obtain the necessary initial skill should vary for different individuals.
   2. Practice teaching facilities should be representative of the better schools in which the graduates will be employed.
   3. Curricula for teachers should aim, in the time available, to make prospective teachers as competent as possible at the beginning of their period of practice teaching.
   4. No teacher should be certificated who has not satisfactorily passed a period of supervised practice teaching.

G. The concept of a "safety minimum" of teaching skill at graduation implies:

1. A period of probation after graduation, during which the prospective teacher demonstrates his ability to add to his teaching skill.
2. A program of in-service education which will stimulate teachers to continued professional development.

H. Aside from having the necessary knowledge and skills a teacher should possess those traits of personality which are usually found among the better teachers and which are associated with leaders in any representative community. Some of the elements in a program for the education of teachers which contribute to personality development are:

1. A comprehensive program of student guidance and welfare.
2. A rich program of extraclass activities especially those which are also found in the elementary or secondary schools.
3. A comprehensive program of health services.
4. The provision of residence and dining facilities which contribute to desirable habits and manners.
5. A generous program for the social and religious activities of students
6. Opportunities to discover and develop latent creative talents.

I. Education should be recognized as one of the major forces responsible for social, political, and economic stability and betterment. A general understanding of this role of education should be a part of the sociological information of all citizens.

J. Preservice curricula for teachers should be largely prescribed—the prescription differing in terms of the positions for which the prospective teachers are preparing. Only in this way can the objectives . . . be realized.

K. Courses in curricula for teachers, whenever the number of students makes it possible, should be "differentiated" for the larger school divisions; that is, teachers preparing for the elementary schools and those preparing for the high schools should have separate courses in the various subjects. . . .

L. Institutions offering curricula for teachers should be approved for and restricted to the preparation of teachers for only those types of positions for which the institutions are satisfactorily equipped in staff, library, and other facilities. . . .

M. The American ideal of equality of educational opportunity is directly related to the preparation of teachers and all programs—state or national—to equalize educational opportunities should include as one of the most important factors the education of the teachers.

N. Institutions offering work on the graduate level for teachers should adapt the courses and the requirements for graduate degrees to the needs of teachers in the various types of positions. . . .

O. The faculty of any institution, the graduates of which are recognized for certification as teachers, should be pervaded by a high degree of contagious enthusiasm for teaching and a sincere interest in the students as prospective teachers. . . .

P. The teacher plays so important a part in the work of the public schools, and so many factors which require years to develop are involved in the increasing efficiency of institutions for the preparation of teachers, that the education of teachers should be classed as one of those essential forms of public service which should be maintained regardless of economic changes.[12]

QUESTIONS FOR DISCUSSION

1. Do you believe that persons who enter the teaching profession are of as high a type as persons entering other professions? In other words, is it true, as George Bernard Shaw has said, "He who can, does; and he who cannot, teaches?" Discuss.

2. What steps, if any, should secondary school teachers take to direct choice students into teaching?

3. What entrance requirements should teacher-preparing institutions have? Compare those more ideal requirements with the requirements now in force. Should teacher-preparing institutions limit their enrollments as do the colleges of medicine? Why or why not?

4. What relation should there be between the supply and the demand of teachers and the requirements for entering the teaching profession? What attitude should teachers take toward raising the requirements for members of their profession? Would raising those requirements be helpful to teachers as well as to the schools? Explain.

5. Should teachers be certificated by state or by local authorities? Why? Should any teacher be given a life certificate? Explain. Should every teacher be required to pass an examination before certification? Why or why not?

6. What provision for the preparation of teachers does your state make? Do you regard these facilities adequate and of a sufficiently high standard? In your state how do the provisions made for the preparation of teachers compare with those made for the preparation of members of other professions, for example, medicine, law, and engineering? What supervision, if any, do you believe the state should give to private colleges which prepare teachers? Discuss.

7. How many years of preparation beyond the secondary school should the teacher have? Should a distinction be made between the amount of college preparation for the elementary school and for the secondary school? Discuss. Should the teacher be required to have as much college preparation as the physician? Why or why not? Account for the much smaller amount of college preparation which teachers have, compared with physicians. Would increasing the amount of college preparation required

[12] *Op. cit.*, Vol. 6, pp. 243–246. See also the publications of the American Association of Colleges for Teacher Education, especially *Teacher Education for a Free People*, Donald P. Cottrell, Editor, published by the Association, 1956.

of teachers cause a better type of person to enter the profession? Explain.

8. Should the teacher go beyond the minimum requirement in obtaining his preparation? Should he work for the master's degree and the doctor's degree when they are not required? Discuss.

9. Do you believe that if a teacher knows his subject matter, he can teach it? Discuss.

10. Is there such a thing as a "teaching personality?" If so, what do you regard as some of its chief characteristics? Do you believe that those characteristics are innate or acquired or both? Explain. What are some personality traits which can be modified?

11. What health requirements should be made of teachers? Should they be required to submit to health examinations periodically? Discuss.

12. Many school systems, especially the city systems, require one or two years of teaching experience before employing a new teacher. Is such a requirement reasonable? Explain.

SELECTED REFERENCES

Bigelow, Karl W., "The American Teachers College," *Journal of Education*, Vol. 137 (January, 1955), pp. 13–14, 18–19, 30.

Here is a short history of the American teachers college together with a factual report of the high character of the average teachers college of today.

Burnett, Ruth Griffith, "Conduct Becoming a Teacher," NEA *Journal*, Vol. 43 (September, 1954), p. 335.

Mrs. Burnett contrasts two fictitious teachers, then asks, "Which teacher had dignity?" Every teacher could look at his own conduct at school and away after reading this article.

Charters, W. W., and Waples, Douglas, *The Commonwealth Teacher-Training Study*, University of Chicago Press, Chicago, 1929, 666 pp.

An analysis of the duties of teachers and of the traits needed by teachers.

Cottrell, Donald P., ed., *Teacher Education for a Free People*, The American Association of Colleges for Teacher Education, Oneonta, New York, 1956, 415 pp.

An interpretative study of current trends and problems in teacher education.

Evenden, E. S., *National Survey of the Education of Teachers*, Vol. 6, U.S. Office of Education, *Bulletin*, 1933, No. 10, 235 pp.

A *Summary of the nation-wide survey of the education of teachers.*

Fuess, Claude M., and Basford, Emory S., *Unseen Harvests*, The Macmillan Co., New York, 678 pp.

An anthology of the literature about teaching, the teacher, and the taught.

Hart, Frank W., *Teachers and Teaching*, The Macmillan Co., New York, 1934, 285 pp.

A report of 10,000 high school seniors on the teacher which they liked best, also the teacher which they liked least; Chapters 3, 5, 7, 8, and 9 present summaries of the investigation.

Research Bulletin of the National Education Association, Vol. 35 (February, 1957), pp. 3–63.

Discusses the status of the American public-school teacher.

Richey, Robert W., *Planning for Teaching*, McGraw-Hill Book Co., Inc., 1952, 422 pp.

Emphasizes the importance and need for planning a career in education.

Robinson, Nina J., "Lift That Teacher Load," *NEA Journal*, Vol. 43 (November, 1954), p. 509.

Mrs. Robinson pleads for a lightened load for the classroom teacher. Extracurricular activities, teachers' meetings, and school affairs, leave the teacher little time to herself.

Russell, William F., "What Criteria Must the Profession Meet?" *School Executive*, Vol. 74 (November, 1954), pp. 70–72.

Discusses the criteria that a group must meet to become a profession.

Russell, William F., as told to Llewellyn Miller, "Should Your Child be a Teacher," *Colliers*, Vol. 132 (August, 1953), pp. 16–17.

Mentions some of the qualifications that a teacher should have.

Sears, Jesse B., and Henderson, Adin D., *Cabberley of Stanford*, Stanford University Press, Stanford, 1957, 301 pp.

A story of a great contribution to American education.

Wells, H. G., *The Story of a Great Schoolmaster*, The Macmillan Co., New York, 1924, 176 pp.

A tribute to one of the teachers of H. G. Wells.

CHAPTER 19

In-Service Education of Teachers

Importance of Education In Service

The preceding chapter pointed out the importance of the preservice preparation of teachers. Although this preservice education can never be neglected, education in service is of even greater importance. The validity of this conclusion will be accepted, if it is remembered that the school has the prospective teacher under its tutelage only a few years, whereas the school of experience "teaches" the teacher as long as he lives. While the prospective teacher is obtaining his preservice preparation, it is not too early for him to direct his attention to the importance of preparation in service and to the means which he may use in obtaining this preparation. Moreover, before any person decides to enter an educational career, he should be informed upon the demands which his profession and society will make upon him for continuing his preparation.

What has just been said applies to other persons as well as to teachers. Although the school performs a large and a necessary service, only a small percentage of the education of the typical person comes through it; by far the largest percentage comes through the school of experience. The fundamental purposes of the school are to provide the individual with the tools and the sources of learning, and to give him an abiding interest in the use of those tools and those sources. If those purposes are accomplished, the individual will be qualified and disposed to continue his education as long as he lives.

That it is possible for a person—particularly a person with good intelligence and ample ambition—to obtain an education when he has little or no schooling is seen in the lives of such persons as Benjamin Franklin and Abraham Lincoln. These eminent Americans had the advantage of only a few weeks of schooling; yet they were well educated—in fact, someone has called Franklin "the first educated American." They were self-educated; the school of experience, of life, of "hard knocks" was their school.

Preparation in service is necessary for school employees [1] who have had a large amount of formal education as well as for those who have had little or no formal education; such in-service preparation is, however, especially necessary for the latter type of school employee. By diligent efforts, although much educational malpractice might ensue in the beginning, it would be possible for persons with little formal preparation to become efficient teachers. One of the best teachers whom the present writer has ever known had not advanced beyond the eighth grade in school; he had become an excellent teacher through thirty years of teaching experience and through constant and well-directed efforts at self-education. Unlike many teachers, who repeat in animal-like fashion the experiences of the previous year or years, this teacher critically "reconstructed his experiences." He had thirty years of invigorating and educative experience instead of having merely one experience which he had repeated thirty times.

Preparation in service for teachers is necessary because teaching efficiency cannot remain static. Teaching is a rapidly developing science and art; moreover, changes in society are being made constantly. Although a teacher may have graduated from a renowned college or university, there is danger that he will become a "back number" or an old fogy within a very few years if he does not take steps to keep abreast of constant changes in his profession and in society. Educational research is constantly ascertaining improved techniques of teaching, more valuable subject matter, and better educational aims, materials, and processes in general. It is a preeminent obligation of the teacher to maintain the spirit of the learner, and to keep in touch with the various improvements in his profession and with the rapidly changing society. A person who is not a constant learner can never accomplish his potentialities in any endeavor.

It is an unfortunate commentary that many teachers do not main-

[1] Since teachers are by far the most numerous of the school employees, the remainder of this chapter will be addressed to teachers.

tain the spirit of the learner; they degenerate into teaching automatons. Many of them early permit themselves to "fall into a rut" where they remain throughout their professional lives. In fact, many of them fall into the rut and then proceed to dig the rut deeper; they regress rather than egress. Whereas teaching is potentially one of the most inspiring and intellectualizing professions, many teachers neglect the opportunity to learn which is ever present; they forget that they are dealing with the most stimulating and precious, yet baffling, materials in the world, namely, the minds of pupils. School officials and teachers must constantly battle that most frequently found and devastating disease of all institutions, namely, "institutional paralysis"; although that disease "creeps" and is painless, it will eventually kill its victims if it is not eliminated.

Needed Aspects of In-Service Education of Teachers

The teacher must keep in mind two aspects of his preparation. In the first place, he must be familiar with the developments and discoveries in the field of professional education; in the second place, he must know what is happening in such worlds as those of commerce, politics, art, religion, science, and international relations. He should keep both of these aspects in mind in his preservice preparation as well as in his preparation in service; and he must keep them in mind throughout his teaching career.

If the teacher is familiar with changes in fields outside education as well as developments in education, he is more likely to be expert in instructing and in guiding his pupils and he is more likely to be highly regarded by the community. A teacher should be able to discuss intelligently with other adults what is happening in the world about him; moreover, he should be able to use this information in instructing and in guiding his pupils. He cannot even be the best citizen, without such information, not to mention being the best teacher. To be the most efficient, the teacher must live in the world of affairs, instead of in a cloister; he must be able to speak the language of the people rather than the language of the cloistered pedagogue—a language which has been facetiously dubbed "pedaguese." He must be a real human being, and not be, as Mark Twain once said, a member of a "third sex."

Agencies for In-Service Education of Teachers

The agencies which the teacher may use in in-service preparation are myriad. Many of these agencies are free to him, and those that are not free are relatively inexpensive. All of the agencies are readily available to teachers who desire to use them. In the following paragraphs the more important and the more available of the agencies will be discussed.

Reading by Teachers. Since the invention and the development of printing, reading has been the greatest intellectualizing agency in the world, and thanks to the schools, the people of the United States have become probably the most avid readers in the world. In the United States, thousands of newspapers, magazines, pamphlets, bulletins, books, and other reading matter are published annually. In the United States, approximately two hundred pedagogical magazines are published, and many new books on the subject of professional education are published annually. There is scarcely a school subject which does not have at least one magazine; likewise, there is scarcely a school subject which does not have at least one book dealing with it. There are magazines and books for all types of teachers. As might be guessed, these magazines and books range from poor to excellent, and the teacher must learn to select the best.

New theories and recent discoveries in education are soon chronicled in the better pedagogical magazines and in the new pedagogical books, and it is difficult to see how the teacher can keep entirely up to date on these new theories and recent discoveries without reading regularly one or more of those magazines, and a few of the new books each year. It is, however, an unfortunate commentary that many teachers do not subscribe for even one pedagogical magazine, and that many teachers do not read even one pedagogical book during the year. Almost as unfortunate as reading no pedagogical magazine or book would be the limitation of one's reading to one magazine or book which presented only one view or philosophy of education and of the social order. Such a diet of reading would be likely to indoctrinate one hopelessly and to aid one in committing intellectual suicide.

The reading of a teacher should not, however, be of a purely professional sort; such emphasis would likely make the teacher a "queer pedagogue." The best newspapers, magazines, and books on other subjects with which intellectual leaders such as teachers should be acquainted should be read. Teachers must be broadly cultured persons.

In many schools and school systems, the teachers have organized a reading club, to which each teacher annually contributes a few dollars for the purchase of magazines and books for the members of the club. In some school systems the board of education co-operates with the teachers by annually making a financial contribution to the teachers' library. The magazines and books are placed on a certain shelf in the school library, in the office of the principal, or in another appropriate place where each teacher may have ready access to them.

Daily Preparation by Teachers. One of the most valuable agencies which the teacher may utilize in improving his proficiency is found in the regular preparation and planning for meeting his classes. Although the teacher may have obtained his bachelor's, his master's, or his doctor's degree from a renowned university and may have taught school several years, he should not be guilty of meeting his classes without having made some special preparation for them. Such daily preparation will give the teacher greater confidence in himself, make him more poised, and give the proper direction to his tutelage.

It is not recommended, of course, that the teacher spend all of the day in the classroom, shop, or laboratory, then devote all his evenings and Saturdays and Sundays in preparing to meet his classes the next day or the next week. Life under such a procedure would be drudgery indeed. Moreover, because it might sap the teacher's vitality, such procedure would likely decrease teaching efficiency rather than increase it. All that is here recommended is that a proper quantum of time be devoted to daily preparation, even though it can be only a few minutes. The teacher who does not devote any time to daily preparation is apt to exemplify the expression of the street, "We don't know where we're going, but we're on our way." An artist teacher will be imbued with the spirit of Thomas Arnold, eminent teacher at Rugby. Arnold was once asked why he spent so much of his time in preparing to meet his classes, and his reply was: "I prefer that my students should drink from a running stream, rather than a stagnant pool."

SUPERVISION OF TEACHERS. In practically every school and school system, classroom supervision of some kind and some amount is provided. The supervision is usually given by the school principal, the superintendent of schools, or assistants to these employees. Frequently, though, and especially in the larger school systems, subject, grade, or department supervisors are provided.

Not always, of course, will this supervision be all that it should be; that unfortunate result obtains because supervisors are not always all that they should be. Sometimes it will go no further than inspection and will not be, in fact, supervision. Sometimes the emphasis is too much on "super" and not enough on "vision." Sometimes it will be arbitrary and expressed in mandates from above; sometimes it will be "snoopervision" rather than supervision; sometimes it will be unfriendly and destructive rather than friendly and constructive. Generally, though, in spite of deficiencies, the wide-awake and sympathetic teacher will be able to profit much from it; this is especially true of the young, the inadequately prepared, and the inexperienced teacher. The inexperienced teacher should not hesitate to request help from the experienced, and the latter should give the help, if at all possible. Supervision has been enormously improved in spirit and techniques in recent years.

RATING BY SCHOOL ADMINISTRATORS AND SUPERVISORS OF TEACHERS. The teacher cannot expect to escape being rated and having his services evaluated. Whether he likes it or not, he is constantly being rated and evaluated by his pupils, parents, patrons, school administrators, and the general public. In the estimation of the members of those groups he is an excellent, an inferior, or a mediocre teacher. Of course, these ratings and evaluations are subjective and are therefore not likely to possess high validity. Nevertheless, they are ratings and evaluations, and accurate or inaccurate, they are being used largely to determine the teacher's salary and the teacher's promotion, and his retention or his dismissal. Several states now require an annual evaluation of the efficiency of each teacher.

During recent years, an attempt has been made by members of the teaching profession to develop more objective methods of measuring educational efficiency to supplant the general-impression and subjective method just described. Numerous score cards and rating scales for teachers have been formulated, and ratings have been given according to the progress made by the teacher's pupils. Although none of these methods of rating has yet reached the stage of perfection, teachers can nevertheless profit much from them. They can especially profit when the ratings are made by sympathetic and intelligent school administrators and supervisors. Prospective teachers should know that only a few school administrators and supervisors are Simon Legrees.

Ratings have the advantage of pointing out to the teacher both his merits and his shortcomings. They should, therefore, lead to the eradication or the amelioration of the shortcomings and the retention of the merits. The teacher cannot completely see his merits or his shortcomings, but must have someone apprise him of them. Few persons have a highly developed power of self-appraisal.

INTROSPECTION AND SELF-MEASUREMENT BY TEACHERS. Difficult though the role is, the teacher should try to be "his own most severe critic." He should examine himself from time to time to ascertain any shortcomings, in order that he may correct them. This introspection should continue throughout life, but the process will be most valuable when the teacher is young; it will be most valuable at that time because shortcomings are more easily corrected in the plastic age of youth, and the handicap which the shortcomings entail will be early eliminated and not be permitted to become a life-time incubus. Of course, such introspection should not be carried so far as to cause the teacher to become an extreme introvert or to lose confidence in himself; the teacher should remember that he has merits as well as shortcomings.

In self-measurement the teacher may use any or all of the measuring instruments and devices which superintendents, principals, and other school administrators are accustomed to use in measuring him and his work, or he may devise his own rating instruments or criteria. Indeed, authorities are agreed that most of the objections to rating by school administrators can be obviated through the practice of the teacher rating himself.

SCHOOL VISITATION BY TEACHERS. In educational practice the factor of imitation has always been very potent. Teachers obtain much of their methods from observing other teachers although many of them unfortunately imitate in a blind and aimless manner without attempting to exercise their critical and constructive faculties on the merit of what they are imitating. Observing something first hand is better than seeing a picture of it, reading about it, or hearing about it. Observing the work of excellent schools may, therefore, be advantageously utilized by teachers who wish to keep abreast of the profession. Such schools may be within or without the local system. Many schools and school systems consider school visitation to be so beneficial that they set aside a certain day or days each year for the purpose of permitting teachers to visit other schools and school systems. In many school systems teachers are paid their regular salaries for the time spent in this visitation.

When visitation is made, it should be made to the best schools or school systems available. It is more beneficial to observe a model or an ideal than merely a sample or a mediocre practice. Before planning a school visit, the teacher should make inquiry from his principal, superintendent, supervisor, fellow teachers, and other competent persons about the best schools to visit; usually, too, he should obtain the approval of his administrators and supervisors regarding the schools which he desires to visit, and he should especially obtain this approval when he is paid for the time spent in the visitation—in fact, such approval is often required.

In many school systems, demonstration and observation lessons in the various classes and subjects of instruction are arranged. For example, a certain school arranges a demonstration and observation lesson in sixth-grade geography, to which the sixth-grade teachers of geography of the whole school system are invited. These lessons are usually conducted on Saturday morning or during the late afternoon of a school day in order that teachers will not have to dismiss their classes in order to attend them.

Participation in School Administration by Teachers. The tendency in school administration is toward democracy between school officials and school employees; there is more sharing of views and a greater willingness on the part of all to sacrifice for the common good. Superintendents, principals, and other school employees in administrative positions are more and more calling upon teachers and other school employees for suggestions regarding, and assistance in, the administration of the school or school system. They are more and more assigning various administrative duties to the teachers; these duties are exercised by the teachers as individuals or as members of committees such as those on the curriculum, teachers' salaries, student welfare, teacher welfare, community relations, school supplies, and textbooks.

This tendency toward democracy in school administration is commendable for two reasons. In the first place, it energizes and makes school employees more co-operative, because employees like to know that they are a vital, recognized, and respected part of the school organization and not merely neglected cogs in it. Teachers like to know that they have a part in the planning for the schools. In the second place, democracy in school administration is helpful to the school or school system. Superintendents, principals, and other school administrators cannot be omnipotent; they need the criticisms and the suggestions of their co-workers. These co-workers will often be able to detect a flaw in the thinking and the planning of school administrators which, if not corrected, is likely to harm not only the schools but the school administrators. Loyalty of a teacher to his administrative and supervisory superiors does not demand that the teacher be an eternal "yes-man"; it requires that he be a "no-man" when he believes that such a position would prevent his superiors from making a mistake. It must be sorrowfully remarked, however, that many school administrators insist upon all teachers always being "yes-men."

Teachers should be looking constantly for ways and means of improving their own work and the work of the whole school or school system as well. Practically all principals, superintendents, supervisors, and other administrative and supervisory officers will be glad to have these suggestions, especially if they are made in a spirit of helpfulness and co-operation and not in the spirit of carping criticism. Unfortunately, however, there will probably always be a few administrative and supervisory employees who regard themselves as educational Solomons, and who believe that they do not need the suggestions of anyone. If the teacher is so unlucky as to have an administrator or supervisor of that sort, it will, of course, be difficult, if not impossible, to make suggestions. In such instances suggestions need not be proffered; if given sufficient "rope," autocratic employees will soon "hang themselves." Moreover, excellent teachers are not tied to the galleys of one position; they need not work for autocrats, because they can go to other and more democratic and better school systems.

Institutes and Other Types of Meetings for Teachers. Institutes, conventions, group conferences, and similar types of meetings have been among the most potent agencies for the preparing of teachers in service. Although these agencies do not always realize their potentialities, and although they are frequently criticized as being boresome by teachers, it cannot be gainsaid that when teachers meet together to discuss educational theories, problems, and practices, or to hear lectures on educational topics, they are benefited.

One important professional obligation of the teacher will have been met when he has become a member of his local and his state education associations, and of the National Education Association. The teacher should have membership in these organizations not only because he will receive large benefit from them, but will be lending his aid toward promoting the excellent work which these organizations are doing to advance the welfare of the profession, and the cause of education. When the small membership fee is considered, it is difficult to understand why a larger percentage of the teachers of the United States do not have membership in their state education association and in the National Education Association. Membership in the National Education Association is only five dollars a year, and the *N.E.A. Journal* which comes monthly to every member of the National Education Association is itself worth the annual fee; this splendid magazine is only one of the many advantages which membership in this association brings.

It is an unfortunate commentary that only approximately one-half of the teachers of the nation are members of the National Education Association which is the foremost educational organization in the world. When this membership is compared with the membership which other professional groups have in their organizations, our chagrin is even greater. Approximately two-thirds of the physicians are members of the American Medical Association, and about two-thirds of the dentists are members of the American Dental Association; and their dues are much higher.

Enrollments in the state education associations are much more numerous than in the National Education Association. The state education associations report a membership which is approximately four-fifths of all the teachers of the nation. Each of the state education associations gives a year's subscription to its magazine with each annual enrollment; as a rule, the annual-enrollment fee does not exceed five dollars. Each association has an annual convention, or district conventions in various parts of the state, or both. These conventions are held for the improvement of teachers and to advance the welfare of the profession and the cause of education. All of the state associations maintain a headquarters, usually in the capital city of the state; most of them employ a full-time secretary, and many of them employ other personnel such as research directors, public-relations agents, and teacher-appointment officers. These employees are usually permanent, and together with the officers of the association, which are usually elected annually, they spend their time promoting the interests of the profession and the cause of education.

The first education associations were local, and these have had a tremendous development. According to the National Education Association, the whole United States now has approximately 5,000 local education associations; approximately one-half of these are affiliated with the National Education Association. When it is remembered that there are approximately 50,000 school districts in the United States, it will be seen that local education associations still have much room for development. The larger of the local organizations usually have divisions for the various types of teachers, such as teachers in the elementary schools and teachers in the secondary schools.

By far the more frequent of teachers meetings are those which are held by the local school system. In practically all school systems, these are held regularly, for example, weekly, bi-weekly, monthly, or at another regular interval. In other schools and school systems, the meetings are held only occasionally, usually upon the call of the principal or the superintendent. In some instances, the meetings are held for all members of the educational staff of the school system; that is, they are general meetings. In other instances, particularly in the large school systems, the teachers meet in smaller groups, these groups being determined by the type of work which the teachers are doing.

Local meetings have two purposes; first, to assist in the routine administration of the school; and second, to give professional preparation to the teachers. While meetings for the first purpose are occasionally necessary, meetings for the second purpose are much more important. The more progressive principals and superintendents frown upon the "bulletin-board" type of teachers' meeting which is so often represented under the first purpose. They, moreover, frown upon meetings of the grumbling or grievance type. More and more they are making their announcements, not through meetings, but through typewritten and mimeographed notices, which are handed to the teachers or posted on the bulletin board of the school. They are reserving meetings for discussion of live educational problems—discussion which is calculated to increase the efficiency of the teachers and of the local school or school system. They are discussing such problems as the following: a guidance program for the local schools, teachers' marks, the curriculum, extraclass activities, the selection of textbooks, the improvement of pupil attendance, ways and means of reducing pupil failure, ways and means of reducing pupil elimination from school, and ways and means of meeting individual differences among pupils. At these meetings, also, demonstration lessons in the teaching of a certain school subject or subjects are frequently conducted by a teacher and a regular class of pupils.

RESEARCH BY TEACHERS. Although it is not recommended that the teacher turn his classroom, shop, or laboratory into an experimental laboratory to investigate all sorts of theories and "isms," it is recommended that he always keep an open mind toward plausible educational theories and practices, and occasionally do some experimentation or some investigation on practical school problems. This interest in research will have a two-fold benefit. In the first place, it will benefit the teacher by keeping him constantly growing. Nothing is so fatal to the teacher as for him to obtain the impression that there are no unsolved problems in education, or that he already knows everything about education. In the second place, an interest in the results of research, and an occasional attempt to do research, will be of value to education by adding something to the total of human knowledge regarding education. Few theories and few practices of education have been scientifically tested and evaluated, and there are few theories and few practices concerning which anyone can be sure. If teachers cannot answer some of the questions or solve some of the problems, they can at least contribute much information on them which eventually may lead to a solution.

The classroom teacher has one of the best opportunities of any member of the profession to conduct research, especially on problems of teaching method and pupil learning. He has the pupils in an environment which is normal—a condition that does not obtain even in the best experimental laboratories of the colleges or universities. In many respects the elementary- and secondary-school teacher is in a better situation to conduct research than the professor in a college or university.

Attending Summer Schools and Extension Courses by Teachers. One of the most significant educational developments during recent years is the large growth of summer schools for college and university students. The growth of these schools has been caused primarily by the increased enrollments of teachers. A large percentage of the teachers are enrolled as students each summer in courses in the teacher-preparing institutions of the United States, and most of these students are experienced teachers who choose to spend their so-called "vacations" in preparing themselves better for their work. Statistics on enrollments in extension and correspondence courses are not available, but observation shows that such courses are popular with teachers.

This large attendance at summer schools and in extension and correspondence courses speaks well for the desire of the teachers of the United States to improve their qualifications. Represented in this huge army of students are persons who are trying to bring their preparation up to standard, and students who are working beyond standards which are normally set for members of the profession. Large numbers of members of the profession are studying for graduate degrees, because more and more a graduate degree or the equivalent is the immediate goal toward which teachers are striving.

It would be possible, of course, for the teacher to pursue summer courses, correspondence courses, and extension courses to the detriment of his health, or to the injury of his vocational efficiency. During the school year, extension courses and correspondence courses are no doubt occasionally pursued on Saturdays and during evenings when the teacher should be spending that time in resting, in recreation, or in preparing to meet his classes, or to do his other work for the next day or the next week.

Many school systems, particularly the larger ones, encourage summer-school study by giving a financial reward for it. This reward is usually given on the basis of the number of credits earned, and there is unfortunately no attempt to ascertain whether the credits actually contribute to teaching efficiency. Many school systems give a bonus of, say, $50, $75, or $100 for teachers who earn a given number of credits at summer school. In other school systems, teachers who are enrolled in summer school are given permanent salary increases. Some school systems also give a financial reward to teachers who take extension courses or correspondence courses during the school year; the amount of financial reward is usually determined by the number of credits obtained by such study.

Participation in Workshops for Teachers. During recent years, thousands of workshops for teachers, school administrators, and other groups of school employees have been conducted, and the movement is still growing. Most of these workshops have been held under the auspices of the colleges and universities, while others have been conducted by local school systems and by state departments of education. They are usually held during the summer months when local schools are not in session, but they are sometimes held on Saturdays and in the evenings.

The *Dictionary of Education* defines a workshop as follows:

> An arrangement under which special facilities, including particularly a wealth of source material and specialized personnel for group and individual conferences, are provided by an educational institution for individualized or small group study of educational problems that are of special interest to advanced students of education or to teachers in service; frequently provided in such areas as curriculum, administration, guidance, higher education, and secondary education.[2]

Exchange Teaching by Teachers. A few school systems permit their teachers, under the rules and regulations of the board of education, to exchange positions with teachers in other school systems for a given period of time, usually a year. For many years the practice of exchanging teachers has been fairly common in the colleges and universities, and is beginning to appear in the elementary and the secondary schools. It is a practice which should be encouraged, because the experience of teaching elsewhere is often a stimulus to the teacher, particularly to one who has been in the same position for several years. Such a teacher can hardly fail to learn much which he could use in improving his own teaching and in improving the local school system.

Travel by Teachers. In the process of learning there is no full substitute for seeing a thing with one's own eyes. Travel gives the

[2] Carter V. Good, ed., *Dictionary of Education*, McGraw-Hill Book Company, 1945, p. 453.

individual that opportunity. By means of the automobile, the railroad, the steamship, and the airplane, teachers are traveling more and more, and are becoming acquainted with geography, history, and other aspects of civilization much more completely than their predecessors could have ever dreamed. Their instruction can hardly fail to be enriched and vitalized from this experience.

Participation by Teachers in Community Life. Through the proper type and the proper amount of participation in churches, clubs, Parent-Teacher Associations, and other activities of community life, the teacher may learn much which will assist him in developing the proper emotional tone and life perspective which are so essential. Such participation should enable the teacher to make another contribution to community welfare and progress. The teacher should not live in a cloister; he should become acquainted with some people. To

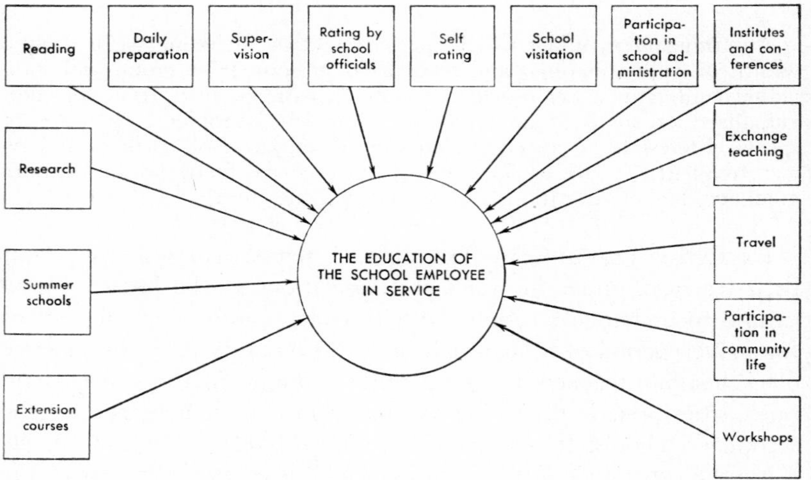

Fig. 63. The chief agencies contributing to the in-service education of the teacher. These agencies are professional education primarily; of course, there are thousands of other agencies for general education.

know his fellow teachers is necessary, but his social and his professional contacts should not be limited to teachers; he needs to "rub elbows" with members of other community groups.

It would be possible for the teacher, of course, to spend too much time in participating in community life. The teacher should never carry such participation so far as to prevent him from spending an ample amount of time in preparing for his classes, or should he permit it to absorb energy and enthusiasm requisite for meeting his classes.

The first obligation of the teacher is to his pupils; his obligation to participate in community life is secondary. Not even so worthy an institution as the church should be permitted by the teacher to take energy and time which may be needed by his pupils. If the teaching of a Sunday-school class, for example, would keep the teacher from doing his best work with his regular school pupils, he should not obligate himself to teach a Sunday-school class.

Miscellaneous Agencies for In-Service Education of Teachers. It has already been remarked that the agencies which the teacher may use in trying to keep abreast of his profession are legion; manifestly every new experience is educational. Within the limits set for this chapter, it has been possible to discuss here only a few of the more important and the more readily available of those agencies. It has not been possible to discuss such important intellectualizing agencies as the radio, television, public lectures, and the theater. It is obvious, however, that these agencies are very potent, and they are available to every teacher who cares to make use of them.

QUESTIONS FOR DISCUSSION

1. What percentage of your experiences and ideas do you estimate that you have obtained from the institutional school, and what percentage from the "school of experience?" Explain.

2. Do you believe that the schools are giving pupils enough preparation for continuing their education after they have left school? Discuss. Briefly outline a school program which you believe would give that preparation in the elementary and the secondary schools.

3. In view of the teacher's association with the immature minds of his pupils, is there danger of the teacher's mind retrogressing? If there is such a danger, how may it be guarded against? Discuss.

4. Account for the fact that some of the best teachers have had little college preparation. Would such preparation have made them even better teachers? Discuss.

5. It has been charged that most school employees reach their maximum efficiency within a few years, say, six to eight years. Do you believe that this is true? Is it easier for the teacher to get into a rut than the workers in other vocations? Explain.

6. Discuss the importance of introspection, self-criticism, and self-

measurement in improving personal efficiency. Discuss also the importance of having the frank criticism of a good friend in correcting one's shortcomings.

7. As a teacher, assume that you have $200 to spend each year in self-improvement. Make a budget for this expenditure. Explain.

8. Do you believe that the dismissing of school for teachers' meetings or for visiting days for teachers is justifiable? Discuss. Should teachers be paid their regular salaries for such time? Explain. Should school administrators indicate the schools which teachers shall visit on visiting days? Why or why not?

9. How do you explain the fact that so small a percentage of the teachers are members of the National Education Association? Is this small percentage a mark against the profession? Why or why not?

10. In many schools and school systems, daily lesson plans are required of teachers. Do you regard such plans as contributing to teacher improvement? Why or why not? How much time do you believe the teacher should spend in preparing to meet his classes the next day? Does this depend? How?

11. Make a list of what you consider to be the five best magazines for elementary-school teachers. Do the same for secondary-school teachers. Also make a list of the five best general magazines from which teachers would profit greatly by reading. What are a few of the great newspapers? Why?

12. It has often been charged that research and literary work cause the teacher to neglect his teaching duties and make him a poorer teacher. Do you agree with such a point of view? Explain.

13. Teachers have been criticized for talking "shop" too much outside school hours. Do you believe that this is a just criticism, or is the practice a compliment? Discuss.

14. Has it been your observation that teachers are "thin-skinned" and resent or are easily "crushed" by any adverse criticism of their work? Discuss.

15. Would you favor a state law which required every teacher to attend summer school from time to time? Why or why not? Should teachers be given extra pay for such attendance? Explain. Should school officials be permitted to choose the college or university which the teacher shall attend? Why or why not?

16. Can you mention other agencies for education in service which teachers may use? What?

SELECTED REFERENCES

Aker, Howard M., "Can In-Service Training Succeed on a Voluntary Basis?" *American School Board Journal,* Vol. 139 (September, 1954), pp. 34–35.

Presents the findings of an evaluation of Milwaukee's in-service education program.

Bruce, William F., and Holden, A. John, *The Teacher's Personal Development*, Henry Holt and Co., New York, 1957, 346 pp.

Discusses the interpersonal relations of the teacher.

Dible, Earl W., "Use Colored Slides to Demonstrate Teaching Techniques," *Nation's Schools*, Vol. 54 (November, 1954), pp. 84, 85, 86.

Describes the contributions which colored slides can make to an in-service training program; tips given on kinds of pictures to take and how to use them.

Hagerman, Rita E., "Visiting Around," *NEA Journal*, Vol. 44 (January, 1955), pp. 28–29.

A teacher can return to his own classroom with new insight and new ideas after spending a half-day or longer visiting in other classrooms.

Hankins, C. F., *Extended Leave for Public School Teachers in Large City School Systems*, George Peabody College for Teachers, Nashville, Tenn., 1939, 10 pp.

Describes practices in cities of 100,000 population and above.

Homier, G. A. Custer, "New Teachers Want Just Treatment, Positive Information," *Nation's Schools*, Vol. 54 (October, 1954), pp. 50, 51.

Discusses some of the common problems encountered by new teachers. These problems were in the following areas: (1) teaching load, (2) philosophy and policy in regard to discipline and discipline problems, (3) administrative policies and personnel, and (4) general orientation.

Hunt, Herold C., "Personal and Family Finances," *Nation's Schools*, Vol. 55 (March, 1955), pp. 48–50.

Describes in-service training program in personal and family finances for teachers.

"Local Education Associations at Work," *Research Bulletin* of the National Education Association, Vol. 26 (October, 1948), pp. 103–139.

Discusses such topics as organization and types of activities.

Lowe, Joe, "5 Steps to Higher Staff Morale," *School Executive*, Vol. 74 (September, 1954), pp. 54–55.

Discusses the administrator's responsibility in building and maintaining staff morale. Five suggestions were listed; they were: (1) administrators should let the staff know they are making worth while contributions, (2) administrators should encourage the staff to share in the development of school policies, (3) administrators should offer sympathetic understanding, (4) administrators should offer the staff help necessary to get the results expected, and (5) staff members want honesty from their administrator.

CHAPTER 20

Public-School Relations

Definition of Public-School Relations

Public-school relations are those activities which seek to bring a harmonious working relationship between the schools and the public which the schools serve. The public relations go on, whether school officials and school employees are conscious of them or not; they are inevitable and go on at all times. A good public-school relations program must meet the four following standards:

1. The program should be planned the same as every phase of the work of the schools.
2. Every school official and every school employee must realize that he is a public-relations agent of the school or school system. He must do his work efficiently, and he must practice good human relations.
3. The public-relations program of the schools should be based on public co-operation with the program. It is not a one-way street.
4. Provisions should be made in the public-relations program for public information about the schools.

Although the term public-school relations is often used interchangeably with the term school publicity, the former is a more appropriate term to use. In the first place, public-school relations has a broader and more accurate connotation, because a large portion of the work of public-school relations falls outside the realm of school publicity. In the second place, the term is more appropriate, because in many quarters the term, school publicity, has acquired an unsavory connotation. To many people, publicity implies selfishness, a cover-up policy, propaganda, press-agentry, or always putting-the-best-foot-forward, irrespective of merit, truth, or ethics.

Importance of Desirable Public-School Relationships

Many school employees neglect to perform their public-relations functions because they are not aware of these functions. Many others deem that what the school does is none of the business of the public. The latter employees act as if they owned the schools. Such an attitude occasionally resembles the public-be-damned attitude, but more often it may be characterized as the public-be-shunned attitude. In the following paragraphs the importance of the school promoting intelligent and harmonious relationships with the home and with all other parts of the community will be discussed.

Ownership of the Schools. The foundation of any worth while public-relations program consists in providing accurate and complete information concerning the school. In providing this information school employees might profitably take some lessons from the practice of private businesses in providing information to their stockholders, their employees, and the public. Every well-managed private business is providing this information largely through advertising, but other means are not being neglected. Companies which are owned by stockholders, as most companies are, are taking steps toward keeping the stockholders regularly informed regarding the earnings and the financial condition of the business; they are giving this information through periodic reports, because they realize that companies which do not make periodic reports of their earnings and their financial condition are likely to be regarded with suspicion by stockholders.

In school affairs all the people are the "stockholders," and they have the same right to have accurate, complete, and continuous information regarding the aims, the progress, the plans, and the needs of the school as do the stockholders of private businesses. The welfare and the progress of the school are determined largely by how the people regard the school. How the people regard the school is determined largely by what they know about it. Abraham Lincoln, who was one of the greatest believers in democracy, once said: "Public sentiment is everything. With public sentiment nothing can fail; without it nothing can succeed."

The schools were established by the people, they have always been financed by the people, and therefore they belong to the people. The schools are regarded by the people as their most precious public possession—a possession concerning which they desire continuous information. In consequence, it is more than an opportunity which school employees have of keeping the people informed about their most precious possession; it is their duty to provide this information. To fail to provide it becomes almost a species of unethical practice on the part of school employees.

Pupil Progress. Since the school exists for the pupils, the test of its efficiency is the extent to which the pupils attain their educational potentialities. To have the most efficient school, there must be co-operation between the school and all community groups. In particular, there must be co-operation between the home and the school. The home should be made to know that the school is working assiduously to advance the welfare of the pupils; it should not be permitted to believe that school employees are demons. Likewise, school employees should keep in mind always the point of view of the home, and they should realize that children are the most precious possession of the home.

Support of the Schools. Expenditures for schools during recent years have increased by leaps and bounds. Since public information regarding the schools has not kept pace with school expenditures, a large percentage of the public has become disgruntled over these expenditures. Many critics of the schools have affirmed that school officials and school employees have engaged in an orgy of expenditure and that there is danger of public bankruptcy unless a halt to the expenditures is called. If school officials and school employees had studiously taken the public into their confidence and had informed it regarding such matters as the importance of education and how the school money was being spent, there would not have been so much adverse criticism of the expenditures for schools.

For the public's moral and financial support of the schools, a public-relations program is necessary at all times. Such a program is necessary in prosperous times as well as in times of adversity. It is especially necessary in times of financial stress or other community difficulty. Because of the growing difficulty of obtaining money for the schools, it will likely be more necessary in the future than it has been in the past.

To summarize, it may be said that the public desires to be informed about the school, and that it is entitled to be informed. Furthermore, the public will be informed in some manner. School employees, therefore, must choose between whether they will provide such information, or whether they will permit the public to obtain the information through hearsay, rumor, or other unreliable sources. School employees should not forget that they serve the general public as well as the pupils and the parents of the pupils.

Growing Difficulties in Providing School Information

At the same time that the task of providing school information to the public has been becoming more important, it has also been growing more difficult. The reasons for this increasing difficulty are not far to seek.

Increasing Size and Complexity of Modern Education. Education is not only the largest public business, but it is also one of the most complex businesses—public or private, and it is constantly growing larger and more complex. The growing size of modern education is shown by school statistics which may be readily obtained from any local, any state, or any Federal school report. Regarding the complexity of education, it may be stated that, contrary to common belief, education is an exceedingly technical and complex enterprise. Education is concerned with the human mind—at once the most baffling and the most precious "mechanism" in the world. Persons who have studied the educative process over a period of many years readily admit that the greater their study, the more baffled they become.

In the early days making provision for schooling was fairly easy. Schooling then was provided in the "little red schoolhouse" having one teacher, a few pupils, and a meager curriculum consisting in many instances of only the "three R's." It is a far cry from those simple provisions to the palatial school buildings of today with their hundreds of teachers, their thousands of pupils, and their curricula of dozens of school subjects. This development has added numerous tasks to the work day of school employees and has made it more difficult for the public to keep informed about the school. In brief, there is much more about the school of modern times to give information concerning, and to obtain information concerning, than ever before, and as the work of the school grows in size and in complexity, this difficulty increases.

Increasing Competition of School Information With Other Interests. At the same time that education has grown in size and in complexity, other phases of life have broadened, have intensified, and have become more complex. Mr. Average Citizen of today has infinitely more interests than his parents and his grandparents had. This is the era of the automobile and the airplane, not the oxcart and the horse and buggy. This is the day of hundreds of activities which were unknown only a few years ago. The individual of today must keep informed on each of the activities if he is to keep abreast of the world of affairs.

School employees should realize that school information competes with the many other types of activities and information, and they must take steps to see that it receives the proper share of the time of the individual. They must keep in mind that by far the major portion of the waking hours of the average person must be used in providing for food, clothing, shelter, and recreation, and in meeting other responsibilities for himself and for his family. They must remember that only a small percentage of those waking hours can be spent by the individual in keeping himself informed and that school information must compete with information on economics, politics, inventions, science, sports, amusements, religion, international relations, and myriad other topics.

Standards for School Information

Truthfulness. The first criterion which information concerning the school should meet is truthfulness. Untruthful information is worse than no information, because it is certain to lessen the confidence of the people in their schools and in school employees. If the people are once given untruthful information, there is danger that they will thereafter be skeptical of the veracity of persons who were responsible for disseminating such information. The people do not like to be "fooled," Barnum notwithstanding.

The truth, though, does not need to be "shouted from the housetops." Some types of information may be ethically withheld. Often "silence is golden." In deciding whether to release certain information concerning the school, the welfare of the pupils should be the criterion. If presenting the information would injure the welfare of any pupil and would serve no useful public purpose, it should not be presented.

There are several types of information pertaining to pupils and to school-employee personnel which should not be disseminated. Among these confidential types of school information are the following: information which school employees have obtained concerning individual pupils and their homes, the marks given by or received by individual teachers on examinations, and the suspension or the expulsion from school of individual pupils. The dissemination of such information would not serve any public purpose except, perhaps, to satisfy idle curiosity; moreover, its dissemination might embarrass some persons unnecessarily. The policy of determining what information to present and what not to present might well be patterned after the motto of an eminent newspaper, namely, "All the news that is fit to print," motto of *The New York Times*.

CONTINUITY. School information consists of two kinds: (1) continuous, and (2) spasmodic. The latter kind is usually provided in publicity campaigns when the schools are making a request for something. Although publicity campaigns are occasionally necessary for the adoption of a new tax rate, a bond issue, or for some other purpose, the emphasis should be on continuous information. If the people are kept in ignorance of their schools until something is wanted from them, they are likely to be suspicious not only of any request which is made but of the persons who make the request. On the other hand, if the people have been taken into the confidence of school employees and have been provided with continuous information concerning the schools, they are likely to support the schools during foul as well as fair weather.

In performing their public-relations function, school employees might well take a lesson from the astute candidate for public office. Such a candidate is likely to be campaigning throughout the 365 days of the year, whereas his less discerning opponent is likely to be ignoring the electorate until a few days or a few weeks before the election. The latter type of candidate is more likely to have something done to him rather than for him.

HUMANIZED INFORMATION. School information should be presented in such manner that all community groups can understand it and would be interested in it. School information, in short, should be humanized. With the proper attention given to its presentation, even somewhat technical information can be presented in such manner that it will meet this criterion. Needless to say, good English should always be used.

In presenting school information, the school personnel should keep in mind the many interests, the various culture patterns, and the different levels of education which are found among the people of the community. In an attempt to meet various culture patterns, some schools of the large cities send out notices and pupil reports written in different languages. There is always danger that information which would be interesting to and understood by a given group would not be interesting to and understood by other groups.

Proper Amount and Desirable Balance in School Information. Although most schools and school systems fail to provide the people with ample information concerning their activities, some school employees spend too much time and energy in providing it. The latter sort of school employees would be more highly regarded by the public if they spent more of their time and energy in performance rather than in publicizing what they have done, are doing, or are planning to do. School information should never appear to be advertising or press-agenting.

In addition to possessing the proper quantity, school information should be balanced, that is, no department or phase of the work of the school should receive more information than that to which it is entitled, and no department or phase of the work of the school should be slighted. In a study made by Belmont M. Farley, it was found that in their public-relations programs school employees have tended to emphasize types of school information in which the people are only secondarily interested, such as athletics, and to neglect providing them with information on other school activities in which they are primarily interested. Farley found that the newspapers gave athletics and other extracurricular activities 47.1 per cent of the space devoted to school information and that this item ranked first in amount of news space; on the contrary, the parents strangely ranked this item at the bottom in their desires for information.[1]

[1] B. M. Farley, *What to Tell the People About the Public Schools*, Columbia University, 1929, pp. 35, 49.

Public-school Relations
Agents and Agencies

Public-school relations agents are the persons who are responsible for planning and for carrying out the program of public-school relations. Among such agents are the members of the board of education, the superintendent of schools and his assistants, the supervisors, the principals, the teachers, and the school janitors. The persons who have just been mentioned may be classified as active agents in the public-school relations program. In addition to these active agents, there are several more or less passive agents; among these passive agents are the alumni organizations, the mothers' clubs, and the Parent-Teacher Associations. Sometimes, though, these passive agents become very active.

Public-school relations agencies are the means or the instruments of public-school relations agents in carrying out the public-school relations program. Among the more widely used of these agencies are the following: student newspapers and magazines, community newspapers, school house organs (that is, employees' magazines), pupils' and teachers' handbooks, school bulletins, letters to pupils and to parents, school catalogues, courses of study, school exhibits, the cinema, the school plant, radio talks, television, talks before various groups, and social contacts.

We shall have to be content in this book to discuss the place of a few of the more important agents and agencies. Since teachers constitute by far the largest group of school employees, they will be emphasized. Teachers have the pupils under their immediate jurisdiction, and the pupils are the connecting link between the school and the home and the community.

Work of the School in Public-school Relations. The first requisite for a desirable public-relations program of the school is an efficient school, and the teacher makes the school largely what it is. If the school is efficient, it will receive desirable word-of-mouth publicity which is the most valuable type of publicity to secure. On the other hand, if the work of the school is inefficient, all of the publicity imaginable cannot make the people believe that it is efficient. To paraphrase an old saying, the people cannot hear what is said about the school, when what the school is constantly dins their ears.

In disseminating information and good will concerning the school, the pupil—at least when taken collectively—is unquestionably the most potent agent. He disseminates such information and good will from the first day of school to the last day. He "hears much, sees much, and says much." At the close of the first day of school, when the pupil reaches home, his parents and other members of his family are certain to ask him how he liked his teacher, and how he liked school. Moreover, they will repeat the question numerous times during the school year, and the same question will be asked by other relatives and other acquaintances. In answering the question, the pupil will compliment the school, or he will condemn it. Since the school is a large part of his world, the pupil will talk about his school even though he has not been questioned about it. He will say that he likes the school, or that he doesn't like it. Moreover, he will be specific; he will relate what goes on in the classroom, on the playground, and in other school activities and affairs.

Since the pupil is the chief dispenser of word-of-mouth information concerning the school, school employees should not only conduct the best school possible but should attempt to give the pupil appropriate information concerning the aims and the progress of the school. The types and the amount of information which the school gives the pupils will be determined by the grade level of the pupils. Information might well be presented on such matters as the following: school expenditures, school curriculum, provisions of the compulsory school-attendance laws, and rules and regulations pertaining to pupil discipline. If pupils are given such information, they will be more efficient and more co-operative in the school, and when they become parents and voters, they are likely to continue to be co-operative.

In his work the school employee must practice good human relations both in school and out. Through this practice he can help to make and to keep friends for both himself and the schools. People who "try giving themselves away"—who are on the alert to extend proper kindnesses to others—have acquired the art of good human relations. The essence of this art is found in the Golden Rule as stated in Luke, 6:31: "And as ye would that men should do to you, do ye also to them likewise."

School Visitation by Parents. In many schools and school systems, particularly those of the larger cities, parents and school employees do not become acquainted. Thousands of parents never enter the school building. This lack of acquaintance between parents and teachers is unfortunate because the school and the home are working for the same aim—namely, the education of the child. This aim can be accomplished only through full co-operation between the home and the school. That co-operation can best be effected when the school and the home are acquainted. There is an old adage which says, "Familiarity breeds contempt," but it can be more truly said that lack of acquaintance breeds suspicion, if not contempt.

School employees should, therefore, encourage visitation to the school. "The latchstring is always out" should be the announced policy of the school. Because of their vital interest in the school, parents should be especially encouraged to visit the school. If they are invited and made to know that they are welcome, many parents will visit the school, but there will be a large percentage which cannot or will not visit unless special inducements are made. Many schools and school systems are making special inducements for visitation through such means as the following: special visiting days, night sessions of school, school exhibits, and school programs by the pupils.

Home Visitation by Teachers. In the early days the practice was for the teacher to visit every home at least once during the school year; in fact, to visit the home was a part of the contract of the teacher, and the teacher did not object to this stipulation because these visits largely provided him with his living accommodations. In those days the teacher "boarded around," staying at one home a few days, then going to another home. Although the plan of "boarding around" had many disadvantages, it had the advantage of permitting the members of the home and of the school to become acquainted. All parties concerned liked the plan.

In more recent years, contrary to early practice, home visitation by teachers has been little practiced. There would, however, be distinct advantages in such visitation. In fact, some school systems consider such visitation to be so important that they require teachers, particularly in the elementary school, to visit, at least once a year, every home represented among their pupils.

In such visitation the aim is not to "spy" on the home, but merely to become acquainted with the parents and to obtain and to give information in order that greater and better service may be given the pupil. Any teacher with intelligence and with tact should be able to make such a visit not only enjoyable and profitable to himself, but helpful to the home and to the pupil as well.

Parent-Teacher Association in Public-school Relations. The Parent-Teacher Association has for its fundamental purpose the bringing of the school and the home into closer acquaintance with the hope that co-operation between them will be obtained. Parent-Teacher Associations on a national basis date back to the National Congress of Mothers, which was founded in 1897. That name was changed in 1907 to the National Congress of Mothers and Parent-Teacher Associations. The name of the present national organization is the National Congress of Parents and Teachers, and was adopted in 1924. The national organization publishes a monthly magazine entitled, *The National Parent-Teacher Magazine*, and this contains much vital information of interest to both teachers and parents.

Local units of Parent-Teacher Associations now exist in thousands of communities and are found in every state of the United States, and in many foreign countries. Anyone who is interested in schools and the education of children is eligible for membership, although the bulk of the membership is made up of school officials, school employees, and parents of school children. Membership in the organization has increased very rapidly, going from 31,642 in 1912 to more than 7,000,000 today. In many communities school officials expect all teachers to be members of the Parent-Teacher Association.

The basic ideals of the organization are altruistic, "nonpolitical," nonsectarian, and noncommercial. The aims of the organization as stated in the National By-Laws, Article II, are as follows:

> First, to promote child welfare in home, school, church, and community; to raise the standards of home life; to secure more adequate laws for the care and protection of children.
>
> Second, to bring into closer relation the home and the school, that parents and teachers may co-operate intelligently in the training of the child; and to develop between educators and the general public such united efforts as will secure for every child the highest advantages in physical, mental, moral, and spiritual education.

In addition to making parents and school employees and school officials acquainted with one another, and in addition to providing the various members of these groups with vital information and with desirable viewpoints, the Parent-Teacher Association can forge ahead and gain other achievements. The following are a few of the achievements which such an organization might have to its credit:

1. Health education may be promoted, particularly in the elementary school. In many schools hot lunches have been sponsored by the association. In many schools, also, the association has promoted campaigns for cleanliness, balanced diets, better teeth, safety, thrift, etc.
2. Many associations have aided the school in obtaining new equipment, supplies, or other materials, conveniences, and facilities. The associations have sometimes obtained the funds for such purposes from entertainments, and other private sources; and at other times, they have stimulated boards of education to provide the funds.
3. When the school system must ask the voters to approve tax levies or bond issues for the school system, the Parent-Teacher Association can do heroic work. The endorsement of the Parent-Teacher Association of a proposal for school funds or for other school purposes should be obtained if at all possible as one of the first, if not the first, acts in a publicity campaign.

Adult-education Programs in Public-school Relations. The largest school development during recent years has been the establishment of adult-education programs in the schools. Thousands of schools and school systems now sponsor these programs in the evening for the adults of the community, and in the whole nation millions of adults are enrolled in the program. In some school systems, the enrollment of adults in the evening-school program is higher than the enrollment of regular pupils in the day schools. In addition to aiding the adult population to extend its education, these programs enable the school to acquaint its adult constituency with its purposes and its procedures. Schools and school systems which have sponsored excellent programs of adult education have found the voters willing to grant ample school revenue and to co-operate with the schools in other ways. Prospective school employees must prepare themselves to aid in the adult-education program of the school.

School-employee Participation in Community Life. Many school employees are dubbed as failures because they do not know how to participate properly in community life; in fact, this is one of the largest causes of teacher failure. Many fail because they do not participate at all; others fail because they overparticipate; and still others fail because certain phases of their participation are offensive to the community or to a portion of it. The problem, therefore, which comes to every school employee is that of participating in the correct amount and in the proper manner.

More and more, the school employee is expected to participate in

FIG. 64. Learning to read English in a class for foreign-born adults. *(Courtesy of the Detroit, Michigan, public schools.)* Adult classes in practically all of the day-school subjects are now organized in small as well as large school systems.

the various phases of community life. When in Rome, people are expected to live as Romans. The school employee cannot always live his life as he would like. He must keep in mind that communities have their mores and their idiosyncrasies, and that each community expects at least a certain amount of conformity to its manners and customs; the Romans do not live exactly as the Athenians.

Shall the school employee dance, play cards, or engage in other types of recreation and amusement over which persons and communities differ? His decision on these matters cannot be based entirely upon his own desires; it must take into account also the mores of the community and the welfare of the school. No school employee has the right to live his life in such a way that his opportunity to obtain the best results with his pupils is injured. If the school employee feels that he must have certain forms of recreation or amusement, and the community in which he is working frowns upon those forms of recreation or amusement, he should consider the advisability of transferring to a community which is in agreement with his beliefs. Better still, of course, the school employee should know those matters before he accepts employment in what later turns out to be a provincial community. Teachers are now offering their services in a seller's market.

Overparticipation in the life of the community is as harmful to the teacher's success as underparticipation. The teacher has only a certain amount of time and energy, and the first drain upon that time and energy should be his school work. To permit the work of his pupils to suffer because of his outside activities is an unpardonable sin. In fact, such a worthy project as teaching a Sunday-school class should not be undertaken by the teacher if the time and the energy devoted to the project results in robbing his regular pupils.

Another warning should be mentioned. The teacher should be tactful and discreet in all his language and all his actions. If he is untactful or indiscreet, he will injure not only his own prestige, but the prestige of his profession and of his school and school system. If he gossips, does not pay his bills promptly, or in other ways does not live appropriately, he will injure not only himself, but the whole cause of education. In the language of the Code of Ethics of the National Education Association the teacher should "adhere to any reasonable pattern of behavior accepted by the community for professional persons."

Student Publications in Public-school Relations. Among the more important types of publicity media of a school are the student publications, such as the daily or weekly paper, the monthly magazine, the annual or yearbook, and the handbook. In addition to their value in mirroring the school's ideals, aspirations, and accomplishments, student publications can be to the teaching of English what the laboratory is to chemistry or to physics, or what a farm plot is to agriculture. Still more, these publications may become one of the most effective agencies in developing and sustaining an excellent morale among the student body of the school.

Most of the student publications are found, as would be expected, in the larger secondary schools. The elementary schools and the smaller secondary schools obviously find it more difficult to edit, to prepare, and to finance them. Because lithographed or mimeographed editions are cheaper, many of the smaller schools have substituted them for printed editions.

In all types of schools, especially in the smaller ones, the tendency during recent years has been away from the publication of school annuals and magazines and toward the publication of school newspapers which appear more frequently. In rural communities many of the secondary schools, which formerly published separate annuals, are now co-operating in the publication of a county annual; by this plan the expense for each school is greatly reduced. Other small secondary schools bind each year the various copies of the school newspaper and make this volume serve as a school annual.

Most of the large secondary schools, and many of the small ones, provide each student with a handbook of the school. Student handbooks are also found in many junior high schools. A handbook serves the purpose of answering questions regarding the curriculum, the school requirements, the traditions, the student organizations, and other vital features of the school. A handbook should be one of the first student publications, because it is a great saver of time both for the students and for the faculty.

In practically all schools the supervision of the student publications is delegated to one or more of the teachers of the school. Because of their preparation in English composition, teachers of English and of journalism are usually delegated this responsibility. Teachers who are qualified to supervise this work are more likely to obtain positions and at a larger salary. They can prepare for the work through such means as taking courses in journalism, serving on the editorial boards of college publications, and reading about student publications.

QUESTIONS FOR DISCUSSION

1. What are the principles of good human relations? Discuss their importance to the school employee.
2. Compare the public-relations problem of the school employee in the small community with that in the large community. Which is more difficult? Why?
3. Discuss the relative importance of each of the following groups as public-relations agents of the school: school officials, teachers, pupils, and parents.
4. Outline your concept of a reasonable social and recreational program for the teacher personnel.
5. What is meant by community personality? Are communities noted primarily for their similarities or for their dissimilarities? Explain.
6. Should the school employee contribute to community projects, such as the Red Cross, community chest, the Y.M.C.A., the Salvation Army, and the churches? Explain.

7. Should the school employee try to "educate" the community to his point of view? Explain. To what extent, if any, is the school employee justified in being a propagandist? Discuss. Is he ever justified in being a propagandist with his pupils? Is propaganda always bad? Discuss.

8. Discuss the importance of the school employees' dress in public-school relations. Discuss also the importance of his personal habits. Should the school employee smoke? Why or why not?

9. Should the school employee teach a Sunday-school class, be a candidate for public office, join the W.C.T.U., attend Sunday baseball games, or dance? Discuss.

10. What are some ways in which a Parent-Teacher Association may assist the school? Should teachers participate in the work of Parent-Teacher Associations? Why or why not? Should school officials require teachers to become members of this organization? Why or why not?

11. Should the school employee live in the community in which he works? Explain. Should he do his shopping in that community?

12. Do you believe that pupils know enough about the school as an institution? Explain. By what appropriate means could they be made better informed?

SELECTED REFERENCES

Brownell, Clifford Lee, *et al., Public Relations in Education,* McGraw-Hill Book Co., 1955, 256 pp.

Says that the school program itself is the most important factor in good public relations.

Carruth, Irby B., "Human Relations Inside the School," *School Executive,* Vol. 71 (June, 1952), pp. 73–74.

Says that a sound public-relations program begins with a fine quality of human relations within the schools.

Curb, Frances, "The Whole Town Was Talking," *NEA Journal,* Vol. 43 (September, 1954), p. 361.

Lawton, Oklahoma, really brought the schools to the attention of the public during American Education Week. Radio, TV, and the press helped greatly. Ministers even gave special sermons on education.

Grinnell, J. E., and Young, Raymond J., *The School and the Community,* The Ronald Press Co., New York, 1955, 444 pp.

Covers various phases of school-community relations.

Hagman, Harlan L., "Seven Concepts of School Public Relations," *Nation's Schools,* Vol. 40 (November, 1947), pp. 23–25.

An excellent statement.

Hedlund, Paul A., "Measuring Public Opinion on School Issues," *American School Board Journal,* Vol. 116 (April, 1948), pp. 29–31, 86.

A discussion of the public-opinion poll.

Hersey, John, "Citizen's Activities," *School Executive*, Vol. 74 (January, 1955), pp. 74–75.

Indicates that citizen groups have progressed from being only money-raising organizations to the point that they influence legislatures.

Horn, Gunnar, *Public-School Publicity*, Inor Publishing Co., New York, 1948, 226 pp.

A guide for teachers and school administrators.

Lane, Bess B., "Corralling Parents," *NEA Journal*, Vol. 43 (October, 1954), pp. 402–403.

Here are some proven methods of getting parents to visit the classroom.

Lippitt, Ronald, "Better Human Relations," *School Executive*, Vol. 67 (January, 1948), pp. 47–49.

Suggests that school administrators, teachers, pupils, and parents be brought closer to the same opinions.

National Scholastic Press Association, University of Minnesota, Minneapolis, Minn.

This association publishes manuals and score cards for student publications and performs many other services for such publications.

"Public Relations in Secondary Schools," *Bulletin of the National Association of Secondary School Principals*, Vol. 32 (February, 1948), 310 pp.

A series of forty-two articles.

Reeder, Ward G., *An Introduction to Public School Relations*, Revised edition, The Macmillan Co., New York, 1953, 287 pp.

A general treatise on the subject.

Sholy, G. I., "Home Visits Break the Ice," *School Executive*, Vol. 74 (September, 1954), p. 53.

A tried-and-true way, but a time-consuming one, is the home visit paid parents by teachers at the beginning of school. The article shows clearly the enthusiasm and co-operation home visits can bring.

Sigband, Norman Bruce, "Make Your Public Relations Letter Perfect," *Nation's Schools*, Vol. 55 (March, 1955), pp. 65–66.

Discusses the use of letters in the public-relations program.

Van Delden, E. H., "The 10 Basic Principles of Sound Human Relations," *Personnel*, Vol. 25 (March, 1949), pp. 313–319.

An interesting discussion by an industrial executive.

Yeager, William A., *School-Community Relations*, The Dryden Press, New York, 1953, 460 pp.

Relates the public-relations work of the school to other institutions of the community.

CHAPTER 21

The Ethics of Teachers and of College Students

Importance and Scope of Ethics

Before any group of workers can emerge into the status of profession it must have evolved a quantum of professional standards for governing the practices of its members, and it must have taken steps to make certain that these standards are known to and are followed by the members. Throughout the centuries, teachers have gradually evolved such standards, and during recent years have crystallized them into codes of ethics. This chapter aims to give teachers and prospective teachers a better acquaintance with these standards and codes and to urge and to point the way to the continuous development and acceptance of more worthy standards and codes. Ethical standards can never be perfect; they must change with times and conditions, and it is hoped that they will always be improved.

Much as he might wish that privilege, no person can live as he pleases. Everyone is an inescapable member of society and in all of his actions must keep in mind the welfare of society as well as his individual welfare. The rule of "the tooth and the claw" is probably inevitable with the beasts of the jungle, but will not suffice to govern the lives of human beings in a civilized society. A society in which each person did as he pleased, or in which each group did as it pleased, would soon fall into anarchy and constant war and could not long survive. The best test of the amount of civilization of any society is the degree of development of ethical standards by and for that society; the same test may be applied to any person or to any group of persons.

People do not inherit ethics, but they must learn them through precept and example. This learning process continues throughout life; through the process some persons come to possess high ethical standards whereas others seem to be content with low ones. Persons who possess the latter standards usually do not acquire them premeditatively; as a rule, they are victims of their environment—of the tutelage of homes, schools, churches, and the many other agencies which sometimes have lax and low standards. If all persons could be taught and would follow ethical standards, through the ubiquity of such standards the selfishness and the strife of the world would be abolished and a Christian millenium would have arrived. The several million present and former college students should accept the challenge of living by, and of inculcating in other persons, those high standards; they should constantly demonstrate that education makes people more ethical.

Among college students, as among the general population, a few individuals of lax ethical standards are found. These lax standards among college students are usually concerned with cheating on examinations, plagiarism in term papers and other school work, poor sportsmanship in athletics and in other contests, and neglect of studying and of meeting other scholastic responsibilities. These and other evidences of perverted vision are, of course, more common among the students of certain colleges than among those of others, and they sometimes exist among college faculties as well as among college students. They are one of the greatest blights upon college life, and they should be eliminated through faculty and student cooperation.

Persons who do not maintain a high regard for ethics when they are college students are not likely to be recommended for, or to be successful in, teaching positions. "Good character" is the most universal requirement for obtaining and keeping a teaching certificate. Students, therefore, who are preparing to enter the teaching profession should be especially solicitous concerning their ethics; they should remember that a devil of today is not likely to be promoted to a saint tomorrow. Nothing will so quickly and so surely handicap one's chances for success in life as failure to abide by the principles of ethics which have been established by society for the conduct of all persons. Until a better one is developed, if ever, the chief code of ethics which everyone should learn and follow is the Decalogue; the superstructure of one's ethical principles can safely be erected on this firm foundation.

Evolution of Ethical Standards. Even primitive man early saw the need for formulating rules to govern the more friction-causing relations among the members of his group (family and tribe) and among his group and other groups. He soon learned that all members of the group must have a certain amount of education and that the selfish members must be throttled in order to assure the happiness and the safety of all the group, and he soon discovered that the protection of his group against other groups could be best found in group solidarity. He developed many ethics, primitive though they were. For example, the punishment which his code of justice decreed for evil doers was "an eye for an eye and a tooth for a tooth." In dealing with other groups his guiding ethic was: "Thou shalt not betray one of thine own to the forces of that other world." His rules, laws, and ethics were brutally realistic, and they kept in mind primarily the welfare of his group; they had not yet been tempered with the spirit of the Golden Rule and the other lofty principles of Christianity.

As he falteringly marched through the dark and devious corridors of time toward the flickering light of civilization, man progressively discovered that he could not have personal safety, security, and happiness without "sweat and tears" and without altruistic co-operation with his group and with all other groups. He gradually learned that "group solidarity" could be carried too far for the welfare of a larger society. His practices and his laws came more and more to have an ethical basis, and constantly the plane of this basis has been raised according to the principles of Christianity. That plane, of course, needs to be raised much further under the tutelage of the home, the school, the church, and the other educational agencies of society, because too many differences among individuals, between capital and labor, among nations, and among other groups are still being resolved by jungle and gangster methods. Members of the teaching profession cannot make their greatest contributions to raising the ethical plane of human relations, unless their own ethics are on a high plane; they must be good examples in all their practices.

As Aristotle says, "Correct thyself first, and if you find yourself perfect, then you may correct others."

Definitions of Ethics. The term ethics is derived from the Greek word *ethos* meaning "the character, sentiment, or disposition of a community or people." According to the original meaning of the term, ethical conduct was customary conduct. During modern times, though, ethics has come to comprehend more than the customary. It has come to comprehend the ideal. It now signifies moral duty. It is now the highest type of law—higher even than statutory law—and should be the basis of all individual and group conduct. Therefore, to define ethics as "the science of moral duty" would be in conformity with the more enlightened theory of today.

The preceding paragraph has defined ethics as "the science of moral duty." What constitutes moral duty? In other words, what is ethical conduct, and what is unethical conduct? Conduct is ethical if it makes for efficient human relations, regards the rights of other persons, and advances the well-being of society. Conversely, conduct which begets friction and social loss is unethical.

Whether an act is ethical or unethical must be determined, therefore, by the effect which the act has upon the well-being of society. The setting of the act has much to do with determining whether the act is ethical or unethical. An act which is ethical under one set of conditions may not be ethical under slightly different conditions. Conversely, an act which is unethical under one set of conditions may be ethical under slightly different conditions. This is only a way of saying that the consequences of an act, that is, the effect of this act upon society, determine the moral quality of behavior. Critical and constructive experience must, therefore, always be the father of ethical standards; it must, in fact, be the father of all worth while standards. That experience must be guided by a belief in the "brotherhood of man and the fatherhood of God"; it must stem from a deep sense of values.

Definition and Purposes of Codes of Ethics

Definition. Civilized man has always had a penchant for organizing his principles and his laws into codes of various kinds. A code of ethics is an organized list of some of the more important "thou shall's" and "thou shall not's" for the members of a given vocation, organization, or other group. It points out examples of ethical and of unethical practice for the members of the group. It states the standards of conduct, for which the group as a whole stands.

Although a code of ethics presents rules or principles of conduct, it is not designed to supplant the Decalogue, or to take the place of statutory law; neither is it designed to cover every practice of the members of the group. There are, of course, thousands of practices for the members of any group, and no usable code of ethics could mention all of the practices. Many volumes would be required to list and to discuss all of the principles of ethics which civilization has evolved.

Purposes. A code of ethics serves two purposes. In the first place, it informs all members of the group regarding some of the more common unethical practices which should be avoided, and regarding some of the more common ethical practices which should be followed. In the teaching profession, for example, the need for serving these purposes becomes more clear when it is realized that many members of the profession are guilty of unethical practices because they are not informed on what constitutes ethical and unethical practice. What has just been said applies particularly to beginning teachers. These neophytes often engage in practices which they would not follow if they were better informed; they are not willingly unethical. They often apply for positions, for instance, without first ascertaining whether the positions are vacant; they are not aware that to engage in such practice might undermine a fellow member of the profession and might injure the prestige of the profession and the welfare of society.

In the second place, a code of ethics serves to warn any careless or venal members of the group who, knowing the difference between ethical and unethical practice might yet be tempted to engage in unethical practice, that the group frowns upon unethical practices. Every profession has its unwelcome quota of Judas Iscariots, and the teaching profession is no exception. A code of ethics serves as a warning to any potential traitors of the profession and of society. It deters such persons, although it may not always thwart them.

It would be possible, of course, for a group to make selfishness rather than altruism the motive of its code. For example, the code might be used as a charter for giving members of the group too many rights and too few obligations; it might be used as an instrument for robbing the public in order that the selfish interests of the members of a group might be advanced. Gangsters often have codes which serve their nefarious purposes the same as righteous groups have codes which point the way to personal sacrifice and service to society. There are Nietzschean philosophies and codes which preach self-assertion, and there are Christian philosophies and codes which invoke brotherly love. There is a *Mein Kampf* as well as a *Holy Bible*. Fortunately, gangster philosophies and codes have never been able to compete successfully with the philosophies and codes of Christianity and democracy; and still more fortunately, gangster philosophies and codes are short-lived.

Few groups which have adopted codes of ethics have abandoned them, and this would seem to be evidence that such codes have served useful purposes. Codes of ethics have frequently been amended or reformulated to keep them up to date, but few groups have abandoned them. Moreover, the rapidly developing tendency for various trades, businesses, professions, and other groups to formulate and adopt codes of ethics gives further evidence that such codes are serving a useful purpose.

Codes of Ethics for Other Groups

The First Code of Ethics. The germ of modern codes of ethics dates back at least to the fourth century B.C. In that century the ancient physician, Hippocrates, promulgated his famous *Oath*. The influence of that oath is fully realized when it is known that the Principles of Medical Ethics of the American Medical Association have long embodied the lofty ideals which the oath expressed. The ending of the oath is quoted herewith:

> While I continue to keep this oath unviolated, may it be granted to me to enjoy life and the practice of the art, respected by all men in all times! But should I trespass and violate this oath, may the reverse be my lot!

The second profession to adopt a code of ethics was the profession of law. In 1836, David Hoffman, of Baltimore, formulated a set of resolutions containing ethical principles which were based on the philosophy of Blackstone, eminent English jurist. The present canons of ethics of the American Bar Association are based largely upon the Hoffman resolutions.

In 1852, the American Pharmaceutical Association formulated its code which, with certain revisions, is still in use. In 1866, the American Veterinary Medical Association adopted a code which, with certain amendments, it still follows.

LATER DEVELOPMENT OF CODES OF ETHICS. Following 1866, few groups adopted codes of ethics until the opening of the twentieth century. Whether the relation was casual or fortuitous is not known, but there was a large movement toward the adoption of such codes immediately following World War I. Perhaps it was the soaring regard for democracy following that war which gave the code-of-ethics movement maximum force, or perhaps it was the business depression of 1921–22 which immediately followed the war and which brought a large amount of unemployment, wage and price cutting, and unfair business practices, that caused codes of ethics to be developed to control professional and business relations. Both causes likely played a part. Whatever the cause of the impetus toward the code-of-ethics movement immediately following that war, certain it is that there was an impetus at that time. In 1921, at least seventeen national groups adopted codes; in 1922, at least twenty-six; and in 1923, at least sixty.

Another large impetus was given the code-of-ethics movement by the National Industrial Recovery Act, voted by the United States Congress and signed by President Franklin D. Roosevelt in 1933. That act was called forth by the severe business depression which started in the latter part of 1929 and continued for several years. It permitted each industry or business to formulate a code of fair business practice which, when it had obtained the approval of the President of the United States, became binding upon all firms doing business in that particular line. The act was declared unconstitutional by the United States Supreme Court in 1935, but during the two years of its life hundreds of industries and other businesses adopted codes of business practice designed to stop any unjustified cutting of wages and prices, and to eliminate other practices of unfair competition.

To summarize, hundreds of industries, trades, professions, and other groups now have some sort of creed, rules of action, or code of ethics. In fact, there are few groups, especially of any size and cohesion, which do not have such a document. Many groups which do not have such codes are considering the formulation and adoption of them. Of course, some of these codes have in mind too much the welfare of the group and not enough the welfare of all the people; many of them merely sloganize the desires of selfish interests.

Codes of Ethics for Teachers

State and Local Codes of Ethics. Compared with other professions, the teaching profession was tardy in developing and adopting codes of ethics. The first codes were developed by state and local education associations. The first state education association to formulate such a code was that of Georgia. On July 14, 1896, the state teachers' association met in annual convention at Cumberland, Georgia, and adopted a code of ethics for the teachers of that state. The preamble of the Georgia code affirmed the purpose of the code to be as follows:

> To assist teachers in settling delicate and difficult questions of professional conduct and propriety, to quicken their sympathies for each other, and for all who are engaged in the work of teaching, to exalt their professional ideals and to increase their love for the profession, this code is devised.

California was the second state whose state education association adopted a code of ethics, such action being taken in 1904. Alabama took similar action in 1908, being the third state. Gradually the good leaven spread to other states and local communities, and at present approximately two-thirds of the state education associations and many local associations have adopted codes of ethics.

An analysis of the various state and local codes shows that there are many matters upon which most of the codes deem it necessary to have pronouncements. Most of the codes have pronouncements on the following matters: (1) preservice and in-service preparation of the members of the profession; (2) salary and other evidences of advancement in the profession; (3) contracts and tenure of teachers; (4) relations between teachers; (5) relations between teachers and school officials; (6) relations of teachers with pupils; (7) relations of teachers with parents and the community; and (8) relations of teachers with publishing and school-supply houses, teachers' agencies, and other private businesses.

Since the adoption in 1929 of the Code of Ethics for the National Education Association of the United States, the state and local education associations have tended to follow that national code and to permit their state and local codes to fall into disuse. The merit of the tendency to follow the national code can be much increased by state and local associations appointing code commissions which would help to publicize and to enforce the national code and to seek its revision where needed. It would probably be better to have one known and enforced code than to have several codes that are unknown and unenforced.

Code of Ethics of the National Education Association. At the 1924 annual meeting of the National Education Association, a report on a code of ethics for teachers was presented to the representative assembly of the Association on behalf of the California State Council of Education. The report memorialized the Association with the following request, among others, "To appoint a committee to formulate and adopt an official body of ethical principles." Acting upon the request just stated, the representative assembly of the Association adopted a motion "providing for the appointment of a committee to formulate for the National Education Association a code of ethics for teachers." [1] That committee was appointed in November, 1924, and its continuance was authorized by the representative assembly at the 1925, 1926, 1927, and 1928 meetings of the Association; it completed its assignment in 1929.

After extensive investigations of the codes of ethics of state and local education associations, and of other professions, and after a questionnaire study of what members of the teaching profession considered to be the more frequent unethical practices of teachers, the Committee on Ethics of the National Education Association formulated a Code of Ethics. This code was recommended for adoption to the representative assembly of the National Education Association in 1929, and was unanimously adopted by the assembly of the Association.

The 1929 code was in effect until 1935 when a slightly revised code was adopted by the representative assembly of the Association. The latter code was amended in 1941, 1944, 1949, and 1952. Although it is not perfect—probably no code could ever be made perfect—it may be regarded as a code worthy of the loyalty of all members of the

[1] May Wade, "Report of Committee on a Code of Professional Ethics for Teachers," Addresses and Proceedings, *National Education Association*, 1924, pp. 285–288.

profession. It should be read critically and constructively by every member of the profession. Equally, each member of the profession should lend his efforts to the improvement of the code where improvement is needed. The code follows:

Code of Ethics of the National Education Association of the United States

We, THE MEMBERS of the National Education Association of the United States, hold these truths to be self-evident—

—that the primary purpose of education in the United States is to develop citizens who will safeguard, strengthen, and improve the democracy obtained thru a representative government;

—that the achievement of effective democracy in all aspects of American life and the maintenance of our national ideals depend upon making acceptable educational opportunities available to all;

—that the quality of education reflects the ideals, motives, preparation, and conduct of the members of the teaching profession;

—that whoever chooses teaching as a career assumes the obligation to conduct himself in accordance with the ideals of the profession.

As a guide for the teaching profession, the members of the National Education Association have adopted this code of professional ethics. Since all teachers should be members of a united profession, the basic principles herein enumerated apply to all persons engaged in the professional aspects of education—elementary, secondary, and collegiate.

First Principle: The primary obligation of the teaching profession is to guide children, youth, and adults in the pursuit of knowledge and skills, to prepare them in the ways of democracy, and to help them to become happy, useful, self-supporting citizens. The ultimate strength of the nation lies in the social responsibility, economic competence, and moral strength of the individual American.

In fulfilling the obligations of this first principle the teacher will—

1. Deal justly and impartially with students regardless of their physical, mental, emotional, political, economic, social, racial, or religious characteristics.
2. Recognize the differences among students and seek to meet their individual needs.
3. Encourage students to formulate and work for high individual goals in the development of their physical, intellectual, creative, and spiritual endowments.
4. Aid students to develop an understanding and appreciation not only of the opportunities and benefits of American democracy but also of their obligations to it.
5. Respect the right of every student to have confidential information about himself withheld except when its release is to authorized agencies or is required by law.

6. Accept no remuneration for tutoring except in accordance with approved policies of the governing board.

Second Principle: The members of the teaching profession share with parents the task of shaping each student's purposes and acts toward socially acceptable ends. The effectiveness of many methods of teaching is dependent upon co-operative relationships with the home.

In fulfilling the obligations of this second principle the teacher will—

1. Respect the basic responsibility of parents for their children.
2. Seek to establish friendly and co-operative relationships with the home.
3. Help to increase the student's confidence in his own home and avoid disparaging remarks which might undermine that confidence.
4. Provide parents with information that will serve the best interests of their children, and be discreet with information received from parents.
5. Keep parents informed about the progress of their children as interpreted in terms of the purposes of the school.

Third Principle: The teaching profession occupies a position of public trust involving not only the individual teacher's personal conduct, but also the interaction of the school and the community. Education is most effective when these many relationships operate in a friendly, co-operative, and constructive manner.

In fulfilling the obligations of this third principle the teacher will—

1. Adhere to any reasonable pattern of behavior accepted by the community for professional persons.
2. Perform the duties of citizenship, and participate in community activities with due consideration for his obligations to his students, his family, and himself.
3. Discuss controversial issues from an objective point of view, thereby keeping his class free from partisan opinions.
4. Recognize that the public schools belong to the people of the community, encourge lay participation in shaping the purposes of the school, and strive to keep the public informed of the educational program which is being provided.
5. Respect the community in which he is employed and be loyal to the school system, community, state, and nation.
6. Work to improve education in the community and to strengthen the community's moral, spiritual, and intellectual life.

Fourth Principle: The members of the teaching profession have inescapable obligations with respect to employment. These obligations are nearly always shared employer-employee responsibilities based upon mutual respect and good faith.

In fulfilling the obligations of this fourth principle the teacher will—

1. Conduct professional business thru the proper channels.
2. Refrain from discussing confidential and official information with unauthorized persons.
3. Apply for employment on the basis of competence only, and

avoid asking for a specific position known to be filled by another teacher.

4. Seek employment in a professional manner, avoiding such practices as the indiscriminate distribution of applications.
5. Refuse to accept a position when the vacancy has been created through unprofessional activity or pending controversy over professional policy or the application of unjust personnel practices and procedures.
6. Adhere to the conditions of a contract until service thereunder has been performed, the contract has been terminated by mutual consent, or the contract has otherwise been legally terminated.
7. Give and expect due notice before a change of position is to be made.
8. Be fair in all recommendations that are given concerning the work of other teachers.
9. Accept no compensation from producers of instructional supplies when one's recommendations affect the local purchase or use of such teaching aids.
10. Engage in no gainful employment, outside of his contract, where the employment affects adversely his professional status or impairs his standing with students, associates, and the community.
11. Co-operate in the development of school policies and assume one's professional obligations thereby incurred.
12. Accept one's obligation to the employing board for maintaining a professional level of service.

Fifth Principle: The teaching profession is distinguished from many other occupations by the uniqueness and quality of the professional relationships among all teachers. Community support and respect are influenced by the standards of teachers and their attitudes toward teaching and other teachers.

In fulfilling the obligations of this fifth principle the teacher will—

1. Deal with other members of the profession in the same manner as he himself wishes to be treated.
2. Stand by other teachers who have acted on his behalf and at his request.
3. Speak constructively of other teachers, but report honestly to responsible persons in matters involving the welfare of students, the school system, and the profession.
4. Maintain active membership in professional organizations and, thru participation, strive to attain the objectives that justify such organized groups.
5. Seek to make professional growth continuous by such procedures as study, research, travel, conferences, and attendance at professional meetings.
6. Make the teaching profession so attractive in ideals and practices that sincere and able young people will want to enter it.

ENFORCEMENT OF CODES OF ETHICS

IMPROVEMENT OF ENFORCEMENT OF CODES. It would be of no avail for a profession to have a code of ethics, if the members of the profession were unfamiliar with the provisions of the code, or if they were familiar with the provisions and did not abide by them. A profession has the obligation of seeing that all of its members become familiar with the provisions of its code of ethics and of obtaining the co-operation of all of its members in abiding by the provisions. Failure of even a small percentage of the members to know and to follow those provisions is likely to bring both the code and the profession into disrepute. A profession has the important and the difficult responsibilities among its members of educating the ignorant and of thwarting the vicious.

WHAT OTHER PROFESSIONS ARE DOING IN CODE ENFORCEMENT. Other professions, including the teaching profession, might profitably take several suggestions from the medical profession in the matter of making their codes of ethics known to all members. For many years the colleges of medicine have taught "The Principles of Medical Ethics of the American Medical Association" to all neophyte physicians before graduation. Not only is formal instruction in the provisions of the physicians' code given early in the course of study, but at every opportunity throughout the course of study the members of the faculty of the college of medicine attempt to inculcate the ideals of this code in the neophyte physician. In consequence, it would seem safe to conclude that the members of the medical profession know the provisions of their code better than the members of any other profession. Colleges of nursing, and of law, during recent years have followed the practice of colleges of medicine in making known the provisions of their codes.

Many professions, moreover, have created local committees on ethical standards and have given these committees the duty of bringing to trial any local members who have been accused of unethical conduct. These committees frequently recommend the disbarment of persons who have been adjudged guilty of breach of professional ethics. Lawyers and physicians have been especially prominent among the members of professions taking such steps to enforce their codes of ethics, and their activities have resulted in building up a large amount of literature dealing with the interpretation of the codes of their professions.

What Teachers Are Doing and Might Do in Code Enforcement. The provisions of the Code of Ethics of the National Education Association are not known by a large number of the members of the teaching profession; in fact, many members have never even heard of this national code or of the code of their state education association. There is, therefore, a large work before the teaching profession in making the provisions of its code of ethics known to every member of the profession and in obtaining the co-operation of every member in abiding by the provisions.

In submitting the Code of Ethics to the representative assembly of the National Education Association in 1929, the Committee on Ethics recommended that steps be taken to acquaint each member of the profession with the provisions of the code. The revised code which was adopted at the meeting of the Association in 1935 made the following recommendations regarding publicizing and enforcing the provisions of the code:

> To be an effective and workable document a code of ethics must be more than words on paper. Like a government constitution, it comes fully alive only when interpreted and construed as specific questions arise. And, usually, only when it has been so interpreted can the need for amendment be determined. Thus, both the fullest use and the improvement of this code depend on the development of a body of code interpretations. In this the NEA membership can be most helpful.
>
> In order to make such interpretations possible, the NEA Committee on Professional Ethics has adopted a program of issuing opinions construing specific sections of the code. The committee issues these opinions on the basis of questions submitted. Members may present questions to the committee in either of two ways: describe the facts in an actual situation, and ask the committee to interpret the code in the light of those facts; or describe a hypothetical case, and ask the committee how the code would apply in such a situation.
>
> Members of the committee hope these opinions not only will serve to inform the profession as to accepted ethical practices, but also along with the code itself will be a valuable source of materials for workshops and courses in professional ethics in schools of education. The American Bar Association has followed a similar plan of issuing opinions with respect to its code for more than 25 years. Study of these opinions constitutes an important part of courses in ethics at leading law schools.
>
> The committee will carefully consider all requests for interpretations, but it reserves the right to determine those matters on which it will

render formal opinions. In any event, neither the names of persons nor school systems involved will be revealed.

Requests for opinions should be addressed to the Committee on Professional Ethics, NEA headquarters.

Inquiry shows that not much has been done by the teaching profession to enforce the observance of ethical standards among its members. When teaching certificates are refused or are revoked because of unethical conduct, the action is almost always taken by school officials and the community. For an offending teacher to be brought to trial by the members of his profession and for a penalty to be recommended for proved guilt are virtually unknown. Until state and local associations of teachers create code commissions or other machinery for publicizing and enforcing their codes of ethics, the teaching profession will not have acquired the full stature of a profession. Such code commissions and similar machinery are almost universal among physicians and lawyers, and are fairly common among the members of a few other professions, but are almost unknown among teachers. Such machinery, well oiled and always ready for use when needed, is a characteristic of every full-grown profession, and the teaching profession should not longer delay acquiring that machinery.

Violations of Ethical Standards by Teacher

Whether teachers more frequently violate the ethical standards of their profession than the members of other professions violate their standards is not definitely known. Considerable observation and some organized research lead, however, to the conclusion that teachers rank favorably with the members of other professions in their regard for ethical standards. When violations occur, they are usually the outcome of ignorance of what constitutes ethical practice; they are seldom the result of malicious intent. Most violations are of the positive sort, that is, they exhibit no action where ethical action is expected. Investigations show that the following violations of ethical standards are fairly common among teachers:

A. *Relations between teachers, and between teachers and school officials*

1. Criticizing and gossiping about associates, predecessors, and suc-

cessors. Investigation shows that this is the most frequent "sin" of teachers.
2. Interfering with the work of other teachers in such matters as pupil discipline and pupil marking.
3. Breaking professional confidences.
4. Failure to expose any corrupt or otherwise unprofessional practice among teachers and school officials. This is probably the most frequent negative violation of ethical standards.
5. Failure to co-operate properly with school officials and to support school policies until they are changed.
6. Use of nepotism and otherwise taking unfair advantage of one's position. Some types of nepotism are illegal in many states.
7. Extending special favors to the children of school officials and other influential persons, and pandering in other ways to persons of influence.
8. "Going over the heads" of one's administrative superiors, especially without notifying them of the action.

B. *Relations with pupils*
1. Tutoring one's regular pupils for extra pay or other special rewards; also selling items to one's own pupils.
2. Embarrassing pupils by gossiping about their I.Q.'s and other confidential matters concerning them.
3. Trying to impose one's political, economic, religious, or other personal beliefs upon pupils.
4. Showing favoritism in marks, discipline, and other matters concerning pupils.
5. Failure to deal with pupils in a spirit of democracy.

C. *Relations with parents and with the community*
1. Showing disregard for the social standards of the community, and failure to participate in any activities for the improvement of the community.
2. Participating in community activities to the extent of harming one's teaching efficiency.
3. Failure to take steps to maintain friendly and otherwise helpful relations with parents.

D. *Salary and professional advancement*
1. Applying for positions not known to be vacant, and otherwise undermining occupants of positions.
2. "Broadcasting" of applications, especially by mimeographed or printed letters.
3. Failure to withdraw outstanding applications for other positions after a contract for a position has been signed.
4. Attempting to obtain or to keep a position through the use of family, political, religious, fraternal, or any other type of "pull."
5. Filing of applications with other than professional officers of the school system.
6. Creating unjust prejudice against competitors for a position.

7. "Kow-towing" to school officials with the expectation of receiving reward.
8. Seeking an offer of a position elsewhere merely to obtain an increase in salary or other promotion in one's present position.
9. Failure to help worthy teachers to obtain positions and promotions. School administrators are frequently guilty of this violation; many of them will not recommend their employees for other positions because they do not want to lose their services or to be put to the bother of obtaining successors.
10. Underbidding for positions.
11. Engaging in, or threatening to engage in, a strike in order to obtain an increase in salary. Strikes of teachers are now illegal in many states.
12. Malingering or otherwise taking unfair advantage of the sick-leave policies of boards of education.

E. *Contracts and tenure*

1. Failure to keep one's contract inviolate until released by the second party to it. Practically all school officials will release employees from their contracts, even though the release frequently means a loss to the efficiency of the school system.
2. Giving so short a notice of resignation that school officials can't readily find a successor for the position vacated.

F. *Relations with business firms*

1. Accepting commissions, royalties, or other favors, from publishing and supply houses, teachers' agencies, and other business firms for contracts over which teachers have exercised or can exercise a decision.
2. Soliciting free books from publishing houses when there is not an expectation of examining them for prospective textbooks. For teachers to sell such gift books is especially heinous.
3. Refusal to pay one's debts, especially when able to do so.

G. *Miscellaneous violations*

1. Slurring the profession and at the same time doing nothing to improve its standards.
2. Failure to keep in mind the necessity for professional growth.

When the number of teachers engaging in them is considered, strikes constitute during recent years one of the most serious violations of the codes of ethics of the teaching profession. Although the number of teacher groups engaging in strikes has not been large, it has been sufficiently large, especially in the larger cities, to cause the legislatures of many states to enact laws prohibiting strikes among all public employees.

Ethics and the College Student

In attempting to develop a higher regard for ethics, college students will be helped by carefully reading and always practicing the following "Code of Ethics for College Students" which was prepared by Professor Harold H. Titus and his students at Denison University. Professor Titus properly suggests, however, that greatest value from the code will come to students who constructively criticize it, revise it where needed, and always adapt it to their local situation.

A Code of Ethics for College Students

General Statement

1. The purpose of education is development, which includes intellectual, spiritual, social, and physical enrichment. While emphasis upon any one phase of life to the exclusion of others is undesirable, the primary purpose of a college is intellectual development; hence this should take precedence over social life, athletics, and mere grades. If a student is not in college for this purpose, his position is ethically indefensible, since he is wasting both his own and other's time and money.
2. The college student should keep mentally alert and be openminded and tolerant, not only of his studies and classes, but in following the affairs of the world at large.

1. Personal Factors

1. A student should regard his personal honor as of supreme importance. He should avoid the philosophy that any means are justifiable to procure good grades. He should be honest and fair, during examinations as at all other times, to himself, to his fellow students, to his professors, and to the school.
2. The student should be prompt in keeping appointments and in class attendance, since delays cause loss of time and inconvenience to others. Promptness in completing assigned work is important for one's own character and self-respect and is also essential for the efficient conduct of a class.
3. Students should remember that they represent a large investment of time and money, which only efficient public service will justify. Later on, human lives may depend upon their knowledge and skill.
4. The college student should, at all times and in every way in his power, keep physically fit, realizing that the best kind of creative living is made possible by good health. A reasonable amount of attention should be given to personal appearance.

2. Inter-Student Relationships

1. Students should recognize the need for student government and should co-operate with the officers of such organizations. Students should realize the purpose of rules and regulations and aid in their enforcement. Where the duties and responsibilities of office call for the enforcement of rules, students should support an officer for rigidly living up to the duties of office. Laxness, rather than faithfulness, should lead to censure.
2. Rules set up by student associations or administrative orders should be respected and obeyed. A student is free to voice his opposition to such rules and to propose changes at any time. His only honorable courses of action are: (1) To obey a rule. (2) While obeying the rule, if he considers it to be unwise or unjust, and of sufficient importance, to study its effect and to present relevant facts, and his own views, to the proper officers of the student association or to the administration of the school, and ask for a reconsideration of the rule. (3) To leave the school and register at an institution where he can be happy and retain his self-respect. He should not resort to the demoralizing practices of secrecy and evasion.
3. A student may help another student where the help is for the purpose of instructing or of clarifying the work. In no case should a student do another's lesson where this merely relieves the other of work and prevents him from receiving the discipline and training which such work brings. It is dishonorable to assist or to permit others to receive help from one's papers.
4. A student should recognize the value of a wide and deep circle of college friendships. He should not judge another student on the basis of money or of clothes, not let fraternity lines prejudice his opinion. Class, fraternity, or sorority prejudice must be avoided. Individuals must be judged on the basis of personal and intrinsic worth alone.
5. Relationships between fraternities and sororities should be that of cordiality and friendly co-operation. A student should not speak disparagingly of another social group; especially should he refrain from talking to prospective students about other social groups in such a manner as to lower them in the eyes of the prospective student. To discriminate against students because of membership or lack of membership in any social group is unethical.

3. Students and Extra-Curricular Activities

1. A student should take responsibilities and co-operate in his college or class activities insofar as these do not jeopardize his scholastic advancement. If he accepts responsibility or membership in a group, he should contribute to it to the best of his ability.
2. A student should not accept more employment or "student aid" than

he can adequately handle along with his studies and extra-curricular activities. He must be thoroughly honest in recording his time.

3. Students should not accept "student aid" if they do not need such financial help, especially if another person who needs the help is thereby deprived of it.
4. Where scholarships and fellowships are granted on the basis of need, and are not merely a recognition of superior scholarship, a student who does not need such help should refrain from applying for it.
5. A student should maintain a high ideal of sportsmanship at athletic contests, whether as a spectator or as a participant, realizing that clean sport and fair play are more important than victories. The decision of referees should be respected by players and by spectators.
6. A student should not play politics in school affairs. Organizations and teams should be free from group politics.

4. Students and the University (Including Faculty and Administration)

1. A student should be courteous and respectful to members of the faculty and regard them as fellow students and advisers. He should, however, have and exercise the right of free thought and open discussion in and out of the classroom.
2. When choosing a course, the subject matter of the course and his own immediate or future need of it should be a student's first consideration, not the fact that it is considered "a snap" or that he may be able to make good grades in it.
3. College property, laboratory equipment, and library books should be handled with the same care that he would give to his own property. Since he is only one of many who may need such books and material, regulations regarding their use should be rigidly observed.
4. The student should refrain from destructive criticism, but he may make any necessary constructive criticism to the responsible parties. He should not criticize the school or its members in public unless real grievances continue which private criticism and discussions have failed to remedy. He should keep the welfare of the school always in mind, and neither by word nor by act reflect upon the good character and high standing of the college.
5. Efforts should be made to cultivate a relationship of mutual friendliness between students and members of the faculty.

QUESTIONS FOR DISCUSSION

1. Do the members of the teaching profession need a code of ethics as much as the members of other professions? Why or why not?

2. Many persons are opposed to all codes of ethics, because they

believe that they place a stricture upon thinking. Do you agree with that view? Explain. Can ethical principles be taught as something inviolable? Why or why not?

3. According to your observation, what are some of the most frequent unethical practices of teachers? Why do you believe these practices to be unethical?

4. What is the difference between an ethical code and a legal code? Would it be ethical for a teacher to violate a legal code? Explain.

5. To what extent may it be assumed that a code of ethics covers all duties and obligations of the members of a group? Explain.

6. Compared with other professions, how may the tardiness of the teaching profession in developing a code of ethics be explained?

7. Since the National Education Association has adopted a code of ethics, is there further need for state and local codes? Why or why not?

8. Does the Code of Ethics of the National Education Association contain any provisions with which you disagree? Does it contain any omissions? Are any of its provisions opposed to the best interests of society? Which ones?

9. How do you account for the fact that physicians always know the provisions of their code of ethics and follow them more carefully than the members of most other groups follow their codes?

10. What means can you suggest whereby members of the teaching profession may be made familiar with the provisions of the Code of Ethics of the National Education Association? By what means may such a code be enforced? What punishment, if any, should be given to violators of the code?

11. Two weeks before the beginning of the school term a teacher received an offer of another position at an increase in salary of $300 annually. She desired to accept the offer, but her employers would not release her from her contract. Should the teacher have broken her contract and accepted the other position?

12. A principal promoted a pupil who had been failed by his teacher. Was the action of the principal ethical?

13. The teachers of a certain school system entered a strike to obtain higher salaries. Is it ethical for teachers to engage in strikes? For what purposes, if any?

14. A teacher published the semester marks and the intelligence quotients of his pupils. Was this action a violation of ethical standards?

15. A wealthy pupil presented his teacher with a new automobile as a Christmas gift. Should the teacher accept the gift? How about a gift of an apple?

16. A student sees another student cheating during an examination. Should he report the student to the instructor or take any other action on the matter?

17. A few years ago a professor wrote a magazine article in which he plagiarized two pages from one of the present author's books. What punishment, if any, should he have suffered?

18. Make a list of a few other cases concerned with the ethics of the teaching profession, and indicate the action which you believe the member of the profession in the case should have taken.

SELECTED REFERENCES

Dewey, John, and Tufts, J. H., *Ethics*, Henry Holt and Co., New York, 1910, 618 pp.

An excellent treatment in the general field of ethics.

Goold, G. Howard, "Responsibility for Enforcing a Code of Ethics," *School Executive*, Vol. 74 (November, 1954), pp. 76–77.

Discusses the lack of teachers' support for enforcing a code of ethics.

Love, Jean O., "Professional Ethics in Education," *Educational Administration and Supervision*, Vol. 40 (November, 1954), pp. 385–394.

This article is mostly a listing of various ethical practices under their general headings, such as "ethical practices in relations with other teachers," "ethical practices in relationships between teachers and administrators," etc., along with the references from which each was taken.

"On Teacher Strikes," *Journal of the National Education Association*, Vol. 36 (February, 1947), p. 38.

Says that the breaking of contracts by teachers violates the code of ethics of the National Education Association.

Perry, Cyrus C., *Annals of the American Academy of Political and Social Science*, (January, 1955).

Discusses ethics of the teaching profession.

1947 Report of the Professional Ethics Committee, National Education Association, Washington, 1947, 64 pp.

Reproduces copies of the codes of ethics of various organizations.

Rogers, Virgil M., "Ethics and Strikes," *School Executive*, Vol. 66 (February, 1947), p. 5.

Condemns strikes of teachers.

Titus, Harold H., *Ethics for Today*, American Book Co., New York, 1936, 470 pp.

Pages 312 to 329 are devoted to the ethics of teachers and students.

CHAPTER 22
Looking Ahead to a Teaching Position

Long before the day for the completion of his teacher-preparing program arrives, the student begins to wonder whether he will be able to obtain a desirable teaching position and how he should go about obtaining it. Moreover, this same problem confronts the experienced teacher who for one reason or another sometimes wants to change positions, especially for a promotion. This chapter, therefore, is designed to make the present as well as the prospective teacher more aware of proper procedures to use in dealing with this problem.

The Competition for Teaching Positions

There is a serious shortage of teachers today, but the supply of teachers graduating from the colleges and universities has over the long term greatly exceeded the demand. At various times prior to World War II, many graduates were compelled to wait one or more years before they were able to find positions. This prewar oversupply of teachers was caused by many factors, among which the following were particularly prominent: (1) the improvement of opportunities (better salaries, pensions, sick-leave provisions, permanent tenure, etc.) in the teaching profession, which caused more persons to desire to enter the profession; (2) an increasing amount of technological unemployment, which caused a larger number of persons to seek public positions; (3) a decline in the birth rate and in immigration which resulted in a smaller number of pupils entering the schools and in fewer teachers being needed, especially in the elementary schools; and (4) a closer approach to the saturation point of school enrollment, which meant less rapid increase in the number of teaching positions, even in the secondary school and the college. In some teaching areas, however, as was pointed out in Chapter 17, the oversupply was much greater than in other areas and in some areas there was an undersupply.

During pre-war years, thousands of the graduates of even the most renowned colleges and departments of education were unable to obtain positions. Many of these graduates no doubt failed to obtain employment, because they did not know how to proceed. Many of them failed in spite of the fact that they were much better qualified for positions than the persons who received the positions.

There is very little teacher unemployment today, and the nation is faced with the largest shortage of teachers in its history. The tendency of the past toward an oversupply of teachers may have been permanently buried. It is hoped that it has been, but whether it has been will be determined by such unpredictables as economic conditions, international affairs and the birth rate; future years will have to answer these questions.

Qualifications for a position do not guarantee the offer of one, though it will greatly help. The position will not necessarily "come to him who waits." The world will not beat a path to the door of the builder of the best "mousetrap" unless the world knows who that builder is and where he lives, and unless the world really wants the best "mousetrap" rather than an inferior product. The teacher's qualifications and services must be marketed the same as "mousetraps" of Emerson lore, and the teacher must assume the chief responsibility for "marketing" his qualifications and his services. Every person is his own public-relations agent; and he determines his own destiny.

PRACTICES FOLLOWED IN SELECTING TEACHERS

VARIATION IN PRACTICE. In the United States, teachers are always selected by local school systems, and there are approximately 50,000 of these school systems. Since the laws of the various states seldom prescribe any of the procedures for teacher selection, local boards of education follow the practices which they desire. As would be expected, therefore, employment practices for teachers vary widely among the thousands of school systems; and in most systems, especially the smaller ones, the practices have never been defined by the boards of education.

The teacher, therefore, who believes that he might be interested in a position in a given school system has the responsibility for becoming acquainted with the practices of employing teachers in that system. In making that acquaintance he will sometimes find practices that are haphazard and unbusinesslike; indeed, he will occasionally find practices that are grossly unethical. For example, he will find that some school systems still appoint their teachers on the basis of "politics," residence, church affiliation, marital status, family relationship to school board members, or some other extraneous consideration. Probably, in no school system will he find perfect employment practices, but conditions have rapidly improved.

Advantages of a Good and Well-defined Practice. The better school systems have seen the advantages of carefully defining their teacher-employment principles and practices and of making the information available in written form to any prospective applicant. Springfield, Massachusetts, for example, has incorporated the information in a 1955 bulletin entitled *Personnel Policies,* and she presents a copy of this bulletin to each person who makes inquiry concerning a teaching position in the Springfield schools; in addition to describing the methods of selecting teachers in Springfield, the bulletin describes the conditions of service and the salaries of the Springfield teaching staff. The Springfield policies pertaining to teacher selection are so forward looking that they are quoted herewith *in extenso:*

> The process of teacher selection in Springfield is free from pressures considered harmful to the best conduct of the schools. Freedom from such pressures is attributable to the long-established and public-approved policy of the School Committee [1] and the administrative officers of observing the following principles in selecting teachers:
>
> 1. *Merit as judged by all pertinent standards is the sole criterion by which teachers are selected.*
> 2. *The use of political, social, or other pressures automatically disqualifies candidates for positions from further consideration.*
> 3. *The immediate relatives of members of the School Committee, of the*

[1] This school governing body is known as the board of education or school board in most states.

members of the Board of Examiners, and of the Superintendent and Assistant Superintendents are not eligible for positions in the Springfield Public Schools. (Immediate relative: parent, wife, husband, child, sister, brother.)

Massachusetts law decrees that the School Committee, selected directly by the people, is responsible for the conduct of the schools in accordance with state and local regulations. . . . Although the superintendent may assign to others certain duties respecting the appraisal of qualifications of candidates, in every case the final decision as to whether the candidate shall be recommended to the School Committee for employment is the Superintendent's alone.

Since 1934 the School Committee of the Springfield Public School System has maintained an official Board of Examiners charged with the responsibility of evaluating the qualifications of all candidates for teaching positions in the public schools and of submitting to the Superintendent of Schools the results of each such evaluation. The Board of Examiners consists of three divisions: (1) a Secondary School Division made up of four junior and senior high school principals, (2) an Elementary School Division made up of four principals of elementary schools, and (3) an Evening School Division made up of evening school principals and the Supervisor of Adult Education. Members of the Elementary and Secondary School divisions are elected by the School Committee upon the nomination of the Superintendent of Schools and serve for overlapping terms of three years each. They are granted an annual salary differential of $100. In the Evening School Division, members hold office during and by virtue of their incumbencies in evening school administrative positions. They are not granted a salary differential. . . .

It is the specific function of this Board, through its several divisions, to make a thorough examination of the qualifications of each candidate in terms of the requirements of the position to which the candidate aspires. This function is discharged through the following processes:

1. Regular meetings of the Board as a whole for the discussion and formulation of general policies and techniques for the selection of teachers.
2. Meetings of the separate division of the Board to study credentials, recommendations, and other written material concerning the qualifications of candidates.
3. Meetings of divisions to interview candidates. These interviews are always given by a full division of the Board, never by individual members.
4. Observation of teaching or other performance of candidates by two or more members of the appropriate division of the Board. At least two members witness the same performance and their judgments, independently arrived at, are carefully considered by the whole division.
5. Conveying to the Superintendent of Schools and to him alone the decisions of the Board as a whole and of its various divisions. No member is ever permitted to discuss these matters with anyone except

other members of the Board, the Superintendent of Schools, or persons designated by the Superintendent. . . .

Of course, many other excellent practices of selecting teachers are found in the various school systems. Although these practices differ in many of their details, they have a common aim, namely, to obtain the best teacher available for the position and for the available salary.

Suggestions on Obtaining a Teaching Position

As has been stated in previous paragraphs of this chapter, each school system uses its own methods of selecting teachers and only a few systems have well-defined methods which they have reduced to writing. The candidate for a teaching position must, therefore, adjust his desires and his practices to the procedures which he finds in a given situation. It is believed that the following suggestions will aid him in making that adjustment:

Making an Early Start for a Teaching Position. Candidates for teaching positions should remember that school administrators usually know several months before the beginning of the next school term whether they will have any vacancies to fill and that they early take steps to fill them. Wide-awake school administrators early begin to search out desirable candidates, because they realize that any delay in the search may result in the loss of a blue-ribbon candidate to another school system. Wide-awake and ethical school administrators are not primarily concerned with obtaining a teacher—they are primarily concerned with obtaining the best teacher for the salary available. They rightly believe that their first obligation is to the pupils and to the public, not to candidates for school positions. Teachers who are ethical will co-operate with the enlightened policy just mentioned.

Since information on many teaching vacancies for the next school year—usually beginning in September in most school systems—becomes known as early as January, February, or March, and since many school administrators take immediate steps to fill those vacancies, that time is not too early for the candidate, especially the beginner, to start exploring the field of opportunities. Of course, most teaching positions become available in the late spring and in the summer months, but it is also true that the competition for those positions becomes more keen as the time for the opening of the next school year approaches.

An early start in the search for a teaching position will give the candidate an opportunity to obtain a position early and thereby to avoid the rush of later months. Assuming that the candidate will be graduated in the following spring or the following summer, January, February, or March is not too early for him to enroll in the appointments division of his college or university and to take other steps toward making contacts with available school positions. These steps will have to be taken sometime, and for the most effective results they should be taken early; to take the steps early will not only be more likely to assure the teacher a position, but the most desirable position under the circumstances.

Making Contacts With Vacancies for Teachers. It would be ideal if the supply of and the demand for teachers always balanced, and it would be ideal also if the position always sought the teacher and the teacher did not have to take the initiative in seeking the position. Such practices are, however, far from realization, and teachers must continue to assume a large part of the responsibility of ascertaining where the vacancies exist and of promoting their candidacies by effective and ethical means; the college which the teacher attended or is attending must also assume its share of this responsibility for helping its graduates in obtaining positions.

The locating of a desirable vacancy is the first step in obtaining a position. To take this step is not always easy, particularly in years when positions are not plentiful. In locating vacancies, such procedures as the following may be used:

1. Enroll in and keep in close contact with the college placement office. Each college which prepares a considerable number of teachers maintains a placement office. The purposes of this office are (1) to aid school officials to find the best qualified employees for any vacancies which they may have, and (2) to aid students and former students to find positions for which they are qualified and which would be acceptable to them. Of course, no placement office can guarantee a position to anyone.

The placement office organizes the credentials of the candidate and sends them to employers who have requested the recommendation of a candidate or candidates; the office will also send the credentials to employers with whom the candidate has made contact on his own initiative.

Most college placement offices do not charge a registration fee; when a fee is charged, it usually ranges from two to five dollars. Commissions for obtaining positions are never charged by college placement offices; the work of such an office is a part of the service extended to the students of the college, and the expense of the office is a regular part of the annual budget of the college.

In a few states the state department of education maintains a placement office, and in a few others, the state education association maintains one. Registration in these offices is available to experienced teachers as well as to prospective ones, especially to those residing in the state.

2. Consider the advisability of enrolling in one or more of the numerous private teachers' agencies. The rapid growth of placement offices in colleges and universities has decreased the work formerly done by private teachers' agencies, but many school employers and teachers still make use of such agencies. Practically all of the private agencies charge a registration fee, usually two dollars; and all of them charge a commission, usually five per cent of the first year's salary for helping the candidate to obtain a position. Under present practice, the employee pays all of the commission of the agency; under ideal practice, however, part or all of the commission would be paid by the employer.
3. Make inquiries of school officials concerning vacancies in their school systems. Inquiries may also be made of other persons regarding vacancies. Of course, such inquiries should always be in good taste, and it should be remembered that the "broadcasting" of inquiries through a form letter is regarded as bad taste, and is condemned by the code of ethics of many education associations.

Since an application for a specific position, unless it is certain that a vacancy exists, might result in displacing a fellow teacher from his position, such practices should be avoided. Even an apparently well-founded rumor of a vacancy should be checked before an application is made for the position. The codes of ethics of teachers' organizations condemn the practice of applying for a specific position until it is definitely known that a vacancy exists. The Code of Ethics of the National Education Association affirms: that a teacher "will apply for employment on the basis of competence only, and avoid asking for a specific position known to be filled by another teacher."

Teachers may ethically, of course, make inquiries of school officials regarding the existence of vacancies. Such communication should not, however, be more than an inquiry; it should not be an application and should never be permitted to embarrass the present occupant of a position.

THE FORMAL APPLICATION FOR A TEACHING POSITION. When the candidate has authentic information that a vacancy in a position exists, assuming that he is interested in the position and is qualified for it, he is privileged to present a formal application. Formal application may be made through a personal interview, through a written communication, or by means of the telephone or the telegraph. The usual practice is, however, to make the application, especially the first application through a written communication. Employers prefer this practice because it gives them a permanent record of the salient qualifications of the applicant; moreover, the practice is usually more convenient and less expensive to the applicant, especially the nonresident one, than to telephone, to telegraph, or to make a personal application.

Most school systems have adopted an application blank which candidates for teaching positions are required to fill out. This blank requests information on such matters as the candidate's teaching experience, his schooling, his references, and his age and other personal characteristics. Unless the candidate has definite information that the school system does not use a formal application blank, his first letter should be largely an inquiry regarding whether such a blank is used by the system and a request for a copy of it. If a blank is received, it should be filled out accurately, completely, and promptly; if the candidate deems that other information would be useful to the employer, he may send that in a letter which will accompany the blank.

When the school system does not use an application blank, the candidate is obliged to write a letter of application. This letter should provide adequate information on such matters as age, marital status, and other personal characteristics, amount and type of schooling, academic and extraclass activities and interests, teaching experience, and references. An informative, correct, and attractive letter should be prepared, because ugly stationery, faulty English, poor mechanical form, indefiniteness, lack of confidence, boasting, and insufficient or irrelevant information are among the factors which are likely to be noticed by the recipient of the letter and to cause the application to be unsuccessful. Although the writer of a magnetic letter may not necessarily be an excellent teacher, "style is usually the man." Employers are prone to begin the process of "separating the wheat from the chaff" on the basis of the letter of application. A good letter always helps a candidate, whereas a poor one is certain to be a poor ambassador for him. If the candidate has any doubt about the mechanical standards which a good letter must meet, he should consult one of the many style books.

The Candidate's Photograph for an Application. When the prospective employer does not know the candidate, a photograph of the candidate should be included with the written application. If the school system to which the candidate is applying provides an application blank, the photograph should be fastened to an appropriate part of the blank; if the school system does not provide such a blank, the photograph should be fastened somewhere on the letter of application. In order that the photograph may be readily identified, in case it should become separated from the application, the name and address of the candidate should be written on the reverse side of the photograph.

The photograph should present an up-to-date likeness of the candidate. It should be unmounted, and its dimensions should permit it to be readily inserted in the ordinary business envelope. Because they are likely to give an unfavorable impression to prospective employers, extremes in such matters as dress, posture, photographic setting, and expression should be avoided. Examples of extremes would be a photograph of the candidate in evening dress or in camping clothes, or a photograph of the candidate playing a game.

References for a Position. As a part of their applications for positions, teachers should give the names, the positions, and the addresses of a few persons who are acquainted with their qualifications and who will provide confidential information upon the request of the employer. The application blank almost always requests the teacher to give a few references, but when it does not make the request, the teacher should present those references in the letter of application. From two to six references will suffice, unless the application blank specifies the number of references to be included.

In the list of references the applicant should include persons who are in the best position to speak of his qualifications as a teacher; among such persons are former and present teachers and former and present employers of the applicant, but the list need not be limited to these persons. The list should not give the employer the impression that the applicant is trying to exercise a "pull" through his acquaintance with prominent "politicians" or other influential persons; to give that impression is likely to blast the applicant's chances of appointment. In brief, the references should be competent to speak of the qualifications of the applicant as a teacher—of such matters as his professional preparation, his moral character, his personal traits, and his general ability as a teacher.

Letters of Recommendation for a Position. The "to-whom-it-may-concern" letter of recommendation—often called the "open letter" or recommendation—should seldom, if ever, be used. Most employers regard the use of such a letter as bad taste and many of them regard its use as unethical; in fact, the codes of ethics of some of the state education associations call the use of such letters an unethical practice. Most employers desire confidential information regarding candidates, and they therefore disdain the open letter of recommendation. To use an open letter is almost certain to handicap the applicant, because there is a general belief that it may not be reliable. The Code of Ethics of the National Education Association enjoins teachers to "be fair in all recommendations concerning the work of other teachers."

The applicant should neither request nor use an open letter of recommendation, but he may properly request and use a letter of introduction to a particular employer. He may also request his former teachers and employers to write confidential letters in his behalf. Of course, he should never impose upon the good nature of his friends by making unjustified requests for confidential letters. He should not make such requests too often, especially when he has registered with a teachers' appointment bureau or agency, because one of the chief functions of such an office is to send copies of such letters and other confidential information to employers.

To Whom to Apply for a Position. Since the welfare of the school and the progress of the pupils are largely determined by the qualifications of the teachers, the selection of the best qualified teachers is one of the most important and most difficult duties of school administrators. Because of the growing recognition of the difficulty of performing the duty, the tendency during recent years has been toward permitting or requiring professionally prepared school administrators to perform the duty; thus, the tendency has been for boards of education to delegate to the superintendent of schools the duty of investigating the qualifications of candidates and of recommending the best qualified candidates for appointment. It is only in some of the isolated rural districts and a few "politically" administered city school systems that boards of education still select the teachers without consulting with the superintendent of schools.

In school systems, therefore, in which the board of education has delegated to the superintendent of schools the duty of selecting teachers, applications for teaching positions should be made to him and all negotiations should be conducted through his office; in such school systems, candidates should not interview or otherwise bother board members, except upon the instruction of the superintendent of schools. When the board of education is the sole selecting agency, teachers are required, of course, to make their applications to it, and not to the superintendent of schools. Some small school systems do not employ a superintendent of schools and in such instances applications must be made to the board of education.

Resident versus Nonresident Teachers as Applicants. In seeking a position in a given community it is well for the teacher to be informed on the policy of the school system regarding the employment of resident versus nonresident teachers. Many school systems give preference to local residents as teachers, and some of them go so far as to dismiss a successful nonresident teacher to make room for the "home-town girl." Many other school systems, on the contrary, give preference to nonresidents as teachers, and some school systems refuse to employ local candidates until they have had one or more years of successful experience in other school systems.

Qualifications should, of course, be the only criterion for determining who shall be selected for, and retained in, a teaching position. General rules, therefore, which limit the choice of teachers to resident or to nonresident persons cannot be sanctioned. Teachers should try to obtain changes in all rules which often levy a protective tariff on qualifications.

Teachers are sometimes advised not to accept positions in their home community because of the belief that their acquaintance with the pupils, the parents, and other adults of the community would tend to make the pupil-discipline and the public-relations functions unduly difficult to perform. Such advice is applied especially to beginning teachers and to the rural and village community. Persons who give that advice readily admit that the advice does not have much merit when applied to experienced teachers and to the large cities.

The question, then, remains whether such advice has merit when applied to the beginning teacher and to the small community. The answer to the question would seem to depend on the particular circumstances, and especially upon the qualifications of the teacher. Assuming that the teacher has proper qualifications, his local acquaintance and his local residence should not militate against him. Indeed, such acquaintance could be used advantageously by him in making the pupil-discipline and the public-relations problems easier, because the nature of such problems would already be known by him.

AVOIDANCE OF NEPOTISM IN POSITIONS. Nepotism may be defined as favoritism of an employer toward his relatives, especially close relatives. Public officials are frequently criticized for practicing nepotism, and many school officials bring that criticism upon themselves. In several states the antagonism toward the practice of nepotism by school-board members has crystallized into statutes which prohibit such practice. A representative statute is that of Ohio which reads as follows:

> Whoever, being a local director or member of a board of education, votes for or participates in the making of a contract with a person as a teacher or instructor in a public school to whom he or she is related as father or brother, mother or sister, or acts in a manner in which he or she is pecuniarily interested, shall be fined not less than twenty-five dollars or imprisoned not more than six months, or both (Section 12932).

Although the state in which the teacher may be seeking employment may not have a statute prohibiting boards of education from employing near relatives, the teacher should hesitate before accepting a position over which a relative, particularly a near relative, has jurisdiction; what has just been said would seem to apply also to the teacher in his relationships with the superintendent of schools who is a near relative. The teacher should hesitate to work under a near relative because of his regard for the welfare of the school, of his relative, and of himself. The teacher may be eminently qualified for his position and may have obtained it without the assistance of his relative; yet, there is always the danger that both he and his relative will be subjected to the charge of favoritism; worst of all, the school may be injured by such criticism. It is worth keeping in mind, too, that many school officials who have relatives in their employment do not promote such relatives as rapidly as their merit deserves because they are afraid of inviting public criticism.

THE PERSONAL INTERVIEW IN APPLICATIONS. Although there is not much evidence to indicate that the personal interview enables school administrators to select better teachers than could be selected without the interview, it is natural for them to insist upon an interview before they will employ a teacher. In fact, it may be said that of all the employment techniques, the personal interview is the most frequently used; it is almost universal. The chief arguments advanced for the personal interview in teacher selection are the following:

1. The interview gives school officials an opportunity to obtain further information regarding the candidate and to evaluate at close range certain qualifications that may or may not be revealed through other sources of data.
2. The interview furnishes another opportunity to acquaint the candidate with the qualifications necessary for the position as well as with the opportunities, if any, for advancement which the position affords. It helps the candidate to decide whether he wants or doesn't want the position.

The initiative in arranging for an interview may be taken by the applicant or by the employer. Always, though, the applicant should respect the wishes of the employer in the matter. If the employer does not wish an interview, probably nothing could be gained by the applicant in requesting it. On the other hand, if an interview is requested by the employer, it should be arranged for by the applicant, provided, of course, that he is interested in the position. As a rule, employers prefer, through correspondence and other means, to eliminate all candidates except a few, then to arrange for interviews with those few. These interviews are usually arranged at the college or university in which the candidate is a student, in the community in which the candidate is then teaching, or in the community which is considering the candidate's employment. Most school systems do not pay the traveling or other expenses of candidates who are interviewed.

In most school systems the superintendent of schools interviews all candidates for teaching positions. In many rural and village school systems the candidates are interviewed by members of the board of education. In other school systems, especially those of the large cities, the interviews are conducted by various other professional workers such as (1) the school principal or other school employee to whom the candidate would be responsible if employed, (2) a personnel employee or an assistant superintendent of schools, and (3) a board of examiners or other committee of the school staff designated for the purpose.

While the candidate should not regard the personal interview as an inquisition, he should look upon it as a serious and businesslike proceeding which is certain to be one of the chief factors in determining whether he receives an offer of the position. The employer will practically always want the candidate to be at ease and to make a favorable impression and he will not be disposed to "place the candidate on the spot."

What can the candidate do during the interview to give a favorable impression and to "sell" himself for what he is really worth? Unfortunately, this question cannot be answered categorically for every situation, because interviews are conducted in various ways, and the applicant must be able to adapt himself to the situation as he meets it. The general purpose of the personal interview is to enable the interviewer to become better acquainted with, and thus better able to evaluate, the candidate's personality. In the interview the interviewer will usually be interested in obtaining information on and insight into the candidate's educational philosophy, his voice, his interests and ambitions, his knowledge of the school subjects that he would be expected to teach, his dress, his manners, his personal habits, and his general culture. Following are a few general suggestions for helping candidates to conduct favorable interviews:

1. Be meticulously careful of personal appearance. Persons who are slovenly in dress are seldom wanted as teachers.
2. Be punctual for the appointment.
3. Answer all questions frankly, clearly, and fully, but do not talk too much. Know the art of being a good listener. Have confidence in yourself, but do not boast. Remember that famous rule: "Do not take yourself too seriously."
4. Although the employer has the responsibility for directing the interview, the applicant need not hesitate to ask the employer a few questions concerning the school, the school system, and the community. The employer usually likes to know whether the applicant is sufficiently interested in the position to obtain further information concerning it.
5. Avoid gossiping about other candidates for the position. If you have had teaching experience, avoid complaining about conditions in the last school, school system, or community in which you taught.
6. Do not necessarily expect a decision from the employer at the close of the interview. Usually, too, the applicant will not be expected to make a decision upon an offer at the close of the interview.
7. Do not prolong the interview, and especially do not prolong it after the employer has given a hint that he has received all needed information.

As a part of the personal interview, a few school systems require the candidate for a teaching position to put on a teaching demonstration either in the practice-teaching classes in the teacher-preparing institution or in the teacher's present position if he happens to be already in service. Demonstrated ability to teach is, of course, the "acid test," and not all teachers can meet that test.

Salary Considerations for a Position. As Chapter 17 has indicated, most school systems have adopted salary schedules for various positions and for various types and amounts of college preparation and teaching experience, and they follow those schedules rigidly. In most teaching positions, therefore, the salary which the applicant would receive is determined automatically. Many of the small school systems, on the other hand, do not have salary schedules, and in these systems the salary of the teacher is determined through bargaining between the teacher and the school officials.

When the salary is determined through bargaining, the teacher should keep in mind not only his own personal needs but the welfare of the profession. He should request an adequate salary, but at the same time he should remember that service cannot be limited on account of small compensation; he should ever keep in mind that the members of a profession are expected to give more than they receive, otherwise they cannot claim that their calling is a profession. In making a decision on what constitutes an adequate salary for himself and for a particular position, the teacher should not underbid a rival for the position.

The Teacher's Contract

Requisites for the Contract. According to the American Law Institute, "a contract is a promise or a set of promises for the breach of which the law gives a remedy, or the performance of which the law in some way recognizes as a duty." In order to form a contract there must be two or more parties who are willing to enter and do enter into contractual relations; in the teacher's contract one of these parties is the teacher, and the other party is the employing board. Figure 65 shows a sample contract for teachers.

The consummation of a contract is *prima facie* evidence that the teacher has obtained a position; it is the act which transforms him from a mere holder of a teaching certificate and a seeker of a position into a *bona fide* teacher. Since the contract is the instrument which vests the teacher with most of his rights, his duties, and his obligations, its importance to him is obvious. He should make certain, therefore, that his contract is in the correct form and that it is legal in every way. He should make certain that both he and the board of education have met all of the contract requirements which have been established by the laws of the state. The following paragraphs discuss briefly the chief requisites for the teacher's contract:

1. The contract must be *mutual*, that is, both the board of education and the teacher must accept all of its provisions.
2. The best type of contract is a *written* one. Most states stipulate that it shall be written, and in those instances the courts have usually held an oral contract to be unenforceable. In the states in which a written contract is not stipulated by law the courts have held an oral contract to be legal, provided it could be substantiated by sufficient evidence, such as correspondence between the teacher and the employer and the minutes of the employer. Since a written contract is more businesslike in every way, both the teacher and the employer should insist upon a written contract.
3. It should be *definite*, that is, its chief terms should be clearly stated. Inclusion of the following matters help to make the contract definite: (1) name of the school district; (2) name of the teacher; (3) statement of the length of the school term during which the teacher is to be employed; (4) amount of salary; (5) time limit for teacher's acceptance; (6) agreement of the teacher to abide by the school laws of the state and by the rules and regulations of the board of education; (7) signatures of the authorized officers of the board of education, and (8) signature of the teacher.
4. It must be *free from illegality*. There are many factors which, if not properly handled, might make the contract illegal; among these are the following: (1) failure by school officials to follow the form of contract prescribed by the laws of the state; (2) failure of the teacher to have the proper certificate or to file it with the proper official; (3) violation by school officials of the taxation or debt limitations of the school district; and (4) personal interest of a school official in the contract, such as permitting himself or a near relative to be employed by the school district. Of course, the laws of the various states differ somewhat on what makes a contract legal or illegal, and the teacher should be informed on the laws of his state governing these matters. Of the factors mentioned above, the second and fourth are entirely under the control of the teacher, while the first and third are largely under his control.

The teacher should remember that a mere promise of a position by the superintendent of schools or by a school board member does

DENVER PUBLIC SCHOOLS
School District No. 1 in the City and
County of Denver and State of Colorado
OFFICE OF THE BOARD OF EDUCATION
414 Fourteenth Street, Denver 2, Colo.

ORIGINAL
(Return to Secretary's Office)

NOTICE OF APPOINTMENT

Date__________

You are hereby notified that the Board of Education has appointed you to a position in the schools of School District No. 1 in the City and County of Denver and State of Colorado, at an initial salary at the rate of $__________ per annum, and thereafter in accordance with the adopted salary schedule of the District, which schedule the District reserves the right to change at the beginning of any District budget year.

Appointment is effective__________if your acceptance is received at the Secretary's office by__________.

TO

This appointment is subject to the laws of the State, and the rules and regulations of the Board of Education. It is expressly subject to the provisions of Chapter 123-17-17, Colorado Revised Statutes 1953, relating to penalties for a teacher's breach of contract. Assignment to work will be made by the superintendent of schools.

Secretary

STATEMENT OF ACCEPTANCE:
I hereby accept the above appointment, agree to its terms, and agree to perform such duties and services as may lawfully be required of me, and to comply with all laws of the State and rules and regulations made by the Board of Education of said School District.

Name__________

Date__________ Address__________

DENVER PUBLIC SCHOOLS
School District No. 1 in the City and
County of Denver and State of Colorado
OFFICE OF THE BOARD OF EDUCATION
414 Fourteenth Street, Denver 2, Colo.

DUPLICATE
(To Be Retained by Teacher)

NOTICE OF APPOINTMENT

Date__________

You are hereby notified that the Board of Education has appointed you to a position in the schools of School District No. 1 in the City and County of Denver and State of Colorado, at an initial salary at the rate of $__________ per annum, and thereafter in accordance with the adopted salary schedule of the District, which schedule the District reserves the right to change at the beginning of any District budget year.

Appointment is effective__________if your acceptance is received at the Secretary's office by__________.

TO

This appointment is subject to the laws of the State, and the rules and regulations of the Board of Education. It is expressly subject to the provisions of Chapter 123-17-17, Colorado Revised Statutes 1953, relating to penalties for a teacher's breach of contract. Assignment to work will be made by the superintendent of schools.

Secretary

STATEMENT OF ACCEPTANCE:
I hereby accept the above appointment, agree to its terms, and agree to perform such duties and services as may lawfully be required of me, and to comply with all laws of the State and rules and regulations made by the Board of Education of said School District.

Name__________

Date__________ Address__________

Fig. 65. A teacher's contract, used in the Denver, Colorado, public schools. *(Courtesy of the Denver, Colorado, public schools.)*

not constitute a legal election to the position. Only the board of education can elect a teacher to a position, and sometimes this board will, as is its prerogative, not endorse the promises of the superintendent or of one or more of its members. A teacher has not been legally elected to a position until the board, at a regular or a special meeting, votes to elect him and records the action in its minutes.

In school systems which do not require a written contract between teacher and employer, the teacher should make certain that he receives a written notice of his election; and he should soon thereafter submit his acceptance in writing. He should file for safe keeping this notice of election and a carbon copy of his letter of acceptance of the position.

Provided the teacher is interested in a position which has been offered him, the teacher should not delay too long in signing the contract or in submitting a letter of acceptance. He should not delay, because the courts have ruled that unless the employer has set a time limit for acceptance of the offer, the employer may rescind the offer at any time before a contract is completed. It should be reiterated that a contract is not complete until it has been endorsed by both the employee and the employer.

TERMINATION OF THE CONTRACT FOR A POSITION. After a contract has been made by the employer and the teacher, it can only be terminated in one of the following ways: (1) by agreement of both parties to the contract to change it or to break it; (2) by complete performance of all the terms of the contract; (3) by breach of one party of the terms of the contract; (4) by an act of God, such as the death or the disability of the teacher; and (5) by the discovery that the contract is illegal in one or more of its parts.

By virtue of entering into a contract, the employer and the teacher give their sacred promise that they will fulfill all provisions of the contract. When one of the parties to the contract does not fulfill all provisions, and is not excused by the other party from fulfilling those provisions, the contract is broken by that party. The courts have invariably ruled that the party breaking a contract is liable for damages to the other party to the contract; this liability to damages is assumed by the teacher who breaks a contract, just as much as the school board that breaks it.

Teachers and boards of education are occasionally guilty of sharp and unethical practices in their contractual relations. Boards of education are sometimes guilty of trying to wriggle out of a contract or out of the unjust and illegal dismissal of teachers under contract. Teachers sometimes treat their contracts as "scraps of paper" and do not hesitate to break a contract when a better contract is offered them by another employer. In fairness, though, it should be stated that such instances as have just been mentioned are the exception. School officials and teachers are preponderantly honest, fair, and ethical.

In addition to incurring the liability of having damages assessed against him for violating his contract, the guilty teacher risks having his teaching certificate revoked. He should remember that several states have enacted statutes which empower the chief state school official, or a local school official, to revoke the certificate of a teacher who is guilty of breaking his contract. Moreover, the Code of Ethics of the National Education Association, and most of the codes of the state education associations, have a pronouncement upon the sacredness of the teacher's contract. The Code of Ethics of the National Education Association has the following to say: The teacher should "adhere to the conditions of a contract until service thereunder has been performed, the contract has been terminated by mutual consent, or the contract has otherwise been legally terminated."

NOTIFICATION OF CHANGE OF POSITION. Teachers and school officials have a reciprocal obligation regarding changes in positions, namely, that of early notification. On this matter the Code of Ethics of the National Education Association says: The teacher should "give and expect due notice before a change in position is to be made."

QUESTIONS FOR DISCUSSION

1. Do you believe that the state should guarantee a position to each certificated teacher? Why or why not? What is the law of supply and demand?

2. Should teachers be "called" to positions, or should they apply for them? Explain.

3. Should teachers enroll with private teachers' agencies? Why or why not? Should employers who obtain teachers from such agencies pay part of the commission? Why or why not?

4. Should a teacher apply for or accept a position from which the previous occupant was dismissed unjustly? What would be your attitude toward applying for a position from which the present occupant is about to be unjustly dismissed?

5. What is your opinion of printed, mimeographed, or carbon copies of letters of application?

6. Under what conditions, if any, would a teacher be justified in requesting and using an open letter of reference? Explain.

7. Do you believe that a teacher is justified in accepting a position in a community in which he has a close relative as a school board member or as school superintendent? Why or why not? What are the laws, if any, of your state on this matter?

8. Should teachers' application blanks request information on political party, war record, church affiliation, religious belief, and race? Why or why not?

9. What value do you attach to the personal interview (a) from the point of view of the applicant, and (b) from the point of view of the employer?

10. What advantages may teachers who are local residents have over nonresidents? What disadvantages? To what extent would the size of the community affect your answer?

11. What information would you want about any teaching position before accepting it? Explain.

12. How do you explain the fact that rural boards of education are more accustomed to select teachers without consulting the superintendent of schools, than urban boards of education?

13. Should teachers be appointed by superintendents or by boards of education? Why? What is the difference between selection and appointment?

14. Under what conditions, if any, would a teacher be justified in breaking his contract? Explain. Would breaking his contract under those conditions be ethical?

SELECTED REFERENCES

Anderson, Earl W., *The Teacher's Contract and Other Legal Phases of Teacher Status*, Teachers College, Columbia University, 1927, 180 pp.

A report of a nation-wide study of the state laws pertaining to teachers' contracts and of the practices of representative school systems.

Armstrong, Earl W., "Suggestions for Securing Teaching Positions," Federal Security Agency, Office of Education, Circular No. 224, Ninth Revision, March, 1950.

Discusses ways of obtaining positions.

Chambers, M. M., "Enforced Celibacy in Schools," *Nation's Schools*, Vol. 18 (August, 1936), pp. 31–32.

A review of court decisions on the employment of married women as teachers.

Coulbourn, John, *Selection of Teachers in Large City School Systems*, Teachers College, Columbia University, 1938, 178 pp.

Reports a survey of practices in thirty-seven large cities and makes recommendations for changes.

Educational Research Bulletin (The Ohio State University).

Each year this periodical summarizes the placement opportunities for teachers of the various school subjects.

Eye, Glen G., and Lane, Willard R., *The New Teacher Comes to School*, Harper and Brothers, New York, 1956, 376 pp.

Discusses such topics as the employment interview, teachers' contracts, and induction responsibilities of the teacher-preparing institution, administrators, and the beginning teacher himself.

Hines, Harlan C., *Finding the Right Teaching Position*, Charles Scribner's Sons, New York, 1920, 200 pp.

A well-rounded discussion of steps to take in obtaining the right teaching position; discusses such matters as the written application and the personal interview.

Institutional Teacher Placement, College of Education, Wayne University, Detroit, 1937, 238 pp.

Describes the practices of colleges and universities in teacher placement.

Morrisett, L. N., *Letters of Recommendation*, Teachers College, Columbia University, 1935, 205 pp.

An analysis and evaluation of such letters.

Tiegs, E. W., *An Evaluation of Some Techniques of Teacher Selection*, Public School Publishing Co., Bloomington, Ill., 1928, 108 pp.

A study of various forms used in teacher selection.

Yauch, Wilbur A., Bartels, Martin H., and Morris, Emmet, *The Beginning Teacher*, Henry Holt and Co., New York, 1955, 339 pp.

Part II emphasizes the importance of getting ready for a teaching position and offers suggestions for securing it.

PART SIX

METHODS OF STUDYING EDUCATIONAL PROBLEMS

CHAPTER 23

The Scientific Study of Education

One of the first facts which the prospective teacher should learn is that progress in professional education can only be obtained by science guided by a sound philosophy of education. The contributions of a sound philosophy to educational progress were discussed in an earlier chapter (Chapter 2). In the present chapter the contributions of science to educational progress will be discussed.

The Place of Research in Education

Technical and Complex Nature of Education. In addition to being one of the most important public businesses, the work of teaching, supervising, and administering the schools is, contrary to common belief, one of the most complex businesses. Because of the size and the complexity of the business, probably no public expenditure, except for the defense of the nation, presents as many and as large opportunities for waste. No informed and fair-minded person will deny that millions of dollars are wasted annually in the teaching and in the management of the schools—seldom maliciously wasted—but wasted either because of ignorance of the best practices or because of oversight and carelessness in adopting and following those best practices.

Lest myopic and unfair critics of the schools attempt to use this testimony on waste as a weapon with which to injure the schools, it should be remarked that, although waste is never condonable, it is not a characteristic peculiar to the schools. Waste exists in all business, whether public or private, whether large or small. Few persons conduct their private affairs with less proportional waste than the schools are conducted.

Although the amount of financial waste in the schools is large, it is a mere bagatelle compared with the pedagogical waste in the schools. By pedagogical waste is meant the waste to the pupil—waste resulting from his not obtaining maximum benefit from the school. Pedagogical waste results from such conditions as teachers not knowing and using the most efficient methods of instruction, the best curriculum, or the best means of classifying and promoting the pupils. If such waste could be measured in dollars and cents, the amount of it would probably stagger the imagination. In spite of the fact that the pedagogical waste cannot be measured in dollars and cents, it is nevertheless real and is sure to be reflected in the ideals, in the attitudes, in the habits, and in the accomplishments of the boys and the girls who will be the citizens of tomorrow. When there is waste in the school, whether the waste is financial or pedagogical, the pupil is being cheated of part of his educational patrimony, and that is the unpardonable sin in teaching and in school administration.

Need for Educational Research. The teaching profession is a long way from knowing the best aims of education and the most effective means of accomplishing those aims; although the profession knows much about those matters, its ignorance regarding them probably exceeds its knowledge of them. The profession is far from knowing the most efficient manner in which to spend the huge amount of school funds which the public entrusts to it; it is far from knowing the way in which the individual pupil learns most effectively and the best teaching procedures to use with the individual pupil. Until two or three decades ago the teaching procedures were dictated largely by tradition, opinion, and rule-of-thumb methods rather than by the facts and the principles of science which were guided by a sound philosophy of education; indeed, the further discoveries of science and of a more profound philosophy of education probably will someday show that the present profession of teaching is largely groping in the dark, so far as its knowledge of those matters is concerned. Writing in 1860, Herbert Spencer, who was an eminent philosopher of England, of the nineteenth century, said:

If there needs any further evidence of the rude, undeveloped character of our education, we have it in the fact that the comparative worth of different kinds of knowledge has been as yet scarcely even discussed—much less discussed in a methodic way with definite results. Not only is it that no standard of relative values has yet been agreed upon, but the existence of any such standard has not been conceived in any clear manner. And not only is it that the existence of any such standard has not been clearly conceived; but the need for it seems to have been scarcely even felt. Men read books on this topic and attend lectures on that; decide that their children shall be instructed in those; and all under the guidance of mere custom, or liking or prejudice; without ever considering the enormous importance of determining in some rational way what things are really most worth learning.[1]

And in 1893, J. M. Rice, sometimes called "the father of the scientific-measuring movement in education," said:

Before pedagogy can be recognized as a science, it will be necessary to discover at least some truths in regard to educational processes which, if ignored by the teacher, will make him fully as liable to prosecution for malpractice as the physician who has bungled in setting a bone. Until an accurate standard of measurement is recognized by which such truth may be discovered, ward politicians will continue to wield the baton, and educational anarchy will continue to prevail.[2]

With such subjective educational procedures as have just been described by Spencer and by Rice, there could not, or cannot, help being a large waste of school funds—and what is still more unfortunate, a waste of the pupil's time, effort, and opportunity. Here is where educational research comes in to help us, because the function of educational research is to provide information which will assist in preventing the financial and the pedagogical waste just mentioned. Such information is always necessary, because our plans and our procedures can never be better than the information upon which they are based. Where information ends, faith, opinion, guessing, and sometimes superstition and prejudice, begin.

Research is a method for finding the solutions of problems. Except as knowledge of its techniques is required, it is not a separate subject. Research is the essence of every live or every growing field. Wherever problems are found, research has a necessary place in their solution.

[1] Herbert Spencer, *Education: Intellectual, Moral and Physical*, Appleton, 1860, pp. 7–8.

[2] J. M. Rice, *Forum*, Vol. 22 (December, 1896), p. 389.

The Place of a Science of Education

Definition of the Science of Education. Since the essence of science is organized knowledge, it is readily seen that the development of a science is dependent upon research. Without knowledge, there is no science, and without research, there can be no development of knowledge. The dependence of science upon knowledge is recognized in every definition of science. For example, Webster's *New International Dictionary* defines science as "accumulated and accepted knowledge which has been systematized and formulated with reference to the discovery of general truths or the operation of general laws; knowledge classified and made available in work, life, or the search for truth; comprehensive, profound, or philosophical knowledge."

Whether, therefore, there is a science of education must be determined by whether there is any systematized knowledge pertaining to professional education. There is already much of such knowledge, and there is, therefore, a science of education. It is the function of the science of education to collect and to organize information on the work of education, in order that such information will be available for the improvement of education.

Definition and Importance of the Scientific Method in Professional Education. One of the outstanding movements in professional education today—indeed, the chief difference between present-day professional education and professional education of yesteryears—is the large dependence today on the scientific method, that is, the method of research, for the solution of educational problems, or for the obtaining of helpful information on the solution of those problems. Contrary to the belief of many persons, the characteristics of the scientific method are not mysterious phenomena which only geniuses are competent to comprehend and to acquire. The scientific method is simply a technique or techniques for finding the truth. It requires, on the part of the persons who use it, the acumen to discern and to solve problems. A scientist, therefore, is a person who searches for the truth, and who has a degree of success in finding the truth and in making it known to his fellow men. According to this definition, it is obvious that the scientist is not merely a person who works in the laboratory with test tubes and with microscopes; the scientist is sometimes found in the guise of a common laborer, a farmer, a mechanic, or a clerk.

If that simple definition of the scientific method is accepted, it will be agreed that the scientific method in education is not, as has been widely claimed, a recent innovation. It is the product of a gradual evolution—an evolution extending back to the beginning of schools. Even a casual knowledge of the history of education will not permit any teacher to conclude that the millions of teachers who have preceded him, and have passed to their great reward, did their work entirely, if even largely, by rule-of-thumb methods. The teacher should prefer to think of his predecessors as possessing, at least to a certain degree, the spirit of inquiry, and as being interested in progress. His predecessors were not robots or automatons. The teacher should choose to think of his predecessors as being intent upon passing down to the succeeding generation a better school and better educational procedures than their predecessors handed down to them. In brief, he should prefer to believe that his predecessors in the teaching profession did employ the scientific method, at least to a certain extent; he should prefer to believe that many of his predecessors were true scientists. How could the school have been constantly improved, as the history of education shows that it has been improved, without the use of scientific method? Progress is seldom a happen-so in any field of endeavor. Guided by a sound philosophy of education, science has always been the handmaid of progress in professional education as well as in all other fields of activity.

Recent Progress of the Scientific Method in Professional Education. It may be safely stated, though, that during the last four or five decades the teaching profession has developed and has used the scientific method more than at any other period in educational history; during this period the teaching profession has become more science-conscious than ever before.

The scientific method in education received its largest impetus from the derivation of the first standardized tests and scales four or five decades ago by such persons as Edward L. Thorndike, Leonard P. Ayres, and Lewis M. Terman. The derivation of standardized tests and scales, measuring for mental ability, aptitudes, and educational accomplishment, marked the beginning of the so-called scientific-measuring movement, without which the science of education could not have made so large an amount of progress. In addition to the development of standardized tests and scales, dozens of other research techniques and research instruments have been developed and used in making thousands of researches of incalculable benefit to the work of the school. Especially noteworthy among these other techniques and instruments has been the development of statistical methods in education which have been valuable in organizing and in presenting information about education. It can be perhaps safely stated that through research the teaching profession has learned more about the educative process during the present century than during all of the previous history of education. Yet in spite of the great progress which has been made, it must be admitted that the science of education is still in its infancy; it is a lusty infant, but it has scarcely outgrown its swaddling clothes. Teachers are still dolefully ignorant about the aims, the means, and the processes of education, but it augurs well for education that teachers today are more aware of their ignorance than ever before. Intelligent or known ignorance is never as unfortunate as unknown ignorance.

A few significant conclusions which educational research has reached and of which use is being made by thousands of teachers and other school employees are the following:

1. Research has shown a large amount of pupil failure and has collected much information on the causes of same and the means of preventing or reducing it. That information is being used to the benefit of millions of pupils, and will continue to be used.
2. Research has informed teachers that it is better to promote the typical pupil to the next grade on trial than to fail him, without giving him another chance. Research has shown that approximately three-fourths of the pupils who are promoted on trial make good, and are in consequence saved the embarrassment and the discouragement of having to repeat a grade.
3. Many studies have shown the large amount of pupil nonattendance and the causes of same, and have suggested ways by which much of the nonattendance may be eliminated.
4. It has been found through research that pupils of the same chronological age vary widely in general intelligence, in special abilities, in interests, in aptitudes, and in other regards. This information is being used by thousands of teachers in attempting to meet the needs of the individual pupil.
5. Numerous studies of the curriculum have been made with the aim of ascertaining the subject matter which is most valuable for pupils to master. Among other benefits, such studies have brought to light the large amount of "dead wood" in the curriculum of the typical school and have suggested the elimination of such material.
6. Hundreds of researches have given us a large amount of useful in-

formation concerning how children learn. These studies, though, have served their chief purpose in making us aware of how little we really know about the working of that most baffling thing in the world, namely, the human mind, and in suggesting to us the need for painstaking and extensive research on this complexity; compared with what we might know and should know, we still know very little about the learning processes of our pupils. But, we already know a great deal that is helpful in teaching.

7. Numerous experiments on different teaching procedures have given us much information which we are now using in improving our teaching procedures. For example, we now know that there are better ways of teaching spelling, arithmetic, reading, and the other school subjects.
8. Several researches have found that small classes are only slightly more efficient than large ones—this, in spite of the fact that small classes are much more expensive than large ones. Some school administrators are using the results of these experiments as an argument for increasing the size of the classes; other school administrators, on the other hand, say that these experiments show only what is, not what ought to be. The evidence is limited to certain types of teaching and certain types of measurement.
9. Many investigations have shown large inequalities in educational opportunities among school districts, counties, and states, and steps have been taken to eliminate or to reduce these inequalities.
10. Many studies have shown that schools and school systems vary, sometimes widely, in the percentage of dropouts which they have.

To list all the truths, all the discoveries, and all the valuable information which educational research has given would require several volumes.[3] The conclusions which have just been mentioned are typical of thousands of facts which have been reported in the educational literature and are now available to every member of the teaching profession. These findings are now known and are being used by thousands of teachers, school supervisors, school administrators, and many other school employees. Facts of this sort have unquestionably been responsible for the prevention or the elimination of millions of dollars of school waste annually; moreover, they have improved teaching techniques greatly with the result that pupils are more and more receiving larger benefits from the school.

[3] For an excellent summary of educational research, see Walter S. Monroe, ed., *Encyclopedia of Educational Research*, Revised edition, Macmillan, 1950.

Value and Improvement of Educational Research

Value and Cost of Educational Research. To obtain such information as has just been mentioned usually requires the expenditure of funds, and someone must provide those funds. Research cannot be financed out of thin air, or on the good wishes of its friends. Either the whole public, through taxation, or private individuals, through free-will contributions, must pay out the "coin of the realm" for it. It is a matter for congratulations during recent years that thousands of dollars from public and private funds have been spent for educational research. Part of this money has been expended for the support of departments or bureaus of educational research in colleges, in universities, and in local and state school systems; other portions of the money have subsidized hundreds of school surveys and thousands of more limited school investigations. Hundreds of persons are now regularly employed in these research activities. These positions provide excellent opportunities for employment, especially for the better prepared and the more experienced persons. The tendency everywhere is to increase the expenditures for research in all fields of endeavor and this evinces a greater public interest in research; in all research endeavors, several billion dollars are spent annually by the whole nation, and more than a million dollars are often spent on only one research project.

No claim is made here that all of the so-called "educational research" is real research, or that all research activities valuably affects school practice. Indeed, it will be readily admitted that much of the so-called "research" is not research, but instead is veritable bunk and quackery; worse still, much of it is vicious in its conclusions and its inferences. There is no field of learning which does not have its quota of quacks and incompetents, and there is no denying the fact that professional education has had its share.

But it is impossible to obtain the wheat without being bothered with the chaff. Persons who sponsor and pay for research cannot expect that every investigator will attack worth-while problems or that the possible precautions may be taken to reduce the "gamble" in research, and it should be realized that all of the "gamble" cannot be entirely eliminated. Even the immortal Edison testified that in many of his epoch-making researches he was compelled to use trial-and-error methods and that hundreds of his researches proved fruitless. In every hundred researches there always has been, and will probably continue to be, a large percentage of waste.

Indeed, it is conceivable that ninety-nine researches in every hundred would be worthless and would show a total loss, but it is also conceivable that the remaining valuable research would pay not only its own way but the way of the ninety-nine worthless researches. One great discovery or invention of an Edison, a Babcock, a Mayo, a Michelson, a Thorndike, a Binet, a Terman, a Bell, a Curie, a Koch, a Marconi, a Pasteur, a Gorgas, a Salk, a Fleming, or an Einstein, will pay large dividends on all expenditures for research during several years. All of these great scientists and inventors, however, would say that they were aided by the researches of other persons. The accomplishments of one genius are worth more to society than the efforts of ten thousand feeble hands. But there is no way of selecting the genius except from the crucible of experiment and proved accomplishment.

Improving Educational Research. Educational research has abundantly proved its value, and it should be increasingly planned for and paid for by society. For several reasons, though, educational research today is not realizing its complete potentialities, and certain improvements are needed to make it function more fully. A few improvements which are needed to make educational research function more fully will be discussed herewith.

In the first place, more educational research should be practical research rather than pure research; this suggestion is made particularly for educational research which is financed by public funds. Practical research is more likely to improve present school procedures than is pure research, because practical research has the aims of ascertaining the truth and of making that truth immediately affect practice. In pure research the practical value of the problem is not necessarily a consideration of the research, nor is the making of the solution of the problem to affect practice a consideration of the research. In final analysis, however, pure research must be regarded as practical because its fundamental aim is to ascertain the truth, and all truth is sure to be, at some time, useful or practical. Michelson's calculations of the speed of light were noted examples of pure research, but they have been of practical value to astronomers and to other scientists, and they have helped the common man better to understand his world.

In the second place, steps should be taken to make the results of educational research known to a larger number of school employees and of the general public. Undoubtedly hundreds of the discoveries of educational research—and many of them are outstanding discoveries—are not being used because school employees are not familiar with them. Thousands of teachers do not know, for example, that teachers' marks given to pupils are somewhat subjective, that much of the curriculum does not meet social needs, that pupils vary widely in native ability, that certain methods of presenting subject matter are better than other methods, that trial promotions of pupils are efficacious, that educational inequalities exist, and that there is a close relation between the mental and the physical health of pupils. Someone has suggested that research workers in education stop conducting research for a few years and spend their time in making people familiar with, and in helping to put into practice, what has already been ascertained. Such a moratorium on educational research will not be necessary, however, if research workers in education will give more attention to the problem of getting their research product properly before the "consumer." *What Research Says to the Teacher* is a valuable series of pamphlets which teachers may obtain from the National Education Association, Washington, D. C.

Educational research could be made to function more fully, if the persons who conducted it would take greater pains in reporting it; the research worker needs to be an efficient "middleman" as well as a producer. Too much educational research today is not functioning because it is reported in such an uninteresting manner that it cannot be read and understood except with great travail. Research should be reported clearly and interestingly to the end that any person with average intelligence could read, and would enjoy reading it. In other words, the reports of research need to be humanized. Too much of the present educational research consists in collecting information which teachers already know and in presenting the information in such manner that no one can understand it. Many persons could make a real contribution to professional education, and incidentally make a good living, by taking theses and similar documents written by other educational research workers, and rewriting them in such a manner that the average teacher could read and understand them.

In the third place, just as fiat money decreases the value of sound money, so pseudo-research tends to cheapen all research in the eyes of the public. The teaching profession will therefore do well to distinguish between real research and pseudo-research, and to place a premium on real research and a penalty or stigma on pseudo-research. Justly or unjustly, scientists in other fields often charge that the science of education is overrun with quacks and incompetents. Whether that charge be true or not, the teaching profession should do everything possible to make impotent the research quack and the pseudo-scientist.

In the fourth place, every school and every school system should have a research program each year, and that program should be based upon the most urgent needs of the local situation; this is sometimes called action research. Often the research program, or at least certain parts of the program, will require several years to consummate. Every teacher, principal, and other educational employee should have an interest, and a part, in planning and in carrying through this program. This program of research should be carefully planned and financed regularly. Such a program could not fail to keep alive in every educational employee the spirit of inquiry, and with this spirit of inquiry the work of the school could not fail to continue to improve. Every prospective teacher should prepare himself to become an effective participant in the program of research of the school or school system which may employ him.

Developing a Scientific Attitude

Importance of the Scientific Attitude for All People. One of the most valuable traits that any person can develop is a scientific attitude, which may be defined as a penchant for "the truth, the whole truth, and nothing but the truth." John Dewey had the following to say of the importance of the scientific attitude:

> One of the only two articles that remain in my creed of life is that the future of our civilization depends upon the widening spread and deepening hold of the scientific habit of mind; and that the problem of problems in our education is therefore to discover how to mature and make effective this scientific habit.[4]

The percentage of the population which has a well-developed scientific attitude is small. The lack of a scientific attitude among people is evidenced in numerous ways. It is evidenced in the manner in

[4] John Dewey, "Science as Subject-Matter and as Method," *Science*, Vol. 21 (January 28, 1910), p. 127.

which the people vote for candidates for public office, make investments, and care for their health. Many people still vote the same political party that was voted by their parents and their grandparents, or they vote for a candidate for public office because of his church, his fraternal connections, or another extraneous reason. Black cats, solar eclipses, sunspots, broken mirrors, and similar signs still carry ill foreboding to millions of people; soothsayers, mediums, palmists, mind readers, and astrologers still make a good living; and thousands of farmers will not risk planting their crops until the "sign of the moon" is right. Such beliefs and such practices indicate that a large percentage of the population does not possess a scientific attitude; they demonstrate that many persons are guided by superstition, tradition, hearsay evidence, and general ignorance or partial truth.

The lack of a scientific attitude on the part of a large portion of the population, and especially on the part of many persons who have responsible political, social, religious, educational, and economic positions, has caused and is causing many of the woes of civilization; it has ever been the chief incubus to the progress of civilization. It has been responsible for financial panics and unemployment, for political and religious revolutions, for plagues, and epidemics, for wars, for famine, and for other woes and miseries among the people. All of these unfortunate happenings can be prevented through straight thinking and sensible acting—in brief, through the use of the scientific attitude in recognizing and in solving problems.

No lesson, therefore, which the teacher can bring to his pupils is of greater importance than the scientific attitude of thinking and of acting. Since the teacher cannot inculcate the scientific attitude in his pupils unless he possesses that attitude himself, a scientific attitude is one of the most valuable traits which the teacher can acquire. If he possesses that trait, the teacher will constantly be trying to push back the frontiers of knowledge, and he will be ever trying to teach that knowledge to his pupils; by precept and by example, he will try to inculcate the scientific attitude into all persons whom he contacts. If he does not possess that trait, the teacher is likely to be completely satisfied with the *status quo*, and he is likely to be guided wholly by tradition and opinion.

CHARACTERISTICS OF THE SCIENTIFIC ATTITUDE. Various persons have attempted to state the characteristics of the scientific attitude. Although those statements are not always in agreement, there is considerable agreement on a few characteristics of them. The characteristics on which there is almost universal agreement are as follows:

1. *Zeal for accuracy and for truth.* A zeal for accuracy and for truth is unquestionably the motivating force of the scientific attitude. It is the force which constantly drives the true scientist; it stimulates him to take infinite pains, to labor long hours, and to make other sacrifices in the pursuit of truth. The true scientist is never satisfied with partial truth or with doubtful accuracy; instead, he constantly seeks to ascertain the whole truth and to obtain complete accuracy, and when he has found what he considers to be the whole truth, he is willing to accept and to announce it, without fear of the consequences. Truth to the scientist is a burning religion; the scientist believes and follows the Biblical precept: "Ye shall know the truth, and the truth shall make you free."
2. *Habits of open-mindedness and of suspended judgment.* A person with the scientific attitude always keeps his mind open for further information on an issue, problem, or question. He tries to see all sides of a question. Not only does he keep his mind open but he avidly seeks new information which will help him to arrive at a better solution or conclusion. He doesn't jump at conclusions, and he is not influenced by prejudices and by preconceived notions; he has hypotheses, but he is willing to change them in the light of further information. If he is a teacher, he doesn't say that general intelligence and subject-matter tests, every new method of teaching, trial promotions, the kindergarten, the junior high school, or other new ideas in professional education are "the bunk" until he has obtained ample information on the issues. He maintains suspended judgment until he has obtained all of the evidence available; even then, he will probably state his conclusions as tentative only and will proceed to try to find new evidence. He holds the view expressed by Gotthold Ephraim Lessing, eminent German critic and dramatist: "If God were to hold in His right hand all truth, and in His left the single everliving impulse to seek for truth, though coupled with the condition of eternal error, and should say to me, 'Choose!' I would humbly fall before His left hand, and say, 'Father, give! Pure truth is, after all, for Thee alone!" [5]

   Persons who possess a scientific attitude in one or more fields of learning often fail to retain such an attitude when they make excursions into other fields of learning; their scientific attitude is channelized rather than generalized. Thus, eminent physicians, chemists, teachers, and inventors often become too sure of themselves on issues which are outside their domain; in fact, many of them have been known to be "laughed out of court" because of their statements on certain controversial questions not in their field of specialization. Persons who possess

[5] Translated by Frank Pierrepont Graves in University of the State of New York *Bulletin*, No. 1100 (September 15, 1936), p. 49.

the highest type of scientific attitude maintain an open mind and suspended judgment in every field of vital thought and activity, and they are wont to maintain such attitudes, especially toward the fields about which they know little or nothing; they agree with Alexander Pope that "A little learning is a dangerous thing," and they refrain from exposing their ignorance.

3. *Desire to make knowledge available to everyone.* A person with the scientific attitude will desire to share his knowledge with all other persons—indeed, he will be willing to make personal sacrifices in order to share his knowledge. He will desire to share it because of his interest in and his desire to improve society. In brief, he will not want to keep his "light under a bushel" but will desire to "shed his light" everywhere. He should not, however, shed his light to individuals and to nations that are known to be "crooked."

A Test of the Scientific Attitude for Teachers. The teacher or the prospective teacher may desire to measure the stage of development of his scientific attitude by means of the following questions:

1. Just to be fashionable, do you not vote with the majority, although you believe the majority to be wrong? Or do you vote your convictions, even though your vote may be unpopular? Are you willing to be a "minority of one?"
2. In school elections do you vote for the best qualified candidates although other candidates might reward you more?
3. Do you ever give a pupil a good mark in a subject merely because he has a pleasing personality or because his parents are influential?
4. Do you believe everything that is told you or everything which you read, or do you check such information against the known facts? Do you go back to the "original or primary" sources of information when possible?
5. Do you "stick to your guns" because you dislike to admit that you are wrong, even though you know that you are? Do you ever change your mind?
6. When your back is turned and some pupil throws a paper wad, do you assume that the "bad boy" of the room has thrown it although you have no evidence that the "bad boy" is guilty this time?
7. When you are expecting an increase in salary and do not receive it, do you conclude that school officials are prejudiced against you?
8. When you make school reports, do you insist upon complete accuracy in statistics and in all other information, or is your aim to get the task over as quickly as possible? Do you avoid approximations in data?
9. Do you ever question the value of the curriculum of the modern school, or do you believe that the curriculum is perfect?

10. Do you always conclude that your methods of teaching are the best methods?
11. Do you indulge in gossip about people without having complete facts about them?
12. Are you careful to avoid overstatements even though they may embellish the story, especially for the unwary?
13. Do you always want the truth, even though the truth may be contrary to your interests and your desires?
14. Do you not conclude that, when a school employee entertains a school official, the employee has an "axe to grind"?
15. Are your conclusions qualified and stated only tentatively, or are they always stated in a cocksure manner?

QUESTIONS FOR DISCUSSION

1. What is a science? What is research?

2. Many persons say that professional education can never be made a science. Do you agree with their view? Do you believe that professional education can be made as much a science as physics, chemistry, and other fields? Why or why not? Is professional education now a science? Why or why not?

3. Do you agree with the following statement of Edward L. Thorndike: "Our ideals may be as lofty and subtle as you please, but if they are real ideals, they are ideals for achieving something; and if anything real is ever achieved it can be measured. I am suspicious of educational achievements which are so subtle and refined and spiritual that they cannot be measured. I fear that they do not exist." [6] Is this statement too idealistic? Why or why not?

4. Do you believe that the placing of professional education on a scientific basis will give the public a greater respect for the teaching profession? Explain.

5. How do you account for the fact that so much of the research in professional education does not sufficiently affect practice?

6. What are a few of the outstanding unsolved problems in teaching? To what extent have practices in the field of these problems been determined by opinion and by tradition? Of what value, if any, are opinion and tradition?

7. To what extent should elementary and secondary school teachers engage in research? List a few practical research problems upon which such teachers might work? What advantages in conducting research do elementary and secondary school teachers have over research specialists in colleges and universities?

[6] Edward L. Thorndike, in *Proceedings* of Indiana University Conference on Educational Measurements, 1914.

8. What contributions have each of the following fields of learning made to the study of teaching problems: biology, psychology, history of education, and sociology?

9. Recall the teachers whom you had, and select the one who had the most highly developed scientific attitude. What were the chief characteristics of the scientific attitude of that teacher? Mention a few evidences of the lack of scientific attitude on the part of teachers whom you have known. What are the characteristics of the scientific attitude?

10. Compare the amount of scientific attitude of the typical teacher with the amount possessed by the typical physician, physicist, and chemist. Account for the difference, and suggest how it might be corrected.

SELECTED REFERENCES

Alexander, Carter, and Burke, Arvid J., *How to Locate Educational Information and Data,* Revised edition, Teachers College, Columbia University, 1950, 441 pp.

A guide to research tools and techniques for the worker in education.

Compton, Arthur H., "What Science Really Is," *Scientific American,* Vol. 146 (January, 1932), pp. 32–33.

Discusses the characteristics of science.

Dewey, John, *Experience and Education,* The Macmillan Co., New York, 1938, 116 pp.

Discusses the implications for education of the scientific method.

Dewey, John, *The Sources of a Science of Education,* H. Liveright, New York, 1929, 77 pp.

Says that the sources of a science of education are the experiences of man.

Good, Carter V., and Scates, Douglas E., *Methods of Research,* D. Appleton-Century Co., New York, 1954, pp. 1–30.

These pages discuss the nature of scientific thinking.

Good, Carter V., ed., *Dictionary of Education,* McGraw-Hill Book Company, Inc., New York, 1945, 495 pp.

Prepared under the auspices of Phi Delta Kappa.

Hillway, Tyrus, *Introduction to Research,* Houghton Mifflin Co., Boston, 1956, 284 pp.

Classifies scholarly research in education into (1) fact-finding investigations, (2) studies of critical interpretation, and (3) complete research processes.

Kelley, Truman Lee, *Scientific Method,* The Macmillan Co., 1932, 234 pp.

Discusses the function of scientific method in research and education.

Monroe, Walter S., ed., *Encyclopedia of Educational Research,* Revised edition, The Macmillan Co., New York, 1950, 1,344 pp.

This is a monumental evaluation, synthesis, and interpretation of the chief studies in the field of education.

Reiser, O. L., *Philosophy and the Concepts of Modern Science,* The Macmillan Co., New York, 1935, 323 pp.

Discusses the relation between science and philosophy.

Review of Educational Research.

Published quarterly by the American Educational Research Association.

Robinson, James Harvey, *The Humanizing of Knowledge,* Doubleday, Doran and Co., New York, 1923, 115 pp.

Discusses the importance of reporting research so that it will be understood by the common man.

Travers, Robert M. W., *Educational Measurement,* The Macmillan Co., New York, 1955, 420 pp.

Discusses the tools of educational measurement and the philosophies determining the use of those tools.

CHAPTER 24

The Observation of School and Class Procedures

School and Class Observations as a Requirement in Teacher Preparation

Universality and Scope of the Observation Requirement. School and class observation is a universal requirement in courses for the preparation of teachers; in fact, with the exception of practice teaching, no requirement in these courses is more frequent and valued more highly than school and class observations. In view of the universality of this phase of teacher preparation, this chapter is devoted to that topic. The chapter will essay to give the student who is preparing to teach an acquaintance with the purposes of school and of class observation and to suggest plans and procedures for conducting those observations.

Since this book is designed for the first course in education, and since most teacher-preparing colleges require the student to begin his school and class observations during that course, the discussion of this chapter will be focused on those first observations. It is hoped, however, that the discussion will have valuable application to the observations in succeeding courses in education as well as to the observations conducted in the first course in education. Since school and class observation is one of the best means which the teacher can use in keeping abreast of developments in his profession, it is hoped also that the discussion will be helpful to the teacher throughout his teaching career.

The curricula of modern teacher-preparing institutions are constituted of three fundamental bodies of knowledge and skills, namely, (1) professional courses (education, psychology, sociology, etc.); (2) subject-matter courses (especially in the school subject or subjects which the student expects to teach, such as mathematics, English, etc.); and (3) field and laboratory experiences (observation, practice teaching, internship teaching, etc.). Arthur R. Mead states that five types of school and class observation are being used by modern teacher-preparing institutions; there are in Arthur R. Mead's words:

1. Observation as a part of theory courses (e.g., with educational phychology).
2. Observation as a part of subject-matter courses (e.g., with English literature or arithmetic).
3. Observation parallel with student teaching, after student teaching, and immediately previous to student teaching.
4. Observation with participation.
5. Observation in a graded series of activities as follows: observation, participation, student teaching.[1]

Most teacher-preparing institutions have their own campus schools in which it is expected that as many of their students as possible will do most of their observing and their practice teaching.[2] These schools have the advantage of possessing demonstration, critic, or supervisory teachers who are especially qualified to assist in a program of teacher preparation; moreover, those schools possess equipment and other facilities which are usually above the average in quality and in amount; still more, they are close at hand.

In many teacher-preparing institutions, though, the campus schools are not large enough to provide observation and practice-teaching facilities for all the students in the teacher-preparing department. This situation has generally been met by making provisions whereby some of the students may do part or all of their observation and their practice teaching in other schools which are conveniently located in the community or in neighboring communities. In fact, most

[1] Arthur R. Mead, *Supervised Student-Teaching,* Johnson, 1930, pp. 160–161. By permission of Johnson Publishing Company, publishers.

[2] These so-called *campus schools* are also occasionally labeled model, practice, training or experimental schools.

teacher-preparing institutions have tried to provide for all their students some observation and some practice-teaching opportunities in those other schools; they have followed that policy, because of desiring to give their students an acquaintance with typical conditions which the students will confront when they become teachers. Since most teachers begin their service in the rural, the village, and the small city school systems, attempt is usually made by the teacher-preparing colleges to provide for some of the observation and some of the practice teaching in such school systems.

Purposes of the Observation Requirement. The belief underlying the observation requirement is that in meeting the requirement the student will learn much from imitation—especially from the imitation of excellent practice—and the student will be assisted in filling the inevitable gap between theory and practice. What the student sees with his own eyes is more likely to make a lasting impression upon him than what he is told or reads about; in other words, "seeing is believing." Experiences obtained by firsthand observation are likely to be clear, complete, and integrated, whereas experiences received vicariously are likely to be vague, lopsided, and "wooden." Not even the best written or the best oral description of excellent schools or of excellent teaching can be a full substitute for seeing such schools and such teaching. Although one picture may not be "worth ten thousand words," as the old Chinese bromide claims it is, the advantage of seeing things with one's own eyes—of having firsthand experience rather than vicarious experience—will not be gainsaid.

Just as no sane person would permit a physician who had never seen an operation to attempt to perform an operation, so the necessity for school and class observation as a prerequisite for teaching is also recognized by all thinking persons. The tendency is to begin these observations soon after the student enters the teacher-preparing curriculum and to continue them to the end of the curriculum. Thus, in the first course in education the tendency is to require a certain number—usually two to six—of directed observations; as a rule, these observations are arranged toward the close of the first course, but advantages are often claimed for beginning them early in the first course and continuing them throughout the first course.

The observations which are made in connection with any course should have the same purposes as the course of which the observa-

FIG. 66. Student teachers observe children's play. (*From Cremin and Borrowman's* Public Schools in Our Democracy, *p. 200. Copyright 1956 by The Macmillan Company.*)

tions are a part; they should work hand in glove with, and should motivate, the course. Thus, the observations which are a part of the first course in education should contribute to a realization of the announced orientation and guidance purposes of the course. More specifically, the purposes of the observations in this first course should be as follows:

1. *To give the student a better firsthand acquaintance with the school as a whole.* This acquaintance should be broad. It should encompass the school's purposes and procedures. It should include the school site, the school building, and the school equipment. It should comprise all grades and as many school subjects as possible. It should extend to the organization and the administration of the school as well as to teaching procedures. In brief, it should attempt to give a telescopic

view of the school and to show something of the relation of each part of the school to the whole school. It should help to prepare the student for his observations in later courses—observations which generally will require a microscopic view rather than a telescopic view.

2. *To help the student decide upon the type of educational service which he wishes to enter.* This is the guidance purpose. That purpose is suggested, because many students have but a meager basis for deciding whether they want to be kindergarten, primary, intermediate, upper grade, or secondary-school teachers, or whether they want to be teachers or school administrators; they lack information on the opportunities and the requirements in the several fields of educational service. The student should observe the various grades, departments, and subjects of the school, in order that he may obtain further information upon which to base his choice of a teaching career. When the student has made his choice, he can emphasize, of course, the observation of that particular grade, department, or school subject, in order that he may better prepare himself for student teaching in that area; if time permits, that emphasis may be begun in the first course in education, but it will, as a rule, have to be postponed until later courses in education.

Making School and Class Observations More Valuable

Preparation for Observations by the Student. Since teaching is one of the largest and most technical endeavors, it is difficult to observe. In fact, teaching is so large and so technical that it is almost baffling, even to the best prepared and the most experienced observer. What, then, of the neophyte observer! Obviously the neophyte cannot make an intelligent and confident beginning in school and class observation without a quantum of preparation. He must be prepared on what and how to observe, and he must realize that school and class procedures which are clear to the practiced observer are often beyond the discernment of the beginning observer. He must be given this preparation in spite of the fact that he has been something of an "observer" for twelve years in the elementary and the secondary schools. Without this preparation the neophyte is like unto the six blind men of Indostan who went to see the elephant:

It was six men of Indostan
To learning much inclined.
Who went to see the elephant
(Though all of them were blind),

That each by observation
Might satisfy his mind.

. . . .

So oft in theologic wars,
The disputants I ween,
Rant on in utter ignorance
Of what each other mean,
And prate about an elephant
Not one of them has seen.[3]

According to Arthur R. Mead, two types of information should be possessed by the student before he begins his school and class observations. The first type is calculated to give the student a background of knowledge concerning school aims and school procedures; the second type is calculated to instruct the student in the techniques of school and class observation, that is, on how to observe, what to observe, and how to analyze, to interpret, and to report the school and class observation. We quote again from Mead:

Two types of learning activity are necessary precedents to the study of teaching by observation. The first type is the preliminary learning of facts, principles, etc., in theory and subject-matter courses (in those types of observation in which the data from observation are not made the basis of the course in theory). This study serves to establish apperceptive bases for use in observation as well as to secure outcomes not so dependent on observation. . . . The first is usually secured by completion of units in such courses. For example, one system of observation begins on an apperceptive basis established through elementary and secondary education and two and one-half years of college education which includes subject matter and theory. Another system begins the observation in the first year of the college course but after the study of a part of the course. It should not be overlooked, also, that there is another type which starts with observation in the first year rather than after the study of a unit in the first year. In this case preliminary preparation for the work is omitted and the student learns primarily through observation and discussion, and study related to the observation. Here actual school conditions are supposed to be the basis of the course.

The second type of preparation consists of learning how to observe, record data, and make analyses of data derived from such a study of teaching. A general conference of all student observers held at the beginning of the work is often used for this purpose. Printed or mimeographed directions, manuals, and guides are supplied for the study. . . .[4]

[3] John Godfrey Saxe, "The Blind Men and the Elephant (A Hindoo Fable)."

[4] Mead, *op. cit.*, pp. 167–168. By permission of Johnson Publishing Company, publishers.

In addition to the two steps of preparation which are suggested by Mead in the foregoing quotation, a third step, namely, preacquaintance with the work of the school or the class exercise which is to be observed, would seem to be helpful. This third step should acquaint the student with the distinctive purposes of the school or of the class exercise, with any unusual teaching procedures, and with any other unusual features of the school or of the class exercise. The aim in taking this step should be merely to give information on the teaching practices to be observed; the aim should not be to propagandize for those practices or for any other practice which has not been found to be the best through experimentation. That acquaintance may be obtained through a general conference of all student observers before the observation of the school or the class exercise, or the student may find the information in a handbook, a manual, or a prospectus of the school, provided, of course, the school is fortunate enough to have such a document.

Co-operating with School Administrators and with the Supervising Teacher. An observation can be most successful only when the observer co-operates with school administrators and with the supervising teacher to obtain that result. The observer should remember that he is a guest of the school; he should, therefore, practice all the proprieties which are expected anywhere and at any time of a guest. He should remember that the school is run for the pupils of the school, not for its observers. The observer can best co-operate with school administrators and with the supervising teacher by being as unobtrusive and as quiet as possible, and he should remember that, even under the most favorable conditions the presence of visitors is likely to be slightly disturbing and burdensome to school administrators, teachers, and pupils. Looking toward reducing such disturbance and burden to a minimum, and looking toward further improvement of school and class observations, especially in the first course in education, the following suggestions are made:

1. Unless the arrangements have already been made for you, present yourself at the office of the principal as soon as you enter the school building and request permission to observe. Obtain there also any directions, and follow them in detail.
2. Arrange your schedule, so that you can remain in the school as many periods of the school day as possible. The purpose of the first observations should be to become acquainted with the school as a whole, and continuous observation throughout the school day will contribute

much to the realization of that purpose. If possible, eat lunch in the school cafeteria to observe whether the lunch period is being conducted as a part of the educational program of the school; see how school intermissions are conducted; visit the school library, shops, laboratories, gymnasium, and similar features of the school.

3. When about to visit a class, present yourself to the teacher before the beginning of the class and request the privilege of observing his class, unless these steps have already been taken for you. It is bad taste to stalk into a classroom before receiving permission. Whenever possible, enter and leave a class exercise only during an intermission. If it is necessary to enter or to leave during a class exercise, do so as quietly and as inconspicuously as possible. If possible, avoid passing in front of the pupils, and try to occupy a seat or to stand where you will not attract the attention of the pupils.
4. Beyond showing a polite interest in the work of the school or a class, refrain from further expression of approval or disapproval while in a classroom or in the school. Try to hear and to see everything, but say or do nothing which will convey your appraisal of any part of the work. Remember that you are a neophyte and not an expert practitioner. Do not offer suggestions, especially when they are not solicited; then, be wary of making adverse criticisms.
5. During a class exercise, avoid talking to other observers or to the pupils. Likewise, avoid laughing, moving about, or similar disturbances.
6. Do your part in trying to make the pupils react in a normal way. If the pupils are distracted by your presence, temporarily turn your attention away from them. Discourage any attempt "to play to the grandstand" by seeming not to notice it.
7. Upon leaving a class exercise, thank the teacher for the privilege of visiting his class, unless this action would interrupt his work. Teachers and school administrators will probably not have time to "visit" with you; don't be a poacher on their time.
8. Don't gossip about school administrators, teachers, pupils, or the school. To do so would violate the ethics of the teaching profession. Good taste doesn't permit us to gossip about our host or hostess, which in the case here mentioned is the school, its administrators, its teachers, and its pupils. Say good, or say nothing, is an excellent rule.

OBTAINING DATA FROM THE OBSERVATION OF A SCHOOL OR OF A CLASS EXERCISE. An observation of a school or of a class exercise may be regarded as having many of the characteristics of a scientific investigation. Just as the scientist must collect, organize, and interpret the data of his investigation, so the observer of a school or of a class exercise must collect, organize, and interpret the data of his observation. Just as the scientist must be on guard lest he fail to obtain complete and accurate data, so the school or class observer must realize that the complexity of the educational process makes it exceedingly difficult for him to obtain complete and accurate information on the observation.

The observer should enter into his work in the spirit of a humble student of the important, the huge, and the complex enterprise of education. He should assume the attitude of a real student rather than the attitude of a carping critic or of an officious inspector. In attempting to study any phase of the work of a school he should have the attitude of a real scientist who tries always to find the truth; he should exhibit the scientific attitude. He should search assiduously for all facts on a problem and should maintain suspended judgment until all the facts are present.

In brief, the student should maintain an open mind toward what he observes. He should not be "taken in" by every new theory, "ism," or practice; on the contrary, he should not look askance at everything that is new. He should worship both the god of what is and the god of what ought to be, but he should worship more devoutly the god of what ought to be. He should be always interested in progress, but he should know that mere change is not necessarily progress and that the labeling of a practice as progressive or efficient does not necessarily make it progressive or efficient.

Alertness to the whole problem of education is a *sine qua non* for the school or the class observer. Although each observation should be organized especially to see certain things, those things should be seen in relation to other things, and the seeing of them should not preclude the seeing of other things. The student must learn to observe more than the details of a class exercise; he should observe also such things as the organization and the administration of the school, the type of curriculum, the mentality and the learning readiness of the pupils, classroom management, health and sanitary conditions, and the school equipment with which the teacher has to work. He should learn to see the "forest in spite of the trees" and to see the relation of the individual tree to the whole forest. This will require that the observer's mind be active in its fringe of consciousness as well as in its center of consciousness. Above all, the observer must look for significant principles, because these principles will be his "anchor" when he becomes a teacher.

In any attempt to observe and to appraise the work of a school or of a class exercise, the observer should proceed first to ascertain

FIG. 67. Student teachers supervising children in classroom recreational activities. *(Courtesy of Austin, Texas, public schools.)*

what aims guide the work, and whether those aims are the most desirable. The presence and the merit of aims having been established, there remains for the observer the task of appraising the efficiency with which the aims are being accomplished. The observer should realize that the taking of those two steps is very difficult, because of the difficulty of receiving complete and accurate data. Even the most experienced observers find difficulty in obtaining complete and accurate data, especially in one observation. What, then, of neophyte observers!

The observation period should be used wholly for the collection of data, reserving for a later time the organization and the interpretation of the data. During the observation, it is, of course, permissible for the observer to take notes.[5] In fact, the taking of notes is suggested, and for subsequent use the notes will be found to be serviceable in proportion to their accuracy, their clarity, and their completeness. The notes may be taken in various ways, and they may vary from brief "running" notes to a complete stenographic record of the observation.

In most instances, provided he wants to hear and to see what is going on, the student will have to be satisfied with brief "running" notes which he will take during the observation. After the observation, and before his impressions have become hazy, he should supplement, organize, and edit his notes in order that they may give a more accurate, a more clear, and a more complete picture of his impressions. In many instances, the period of the observation will not provide all the data necessary for the observation report, and the student will have to supply the missing data through an individual conference with the supervising teacher, or through reading; he should never guess at the missing data.

Most teacher-preparing institutions provide the observer with directions to follow in making his observations. Many institutions also have a report blank, or a series of report blanks, which the observer is expected to use in reporting his observations.[6] Directions and report blanks, especially directions, are recommended, provided they are not permitted to degenerate into stereotyped affairs and thus to interfere with broad observations and student thinking. Re-

[5] A few teachers are opposed to the taking of notes during an observation, because they claim that it disturbs the teacher and the pupils. The desires of such teachers must, of course, be respected.

[6] For samples of such report blanks, see the Selected References at the close of this chapter; see especially Mead, *op. cit.*, pp. 160–217.

port blanks which contain long lists of rambling and unrelated questions are likely to interfere with broad observations and thinking and are, therefore, to be frowned upon. Such items of information as the following should be obtained for each observation of a class exercise: [7]

Name of the school.................. Name of the teacher observed .... Date of observation................ Hour or period observed.................. Subject or grade.................. Number of pupils in class or group.................. Brief description of the classroom (Adequacy of equipment, decorations, etc.)..........
....
....

Brief description of the pupils (age, sex, race, etc.)..................
....
....

Other descriptive data..
....

Secure answers to as many of the following questions as possible:

1. What were the materials of instruction? What subject matter did the teacher emphasize and what did he neglect?...............
....
....
2. *What was the function of the subject matter?* So far as you could see, what was the teacher trying to accomplish?...............
....
3. *What methods of instruction were emphasized?* What methods were used over and over, and what appropriate methods were neglected?...
....
....
4. *How effective did the teacher's materials and methods seem to be?*
....
....
5. *How did the teacher help students with their personal problems?* Did he neglect such opportunities? Did he help certain pupils and neglect others? What kinds of problems were emphasized, and how effectively were they handled?......................
....
....
6. *What did the teacher do to promote better school-community relations?* What did he emphasize, and what did he overlook?........
....
....

[7] This report blank is based largely upon *The Ohio Teaching Record: Anecdotal Observation Form*, The Ohio State University, 1941. By permission of the College of Education, The Ohio State University, publishers.

7. *To what extent and by what means were democratic attitudes and relationships fostered?* Did the teacher practice democracy? Did the teacher make the students conscious of democratic and authoritarian tendencies in their daily living? . . . .

. . . .

. . . .

8. *What evidence did the teacher show of having specialized training in the subject or area in which he was teaching?* Was the teacher competent or incompetent? Why? . . . .

. . . .

. . . .

Unless the student is an accomplished stenographer, which he will probably not be, he will have difficulty in obtaining a "black-and-white record" of everything seen and heard in the class observation. Moreover, an attempt to obtain such a record would probably prevent him from seeing some of the more important matters such as educational principles, the personal relations existing between the teacher and the pupils, and the educational setting or environment; in brief, the attempt to take verbatim notes might well prevent the student from "seeing the forest because of the trees."

A few teacher-preparing colleges make provision from time to time for an accomplished stenographer to accompany a group of observers to a class exercise and to take a stenographic record of everything that happens, especially everything that is said by the teacher and by his pupils. This record is then mimeographed and placed in the hands of each observer, first for his individual study and later for group discussion. Although he admits that a stenographic record is nothing more than a "black-and-white lesson" and that it has such limitations as failing to reproduce the personal relations existing between the teacher and his pupils, Romiett Stevens claims the following advantages for such a record:

With all these limitations, however, the stenographic report has distinct uses. Shorn thus of all embellishments it is of importance to the student to see what the lesson offers in intellectual and educational substance. It is this residue that furnishes him material for study. It not infrequently happens that groups of students come from a class observation completely dominated by the personality of the teacher, in some instances where there is little to commend except a charming and dramatic manner on the part of the teacher. The stenographic lesson report soon reveals the actual strength or weakness in the content of the lesson and in the psychology of its presentation. It gives the *facts* of the lesson for analysis and study, and for repeated analysis and study as the student grows in the power to observe; whereas from the general observation he has only *impressions* to work upon, impressions that are easily obscured or effaced. With the manuscript as a basis, or point of departure, it is also possible to do constructive work on content, plan, questioning, application, etc.[8]

Reports and Conferences on Observations by Students. After the student has collected the data on the observation, he has the further task of organizing, interpreting, evaluating, and reporting the data. Without these steps, the value of the observation is largely lost. Most teacher-preparing institutions require student observers to make either an oral or a written report of each observation.

Following each observation most teacher-preparing institutions make provision for group or for individual conferences on the observation. The purpose of these conferences is to bring into clearer view the principles and the practices found operating in the school or the class exercise observed. These conferences afford an opportunity for the observer to ask questions, to make suggestions, and to receive suggestions regarding the work of the school or the class observed. Moreover, the conferences provide opportunity for giving preparation in the making of further observations and in reporting them. In brief, the conferences are generally regarded as a vital part of the observation program and a wise student will not neglect the opportunity which they afford.

The report of, and any conferences on, the observation should follow fairly closely the observation. The longer the delay in writing the report or in holding the conference, the more hazy the impression of the observation is likely to be. On the contrary, there is a possibility that a report made, or a conference held, too soon after the observation will lead to snap judgment on the observation. Good practice, therefore, should steer between those two dangers and should recognize that the first danger is far greater than the second danger.

In making any written reports, the student should always follow an acceptable style regarding footnotes, bibliographies, tables, illustrations, organization, and English; acceptable standards in those details should be regarded as part of his preparation for teaching. Illustrations of good style may be found in this book, and unless

[8] Romiett Stevens, "Stenographic Reports of High School Lessons," *Teachers College Record*, Vol. 2 (September, 1910), p. 2.

the instructor requires other styles, the styles herein illustrated may well be followed by observers; it is recognized, though, that the merit of styles is a matter of opinion.

Other Types of Direct Experiences for Prospective Teachers

Students who are preparing for some phase of teaching service will be helped by supplementing their school and their classroom observations with other types of experiences related to teaching. Many teacher-preparing institutions make provisions for these other types of direct experience, and some of them require those experiences of all prospective teachers. Such experiences, especially of an observational nature, can be begun early in the student's preservice preparation for teaching and can be continued throughout his professional career. Although there are hundreds of others, some of the most ubiquitous and valuable of these experiences are the following:

1. Observation and group leadership in child welfare and similar activities such as Boy and Girl Scouts, Campfire Girls, Y.M.C.A., Y.W.C.A., Sunday school, camps, and playgrounds.
2. Case studies of pupils.
3. Visits to governmental, civic, and social agencies such as juvenile courts, detention homes, legislative assemblies, health departments, institutions for mentally deficient or handicapped persons, guidance centers, children's hospitals, and clinics of various kinds.
4. Community studies.
5. Practice teaching; also internship teaching.
6. Attending P.T.A. meetings; also school board meetings, and school board meetings are usually open to the public.

QUESTIONS FOR DISCUSSION

1. In the conduct of observation and in practice teaching, do you believe that teacher-preparing institutions could learn anything from the methods of colleges of medicine? What? Compare the emphasis upon and the facilities for school and class observations and practice teaching with the emphasis upon and the facilities for clinics and internships in colleges of medicine. Why the difference?

2. In view of the influence of imitation in teacher preparation, why should the observation of the best practices be stressed? Would there be any advantage in observing an inefficient school or class exer-

cise? What, if any? What danger might there be in observing an inefficient example?

3. Do you believe that school and class observations should be begun with a telescopic view, or with a microscopic view? Why? Define each view.

4. Discuss the importance of the school or the class observer possessing the scientific attitude. What are the chief characteristics of such an attitude?

5. Why do many parents object to having their children taught by practice teachers? Are such objections valid, and how may the objections be minimized? What standards should the student meet before he is permitted to do his practice teaching? Is it legitimate to require him to have a certain standard of scholarship as evidenced by his school marks? Why?

6. Compare the advantages of observing in a training school with those of observing in a regular school such as the student will probably first find employment in.

7. Discuss the advantages and the shortcomings of stenographic reports of class exercises as material for the study of teaching procedures.

8. In making an observation of a class exercise, what should be the test of teaching efficiency?

9. List a few outstanding standards which you would expect an excellent school to meet. List similar standards for a class exercise. Be able to justify each standard.

SELECTED REFERENCES

Alcorn, Marvin D., *et al., Better Teaching in Secondary Schools,* Henry Holt and Co., New York, 1954, 512 pp.

A discussion for student teachers.

Dewey, John, *The Relation of Theory and Practice in Education,* Part I of the *Third Yearbook* of the National Society for the Study of Education, Public School Publishing Co., Bloomington, Ill., 1926.

Contains many valuable suggestions on the conduct of school and class observations.

Raths, Louis, *et al., The Ohio Teaching Record: Anecdotal Observation Form,* The Ohio State University, Columbus, rev. ed., 1941, 30 pp.

Designed for co-operative use by teachers and observers.

Richey, Robert W., "Some Types of Direct Experiences Utilized in Teacher Education," *Educational Research Bulletin,* Vol. 21 (January 14, 1942), pp. 13–18.

Describes the practices of several typical institutions.

Schorling, Raleigh, and Wingo, G. Max, *Elementary-School Student Teaching*, McGraw-Hill Book Co., Inc., New York, 1952, 456 pp.

Discusses the teaching method and the aims of the elementary school.

Schorling, Raleigh, *Student Teaching: An Experience Program*, McGraw-Hill Book Co., New York, 1940, 520 pp.

Contains suggestions for the student observer as well as the student teacher.

Wrinkle, William L., and Armentrout, Winfield D., *Directed Observation and Teaching in Secondary Schools*, The Macmillan Co., New York, 1932, 399 pp.

Approaches the problem from an analytical point of view; contains a complete bibliography and many exercises.

INDEX